INTERVIE

Principles and Practices

FOURTEENTH EDITION

INTERVIEWING

Principles and Practices

FOURTEENTH EDITION

Charles J. Stewart

Purdue University

William B. Cash, Jr.

INTERVIEWING: PRINCIPLES AND PRACTICES, FOURTEENTH EDITION

Published by McGraw-Hill Education, 2 Penn Plaza, New York, NY 10121. Copyright © 2014 by McGraw-Hill Education. All rights reserved. Printed in the United States of America. Previous editions © 2011, 2008, and 2006. No part of this publication may be reproduced or distributed in any form or by any means, or stored in a database or retrieval system, without the prior written consent of McGraw-Hill Education, including, but not limited to, in any network or other electronic storage or transmission, or broadcast for distance learning.

Some ancillaries, including electronic and print components, may not be available to customers outside the United States.

This book is printed on acid-free paper.

2 3 4 5 6 7 8 9 0 DOC/DOC 1 0 9 8 7 6 5 4

ISBN 978-0-07-803694-1
MHID 0-07-803694-1

Senior Vice President, Products & Markets: *Kurt L. Strand*
Vice President, General Manager: *Michael Ryan*
Vice President, Content Production & Technology Services: *Kimberly Meriwether David*
Executive Director of Development: *Lisa Pinto*
Managing Director: *David Patterson*
Director: *Susan Gouijnstook*
Marketing Specialist: *Alexandra Schultz*
Managing Development Editor: *Pennia Braffman*
Brand Coordinator: *Adina Lonn*
Director, Content Production: *Terri Schiesl*
Content Project Manager: *Jolynn Kilburg*
Buyer: *Susan K. Culbertson*
Cover Designer: *Studio Montage, St. Louis, MO*
Compositor: *Cenveo® Publisher Services*
Typeface: *10/12 Times LT Std Roman*
Printer: *R. R. Donnelley*

All credits appearing on page or at the end of the book are considered to be an extension of the copyright page.

Library of Congress Cataloging-in-Publication Data

Stewart, Charles J.
  Interviewing : principles and practices / Charles Stewart, Purdue University, William B. Cash, Jr. —
14 Edition.
    pages cm
  Includes index.
  ISBN 978-0-07-803694-1 (pbk.)
  1. Interviewing—Textbooks. 2. Employment interviewing—Textbooks. 3. Counseling—Textbooks.
I. Cash, William B. II. Title.
BF637.I5S75   2013
158.3'9—dc23   2013020015

The Internet addresses listed in the text were accurate at the time of publication. The inclusion of a website does not indicate an endorsement by the authors or McGraw-Hill Education, and McGraw-Hill Education does not guarantee the accuracy of the information presented at these sites.

www.mhhe.com

*To the memory of William "Bill" Cash, Jr., student,
co-author, and friend*

Charles J. Stewart

Charles J. "Charlie" Stewart is the former Margaret Church Distinguished Professor of Communication at Purdue University where he taught from 1961 to 2009. He taught undergraduate courses in interviewing and persuasion and graduate courses in such areas as persuasion and social protest, apologetic rhetoric, and extremist rhetoric on the Internet. He received the Charles B. Murphy Award for Outstanding Undergraduate Teaching from Purdue University and the Donald H. Ecroyd Award for Outstanding Teaching in Higher Education from the National Communication Association. He was a Founding Fellow of the Purdue University Teaching Academy. He has written articles, chapters, and books on interviewing, persuasion, and social movements.

Charlie Stewart has been a consultant with organizations such as the Internal Revenue Service, the American Electric Power Company, Libby Foods, the Indiana University School of Dentistry, and the United Association of Plumbers and Pipefitters. He is currently a Court Appointed Special Advocate (CASA) for children.

William B. Cash, Jr.

The late William "Bill" Cash began his work life in his father's shoe and clothing store in northern Ohio. While still in high school, he began to work in broadcasting and advertising, and this led to bachelor's and master's degrees in broadcasting and speech communication at Kent State University. After completing his academic work at Kent State, he joined the speech communication faculty at Eastern Illinois University and began to consult with dozens of companies such as Blaw-Knox, IBM, and Hewitt Associates. Bill took a leave from Eastern Illinois and pursued a PhD in organizational communication under W. Charles Redding. He returned to the faculty at Eastern Illinois and created and taught a course in interviewing.

Bill Cash left college teaching and held positions with Ralston Purina, Detroit Edison, Baxter, and Curtis Mathis, often at the vice president level. After several years in industry, he returned to teaching and took a faculty position at National-Louis University in Chicago. He became the first chair of the College of Management and Business and developed courses in human resources, management, and marketing.

BRIEF CONTENTS

CONTENTS

6 The Survey Interview 137

9 The Performance Interview   259

10 The Persuasive Interview   285

11

The Counseling Interview   331

12
The Health Care Interview   357

PREFACE

This fourteenth edition of *Interviewing: Principles and Practices* continues a tradition started with the first edition that appeared in 1974. It focuses on the fundamental principles applicable to all forms of interviewing and to seven specific types of interviewing while incorporating the latest in research, interpersonal communication theory, the uses of technology and social media, the role of ethics in interviewing, and EEO laws that affect employment and performance interviews. While we have included recent research findings and developments, we continue the emphasis on building the interviewing skills of both interviewers and interviewees. Several chapters address the increasing diversity in the United States and our involvement in the global village as they impact the interviews in which we take part.

We have continued our quest to make each edition more reader-friendly by tightening up the writing style, eliminating unnecessary materials and redundancies, making explanations and definitions more precise, reducing the frequency of lists and using a variety of print types to call attention to important words, terms, and concepts. Portions of several chapters have been restructured to take readers through each in a clearer and more natural progression. A list of objectives now appears at the start of each chapter to orient students to the major topics and purposes of the chapter. Notes in the margins provide guidelines, cautions, and observations. Lists of key terms appear at the end of each chapter, and a glossary of important terms is provided at the end of the book.

Changes in the Fourteenth Edition

Each chapter includes new or revised examples and illustrations, student activities, suggested readings, research findings, and an interview that challenges students to apply theory and principles to a realistic interview. In each interview, the parties do some things well and others poorly. We want students to be able to identify strengths and weaknesses and to offer alternatives that would have made the interview more effective for each party.

Major changes include:

- Chapter 1 includes a restructured development of our definition of interviewing to help students understand how it is similar to and different from other forms of interpersonal communication. The emphasis is on a collaborative effort by both parties. There is a more detailed discussion of technology and the interview, including the use of Skype and Webinars.

- Chapter 2 includes new or expanded treatments of intra-personal communication, trust, self-concept, self-identity, self-esteem, self-disclosure, active listening, and the differing notions of place for women and men.

- Chapter 3 includes sharper and fewer words to explain the types of questions and the uses and misuses of questions. It includes a discussion of the

differences of question use and question pitfalls in formal, professional interviews as compared to everyday conversations.

- Chapter 4 includes clearer and expanded explanations of the interview guide and
  interview schedules. The notion of territoriality is expanded, particularly for men
  and women.

- Chapter 5 is restructured with strong emphases on studying the interview situation,
  becoming aware of the relationship of the interviewer and interviewee, and choosing the best location and setting. It includes expanded treatments of the press conference and the broadcast interview.

- Chapter 6 now includes new discussions of qualitative and quantitative interviews, probability and non-probability sampling, convenience sampling,
  coverage bias, and using monetary and non-monetary incentives to increase
  participation in surveys. There is an expanded treatment of telephone and cell-
  phone interviews.

- Chapter 7 has expanded treatments of reaching and attracting qualified applicants, working career/job fairs, selecting staffing firms, using software to scan
  résumés, the problem of applicants cheating on résumés, the use of standardized
  tests, and the pluses and minuses of checking applicant use of social media. Other
  areas of increased emphasis include the atmosphere and setting of the recruiting
  interview, types of interview parties in chain, team, panel, group, seminar, and
  board interviews.

- Chapter 8 is restructured and introduces students to the notions of branding that
  differentiates you from other applicants, proper interview etiquette, and structuring answers using the STAR and PAR methods. It includes more detailed treatments of researching the position and organization, using networking and social
  media, developing traditional and scannable résumés, and appropriate dress and
  appearance.

- Chapter 9 places a strong emphasis on approaching the performance review
  interview as a coaching opportunity. It includes expanded treatments of con-
  forming to EEO laws, selecting appropriate review models, and determining just
  cause in performance problem interviews.

- Chapter 10 combines in a single chapter the discussions of both the interviewer
  and interviewee in the persuasive interview for a more cohesive treatment of the
  persuasive interview. There is an expanded treatment of the ethics of persuasion
  pertaining to both parties.

- Chapter 11 includes a new emphasis on ethics and the counseling interview
  that focuses on establishing and maintaining trust, acting in the interviewee's
  best interests, understanding your limitations, not imposing your beliefs, attitudes, and values on the interviewee, respecting diversity, maintaining relational
  boundaries, and doing no harm. The treatment of structuring the interview rein-
  corporates the "sequential phase model" created by Hartsough, Echterling, and
  Zarle. This chapter includes an expanded discussion of self-disclosure and its
  importance to counseling.

- Chapter 12 includes a new emphasis on ethics in the health care interview that focuses on the critical importance of the relationship between health care provider and patient. The focus throughout this chapter is on Patient-Centered Care (PCC). The treatment of self-disclosure is expanded with a strong emphasis on establishing and maintaining trust. A new topic in this chapter is "health literacy" and its effects on information giving and processing.

Chapter Pedagogy

We have included a **sample interview at the end of each chapter,** not as a perfect example of interviewing but to illustrate interviewing types, situations, approaches, and mistakes and to challenge students to distinguish between effective and ineffective interviewing practices. We believe that students learn by applying the research and principles discussed in each chapter to a realistic interview that allows them to detect when interview parties are right on target as well as when they miss the target completely. The **role-playing cases** at the ends of Chapters 5 through 12 provide students with opportunities to design and conduct practice interviews and to observe others' efforts to employ the principles discussed. **Student activities** at the end of each chapter provide ideas for in- and out-of-class exercises, experiences, and information gathering. We have made many of these less complex and time-consuming. The **up-to-date readings** at the end of each chapter will help students and instructors who are interested in delving more deeply into specific topics, theories, and types of interviews. The glossary provides students with definitions of key words and concepts introduced throughout the text.

Intended Courses

This book is designed for courses in such departments as speech, communication, journalism, business, supervision, education, political science, nursing, criminology, and social work. It is also useful in workshops in various fields. We believe this book is of value to beginning students as well as to seasoned veterans because the principles, research, and techniques are changing rapidly in many fields. We have treated theory and research findings where applicable, but our primary concern is with principles and techniques that can be translated into immediate practice in and out of the classroom.

Ancillary Materials

For the Student

Student's Online Learning Center (OLC)

The Student's Online Learning Center Web site that accompanies this text offers a variety of resources for students, including—for each chapter—a chapter summary; an interactive quiz with multiple-choice, fill-in, and/or true/false questions; and flashcards of key terms. Please visit the *Interviewing* OLC at www.mhhe.com/Stewart14e.

For the Instructor

The Instructor's Manual, written by Charles Stewart, Test Bank, and PowerPoint slides are available to instructors on the password-protected Instructor's section of the Online Learning Center Web site.

Acknowledgments

We wish to express our gratitude to students at Purdue University and National-Louis University College of Management, and to past and present colleagues and clients for their inspiration, suggestions, exercises, theories, criticism, and encouragement. We thank Suzanne Collins, Ellen Phelps, Mary Alice Baker, Jeralyn Faris, Vernon Miller, Dana Olen, Kathleen Powell, Garold Markle, and Patrice Buzzanell for their resources, interest, and suggestions.

We are very grateful to the following reviewers for the many helpful comments and suggestions they provided us:

Suzanne Collins, Purdue University

Judith Fahey, Ohio University Eastern Campus

Diane Ferrero-Paluzzi, Iona College

Dirk Gibson, University of New Mexico

Diane Hagan, Ohio Business College

Emily Holler, Kennesaw State University

Rosalind Kennerson-Baty, Baylor University

CHAPTER 1

An Introduction to Interviewing

When you participate in an interview, you take part in the most common form of purposeful, planned, and serious communication. It may be formal or informal, minimally or highly structured, simplistic or sophisticated, supportive or threatening, and last for a few minutes or hours. Your purpose may be to give or get information, seek employment or recruit employees, review the behavior of another or of yourself, persuade or be persuaded, counsel or seek counsel. Interviews share characteristics with brief interactions, social conversations, small groups, and presentations, but they differ significantly from each of these communication forms.

> **Interviews are daily occurrences.**

The objectives of this chapter are to identify the essential characteristics of interviews, set interviews apart from other types of communication, discuss traditional forms of interviews, and examine the growing role of technology in conducting interviews during the twenty-first century.

The Fundamental Characteristics of Interviews

Two Parties

The interview is a dyadic—*two party*—process that typically involves two people such as a reporter and a voter, attorney and client, nurse practitioner and patient, sales representative and customer. An interview may involve more than *two people* but never more than *two parties*. For instance, three college recruiters may be interviewing a prospective student, a computer sales person may be interviewing a husband and wife, or four college students may be interviewing an apartment manager about housing for next semester. In each case, there are *two distinct parties*—an interviewer party and an interviewee party. If there is a single party involved (three students discussing a field project) or three or more parties involved, it is a small group interaction with multiple parties, not an interview.

> **Dyadic means two parties.**

Purpose

One or both of the two parties must come to an interview with a *predetermined* and *serious purpose*, a characteristic that sets the interview apart from social conversations or informal, unplanned interactions. While conversations and happenstance meetings are rarely organized in advance, interviews must have a degree of planning and structure. Interviewers typically plan openings and closings, select topics, prepare questions, and gather information.

> **Interviews are structured.**

More than two people may be involved in an interview, but never more than two parties—an interviewer party and an interviewee party.

Interactional

An interview is *interactional* because there is *sharing* and *exchanging* of roles, responsibilities, feelings, beliefs, motives, and information. If one party does all of the talking and the other all of the listening, it becomes a speech to an audience of one, not an interview. John Stewart writes that communication is a "continuous, complex collaborative process of verbal and nonverbal meaning-making."[1] *Collaborative* means a mutual creation and sharing of meanings that come from words and nonverbal signals—touches, hugs, handshakes, and facial expressions—that express interest, concerns, reactions, and a willingness to take risks entailed in close interpersonal interactions such as interviews.

> **Parties exchange and share.**

Communication interactions are not static. Role changes, information exchanges, and revelations of feelings and motives produce reactions and insights that lead to new and unexpected areas. The interview as a *process* is a dynamic, continuing, ongoing, ever-changing interaction of variables with a degree of *system* or *structure*. "Human communicators are always sending and receiving simultaneously. As a result each communicator has the opportunity to change how things are going at any time in the process."[2] Like most processes, once an interview commences, we "cannot not communicate."[3] We may do it poorly, but we will communicate something.

Questions

Asking and answering **questions** are important in all interviews. Some interviews, such as market surveys and journalistic interviews, consist entirely of questions and answers. Others, such as recruiting, counseling, and health care, include a mixture of questions and information sharing. And still others, such as sales, training, and performance review, involve strategic questions from both parties designed to obtain or clarify information and to change another person's way of thinking, feeling, or acting.

> **Questions play multiple roles in interviews.**

Questions are the tools interview parties employ to obtain information, check the accuracy of messages sent and received, verify impressions and assumptions, and provoke feeling or thought. Chapter 3 introduces you to a variety of question types and their uses and misuses.

An interview, then, is an interactional communication process between two parties, at least one of whom has a predetermined and serious purpose, that involves the asking and answering of questions.

With this definition as a guide, determine which of the following interactions constitutes an interview and which does not.

Exercise #1—What Is and Is Not an Interview?

1. A professor is asking students in her class about the practical applications of games in economics.

2. A volleyball player is meeting with two surgeons about her torn ACL.

3. A reporter is speaking with an eyewitness to a drive-by shooting.

4. Two members of a law firm are discussing how to handle an intellectual properties case.

5. A committee of teachers is reviewing the School Board's proposal for mandatory student-teacher evaluations of all classes, grades one to twelve.

6. A student is talking to his academic counselor about a grade.

7. A car salesperson is discussing a hybrid model with a husband and wife.

8. An associate runs into his supervisor in the hallway and remembers to ask about getting off early on Friday for a family gathering.

9. A member of a survey research team is making calls to registered voters to learn their attitudes toward a "right to work" law being proposed by the governor.

10. A college recruiter is meeting with a family about a football scholarship for Jack.

Traditional Forms of Interviewing

Our definition of interviewing encompasses a wide variety of interview types, many of which require specialized training and specific abilities. Nearly 30 years ago, Charles Redding, a professor at Purdue University, developed a situational schema of traditional forms of interviewing according to their functions. Let's use Redding's schema as a way of introducing the many types and uses of interviewing, both formal and informal.

Information-Giving Interviews

When two parties take part in orienting, training, coaching, instructing, and briefing sessions, they are involved in information-giving interviews, the primary purpose of which is to exchange information as accurately, effectively, and efficiently as possible. Information-giving interviews may seem simple when compared to others—merely transferring facts, data, reports, and opinions from one party to another, but they are deceptively difficult. Because this type is so common and critical in health care interviews, Chapter 12 will discuss the principles, problems, and techniques of information giving.

> **Information giving is common but difficult.**

Information-Gathering Interviews

When two parties take part in surveys, exit interviews, research sessions, investigations, diagnostic sessions, journalistic interviews, and brief requests for information, the interviewer's primary purpose is to gather accurate, insightful, and useful information through the skillful use of questions, many created and phrased carefully prior to the interview and others created on the spot to probe carefully into interviewee responses, attitudes, and feelings. Chapter 5 discusses the principles and practices of moderately structured informational interviews such as journalistic interviews and investigations.

> **Information gathering is pervasive in our world.**

Chapter 6 introduces you to the principles and practices of highly structured surveys and polls. And Chapter 12 discusses information gathering in the health care setting.

Focus Group Interviews

Focus group interviews, usually consisting of eight to twelve *similar interviewees* and a single interviewer, are designed to focus on a specific issue guided by a set of carefully selected questions. The interactions among interviewees generate a range of information and opinions different from a single interviewee.[4] Melinda Lewis writes that the focus group interview "taps into human tendencies where attitudes and perceptions are developed through interaction with other people."[5]

Selection Interviews

The most common form of the selection interview takes place between a recruiter attempting to select the best qualified applicant for a position in an organization and an applicant attempting to attain this position. Another form, the placement interview, occurs when an interviewer is trying to determine the ideal placement of a staff member already a part of the organization. This interview may involve a promotion, a restructuring of an organization, or a reassignment such as from sales to management. Because the selection or employment interview plays such a major role in all of our personal and professional lives, we will focus in detail on the recruiter in Chapter 7 and the applicant in Chapter 8.

> Selection is critical in the lives of people and organizations.

Performance Review

When two parties focus on the interviewee's skills, performance, abilities, or behavior, they take part in scheduled or nonscheduled performance reviews (what once were referred to commonly as the annual or semiannual appraisal interview). The emphasis is on coaching a student, employee, or team member to continue that which is good and to set goals for future performance. Chapter 9 focuses on models for conducting performance reviews and the principles essential for the performance problem interview.

> Performance review is essential to employee and employer.

Counseling

If an interviewee has a personal or professional problem, the parties may take part in a counseling interview in which the interviewer strives to help the interviewee attain insights into a problem and possible ways of dealing with this problem. Chapter 11 addresses the principles and practices of conducting and taking part in counseling interviews.

Persuasion

The persuasive interview occurs when one party attempts to alter or reinforce the thinking, feeling, or acting of another party. The sales interview comes immediately to mind, in which one person is trying to sell a product or service to another person. We are involved in one-on-one persuasive interactions on a daily basis. The persuasive interview may be as informal as one friend trying to persuade another friend to attend a concert or as formal as a developer trying to persuade a couple to purchase a lake home. Chapter 10 addresses the highly complex nature of the persuasive interview.

> Persuasion is more than selling a product or service.

Technology and Interviewing

Technological developments, beginning with the telephone in 1876 and exploding in the twentieth and twenty-first centuries with electronic media and the Internet, have altered how we conduct and take part in interviews. Parties no longer have to be in the physical presence of one another in a face-to-face encounter but may be ear-to-ear, keyboard-to-keyboard, or screen-to-screen.

The Telephone Interview

Telephone interviews have become so commonplace and irritating that many states and the federal government created "Don't Call" lists to protect our privacy and sanity. Organizations have turned to the telephone to conduct initial employment screening interviews, fund-raising campaigns, and opinion polls to save time, reduce monetary expenses, and eliminate the time necessary to send staff to numerous locations. They use conference calls to enable several members of an organization to ask questions and hear replies from staff and clients in multiple locations scattered over a wide geographical area. Interviewers and interviewees can talk to several people at one time, answer or clarify questions directly, be heard while responding, and receive immediate feedback.

> The telephone interview is convenient and inexpensive.

A major problem with telephone interviews is the lack of "presence" of parties. Hearing a voice is not the same as being able to observe an interviewer's or interviewee's appearance, dress, manner, eye contact, face, gestures, and posture. Some studies comparing telephone and face-to-face interviews suggest that the two methods produce similar communicative results, with respondents giving fewer socially acceptable answers over the telephone and preferring the anonymity it provides.[6] Other studies urge caution in turning too quickly to the telephone. One study found that interviewers do not like telephone interviews, and this attitude may affect how interviewees reply. Another study discovered that fewer interviewees (particularly older ones) prefer the telephone, and this may lower degree of cooperation.[7] People may feel uneasy about discussing sensitive issues with strangers they cannot see, and it is difficult to make convincing confidentiality guarantees when not face-to-face. On the other hand, interviewees such as job applicants may take the telephone interview, what one source refers to as the "fuzzy slipper" interview, less seriously than a face-to-face interview, perhaps not as an interview at all.[8] These attitudes may lead to casual dress, speaking manner, and choice of words, including slang and vocal fillers such as "you know," "know what I mean," and "you betcha."

The widespread use of the cell phone has created a new world of "talking," and we assume some listening, that seemingly takes place everywhere, from dorm rooms, kitchens, and backyards to restrooms, parks, and classrooms. When we walk through our campuses at 7:00 in the morning and see, and hear, students on their cell phones, we wonder whom they are talking to so early in the morning. Only one in ten households now rely solely on a landline phone, and the young and single are the largest group to abandon landlines altogether. Be cautious in relying only on cell phones for conducting and taking part in interviews because they are subject to dropped calls, spotty service, and dead batteries, non-factors with landlines.[9]

The growing sophistication of two-way video technology may reduce the problems and concerns caused by critical nonverbal cues missing from the telephone interview. Cell phone technology that allows parties to send visual images of one another while they are talking is an important development. Tiny headshots, of course, are far from the presence of face-to-face interviews, but they are a step forward in the electronic interview process.

Not many years ago, we would seek the privacy of a telephone booth when making a personal or business call and take precautions that would prevent us from being overheard. Times have changed, and today there is a growing concern for the **privacy** not only of the interview parties but of those who cannot avoid being part of the interviewing process. Cell phone users, apparently feeling they must talk loud enough for all of us within 75 feet to hear, shout to the person on the other end. You can go to any restaurant, lounge area, or airport boarding area today and hear complete conversations that otherwise would be held behind closed doors to ensure confidentiality. We have heard executives discussing mergers, profit margins, and personnel changes; patients discussing their diagnoses and prescriptions with medical practitioners; and students requesting help with assignments, grade adjustments, and personal problems.

There are ways to avoid irritating the 81 percent of adults in the United States who are bothered by cell phone use in public places.[10] Suggestions include speaking quietly, keeping calls brief, turning away from others, finding a more appropriate location such as a booth, or taking calls without a central focus such as stores or sidewalks. Taking calls in theaters, churches, classrooms, restaurants, and crowded waiting areas such as airports are most irritating.

The Videoconference

Videoconference technology, including the use of Skype, enables interview parties to interact visually over long distances, point-to-point or multiple points, faster, and with less expense. For instance, physicians in New Jersey are using "telepsychiatry" to treat patients more quickly and to counter the national shortage of psychiatrists, particularly child psychiatrists.[11] Although this technology would seem to be as good as "being there in person," there are significant differences from face-to-face interviews.

Since visual cues are limited to the top half or faces of participants, or group shots in the case of multiple-person interview parties, there are fewer nonverbal cues. One result is fewer interruptions that lead to longer and fewer turns by participants. It is more difficult to interact freely and naturally with people on a screen. Perhaps this is why participants provide more negative evaluations of others in the interview who appear to dominate the process. One study showed that interviewers liked the videoconference because they could "unobtrusively take more notes, check their watches, or refer to resumes without disrupting the flow of the interview" or, perhaps, being noticed by the other party. On the other hand, they had trouble "reading nonverbal behaviors such as facial expression, eye contact, and fidgeting" and telling "whether a pause was due to the technology, or the applicant being stumped." Although a significant majority of interviewers (88%) indicated a willingness to use videoconferencing for interviews, a significant majority (76%) said they preferred face-to-face interviews.[12]

> **Both parties must focus attention on the interaction.**

Interviewees in teleconference interviews should be aware of the length of their answers to enhance turn-taking and avoid the appearance of trying to dominate the interview. They, too, can check their lists of questions, take notes, and watch their time without being noticed. Above all, interviewees should be aware of the importance of upper-body movement, gestures, eye contact, and facial expressions that will attract favorable and unfavorable attention. With technology, there is no traditional handshake and the interviewee is alone in a room, factors that may generate tension for some. Follow these suggestions for a more effective and enjoyable interview: speak up so you can be heard easily, dress conservatively in solid colors, look at the camera full-face, limit movements, try to forget about the camera, expect some lag time between questions and responses.[13] One study indicated that applicants in recruiting interviews were more satisfied with their performance in face-to-face interviews when the interviews were less structured and more satisfied with their performance in videoconference interviews when the interviews were highly structured.[14] Since questions in highly structured interviews tend to require shorter answers, interviewees may feel less pressured to determine length and content of answers and turn-taking.

E-Mail

> The Internet lacks the nonverbal cues critical in interviews.

With the introduction of the Internet, many interviews went from face-to-face and ear-to-ear to finger-to-finger. It enabled large numbers of people to make inquiries, send and receive information, and discuss problems at any time of the day or night and nearly anywhere in the world. But are these interactions electronic mail rather than interviews? If two parties use the Internet to interact in real time so it is truly an interaction, it meets our definition of an interview. Small video cameras mounted on computers that send live pictures and sound between interview parties make electronic interactions superior to the telephone and ever closer to the face-to-face interview. One obstacle to overcome is the reluctance of parties to type lengthy answers to questions that they can provide easily in person or over the telephone. The Internet's potential seems unlimited and, as it becomes more visually interactive, it will take on more of the properties of the traditional interview in which both parties not only ask and answer questions but also communicate nonverbally.

Although much emphasis has centered on using e-mail in the employment selection process, the e-mail interview is gaining use in other fields. For instance, physicians are finding the Internet efficient, timely, and effective when interacting with patients; it is a modern-day e-house call.[15] The American Medical Association recently issued guidelines for physician-patient

Mike Harrington/Getty Images

■ *The Internet can provide important information on positions and organizations and background on interviewers and interviewees.*

electronic communications, warning that technology must not replace face-to-face inter-actions with patients. To ensure privacy and security, some physicians are using voice recognition software.

Studies have focused on the use of e-mail in conducting sophisticated research inter-views. The authors indicate that disadvantages such as difficulty in opening interviews (frequent false starts), establishing rapport with interviewees, determining emotional reactions, and translating unusual symbols and acronyms interviewees may use are out-weighed by reduced cost and time, wider geographical and individual diversity, enhanced self-disclosure due to a greater degree of anonymity, elimination of interviewer interrup-tions, ease of probing into answers, ease of transcription of responses, and streamlined data analysis.[16] One researcher concluded, "While a mixed mode interviewing strategy should always be considered when possible, semi-structured e-mail interviewing can be a viable alternative to the face-to-face and telephone interviews, especially when time, financial constraints, or geographical boundaries are barriers to an investigation."[17]

Webinars

So-called webinars are becoming popular for conferences, lectures, training sessions, seminars, and workshops.[18] When a webinar is conducted by a presenter to an audi-ence on the web, it is not an interview but a speech, lecture, or webcast. However, if a webinar becomes more collaborative with questions and answers over a telephone line or voice over technology and there are two distinct parties, it may be an interview. It is more spontaneous and in real time than an e-mail interview.

The Virtual Interview

The meaning of the term "virtual interview" varies according to the organization using it, but it refers most often to a selection interview, real or simulated, that involves some form of electronic means—computers, the Internet, or digital video.[19] Even though an interview may be simulated—make believe—interviewees must take these interviews seriously by paying careful attention to appearance and answering questions correctly, smoothly, and confidently.

Organizations are conducting virtual job fairs because they are cheaper and recruit-ers need not spend time traveling to locations around the country.[20] In the mode of the electronic game, interviewers and applicants may attend in the form of avatars.

ON THE WEB

Learn more about the growing uses of electronic interviews in a variety of settings. Search at least two databases under headings such as telephone inter-views, conference calls, and video talk-back. Try search engines such as ComAbstracts (http://www.cios.org), Yahoo (http://www.yahoo.com), Infoseek (http://www.infoseek.com), and ERIC (http://www.indiana.edu/~eric_rec). In which interview settings are electronic interviews most common? What are the advantages and disadvantages of electronic inter-views? How will new developments affect electronic interviews in the future? How will the growing use of electronic interviews affect the ways we conduct traditional face-to-face interviews?

Organizations report that applicants seem to relax when appearing in the form of an avatar, but they warn that applicants still need to know how to dress, act, and respond. Interviews are conducted in the form of instant-messaging chats.

Some organizations are using virtual job interviews in place of face-to-face interactions in the screening process that may involve hundreds of interviews. One source warns that in this age of the video game, virtual interviews may not be taken 100 percent seriously by one or both parties; it seems like a game instead of reality.[21] Some sources use an innovative "asynchronous" approach in which the interviewer need not be present in real time. One recommends this approach for marketing, sales, customer service, and other positions that require excellent communication and presentation skills and you need to see them.[22]

Wake Forest University has experimented with virtual admissions interviews in which applicants may sit in their living rooms with a webcam, microphone, and Internet and have a distant face-to-face interview with an admissions officer. An admissions officer reports that they can interview students who cannot travel to the Winston-Salem, North Carolina, campus, and "This allows us to have personal contact with every applicant. We can get a sense of who the applicant is beyond academic credentials. The interview helps decide if the student is a good fit for Wake Forest."[23] Applicants have responded positively, and Wake Forest plans to extend the virtual interview offer to a wider variety of prospective students.

The virtual interview most similar to gaming is being experimented with in the medical profession in which interviews can take place in simulated operating rooms and other selected venues. In one application of this software in London, "most students were positively surprised at the level of realism" achieved for "specific objects."[24] The emphasis at present is on the teaching possibilities of virtual interviews for training physicians and nurses.

Summary

Interviewing is an interactional communication process between two parties, at least one of whom has a predetermined and serious purpose, that involves the asking and answering of questions. This definition encompasses a wide variety of interview settings that require training, preparation, interpersonal skills, flexibility, and a willingness to face risks involved in intimate, person-to-person interactions. Interviewing is a learned skill and art, and perhaps the first hurdle to overcome is the assumption that we do it well because we do it so often. The increasing flexibility of technology is resulting in significant numbers of interviews no longer occurring face-to-face, and this is posing new challenges and concerns.

There is a vast difference between skilled and unskilled interviewers and interviewees, and the skilled ones know that practice makes perfect only if you know what you are practicing. Studies in health care, for example, have revealed that medical students, physicians, and nurses who do not receive formal training in interviewing patients actually become less effective interviewers over time, not more effective.

The first essential step in developing and improving interviewing skills is to understand the deceptively complex interviewing process and its many interacting variables. Chapter 2 explains and illustrates the interviewing process by developing a model step-by-step that contains all of the fundamental elements that interact in each interview.

Key Terms and Concepts

The online learning center for this text features FLASHCARDS and CROSSWORD PUZZLES for studying based on these terms and concepts.

Beliefs	Information-giving	Questions
Collaborative	interviews	Selection interview
Conversation	Interactional	Serious purpose
Counseling	Internet	Structure
Dyadic	Interpersonal	System
Electronic interviews	Meaning making	Technology
E-mail interviews	Motives	Telephone interview
Exchanging	Parties	Two-party process
Feelings	Performance review	Videoconference interview
Focus group interviews	Persuasion	Virtual interview
Information-gathering	Predetermined purpose	Webinar
interviews	Process	

An Interview for Review and Analysis

The New Ross Neighborhood Association was formed several years ago as the large university located next to it began to crowd the historic neighborhood and several large, older homes were converted into apartments for students. Its goal was to preserve the nature of the neighborhood and its traditional single-family dwellings. Over the years, the Association became inactive as some of its initial concerns were addressed and members who established the Association retired or moved to other cities. Joe and Carol Stansberry have become concerned about plans being floated by developers for high rise apartments that would loom over the homes at the edge of the neighborhood. They have decided to talk to residents in the area to discover what they know about the New Ross Neighborhood Association and their major concerns as residents.

As you read through this interaction, answer the following questions: Is this an interview or a small group discussion? How is this interaction similar to and different from a speech or social conversation? If this is, in fact, an interview, what traditional form does it take? What is the predetermined purpose of this interaction? What is the approximate ratio of listening and speaking between the parties, and how appropriate is it? When, if ever, do the principal roles of interviewer and interviewee switch from one party to the other? What makes this interaction a collaborative process? What roles do questions play?

1. **Joe:** Hi. I'm Joe Stansberry and this is my wife Carol. We live at 612 Eaton, about two blocks east of here.

2. **Carol:** We're members of the New Ross Neighborhood Association that was formed several years ago to preserve the nature of this neighborhood and its traditional single-family dwellings. Is this the Zimmer home?

3. **Ada:** Yes, it is; I'm Ada Zimmer. I didn't think the Ross Association existed anymore. Some of our older neighbors have mentioned it occasionally.

4. **Carol:** It has been very inactive for a number of years, and, along with some of our friends, we're talking to people about making it a more active voice for all of us in issues that affect all of us.

5. **Frank:** I'm Frank Zimmer. Did I hear something about the New Ross Neighborhood Association? That's a name from the past.

6. **Joe:** Hi Frank. I'm Joe and this is my wife Carol. Don't you have a daughter in gymnastics? I think we've seen you at meets.

7. **Frank:** Yes, we do. Our daughter Heather is now a level seven and competes with the Star City Gymnastics Club.

8. **Carol:** Our daughter Wendy is a level five with Star City. Unfortunately the Association is thought of in the past tense when we are facing a number of issues that affect us in the present.

9. **Ada:** What plans do you have for the Association?

10. **Frank:** We hope to restore the Association as an organized voice for all of us who live in the neighborhood. First, however, we thought it would be helpful to discover the concerns our neighbors have; and then, second, to think about what sort of Association we feel is best suited for us.

11. **Ada:** That makes sense. We're not joiners and generally do our own thing, but sometimes we don't have much clout as individuals.

12. **Joe:** That's exactly how we feel. If you were to identify the most important concern you have as residents of the Ross neighborhood, what would it be?

13. **Ada:** People allowing cars to park in their yards during home football and basketball games. It often leaves an unsightly mess?

14. **Frank:** Yeah, that irritates me too, but my major concern is the developers trying to build high-rise apartment buildings for students right up to our backyards. One developer proposes that that they would provide a parking lot for students two miles away. Fat chance students will park two miles from where they live.

15. **Carol:** Those are issues we hear a lot about. What other concerns do you have?

16. **Frank:** Parking is always a problem during the day when classes are in session. Loud music and parties tend to be limited to spring and fall.

17. **Ada:** Yeah, but the university recently announced a plan to go to trimesters in a couple of years, so parking and noise could be with us for much of the year.

18. **Joe:** What other concerns do you have?

19. **Ada:** Beer cans on our lawn.

20. **Frank:** I'm concerned with the growing number of absentee landlords who own homes in the area and are letting them deteriorate. Renters don't take care of the yards or clear sidewalks in the winter.

21. **Joe:** What would you like to see the New Ross Association become in the future?

22. **Frank:** I'd like for you to answer that question since you're members now and are talking to people in the Ross neighborhood.

23. **Ada:** Yeah, what are you guys thinking?

24. **Carol:** Well, first, we want to identify the problems that concern residents the most. Then, we would like to have a meeting at the high school for everyone interested in joining and strengthening the Association.

25. **Joe:** We don't feel that we as residents have much of a say in decisions that affect us directly, such as the high rises the university plans to build into the edges of the neighborhood.

26. **Frank:** That makes sense. Who would run the Association?

27. **Joe:** We have a constitution and bylaws that call for elections every two years with term limits for officers.

28. **Carol:** The New Ross Neighborhood Association is designed to involve everyone in neighborhood decisions and actions and avoid a few people dominating what we do.

29. **Ada:** That sounds good, and we are proud to live in this historical neighborhood.

30. **Carol:** It's been great having a chance to talk to you this evening. After we've gathered some information and input from residents, we hope to have a meeting at the high school to plan the future. Our e-mail address is nrossassoc@hood.org. If you would contact us with your e-mail address and telephone number, we will add you to our address list and contact you well in advance of our next meeting.

31. **Frank:** That sounds great. We look forward to hearing from you.

32. **Joe:** Thanks for talking to us this evening, and we hope your daughter has a good season.

33. **Ada:** Thanks. Have a good evening.

Student Activities

1. Keep a journal of interviews in which you take part during a week. How many were traditional, face-to-face interviews and how many were electronic? Which types tended to be traditional and which electronic? How were they similar and different? How did interactions vary? How did lack of presence, eye contact, appearance, facial expressions, and gestures appear to affect electronic interviews? How did you and the other parties try to compensate for this?

2. Make a list of what you consider to be essential characteristics of good interviews and then observe two interviews on television. How well did the interviewers and interviewees meet your criteria? What did they do best? What did they do poorly? How did the settings and situations seem to affect the interactions? If one or both parties were what we currently consider "celebrities," how did this factor appear to affect interactions, roles played, amount of time each asked and answered questions, and content of responses?

3. Select a person you know superficially (classmate, co-worker, member of a fitness club) who is willing to interview you and be interviewed by you. Take part in two seven-minute interviews and try to discover everything you can about the other party. Which topics were covered and which avoided? How did the phrasing of questions seem to affect answers? How did your relationship with the other party affect the

openness with which the two of you shared and revealed information? Did you ever switch the roles of interviewer and interviewee during an interview?

4. Take part in a traditional job fair and a virtual job fair on or near your campus. After you have taken part in each, list what you liked and disliked about each. What did the face-to-face encounter with a prospective employer offer that an electronic encounter could not? And what did the electronic encounter offer that a face-to-face encounter could not? If you played the role of avatar in a virtual job fair, how comfortable were you with this role? How did you prepare for each encounter? If the virtual job fair experience entailed simulated interviews, how did you react to these encounters?

Notes

1. John Stewart, ed., *Bridges Not Walls,* 11th ed. (New York: McGraw-Hill, 2012), p. 16.

2. Stewart, p. 20.

3. Michael T. Motley, "Communication as Interaction: A Reply to Beach and Bavelas," *Western Journal of Speech Communication* 54 (Fall 1990), pp. 613–623.

4. "Effective Interviewing: The Focus Group Interview," Virtual Interviewing Assistant, http://www2.ku/~coms/virtual_assistant/via/focus.html, accessed October 12, 2006; Program Development and Evaluation, *Focus Group Interviews, Quick Tips #5,* University of Wisconsin-Extension, Madison, WI, 2002; "Focus Group Approach to Needs Assessment," Iowa State University Extension, 2001, http://www.extension.iastate.edu/communities/tools/assess/focus.html, accessed December 2, 2008.

5. M. Lewis, "Focus Group Interviews in Qualitative Research: A Review of the Literature," *Action Research E-Reports,* 2 (2000). Available at http://www.fhs.usyd.edu.au/arow/arer/002.htm.

6. Theresa F. Rogers, "Interviews by Telephone and in Person: Quality of Responses and Field Performance," *Public Opinion Quarterly* 39 (1976), pp. 51–65; Stephen Kegeles, Clifton F. Frank, and John P. Kirscht, "Interviewing a National Sample by Long-Distance Telephone," *Public Opinion Quarterly* 33 (1969–1970), pp. 412–419.

7. Lawrence A. Jordan, Alfred C. Marcus, and Leo G. Reeder, "Response Style in Telephone and Household Interviewing," *Public Opinion Quarterly* 44 (1980), pp. 210–222; Peter V. Miller and Charles F. Cannell, "A Study of Experimental Techniques in Telephone Interviewing," *Public Opinion Quarterly* 46 (1982), pp. 250–269.

8. Martin E. Murphy, "The Interview Series: (1) Interviews Defined," The Jacobson Group, http://www.jacobsononline.com.

9. David J. Critchell, "Cell Phones vs. Landlines: The Surprising Truths," http://www.mainstreet.com/print/4130, accessed January 10, 2012.

10. Scott Campbell, "Perceptions of Mobile Phone Use in Public: The Roles of Individualism, Collectivism, and Focus of the Setting," *Communication Reports* 21 (2008), pp. 70–81.

11. "Videoconferencing," http://en.wikipedia.org/wiki/videoconferencing, accessed January 6, 2012; Lorraine Ash, "Doctors Turning to Telepsychiatry," Lafayette/West Lafayette, Indiana *Journal & Courier,* C6, 1 January 2012; "Skype," http://en.wikipedia.org/wiki/Skype, accessed January 6, 2012.

12. Derek S. Chapman and Patricia M. Rowe, "The Impact of Videoconference Technology, Interview Structure, and Interviewer Gender on Interviewer Evaluations in the Employment Interview: A Field Experiment," *Journal of Occupational and Organizational Psychology* (2001), p. 279–298.

13. Carole Martin, "Smile, You're on Camera," Interview Center, http://www.interview.monster.com/articles/video, accessed September 30, 2006.

14. Derek S. Chapman and Patricia M. Rowe, "The Influence of Video Conference Technology and Interview Structure on the Recruiting Function of the Employment Interview: A Field Experiment," *International Journal of Selection and Assessment* (September 2002), p. 185.

15. Susan Jenks, *Florida Today,* "Forget the Office, the Doctor Will 'e' You Now," Lafayette, Indiana *Journal & Courier,* January 6, 2009, pp. D1–2.

16. Kay A. Persichitte, Suzanne Young, and Donald D. Tharp, "Conducting Research on the Internet: Strategies for Electronic Interviewing," U.S. Department of Education, Educational Resources Information Center (ERIC), ED 409 860.

17. Lokman I. Meho, "E-Mail Interviewing in Qualitative Research: A Methodological Discussion," *Journal of the American Society for Information Science and Technology* 57(10) (2006), pp. 1284–1295.

18. "Web Conferencing," http://wikipedia.org/wiki/web/webconferencing, accessed January 6, 2012.

19. "Interview Preparation: The Virtual Interview," Western State College of Colorado Career Services, http://www.western.edu/career/Interview_virtual/Virtual_interview.htm, accessed December 11, 2008; "Virtual Interview," 3M Careers: Virtual Interview, http://solutions.3m.com/wps/portal/3M/en_US/Careers/Home/Students/VirtualInterview/, accessed December 16, 2008. "Virtual Interviews," http://www.premierhealthcareers.com/1/434/virtualinterviews.asp?printview=21, accessed January 21, 2012; "Virtual Interviews," North Carolina Resource Network, 2008, http://www.soicc.state.nv.us/soicc/planning/virtual.htm, accessed January 21, 2012.

20. Eric Chabrow, "Second Life: The Virtual Job Interview," posted June 20, 2007, http://blogs.cioinsight.com/parallax_view/content/workplace/second_life_the_virtual_job, accessed December 16, 2008.

21. "Virtual Interviews Less Serious?" http://blog.recruitv.com/2008/09/virtual-interviews-less-serious/, accessed December 16, 2008.

22. "Interview Connect: The Virtual Interview Management Solution," http://www.interviewconnect.com/, accessed December 15, 2008.

23. "Wake Forest University offers virtual interviews for admissions," Wake Forest University New Service, December 1, 2008, http://www.wfu.edu/news/release/2008.12.01.i.php, accessed December 11, 2008.

24. Bertalan Mesko, "Interview with Dr. James Kinross: Simulation in Second Life," *Medicine Meets Virtual Reality* 17, November 27, 2008, http://mmvr17.wordpress.com/2008/11/27/interview-with-dr-james-kinross-simulation-in . . . , accessed December 16, 2008.

Resources

Anderson, Rob, and G. Michael Killenberg. *Interviewing: Speaking, Listening, and Learning for Professional Life*. New York: Oxford University Press, 2008.

Gubrium, Jaber F., James A. Holstein, Amir B. Marvasti, and Karyn D. McKinney, eds. *The SAGE Handbook of Interview Research: The Complexity of the Craft*. Thousand Oaks, CA: Sage, 2012.

Holstein, James A., and Jaber F. Gubrium, eds. *Inside Interviewing: New Lenses, New Concerns*. Thousand Oaks, CA: Sage, 2003.

Martin, Judith N., and Thomas K. Nakayama. *Experiencing Intercultural Communication*. New York: McGraw-Hill, 2011.

Stewart, John. *Bridges Not Walls: A Book about Interpersonal Communication*. New York: McGraw-Hill, 2012.

Trenholm, Sarah, and Arthur Jensen. *Interpersonal Communication*. New York: Oxford University Press, 2013.

2 An Interpersonal Communication Process

The essential first step in developing and improving your interviewing skills is to broaden your understanding of the **deceptively complex interviewing process** and its many interrelated and interacting variables. You must appreciate the total process, not merely the questions and answers that are its most visible characteristics. **The goal of this chapter** is to develop step-by-step a summary model of the interview that explains and portrays the intricate and often puzzling interview process so that, by the time you reach Figure 2.8, you will anticipate and not be surprised by the complexity of the process portrayed.

> Interviewing is more than asking and answering questions.

Two Parties in the Interview

The two circles in Figure 2.1 represent the two parties in the interviewing process. Each is a unique product of culture, environment, education, training, and experiences. Each is a mixture of personality traits. A person may be optimistic or pessimistic, trusting or suspicious, flexible or inflexible, sociable or unsociable. Each adheres to specific beliefs, attitudes, and values and is motivated by an ever-changing variety of expectations, desires, needs, and interests. And each party communicates **intra-personally**, literally talks to oneself. What each says to oneself and how each says it influences verbal and nonverbal patterns and how each experiences the interview because "communication always involves identities or selves."[1] In a very real sense, the whole person speaks and the whole person listens in interactions we call interviews.[2]

> Each party consists of unique and complex individuals.

Although each party consists of unique individuals, both must collaborate to produce a successful interview. Neither party can **go it alone.** The overlapping circles in Figure 2.1 symbolize the relational nature of the interview process in which two parties do something **with, not to** one another. The parties are connected interpersonally because each has a stake in the outcome of the interview. Their relationship may commence with this interview or have a **relational history** that goes back hours, days, weeks, months, or years. Interactions between parties with no prior history may be difficult because neither party may know what to expect from the other, how to get the interaction started, when to speak and when to listen, and what information may and may not be shared. In some cultures, "all strangers are viewed as sources of potential relationships; in others, relationships develop only after long and careful scrutiny."[3] Stereotypes such as age, gender, race, and ethnicity may play significant negative roles in zero-history situations, particularly during the anxious opening minutes of an interaction.[4] On the other hand, negative expectations and attitudes may exist because previous interactions between the parties did not go well.

> Each interview contributes to a relational history.

Figure 2.1   *The interview parties*

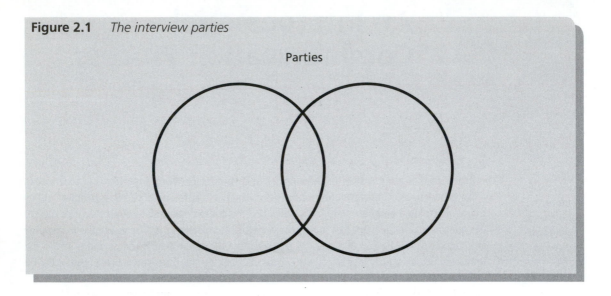

Parties

A relationship may be **intimate** with a close friend, **casual** with a co-worker, **distant** with a sales associate, **formal** with a college dean, or **functional** with a physician. This relationship may change over time or during an interaction. What may start out as a purely functional relationship may evolve into a close, personal friendship for a lifetime. John Stewart and Carole Logan write that "each time they communicate, relational partners construct and modify patterns that define who they are for and with each other."[5]

A situation may alter a relationship.

Your relationships change as situations change. For instance, you may have a pleasant, supportive relationship with a supervisor until this person gives you a less than favorable performance review. As a journalist you may have developed a friendly relationship with a politician that continues as you ask routine, easy-to-answer questions but deteriorates rapidly when the person becomes "rattled" when confronted with potentially embarrassing or controversial inquiries. Sarah Trenholm and Arthur Jensen claim that you must acquire **relational competence** to know "the parts you and your partner will play in the relationship," develop "workable rules and norms," and know "when to adapt and when not to."[6]

Relational Dimensions

All of your relationships are multidimensional, and five are critical to interviews: similarity, inclusion, affection, control, and trust.

Similarity

A few similarities do not equal relational peers.

Relationships are fostered when both parties share cultural norms and values, education, experiences, personality traits, beliefs, and expectations. You may find it easier to interact with people of the same gender or race, who share your political views, have the same academic major, and love classical music. Awareness of such similarities enables interview parties to understand one another and establish common ground—literally to expand the overlap of the circles until perceived similarities overcome perceived dissimilarities. Be cautious, however, because surface similarities such as age, dress, and ethnicity may be all that you have in common. Judith Martin and Thomas Nakayama write that "similarity is based not on whether people actually are similar but on the perceived (though not necessarily real) recognition or discovery of a similar trait."[7]

Inclusion

> **Wanting to take part leads to collaboration.**

Relationships are enhanced when both parties are motivated to take part actively as speakers and listeners, questioners, and respondents. The more you are involved and share, the more satisfied you will be with the relationship and look forward to future interactions. Degree of satisfaction may be apparent in each party's words, gestures, face, eyes, and actions. Effective relationships develop when interviewer and interviewee become interdependent, when "Each becomes aware that what" they do and not do "will have an impact on the other" and each begins to act with the other person in mind. Their behaviors are no longer individual actions but instead are what John Shotter calls "**joint actions.**"[8] Do not come to an interview with expectations that are either too high and unattainable or too low and unrewarding and unfulfilling.

Affection

> **We interact more freely with persons we like.**

Interview relationships are cultivated when the parties like and respect one another and there is a marked degree of warmth or friendship. Affection occurs when there is a "we" instead of a "me-you" feeling and you communicate in a way the other party finds pleasant, productive, and fair. It is important that both parties know whether feelings toward one another in an interview are likely to be positive, ambivalent, or negative. Signals of affection and hostility are inconsistent, however. In one study, parties lowered their loudness to express disliking as well as liking for one another. In others, decreased talk time seemed to indicate liking by showing greater attentiveness or disliking by exhibiting disengagement from the interaction.[9] Some of us find showing affection to be difficult, particularly in formal or public settings, and prefer to keep acquaintances and strangers at a safe distance.

You may come to an interview with an ambivalent or hostile attitude toward the other party, perhaps due to relational history or what James Honeycutt calls **relational memory.** He writes that "even though relationships are in constant motion, relationship memory structures provide a perceptual anchor [so that] individuals can determine where they are in a relationship."[10] Relational memory may aid parties in dealing with what researchers call **dialectical tensions** that result from conflicts between "important but opposing needs or desires," or "between opposing" or contrasting "'voices,' each expressing a different or contradictory impulse."[11] Kory Floyd writes that such dialectical tensions are not necessarily bad because "researchers believe" they are a "normal part of any close, interdependent relationship, and they become problematic only when people fail to manage them properly."[12]

Control

Because each party participates in a continuous process, each is responsible for its success or failure. John Stewart introduced the concept of "nexting" that he labels, "The most important single communication skill" because whenever "you face a communication challenge or problem, the most useful question you can ask yourself is, 'What can I help to happen next?'"[13] He claims that "since no one person determines all the outcomes of a communication event, you can help determine some outcomes, even if you feel almost powerless. Since no one person is 100 percent to blame or at fault, and all parties share response-ability, your next contribution can affect what's happening."[14]

Who controls what and when poses problems in interviews because interviews frequently involve organizational hierarchies or chains of command: president over vice president, professor over student, supervisor over intern. This **upward** and **downward** communication may encumber each party, perhaps in different ways. Edward Hall observes, "One's status in a social system also affects what must be attended. People at the top pay attention to different things from those in the middle or the bottom of the system."[15] What you look for and value as a student may be quite different from what a professor looks for and values.

Hierarchy may hinder the flow of information and self-disclosure.

Trust

Fisher and Brown claim that trust is the "single most important element of a good working relationship."[16] Trust is essential because potential outcomes affect each party directly—your income, your career, your purchase, your profits, your health, and your understanding. Relationships are cultivated when parties trust one another to be honest, sincere, reliable, truthful, fair, even-tempered, and of high ethical standards—in other words **safe.** William Gudykunst and Young Kim write, "When we trust others, we expect positive outcomes from our interactions with them; when we have anxiety about interacting with others, we fear negative outcomes from our interactions with them."[17]

Creating trust is a delicate process and may take months or years to develop with another party, but it can be destroyed in an instant if you feel betrayed by a friend, colleague, or co-worker.[18] "Trust provides a context in which interaction can be more honest, spontaneous, direct, and open."[19] Disclosure is critical to the success of interviews, and uninhibited disclosure requires trust. Unpredictable persons and outcomes lead to cautious questions and responses and sharing of information and attitudes—risk is too high. Unfortunately, trust is in a free fall in this country. A generation ago two-thirds of Americans said they trusted other persons; now two-thirds say they do not trust others. The result is that there is a greater effort to protect ourselves when communicating with other people.[20]

Trust is essential in every interview.

Global Relationships

Since your social, political, and work worlds will be increasingly global, you need to understand how relationships come about and are fostered in different countries and cultures. Martin, Nakayama, and Flores warn, for instance, that "in intercultural conflict situations, when we are experiencing high anxieties with unfamiliar behavior (for example, accents, gestures, facial expressions), we may automatically withhold trust."[21] "(Some anxiety already exists in the early stages of any relationship.) This anxiety stems from fears about possible negative consequences of our actions. We may be afraid that we will look stupid or will offend someone because we're unfamiliar with that person's language or culture."[22]

In the United States, we tend to have numerous friendly, informal relationships and place importance on how a person looks, particularly early in relationships.[23] We create and discard relationships frequently, while Australians make deeper and longer-lasting commitments. Arabs, like Americans, develop relationships quickly but, unlike Americans who dislike taking advantage of relationships by asking for favors, Arabs believe friends have a duty to help one another.

The Chinese develop strong, long-term relationships and, like Arabs, see them involving obligations.[24] In Mexico, trust in relationships develops slowly, is given sparingly, and must be earned. Betrayal of trust results in the greatest harm possible to a relationship.[25] Germans develop relationships slowly because they see them as very important, and using first names before a relationship is well-established is considered rude behavior. Japanese prefer not to interact with strangers, want background information on parties before establishing relationships, prefer doing business with people they have known for years, and take time establishing relationships.

> **Relationships develop differently in different cultures.**

Gender in Relationships

Researchers have generally concluded that men and women are more similar than different in their communication and relationships, and Kathryn Dindia argues that rather than men being from Mars and women from Venus, as a recent best-selling book proclaimed, an accurate metaphor is "Men are from North Dakota, and women are from South Dakota."[26] Brant Burleson and Adrienne Kunkel found, for instance, "substantial similarity—not difference—in the values both sexes place on supportive communication skills, such as comforting and listening."[27]

Regardless of similarities, however, gender differences of interview parties may be critical in establishing and refining relationships. Men's talk tends to be directive and goal-oriented with statements that "tend to press compliance, agreement, or belief." Women's talk may be more polite and expressive, containing less intense words, qualifiers (perhaps, maybe), and disclaimers ("Maybe I'm wrong but . . ." "I may not fully understand the situation, but . . .").[28] Women, for instance, use communication as a primary way of establishing relationships, while men communicate "to exert control, preserve independence, and enhance status."[29] Women give more praise and compliments and are reluctant to criticize directly in the workplace while men remain silent when a co-worker is doing something well and take criticism straight.[30] Researchers have discovered that women report "greater satisfaction with their interactions than do men.[31] On the other hand, researchers have found that "women are more likely to betray and be betrayed by other women." Men report they are more often betrayed by other men with whom they are competing.[32] Each of these differences may impact the critical interview relationship.

> **Gender differences have evolved but not disappeared.**

Interchanging Roles during Interviews

While one party may control an interview, both speak and listen from time to time, ask and answer questions, and take on the roles of interviewer and interviewee. Neither party can sit back and expect the other to make the interview a success single-handedly. John Stewart writes that "human communicators are always sending and receiving simultaneously. As a result, each communicator has the opportunity to change how things are going at any time in the process."[33] The small circles within the party circles in Figure 2.2 portray the interchange of roles in interviews.

> **A single party cannot make an interview a success but can ensure its failure.**

Figure 2.2   *The switching of roles*

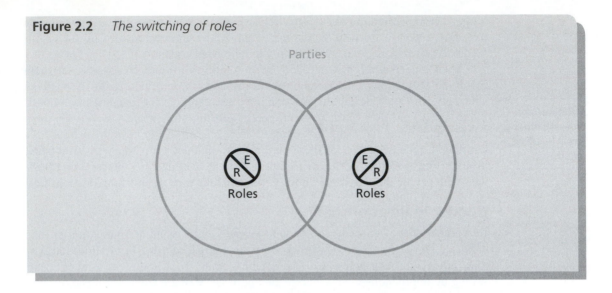

The degree to which roles are exchanged and control is shared is often affected by the status or expertise of the parties, who initiated the interview, type of interview, situation, and atmosphere of the interaction—supportive or defensive, friendly or hostile. These factors determine which of two fundamental approaches an interviewer selects—**directive** or **nondirective.**

> **A directive approach allows the interviewer to maintain control.**

Directive Approach

In a directive approach, the **interviewer** establishes the purpose of the interview and attempts to control the pacing, climate, and formality of the interview. Questions are likely to be closed with brief, direct answers. Although an aggressive interviewee may assume some control as the interview progresses, the interviewer intends to control the interview. Typical directive interviews are information giving, surveys and opinion polls, employee recruiting, and persuasive interviews such as sales. The directive approach is easy to learn, takes less time, enables you to maintain control, and is easy to replicate.

The following exchange illustrates a directive interviewing approach:

1. **Interviewer:** Did you vote in today's election?
2. **Interviewee:** Yes, I did.
3. **Interviewer:** Did you vote for or against the school referendum?
4. **Interviewee:** I voted for it.
5. **Interviewer:** What was the primary reason for your vote?
6. **Interviewee:** I believe it is critical to maintain the quality of our schools.

Nondirective Approach

In a nondirective approach, the **interviewee** has significant control over subject matter, length of answers, interview climate, and formality. Questions are likely to be open-ended and neutral to give the interviewee maximum opportunity and freedom to respond. Typical nondirective interviews are journalistic, oral history, investigations, counseling, and performance review. The nondirective approach allows for greater flexibility and adaptability, encourages probing questions, and invites the interviewee to volunteer information.

> **A nondirective approach enables the interviewee to share control.**

The following is a nondirective interview exchange:

1. **Interviewer:** I understand that you just returned from Haiti. Where did you go in Haiti?

2. **Interviewee:** We flew to Port-au-Prince and stayed over-night in a facility designed as a way station for missionaries. The next morning we drove for nearly three hours up in the mountains to our sister parish in Boudain. From there we visited a number of medical clinics in the area.

3. **Interviewer:** What did you do?

4. **Interviewee:** I checked in patients, helped to distribute a variety of medicines, and sterilized instruments for the physicians who went with us.

5. **Interviewer:** What were your impressions?

6. **Interviewee:** The poverty everywhere is almost overwhelming, but the people are amazingly happy and friendly. They were so appreciative of the little things we could do. I saw children walking miles without shoes to get to school.

Combination of Approaches

> **Be flexible and adaptable when selecting approaches.**

You may select a combination of directive and nondirective approaches. For instance, as a recruiter, you may use a nondirective approach at the start of an interview to relax an applicant, then switch to a directive approach when giving information about the organization and position, and return to a nondirective approach when answering the applicant's questions.

> **The roles we play should guide but not dictate approaches.**

Be flexible in choosing the most appropriate approach. Often the choice of interviewing approach is governed by societal or organizational rules and expectations. For instance, an employee, applicant, client, or patient "enters an interview expecting that the interviewer will direct and influence one's conversational behaviors much more extensively than one will influence the interviewer's behavior. You both make it happen that way."[34] Adherence to societal roles and expectations may produce an ineffective interview.

Perceptions of Interviewer and Interviewee

> **Four perceptions drive our interactions.**

Each party comes to an interview with perceptions of self and of the other party, and these perceptions may change positively or negatively as the interview progresses. Our relationships are largely due to these perceptions and determine how we communicate. Four critical perceptions are portrayed by the double-ended arrows in Figure 2.3.

Perceptions of Self

Our self-perception—**self-concept**—emerges from our experiences, activities, attitudes, accomplishments and failures, interactions, and the superior and subordinate

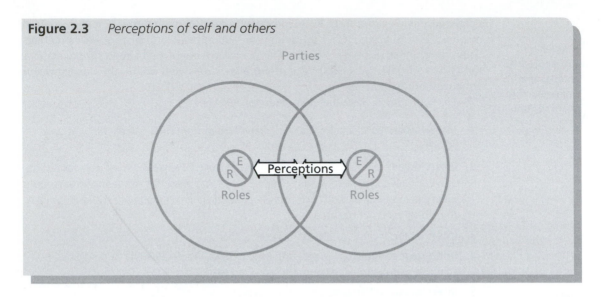

Figure 2.3   *Perceptions of self and others*

roles we play. It is "a demanding and assertive personal view of who we are and how we want to be seen and taken, of the kind of person we feel ourselves to be or the kind of person we think we *ought* to be."[35] Our self-concept is a mutual creation of interpretations—how we interpret and think others interpret who we have been, are, and will be. It's through these interpretations that we create a **self-identity**. John Stewart writes that we "come to each encounter with an identifiable 'self,' built through past interactions, and *as we talk,* we adapt ourselves to fit the topic we're discussing and the people we are talking with, and we are changed by what happens to us as we communicate."[36]

> **What we perceive ourselves to be may be more important than what we are.**

Our self-concept and self-identity are affected by the expectations family, society, professions, and organizations place upon us. We may experience different self-concepts as we move from one situation or role to another.

Self-esteem—how we perceive our self-worth—is a critical element of self-concept and self-identity. Theorists claim that we exert a great deal of mental and communicative energy attempting to gain and maintain recognition and approval from family members, friends, peers, and others because we have a "persistent and compelling" need to give an accounting of ourselves.[37] If we feel respected and taken seriously—have high self-esteem—we may be more perceptive, confident, and likely to express attitudes and ideas that are unpopular. On the other hand if we see ourselves to be of little value or significance—have low self-esteem—we may be so self-critical that we cannot interpret accurately the behavior and communication of others. Our self-esteem may determine the

> **Self-esteem is closely related to self-worth.**

success or failure of an interview or whether an interview takes place at all. We may succeed or fail because we convince ourselves that we will—a **self-fulfilling prophecy** that influences messages sent and received, risks taken, confidence, and self-disclosure.

Culture and Gender Differences

Self-concept, self-identity, and self-esteem are central in American and Western cultures because they emphasize the individual. They are not central in Eastern cultures and South American countries. Japanese, Chinese, and Indians, for example, are collectivist rather than individualist cultures and are more concerned with the image, esteem, and achievement of the group. Attributing successful negotiations to an individual in China would be considered egotistical, self-advancing, and disrespectful. Success is attributed to the group or team. Failure to appreciate cultural differences causes many communication problems for American interviewers and interviewees.

Many citizens of the global village are less concerned with self than with group.

Kory Floyd reminds us that gender matters in self-concept because "gender roles are socially constructed ideas about how women and men should think and behave."[38] Men are expected to be more assertive, in charge, and self-sufficient while women are taught to be "feminine," submissive, and to show empathy and emotional expressiveness. Not all men and women act this way, of course, but we cannot ignore the role of society on gender and self-concept and its potential impact on an interview.

Perceptions of the Other Party

How you perceive the other affects how you approach an interview and how you react during the interview. For instance, you may be in awe of the other's reputation or position—a leading journalist, the CEO of your company, a surgeon. Previous encounters with a party may lead you to look forward to or dread an interview. Your **perceptions** may be influenced by the other's age, gender, race, ethnic group, size, and physical attractiveness—particularly if the person differs significantly from you. A positive endorsement of a third party may alter the way you perceive a person. If you are flexible and adaptable, perceptions of the other party may change as an interview progresses by how the interview begins; the other party's manner, attitudes, dress, and appearance; listening and feedback; verbal and nonverbal interactions; questions and answers; and how the interview ends. Warmth, understanding, and cooperation on the part of both parties can enhance perceptions of each.

Perceptions are a two-way process.

Allow interactions to alter or reinforce perceptions.

Communication Interactions

The curved arrows in Figure 2.4 that link the two parties symbolize the communication levels of verbal and nonverbal interactions that occur during interviews. The three levels differ in relational distance, self-disclosure, risk encountered, perceived meanings, and amount and type of content exchanged.

Levels of Interactions

Level 1 interactions are relatively safe, nonthreatening exchanges about such topics as hometowns, professions, sporting events, college courses, and families. They generate safe, socially acceptable, comfortable, and ambiguous answers such as "Pretty good," "Not bad," and "Can't complain" that do not reveal judgments, attitudes, or feelings.

Level 1 interactions avoid judgments, attitudes, and feelings.

Each level is a metaphorical door, with the door being slightly open in Level 1 interactions. General ideas, surface feelings, and simple information pass through, but either party may close the door quickly and safely if necessary. The thickness of the arrow indicates that Level 1 communication exchanges are most common in interviews, and the length of the arrow symbolizes **relational distance.** Level 1 interactions dominate interviews in which there is no relational history, trust, the issue is controversial, or

Level 1 interactions are safe and superficial.

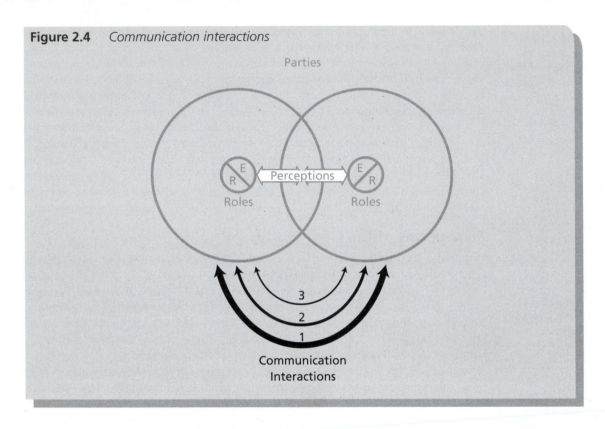

Figure 2.4 *Communication interactions*

the role relationship is between high-status and low-status parties. The following inter-action is a typical Level 1 communication:

1. **Interviewer:** How do you feel about the early retirement packages being offered to senior staff?

2. **Interviewee:** They seem to be attractive to some senior staff interested in retiring earlier than planned.

3. **Interviewer:** And what about you?

4. **Interviewee:** I'm looking them over.

Level 2 interactions deal with personal or controversial topics and probe into beliefs, attitudes, values, and positions. Responses tend to be half-safe, half-revealing as parties seek to cooperate without revealing too much. The metaphorical door is half open (the optimist's view) or half closed (the pessimist's view) as more specific and revealing ideas, feelings, and information pass through. Though willing to take more risk, parties retain the option to close the door quickly. The thickness of the arrow signifies that Level 2 interactions are less common than Level 1, and the length of the arrow indicates that a closer relationship between parties is necessary to move from

> Level 2 interac-tions require trust and risk-taking.

superficial to more revealing exchanges. This interaction is a typical Level 2 communication. The parties, though cautious, are more specific and revealing.

1. **Interviewer:** How do you feel about the early retirement packages being offered senior staff?
2. **Interviewee:** It may help to reduce the personnel budget, but I am concerned about losing some of our key people.
3. **Interviewer:** I appreciate your concern. And how do you feel about these packages?
4. **Interviewee:** I know we must reduce our personnel budget, but I'm not sure I'm ready for early retirement.

> Level 3 interactions involve full disclosure.

Level 3 interactions deal with more personal and controversial areas of inquiry. Respondents fully disclose their feelings, beliefs, attitudes, and perceptions. Little is withheld, and sometimes questioners get more than they bargained for. The metaphorical door is wide open. Risks and benefits are considerable for both parties. The thin, short arrow indicates that Level 3 interactions are uncommon, particularly in initial contacts, and the relationship between parties must be trusting with a sharing of control. This exchange illustrates a Level 3 interaction.

> A positive relationship is essential for Level 3 interactions.

1. **Interviewer:** How do you feel about the early retirement packages I developed to reduce expensive senior staff positions?
2. **Interviewee:** I can understand the motivation for developing these retirement incentives, but I believe it is short-sighted because losing key senior staff may have significant long-term consequences.
3. **Interviewer:** I can see how you as a senior staff member could feel that way, but we need to bring in new blood to energize this company.
4. **Interviewee:** I felt that way years ago and even resented what some derisively called "gray beards" because they were considerably older than us. Over the years, however, I've come to realize how much I gained from their experiences and their mentorship.

Self-Disclosure

> We are on the line in many interview settings.

In most interviews, you must move beyond Level 1 to Level 2 to Level 3 to obtain information, detect feelings, discover insights, and attain commitments. This requires varying degrees of **self-disclosure**, and this may not be easy to do. Unlike being a member of a group or audience into which you can blend or hide, the interview often places your social, professional, financial, psychological, or physical welfare on the line. Interviews deal with *your* behavior, *your* performance, *your* reputation, *your* decisions, *your* weaknesses, *your* feelings, *your* money, or *your* future. David Johnson writes:

> Yet self-disclosure does carry a degree of risk. For just as knowing you better is likely to result in a closer relationship, sometimes it could result in people liking you less. To build a meaningful relationship you have to disclose yourself to the other person and take the risk that the other person may reject rather than like you.[39]

Because of the risks of self-disclosure, communication theorists have offered suggestions for reducing risk. Be aware of the nature of your relationship with the other party, begin with a safe level of disclosure, be sure disclosure is relevant and appropriate, be sensitive to the effect your disclosure will have on the other party and persons not involved in the interview, continue to disclose at a level at which the other party reciprocates.[40] We tend to have fewer inhibitions when interacting online and may disclose too much information, what some refer to as "hyperpersonal" revelations, and this information may come earlier ("fast-tracked") in online interactions.[41] We have experienced people using antagonistic words and making accusations online they would never make face-to-face or on the telephone.

Women disclose more freely than men.

Gender

Generally speaking women disclose more than men and, except for anger, are allowed to express emotions (fear, sadness, sympathy) more than men. Because women are perceived to be better listeners and more responsive than men, disclosure is often highest between woman-to-woman parties (perhaps because talk is at the very heart of women's relationships), about equal in woman-to-man parties, and lowest among man-to-man parties.[42]

Culture

Culture may determine what is disclosed to whom and how. For example, Americans of European descent may disclose a wider range of topics, including personal information, than Japanese and Chinese, disclose more about their careers and less about their families than Ghanians, and disclose to more different types of people than Asians. Asians disclose more to those with expertise and ability to exhibit honest and positive attitudes than to those who like to talk and show more emotional feelings. Research suggests that people in high-context, collectivist cultures, such as Japan and China, in which they are expected to work for the good of the group and to know and follow cultural norms, disclose less than those in low-context, individualist cultures, such as the United States and Great Britain, in which they strive to succeed as individuals and cultural norms are less well known and more flexible. Conflict may result if we overdisclose, underdisclose, or disclose to the wrong person in differing cultures. Regardless of culture, however, important ingredients determine degree of self-disclosure, including perceived similarity, competence, involvement, and self-disclosures that may take the relationship to a higher level.[43]

Culture may dictate what we disclose and to whom.

While cultures vary in how, when, and to whom self-disclosure is appropriate, some theorists claim that the notion of politeness—maintaining positive rather than negative face—is universal. According to **"politeness theory,"** all humans want to be appreciated and protected. Littlejohn writes:

Positive and negative face are universal motives.

> *Positive face* is the desire to be appreciated and approved, to be liked and honored, and *positive politeness* is designed to meet these desires. Showing concern, complimenting, and using respectful forms of address are examples. *Negative face* is the desire to be free from imposition or intrusion, and *negative politeness* is designed to protect the other person when negative face needs are threatened. Acknowledging the imposition when making a request is a common example.[44]

You encounter situations in which politeness is essential not only when dealing with persons from other cultures but whenever you are involved in challenging, complaining, evaluating, disciplining, advising, and counseling. Guerrero, Andersen, and Afifi write that "people face a constant struggle between wanting to do whatever they want (which satisfies their negative face needs) and wanting to do what makes them look good to others (which satisfies their positive face needs)."[45] They identify several severe "face threatening acts," such as behavior that violates an important cultural, social, or professional rule; behavior that produces significant harm; behavior for which the party is directly responsible; and the more power or authority the other party has over the offending party. The desire to be polite—to avoid hurting or upsetting another and to show appreciation, understanding, or agreement—is one of the most common causes of deception.[46] A misleading statement or answer may seem warranted to sustain politeness and harmony in an interview.

Verbal Interactions

Interactions in interviews involve intricate and inseparable combinations of verbal and nonverbal symbols, some intentional and some not. We will separate them for instructional purposes only.

> **Never assume communication is taking place.**

Verbal interactions, words, are merely arbitrary connections of letters that serve as symbols for people, things, events, ideas, beliefs, and feelings. Their imperfect nature is experienced every day in misunderstandings, confusions, embarrassments, antagonisms, and hurt feelings over what seem to be common and neutral words. Perhaps *the greatest single problem with human communication is the assumption of it,* and the use and misuse of words cause many problems in interviews. Journalism professor Michael Skube writes about the lack of familiarity many college students have with what are *assumed* to be commonly understood words, including impetus, lucid, advocate, derelict, and brevity.[47]

What if we all used words "properly"? Would this end our misunderstandings? The answer is "no" because it's the arbitrary nature of language and not misuse that causes most problems.

Multiple Meanings

> **A word rarely has a single meaning.**

Words have many meanings. Those for *argue* range from giving reasons or evidence to disagreeing in words and persuading. *Game* may refer to a basketball game, a wild animal, or a person willing to try new things. To *reveal* may mean to tell, disclose, make known through divine inspiration, or violate a confidence.

Ambiguities

Words may be so ambiguous that two parties may assign different meanings to them. What are a "nice" apartment, an "affordable" education, a "simple" set of instructions, a "small" college, and a "living" wage? When is a person "middle-aged"? How do you know that something is "one of the best" or "one of the rarest"?

Sound Alikes

> **Beware of words that sound alike.**

Similar sounding words may cause confusion in interviews because you usually hear rather than see words. Examples are see and sea, do and due, sail and sale, and to, too, and two. Pronunciation or enunciation may add to this problem. A banker in Los Angeles related an incident in which she was talking to a banking associate in Chicago and thought she heard the other say, "We're axing John." The associate had meant "asking John," not firing him.

Connotations

> Words are rarely neutral.

Words have positive and negative connotations. Is a suit "inexpensive" or "cheap," a car "used" or "preowned," the purchase of a computer a "cost" or an "investment." Persuasion may mean to inspire or to contrive; execution may mean to perform or to hang.

Jargon

Parties may cause problems by altering or creating words. Every profession has its specialized jargon: "vehicular control devices" are stoplights, "spin doctoring" is explaining or defending issues, a hammer in the military is a "manually powered fastener-driving impact device." Use the simplest, clearest, most appropriate words in each interview.

Slang

> Slang comes and goes and often determines who's in and who's out.

Each generation has an unofficial jargon called *slang*. Fast, powerful cars went from "keen" in the 1940s and 1950s, to "cool," and "far out" in the 1960s and 1970s, to "decent," and "mean" in the 1980s, to "awesome," in the 1990s. Today cars are "hot."

Euphemisms

A euphemism is a substitution of a better-sounding word for a common word. You are likely to purchase a lifelike Christmas tree rather than an artificial one, inquire about the location of the powder room rather than the toilet, purchase an appliance from an associate rather than a clerk, and experience discomfort rather than pain from an invasive procedure rather than surgery.

Naming

> Naming is an effort to alter social reality.

You may label a person, place, or thing to alter how you and the other party **see reality**. You may purchase a diet cola but not a diet beer, experience a downturn rather than a recession, and order a quarter-pound hamburger but not a four-ounce hamburger. When substituting woman for girl, or firefighter for fireman, you are not being "politically" correct but are addressing the reality that men and women perform professional roles, not girls and boys. Words matter.

Power Words

> Words may be powerful or not.

There are power and powerless speech forms.[48] Power forms include certainty, challenges, orders, leading questions, metaphors, and memorable phrases such as "Read my lips!" "Make my day!" "Take your best shot!" and "Get a life!" Powerless forms include apologies, disclaimers, excuses, indirect questions, nonfluencies such as "Uh" and "Umm," and meaningless fillers such as "Know what I mean" and "You know." They are powerless, meaningless distractions that communicate the inability of a person to articulate thoughts and sentences.

Regional and Role Differences

Most Americans speak "English," but there are regional and role differences. People in New Jersey go to the shore, while those in California go to the beach. A person in

New England asks for a soda, a person in the Midwest for pop, and a person in the South for a coke. A government entitlement program such as Social Security has different meanings for 24-year-old and 64-year-old interview parties. Employees and management view downsizing and outsourcing differently.

Gender Differences

Gender differences may lead to power differences.

Studies of gender and communication have identified differences in language use among men and women. For example, men tend to be socialized into developing and using power speech forms and to dominate interactions, while women tend to be socialized into developing powerless speech forms and to foster relationships and exchanges during interactions. Research indicates that women's talk is more polite and expressive, contains more qualifiers and disclaimers, includes more second- and third-person pronouns (such as we and they rather than I or me), makes more color distinctions, includes fewer mechanical and technical terms, and is more tentative than men's talk.[49] Men not only use more intense language than women, but also they are often expected to do so because it is considered masculine. If a woman uses the same language, she may be termed bitchy, pushy, or opinionated.

Stereotypes are dangerous assumptions.

Be cautious when stereotyping language and interaction differences among genders. Julia Wood writes that "despite jokes about women's talkativeness, research indicates that in most contexts, men not only hold their own but dominate the conversation."[50] In addition, men tend to interrupt women more than other men and do so to state opinions; women tend to interrupt to ask questions. Recent studies also indicate that both men and women use tentative forms of speech. Several factors may affect how men and women use language, including context of the interview, subject matter, length of the interaction (affecting how much parties become comfortable with one another), status differences between the parties, and roles being played.[51]

Global Differences

Global use of words may be more significant than foreign words.

Language differences are magnified in the global village, even when parties are speaking the same language. North Americans value precision, directness, explicit words, power speech forms, use "I" to begin sentences, and straight talk.[52] Other cultures value the group or collective rather than the individual and rarely begin with "I" or call attention to themselves. Chinese children are taught to downplay self-expression. Japanese tend to be implicit rather than explicit and employ ambiguous words and qualifiers. Koreans prefer to avoid negative or "no" responses and imply disagreements to maintain group harmony. Arab-speaking peoples employ what is referred to as "sweet talk" or accommodating language with elaborate metaphors and similes.

Idioms such as "bought the farm," "get your feet wet," "wild goose chase," "stud muffin," and "hit a home run" are unique to us and may pose serious problems for those with varying degrees of expertise in a language or culture. Wen-Shu Lee writes of her experiences as a new graduate student in the United States. Although she was fluent in English, she was taken aback when a fellow student looked at her notes in Chinese and remarked, "That's Greek to me." When she said that it was Chinese, not Greek, the student thought this was funny. Only then did Lee realize that she had misunderstood a common idiom in the United States. She warns that some people will remain silent when hearing an idiom rather than risk appearing stupid, and recommends that "speakers need to work together to establish a conversational decorum in which it is all right or socially acceptable to bring up problems."[53]

Guidelines for Reducing Language Problems

Famous linguist Irving Lee wrote years ago that we often "talk past" one another instead of with one another.[54]

> Language problems are avoidable.

You can reduce the likelihood of talking past a party by choosing words with care, expanding your vocabulary, ordering words clearly, listening to the context in which another party uses words, being aware of common and professional jargon, and keeping up to date with changing uses of language. Always be cognizant of how gender, age, race, culture, and ethnic group of both parties may alter how words are processed and meaning determined.

Nonverbal Interactions

> Nonverbal signals send many different messages.

Because of the interactive nature of the interview, each party relies on nonverbal signals to interpret the other's verbal expressions and to know when it is time to talk and listen. A head nod, pause, voice, or leaning back may invite turn taking or a role change because we rely on nonverbal cues to express ourselves and interpret the expressions of others.[55] Since the parties are in such close proximity, they are likely to detect and interpret what the other **does** and **does not do** nonverbally: eye contact, facial expressions, winks, touches, glances.

A single behavioral act may convey a message. Poor eye contact may tell the other party that you have something to hide, a limp handshake that you are timid, a serious facial expression that you are sincere, or a puzzled expression that you are confused. Your speaking rate may communicate urgency (fast speed), the gravity of the situation (slow speed), lack of interest (fast speed), lack of preparation (slow speed), nervousness (fast speed and breathless voice), or indecision (halting voice). **Silence** may encourage the other to talk, signal that you are not in a hurry, express agreement with what is being said, and keep the other party talking.[56]

> Any behavioral act, or its absence, can convey a message.

A combination of nonverbal acts may enhance the impact of the message. For instance, you may show interest by leaning forward, maintaining good eye contact, nodding your head, and having a serious facial expression. When you fidget, cross and uncross arms and legs, sit rigid, look down, furrow brows, and speak in a high-pitched voice, you may reveal a high level of anxiety, fear, or agitation. A drooping body, frown, and slow speaking rate may reveal sadness or resignation. Leaning backward, staring at the other party, and raising an eyebrow may signal disagreement, anger, or disgust. The way you shake hands and look the other in the eye may signal trustworthiness. Body movements, gestures, and posture show dynamism or lack of it. Any behavioral act may be interpreted in a meaningful way by the other party. Your message may be intentional or unintentional, accurate or inaccurate, but it will be interpreted.

Physical appearance and dress are particularly important during the first few minutes of interviews as you get to know and respect one another. People respond more favorably to attractive persons who are neither too fat nor too thin, tall rather than short, shapely rather than unshapely, pretty and handsome rather than plain or ugly. They see attractive persons as more poised, outgoing, interesting, and sociable. How you dress and prepare yourself physically for an interview may reveal how you view yourself, the other party, the situation, and the importance of the interview.[57]

Verbal and Nonverbal Intertwined

> In mixed messages, the *how* may overcome the *what*.

Although we have separated verbal and nonverbal interactions for instructional purposes, it is nearly impossible to isolate one from the other. The nonverbal often **complements** the verbal such as when we call attention to important words or phrases through vocal emphasis (like underlining, italicizing, or highlighting in print). We complement words with tone of voice, speaking rate, facial expression, and eye contact. The nonverbal may **reinforce** words with a head nod or head shake. The nonverbal may serve as a **substitute** for words, such as when we point to a chair without saying "Sit here." Silence can signal disagreement more tactfully than words even when the meaning is the same.

> Verbal and nonverbal messages are intricately intertwined.

Research indicates, however, that the nonverbal may be more powerful than the verbal in some circumstances. Nonverbal may exchange feelings and emotions more accurately; convey intentions relatively free of deception and confusion; be more efficient; and impart ideas indirectly. Subjects in studies indicated they thought nonverbal behaviors were more truthful than verbal messages and, if the messages conflicted—mixed messages, they were more likely to believe the nonverbal. *How* trumps the *what*.

Gender and Culture Differences

> Women are more adept at nonverbal communication.

Gender differences affect interviews because women are more skilled at and rely more on nonverbal communication than men. For instance, facial expressions, pauses, and bodily gestures are more important in women's interactions than men's, perhaps because women are more expressive than men. Women tend to gaze more and are less uncomfortable when eye contact is broken. Men's lower-pitched voices are viewed as more credible and dynamic than women's higher-pitched voices. Female parties stand or sit closer than opposite-sex parties, and males maintain more distance than opposite-sex or female parties.

Stock4B–RF/Getty Images

■ *Be aware of cultural differences in nonverbal communication.*

Differing cultures share many nonverbal signals. Around the world people nod their heads in agreement, shake their heads in disagreement, give thumbs down for disapproval, shake fists in anger, and clap hands to show approval. On the other hand, nonverbal communication differs significantly among cultures.

In the United States, African-American participants maintain eye contact more when speaking than when listening. They give more nonverbal feedback when listening than European-Americans. In general, African-Americans are more animated and personal, while European-Americans are more subdued. They avoid eye contact with superiors out of respect, a trait often misinterpreted by European-Americans who see lack of eye contact as a sign of disinterest, lack of confidence, or dishonesty. And African-Americans tend to touch more and stand closer together when communicating than do European-Americans.[58]

> **Black and white Americans use different non-verbal signals.**

On the global scene, Americans are taught to look others in the eye when speaking, while Africans are taught to avoid eye contact when listening to others. An honest "look me in the eye" for a Westerner may express a lack of respect to an Asian. An American widens his or her eyes to show wonder or surprise, while the Chinese do so to express anger, the French to express disbelief, and Hispanics to show lack of understanding. Americans are taught to smile in response to a smile, but this is not so in Israel. Japanese are taught to mask negative feelings with smiles and laughter. Americans are taught to have little direct physical contact with others while communicating, but Mediterranean and Latin countries encourage direct contact. On a loudness scale of 1 to 10, with 10 being high, Arabs would be near 10, Americans would be near the middle, and Europeans would be near 1. Arabs perceive loudness as signs of strength and sincerity and softness as signs of weakness and deviousness. Not surprisingly, many Americans and Europeans see Arabs as pushy and rude. A firm handshake is important in American society but signals nothing in Japan.

> **Be aware of the diversity of nonverbal messages in different parts of the world.**

Many gestures you observe in different cultures and countries have different meanings. A simple wave means "hello" in the United States and "come here" in Algeria. A finger to the forehead means smart in the United States and stupid in many European cultures. A thumb up means "way to go" in the United States and "screw you" in Iran. A circular motion of a finger around the ear means crazy in the United States and "you have a telephone call" in the Netherlands. Fingers in a circle means "okay" in the United States but is an obscene gesture in Brazil.[59]

Feedback

Feedback is immediate and pervasive in interviews, and is essential to verify what is being communicated and how. The large, double-ended arrow that links the top of the party circles in Figure 2.5 symbolizes the heavy stream of feedback between interview parties. Feedback is both verbal (questions and answers, arguments and counterarguments, agreements and disagreements, challenges and compliances) and nonverbal (facial expressions, gestures, raised eyebrows, eye contact, vocal utterances, and posture).

You can detect critical feedback and assess how an interview is progressing by observing and listening to what is and is not taking place or being said. During the interview, does the other party select a power position and move closer or farther apart? Are there changes in tone or attentiveness? Are there changes in eye contact, voice, or posture? Is there more or less willingness to disclose information, feelings, and attitudes?

> **Be perceptive, sensitive, and receptive.**

Do not read too much into small nonverbal actions and changes. A person may fidget because a chair is hard, not because of a question or answer; pay less attention because of noise and interruptions, not disinterest; speak loudly because of habit, not because of a hearing impairment. Poor eye contact may indicate shyness or culture, not deceptiveness or mistrust.

Figure 2.5   *Feedback*

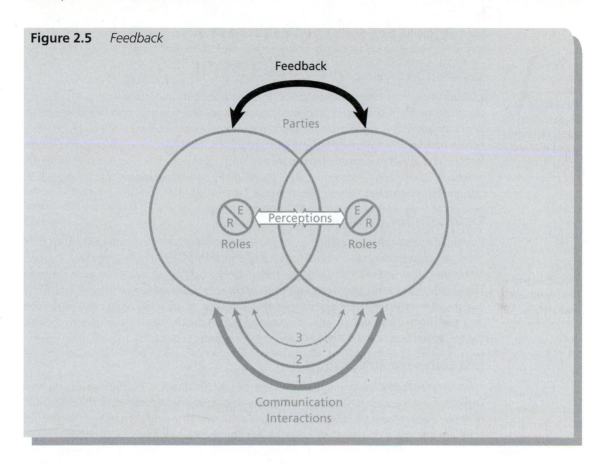

Listening skills are essential to obtaining information, detecting clues, and generating Level 2 and Level 3 responses. Few people listen well. Surveys of hundreds of corporations in the United States reveal that poor listening skills create barriers in all positions from entry level to CEO.

> **It is difficult to listen with your mouth open and your ears closed.**

An interviewee may not listen carefully to a question, while the interviewer may not listen carefully to the answer. Parties may be so absorbed in their primary roles as questioner or respondent that they do not listen well. Unfortunately, most of our educations prepare us to talk, not listen. There are four approaches to listening—for comprehension, for empathy, for evaluation, for resolution—and each plays a specific role in giving, receiving, and processing information accurately and insightfully.

Listening for Comprehension

> **The intent of listening for comprehension is to understand content.**

Listening for comprehension is designed to receive, understand, and remember an interchange as accurately and completely as possible by concentrating on a question, answer, or reaction to understand and remain objective, not to judge. This approach is essential when giving and getting information and during the first minutes of interviews when determining how to react. Use these guidelines for listening for comprehension. Listen carefully and patiently to each question and answer. Listen to content and ideas as well as tone of voice and vocal emphasis for subtle meanings. Ask questions to clarify and verify.

Listening for Empathy

> The intent of empathic listening is to understand the other party.

Listening for empathy communicates genuine concern, understanding, and involvement. Empathic listening reassures, comforts, expresses warmth, and shows regard. It is not expressing sympathy or feeling sorry for someone but the ability to place one's self in another's situation. Follow these guidelines for listening with empathy. Show interest and concern nonverbally and by not interrupting. Be comfortable and nonjudgmental with displays of emotion. Reply with tact and understanding and by providing options and guidelines.

Listening for Evaluation

> The intent of evaluative listening is to judge content and actions.

Listening for evaluation (*critical listening*) judges what you hear and observe. It may follow comprehension and empathy because you are ready to judge when you comprehend the verbal and nonverbal interactions. Openly expressing criticism may diminish cooperation and level of disclosure. Follow these guidelines for evaluative listening. Make judgments only after listening carefully to content and observing nonverbal cues. Ask questions for clarifications of exchanges and validations of your interpretations. Do not become defensive when an interview party reacts critically to your criticisms.

Listening for Resolution

> The intent of dialogic listening is to resolve problems.

John Stewart has developed a fourth type of listening called **dialogic listening** that focuses on *ours* rather than *mine* or *yours* and believes the agenda for resolving a problem or task supersedes the individual.[60] Dialogic listening is most appropriate for problem-solving interviews when the goal is the joint resolution of a problem or task. Stewart likens dialogic listening to adding clay to a mold together, to see how the other person will react, what the person will add, and how this will affect the shape and content of the product. Follow these guidelines when listening for resolution. Encourage interaction and trust the other party to make significant contributions. Paraphrase and add to the other party's responses and ideas while focusing on the present. Center your attention on the communication taking place rather than the psychology of the interview.

> Listening, like speaking, is a learned skill.

Active and insightful listening is critical to interviews, but it is a difficult, invisible skill to attain, partly because our educations and experiences as children, students, employees, and subordinates prepare us to be passive listeners. You can become a more effective listener, first, by being as satisfied as a listener as you are a talker. Second, be an active listener by attending carefully and critically to both verbal and nonverbal signals. Third, learn to ignore distractions such as surroundings, appearances, and interruptions. And fourth, know which is the most appropriate listening approach to use.

The Interview Situation

Every interview takes place at a specific *time*, in a specific *place*, and with specific *surroundings*, and these variables—and how each party *perceives* them—impact every aspect of the interactions that take place. The enveloping circle in Figure 2.6 portrays

Figure 2.6 *Situational variables*

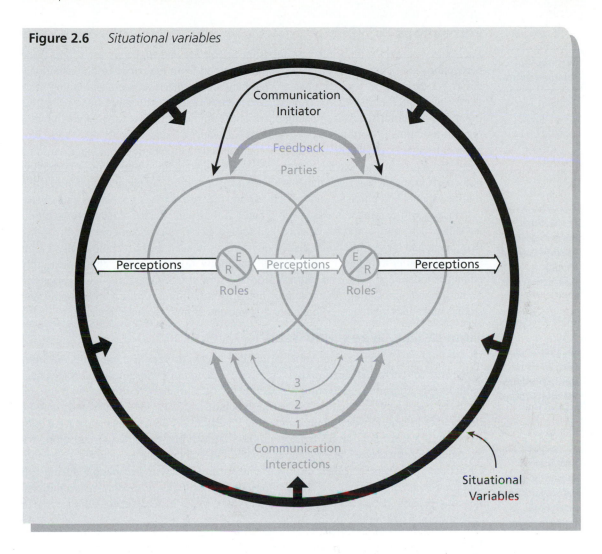

the interview situation and the imploding arrows represent the variables that influence the process within.

Initiating the Interview

Who initiates
an interview
and how may
affect control,
roles, and
atmosphere.

Either party may initiate an interview, as shown by the arrows in Figure 2.6 that emerge from the top of the circle and touch each party. You may initiate an interview with a recruiter, or the recruiter may initiate an interview with you. On the other hand, the situation may determine who initiates an interview and with whom. For instance, an insurance claims adjuster must interview the owner of a computer that was stolen from an apartment. You can enhance the climate of an interview by initiating it directly rather than through a third party and by informing the interviewee about the purpose, nature, and use of the information to be exchanged.

Perceptions

Settings are seldom neutral.

Each party perceives the interview situation in *similar* and *different* ways, and these perceptions are symbolized by the arrows that extend from the parties to the situational circle. For example, a recruiter and applicant may see the purpose, need, and timing of an employment interview similarly. However, the recruiter may see the interaction as a routine event that is neither special nor exciting, while the applicant may see the interaction as a once-in-a-lifetime opportunity to advance a career, achieve financial goals, and secure professional status. A physician may see nothing unusual or threatening about an examining room, but a patient may see the instruments, sterile surroundings, and pictures portraying body parts as menacing. Each may have very different goals, the physician to complete a routine examination efficiently and effectively and the patient to get good news and escape.

Perceptions are critical in moving beyond Level 1 interactions.

Parties will communicate at Levels 2 and 3 if they perceive the situation to be familiar rather than strange, informal rather than formal, warm rather than cold, private rather than open, and close rather than distant physically, socially, and psychologically. Organizations attempt to enhance concentration and motivation with well-lighted, pleasantly painted, moderate-sized rooms with comfortable furniture, temperature, and ventilation. Some professional settings that resemble living rooms, dining rooms, family rooms, and studies make interview parties feel more at home and willing to communicate.

Time of Day, Week, and Year

Each of us has optimum times for interactions.

We may interact best at certain times of the day, week, or year. For example, our optimum time for performance, thinking, creativity, and dealing with important issues may be morning, afternoon, or evening. It may be counter-productive to talk about critical issues or exchange information just before lunch or late in a work day. Moods may be dark and motivation low on Monday morning, Friday afternoon, or during dreary winter days. Holidays are good times for some interviews and bad for others. Counselors, for

Take into account events before and after interviews.

example, report increases in crisis interviews with lonely people around Thanksgiving, Christmas, and Passover. Police officers cite strange behaviors of people during full moons. Events that precede or follow interviews—academic or medical examinations, possible layoffs, drops in the stock market—may make it difficult for either party to concentrate, listen, or answer questions.

Place

Don't underestimate the importance of place.

Consider whose turf is best for an interview. For instance, you may feel more comfortable and less threatened in your home, room, office, business, or in a neutral place such as a lounge area or restaurant. We protect our turf. Think of your reactions when you walked into your room or office and found another person in your chair or at your desk. Judy Pearson writes that "Few women have a particular and unviolated room in their homes while many men have dens [often referred to as man caves], studies, or work areas that are off limits to others."[61]

Surroundings help create a productive climate.

Surroundings

Objects and decorations may create an appropriate atmosphere and interview climate. Trophies, awards, degrees, and licenses attractively displayed communicate achievements, professional credibility, and stature in a field. Pictures, statues, and busts of leaders or famous persons communicate organizational and personal history, success, recognition, endorsement, and contacts. Models or samples may display state-of-the-art products and services. Colors of walls, types of carpeting, wall hangings, wallpaper, and curtains can provide a warm, attractive atmosphere conducive to effective communication.

Noise in an interview is anything that interferes with the communication process, including background noise, doors opening and closing, music, others talking, objects being dropped, and traffic. The interview may be interrupted by a cell phone or a text message. People coming in and out of the room, walking by an open door, or asking for assistance are common distractions.

> **Control noise to focus attention on the interaction.**

Eliminate negative influences of noise by selecting locations free of background noise or taking simple precautions: close a door, window, or curtain; turn off a cell phone, television, or CD player. Inform others you do not wish to be disturbed. Limit self-generated noise by coming to each interview physically and psychologically ready to concentrate. During the interview, strive to blot out noise by focusing your attention on the other party, questions, answers, and nonverbal signals.

Territoriality

You may select a seat, arrange books and papers, and place coats and hats strategically around you to stake out your physical and psychological space. You may resent those who invade this carefully crafted space with their choice of seating, possessions, eyes, voices, or bodies. Think of how you have reacted to common invasions of territory such as another student walking into a professor's office while you were discussing a problem, a nearby diner listening to your conversation with a recruiter, or a colleague talking loudly at the next desk while you were talking to a client.

Proximity of interview parties affects comfort level. You may feel uncomfortable with persons who insist on talking nose-to-nose, and may react by backing up, placing furniture between you, or terminating the interview. Trenholm and Jensen write about "**territorial markers**" and use the term "**personal space**" to describe an "imaginary bubble" around us that we consider to be "almost as private as the body itself."[62] Researchers have identified intimate distance (touching to 18 inches), personal distance (1½ to 4 feet), and social distance (4 to 12 feet).[63] Two to four feet—approximately an arm's length or on opposite sides of a table or desk—is an optimum distance for most interviews.

> **Relationship affects territorial comfort zones.**

Relationship, status, situation, and feelings of parties toward one another, influence the size of the bubble with which you are comfortable. High-status people stand or sit closer to low-status people, while low-status people prefer greater distances when dealing with superiors. We maintain a greater distance with a stranger than with close associates, peers, and friends. Some people want to "get in your face" when angry, while others widen the space because their anger is translated into distancing themselves from you physically, socially, and psychologically.

> **Age, gender, and culture influence territorial preferences.**

Age, gender, and culture determine space preferences. People of the same age stand or sit closer together than those of mixed ages, particularly when the age difference is significant. All-male parties tend to arrange themselves farther apart than all-female or mixed-gender parties. North Americans prefer greater personal distances than do Middle Eastern and Latin American peoples. Arabs and Latin Americans

Stockbyte/Getty Images

■ *A corner seating arrangement is preferred by many interviewers and interviewees.*

see us as distant and cold, while we see them as intruding into our space. Northern Europeans prefer greater personal distance than Southern Europeans.[64]

Where you sit and on what you sit is often determined by status, gender, furnishings, cultural norms, relationship, and personal preferences. For example, a superior and a subordinate may sit across a desk from one another, arrangement A in Figure 2.7, with one sitting in a large leather swivel chair while the other sits on a simple chair. This provides distance in a formal setting in which one party maintains a superior position. Two chairs at right angles near the corner of a desk or table, arrangement B, creates a less formal atmosphere and a greater feeling of equality between parties. Students often prefer this arrangement with college professors.

> **Seating may equalize control and enhance the interview climate.**

You may remove physical obstacles and reduce the superior-subordinate atmosphere further by placing chairs at opposite sides of a small coffee table or by omitting the table altogether, arrangements C and D. A circular table, arrangement E, is growing in popularity in counseling ones or interviews involving more than two people, because it avoids a head-of-the-table position, allows participants to pass around materials, and provides a surface on which to write, review printed items, and place refreshments. The circular table or chairs around a small table work well for panel interviews. Arrangement F is most suitable when one or both parties consist of several persons such as a focus group.

Outside Forces

> **Outside forces determine roles in many interviews.**

The addition of outside forces in Figure 2.8 completes the summary model of the interview that incorporates two parties, role exchanges, perceptions of self and other, levels of communication interactions, feedback, communication initiator, situational variables, perceptions of the situation, and outside forces. **This model *appears* very complicated because the interview *is* very complicated.** Every interview in which you take part is a **complex process** and you need to understand the interacting variables and the roles you play each time you take part in a purposeful, planned, and serious interaction with another party.

Figure 2.7 *Seating arrangements*

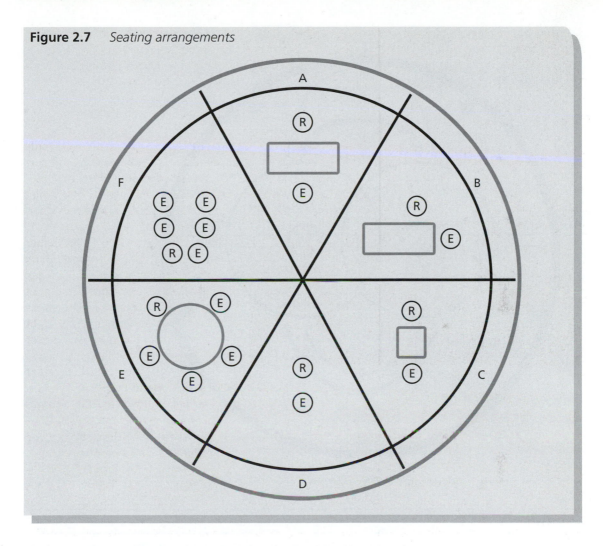

We are not really alone with the other party.

Outside forces such as those identified in the model may suggest or dictate who takes part, when, and where; attitudes assumed; topics covered; structure followed; questions asked; and answers given. Organizational policies, union contracts, pressures of a political campaign, Equal Employment Opportunity (EEO) laws, and competitors influence perceptions, levels of exchanges, self-disclosure, and interviewing approach. What may take place *following the interview*—a report you must submit, accounts in the media, possible grievances or lawsuits, reactions of peers—may make parties careful and wary or headstrong and hasty. You may feel pressure to relate that you "followed the rules," "drove a hard bargain," "got a deal," or told the other party "where to get off." Remember that the two interview parties are seldom truly alone in the process.

Figure 2.8   *Outside forces*

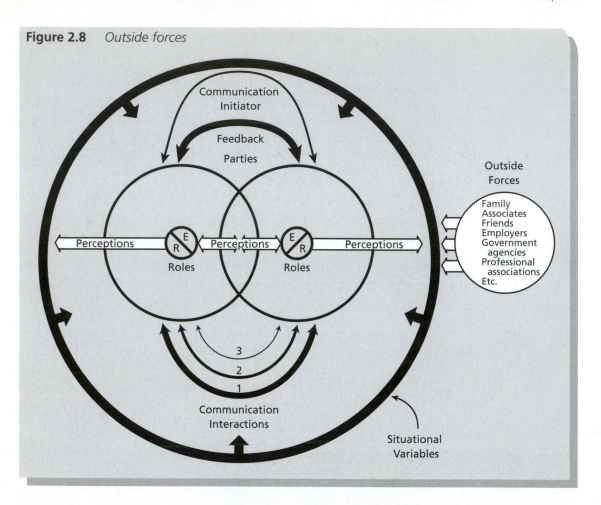

Summary

This chapter developed a summary model of the process that contains the many interacting variables present in each interview: two parties, exchanging of roles, perceptions, levels of exchanges, verbal and nonverbal messages, relationships, feedback, listening, situation, and outside forces. Interviewing is a dynamic process between two complex parties operating with imperfect verbal and nonverbal symbols guided and controlled by perceptions and the situation. The ability to listen (for comprehension, empathy, evaluation, and resolution) and to employ silence strategically are often more important than what you have to say.

A thorough understanding of the process is a prerequisite for successful interviewing. Be aware that perceptions of self, the other party, how the other party sees you, and the situation are critical in determining how interviews progress and whether desired outcomes are achieved. Acknowledge and adapt to the influence of outside forces.

Interviewer and interviewee must be flexible and adaptable in choosing which approach to take (directive, nondirective, or a combination) not only because each party is unique and each situation is different, but because each party is molded and affected by demographics such as age, gender, race, and culture. This chapter has tried to enhance your awareness of how demographics and culture affect self-esteem, disclosure, levels of communication, language, nonverbal communication, and territoriality. In the global village of the twenty-first century, be aware of how different people and different cultures communicate.

Key Terms and Concepts

The online learning center for this text features FLASHCARDS and CROSSWORD PUZZLES for studying based on these terms and concepts

Complex communication process	Levels of interactions	Role competence
Control	Listening	Self-concept
Culture	Noise	Self-disclosure
Defensive climate	Nondirective approach	Self-esteem
Dialectical tensions	Nonverbal interactions	Self-fulfilling prophecy
Dialogic listening	Outside forces	Self-identity
Directive approach	Perceptions	Silence
Downward communication	Personal space	Situation
Feedback	Politeness theory	Supportive climate
Gender	Proximity	Territorial markers
Global relationships	Relational dimensions	Territoriality
Idioms	Relational distance	Upward communication
Initiating	Relational history	Verbal interactions
	Relational memory	

An Interview for Review and Analysis

Joe is a production supervisor with 20 years of experience and a good record.[65] The plant manager is considering him for promotion and this interview is a first step in that process. It is exploratory rather than decision making. Company policy stipulates that employees are *not* to be informed when being actively considered for promotion, so Joe is unaware that a promotion may be in the offing. Company policy does allow mentioning overall considerations related to the current workforce situation and to established company criteria for promotions. Two hours prior to the interview, Joe received a call from the manager's secretary asking him to report to the manager. No reason is given. Joe enters the manager's office at 4:30 p.m. (his shift ends at 5:00 p.m.) and is seated across the desk from the manager.

What *perceptions* do Joe and the manager have of themselves, of one another, and of the situation? How would you assess the relationship between Joe and the manager? When, if ever, do the parties *exchange roles* of interviewer and interviewee? At which *communication levels* do most interactions occur? How do *words* influence the interview? How does *nonverbal behavior* affect the interview? Which *listening approaches* do Joe and the manager employ most often and with what effect? Which *interviewing approach* does the manager employ? How do *situational variables* influence this interview? What role do *outside forces* play in this interview? What suggestions would you offer the manager and Joe for handling such situations more effectively and for improving their interviewing skills?

1. **Manager:** Joe, come in. (smiling) Have a seat. It's been awhile since we've had time for a chat.

2. **Joe:** (sitting facing the manager) Thank you, sir. (soft voice)

3. **Manager:** (serious facial expression and tone of voice) How are things moving along these days, Joe? *Everything* under control in your section?

4. **Joe:** Fine, sir. No complaints. (fast speaking rate)

5. **Manager:** I'm *glad* to hear there are no *complaints*. (pause) You think you're doing okay?

6. **Joe:** As good as I know how, sir. (shifts weight in chair)

7. **Manager:** Good. (pause; looks Joe directly in the eyes) By the way, have you ever thought of uh, (pause) doing *something else?*

8. **Joe:** (pause; speaks slowly) Well (pause) uh, yes and no. I do like my job a lot. (rapidly)

9. **Manager:** Hmmm, I see. You don't want to change your job?

10. **Joe:** Uh (pause) no. (pause) I don't think so.

11. **Manager:** (looking closely at Joe; measuring his words) I see. Why do you want to stay on this job?

12. **Joe:** Well, I know the work real well. And everybody seems to like me.

13. **Manager:** Seems to like you? (looks Joe directly in the eyes)

14. **Joe:** Oh (pause) there may be one or two people who don't like me. But we manage to get along.

15. **Manager:** Some people don't like you, then? (sounds accusatory)

16. **Joe:** Well, I wouldn't exactly say *that*. Occasionally someone gets sore because I won't give him overtime.

17. **Manager:** That's the *only* reason?

18. **Joe:** Yes, sir! That's the only thing of importance I can think of. (firm voice, direct eye contact)

19. **Manager:** I see. (pause) Uh, Joe, do you ever think of (pause) *bettering* yourself?

20. **Joe:** Everyone wants to do better. Know what I mean?

21. **Manager:** What do you mean?

22. **Joe:** Well, I mean, almost anyone can find ways to improve. (looks down)

23. **Manager:** You think, then, you could handle your job better?

24. **Joe:** Oh, there's always room for improvement.

25. **Manager:** Joe, have you ever thought of bettering yourself on (pause) *another* job?

26. **Joe:** I like this job and company very much, sir! I know this job well, and you and the company have been very good to me.

27. **Manager:** I don't think you listened *carefully* to my question, Joe. Have you ever thought of *bettering* yourself on *another* job?

28. **Joe:** Well, everybody daydreams about how things might be at another company or even owning your own business. But I haven't given it much serious thought, really.

29. **Manager:** I take it, then, that you prefer definitely to stay on your *present job*.

30. **Joe:** Yes, sir. (pause) Do you have something specific in mind, sir? (rapid speaking voice)

31. **Manager:** Oh, don't worry about that, Joe. I'm glad we had time for this little chat. We'll have to get together again soon. Good luck. (shakes Joe's hand firmly without meeting his eyes)

Student Activities

1. Interview four students on your campus: one from Central America, one from southern Europe, one from the Near East, and one from Asia. Ask them to identify and illustrate verbal and nonverbal communication problems they have encountered since coming to the United States. What relational similarities and differences have they experienced? How have they attempted to work through these problems and differences?

2. Watch a 10–15 minute television interview with a person who had been accused of a crime or unethical behavior. How effective was the interviewer in getting to Level 2 and 3 interactions? How did the interviewee attempt to avoid disclosing potentially damaging information?

3. Research indicates measurable differences in communication between genders. Observe interactions between two males, two females, and a male and a female to see what differences if any you can detect in proximity, eye contact, gestures, body movements, and territoriality. What influence do you believe the prior relationship of the parties had on these nonverbal and situational factors?

4. Watch three 10–15 minute interviews between sportscasters and professional athletes, one in which an athlete is about to take part in a game, one in which an athlete just won a game, and one in which an athlete just experienced a loss. Which forms of listening did the participants in these interviews use most often? How did the situations appear to have affected the participants' abilities to listen?

Notes

1. John Stewart, ed., *Bridges Not Walls: A Book about Interpersonal Communication* (New York: McGraw-Hill, 2012), p. 73.

2. Robert S. Goyer, W. Charles Redding, and John T. Rickey, *Interviewing Principles and Techniques: A Project Text* (Dubuque, IA: Wm. C. Brown, 1968), p. 23.

3. Judith N. Martin and Thomas K. Nakayama, *Intercultural Communication in Contexts* (New York: McGraw-Hill, 2007), p. 371.

4. Judith N. Martin and Thomas K. Nakayama, *Experiencing Intercultural Communication* (New York: McGraw-Hill, 2011), pp. 255–256.

5. John Stewart and Carole Logan, *Together: Communicating Interpersonally* (New York: McGraw-Hill, 1998), p. 277.

6. Sarah Trenholm and Arthur Jensen, *Interpersonal Communication* (New York: Oxford University Press, 2013), pp. 38–39.

7. Judith N. Martin and Thomas K. Nakayama, *Experiencing Intercultural Communication Experiencing* (New York: McGraw-Hill, 2011), p. 259.

8. Sarah Trenholm and Arthur Jensen, *Interpersonal Communication* (New York: Oxford University Press, 2013), p. 30.

9. George B. Ray and Kory Floyd, "Nonverbal Expressions of Liking and Disliking in Initial Interaction: Encoding and Decoding Perspectives," *Southern Communication Journal* 71 (March 2006), p. 60.

10. Trenholm and Jensen (2013), p. 31.

11. Kory Floyd, *Interpersonal Communication: The Whole Story* (New York: McGraw-Hill, 2011), p. 317; Trenholm and Jensen (2013), pp. 29, 276–277.

12. Floyd, p. 317.

13. Stewart, p. 18.

14. Stewart, p. 30.

15. Edward T. Hall, "Context and Meaning," in Larry A. Samovar and Richard E. Porter, eds., *Intercultural Communication: A Reader* (Belmont, CA: Wadsworth, 2000), p. 35.

16. R. Fisher and S. Brown in Judith N. Martin, Thomas K. Nakayama, and Lisa Flores, *Intercultural Communication: Experiences and Contexts* (New York: McGraw-Hill, 2002), p. 334.

17. William B. Gudykunst and Young Yun Kim, *Communication with Strangers* (New York: McGraw-Hill, 2003), p. 339.

18. Trenholm and Jensen, pp. 275–276.

19. Larry A. Samovar, Richard E. Porter, and Edwin R. McDaniel, *Intercultural Communication: A Reader* (Boston, MA: Wadsworth CENGAGE Learning, 2009), p. 391.

20. Stewart, p. 487.

21. Judith N. Martin, Thomas K. Nakayama, and Lisa A. Flores, *Intercultural Communication Experiences and Contexts* (New York: McGraw-Hill, 2004), p. 334.

22. Martin and Nakayama (2011), p. 255.

23. Donald W. Klopf, *Intercultural Encounters* (Englewood, CO: Morton, 1998), pp. 176–193; Carley H. Dodd, *Dynamics of Intercultural Communication* (New York: McGraw-Hill, 1995), pp. 21–24.

24. Martin and Nakayama (2011), p. 323.

25. Samovar, Porter, and McDaniel, p. 261.

26. K. Dindia and D. J. Canary, eds., *Sex Differences and Similarities in Communication* (Mahwah, NJ: Lawrence Erlbaum, 2006), pp. 3–20; Floyd, p. 58; Cynthia Burggraf Torppa, "Gender Issues: Communication Differences in Interpersonal Relationships," *FACT SHEET: Family and Consumer Sciences*, The Ohio State University, 2010.

27. Brant Burleson and Adrienne Kunkel, "Revisiting the Different Cultures Thesis: An Assessment of Sex Differences and Similarities in Supportive Communication," in K. Dindia and D. J. Canary, eds., *Sex Differences and Similarities in Communication* (Mahwah, NJ: Lawrence Erlbaum, 2006), pp. 137–159.

28. Trenholm and Jensen (2013), pp. 95–97.

29. Stewart and Logan, p. 84.

30. Trenholm and Jensen (2013), p. 315.

31. Stewart (2012), p. 293.

32. Stewart (2012), p. 334.

33. Stewart (2012), p. 20.

34. Stewart and Logan, p. 277.

35. Stewart (2009), p. 97.

36. Stewart (2012), p. 26.

37. Trenholm and Jensen (2013), pp. 85 and 270; Stewart (2012), pp. 455–457.

38. Floyd, p. 77.

39. David W. Johnson, "Being Open with and to Other People," in Stewart (2012), pp. 210–211.

40. Stewart (2012), pp. 214-215; Trenholm and Jensen (2013), pp. 193–194; Floyd, pp. 98–99.

41. Floyd, pp. 97–98.

42. Diana K. Ivy and Phil Backlund, *Exploring Gender Speak: Personal Effectiveness in Gender Communication* (New York: McGraw-Hill, 1994), p. 219; Floyd, p. 99.

43. Martin and Nakayama (2011), p. 268.

44. Stephen W. Littlejohn, *Theories of Human Communication* (Belmont, CA: Wadsworth, 1996), p. 262.

45. Laura K. Guerrero, Peter A. Andersen, and Walid A. Afifi, *Close Encounters in Relationships* (New York: McGraw-Hill, 2001), p. 46.

46. Floyd, pp. 386–387.

47. Michael Skube, "College Students Lack Familiarity with Language, Ideas," Lafayette, IN, *Journal & Courier,* August 30, 2006, p. A5.

48. Sik Hung Ng and James J. Bradac, *Power in Language: Verbal Communication and Social Influence* (Newbury Park, CA: Sage, 1993), pp. 45–51.

49. Guerrero, Andersen, and Afifi, pp. 297–298; Ivy and Backlund, pp. 163–165.

50. Julia T. Wood, "Gendered Interaction: Masculine and Feminine Styles of Verbal Communication," reprinted in Kathleen S. Verderber, ed., *Voices: A Selection of Multicultural Readings* (Belmont, CA: Wadsworth, 1995), p. 24.

51. Trenholm and Jensen (2013), p. 96.

52. William B. Gudykunst, *Bridging Differences: Effective Intergroup Communication* (Newbury Park, CA: Sage, 1991), pp. 42–59.

53. Wen-Shu Lee, "That's Greek to Me: Between a Rock and a Hard Place in Intercultural Encounters," in Larry A. Samovar and Richard E. Porter, eds., *Intercultural Communication: A Reader* (Belmont, CA: Wadsworth, 2000), pp. 217–219.

54. Irving J. Lee, *How to Talk with People* (New York: Harper & Row, 1952), pp. 11–26.

55. Stewart (2012), pp. 152–153.

56. Stewart (2012), p. 113.

57. Floyd, pp. 283–284.

58. Trenholm and Jensen (2012), pp. 331–333; Donald W. Klopf, *Intercultural Encounters* (Englewood, CO: Morton, 1998), pp. 232–233.

59. Martin and Nakayama (2011), pp. 174–188.

60. Stewart (2012), p. 192–194.

61. Stewart (2012), p.118.

62. Trenholm and Jensen (2013), p. 55.

63. Trenholm and Jensen (2013), pp. 53–55.

64. Martin and Nakayama (2011), pp. 176–178.

65. This interview is loosely based on pp. 24–25 in *The Executive Interview* by Benjamin Balinsky and Ruth Burger. Copyright 1959 by Benjamin Balinsky and Ruth Burger. It is reprinted by permission of HarperCollins.

Resources

Martin, Judith N., and Thomas K. Nakayama. *Experiencing Intercultural Communication.* New York: McGraw-Hill, 2011.

Samovar, Larry A., Richard E. Porter, and Edwin R. McDaniel. *Intercultural Communication: A Reader.* Belmont, CA: Wadsworth CENGAGE Learning, 2009.

Stewart, John, ed. *Bridges Not Walls: A Book about Interpersonal Communication.* New York: McGraw-Hill, 2012.

Trenholm, Sarah, and Arthur Jensen. *Interpersonal Communication.* New York: Oxford University Press, 2013.

Wood, Julia T. *But I Thought You Meant . . . Misunderstandings in Human Communication.* Mountain View, CA: Mayfield, 1998.

Questions and Their Uses

Q uestions are the tools of the trade for both parties in interviews and, like all tools (hammers, screwdrivers, golf clubs, paint brushes), each type has a name, unique characteristics, performs specific functions, and enables us to complete tasks efficiently and effectively. Technology editor Jamie McKenzie writes, "Questions may be the most powerful technology we have ever created" because "they allow us to control our lives and allow us to make sense of a confusing world" by leading "to insight and understanding."[1] A question need not be a complete sentence with a question mark at the end. It is *any word, phrase, statement, or nonverbal act that invites an answer or response.*

> **A question is any action that solicits an answer.**

The objectives of this chapter are to introduce you to the many types of questions, their specific uses and limitations, and common question pitfalls into which we all tumble from time to time. Let's begin with the most fundamental types of questions: open and closed.

Open and Closed Questions

Open and closed questions vary in the amount of information they solicit and degree of interviewer control. Information may range from a single word to lengthy descriptions, narratives, and reports of statistical data. Control may range from minimal for open ended questions to maximum with closed questions.

Open Questions

> **Open questions invite open answers.**

Open questions vary in degree of openness ranging from a topic or area of inquiry to more specified subject matter. Regardless, respondents have considerable freedom to determine the amount and kind of information to give.

Highly Open Questions

Highly open questions place virtually no restrictions on the interviewee.

What do you recall about the blizzard of 1978?

What was it like fighting in the mountains of Afghanistan?

Tell me about your safari in Kenya.

■ *Open questions let the respondent do the talking and allow the interviewer to listen and observe.*

Steve Mason/Getty Images

Moderately Open Questions

Moderately open questions are more restrictive but give respondents considerable latitude in answers. The highly open questions above might be narrowed to:

How did you manage to dig out your car after the blizzard of 1978?

Tell me about your most frightening experience while fighting in the mountains of Afghanistan.

What was it like visiting the Masai village during your safari in Kenya?

Advantages of Open Questions

> Interviewees can volunteer and elaborate.

Open questions encourage respondents to talk, determine the nature and amount of information to give, and volunteer information. Lengthy answers reveal what respondents think is important and motivate them to provide details and description. Open questions communicate interest and trust in the respondent's judgment, are usually easier to answer, and pose less threat. Longer answers reveal a respondent's level of knowledge, uncertainty, intensity of feelings, perceptions, and prejudices.

Disadvantages of Open Questions

> Interviewees can pick and choose, reveal and hide.

A single answer may consume a significant portion of interview time because the respondent determines the length and nature of each answer. On the one hand, respondents may give unimportant or irrelevant information, and on the other may withhold important information they feel is irrelevant or too obvious, sensitive, or dangerous. Keep respondents on track and maintain control by tactfully intervening to move on. Lengthy, rambling answers are difficult to record and process.

Closed Questions

Closed questions are narrow in focus and restrict the interviewee's freedom to determine the amount and kind of information to provide.

Moderately Closed Questions

> Restricted questions lead to restricted answers.

Moderately closed questions ask for specific, limited pieces of information, such as:

What are your favorite places to eat?

On which airlines have you flown during the past year?

What was the first thought that came to mind when the principal announced over the PA system that the school was in lockdown?

Highly Closed Questions

Highly closed questions are very restrictive and may ask respondents to identify a single bit of information.

Which cruise line did you take on your Alaska trip?

How much does it cost per credit hour for your online courses?

What is your e-mail address?

Bipolar Questions

Closed questions may be **bipolar** because they limit respondents to two polar choices. Some ask you to select an answer from polar opposites.

Are you going to the Sunday afternoon or Sunday evening service?

Do you usually work the day or night shift?

Are you a Democrat or a Republican?

Other bipolar questions ask for an evaluation or attitude.

Are you for or against compulsory health insurance?

Do you approve or disapprove of the new library closing hours?

Do you like or dislike the new traffic circle at Cumberland and Kent?

The most common bipolar questions ask for yes or no responses.

Have you voted yet?

Are you going to the staff meeting this afternoon?

Do you have an E-Z Pass for the toll road?

Advantages of Closed Questions

Closed questions permit interviewers to control the length of answers and guide respondents to specific information needed. Closed questions require little effort from either party and allow you to ask more questions, in more areas, in less time. Answers are easy to replicate, tabulate, and analyze from one interview to another.

Disadvantages of Closed Questions

Answers to closed questions often contain too little information, requiring you to ask several questions when one open question would do the job. And they do not reveal why a person has a particular attitude, the person's degree of feeling or commitment, or why this person typically makes choices. Interviewers talk more than interviewees when asking closed questions, so less information is exchanged; interviewees have no opportunity to volunteer or explain information; and they can select an answer or say yes or no without knowing anything about a topic.

Figure 3.1 illustrates the major advantages and disadvantages of open and closed questions. As you narrow a question, the amount of data decreases. As the

Figure 3.1   *Question options*

Advantages and Disadvantages of Question Types	Type of Questions			
	Highly Open	Moderately Open	Moderately Closed	Highly Closed
Breadth and depth of potential information	10	7	4	1
Degree of precision, reproducibility, reliability	1	4	7	10
R's control over question and response	1	4	7	10
Interviewer skill required	10	7	4	1
Reliability of data	1	4	7	10
Economic use of time	1	4	7	10
Opportunity for E to reveal feelings and information	10	7	4	1
	10 High	7 Above average	4 Average	1 Low

amount of data decreases, your control increases, less time and skill are required, and the degree of precision, reliability, and reproducibility increases. On the other hand, as you open up a question, the amount of data increases and interviewees may reveal knowledge level, understanding, reasons for feeling or acting, attitudes, and hidden motives.

Interviewers may include open and closed questions with varying degrees of constraint to get the information desired. For instance, an interviewer might follow up a bipolar question such as "Are you familiar with the president's jobs plan?" with an open-ended question such as "What do you know about this plan?" An open-ended question such as "Tell me about your study abroad semester in Poland" may be followed up with a more closed question such as, "What was your first impression of Poland?"

Combinations often lead to the best results.

Primary and Probing Questions

**Primary ques-
tions make
sense out of
context.**

Primary questions introduce topics or new areas within a topic and can stand alone even when taken out of context.

Tell me about your trip to western Canada.

Who was the most influential person in your professional life?

How did you prepare to run the Boston Marathon?

All examples of open and closed questions presented earlier are primary questions.

**Probing
questions make
sense only in
context.**

Questions designed to dig deeper into answers that appear to be incomplete, superficial, suggestive, vague, irrelevant, or inaccurate are called **probing questions.** Unlike primary questions that can stand alone and make sense, probing or follow-up questions make sense only when connected to the previous question or series of questions.

Types of Probing Questions

Silent Probes

**Be patient and
be quiet.**

If an answer is incomplete or the respondent seems hesitant to continue, use a **silent probe** with appropriate nonverbal signals such as eye contact, a head nod, or a gesture to encourage the person to continue. Silence shows interest in what is being said, and is a tactful way to respect the answer and the respondent if you communicate disbelief, uncertainty, or confusion. An exchange might go like this:

1. **Interviewer:** What did you think of the President's State of the Union speech?
2. **Interviewee:** It was about what I expected.
3. **Interviewer:** (silence)
4. **Interviewee:** Most of his ideas have appeared in the news or in other speeches over the past two months, so I was not surprised by anything he said.

Nudging Probes

**A nudge
replaces silence
with a word or
phrase.**

Use a **nudging probe** if a silent probe fails and words seem necessary to get what is needed. It nudges the interviewee to reply or to continue. The nudging probe is usually simple and brief.

I see.	And?
Go on.	So?
Yes?	Uh-huh?

A common mistake is the assumption that all questions must be multiple-word sentences. A lengthy probing question may stifle the interchange or open up a new area or topic, the opposite of what you want. Valuable information and insights may be lost.

Clearinghouse Probes

**Ask rather than
assume.**

A **clearinghouse probe** is an essential tool for discovering whether a series of questions has uncovered everything of importance on a topic or issue. It encourages respondents to volunteer information you might not think to ask for and to fill in gaps your questions did not elicit. This probing tool literally clears out an area or topic, such as the following:

What have I not asked that you recall about this incident?

Is there anything else you would like for me to know?

A clearinghouse probe enables you to proceed, confident that you have gotten all important information. You cannot anticipate or plan for all information a party might be willing to reveal, so what you do not ask may be more important than what you do ask.

Informational Probes

Informational probing questions are used to get additional information or explanations. For example, if an answer is superficial, ask a probing question such as:

What specifically did she say?

Tell me more about your encounter with the Senator.

If an answer is vague or ambiguous, perhaps inviting different interpretations, ask an informational probe.

You say you are from a small town. What was its population?

If an answer suggests a feeling or attitude, ask an informational probe.

You still appear to be depressed about that three overtime loss.

Would you be willing to accept your student's comments about you on his Facebook page?

> Pry open vague, superficial, and suggestive answers.

Restatement Probes

Respondents may not answer the question you ask. Rather than create a new probing question, restate all or part of the original question, perhaps using vocal emphasis to draw attention to the original concern. Rephrasing an original question tactfully may avoid embarrassing an interviewee. The following illustrates a **restatement probe:**

> Restate or rephrase to get complete answers.

1. **Interviewer:** How do you feel about the company's new health care options?
2. **Interviewee:** I'm not in favor of finding my own plan; that's for sure.
3. **Interviewer:** I know how you feel, but what about the company's new health care options?

If an interviewee *makes a mistake* in an answer, restate your question tactfully, perhaps with vocal emphasis, to avoid the appearance of questioning the person's honesty or intelligence. For example:

1. **Interviewer:** Who do you think was the best Democratic President during the past fifty years?

2. **Interviewee:** Ronald Reagan without a doubt.

   Interviewer: Who do you think was the best *Democratic* President during that time?

If a person seems hesitant to answer a question, the question may be unclear or seem to demand what is difficult to provide. Restate the question in a clearer, easier to answer fashion.

1. **Interviewer:** As a political consultant, what is your ethical stance on negative political ads on television?

2. **Interviewee:** I think ethical stances are up to the individual.

3. **Interviewer:** I see, but what is *your* ethical stance on negative television ads?

If you ask a question with more than one part, a respondent may answer one part. Restate the portion or portions left unanswered.

1. **Interviewer:** What were your first impressions of Beijing and China?

2. **Interviewee:** I was very impressed with the airport and how modern the city had become in such a short time. The traffic was amazing, and I was surprised by the number of American SUVs on the streets. The people were very helpful and friendly, and the majority of people in Beijing seem to live in high-rise apartment buildings.

3. **Interviewer:** And what were your impressions of China?

Reflective Probes

Reflective questions verify and clarify.

A **reflective probe** literally reflects the answer just received to *verify* or *clarify* it so you know you have interpreted it as the respondent intended. Make it obvious that you are seeking verification and clarification, not attempting to lead or trap the interviewee into giving a desired answer or to question honesty or intelligence. Be tactful verbally and nonverbally. If an answer seems inaccurate (wrong date or figure, inaccurate quotation, mix-up in words), ask a reflective probing question such as the following:

That was *after* the fire was first detected?

That was *gross* profits from the fund-raiser?

By former President Bush, you are referring to President George H. W. Bush?

If unsure about what a respondent has said or implied, a reflective question may resolve uncertainty, such as the following:

1. **Interviewer:** Do you believe the candidate's wife has a good grasp of what life is like for most citizens?

2. **Interviewee:** No, I don't. She hasn't worked a day in her life.

3. **Interviewer:** Are you saying that being the mother of four children is not work?

A reflective probe differs from a restatement probe in that the first seeks to clarify or verify an answer while the second seeks to obtain more information following a primary question.

Mirror Probes

The **mirror question,** unlike the reflective question, *summarizes* a series of answers or interchanges to ensure accurate understanding and retention. It may mirror or summarize a large portion or an entire interview, to be certain of instructions, elements of a proposal, prescribed regimens, agreed-upon procedures, and so on. For instance, a physician might use a mirror question to verify understanding of a patient's symptoms.

> If I understand what you're saying, you first experienced pain in your left knee when you were painting your apartment and spent a lot of time kneeling on the floor. The discomfort seemed to go away after a few days but then returned after you played a pickup basketball game at the gym. This time it seemed to continue and grow more uncomfortable when you drove home, about a three-hour drive. Over-the-counter painkillers have not helped. Correct?

Reflective and mirror questions can help you avoid errors caused by faulty assumptions, poor memory, or misinterpretations.

Skillful Interviewing with Probing Questions

The use of probing questions separates skilled from unskilled interviewers. The unskilled person sticks with a prepared list of questions, anticipates questions prematurely, or is impatient. The skilled person listens carefully to each response to determine if the answer is satisfactory. If it is not, the questioner determines the probable cause within seconds and phrases an appropriate probing question. Skillful probing discovers more relevant, accurate, and complete information and may heighten the other party's motivation because you appear to be interested and listening.

Probing questions may cause problems. If a person does not respond immediately, you may jump in with a probing question when none is needed. Phrase probing questions carefully and be aware of vocal emphasis. Stanley Payne illustrates how the meaning of a simple "Why" question can be altered by stressing different words.[2]

Why do you say that?

Why *do* you say that?

Why do *you* say that?

Why do you *say* that?

Why do you say *that?*

A "simple" why question may unintentionally communicate disapproval, disbelief, mistrust, and make the other party defensive and reluctant to disclose openly. A poorly phrased probing question may alter the meaning of the primary question or bias the reply. Be tactful and not demanding. Do not misquote or put words into the person's mouth.

Exercise #1—Supply the Probing Question

Supply an appropriate probing question for each of the following interactions. Be sure the question probes into the answer and is not a primary question introducing a new facet of the topic. Watch assumptions about answers, and phrase probing questions tactfully.

1. **Interviewer:** How was the Super Bowl?

   Interviewee: It was awesome!

   Interviewer:

2. **Interviewer:** What is your teaching philosophy?

   Interviewee: (silence)

   Interviewer:

3. **Interviewer:** Are you going to college after you get out of the Air Force?

   Interviewee: Perhaps.

   Interviewer:

4. **Interviewer:** What do you do in your free time?

   Interviewee: Oh, I hang out with friends, play video games, and things like that.

   Interviewer:

5. **Interviewer:** How much did your trip to New Zealand cost?

   Interviewee: It was pretty expensive.

   Interviewer:

6. **Interviewer:** Why did you join the Peace Corps?

   Interviewee: My coach suggested it.

   Interviewer:

7. **Interviewer:** What did you think of the chaplain's sermon?

   Interviewee: It was typical.

   Interviewer:

8. **Interviewer:** Who did you vote for in the 2012 presidential election?

   Interviewee: Governor Christie.

   Interviewer:

9. **Interviewer:** Which movie do you think should win the Academy Award this year?

   Interviewee: I don't know.

   Interviewer:

10. **Interviewer:** I understand that you think global warming is a hoax.

    Interviewee: You might say that.

    Interviewer:

Neutral and Leading Questions

Neutral questions allow respondents to decide upon answers without direction or pressure from questioners. For example, in open, neutral questions, the interviewee determines the length, details, and nature of the answers. In closed, neutral questions, a person may choose between equal choices. All questions discussed and illustrated so far have been neutral questions.

Neutral
questions
encourage
honest
answers.

Leading questions suggest the answer expected or desired because the questioner leads the respondent toward a particular answer by making "it easier or more tempting for the respondent to give one answer than another."[3]

Interviewer bias occurs whenever respondents provide answers they *feel* interviewers prefer to hear. Such bias may be *intentional* or *unintentional*. Leading questions are a major source of interviewer bias, but others are status difference between the parties, an interviewee's perceptions or assumptions, word choice, dress, symbols such as political buttons, and nonverbal signals.

Leading ques-
tions direct
interviewees
to specific
answers.

The varying degrees of leading and the distinction between neutral and leading questions are illustrated in the following questions.

Neutral Questions	Leading Questions
1. Do you enjoy fly fishing?	1. You like fly fishing, don't you?
2. Are you going to the conference?	2. You're going to the conference, aren't you?
3. How did this class compare to the last one?	3. Wasn't this class better than the last one?
4. How do you feel about working out?	4. Do you hate to work out like most of us?
5. What were your reactions to the new scheduling system?	5. What were your reactions to the stupid new scheduling system?
6. Have you ever gotten drunk?	6. When was the last time you got drunk?
7. Have you ever cheated in class?	7. Have you stopped cheating in class?
8. Do you consider yourself to be a conservative or a liberal?	8. Do you consider yourself to be a conservative or a socialist?
9. How do you feel about gun control laws?	9. How do you feel about gun control laws that violate our second amendment rights and will lead to a police state?
10. Do you want a diet soft drink?	10. I assume you want a diet soft drink.

Interviewer
bias leads
to dictated
responses.

All 10 leading questions make it easier for a person to reply in a specific way. If you are in a nonthreatening, informal, pleasant situation with a friend or equal in an organizational or social situation, you might ignore or object to a leading question. However, if you are in a threatening, formal situation with a higher status party, you might feel obligated to answer as the interviewer prefers. At other times, you might go along with the direction because you don't care, want to cooperate, avoid upsetting a person, or "not make a scene." If that's the answer a person wants, you give it.

An apparent
bipolar ques-
tion may in
reality have
only one pole.

The first four and the last two leading questions are mild in direction. Each appears to be bipolar. However, the phrasing of each guides the respondent toward one pole; they are actually *unipolar* questions.

Respondents could ignore the direction of questions 1, 2, 3, and 10 if their relationship did not seem to depend on yes answers. Question 4 uses a bandwagon (follow-the-crowd) technique, and a respondent's answer might depend on past experiences with this interviewer and whether the respondent wants to follow the majority. Question 10 suggests that the respondent will want a diet soft drink. A person with ambivalent or apathetic feelings might just give the answer the interviewer seems to want.

Loaded Questions

Loaded questions are extreme leading questions. Questions 5 to 9 provide strong direction, virtual dictation of the correct answer; that's why they are called *loaded* questions. Questions 5 and 9 are loaded because of name-calling and emotionally charged words. In response to question 8, a person is likely to choose the least onerous of the choices provided, conservative, because few Americans see themselves as socialists. Questions 6 and 7 entrap the respondent. Question 6 implies that the respondent has been drunk. Question 7 charges the person with cheating. A yes or no may get the person in trouble.

> Loaded questions dictate answers through language or entrapment.

Since leading questions, particularly loaded ones, have potential for severe interviewer bias, avoid them unless you know what you are doing! Introductory phrases such as "According to the law," "As we all know," "As witnesses have testified," and "As the coach warned" may lead respondents to give acceptable answers rather than true feelings or beliefs. You can turn a neutral question into a leading question by the nonverbal manner in which you ask it. For example, you might appear to demand a certain answer by leaning toward the respondent, looking the person directly in the eyes, or raising an eyebrow. You might place vocal emphasis on a key word, such as:

> Leading questions have legitimate functions.

Did you *like* that pizza?

When did you *show up* for work?

You're going to vote for *her*?

Regardless of their potential for mischief, leading questions have important uses. Recruiters use them to see how interviewees respond under stress. Sales representatives use leading questions to close sales. Police officers ask loaded questions to provoke witnesses. Journalists ask leading questions to prod reluctant interviewees into responding. Counselors use a loaded question such as "When was the last time you used meth?" to show that a range of answers is acceptable and that none will shock the interviewer.

Do not confuse neutral mirror and reflective probing questions with leading questions. Mirrors and reflectives may *appear* to direct respondents toward particular answers, but their purposes are *clarification and verification,* not leading or direction. If they lead by accident, they are failures.

Figure 3.2 compares types of questions available to interviewers and interviewees, including open and closed, primary and probing, and neutral and leading questions.

Exercise #2—Identification of Questions

Identify each of the following questions in four ways: (1) open or closed, (2) primary or probing, (3) neutral or leading, and (4) whether it is a special type of question

Figure 3.2   *Types of questions*

	Neutral		**Leading**	
	Open	**Closed**	**Open**	**Closed**
Primary	How do you feel about the new core requirements?	Do you approve or disapprove of the new core requirements?	Most top students favor the new core requirements; how do you feel about them?	Do you favor the new core requirements like most top students I've talked to?
Probing	Why do you feel that way?	Is your approval moderate or strong?	If you favor the core requirements, why did you initially oppose them?	I assume you favor the new core requirements because you're graduating in two months.

tool: bipolar, loaded, nudging probe, clearinghouse probe, informational probe, restatement probe, reflective probe, or mirror probe.

1. What did you do during your internship?

2. Are you saying that you joined the Army for the college scholarship?

3. Did you vote in the last primary election?

4. Is there anything else you would like to tell me about your position with the NCAA?

5. Quitting your job in the middle of a recession was pretty dumb, wasn't it?

6. I see.

7. You are concerned about this situation, aren't you?

8. **Interviewer:** What did you see first when you came upon the accident?

   Interviewee: A lot, believe me.

   Interviewer: I'm sure. What did you see first?

9. Okay, it sounds like planning for the lecture is set. As I understand, you are taking care of publicity, Jane is handling travel and housing, Fallon is arranging for a dinner prior to the lecture, I will introduce the speaker and handle the Q and A session, and Zack is setting up the reception in the atrium immediately following the lecture. Is all of this correct?

10. And what happened after that?

Common Question Pitfalls

Because interviews are often minimally structured and we must create both primary and probing questions on the spot, it is easy to stumble into common **question pitfalls** without being aware of it. These pitfalls include the bipolar trap, the tell me everything, the open-to-closed switch, the double-barreled inquisition, the leading push, the guessing game, the yes (no) response, the curious probe, the quiz show, and the don't ask, don't tell question. In informal interactions with friends, family, and associates, the other party may help you out by providing more information and insights than a closed or bipolar question is designed to elicit, by ignoring a leading question or forgiving a loaded question, or by answering both parts of a double-barreled question. In structured, purposeful interviews, however, parties may have little to no motivation to help you out. They may provide only what you ask for with the intent to volunteer as little as possible (perhaps a yes or no), to reply to only one part of a double-barreled question, and to take offense at a leading or loaded question. This book and your course are designed to prepare you for taking part in *formal, professional interactions* we call interviews and you must be aware of question pitfalls and how to avoid them if you are to be a successful interviewer and interviewee.

The Bipolar Trap

You fall into a **bipolar trap** when you ask a bipolar question designed to elicit a yes or no answer when you really want a detailed answer or specific information. This pitfall is obvious in questions that begin with words such as *do you, did you, are you, have you, were you, can you, is there, would you,* and *was it.* If all you want is a yes or no, each may be satisfactory, but a yes or no tells you little.

Bipolar questions assume there are only two possible answers and that the answers are poles apart: conservative–liberal, like–dislike, approve–disapprove, agree–disagree, high–low, yes–no.

Eliminate bipolar traps by reserving bipolar questions for situations in which only a yes or no or a single word is desired. Begin questions with words and phrases such as *what, why, how, explain,* and *tell me about* that ask for detailed information, feelings, or attitudes.

The Tell Me Everything

The **tell me everything** question is at the opposite end of the scale from the bipolar trap. Instead of a simple yes–no or agree–disagree, this question trap occurs when the interviewer asks an extremely open question with no restrictions or guidelines for the interviewee. The interviewee may have a difficult time determining where to begin, what to include, what to exclude, and when to end. The tell me everything pitfall occurs in an employment interview when a recruiter asks "Tell me about yourself," in a journalistic interview when a reporter asks "What was it like in Afghanistan," or a health care provider asks "Tell me about your medical history."

Ask open-ended questions rather than closed and bipolar questions, but don't make them too open. In the examples above, let the interviewee know what part of self, the

Afghanistan deployment, and the medical history you are most interested in. If an interviewee were to respond as directed, the answer could take an hour and you might have difficulty shutting the person off tactfully.

The Open-to-Closed Switch

Think before asking and know when to stop asking.

The **open-to-closed switch** question occurs when you ask an open question but, before the interviewee can respond, you rephrase it into a closed or bipolar question. This trap is readily apparent in interviews, such as:

Tell me about your trip to Seattle. Did you see the new Boeing Dreamliner?

Why did you purchase a new pickup truck at this time? Was it because of the rebate?

The open-to-closed switch occurs when you are still phrasing a question in your mind. This rummaging about for the right phrasing often changes a perfectly good open question into a narrow, closed question. The respondent is likely to address only the second question, perhaps with a yes or no. Avoid the open-to-closed switch by *preparing* questions prior to the interview and *thinking through* questions before asking them.

The Double-Barreled Inquisition

Ask one question at a time.

The **double-barreled inquisition** question occurs when you ask two (or more) questions at the same time instead of a single, precise question.

Which charities do you give to most often and how did you choose these?

Tell me about your positions at Penney's and at Macy's.

Respondents may react in a variety of ways to double-barreled questions. They may answer both parts, answer both parts superficially, answer the part they can remember, select the part they want to answer, or react negatively to a perceived inquisition. You may find it necessary to repeat a portion of the initial question to get all of the information wanted, or you may be unaware of missing information and go to another primary question prematurely.

Avoid the double-barreled trap and its dangers by asking one question at a time. If you ask a double-barreled question, repeat the part the interviewee does not answer.

© MBI/Alamy

■ *How you ask a question may bias the answer you receive.*

The Leading Push

The **leading push** occurs when you ask a question that suggests how a person ought to respond. The push may be intentional (you want to influence an answer) or unintentional (you are not aware of the push). It is easy to interject feelings or attitudes in questions through language and nonverbal signals.

> **Push only when there is a need to push.**

You're going to the help session, aren't you?

You chose a college because *your girl friend* went there?

You may not realize you have asked a leading question and remain unaware that you received a skewed answer to please you. The interviewee may go along with whatever answer you seem to want, particularly if you are in a superior role. Avoid the leading push trap by phrasing questions neutrally and listening carefully to each question you ask.

The Guessing Game

> **Don't guess; ask!**

The **guessing game** pitfall occurs when you try to guess information instead of asking for it. Guessing is common in interviews. Strings of closed, guessing questions fail to accomplish what a single open-ended question can. Observe the failure of this guessing spree to gain detailed information.

1. **Interviewer:** Were you the first on the scene?
2. **Interviewee:** No.
3. **Interviewer:** Were you with the first responders?
4. **Interviewee:** No.
5. **Interviewer:** Were you with the second responders?
6. **Interviewee:** No.
7. **Interviewer:** Did you arrive before they brought out the first children?
8. **Interviewee:** No.

This long list of guesses would not have been necessary if the first question had been, "When did you arrive?" **Ask** rather than **guess,** and rely on open rather than closed questions to avoid the guessing game pitfall.

The Yes (No) Response

> **An obvious question will generate an obvious answer.**

The **yes (no) response** pitfall occurs when you ask a question that has only one obvious answer, a yes or a no. Each of the following questions is likely to get a predictable response:

(asked of a student) Do you want to pass this course?

(asked of a medical patient) Do you want to die?

Avoid the yes (no) question pitfall by opening up your questions and avoiding the obvious.

The Curious Probe

> **Curiosity may be fatal to interviewers.**

Curious probes delve into information you **do not need.** Make sure every question you ask probes into information that is relevant and important to the purpose of your interview. If there is a likelihood that a question **may appear to the interviewee** to be irrelevant or none of your business, explain why it is important and how you will use the information you receive. For example, ask for demographic data such as age, income, educational level, and marital status only when such information is clearly *necessary* and *relevant,* after you have *established trust,* and at the *end* of the interview.

As an interviewee, do not assume a question is irrelevant; the interviewer may have a legitimate reason for asking. Other cultures ask questions that might appear irrelevant. Japanese may ask personal questions early in interactions to learn important characteristics about you, such as where you were born, where you went to school, how you feel about Japanese food, what Japanese you speak, and what hobbies you have.

The Quiz Show

> What does the interviewee know of relevance to this topic?

Interviews are not **quiz shows** between interviewers and contestants. The parties you interview should have a store of knowledge that enables them to answer comfortably and intelligently. Questions above a respondent's information level may cause embarrassment or resentment because no one wants to appear uninformed, ill-informed, uneducated, or unintelligent. Respondents may fake answers or give vague answers rather than admit ignorance. On the other hand, questions beneath a respondent's level of information may be insulting.

Avoid the quiz show pitfall by asking for information in common categories or frames of reference such as pounds rather than ounces, cups rather than pots of coffee, or number of hours watching television per day rather than month or year. Know if a respondent is a layperson, novice, or expert on the topic.

Complexity vs. Simplicity

Ask questions that are simple, clear requests for reasonable amounts of information. Avoid overly complex questions that challenge respondents to figure out what you want. The following is a common type of survey question asked over the telephone:

> Now, I would like your opinion on some leading brands of detergent. I would like you to rate these brands by using the numbers from plus five to minus five. If you like the brand, give it a number from plus one to plus five. The more you like it, the bigger the plus number you should give it. If you dislike the brand, give it a number from minus one to minus five. The more you dislike it, the bigger the minus number you should give it. If you neither like nor dislike the brand, give it a zero.

If you must ask a complex question, explain the scale and provide opportunities for interviewees to try out the scale to determine if they understand the question and how to answer it. If interviews are face-to-face, hand a small card to interviewees that contains the scale and answer options so they need not remember all of the complex question. Phrase questions carefully by avoiding a mixture of negatives, positives, maybes, and unnecessary detail.

The Don't Ask, Don't Tell

Don't ask, don't tell questions delve into information and emotions that respondents may be incapable of addressing because of social, psychological, or situational constraints. You learn from an early age, for instance, that it is more socially acceptable to be humble than boastful. If an interviewer asks you to assess your beauty, intelligence, creativity, generosity, or bravery, you are likely to pose an "Aw shucks" attitude or say "Yes" with a flourish that treats your answer as a joke. You also learn that "there is a time and a place for everything," so you do not discuss certain topics in mixed groups, in public, or in political, religious, or social settings. Some areas are often taboo: sex, personal income, religious convictions, and certain illnesses.

> **Delve into inaccessible areas only when necessary.**

Explain why a question is essential to ask, and delay "touchy" or "taboo" questions until you have established a comfortable climate and positive relationship. Phrase questions carefully to lessen social and psychological constraints and to avoid offending interviewees.

Gender and cultural differences may affect social and psychological *accessibility*. Research indicates that women disclose more information about themselves, use more psychological or emotional verbs, discuss their personal lives more in business interactions, have less difficulty expressing intimate feelings, talk more about other people's accomplishments and minimize their own, and appear to be more comfortable when hearing accolades about themselves.[4] Cultures also differ in readily accessible areas. Learn as much as you can about an interviewee prior to an interview to determine what can and cannot be asked and how it should be asked.

> **Avoid pitfalls by preparing and thinking.**

Avoid common question pitfalls by planning questions prior to the interview so you do not have to create them on the spot in the give-and-take of the interaction. Think before uttering a question, stop when you have asked a good open question instead of rephrasing it, use bipolar questions sparingly, avoid questions that are too open-ended, ask only necessary questions, ask for information at the interviewee's level, avoid complex questions, and be aware of the accessibility factor in questions and answers. Know the common question pitfalls well enough that you can catch yourself before tumbling into one.

Exercise #3—What Are the Pitfalls in These Questions?

Each of the following questions illustrates one or more of the common question pitfalls: bipolar trap, open-to-closed switch, double-barreled inquisition, leading push, guessing game, yes (no) response, tell me everything, curious probe, complexity vs. simplicity, quiz show, and don't ask, don't tell. Identify the pitfall(s) of each question and rephrase it to make it a good question. Avoid a new pitfall in your revised question.

1. Tell me about your trip to Alaska; was it what you expected?
2. (asked in a college recruiting interview) Are you a registered Democrat or Republican?
3. Tell me about your study abroad experience in Paris and the courses you took.
4. Did you like the play?
5. You're concerned about your job, aren't you?
6. Do you consider yourself to be a genius?
7. (asked of a parent) Do you want your child to have a good education?
8. Did you join Air Force ROTC for the college scholarship?
9. Tell me about Ford Motor Company.
10. Do you like or dislike scallops?

ON THE WEB

Browse an Internet site to locate a variety of question–answer interactions that vary in intensity from happy to sad, cooperative to uncooperative, friendly to hostile, and understanding to patronizing. Identify the different types of primary and probing questions in these interactions. Which question pitfalls can you identify? Which of these pitfalls were accidental and which purposeful? Use search engines such as the Knight Ridder Newspapers (http://www.kri.com), CNBC (http://www.cnbc.com), and CNN (http://cnn.com).

Summary

You have a limitless variety of question tools to choose from, and each tool has unique characteristics, capabilities, and pitfalls. Knowing which question to select and how to use it is essential for interviewing effectively and efficiently. Each question has three characteristics: (1) open or closed, (2) primary or probing, and (3) neutral or leading. Open questions are designed to discover large amounts of information, while closed questions are designed to gain specific bits of information. Primary questions open up topics and subtopics, while probing questions probe into answers for more information, explanations, clarifications, and verifications. Neutral questions give respondents freedom to answer as they wish, while leading questions nudge or shove respondents toward specific answers.

Phrasing questions is essential to get the information needed. If you phrase questions carefully and think before asking, you can avoid common question pitfalls such as the bipolar trap, tell me everything, open-to-closed switch, double-barreled inquisition, leading push, guessing game, yes (no) response, curious probe, quiz show, complexity vs. simplicity, and don't ask, don't tell.

Key Terms and Concepts

The online learning center for this text features FLASHCARDS and CROSSWORD PUZZLES for studying based on these terms and concepts.

Bipolar question	Informational probe	Primary question
Bipolar trap	Leading push	Probing question
Clearinghouse probe	Leading question	Question pitfalls
Closed question	Loaded question	Quiz show
Complexity vs. simplicity	Mirror probe	Reflective probe
Curious probe	Neutral question	Restatement probe
Don't ask, don't tell	Nudging probe	Silent probe
Double-barreled inquisition	Open question	Tell me everything
Guessing game	Open-to-closed switch	Yes (no) response

An Interview for Review and Analysis

The interviewer is conducting oral history interviews with residents of a newly designated historic district in Springfield to learn about the homes in the district, some more than 150 years old. This interview is with an 80-year-old resident who has resided all of his life on "The Hill," as the area is known locally. It is taking place in the interviewee's home.

As you read through this interview, identify the questions as open or closed, primary or probing, and neutral or leading. Look for specific types of questions such as bipolar, loaded, silent probe, nudging probe, clearinghouse probe, informational probe, restatement probe, reflective probe, and mirror probe. Does the interviewer stumble into common question pitfalls such as leading push, bipolar trap, yes or no response, tell me everything, open-to-closed switch, guessing game, double-barreled inquisition, curious probe, quiz show, complexity vs. simplicity, and don't ask, don't tell?

1. **Interviewer:** Hi Mr. Mullins. I'm Jackie Li from the Springfield Historical Society.

2. **Interviewee:** Hi Jackie, please call me Ed.

3. **Interviewer:** As I mentioned on the phone, I'm conducting oral history interviews with residents of the new historic district. It will take about an hour.

4. **Interviewee:** I'm glad you're interested in our area. Please come in and sit down.

5. **Interviewer:** This is a beautiful home. When was it built?

6. **Interviewee:** It was first built in 1856 in what was called the Federal style.

7. **Interviewer:** You said "first built," what do you mean by that?

8. **Interviewee:** Well, the initial structure contained a living room and kitchen on the first floor and four bedrooms on the second.

9. **Interviewer:** And then what happened?

10. **Interviewee:** Shortly after the Civil War, in about 1867, a wing was added on the north side that contained a sitting room and a library on the first floor.

11. **Interviewer:** And this was only a one-story addition?

12. **Interviewee:** No.

13. **Interviewer:** There was a second floor?

14. **Interviewee:** Yes.

15. **Interviewer:** Tell me about that and the summer kitchen.

16. **Interviewee:** It contained a fifth bedroom for guests and what was then called a modern bathroom with a sink, tub, and running water from a tank in the attic.

17. **Interviewer:** And when did your family first move into this home?

18. **Interviewee:** My grandparents purchased the home in 1905 shortly after my father was born.

19. **Interviewer:** And how long have you lived here?

20. **Interviewee:** All my life.

21. **Interviewer:** *All* (vocal emphasis) of your life?

22. **Interviewee:** Yes.

23. **Interviewer:** You weren't born in this house, were you?

24. **Interviewee:** Yes.

25. **Interviewer:** Where?

26. **Interviewee:** In my parents' bedroom.

27. **Interviewer:** And you've never lived anywhere else?

28. **Interviewee:** That's right.

29. **Interviewer:** Where did you live while in college?

30. **Interviewee:** I commuted from here.

31. **Interviewer:** Why do people in Springfield refer to this area as "the Hill;" is it simply because it's on a high hill?

32. **Interviewee:** No.

33. **Interviewer:** When did they start referring to it as "the Hill?"

34. **Interviewee:** My dad said they often referred to it as "the Hill" when he was a kid and people came from all over town to sled down the streets during snowfalls. There was a toboggan run on the west side for many years.

35. **Interviewer:** What have I not asked about that you think I ought to know?

36. **Interviewee:** Well . . . I got married in this house, and my wife and I raised our family of five children here.

37. **Interviewer:** That's very interesting. Do any of your children live here now?

38. **Interviewee:** No, they all live in other states.

39. **Interviewer:** Do you foresee selling the house to another family in a few years?

40. **Interviewee:** Perhaps.

41. **Interviewer:** Thanks for meeting with me. This has been a very interesting project.

42. **Interviewee:** You're welcome. Let me know if I can be of more help.

Student Activities

1. Watch an interview on C-SPAN that lasts at least 15 minutes. Which types of questions does the interviewer employ? Which seem to be the most effective? How does the relationship between interviewer and interviewee appear to affect question types and responses? How does the situation appear to affect question selection and responses?

2. Prepare two sets of 10 questions each, one with all neutral questions and one with four of the questions rephrased as leading questions. Conduct six interviews, three with all-neutral questions and three with the mixture of neutral and leading questions. Compare the answers you received and determine how types of questions may have influenced these answers. Why do you think some interviewees ignored the direction you provided in leading questions while others did not?

3. Create a list of closed questions, including bipolar questions, on a topic of importance in your state. Interview four people: a friend, a family member older than you, an acquaintance, and a stranger selected at random. Which ones gave you the shortest, least revealing answers? Which ones volunteered the most information regardless of question type? What does this tell you about using closed questions and the relationship between parties?

4. Listen to several interviews on television, including ones with politicians, company representatives, sports figures, and people who have experienced a crisis. Identify the question pitfalls exhibited in the questions asked and how they seemed to affect responses. Which were the most common pitfalls? Did you identify question pitfalls not covered in this chapter?

Notes

1. Joyce Kasman Valenza, "For the best answers, ask tough questions," *The Philadelphia Inquirer,* April 20, 2000, http://www.joycevalenza.com/questions.html, accessed September 26, 2006.

2. Stanley L. Payne, *The Art of Asking Questions* (Princeton, NJ: Princeton University Press, 1980), p. 204.

3. Robert L. Kahn and Charles F. Cannell, *The Dynamics of Interviewing* (New York: John Wiley, 1964), p. 205.

4. Lillian Glass, *He Says, She Says: Closing the Communication Gap between the Sexes* (New York: Putnam, 1993), pp. 45–59; Kory Floyd, *Interpersonal Communication* (New York: McGraw-Hill, 2011), p. 99.

Resources

Barone, Jeanne Tessier, and Jo Young Switzer. *Interviewing: Art and Skill*. Boston: Pearson Education, 1995.

Devito, Joseph A. *Interviewing Guidebook*. Boston: Pearson Education, 2010.

Payne, Stanley L. *The Art of Asking Questions*. Princeton, NJ: Princeton University Press, 1980.

Powell, Larry, and Jonathan H. Amsbary. *Interviewing: Situations and Contexts*. Boston: Pearson Education, 2006.

Structuring the Interview

Every interview has a degree of structure, the nature of which is determined by purpose, length, and complexity. Different types of interviews require different structures, but fundamental principles and techniques apply to all. **The objectives of this chapter** are to introduce you to the principles and techniques of structuring and explain how they apply to the opening, body, and closing of interviews. This chapter begins with the **body** of the interview because that is where you should start your preparation.

The Body of the Interview

The first step in preparing for an interview is to determine a **clear purpose**. What specifically do you want and need to accomplish during this interview? Go no further until you have a clearly delineated purpose.

Interview Guide

> An interview guide contains topics, not questions.

The second step is to prepare an **interview guide**—a carefully structured outline of topics and subtopics to be covered, not a list of questions. A guide enables you to identify specific areas of inquiry that ensures coverage of important topics during the heat of the interview and helps you to distinguish relevant from irrelevant information. It will assist you in phrasing questions, recording answers, and recalling information at a later date.

Outline Sequences

Since the interview guide is an outline, review the fundamentals of outlining learned over the years to impose a clear, systematic structure on your interview. **Outline sequences** are quite useful for interviews.

A **topical sequence** follows natural divisions of a topic or issue. For example, if you are planning to interview a number of attorneys about law schools you might attend, your guide would include such topics as ranking among law schools, areas of specialization, quality of the law school review, number and type of law firms that come to campus for interviews, and cost. The traditional **journalist's guide** consisting of six key words—who, what, when, where, how, and why—is useful in many interview settings.

> Sequences help organize topics and impose a degree of structure on interviews.

A **time sequence** treats topics or parts of topics in chronological order. For instance, a conference on solar-powered vehicles may start with registration from 8:30 to 9:30 a.m., proceed to a general session on the history of solar-powered vehicles at 10:30 a.m., a session on recent developments in solar powering of vehicles at 11:30 a.m., lunch from 12:30 to 1:30 p.m., a demonstration of solar-powered vehicles on the nearby county fairgrounds race track from 1:30 to 3:30 p.m., and a closing session from 3:30 to 4:30 p.m.

A **space sequence** arranges topics according to spatial divisions: left to right, top to bottom, north to south, or neighborhood to neighborhood. A person conducting tours of a resort might begin with the restaurants and bars, and then proceed to the pool area, sauna, fitness facility, golf course, and marina.

A **cause-to-effect sequence** explores causes and effects. An interviewer might begin with a cause or causes and then proceed to effect, or discuss an apparent effect and then move to possible causes. For example, if you were investigating the collapse of a stage during a violent thunderstorm, you might interview persons in the area during the collapse to determine effects of the storm followed by interviews with structural engineers to determine the cause or causes of the collapse.

A **problem-solution sequence** consists of a problem phase and a solution phase. You might conduct interviews with recruiters to discuss a serious problem with lack of diversity among an organization's workforce and then identify and discuss possible solutions.

Developing an Interview Guide

You are majoring in health sciences and, after talking to several of your professors and fellow students, have decided to spend a semester studying abroad. After looking at a number of universities in several countries, you have arranged an interview with a representative of the University of Canterbury in Christchurch, New Zealand, when she comes to visit your campus early next month. As you start your interview guide, begin with major areas of information you need to make your decision, such as the following:

I.   Courses related to health sciences

II. Teaching/learning facilities

III. Research facilities

IV. Housing

With major areas identified, place possible subtopics under such as the following:

> A guide ensures the consideration of all important topics and subtopics.

I.   Courses related to health sciences
    A.   Psychological sciences
    B.   Audiology and speech sciences
    C.   Foods and nutrition
    D.   Biology
    E.   Health and kinesiology

II. Teaching/learning facilities
    A.   Learning and support services
    B.   Learning and teaching plan
    C.   Resources for teaching and learning
    D.   Electronic learning media
    E.   Learning skills center

III. Research facilities
  A. Laboratories
  B. Libraries
  C. IT and computing facilities
  D. Survey research center
  E. Research-teaching link

IV. Housing
  A. Cost
  B. Type
  C. Availability
  D. Relationship to campus
  E. Transportation

> **Interviews may include more than one sequence or none at all.**

Finally, with major areas and subtopics listed, determine if there are important subtopics of subtopics. For example, you might want to know about different types of research laboratories, research monographs available in the libraries and on-line, how IT and computing facilities are available to undergraduate students, health sciences research conducted at the survey research center, and how involved faculty are in both teaching and research. You may not know enough prior to the interview to develop subtopics under certain areas and subtopics or you may discover additional subtopics during the interview. The interview guide enables you to add and delete as necessary. You may employ more than one outline sequence in an interview. Selection of areas and appropriate subtopics will determine which sequences are most appropriate.

Interview Schedules

A Nonscheduled Interview

> **A nonscheduled interview is merely an interview guide.**

After completing an interview guide, decide if additional structuring and preparation are needed. The guide may be sufficient to conduct a **nonscheduled interview** with no questions prepared in advance. The nonscheduled interview is most appropriate when interviews will be brief, interviewees and information levels differ significantly, interviewees are reluctant to respond or have poor memories, or there is little preparation time.

A nonscheduled interview gives you unlimited freedom to probe into answers and adapt to different interviewees and situations because it is the most flexible of interview schedules. However, nonscheduled interviews require considerable skill and are difficult to replicate from one interview to another. You may have difficulty controlling time. And interviewer bias may creep into unplanned questions.

A Moderately Scheduled Interview

> **A moderately scheduled interview lessens the need for instant question creation.**

A **moderately scheduled interview** consists of all major questions with possible probing questions under each. The sentences and phrases in a guide become questions. The moderate schedule, like the nonscheduled interview, allows freedom to probe into answers and adapt to different interviewees, but it also imposes a greater degree of structure, aids in recording answers, and is easier to conduct and replicate. You need not create every question on the spot but have many thought out and carefully worded in advance. This lessens pressures during the interview. Since interview parties tend to wander during unstructured interviews, listing questions makes it easier to keep on track and return to a structure when desired. Journalists, medical personnel, recruiters, lawyers, police officers, and insurance investigators, to name a few, use moderately scheduled interviews. A moderately scheduled interview would look like this:

I.   Why did you decide to move your company from Illinois to Indiana?
    A.   When did you decide to do this?
    B.   What influenced you most in your decision?
    C.   Who influenced you most in your decision?

II. Why did you choose to relocate near Rensselaer?
    A.   How important was location near the Illinois border?
    B.   How did Rensselaer compare in cost of construction to other locations?
    C.   What role did your current corporate staff play in this decision?
    D.   How important was Rensselaer's being on the same time zone as Chicago?

III. What concerned you most about relocating to Indiana?
    A.   What about availability of qualified workers?
    B.   What about Indiana's history, until recently, of allowing union shops?
    C.   What about transportation?

A Highly Scheduled Interview

On paper a **highly scheduled interview** may look no different from the moderately scheduled interview illustrated above, but they are very different in execution. Unlike those in a moderate schedule, all questions in a highly scheduled interview are asked exactly in the order they are listed and worded in the schedule. It permits no unplanned probing, word changes, or deviation from the schedule. Questions may be closed so respondents can give brief, specific answers. Highly scheduled interviews are easy to replicate and conduct, take less time than nonscheduled and moderately scheduled interviews, and prevent parties from wandering into irrelevant areas or spending too much time on one or two topics. Flexibility and adaptation are not options, however. Probing questions must be planned. Researchers and survey takers use highly scheduled interviews.

> Highly scheduled interviews sacrifice flexibility and adaptability for control.

A Highly Scheduled Standardized Interview

The **highly scheduled standardized interview** is the most thoroughly planned and structured. All questions and answer options are stated in identical words to each interviewee who then picks answers from those provided. There is no straying from the schedule by either party. Highly scheduled standardized interviews are the easiest to conduct, record, tabulate, and replicate, so even novice interviewers can handle them. However, the breadth of information is restricted, and probing into answers, explaining questions, and adapting to different interviewees are not permitted. Respondents cannot explain, amplify, qualify, or question answer options. **Built-in interviewer bias** may

> Highly scheduled standardized interviews provide precision, replicability, and reliability.

be worse than **accidental bias** encountered in nonscheduled and moderately scheduled interviews.

Researchers and survey takers use highly scheduled standardized interviews because their procedures must produce the same results in repeated interviews by several interviewers. The following is a highly scheduled standardized interview:

I. Which one of the following often-mentioned causes of high gasoline prices do you think is the most important?
    A. Shortage of oil
    B. Too little domestic production
    C. Oil companies increasing prices to raise profits
    D. Foreign countries purposely raising cost of oil
    E. Speculators on the oil market
    F. Increasing demand for oil in countries such as China and India

II. Which one of the following solutions do you feel has the best potential for lowering the cost of gasoline?
    A. Increased drilling in the wilderness areas of Alaska
    B. Increased drilling along the Atlantic, Gulf, and Pacific coasts of the United States
    C. A pipeline from Canada to Texas to bring oil sands to refineries
    D. Opening up the strategic reserves of oil held in the United States
    E. Increased use of all electric and hybrid vehicles in the United States
    F. Development of alternate fuels from corn, sugar cane, and waste

III. How likely do you feel this solution will be implemented within the next three years?
    A. Highly likely
    B. Likely
    C. Unsure
    D. Unlikely
    E. Highly unlikely

IV. If gasoline prices continue to increase, which of the following results do you expect to see this summer?
    A. Vacations closer to home
    B. A significant drop in driving
    C. A significant increase in use of public transportation
    D. A significant rise in food costs
    E. A slowing down of the economic recovery

Each interviewing schedule has unique advantages and disadvantages. Choose the schedule best suited to your needs, skills, type of information desired, and situation. One type of schedule does not fit all interview types and situations. A schedule designed for a survey would be a terrible schedule for an employment interview. Be aware of the options available and which one or ones seem most appropriate for each interview. Figure 4.1 summarizes the advantages and disadvantages of each schedule.

Figure 4.1 *Structural options*

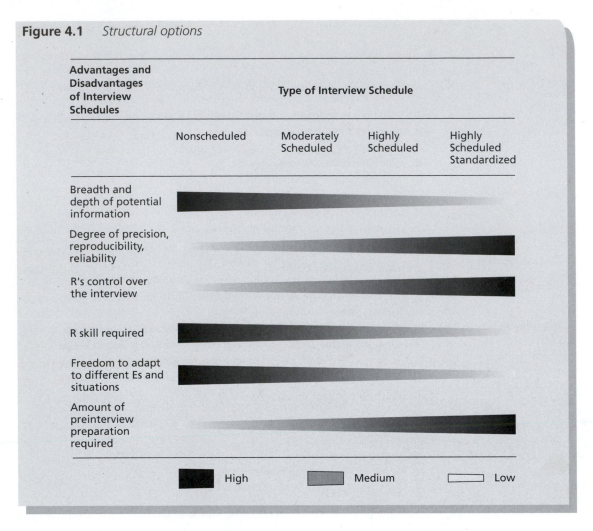

Combination of Schedules

> Combined schedules enable interviewers to satisfy multiple needs.

Consider strategic combinations of schedules. For example, use a nonscheduled approach during the opening minutes, a moderately scheduled approach when it is necessary to probe and adapt to interviewees, and a highly scheduled standardized approach for easily quantifiable information such as age, religion, formal education, and marital status. Schedules range from a topic outline to a manuscript. For instance, you might write major arguments for a persuasive interview, instructions for an information-giving interview, and the opening and closing for a survey interview.

Exercise #1—Interview Schedules

Which schedule would be most appropriate for each of the situations below: nonscheduled, moderately scheduled, highly scheduled, highly scheduled standardized? Explain why you would select this schedule.

1. You are a journalist interviewing witnesses to a hit and run on campus resulting in critical injuries to two students.

2. You are a recruiter for a computer software firm conducting interviews at a job fair arranged by a member of Congress.

3. You are conducting a survey of graduating seniors as part of a nationwide study of the status of the job market for college graduates.

4. You are a developer of an apartment complex near a college campus and are attempting to persuade a member of the city council to vote for your proposal.

5. You are a member of the Parks and Recreation Board but missed the last meeting because of a family emergency. You are interviewing another board member to learn what was discussed and agreed upon at that meeting.

Question Sequences

Earlier we introduced you to a variety of question schedules, and now it's time to identify question sequences. Common **question sequences** are tunnel, funnel, inverted funnel, hourglass, diamond, and quintamensional design.

Tunnel Sequence

> **A tunnel sequence works well with informal and simple interviews.**

The **tunnel sequence**, or string of beads, is a similarly phrased string of open or closed questions. See the illustration in Figure 4.2. Each question may cover a specific topic, ask for a specific piece of information, or identify an attitude or feeling. A tunnel sequence might look like the following.

I understand that you took part in the "Occupy Wall Street" demonstrations that started the "occupy movement" in 2011.

1. When did you initially get involved?
2. Where did you initially get involved?
3. What was the most important factor in your decision to get involved?
4. At first, were you an organizer or a protestor?
5. What was your major role in occupying Wall Street?

The tunnel sequence is common in polls, surveys, journalistic interviews, and medical interviews designed to elicit information, attitudes, reactions, and intentions. When the questions are closed, information is easy to record and quantify.

Figure 4.2 *The tunnel (string of beads) sequence*

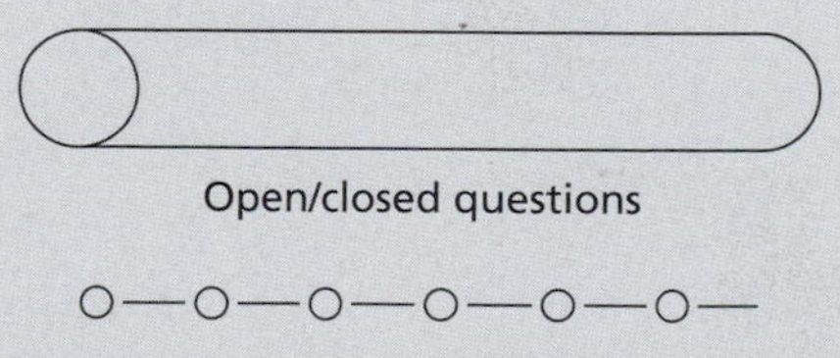

Open/closed questions

Funnel Sequence

A **funnel sequence** begins with broad, open-ended questions and proceeds with more restricted questions. See Figure 4.3. The following is a funnel sequence.

1. Tell me about your recruiting trip to the 21st Century Advertising agency in Raleigh.
2. What were the interviews like?
3. What were your impressions of 21st Century Advertising from these interviews?
4. Where did the interviews take place?
5. How long were you at the agency?
6. Will there be more interviews with this agency?

A funnel sequence begins with open-ended questions and is most appropriate when respondents are familiar with a topic, feel free to talk about it, want to express their feelings, and are motivated to reveal and explain attitudes. Open questions are easier to answer, pose less threat to respondents, and get people talking, so the funnel sequence is a good way to begin interviews.

The funnel sequence lessens possible conditioning or biasing of later responses. For example, if you begin an interview with a closed question you may force a respondent to take a polar position or appear to signal that you want only brief answers. An open question does not force respondents to take polarized positions and enables them to explain and qualify positions.

Inverted Funnel Sequence

The **inverted funnel sequence** begins with closed questions and proceeds toward open questions. It is most useful when you need to motivate an interviewee to respond or an interviewee is emotionally involved in an issue or situation and cannot readily reply to an open question. See Figure 4.4. The following is an inverted funnel sequence.

1. When did you start working for Alcoa?
2. What was your first job with the company?

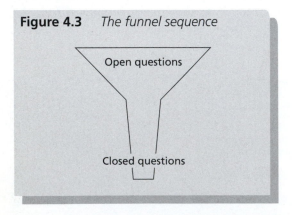

Figure 4.3   *The funnel sequence*

Open questions

Closed questions

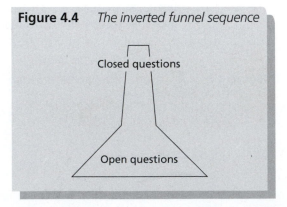

Figure 4.4   *The inverted funnel sequence*

Closed questions

Open questions

3. How long were you in this position?

4. How did this position prepare you for a supervisory position?

5. Tell me about your current position.

6. Walk me through a typical day for you in your current position.

The inverted funnel sequence is best when interviewees feel they do not know much about a topic or do not want to talk. A respondent's memory or thought processes may need assistance, and closed questions can serve as warm-ups when open-ended ones might overwhelm a person or result in disorganized and confused answers. This sequence may end with a clearinghouse question such as "Is there anything else you would like to tell me?"

Combination Sequences

A situation may call for a combination of question sequences. For instance, the **hourglass sequence** begins with open questions, proceeds to closed questions, and ends with open questions. Employ it when you wish to begin with a funnel sequence and then proceed in your line of questioning to an inverted funnel sequence. This combination enables you to narrow your focus and then proceed to open it up when the interviewee or topic warrants it. See Figure 4.5.

A second combination sequence places funnel sequences top-to-top, what some writers call a **diamond sequence.**[1] This sequence enables interviewers to begin with closed questions, proceed to open questions, and end with closed questions. See Figure 4.6.

Each combination sequence offers different arrangements of open and closed questions that enable you to approach specific interview situations and interviewees with flexibility and adaptability.

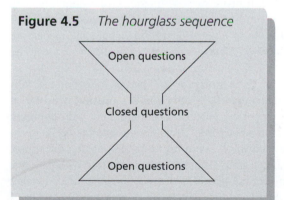

Figure 4.5   *The hourglass sequence*

Open questions

Closed questions

Open questions

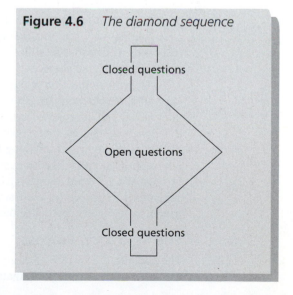

Figure 4.6   *The diamond sequence*

Closed questions

Open questions

Closed questions

Quintamensional Design Sequence

George Gallup, the famous poll designer, developed the **quintamensional design sequence** to assess the intensity of opinions and attitudes.[2] This five-step approach proceeds from an interviewee's awareness of the issue to attitudes uninfluenced by the interviewer, specific attitudes, reasons for these attitudes, and intensity of attitude. For example:

> The quinta-
> mensional
> design is
> effective at
> assessing
> attitudes and
> beliefs.

1. *Awareness:* What do you know about the new state law banning smoking in some facilities?
2. *Uninfluenced attitudes:* How might this ban affect you?
3. *Specific attitude:* Do you approve or disapprove of the statewide ban on smoking?
4. *Reason why:* Why do you feel this way?
5. *Intensity of attitude:* How strongly do you feel about this—strongly, very strongly, not something you will change your mind on?

You can use this sequence, or modify it by creating questions most suitable for specific interview situations.

Once you have determined a specific purpose for your interview and developed a structure appropriate for your interview, you are ready to create an opening adapted to the parties in the interview, the situation, and your purpose. The few seconds or minutes spent in the opening are critical to the success of your interview.

Opening the Interview

> It takes two
> parties to
> launch an
> interview
> successfully.

What you do and say, or fail to do and say, in the opening influences how the other party perceives self, you, and the situation. The **opening** sets the tone and mood of the interview and affects willingness and ability to go beyond Level 1 interactions. The tone may be serious or lighthearted, optimistic or pessimistic, professional or non-professional, formal or informal, threatening or nonthreatening, relaxed or tense. A poor opening may lead to a **defensive climate** with superficial, vague, and inaccurate responses. If dissatisfied with the opening, a party may say no, walk away, close the door, or hang up the phone.

The primary function of the opening is to **motivate** both parties to participate willingly and to communicate freely and accurately. Motivation is a **mutual product** of interviewer and interviewee, so every opening must be a **dialogue,** not a **monologue.** It is *done with* the other party, not *to* the other party. Too often the interviewee is given little opportunity to say anything beyond single-word responses to opening questions. Interrupting an interviewee is common. A study of physicians interacting with patients, for instance, revealed that physicians did not permit patients to complete their closing statements 69 percent of the time. And when this happened, fewer than 2 percent of patients attempted to complete their statements.[3]

The Two-Step Process

The opening is a two-step process of establishing rapport and orienting the other party that encourages active participation and willingness to continue with the interview.

What is included and how content is shared depends upon interview type, situation, relationship, and preference.

Establish Rapport

Rapport is a process of establishing and sustaining a relationship between interviewer and interviewee by creating feelings of goodwill and trust. You may begin with a self-introduction or a simple greeting if the relationship is established and positive accompanied by appropriate nonverbal actions such as a firm handshake, eye contact, a smile, a nod, and a pleasant, friendly voice. The rapport step may include personal inquiries or small talk about the weather, mutual acquaintances, families, sports, or news events. Consider flavoring a personal inquiry and small talk with tasteful and appropriate humor. Do not prolong the rapport stage; know when enough is enough.

> Do not overdo small talk or compliments.

Customs of a geographical area, organizational traditions or policies, culture, status differences, relationship, formality of the occasion, interview type, and situation may determine the appropriate verbal and nonverbal rapport-building techniques of each interview. Do not refer to strangers, superiors, or high-status persons by first names unless asked to do so. Limit humor or small talk when a party is busy or the situation is highly formal or serious. Do not overdo sweet talk such as congratulations, praise, and expressions of admiration. Be sincere.

Mash/Getty Images

■ *What you do and say in the opening seconds sets the tone for the remainder of the interview.*

Orient the Other Party

Orientation is an essential second step in the opening. You may explain the purpose, length, nature of the interview, how the information will be used, and why and how you selected this party to interview. Study each situation carefully to determine the extent and nature of orientation.

Do not assume that because you and the other party appear to be similar (gender, age, appearance, language, educational background, or culture) that you are similar in ways critical to the success of the interview. LaRay Barna warns that "The aura of similarity is a serious stumbling block to successful intercultural communication. A look-alike facade is deceiving when representatives from contrasting cultures meet, each wearing Western dress, speaking English, and using similar greeting rituals."[4] You may falsely assume that you share similar nonverbal codes, beliefs, attitudes, or values. "Unless there is overt reporting of assumptions made by each party, which seldom happens, there is no chance of comparing impressions and correcting misinterpretations."

Rapport and orientation are often intermixed and reduce **relational uncertainty.** By the end of the opening, both parties should be aware of important

Be careful of
assuming too
much or too
little about the
other party.

similarities, the desire of each to take part in the interview, degree of warmth or friendliness, how control will be shared, and level of trust. A poor opening may mislead and create problems during an interview. Recall how you felt when you discovered that an appeal for assistance from a person at your door turned out to be a ruse to sell you a product.

The rapport and orientation steps are illustrated in the following opening.

1. **Interviewer:** Hi, I'm Loretta Pinkston from Brewer Insurance Agency.
2. **Interviewee:** Oh hi. I'm Kyle Zimmer. You're the person I talked to on the phone about our homeowner's policy.
3. **Interviewer:** Yes, that's me. You have a lovely home in a beautiful rural setting.
4. **Interviewee:** Thanks. We love living out here but we're a bit concerned about fire protection from an all volunteer fire department and security with a sheriff's department nearly ten miles away.
5. **Interviewer:** I can certainly understand that. We live in the south part of the county in a similar area and faced some of the same concerns.
6. **Interviewee:** Then we're on the same wavelength.
7. **Interviewer:** I'd like to ask you some questions about your concerns, what you feel you need to cover most with insurance, and then talk to you about several options available to you.
8. **Interviewee:** That sounds good. Let me get my wife from the greenhouse.

Verbal Opening Techniques

Be creative and adapt the opening to the interviewee and the situation. Don't fall into the habit of using an "all occasions" opening for interviews regardless of specific type, such as employment interviews or information-gathering interviews. The following **verbal opening techniques** may build rapport, orient the other party, or both.

State the Purpose

Explain *why* you are conducting the interview.

Adapt the
opening
to each
interviewee
and situation.

Example: (A student to a professor) Hi Professor Dinwiddie. I'd like to talk to you about the internship in marketing that you mentioned in class yesterday. I've thought about an internship for some time but I don't know much about getting one that is suitable to my major in agricultural sales.

Stating a detailed purpose may make its achievement difficult. This is the case in some research, survey, and sales interviews. You may need to withhold a specific purpose until later in the interview to get honest, unguarded answers, to motivate the interviewee to take part, or to avoid defensiveness.

Example: (A research study funded by a religious organization for a group of politically conservative candidates) Good evening. I'm conducting a survey of potential voters in this fall's election to see how they feel about candidates who talk a great deal, some, very little, or not at all about their religion and religious issues.

Summarize a Problem

Begin with a summary when an interviewee is unaware of a problem, vaguely aware of it, or unaware of details. The summary should **inform** the interviewee but not spill into the body of the interview.

> **Example:** (A physician to a patient) As you know, you have been struggling with dangerously high cholesterol levels for a number of years. They remain high in spite of your exercise program, strict diet, and weight loss. You come from a family that shares these high levels. We need to talk about other means to bring down this troubling cholesterol level.

Explain How a Problem Was Discovered

You may explain *how* a problem was detected and perhaps *by whom*. Be honest and specific in revealing sources of information without placing the interviewee on the defensive.

> **Example:** (An employee to a supervisor) I was checking my work schedule on the Web site last night and discovered that I have been scheduled to work during the first week of June. That is the first week of my Air Force Reserve summer training at George Air Force Base in California.

Offer an Incentive or Reward

An incentive may motivate an interviewee, if it is significant enough and appropriate for the situation. Because many sales pitches include an incentive, it may be difficult to convince a respondent that you are conducting a research, journalistic, or survey interview rather than a sales interview.

> **Example:** I'm conducting a survey of student attitudes toward the current fall break that essentially gives students a four-day weekend. My results will be given to the Student Affairs Committee of the University Senate that is considering changes that would provide a better fall break for students like you.

Request Advice or Assistance

This opening is common because interviewers often need help. The need must be clear, precise, and one the interviewee can satisfy. Do not use this opening as a technique for networking, climbing the ladder, or boosting one's ego.

> **Example:** I'm working on my senior class project and wonder if you would help me with some problems I am encountering.

Refer to the Known Position of the Interviewee

This technique identifies the interviewee's position on an issue or problem. Be tactful and positive in manner and accurate and complete when interpreting an interviewee's position.

Example: Sally, I appreciate the position you are in with the small amount of merit raise money available this year and the restrictions handed down by the administration, but I would like to talk to you about some of the things I have accomplished this year.

Refer to the Person Who Sent You

A referral is a way to connect positively with another party. Never use a person's name without permission. Discover if the interviewee knows, respects, and likes the person you intend to name. It can be embarrassing or disastrous to discover that the interviewee does not recall or dislikes the reference.

Example: I'm writing a story about the pending retirement of Alex Madder, who has been on the staff for over 40 years. Marcie Dumont said that you worked closely with Alex for many years and knew him well personally and professionally.

Know what to do if references to an organization generate negative reactions.

Refer to Your Organization

Often you must refer to an organization you represent (company, hospital, government agency, religious group) for identity and legitimacy as an interviewer. Realize that an interview party may not be a fan of your organization, particularly if you represent possible negative publicity, lawsuits, regulatory enforcement, or legal investigations.

Example: Good evening. I'm Chad McMasters of Keystone Development. We're interested in developing a community center on the old motel property that borders this neighborhood and would like to get your input on what you would like to see in such a center.

Request a Specific Amount of Time

Make an appointment for interviews of more than 5 or 10 minutes.

When asking for a specific amount of time, be realistic in your request. "Got a second?" is probably the most overused and misused interview opening. You can't ask a question in one second.

Example: Professor Williams, do you have about 10 minutes to talk to me about my field project?

Ask a Question

An open-ended, easy to answer question may establish rapport or begin to orient the interviewee.

Example: I'm Kristen Sullivan with Maple Realty. We have a variety of apartments available in several complexes. What are you looking for in an apartment?

Be careful of closed questions that can be answered with a quick no or rejection. Common closed questions are dead ends.

Examples: Can I help you?
Looking for something?

Interviewees may be turned off by an obvious yes-no question.

Examples: Are we going to do anything important in class today?
Are you busy?

These 10 verbal opening techniques provide a variety of ways to open interviews effectively.

Most openings, of course, include a strategic combination of techniques. Create an opening that is most appropriate for each interview and situation. **Above all, involve the interviewee in the opening.** As an interviewee, insist on playing an active role from the beginning. Don't be a mere bystander.

Nonverbal Communication in Openings

Verbal opening techniques are accompanied by appropriate **nonverbal communication.** An effective opening depends upon *how* you look, act, and say *what* you say. Nonverbal communication is critical in creating a good first impression and establishing your legitimacy. It signals sincerity, trust and trustworthiness, warmth, and interest.

Territoriality

Knock before entering a room, even if the door is open, you are a superior, or you are in your own home, building, or organization. You are entering another's *space,* and any perceived violation of this territory may begin an interview poorly. In some cultures, women enjoy less territoriality than men. For instance, Judy Pearson writes that in the United States, "Few women have a particular and unviolated room in their homes while many men have dens, studies, or work areas which are off limits to others. Similarly, it appears that more men than women have particular chairs reserved for their use."[5] Regardless of gender wait until the other party signals to enter with a smile, head nod, wave, or by pointing to a chair. Maintain eye contact without staring to show trust and enable you to pick up nonverbal signals that say "come in," "be seated," "sit there," and "I'm willing to talk to you," or "Not now," or "I'm very busy."

Face, Appearance, and Dress

Appearance and dress contribute a great deal to first impressions. They may communicate interest, sincerity, warmth, urgency, attractiveness, neatness, maturity, and professionalism. Do not signal catastrophe when the interview will be routine, friendliness when you are about to discipline a person, warmth when you are angry, happiness when a major problem needs urgent attention, or closeness when you have never met.

Touch

If shaking hands is appropriate for the relationship and the situation, give a firm handshake. Be careful of overdoing handshaking with acquaintances and colleagues or during informal interviews. Touching is generally appropriate only when both parties have an established and close relationship.

Reading Nonverbal Communication

Do not underestimate the importance of verbal and nonverbal communication in openings, but do not read too much into simple words and nonverbal acts or try to read everyone the same. People of apparently similar backgrounds may differ significantly in communicative behavior.

Interpersonal communication theorists emphasize the importance of nonverbal clues. For instance, Trenholm and Jensen write, "People read a lot in our facial expressions. They infer some personality traits and attitudes, judge reactions to their own messages, regard facial expressions as verbal replacements, and, primarily, use them to determine our emotional state."[6] Regarding first impressions, Floyd notes that "the quality of a person's clothing is a relatively reliable visual cue to his or her socioeconomic status" and type or style of clothing may enable us, often quite accurately, to identify an interview party with a particular cultural or political group.[7] Stewart warns us, however, that we "tend to *notice* those behaviors [and possibly appearance and dress] that are consistent with the beliefs we have about another and ignore those that are inconsistent."[8]

Lillian Glass has catalogued 105 "talk differences" between American men and women in basic areas of communication: body language, facial language, speech and voice patterns, language content, and behavioral patterns. She has found that men touch others more often, tend to avoid eye contact and not look directly at the other person, sound more abrupt and less approachable, make direct accusations, and give fewer compliments.[9] Some research indicates that women are more skilled at "rapport talk" that establishes and strengthens relationships while men are more skilled at "report talk" that analyzes issues and resolves problems.[10]

Americans share rules for greeting others, but these rules may not be shared with other cultures. Shaking hands, for instance, is a Western custom, particularly in the United States, so do not ascribe meaning to firmness or lack of firmness when interviewing persons from other cultures who may see handshaking as merely a quaint Western custom of little importance. While Americans expect persons to look them in the eyes to exhibit trust, openness, and sincerity, other cultures consider such eye contact to be impolite and insulting. The United States is not a touching society, but do not be shocked if a party from Italy or Latin America touches you during an opening.

Exercise #2—Interview Openings

How satisfactory is each of the following openings? Consider the interviewing situation and type, the techniques used, and what is omitted. How might each be improved? Do not assume that each opening is unsatisfactory.

1. This is a recruiting interview for a logistics specialist with a large trucking firm.

    Interviewer: Hi, I'm Tyler (points to chair). When did you get to town?

    Interviewee: About ten this morning.

    Interviewer: Great. Tell me about yourself.

2. This is an interview taking place in a large law firm between two partners.

    Interviewer: Are you busy?

Interviewee: No, I'm just sitting here with my laptop.

Interviewer: Okay, you got me. I'd like to talk to you about the Warren contract.

3. This is an interview between a student and a professor in his office.

Interviewer: Professor Cho, got a second?

Interviewee: (brief pause) Time's up!

Interviewer: Could we talk for about ten minutes?

4. This is an interview in the hallway near the U.S. Senate Chamber between an ABC Capitol Hill correspondent and a senator. The senator is arriving for a roll call vote.

Interviewer: Senator Hernandez! (waving and shouting) What's your reaction to the President's nominee for Commerce Secretary?

Interviewee: I'm looking into it.

Interviewer: Are your initial feelings positive or negative?

5. This is an interview between the offensive line coach and the head coach.

Interviewer: I just heard you're benching Jablonski for the opening game on Saturday without informing me first.

Interviewee: Sorry, but yes I did.

Interviewer: Can't we talk about this?

Closing the Interview

The closing is critical because it not only affects this interview but also your relationship with a party and the nature, atmosphere, cooperation, and expectations of future contacts. Each interview creates or alters a relational history. An abrupt closing may make the other party feel used, important only as long as needed.

> Take your time and be tactful in what you say and do in the closing.

It is natural to relax and let your guard down when an interview is coming to a close. Don't be in a rush to get to your next task or appointment. Be attentive to everything you do and say and don't do and say during these final seconds or minutes of an interaction because the other party will be watching and listening for signals about your relationship, appreciation, interest, and sincerity. Both parties should be aware that a closing is commencing.

Closings are signaled nonverbally before any words are exchanged. Mark Knapp and his colleagues, in their classic study of "leave-taking" in interpersonal interactions, identified a variety of nonverbal closing actions, some of them rather subtle.[11] For instance, you may straighten up in your seat, lean forward, uncross your legs, place your hands on your knees as if preparing to rise, look at your watch, pause briefly, or break eye contact. Other more obvious actions are standing up, moving away from the other party, or offering to shake hands. Whether subtle or not, nonverbal actions signal that you want to close the interview. As an interviewee, watch for signals to detect when a closing is commencing so you are not taken by surprise or experience an awkward ending to the interaction. At the same time, be aware that a person may be checking a watch to see that there is adequate time remaining for additional questions or information sharing, uncrossing legs to get more comfortable, or breaking eye contact to think of a new question. Your authors placed small clocks inconspicuously on their desks because they discovered that every time they checked their watches, students started into leave-taking, assuming this was a signal for them to leave.

Both parties make closings successful.

Guidelines for Closing Interviews

Follow simple rules for conducting closings. First, the closing, like the opening, is a **dialogue,** not a **monologue.** When you are the interviewer, encourage the interviewee to take part by employing verbal and nonverbal signals, including silence. As an interviewee, take an active part in the closing by responding to questions, adding a few important comments or facts not covered, and expressing appreciation when appropriate.

Second, be sincere and honest in the closing. Make no promises or commitments you cannot or will not be able to keep.

Third, pace the interview so you do not have to rush the closing. The **law of recency** suggests that people recall the last thing said or done during an interview, so being rushed or dismissed with an ill-chosen nonverbal action or phrase may jeopardize the effects of the interview, your relationship, and future contacts with this party.

Fourth, be aware that the other party will be observing and interpreting everything you say and do, and everything you don't say and don't do, until you are out of sight and sound of one another. A slip of the lip or an inappropriate nonverbal act may negate all that you accomplished during the interview.

Be careful of what you do and say.

■ *Remember that the interview is not completed until the interviewer and interviewee are out of sight and sound of one another.*

Keith Brofsky/Getty Images

Fifth, leave the door open, and perhaps set the groundwork, for future contacts. If an additional contact is planned (common in health care, employment, counseling, and sales interviews), explain what will happen next, where it will happen, when it will happen, and why it will happen. When possible, make an appointment before leaving.

Sixth, don't introduce new topics or ideas or make inquiries when the interview has in fact or psychologically come to a close. A **false closing** occurs when your verbal and nonverbal messages signal that the interview is coming to a close only for you to open it back up. This may be awkward for both parties and such after-the-fact interactions are likely to be superficial and add little to the interview.

Seventh, avoid what Erving Goffman called **failed departures** that occur when you have brought an interview to a close and taken leave from the other party. Then a short time later you run into the party in the hall, parking lot, or restaurant.[12] The result is awkward because both of you have said your good-byes, and now you try to think of something appropriate to say when there is nothing to say. Practice situations to determine what you might say when this happens to avoid awkward and embarrassing moments.

Closing Techniques

Be creative and imaginative when closing interviews. Adapt each closing to the interviewee and the situation. The following techniques may serve as entire closings, begin the closing process, or complete the closing.

Offer to Answer Questions

Regardless of technique, involve the interviewee in the closing.

Be sincere when offering to answer questions, and give the other party adequate time to ask them. Do not give a brief answer to one question and then end the interview.

What questions do you have?

What questions have I not answered?

Use Clearinghouse Questions

Questions, intentions, and inquiries allow you to close effectively.

A clearinghouse question enables you to determine if you have covered all topics, answered all questions, or resolved all concerns. The request must be an honest and sincere effort to ferret out unaddressed questions, information, or areas of concern.

Have I answered all of your questions about the new software?

What important information have I not covered in this interview?

Declare Completion of the Intended Purpose

State that the task is completed. The word *well* signals more closings than any other word or phrase. When we hear it, we automatically assume that leave-taking is commencing and begin to wind things up. Is this what you want to happen?

Well, I think that covers everything.

Okay, that's all the questions I have.

Make Personal Inquiries

Be genuinely interested in the other party.

Personal inquiries are pleasant ways to end interviews and to enhance relationships. Be sincere and give the interviewee adequate time to address an inquiry or concern.

What are your plans for the summer?

How is your father doing after his surgery?

Make Professional Inquiries

Professional inquiries are more formal than personal ones, and they must be sincere and show genuine interest. We appreciate interest in our careers.

How is your research into alternative fuels going?

When do you leave for your assignment in Singapore?

Signal That Time Is Up

Do not rush the closing but end the interview when most appropriate.

Set a time limit in advance or during the opening. Be tactful, and avoid the impression that you are running an interview assembly line.

Well, our time's up for this session.

I see we're out of time.

Explain the Reason for the Closing

Explain why the interview must end. A phony-sounding reason can harm the interview and relationship.

You have another student waiting to talk with you.

I have an appointment downtown, so I'll have to close for now.

Express Appreciation or Satisfaction

Express appreciation or satisfaction because you have usually received something—information, assistance, evaluation, a story, a sale, a position, a recruit, time. Be sincere.

Thanks so much for meeting with me on such short notice.

Thanks for taking part in my survey.

Arrange for the Next Meeting

If a subsequent interview is necessary, arrange it now.

When appropriate, set up the next meeting or reveal what will happen next, including date, time, place, topic, content, or purpose.

I have several more questions to ask; could we meet later today?

I've enjoyed talking to you about your career interests. When might you be available to meet other members of our staff?

If it is unnecessary to set a specific time for another interview, simple phrases may communicate a likely interval between interactions. For instance, "See you," or "Until next time" signal short intervals. "Let's stay in touch" and "Don't be a stranger" signal moderate intervals. "Good-bye" and "So long" tend to signal lengthy or forever intervals. "We'll be in touch" and "Don't call us; we'll call you" may signal the traditional "brushoff" that means never. Be aware of cultural differences and expectations between parties. Interviewees from other cultures not familiar with the "Don't call us; we'll call you" phrase have been known to quit their current positions in anticipation of immediate job offers that never came.

Summarize the Interview

A summary closing is common for informational, performance, counseling, and sales interviews. Repeat important information, stages, or agreements or verify accuracy and agreement. Be sure the summary is accurate and complete.

I've enjoyed talking to you about your experiences in Japan right after the tsunami struck last year. As I understand it, you will be in the United States from June 15 through July 24 this summer and will be able to attend the Middle American First Responders conference on natural disasters on July 14 or 15. Your address will focus on the critical first 24 hours. We will take care of your travel and housing expenses and pay an honorarium of $2,500.

> **Plan the closing as carefully as you do the opening and body of the interview.**

Understand what words and actions are *saying* to the other party. Decide which closing techniques are most suitable. Your role in an interview and your relationship with the other party may require some techniques, rule out others, and determine who will initiate the closing and when. Usually you will combine several verbal and nonverbal techniques into effective closings.

Exercise #3—Interview Closings

How satisfactory is each of the following closings? Consider the interviewing situation and type, relationship, the techniques used, nonverbal communication, and what is omitted. How might each be improved? Do not assume each closing is unsatisfactory.

1. This is a recruiting interview for an HR position with a national chain of home improvement stores. The applicant will soon graduate with a degree in management.

    Interviewer: Well, it's been a productive interview. We appreciate your interest in our position and the organization.

    Interviewee: Thank you.

    Interviewer: (Looks at notes but not at the applicant) We'll be in touch. Good luck with your search.

2. This is an interview with Zach and Marge who are looking for a lakeside cottage to rent for the summer.

    Interviewer: This cottage seems to meet your needs and is a good price because of the recession.

    Interviewee: Yes (looking at Marge), well, we need to think about it as we are just beginning to look around.

    Interviewer: Okay.

3. This is a performance review of Darrell Smythe who works as a claims adjuster for an insurance company.

    Interviewer: You're doing a great job Darrell, just keep in mind some of my suggestions. How's your son doing on the high school baseball team?

    Interviewee: He threw a no hitter last week against Deer Creek.

    Interviewer: Good. See you soon.

4. This is an interview between a journalist and a whistle blower who has been working for a defense contractor developing a new attack aircraft for the Army.

    Interviewer: Well (leaning forward and looking at the interviewee), this has been a very disturbing revelation of the cost overruns being ignored by both the contractor and the Army. Can I get in touch with you at the same cell phone number?

ON THE WEB

This chapter has presented guidelines and techniques for developing effective openings and closings. Use the Internet to locate sample interviews on issues such as education, the economy, foreign affairs, and medicine. Critique the openings and closings used in these interviews. Two useful Internet resources for locating interviews are CNN (http://cnn.com) and C-SPAN (http://indycable .com/cabletv/comastindyupgrade/ch24.htm).

Interviewee: Yes you can.

Interviewer: Good. (leaning back) Let me ask you about the engine tests you alluded to.

Interviewee: Okay.

5. This is a telephone survey interview being conducted by a survey research organization on an upcoming primary election.

Interviewer: That's all the questions I have.

Interviewee: When will the results be announced?

Interviewer: We'll release our findings within a few days on the Internet.

Interviewee: Okay.

Summary

Each part of the interview—opening, body, and closing—is vital to its success. Do not underestimate the importance of both words and nonverbal actions and reactions during all three stages. Be conscious of cultural differences that affect the meaning of actions such as handshaking, eye contact, voice, touch, and gestures.

The opening influences how both parties perceive themselves and one another. It sets the tone for the remainder of the interview, orients the interviewee, and influences the willingness of both parties to communicate beyond Level 1. The opening often determines whether the interview will continue or end prematurely. Select opening techniques most appropriate for each interview.

The body of the interview must be carefully structured with an appropriate sequence that guides the interviewer's questions, areas of information, or points systematically and allows the interviewee to understand where the interview is going and why. A nonscheduled interview is simply an interview guide with topics and subtopics an interviewer wants to cover. A moderately scheduled interview contains all major questions and possible probing questions under each. A highly scheduled interview includes all questions to be asked during an interview. A highly scheduled standardized interview contains all questions to be asked with prescribed answer options under each. Question sequences allow strategic structuring of questions within scheduled interviews.

The closing brings the interview to an end and may summarize information, verify agreements, arrange future contacts, and enhance relationships. A good closing should make both parties glad they took part and pleased with the results. Be sincere and honest by not rushing the closing, by making promises and commitments that you can and will keep, and by making sure that both parties are actively involved.

Key Terms and Concepts

The online learning center for this text features FLASHCARDS and CROSSWORD PUZZLES for studying based on these terms and concepts.

Accidental bias
Built-in interviewer bias
Cause-to-effect sequence
Closing
Closing techniques
Combination schedule
Culture
Defensive climate
Diamond sequence
Failed departures
False closings
Funnel sequence
Highly scheduled interview
Highly scheduled
   standardized interview

Hourglass sequence
Interview guide
Interview schedules
Inverted funnel sequence
Journalist's guide
Law of recency
Moderately scheduled
   interview
Nonscheduled interview
Nonverbal closing actions
Nonverbal communication
Opening
Orientation
Outline sequences
Problem-solution sequence

Question sequences
Quintamensional design
   sequence
Rapport
Relational uncertainty
Space sequence
Territoriality
Time sequence
Topical sequence
Tunnel sequence
Verbal opening techniques

An Interview for Review and Analysis

This interview is between a student majoring in communication and political science and a faculty member who ran for a city council seat a few years ago. The interview is part of the student's field project for a course in county and municipal government and elections. The interviewee is currently teaching a course in persuasion in which the interviewer is a student.

How satisfactory is the opening? Which type of schedule does the interviewer appear to be using? Which structural sequence(s) can you detect? Which question sequence(s) can you detect? How satisfactory is the closing? How does nonverbal communication affect this interview?

1. **Interviewer:** Professor Prohaska, got a minute?

2. **Interviewee:** A minute? Sure. I do have a class in about 15 minutes.

3. **Interviewer:** Well, this shouldn't take too long. (standing and appearing nervous)

4. **Interviewee:** Please sit down. (pointing to a chair and smiling) What can I do for you?

5. **Interviewer:** I'm doing a field project for my poly sci class on local government and elections.

6. **Interviewee:** Yes, I'm familiar with that class and its field projects.

7. **Interviewer:** Good. Professor Clair mentioned that you had run for a local office a few years ago.

8. **Interviewee:** That's right. I often talked to her about my campaign for a city council seat.

9. **Interviewer:** I'd like to discuss your campaign and experiences in the local political process.

10. **Interviewee:** Okay.

11. **Interviewer:** Why did you decide to run for political office?

12. **Interviewee:** The mayor talked me into it.

13. **Interviewer:** Why did he do that?

14. **Interviewee:** Actually it was a she, Mayor Jackie Jensen. We had known each other for several years, and I had been involved in a variety of community activities.

15. **Interviewer:** So, you said yes because of your relationship with Mayor Jensen and interest in your community?

16. **Interviewee:** No.

17. **Interviewer:** Why did you say yes?

18. **Interviewee:** I told her no and that I was not much of a party person and would not run "against" the incumbent that I liked.

19. **Interviewer:** What did she say?

20. **Interviewee:** She said that local elections were more about the people and not about the political party. The mayor also referred to her previous campaigns and those of others in her party that were always positive. She said my active part in a year-long strategic planning process for the city made me an ideal candidate.

21. **Interviewer:** Then you said yes?

22. **Interviewee:** That's correct.

23. **Interviewer:** Tell me about the campaign.

24. **Interviewee:** I enjoyed campaigning because local elections in smaller cities are very interpersonal in nature. I spent most of my time going door-to-door meeting and talking to voters about the future of the city. It was time consuming and rewarding.

25. **Interviewer:** How was it rewarding?

26. **Interviewee:** I got to meet a lot of great people in our city, and it gave me insights into the political process of this country and how we pick our representatives. I cannot imagine how difficult it is to run a state-wide or national campaign. I do not agree with many candidates and their agendas, but I do respect the dedication they have to run for a major office.

27. **Interviewer:** Did you do any television ads?

28. **Interviewee:** No, those are very expensive and don't have much effect in local elections.

29. **Interviewer:** Did you debate your opponent on television?

30. **Interviewee:** No, but we did have a joint appearance on the local cable channel. It was the strangest experience of the campaign.

31. Interviewer: Tell me about that.

32. Interviewee: Well, my opponent and I showed up at the studio for the interview, but the moderator did not. The camera operator read questions to us from his position behind the camera, and we answered as if we were talking to a moderator.

33. Interviewer: How did that work when it was televised?

34. Interviewee: The cable system hired a local retired television teacher with broadcast experience to come in and pretend my opponent and I were actually answering his questions. The cable people then put it all together and it came out like a moderated political exchange.

35. Interviewer: Did you win the election?

36. Interviewee: No, I was running in a district that always voted heavily for the other party and knew all along that I was virtually certain to lose. (looks at his desk clock) I need to leave for class.

37. Interviewer: Oh, okay, uh (looking at a schedule of questions), let me see. I do have several questions left. Can we get together in a few days?

38. Interviewee: Sure.

39. Interviewer: (standing and walking toward the door) Well, thanks for your help Professor Prohaska, I'll see you later.

40. Interviewee: Good luck with your project.

Student Activities

1. Select an interview topic and a person you would choose to be the interviewee. Proceed through developing the body of the interview you would conduct. Develop a carefully phrased and limited purpose. Create an interview guide (beginning with major topics, proceeding to subtopics) and select one or more outline sequences. Turn your guide into an appropriate question schedule: moderately scheduled, highly scheduled, or highly scheduled standardized. Determine which question sequences you would employ. Looking back over what you have created, ask yourself how you determined the appropriateness of each stage of this process.

2. Watch a complete televised interview of at least 15 minutes in length. How was the interview opened verbally and nonverbally? How involved was the interviewee? Which type of schedule did the interviewer employ? Which question sequences did the interviewer employ? How was the interview closed verbally and nonverbally? How involved was the interviewee? Rate the effectiveness of each stage of the interview according to the guidelines presented in this chapter.

3. Watch a complete televised interview of at least 15 minutes in length. Try to construct an interview guide of topics from this interview. From this guide, see if you can detect one or more question schedules and question sequences. From your reconstruction of this interview, what conclusions would you draw about the interviewer's preparation? How would you improve the guide and schedule(s)?

4. Make arrangements to interview an experienced interviewer: for example, a journal-ist, police officer, counselor, recruiter, insurance investigator, fund raiser. How does this person determine which opening techniques to employ? How does this person determine the degree of preparation from creating an interview guide through a highly scheduled interview? How does this person determine which closing tech-niques to employ? What roles do purpose, relationship, situation, and time play in the interviewer's decisions?

Notes

1. http://scit.ac.uk/university/scit/modules/cp4414/lectures/week3interview/sid021, accessed September 28, 2006.

2. George Gallup, "The Quintamensional Plan for Question Design," *Public Opinion Quarterly* 11 (1947), p. 385.

3. H. B. Beckman and R. M. Frankel, "The Effect of Physician Behavior on the Collection of Data," *Annals of Internal Medicine* (1984), pp. 692–696.

4. LaRay M. Barna, "Stumbling Blocks in Intercultural Communication," in Larry A. Samovar and Richard E. Porter, eds., *Intercultural Communication: A Reader* (Belmont, CA: Wadsworth, 1988), pp. 323–324.

5. Judy C. Pearson, *Communication in the Family* (New York: Harper & Row, 1989), p. 78.

6. Sarah Trenholm and Arthur Jensen, *Interpersonal Communication* (New York: Oxford University Press, 2013), p. 59.

7. Kory Floyd, *Interpersonal Communication: The Whole Story* (New York: McGraw-Hill, 2011), p. 188.

8. John Stewart, *Bridges Not Walls: A Book about Interpersonal Communication* (New York: McGraw-Hill, 2009), p. 186.

9. Lillian Glass, *He Says, She Says: Closing the Communication Gap between the Sexes* (New York: Putnam, 1993), pp. 45–59.

10. Cynthia Burggraf Torppa, "Gender Issues: Communication Differences in Interper-sonal Relationships," FACT SHEET: Family and Consumer Sciences (Columbus, OH: The Ohio State University, 2010), p. 1.

11. Mark L. Knapp, Roderick P. Hart, Gustav W. Friedrich, and Gary M. Shulman, "The Rhetoric of Goodbye: Verbal and Nonverbal Correlates of Human Leave-Taking," *Speech Monographs* 40 (1973), pp. 182–198; John Stewart, *Bridges Not Walls* (New York: McGraw-Hill, 2012), p. 153.

12. Erving Goffman, *Relations in Public* (New York: Basic Books, 1971), p. 88.

Resources

Adler, Ronald B., and Jeanne Marquardt Elmhorst. *Communicating at Work: Principles and Practices for Business and the Professions*. New York: McGraw-Hill, 2008.

"Conducting the Information Interview: Module 5: Conducting the Interview," http://www.rogue.com/interview/module5.html, accessed April 21, 2009.

Knapp, Mark L., Roderick P. Hart, Gustav W. Friedrich, and Gary M. Shulman. "The Rhetoric of Goodbye: Verbal and Nonverbal Correlates of Human Leave-Taking." *Speech Monographs* 40 (1973), pp. 182–198.

Krivonos, Paul D., and Mark L. Knapp. "Initiating Communication: What Do You Say When You Say Hello?" *Central States Speech Journal* 26 (1975), pp. 115–125.

Sandberg, Anne. "Build an Interview: Interview Questions and Structured Interviewing," http://www.buildaninterview.com/interviewing_opening_and_closingremarks:asp, accessed April 21, 2009.

Zunin, Leonard, and Natalie Zunin. *Contact: The First Four Minutes*. London: Random House, 1986.

CHAPTER 5

The Informational Interview

The informational interview is the most common of interviews.

The **informational interview** is the most common of interviews because you participate in informational interviews nearly every day. Journalists, recruiters, police officers, attorneys, counselors, supervisors, consumers, professors, and students, to name only a few, rely on them to obtain or transmit facts, opinions, attitudes, feelings, and observations. The informational interview may be as brief and informal as a student asking a professor for clarification of a project or as lengthy and formal as a journalist talking to a CEO about a company's hiring plans.

Regardless of length, formality, or setting, the **purpose** of every informational interview is to obtain relevant and timely information as accurately and completely as possible in the shortest amount of time. This requires skillful and insightful questioning, listening, observing, and probing into superficial and perhaps inaccurate answers. Unfortunately, few of us, including professional journalists, are trained in interviewing. For instance, Chip Scanlon (author of *Reporting and Writing: Basics for the 21st Century*) writes that "journalists get little or no training in this vital aspect of their job. Most learn by trial and error."[1] Likewise, journalist Sarah Stuteville claims that "It's odd that so much emphasis is put on teaching journalists how to write an article when that skill is useless without also teaching journalists how to develop strong interview techniques."[2]

The objectives of this chapter are to introduce you to the fundamentals of how to conduct and take part in informational interviews. These fundamentals include thorough preparation, selecting interviewers and interviewees, choosing a setting, opening interviews, motivating interviewees, asking questions, note taking and recording, handling special situations and difficult parties, and closing interviews.

Preparing the Interview

Thorough preparation is the essential first step in conducting and taking part in informational interviews. Unfortunately, there is no simple formula or model to follow. As Eric Nadler, the Pulitzer Prize–winning chief investigative reporter for the *Seattle Times,* writes, they are as varied as the conversations we have and the people we talk to.[3] Preparation consists of determining your goal, researching the topic, and structuring the interview. Scanlan describes interviewing as "a process, like writing, that involves a series of decisions and actions designed to get the best possible information."[4] The first step in this process is to determine your goal.

Determine Your Purpose

Begin your preparation by asking a series of questions. Why are you going to conduct this interview? What information do you need: feelings, attitudes, opinions, facts, eye-witness accounts, expert or lay testimony? How quickly do you need this information? How will you use this information: to make a decision, take an action, write a research report, prepare a feature story for the 10:00 p.m. news show, prepare a court case? Ken Metzler, a long-time professor of journalism at the University of Oregon, claims that when you know exactly what you want, "you're halfway there."[5]

Study the Situation

Consider situational variables that may affect your interview. When and where will the interview take place? How might events before and after affect the interview? Will invited or uninvited audiences be present? What outside influences should you be aware of? Will the interview be broadcast? How much time do you have to prepare? Are you responding to an emergency or crisis that gives you little time to prepare? Is there a deadline for obtaining the information you need? Will the setting such as a news conference or briefing limit the number and types of questions you can ask and the information you can use? Should you defer an interview until you are better informed and ready to manage difficult questions in a difficult situation?

Prepare yourself for human suffering, emotional outbursts, scenes of destruction, threats to health and safety, and filthy conditions. We have all observed journalists, first responders, police officers, and government officials having to deal with the aftermaths of tornados, forest fires, crashes on highways, shootings, and the removal of children from living conditions that defy the imagination. Too often we see interviewers intruding into people's lives at the wrong time and in the wrong place.

Research the Topic

A thorough research of the topic serves five functions for the informational interview. First, research enables you to determine what information is readily available from other sources so you do not waste valuable interview time. Why, for instance, would you ask simple biographical questions when such information is readily available on a Web site or in organizational literature? Helpful sources may include a course syllabus, journal or newspaper articles, the Internet, databases, annual reports, instructional manuals, court documents, archives, reference works, organizational records, and previous interviews. Some journalists claim that research time should be 10 times the actual interview time.[6]

Second, research may reveal areas of the topic that remain unaddressed and of particular interest to you, such as explanations, personal experiences, interpretations of data, the many sides of an issue, attitudes, and feelings. Research enables you to ask insightful questions and avoid **false assumptions** about events, causes and effects, and the willingness and ability of an interviewee to give accurate information.

Third, be perceptive and critical about the pre-interview information you discover. Not everything in print, particularly on the Internet, is accurate and truthful. Many sources have hidden agendas that lead to shoddy data. Is the information you have the most recent available? Have sources changed their minds because of changing

ON THE WEB

Use the Internet to research your college or one that you might select as a graduate or professional school. Focus first on the college or university, then on the school or college within this larger structure, and finally on the department. What kinds of information are readily available? How up-to-date is the information? What kinds of information are not included that you would have to discover through interviews with faculty or students?

circumstances or experiences? Are newer studies available? What anecdotes or quotations might be important for your study, report, or story? Are quotations cited in sources taken out of context? Are there apparent inaccuracies, even in usually reliable sources? Journalist Jaldeep Katwala warns, "Be sure of your facts. There's nothing worse than being told you are wrong by an interviewee—especially when it's live."[7]

> **Show interest in me, and I'll show interest in you.**

Fourth, your questions must reveal that you have done your homework to establish credibility with the interviewee. Eric Raymond and Rick Moen recommend that "when you ask your question, display the fact that you have done these things first; this will help establish that you're not being a lazy sponge and wasting people's time. Better yet, display what you have *learned* from doing these things."[8] Failure to do your homework and a show of ignorance during an interview can destroy your credibility and embarrass you and your organization. Don't try to impress a person with your knowledge; let your knowledge and understanding of a topic reveal itself in your questions and reactions. You may phrase initial questions to reveal your familiarity with an area such as medicine, technology, the economy, military affairs, or history. Thorough research enables you to ask insightful questions less prepared interviewers would fail to ask. Your research may provide more information than you can use in any one interview, and you may hate to leave out statistics, revelations, or stories that you find interesting or provocative. Resist the temptation to ask too many questions or to cram too much information into the questions you ask.

Fifth, evidence of your research shows you cannot be easily fooled and motivates interviewees to respond honestly, insightfully, and in depth. We are flattered when others take the time to learn about us, our interests, fields, accomplishments, and opinions. We take pride in what we do and who we are. Know appropriate jargon and technical terms and use and pronounce them correctly. Know the respondent's name (and how it is pronounced), title, and organization. You should know if a person is a professor or an instructor, an editor or a reporter, a pilot or a navigator, a CEO or CFO, and a doctor with a PhD, MD, DVM, DDS, DO, or EdD degree.

Structure the Interview

Interview Guide

As you research a topic, jot down areas and subareas that will evolve into an **interview guide.** The guide may be an elaborate outline, major aspects of a topic, or key words in a notebook. The traditional journalistic interview guide may be all you need for an interview, and these six words may become the primary questions you ask in a moderately scheduled interview.

- *Who* was involved?
- *What* happened?
- *When* did it happen?
- *Where* did it happen?
- *How* did it happen?
- *Why* did it happen?

Length, sophistication, and importance of the interview will dictate the nature and details of the guide.

Plan a structural sequence but remain flexible.

Refer to the structural sequences discussed in Chapter 4. Chronological sequences are effective in moving through stories or happenings that occur in time sequences. A logical sequence such as cause-to-effect or problem-to-solution is appropriate for dealing with issues and crises. A space sequence is helpful when an interview deals with places. Remain flexible because few informational interviews go exactly as planned.

Interview Schedule

A moderate schedule is a useful tool for long interviews.

If your interview will be brief or you are skilled in conducting informational interviews, you may need only a guide to conduct a nonscheduled interview. If not, develop a moderate schedule that turns topics and subtopics into primary questions and provides possible probing questions under each.

A moderate schedule eliminates the necessity of creating each question at the moment of utterance and allows you to phrase questions carefully and precisely. At the same time, the moderate schedule allows **flexibility** to delete questions or create new ones as the need or opportunity arises. For instance, you may accidentally discover an issue or topic not detected during research or planning that warrants a detour. You needn't fear if you digress from a planned schedule, and the risks are worth taking. You can return to your schedule and pick up where you left off. Thomas Berner recommends that if a good question comes up in answer to another question, jot it down in the margin of your schedule and return to it when most appropriate.[9] The freedom to adapt and improvise makes the moderate schedule ideal for informational interviews.

Selecting Interviewees and Interviewers

Once you have determined your purpose, studied the situation, conducted the necessary research, and structured a guide or schedule, select interviewees and decide who should conduct the interviews.

Selecting Interviewees

Your purpose and the situation may determine the party you must interview: a specific injured police officer, a witness to a fire at an oil refinery, member of the state legislature, or a cancer survivor. If so, all you need to do is *review* what you know about

■ *Select interviewees with several criteria in mind.*

© Realistic Reflections

this person's background, positions on issues, ability as an interviewee, and relationship with you and then *look into* what you don't know. You may need to select from among several police officers injured while on duty, witnesses to an oil refinery fire, members of a state legislative committee, or cancer survivors. Your purpose may require you to interview established experts on your topic such as scientists, physicians, professors, or attorneys. Or it may require you to interview laypersons not skilled in specific professions such as voters, football fans, witnesses to an accident, or shoppers at a mall. Once you know the person or type of persons you must interview, use four criteria to select interviewees: level of information, availability, willingness, and ability.

Level of Information

Make sure your interviewee possesses the information you need.

The most important criterion is whether a party has the information you need. If so, what is the party's level of expertise through experiences, education, training, and positions? For instance, **primary sources** are those directly involved with the information you want, **support sources** are those with important connections to primary sources, and **expert sources** are those with superior knowledge or skills relating to the information you need.[10] Your goal may be to assess a person's level of expertise. As an oral historian, you may want to interview a person who was actively involved in organizing a political rally for President John Kennedy, not merely a person who attended the rally. As a journalist, you may interview a CEO about a proposed merger, not an employee.

Raymond Gorden writes about **key informants** who can supply information on local situations, assist in selecting and contacting knowledgeable interviewees, and aid in securing their cooperation.[11] Identify these people and how they might assist in selecting respondents. A key informant might be a family member, friend, fellow student, employer, or aide.

Availability

Do not assume a potential interviewee is unavailable; ask.

A source might be too far away, available only for a few minutes when you need an in-depth interview, or unavailable until after a deadline. Consider the telephone, videoconference, or e-mail before giving up on a source. And never assume a person is unavailable. Stories abound among journalists and researchers about famous interviews that occurred merely because interviewers asked for interviews or were persistent in asking. You may talk yourself out of an interview by being certain the person will not talk—a self-fulfilling prophecy: "You don't have time to talk, do you?"

Consider a possible go-between, Gorden's key informant, such as a mutual friend or associate, or the public relations department. You might go to where a person works, lives, or plays rather than expect the person to come to you. Sometimes an interviewee will ask to see some or all of your questions in advance. As a general rule, "Don't do it." Giving questions to an interviewee in advance may limit the questions you can ask during the interview to those you list, prevent you from adapting to changing circumstances and events, and enable the interviewee to phrase and rehearse answers in advance. At a minimum, agreeing to such requests may destroy the spontaneity of the interview. Be careful of excessive demands about topics and questions being off-limit and off-the-record, which may make a person no longer a viable interviewee.

Willingness

Potential respondents may be unwilling to meet with you for a variety of reasons, including mistrust of you or your organization, profession, or position. Some information they give might harm them, their organizations, or significant others, particularly because of inaccurate reporting, hidden agendas, or sensationalism prevalent in news sources. They may feel the information you want is no one else's business or a waste of time.[12] In short, a respondent may see nothing in the interview that warrants the time and risks involved. Lawsuits materialize today over almost anything a person says or does not say, and organizations are fearful of being sued for millions. They control who can speak for them.

> Fear of what may be revealed in an interview might make participants reluctant.

You may have to convince interviewees that you can be trusted for confidentiality, accuracy, thoroughness, and fair reporting. Parties will cooperate if they have an interest in you, the topic, or the outcome of the interview. Point out why their interests will be better served if information and attitudes are known. Sometimes you may have to employ a bit of arm-twisting such as "If you don't talk to us, we'll have to rely on other sources" or "The other parties involved have already told their sides of the incident. Are you certain you do not want us to hear yours?" Be careful of threats. They can ruin an interview, damage a relationship, and preclude future contacts. Be equally wary of persons who are too eager to be interviewed.

> Resort to arm-twisting as a last resort.

Ability

Is the potential interviewee able to transmit information freely and accurately? Poor memory, failing health, state of shock, biases or prejudices, habitual lying, proneness to exaggeration or oversimplification, and repression of horrific memories may make a person unacceptable. Elderly witnesses may remember events very differently than they really were. A father or mother grieving over the loss of a child (and confronted with recorders, interviewers, lights, and cameras) may be unable to focus on details. Interviewers often expect persons to relate minute details and exact timing of events that took place months or years before, when most of us have trouble recalling what we did yesterday.

> Many potential interviewees are willing but unable.

When time permits, become familiar with the interviewee ahead of time. Learn about the person's accomplishments, personality, reputation, biases, interests, and interviewing traits. Copywriter Star Zagofsky notes that "The truth is that some people have a good story to tell on a subject, and others don't. Some people are naturally talented at being interviewed, and others aren't."[13] How skilled is the person at responding

> Some interviewees study how to respond, evade, and confront.

to (and evading) questions? Many persons are interviewed daily, and a growing number have taken intensive courses in which they have learned how to confront interviewers, use humor to evade questions, and phrase ambiguous answers that reveal little or nothing. Eugene Webb and Jerry Salancik write that the interviewer "in time, should know" a "source well enough to be able to know when a distortion is occurring, from a facial expression that doesn't correspond to a certain reply."[14]

Selecting Interviewers

Eric Nalder claims that the number one trait of an ideal journalist, or any informational interviewer, is curiosity about everyone and everything. Similarly, Ken Metzler claims "the best interviewers are those who enjoy people and are eager to learn more about the people they meet—and who are eternally curious about darned near everything."[15] Along with curiosity, the interviewer should be friendly, courteous, organized, observant, patient, persistent, and skillful.

A situation may require an interviewer of a certain age, gender, race, ethnic group, religion, political party, or educational level. A 70-year-old interviewer might find it as difficult to relate to a teenager as a teenager would to the 70-year-old. A woman might confide more readily to a female interviewer than to a male interviewer. An interviewer of Haitian ancestry might be more effective with Haitian immigrants because of common culture, traditions, and communication customs.

Relationship of Interviewer and Interviewee

Once you have selected an interviewee and interviewer, you should be aware of the **relationship** that exists between the two. Robert Ogles and other journalism professors note that informational interviews rely on "secondary relationships" that are not intimate and rely on few relational dimensions.[16] These dimensions are more functional than emotional and rely on surface cues such as obvious similarities, appearance, and nonverbal behavior. Review these questions:

- To what degree does each party want to be *included* in this interview?
- To what degree does each party *like and respect* the other?
- What degree of *control or dominance* will each party exert or try to exert in this interview?
- What is the degree of *trust* between the interview parties?

Know the relational history of the parties.

Be aware of the **perceived** similarities and differences of both parties. A positive relationship is critical to successful informational interviews because interviewers probe into beliefs, attitudes, values, feelings, and information a source may prefer not to reveal, let alone in depth. The **status difference** between interviewer and interviewee offers advantages for each party.

Status difference and similarity affect motivation, freedom to respond, control, and rapport.

When an interviewer is *subordinate* to an interviewee (student to professor, associate to manager, vice president to president):

- The interviewer need not be an expert.
- The interviewee will not feel threatened.

- The interviewee will feel freer to speak.
- The interviewee might want to help the interviewer.

Famous NBC news correspondent, anchor, and host David Brinkley remarked in a PBS interview that he welcomed the opportunity to meet with journalism students and young reporters in his office, to show them around the studio, and to discuss the academic background needed to be effective reporters.

When an interviewer is *superior* to the interviewee (lieutenant to sergeant, CEO to division head, physician to nurse practitioner):

- The interviewer can control the interview.
- The interviewer can reward the interviewee.
- The interviewee may feel motivated to please the interviewer.
- The interviewee may feel honored to be a participant.

Some organizations give high-status-sounding titles to representatives to enhance their superior aura: chief correspondent rather than correspondent, vice president instead of sales director, editor rather than reporter, executive rather than supervisor.

When the interviewer is *equal* to the interviewee (student to student, associate to associate, researcher to researcher):

> **Status is a critical criterion for some interviewees.**

- Rapport is easily established.
- There are fewer communication barriers.
- There are fewer pressures.
- A high degree of empathy is possible.

In many situations, interviewees prefer interviewers similar to them in a variety of ways, including gender, age, education level, and professional field. Some will not grant interviews to organizations or people they perceive to be of lower status. If they are senior members of Congress, for instance, they expect the media to send their senior correspondents.

Choose the Location and Setting

> **Choose the best possible setting.**

Although some sources state that the interviewer should "take control of the location" because "it's your interview" and "you should decide what the background should be," your choice is not always that simple.[17] If an attorney says she will grant an interview only in her office, a political campaign manager says he will agree to an interview only at campaign headquarters, or if a mother and father agree to an interview only at a neutral location such as a coffee shop, that's where you will conduct the interview. You might prefer to be seated on comfortable chairs facing one another with no barriers separating you, but the interviewee may insist on sitting behind a desk with its status symbols readily apparent. Do the best with what you have.

Sarah Stuteville recommends that "if there is any way you can interview in a place that has some relevance to the story of your subject you'll have much greater success . . . not only because you'll gain a further sense of context" but because "people are often more comfortable (and open) when they're in a familiar place or what feels like 'their territory'."[18] Many of the best interviews are conducted at hospitals, prisons, and factories; on locations of accidents, protest rallies, and natural disasters; and with police officers, EMTs, and sales representatives on "ride alongs" to experience the situation as well as the interview.

Eric Nalder claims that it is essential to interview people "at the place where they are doing the thing that you are writing about." It is important not only to *hear* answers but to *see* and get the *feel* of things.[19] When Nalder was writing a book on oil tankers, a member of a crew told him that he could not understand crews and life on oil tankers until he'd been aboard in the Gulf of Alaska during the violent January seas "puking your guts out." Nalder took this advice and gained exceptional insights from his experiences and those of his interviewees.

Opening the Interview

You are now ready to create an effective opening. Plan the opening with great care because the level of trust between and your interviewee begins immediately with the way you look, the way you act, how you sound, the words you use, the comments you make, and the questions you ask.[20] Journalist Sarah Stuteville reminds us that a good report or story may depend "on a total stranger's cooperation and participation." Be respectful and strive for a pleasant professional conversation rather than a confrontation. Small talk, easy to answer icebreaker questions, and friendly comments establish rapport and serve as transitions to the body of the interview.

Be careful of preparing small talk to the point at which it sounds trite, mechanical, or staged. Do not be too familiar with the interviewee. Are you really on a first name or nickname basis? If you are a stranger, identify yourself, your position, and the organization you represent. Even if you are well known to another, explain *what* you wish to discuss and *why*, reveal how the information will be *employed*, and state *how long* the interview will take. Don't pull out a notebook or produce a recorder immediately because these can threaten an interviewee.

> A solid opening is essential in motivating an interviewee.

Ask a question about something you have noticed in the interviewee's office or about hobbies, interests, or a news item. Congratulate the person on a recent recognition or accomplishment. Insert something humorous that you discovered in your research or encountered in planning the interview. Refer tactfully to the interviewee's position on an issue. Consider telling your own story to open up the interviewee. Don't begin with difficult or embarrassing questions. Raymond and Moen warn, "Beware of asking the wrong question." Prepare the opening question carefully: "Think it through. Hasty sounding questions get hasty answers, or none at all. The more you do to demonstrate that having put thought and effort into solving your problem before seeking help, the more likely you are to actually get help."

Review the opening techniques discussed in Chapter 4 and select one or a combination best suited for this interview.

Design the opening to fit each occasion and interviewee.[21] A casual compliment, friendly remark about a topic or mutual friend, or a bit of small talk might create a friendly, relaxed atmosphere with one person and produce the opposite effect with a busy, hassled interviewee who neither likes nor has time for small talk. As discussed in Chapter 2, establishing a positive relationship between interviewer and interviewee is critical to the success of every interview. Try to establish a "friendly conversational rapport, like old friends talking" without seeming to be too friendly or close. Enhance the relationship, but don't try to leap beyond it.[22] Avoid any semblance of artificiality in the opening.

Know what "off the record" means to both parties.

Be sure both parties have a mutual understanding of **ground rules** governing the interaction before proceeding past the opening. This is particularly important in investigative interviews conducted by police officers, journalists, and supervisors. If everything of importance is **off the record,** however, why conduct the interview? Make it clear there can be no retroactive off-the-record demands. Both parties must understand what "off the record" means. If a person does not want to be quoted, try to get agreement that quotations may be attributed to an unnamed source or worked into the text of a report without attribution.

Conducting the Interview

The goal of the informational interview is to get in-depth and insightful information that only an interviewee can offer. It is essential, then, to get beyond superficial and safe Level 1 interactions to riskier and deeper Level 2 and Level 3 interactions. You must **motivate** an interviewee to disclose beliefs, attitudes, and feelings as well as unknown facts.

Motivating Interviewees

There are many reasons why a person might be reluctant to talk to you or to communicate beyond Level 1.[23] An interviewee may have been "burned" in previous interviews such as this one. A negative or threatening reputation may precede you. An interviewee may see the interview as a risk to self-image, credibility with others, or a career. Perhaps the interview is seen as an invasion of privacy or posing the danger of opening up areas the interviewee may prefer to remain forgotten or unknown. And the interviewee may not want to be interviewed on any subject. On the other hand, be careful of interviewees who appear to be too eager to take part and reveal secrets. They may be after publicity, exposure, an ego-trip, a chance to sell a product or idea, or to get even with someone or an organization.

Know what motivates each interviewee.

Trust is essential for informational interviews.

Interviewees are likely to communicate beyond Level 1 if you adhere to simple guidelines that follow the golden rule: *do unto others as you would have them do unto you.* This rule applies to the most difficult of interview situations. A report about interrogation interviews with insurgents in Iraq and Afghanistan noted that "the successful interrogators all had one thing in common in the way they approached their subjects. They were nice to them."[24] Parties will communicate freely and accurately if they trust you to react with understanding and tact, maintain confidences, use the information fairly, and report what they say accurately and completely. Ken Metzler recommends that we avoid the term *interview* and call it a conversation, talk, discussion, or chat. He also advises to "drop names" of people the interviewee respects that may serve as credibility enhancers and motivators.

Don't have an *attitude*. From the opening until the interview ends, show sincere interest in and enthusiasm for the interviewee, the topic, and answers. Don't reveal how you feel about answers and issues; remain neutral. Control the interview without interrupting and look for natural pauses to probe or to ask primary questions. Ask questions rather than make statements. Listen not only with your ears but also with your eyes, face, nods, and attentive posture. Metzler writes, "It's not the questions you ask that make for a successful interview but the attention you pay to the answers you receive." Some experienced interviewers recommend listening to the interviewee 100 percent of the time.[25]

Asking Questions

Questions are tools of the trade that motivate interviewees to provide information and insights. Unfortunately, interviewers tend to ask too many questions, and this limits their opportunities to listen, observe, and think. Interviewers may appear arrogant or assume they "are *entitled* to an answer." Raymond and Moen declare, "You aren't, after all, paying for the service. You will earn an answer, if you earn it, by asking a substantial, interesting, and thought-provoking question—one that implicitly contributes to the experience of the community rather than merely passively demanding knowledge from others."

Ask Open-Ended Questions

> Listening is as important as asking.

Open questions motivate and encourage interviewees to communicate. Thorough answers to open-ended questions allow you to listen appropriately (for comprehension, empathy, evaluation, resolution) and observe the interviewee's mannerisms, appearance, and non-verbal communication. Listening and observing help determine the accuracy and relevance of answers and the interviewee's feelings. A raised eyebrow or a slight hesitancy of a respondent from another culture, for instance, may signal that you used a slang phrase, colloquialism, or oxymoron with which this person is unfamiliar or that sounds strange.

> Make the interviewee the star of the show.

Ask Probing Questions

> Be an active listener, not a passive sponge.

Be patient and persistent. Do not interrupt a respondent unless the person is obviously off target, evading a question, or threatens to continue answering forever. The flexible nature of the informational interview requires a full range of probing questions. Metzler writes that "probes—followup questions—are essential. It's seldom the first question that gets to the heart of the matter, it's the seventh, or maybe 16th question you didn't know you were going to ask but have chosen to ask because of your careful, thoughtful listening." Use **silent** and **nudging probes** to encourage an interviewee to continue. Tolerate silences because the interviewee might want to say something important about which you did not plan to ask. Use **informational probes** to detect cues in answers or to get additional information or explanations. Use **restatement probes** to obtain a direct answer. Use **reflective** and **mirror questions** to verify and clarify answers and to check for accuracy and understanding. Use **clearinghouse probes** to be sure you have obtained everything of importance to your story or report. Metzler suggests asking **metaphorical questions,** such as "Governor, do you hope to hit a home run with this legislative proposal?" to motivate interviewees to expand answers in an interesting and understandable manner.

You cannot plan for every piece of information or insight an interviewee might have. Some journalists claim that "even if you go into an interview armed with a list of questions, the most important probably will be ones you ask in response to an answer."[26] For instance, if an interviewee says something surprising or reveals a secret, follow this lead to see where it takes you. Then you can go back to your schedule and continue as planned until the next lead comes along. Inflexible interviewers miss opportunities to gain valuable insights and information.

Be courteous, friendly, tactful, and nonargumentative. Be understanding when delving into sensitive or personal areas. Be prepared to back off if an interviewee becomes emotionally upset or angry. There are times when you need to pry into potentially embarrassing areas such as the nature of an illness, marital problems, organizational finances, or an arrest.

Persistent probing is essential in informational interviews, but you must know when to stop. An interviewee may become agitated, confused, or silent if you probe too far. This exchange occurred between an attorney and a physician:[27]

> **Know when enough is enough.**

Attorney: Doctor, before you performed the autopsy, did you check for a pulse?

Physician: No.

Attorney: Did you check for blood pressure?

Physician: No.

Attorney: Did you check for breathing?

Physician: No.

Attorney: So, then it is possible that the patient was alive when you began the autopsy?

Physician: No.

Attorney: How can you be so sure, Doctor?

Physician: Because his brain was sitting on my desk in a jar.

Attorney: But could the patient have still been alive nevertheless?

Physician: It is possible that he could be alive practicing law somewhere.

Be persistent, even relentless, but know when enough probing is enough.

Phrasing Questions

Phrase each question carefully, particularly unplanned probing questions that you create on the spot. Review thoroughly the common question pitfalls discussed in Chapter 3 so you can catch yourself before stumbling into one. These include the bipolar trap, the tell me everything, the open-to-closed switch, the double-barreled inquisition, the leading push, the guessing game, the yes (no) response, the curious probe, the quiz show, the don't ask, don't tell, and complexity vs. simplicity. Make each question brief and to the point, and then give the interviewee your full attention.

> **All rules are made to be broken, but you must know when and how.**

Sometimes you must break the rules to get information you want. It may be necessary to ask an obvious question even when you know the answer in advance, such as "I see you were in Iran last spring." Seemingly obvious questions can relax respondents by getting them to talk about things that are well known and easy to talk about, showing interest in topics important to interviewees, and revealing that you have done your homework. A leading push such as "You surely don't believe that?" may provoke a respondent into a revealing interchange. Be cautious when asking leading questions of children. Studies have shown that children are susceptible to such questions because they "are very attuned to taking cues from adults and tailoring their answers based on the way questions are worded."[28] You may ask a double-barreled question at a press conference to get two or three answers because it may be the only question you get to ask. A bipolar question will produce a yes or no for the record, a common need in journalistic interviews.

Phrase questions carefully to avoid confusion. The following interaction between a patient and a physician illustrates the dangers of jargon and sound-alike words:

Know what you are doing and why.

Physician: Have you ever had a history of cardiac arrest in your family?

Patient: We never had no trouble with the police.

Some interviewees will answer questions about which they have no knowledge, faking it rather than admitting ignorance. Others are experts on everything and nothing. Listen to call-in programs on radio to hear people make incredibly uninformed or misinformed claims, accusations, and observations. Sometimes interviewees will play funny games, such as this exchange that took place during an election campaign in New Hampshire:

Reporter: How are you going to vote on Tuesday?

Resident: How am I going to vote? Oh, the usual way. I'm going to take the form they hand me and put x's in the appropriate boxes (laughing).

Reporter: (pause) Who are you going to vote for on Tuesday?

Think before asking.

Listen to answers to avoid embarrassments such as the following exchange between an attorney and a witness:

Attorney: Now, Mrs. Johnson, how was your first marriage terminated?

Witness: By death.

Attorney: And by whose death was it terminated?

It can be embarrassing and insulting to repeat a question during an interview because you forgot you already asked it. Think before asking questions you have not prepared in advance. For instance, Ken Metzler recommends avoiding the "how do you feel about that" question because "It's the most trite, overused question in American journalism and sources begin to hate it after time." Interviewees often respond with brief answers such as "Okay," "Not bad," or "As good as might be expected" that tell you nothing. It's a vague answer to a routine question.[29] Metzler suggests substituting "What were you thinking when . . . ?" for the "feel" question.

Effective note taking entails maintaining eye contact as much as possible.

© David Buffington/Blend Images LLC

Note Taking and Recording

Although experts disagree on the extent of note taking and the use of electronic recorders because each can be intrusive and unreliable, it is wise to use the means best suited to you, the interviewee, the situation, and the report you will prepare. Lack of note taking or recording may make it impossible to recall figures, dates, names, times, details, and quotations accurately.

Note Taking

Note taking increases your attention to what is being said and how, and this enhanced attention shows respondents you are interested in what they are saying and are concerned about accuracy. William Zinsser writes that this direct involvement allows the interviewee to see you working and doing your job.[30] If you take notes according to the structure of the interview, you have your notes clearly organized when the interview ends and can easily locate information you need when writing your report or story.

> **Weigh carefully the pros and cons of note taking prior to the interview.**

Note taking has disadvantages. Because respondents tend to speak rapidly, it may be impossible for you to record in writing exactly what was said. It is difficult to concentrate on questions and answers and to maintain eye contact while writing notes, so you may fail to hear or probe into an answer because you are busy writing rather than listening. Note taking may hamper the flow of information because the interviewee may become anxious or curious about what you are writing. People may be reluctant to talk while you are writing or feel a break in communication while you are focusing on your pad instead of them. In an in-depth interview with a newspaper publisher, one of our students discovered that whenever she began to write, the interviewee would stop answering until she stopped writing, apparently to let her catch up. Before long, he arranged his chair so he could see what she was writing.

Follow these guidelines when taking notes during interviews.[31]

> **Note taking should not threaten the interviewee.**

- Ask permission to take notes and explain why note taking is beneficial to both parties.
- Show your notes occasionally to the interviewee to reduce curiosity and anxiety, check for accuracy, and enable the interviewee to fill in gaps and volunteer information.
- Preserve communication by maintaining eye contact and making note taking as inconspicuous as possible.
- Instead of writing full sentences and every word, use abbreviations or a personal shorthand like when sending text messages.
- Reduce the time it takes by writing down only important information, key words, and the gist of some quotes.

Maintain communication while taking notes.

- Take notes throughout rather than sporadically during the interview to avoid signaling that the interviewee just dropped a "bombshell" quote or causing the interviewee to become cautious in revealing important information.

- Note taking tends to slow the pace of interviews but, if an interviewee is answering too rapidly for adequate note taking, ask the person tactfully to slow down, repeat an answer, or ask a stalling question such as "Tell me more about that" to give you time to get caught up.

- Review your notes immediately following the interview to fill in gaps, check for accuracy and objectivity, complete abbreviations, translate your handwriting, and determine if another interview is necessary.

Recording

Recording allows interviewers to listen and probe more effectively.

Only a recorder can provide a complete record of *how, when,* and *what* an interviewee says. A recorder enables you to relax, concentrate on what is being said and implied, and then create effective probing questions. You can hear or watch what was said and how it was said hours or days afterward. A recorder may pick up inaudible answers and give you a complete and accurate record of the content of the interview.

A recorder may add an intrusive element to the interview.

Recording has potential disadvantages. Recorders can malfunction or prove tricky to use. Batteries can go dead. A number of our students have used recorders during lengthy interviews for class projects only to discover disks or memory sticks were blank when they tried to review them later. Some subjects view recorders as intruders in intimate interviewing situations, and they provide permanent, undeniable records that threaten them with unknown future consequences. It takes time to review a lengthy recording to locate facts, reactions, and ideal quotes.

Follow these guidelines when recording interviews.[32]

Ask permission before using a recorder.

- Reduce interviewee fears and objections by explaining why the recorder is advantageous to the interviewee, why you want or are required to use a recorder, how the recording will be used, and offering to turn off the recorder when desired.

- Reduce mechanical difficulties by testing the recorder prior to the interview.

- Be familiar with the recorder and practice with it in a simulated interview setting.

- Research appropriate state laws before using a hidden recorder or recording interviews over the telephone. The law generally allows one party to record a second party (no third parties) without permission, but 12 states prohibit the recording of conversations without the consent of both parties, including California, Connecticut, Florida, Illinois, Maryland, Massachusetts, Michigan, Montana, Nevada, New Hampshire, Pennsylvania, and Washington.[33] Twenty-four states have laws that pertain to the use of hidden cameras. An excellent source on legal aspects of interviewing is a guide published by the *Reporters Committee for Freedom of the Press* (http://www.rcip.org).

- Ask permission before recording an interview to avoid possible lawsuits and to establish goodwill.

- Set ground rules with the interviewee ahead of time such as wearing a microphone, having a recorder nearby, looking at the lens of a camera instead of the light, limiting background noise and interruptions, speaking loud enough for the recorder.

Handling Special Situations

There are three special situations that place both parties in somewhat unique situations that affect role relationships and necessitate changes in the ways each party usually prepares for and participates in interviews. These situations are the press conference, the broadcast interview, and the videoconference interview.

The Press Conference

The press conference is unique in that several interviewers are involved simultaneously and the *interviewee* determines purpose, subject matter, time, place, length, and ground rules for the interview. A press conference may be called with little warning and offer minimal indication about what will be addressed. It is likely to start with a prepared statement or presentation and then go to questions from the interviewers present. Ground rules may include which topics or issues are off limits to questioning, whether answers may be quoted and the interviewee cited, or whether only background or unattributed materials can be used in your report of the conference.

If you have little notice of a press conference, try to determine from your records and experiences and contacts with other sources which issue or topic is likely to be addressed and the interviewee's position.[34] The result might be a simple interview guide. If possible, prepare some questions in advance knowing that some may prove to be irrelevant, declared off limits, or asked by other interviewers who are recognized before you. Assess your relationship with the interviewee. If the person likes and trusts you, you may be chosen to ask the first question or be one of a few who are recognized during the question period. If your relationship is negative, the interviewee may refuse to recognize you, give a superficial or hostile response to your question, or say "No comment" and turn quickly to another interviewer.

Always be on time for a press conference and make yourself visible by sitting as near the interviewee as possible and in the center so you are less likely to be overlooked during the question period. Be close enough to hear what is said and any possible whispers between the interviewee and aides. Note what is said and not said in the statement and answers to questions. Be aware that your purpose and that of the interviewee may not only be different but also at odds. The interviewee may want to use the situation and interviewers for self-promotion, promotion of a new product, public relations, free advertising, or to place a positive spin on an issue or action and want you to do the same. Your job is to get to the truth of the matter and to cut through the "smoke and mirrors" presented in statements and vague generalities, allegations, and unsupported claims in answers. The interviewee *needs you* and this gives you some control of the situation.

> The interviewee controls the press conference.

Don't be intimidated by the situation or the status of the interviewee. Journalist Tony Rogers writes that "It's your job to ask tough questions of the most powerful people in our society."[35] Once the question period begins, it is likely to be a free-for-all with raised hands, interviewers jumping to their feet, and shouted questions. Ask your most

■ *The broadcast interview presents unique problems for both parties.*

© Digital Vision Ltd. / SuperStock

important question first because it may be the only question you get to ask. It is unlikely that you will be able to probe into answers. You may ask a double-barreled question in an effort to get two answers in one. You may not get to your prepared questions, and this can be an advantage. Listen carefully to answers to other interviewers' questions for valuable information and a follow-up you might ask. Your best questions may be aimed at clarifying and getting new information from these answers or the interviewee's statement. Remember that interviewer questions need not be on the topic of the press conference. Protocol enables the interviewee or a staff member to end the press conference without warning, perhaps to avoid or escape unwanted exchanges and issues.

The Broadcast Interview

> **Outside forces influence broadcast interviews.**

The broadcast interview poses unique challenges to both parties. It may be on a real or figurative stage in which both must engage in "performing" for outside forces such as live audiences, viewers, and listeners that may constitute "a three-way interaction."[36] This virtual third party may cause nervousness and lead the interviewer and interviewee to adapt questions and answers to it. The interviewer not only needs to attain answers and reactions but also sound and pictures that play well on the air. The interview may be live or pre-recorded and, if live, anything can and frequently does happen. There are no "do-overs" in live broadcasting, and interactions may be in full view verbally and nonverbally of those who have tuned in. The interviews may take place in the field or in studios, and interviewer and interviewee may be in separate locations many miles and time zones apart.[37]

> **Being familiar with the physical setting can eliminate many surprises.**

Take advantage of ways to enhance your efficiency and performance and reduce nervousness. Practice and simulations in pre-recorded situations that emulate the real thing followed by a thorough debriefing will help you to determine what you did well and where you need more practice. Do your homework before every interview by knowing who you will interview, when, and where and by becoming acquainted with the program format and targeted audience. Become thoroughly familiar with the physical setting, including seating for interviewer and interviewee, technicians and other support staff who will be present, and audio and video equipment. When appropriate and possible, test out the equipment. Pay close attention to the briefing concerning time limits, opening and closing signals, microphone use, and camera locations.

Help the interviewee to make the interview a successful interaction for both parties. Brief the person (or persons if a group interview) in advance of what is expected during the interview. Explain ground rules such as wearing a microphone, having a recorder nearby, looking at you rather than the camera or broadcasting staff, speaking loud enough to be heard easily, and if more than one interviewee is present, the importance of only one person speaking at a time. Caution the interviewee about content or responses that may result in negative reactions from third parties.

The "staging" of the broadcast interview is critical to its success. The interviewer or director will determine the framing of shots—whether the interviewer or interviewee will face the camera left or right, eyelines (interviewee's eye level with the interviewer's), whether shots will be mid-shot or medium close-ups, and whether to select a sequence of shots. Other decisions involve lighting (in front of a window if lighting is inadequate), props, background (not dark clothing on a dark backdrop, not an overly busy background), and limiting noise such as shuffling of papers, heating and cooling systems, bell towers, nearby interactions, and foot traffic. These decisions make the broadcast interview far more complex than a simple face-to-face interview.[38]

Know and play your role in the interview.

As you conduct the broadcast interview, make it seem that the interviewee is conversing only with you by maintaining eye contact and taking only limited and necessary notes. Let the recorder do its job. Put the interviewee at ease from the start, perhaps by some informal conversation before the recording or broadcast begins. Open with easy first questions, preferably open-ended ones when time allows. Deadlines and time limitations may dictate that questions be direct, to the point, and moderately open. Fred Fedler notes that "the live interview may last no more than seconds or a few minutes and allows little time to ask challenging questions."[39] Ask questions and don't make statements; your job is to get information, not to give it. Know your questions well enough to ask from memory or a few small cards to make the interview look and sound spontaneous and professional. You want to avoid "dead air space" for any length of time but you must also tolerate silence that gives the interviewee time to think and answer your question. Avoid the sin of jumping in too quickly with another question.

You must be persistent in getting at the information you need, particularly when an interviewee is purposely being vague or evasive or by answering a question you did not ask. There is a big difference between tenacity and incivility. Sparks recommends that interviewers should be aggressive with charm. Realize, however, that no matter how civil and charming you might try to be, some interviewees and their advocates will accuse you of bias and rudeness.[40] Strive to make the interview worthwhile for the interviewee by showing respect and making your questions relevant and neutral. Pay close attention to the interviewee's physical and mental well-being by detecting nervousness, anger, confusion, and emotional reactions. It may be time for a break or to draw the interview to a close.

Spontaneous questions generate spontaneous answers.

Some utterances and actions cannot be broadcast or may be embarrassing, such as profanities, obscene gestures, poor grammar, too many "uhs," "you knows," "know what I means," and excessive "blood and gore." Some newspaper reporters, when being crowded out by cameras and microphones, shout obscenities to shut down their electronic counterparts and get closer to the action. A state legislator told one of the authors that he would purposely insert profanities into answers to prevent reporters from using them on the air.

The Videoconference Interview

As discussed in Chapter 1, the videoconference interview is becoming increasingly common as a means of communicating long distances quickly, efficiently, and inexpensively. Videoconferences share similarities with face-to-face interviews, but there are differences you need to understand and practice. A Boston College Web site offers these suggestions for video interviewing.[41]

- **Hesitate slightly** before asking or answering questions because there is typically a slight delay in receiving the audio and video.
- **Look straight into the monitor** or camera so you appear to be looking into the interviewer's or interviewee's eyes.
- **Focus on the interviewer or interviewee** so you can become comfortable with the video interview situation.
- **Avoid excessive motion or stiffness** so you appear relaxed and enjoying a pleasant conversation.
- **Speak naturally** without shouting because the microphone will pick up your voice, and you need not lean into the microphone to be heard.
- **Show energy and enthusiasm** through your voice and face (including smiling) because you will appear as a "talking head," no more than from the waist up.

Other suggestions include wearing solid and neutral color clothing. Both cameras and interview parties have problems focusing on the interview when parties are wearing plaids, stripes, or white shirts and jackets. Avoid noises that are particularly distracting in videoconferences, such as tapping on a desk, moving papers, or jewelry that makes audible sounds. Glittery jewelry may catch light and be distracting to interview parties. Remember to smile because the videoconference enables you to talk face-to-face.[42] We will return to preparing for and taking part in videoconference interviews in Chapter 8 that focuses on the applicant in the employment interview.

Handling Difficult Interviewees

Informational interviews delve into feelings, attitudes, and reasons for actions and may hit raw nerves and evoke reactions ranging from tears and hostility to an interviewee stopping the interview. The settings of disasters, crimes, election defeats, losses in sporting events, memorial ceremonies, deaths, and scandals are tense, emotional, and embarrassing. Be prepared to handle difficult interviewees in difficult situations. As journalist Bob Steele warns, "If we aren't proficient at asking the right questions at the right time, we'll miss on accuracy, fall short on context, and stumble on fairness."

Emotional Interviewees

Silence is often better than talk with emotional interviewees.

Respondents may burst into tears during interviews. The problem is not helped when an interviewer blurts out, "I know just how you feel." Tactful and sincere reactions such as the following may help.

It's okay to cry.
Take your time.
Do you need a few minutes?

Remain silent until a person regains composure and is ready to continue. If you have a close relationship with an interviewee, you may hold the person's hand or place an arm across the shoulders as comforting gestures.

Treat others as you would like to be treated.

Be sensitive to people who have experienced tragedies by not invading their privacy for pictures or tearful comments for news broadcast. How you broach a sensitive topic at a sensitive time is a serious ethical issue for informational interviews.[43] Reporters are notorious for asking thoughtless questions such as, "How do you feel about your child's death?" or "Is the family devastated by this tragedy?" John and Denise Bittner suggest that you ask only direct and necessary questions. "Remember, people in crisis situations are under a great deal of stress," they write. "A prolonged interview won't provide additional information; it will only upset people."[44] The dangers of insensitive interviewing were illustrated when a CNN interviewer grilled the mother of a missing boy on national television. She challenged her alibi, demanding to know where she was at the time, what she was doing, and why she wasn't providing specifics about stores she visited and items she purchased. Shortly after the interview, the mother committed suicide. Local media speculated that the CNN interviewer had "pushed her over the edge."[45]

Hostile Interviewees

Determine if hostility is real or imagined. If it is real, discover why. A person may feel angry, depressed, helpless, or frightened because of circumstances beyond his or her control, and you become a convenient target for prying into and releasing feelings. Hostility may be toward you, your organization, your position, or your profession. Bad experiences with interviewers, particularly ones from your organization, may lead an interviewee to expect the worst from you. The person may simply be having a bad day because of traffic, a headache, a computer glitch, a late appointment.

A *nondirective interviewing approach* such as the following might reveal the source or cause of hostility.

> You appear to be very angry this morning.
> You seem very upset.
> I detect hostility; would you like to talk about it?

Large male interviewers often appear threatening to interviewees.

You may avoid hostility by *not* making unwarranted demands, invading a person's territory or personal space, or allowing your physical presence and manner to appear threatening.

- Do not intentionally or unintentionally mislead the interviewee about who you are, what you want, why you want it, how you will use it, and whether the interviewee will be identified in your story or report.
- Substitute better sounding words for potentially antagonizing ones: aides for handlers, damage control for spin doctoring, negative campaigning for mudslinging.
- Use neutral, open-ended questions.
- Use silence to allow the interviewee time to explain or to blow off some steam.
- Proceed to a new topic.

Phillip Ault and Edwin Emery offer this simple rule: "Treat the average person with respect, and he [she] will do the same."[46]

Reticent Interviewees

Be prepared for the "silent types."

If a person appears unwilling or unable to talk, discover why. The person may be inhibited by you or your position, the situation, the topic, the surroundings, people, or lack of privacy. Many people are reticent around authority figures, supervisors, investigators, and journalists. Think of a time when you went to a professor or supervisor with a personal problem and the setting was a small cubicle or open area in which other persons could easily overhear. Reticence may be a personal trait that has nothing to do with the interview and cannot be altered during the interview.

When interviewing reticent persons, use conversation starters by asking about pictures, awards, or arrangement of furnishings in the room. Begin with easy-to-answer questions on nonthreatening topics. Become less formal. If open questions do not generate in-depth answers, use closed questions (an inverted question sequence) until the party is ready to talk. Use silent and nudging probes. Realize that no tactic can get some reticent people to talk openly and freely; they simply don't talk much.

Talkative Interviewees

Controlling talkative persons may be more difficult than getting reticent ones to open up.

If you think a *reticent interviewee* is difficult, meet the *talkative interviewee*. Some people love to talk and can do so at length without taking a breath. They give lengthy answers to highly closed questions and seemingly unending answers to open questions. They want to be helpful to a fault.

Use targeted, closed questions that give talkative interviewees less verbal maneuverability and more direction. Look for natural openings or slight pauses to insert a question or redirect the interview:

> I'm glad you mentioned that. Tell me about . . .
>
> Speaking of the opening day at the track, what are your plans for . . .
>
> That's really interesting. Now, what about . . .
>
> Thanks for elaborating on that. Let's turn our attention to . . .

Be tactful and sensitive in using nonverbal signals.

Avoid awkward interruptions by using signaling that you need to move on: look at your notes, lean forward, nod your head as if to say "That's enough," stop note taking, or glance at your watch. Telephone and other electronic interviews pose problems because you have few nonverbal signals to halt answers, so interviewees may give long, rambling answers.

Evasive Interviewees

Discover why a person may be evasive.

Interviewees may evade questions that require them to reveal feelings or prejudices, make them take stands, give specific information, or may incriminate them in some way. Evasive strategies include humor, fake hostility, counter questions, ambiguous language, or rambling answers that never get to the point. Interviewees may quibble over the wording of questions or the definitions of key words. A common tactic is to counter a question with a question, perhaps revolving the question onto the interviewer:

> Well, how would *you* answer that?
> What do *you* think we should do?
> Tell me about *your* private life.

Be patient and persistent.

Interviewees may answer a question not asked but one they want to answer. You can deal with evasive interviewees by being persistent in questioning. For instance:

- Repeat or rephrase a question.
- Laugh and continue with your questions.
- Go to other questions and come back to this one later.
- Resort to leading or loaded questions to evoke meaningful responses.

An interviewee may be dishonest. Listen carefully to answers to determine if they square with the facts from your research and previous interviews. Observe nonverbal cues to detect dishonesty but be aware that clever respondents know how to *appear* honest, including excellent eye contact. Pat Stith writes that when an interviewee "says 'to be honest' or 'to be perfectly candid' the hair ought to stand up on the back of your neck. Almost always these phrases are followed by fibs."[47]

Two experienced FBI agents, Joe Navarro and John R. Schafer, offer detailed suggestions on how to detect dishonesty during interviews but warn that "lie detection" is a "50/50 proposition even for experienced investigators."[48] They recommend that interviewers look for "clusters of behavior, which cumulatively reinforce deceptive behaviors unique to the person being interviewed." Nonverbal behaviors include fidgeting feet, increased eye contact, rapidly blinking eyes, leaning away, irregular breathing, folding arms or interlocking legs to use less space, and lack of gesturing or finger pointing. Verbal cues include what Navarro and Schafer call "text bridges" such as "I don't remember," "The next thing I knew," and "After that." Stalling tactics may include asking an interviewer to repeat a question or using phrases such as "It depends on what you mean by," "Where did you hear that," and "Could you be more specific?" As an informational interviewer, strike a balance between being gullible and suspicious.

Confused Interviewees

Respondents may become confused by topics or questions, particularly in tense situations. Be prepared to handle confused persons without embarrassing them or creating hostility. Restate or rephrase a question tactfully. Return to the question later in the interview. Be conscious of jargon and similar sounding words. This exchange took place between an attorney and a witness.[49]

Be understanding, helpful, and adaptive to confused interviewees.

Attorney: Is your appearance here this morning pursuant to a deposition notice which I sent to your attorney?

Witness: No, this is how I dress when I go to work.

Be careful of your nonverbal reactions. Broadcast journalists who get strange responses rarely exhibit a smile or shock when that happens. They go on to the next question or topic as if nothing embarrassing has happened.

Dissimilar Interviewees

Gender and cultural characteristics are generalities and may not apply to a particular interviewee.

Adapt carefully to interviewees who are dissimilar to you. Journalist Wendell Cochran asks, "How do you deal fairly with someone whose views are anathema to you?"[50] Observe interviews in the media to see how interviewers deal with interviewees they clearly do not like such as a person convicted of molesting children, a captured terrorist, a CEO who deceived workers and investors, or one with very different political, social, or religious beliefs.

Previous chapters have identified important communicative characteristics unique to males and females and different cultures. Gender differences are important in informational interviews. For example, men tend to talk more, monopolize conversations, make more direct statements ("beat around the bush" less often), answer questions with declarations (while women tend to answer questions with questions), get to the point sooner in answers, and respond to questions with minimal responses (yeah, nope, fine, okay, sure). Elderly respondents may be less trusting because of experiences and insecurity, but are often communication starved and may be *very* talkative in interviews.

Interviewers may stereotype ethnic groups such as Irish-Americans, Asian-Americans, African-Americans, Arab-Americans, and Hispanic-Americans and expect them to act in certain ways during interviews. On the other hand, interviewees may stereotype interviewers because of their ethnic backgrounds or the organizations or professions they represent. When one of the authors was conducting interviews with funeral directors in preparation for a book and course on grief counseling, some directors assumed that, as a college professor, the author must be an atheist or at least a "nonbeliever." Interviewees may have developed solidarity through in-group codes, symbols, expectations, and enemies that outsiders neither share nor understand. Research indicates that African-Americans prefer indirect questions, consider extensive probing to be intrusive, and prefer more frequent and equal turn taking. Mexican-American respondents rely more on emotion, intuition, and feeling than midwestern European-Americans. Persons of rural backgrounds value personal know-how, skills, practicality, simplicity, and self-sufficiency more than those of urban backgrounds. Adapt your questions and structure to different interviewees and be aware of gender and cultural differences that may motivate interviewees and explain the answers you receive.

Closing the Interview

Close the interview when you have the information you need or your allotted time runs out. If the interviewee has agreed to a 15-minute interview, complete the interview within this time or prepare to close the interview. Do not ignore a time limit or press the interviewee for additional time. The **interviewee** may grant additional minutes when you signal that your time is up or you obviously need only a few more minutes. If the interviewee appears reluctant to expand the time, close the interview positively and arrange for another appointment.

Review the closing guidelines and techniques discussed in Chapter 4, particularly the use of clearinghouse probes. It is wise to begin a closing with a clearinghouse question—such as "Is there anything else you would like to add?" or "What have I not asked that you think is important?"—to be sure you have asked for all important information. The most thoroughly prepared interview may miss something important that did not occur to you before or during the interview. Express appreciation for the interviewee's assistance. Make the closing a dialogue with the interviewee, not a monologue in which you recite a prepared closing statement. **The interviewee must be an active party from opening through closing.**

Be sure you understand the information you have obtained; can reproduce names; position titles, dates, quotations, facts, and statistics accurately; and can interpret attitudes, feelings, and beliefs as meant by the interviewee. Remember that the interview is not over until both parties are out of sight and sound of one another. An interviewee may relax and be less on guard when the interview appears to be coming to an end and reveal important information, insights, and feelings, some of which may alter your understandings and impressions established during the body of the interview. Journalist Pat Stith writes that "some of the best stuff you're going to get will come in the last few minutes, when you're wrapping up the interview, packing your stuff, and getting ready to leave."[51] Observe and listen.

Preparing the Report or Story

Make it a habit to check all sources.

The final stage in the informational interview is to prepare the necessary **report** or **story.** Review the information and observations obtained through your interviews to see if you have obtained the information necessary to satisfy your purpose. This means remembering interchanges, reading notes, and listening or viewing recordings. Sift through hundreds or thousands of words, statements, facts, opinions, and impressions to locate what is most important to include in a report or story. Check answers with other sources, especially if there is reason to suspect an interviewee gave inaccurate information.

A critical decision is what to include and not to include in your report or story. If the interview or press conference covers several topics or raises a number of issues, you must decide if your information warrants several stories or one lengthy one that covers all or several of them. The time and space you have to report are key determiners. What is truly important for others to know? Include important announcements, revelations, allegations, denials, and positions as well as significant quotations, stories, sound bites, and changes in labels: from accidental death to murder, explosion to terrorism, malfunction to sabotage, civil union to gay marriage. Once you know what you have obtained from the interview stage, editing begins. If the report is a verbatim interview for publication or dissemination, determine if grammatical errors, mispronounced words, expletives, slang, and vocalized pauses such as "uh," "and uh," and "you know" should remain. What about repetitious statements, long and rambling explanations, and simple, unintentional errors? Readers and listeners may enjoy the account with all of the warts showing, but both interview parties may be embarrassed and lose credibility, and the relationship may be damaged beyond repair and place future interviews in jeopardy.

Be honest, accurate, and fair in reporting interview results.

Preface answers and questions so readers and listeners will have a clear understanding of each. Edit questions to make answers more pointed and meaningful. When quoting from notes or memory, strive for accuracy. Do not put words into an interviewee's mouth. Be sure proper qualifiers are included. Do not understate or overstate an interviewee's opinions, attitudes, intentions, or commitments. Be sure both questions and answers are reported in proper context.

The technical steps of report or story preparation are beyond the scope of this book (see the resources at the end of this chapter), but here are a few precautions.

- Remember the ground rules agreed to and what information is "off the record."
- Be careful of assumptions.
- Strive for accuracy and fairness in every fact and interpretation.
- Check carefully all sources and reports.
- Arrange information in order of importance.
- Use quotations to enliven and support the story or report.
- Include several points of view to achieve balance.

A few years ago Ted Mann, the former sports publicist for Duke University, picked up the morning paper and discovered to his surprise that he was dead. It had all started when a friend of a reporter who worked for a rescue squad told the reporter Mann had died. The reporter called the Mann home to verify the report, and the woman who answered the phone said, "Mr. Mann's not here. He's gone." The reporter assumed this phrase was a euphemism for dead and that the woman had verified Mann's death. He wrote an obituary on this false assumption.[52]

The Interviewee in the Probing Interview

Interviewing books typically focus on the interviewer because most readers are concerned with learning how to conduct interviews effectively. But all of us are interviewees at least as often as we are interviewers. Let's turn our attention, then, to becoming more effective respondents in interviews.

Do Your Homework

Get to know the interviewer as well as the interviewer knows you.

Before taking part in an informational interview, become thoroughly briefed on topics that might come up, including recent events, accidents, controversies, innovations, decisions, and laws. Have you played roles in any of these? Check organizations to be sure you understand organizational policies, positions, and involvements and what authority you have to speak for the organization. Is there a more knowledgeable or authoritative person who should be the interviewee?

Learn everything available about the interviewer, including age, gender, ethnic group, education and training, special interests, and experiences. What are the interviewer's attitudes toward you, your organization, your profession, and the topic: friendly or hostile, trusting or suspicious, interested or disinterested. Some interviewers will have little to no knowledge or expertise on a topic while others have engineering, management, economics, law, or science degrees or have developed a high level of expertise on topics such as energy, stem cell research, or foreign policy. What is the interviewer's reputation for fairness and honesty? What questioning techniques does the interviewer usually employ? Observe the interviewer in action by watching the person reporting on news shows, reading print reports of interviews, and reviewing story angles the person likes to take.

Interviews often take place without warning. A person may call, stop by your office, appear at your front door, or approach you on the street. When this happens, be sure the opening reveals the identity of the interviewer, the interviewer's organization, length of the interview, information desired, and how the information will be used. A thorough opening, including small talk, orients you about the topic, purpose, and relationship and gives you time to think and prepare answers strategically.

Understand the Relationship

Appreciate the impact of upward and downward communication in interviews.

The relationship between interviewer and interviewee is a major concern in informational interviews because one or the other is likely to be in a superior position: a young accountant interviewing the CFO or the president of the university interviewing a young assistant professor. This upward and downward communication may lead either party to be overawed by the other. Feelings of subordination, obligation, or flattery may lead you to answer any question asked, particularly in the presence of cameras, microphones, technicians, or audiences. Determine whether to speak to a particular person at a particular time. Realize that refusals of interviews may lead interviewers to state ominously at a later date that "Joe Smoe was unavailable for comment" or "refused to talk to us." Such statements imply guilt, but may be preferable to foolish comments that become headlines.

Assess the relationship between parties prior to the interview for indicators of what might take place during the interview.

Understand the relationship prior to the interview.

- What is your relational history?
- How similar are you?
- How willing and eager are both parties to take part?
- How much control will you have?
- Do the parties perceive one another to be trustworthy, reliable, and safe?

Be Aware of the Situation

Assess the many situational variables that will impact the interview.

Be thoroughly aware of the interview situation, particularly if it is a broadcast interview. Become familiar with the media format and how you might help by providing good visuals. Diana Pisciotta, an expert in strategic communication, warns that "An appearance on CNBC or an interview on NPR can help to make or break your company's reputation."[53] She suggests that if the interview is not "live," you should pretend it is because your interview might be picked up by the Internet or other media outlets. There is no substitute for practice, rehearsal, and role playing to prepare you for the broadcast interview. Dress for the camera; appear to be excited and engaged; be animated because body language enhances your voice, credibility, expertise, and authority; keep your eyes on the interviewer rather than the camera.[54]

Consider establishing ground rules such as time, place, length, which topics are off limits or off the record. Be realistic in demands. If you demand that all important topics be off limits, there is no interview. Occasionally you may request to see questions in advance to prepare well-thought-out answers with accurate and substantial data. If Diane Sawyer of ABC wants to interview you, you would be foolish to demand a different interviewer. How much control you have depends upon your importance as a source, your relationship with the interviewer, the situation, and how eager you are to serve as an interviewee.

Anticipate Questions

Be as prepared to answer as the interviewer is prepared to ask.

Anticipate questions and think through possible responses. What might be the most important information to divulge or conceal? How should you qualify answers? What evidence can you provide for assertions and claims? How might you reply to questions you cannot answer because of lack of information, need for secrecy, protection of sources, legal consequences, or organizational policies and constraints?

In this age of litigation and media involvement in every issue, increasing numbers of interviewees are undergoing training in how to handle questions. For instance, prosecutors, attorneys, and aides prepare witnesses and clients (including presidents of the United States and CEOs) to answer questions in court, congressional hearings, board meetings, and press conferences. Seek help if you are facing a difficult encounter with a trained and experienced interviewer.

Listen to Questions

While listening carefully to each question, follow these guidelines for responding effectively.

Listen and Think before Answering

Fully engage the brain before opening the mouth.

At scenes of accidents, crimes, or controversies, persons make statements they soon regret. African-Americans and Hispanic-Americans are often accused of crimes they did not commit because interviewees claimed to see a black or Hispanic man in the area where a crime took place. False statements and reports may lead to lawsuits, reprimands, or embarrassment. *Listen* carefully to what is being asked. Listen for words you do not know or may misinterpret. Two pieces of advice are worth taking: Keep it simple (particularly in broadcast interviews that operate under tight deadlines and think in terms of 2–3 minute segments and 7-second sound bites) and if you don't know an answer, don't try to make something up.

Be Patient

Do not assume you know a question before it is completed. React only after fully hearing and understanding each question. Do not interrupt the interviewer.

Focus Attention on the Question of the Moment

Do not continue to replay a previous answer that is history or anticipate a future question because you will fail to hear the current question.

Concentrate on the Interviewer and the Question

Watch for nonverbal signals that complement the verbal and reveal the interviewer's feelings, attitudes, and beliefs. Focus eyes and ears on the interviewer. This is particularly important in broadcast interviews that involve several persons, studios, cameras, monitors, and microphones and field interviews that involve spectators, noise, traffic, and distracting objects.

Do Not Dismiss a Question Too Quickly as Irrelevant

The interviewer may have a very good reason for asking a question, and it may be one in a series leading up to a highly important question. An interviewer may be using an inverted funnel sequence, and you will get an opportunity to respond at length later.

Answer Strategically

A good answer is concise, precise, carefully organized, clearly worded, logical, well supported, and to the point. There are many strategies for responding to questions.

> **Becoming hostile reduces you to the level of the interviewer.**

- Avoid defensiveness or hostility.
  - —Give answers, not sermons.
  - —Give reasons and explanations rather than excuses.
  - —Be polite and tactful in words and manner.
  - —Use tasteful, appropriate humor.
  - —Do not reply in kind to a hostile question.
- Share control of the interview.
  - —Insist on adequate time to answer questions.
  - —Do not allow the interviewer to "put words in your mouth."
  - —Challenge the content of questions that contain unsupported assertions or inaccurate data or quotations.
  - —If a question is multiple-choice, be sure the choices are fair and include all reasonable options.
  - —Ask the interviewer to rephrase or repeat long, complicated, or unclear questions.
  - —Answer a question with a question.
  - —Search reflective and mirror questions for accuracy and completeness.
- Explain what you are doing and why.
  - —Preface a lengthy answer by explaining why it must be so.
  - —Preface an answer by explaining why a question is tough or tricky.
  - —Provide a substantial explanation why you must refuse to answer a question or simply say "No comment."
  - —Rephrase a question: "If what you're asking is . . ." or "You seem to be implying that . . ."

- Take advantage of question pitfalls,

  —Reply to the portion of a double-barreled question you remember and can answer most effectively.

  —Answer a bipolar question with a simple yes or no, when it suits you.

  —Reply to the open or closed portion of an open-to-closed switch question that is to your advantage.

- Avoid common question traps.

  —If a question is leading, such as "Don't you agree that . . . ," do not be led to the suggested answer.

  —If a question is loaded, such as "Are you still cheating on your exams?," be aware that either a yes or a no will make you guilty.

  —If an apparent bipolar question offers two disagreeable choices, such as "Did you go into medicine for the prestige or for the money," answer with a third option.

  —Watch for the yes-no pitfall, such as "Do you want to die?" and answer or refuse to answer politely.

- Support your answers.

  —Use stories and examples to illustrate points.

  —Use analogies and metaphors to explain unknown or complicated things, procedures, and concepts.

  —Organize long answers like mini-speeches with an introduction, body, and conclusion.

- Open your answers positively rather than negatively. The authors of *Journalistic Interviews: Theories of the Interview* offer these examples of interviewee responses:[55]

Negative	**Positive**
You failed to notice	May I point out
You neglected to mention	We can also consider x, y, z
You overlooked the fact	One additional fact to consider
You missed the point	From another perspective

Summary

The informational interview is the most common type of interview because it is used daily by persons ranging from journalists, police officers, and health care professionals to students, teachers, and parents. Length and formality vary, but the purpose and method are the same: to get needed information as accurately and completely as possible in the shortest amount of time. The means are careful questioning, listening, observing, and probing.

Although preparation of an interview guide or schedule is important, the interviewer must remain flexible and adapt to each interviewee, situation, and response. This chapter has presented guidelines for structured informational interviews that call for thorough preparation and flexibility. The nature of each stage depends upon the situation and the relationship between the interviewer and interviewee.

Interviewees need not be passive participants in informational interviews. When given advance notice, interviewees should prepare thoroughly. They should share control with the interviewer and not submit meekly to whatever is asked or demanded. And they should know the principles and strategies of effective answers. Good listening is essential.

Key Terms and Concepts

The online learning center for this text features FLASHCARDS and CROSSWORD PUZZLES for studying based on these terms and concepts.

Broadcast interview	Hostile interviewees	Reticent interviewees
Confused interviewees	Icebreaker questions	Status difference
Dishonesty	Key informants	Strategic answers
Dissimilar interviewees	Metaphorical questions	Talkative interviewees
Emotional interviewees	Off the record	Videoconference
Evasive interviewees	Press conference	
False assumptions	Research	

A Probing Interview for Review and Analysis

The interviewer is a reporter for the *Courier-Times,* a Gannett newspaper published in a city of 150,000 and the home of a major state university. He is developing a feature story on cheating in college classrooms that will appear just before finals week in the spring semester. His interviewees will be state university students chosen at random in areas such as the food court in the Memorial Union, outdoor seating areas around campus, and apartment complexes adjacent to campus. The interviewee is having lunch at the food court and listening to music on her iPod.

As you review this informational interview, ask such questions as: How satisfactory is the opening, including involvement of the interviewee? How effective are the interviewer's primary questions? How effectively does the interviewer listen and probe into answers? How well does the interviewer avoid common question pitfalls? How well does the interviewer cover major topics on college cheating and elicit valuable and insightful information? What important information does the interviewer fail to discover? How satisfactory is the closing, including involvement of the interviewee? How effectively does the interviewee employ answer strategies? How effectively does the interviewee share control of the interview?

1. **Interviewer:** Hi. I'm Zack Irwin, a reporter for the *Courier-Times*.

2. **Interviewee:** Hi. I'm Zelda Zwier. What are you doing on campus?

3. **Interviewer:** Well, I'm in the early stages of preparing a feature story on cheating in college classrooms, and I'm talking to students about their views of cheating on

campus, its significance, and their personal experiences. Could I talk to you for 10–15 minutes while you eat lunch?

4. **Interviewee:** I suppose so, but I've not had a lot of experience with cheating.

5. **Interviewer:** Are you a junior or senior?

6. **Interviewee:** I'm a second semester junior in finance.

7. **Interviewer:** Good. Let's begin with the cheating problem.

8. **Interviewee:** Will I be identified by name or picture in your story?

9. **Interviewer:** No, I will not use names or pictures and will respect your privacy. (takes out a small recorder and places it on the table)

10. **Interviewee:** Wait! You're going to tape this conversation?

11. **Interviewer:** Yes, but only so I have a complete and accurate set of notes. Your identity will remain secret.

12. **Interviewee:** Okay, but I want that in writing.

13. **Interviewer:** No problem. We can take care of that when we finish. How significant is the problem of cheating on your campus?

14. **Interviewee:** I think it depends on the course and instructor.

15. **Interviewer:** What do you mean by that?

16. **Interviewee:** Well, if the professor makes it clear that cheating will not be tolerated and that the penalty will be severe, such as flunking the course, students will be reluctant to run the risk.

17. **Interviewer:** I see, and that takes care of the problem?

18. **Interviewee:** No, that's the start. The professor must make cheating as difficult as possible by creating different versions of exams and having them printed in different colors, patrolling the room, making sure there are no laptops or cell phones available. That sort of thing.

19. **Interviewer:** How widespread is cheating on your campus? Have you actually witnessed cheating in the classroom?

20. **Interviewee:** Yes, I have.

21. **Interviewer:** Did it involve electronic sources such as laptops or iPads?

22. **Interviewee:** No.

23. **Interviewer:** What about cell phones?

24. **Interviewee:** No.

25. **Interviewer:** How did a student cheat?

26. **Interviewee:** It involved more than one student.

27. **Interviewer:** Tell me about it.

28. **Interviewee:** Three students from the same Greek house sat together in the lecture hall and whispered answers to one another.

29. **Interviewer:** Did you or another student report this to the professor?

30. **Interviewee:** Not that I know of.

31. **Interviewer:** So this didn't pose a problem for you or others?

32. **Interviewee:** Oh yeah. Successful cheating can raise the grades for an exam and affect the curve for those of us not cheating.

33. **Interviewer:** Why didn't you report this cheating to the professor?

34. **Interviewee:** It ticked me off, but none of us want to get other students in trouble or be snitches.

35. **Interviewer:** I see. When was the last time you cheated in a class?

36. **Interviewee:** What makes you think I've cheated? When did you cheat in college?

37. **Interviewer:** I am not part of this study, so my background is unimportant. Besides, I went to college a long time ago.

38. **Interviewee:** Your background is important, and college hasn't changed that much. When you were in college, did you and others cheat?

39. **Interviewer:** I'm sure there was cheating. (laughing) I guess I have to say "No comment."

40. **Interviewee:** Then I guess my answer is also "No comment." The 5th amendment works for me.

41. **Interviewer:** I guess that's fair. How can colleges reduce if not eliminate the problem of cheating that has probably always been with us?

42. **Interviewee:** First, professors must make it as difficult as possible to cheat. Simple multiple-choice exams are open invitations to cheat.

43. **Interviewer:** You mentioned earlier that professors could rearrange questions and print exams on different color paper with no two students sitting side-by-side with the same exam. How does that work?

44. **Interviewee:** I think that's pretty effective, particularly if seats are assigned for exams to keep friends from sitting together.

45. **Interviewer:** You suggest that there are other means?

46. **Interviewee:** Yes, I think the penalty should be severe such as failing an entire course, not just one exam or project. The possibility of getting caught and paying a significant price are strong motivators.

47. **Interviewer:** What have I not asked that you think would be important for my feature article in the *Courier-Times*?

48. **Interviewee:** I believe any real solution must begin with an effort to change the attitude of college students today. The overriding concern is getting a degree, a piece of paper, to get a job. Learning something is secondary, and too many students see it as a big game in which anything goes to get that all-important diploma.

49. **Interviewer:** Okay. Thanks, Zelda, for talking to me candidly about cheating. My article should appear in about two weeks, the weekend before finals.

50. **Interviewee:** Don't forget that paper you agreed to sign that I would not be identified in any way.

51. **Interviewer:** Oh yes. Here's a form that I have prepared for such requests. Thanks again for your help and good luck on your finals.

Probing Role-Playing Cases

Iraq and Afghanistan Veterans Seeking Disability

The Department of Veterans Affairs recently discovered that a staggering 45 percent of military veterans returning from duty in the wars in Iraq and Afghanistan were seeking compensation for service-related injuries. In addition, they are claiming as many as 11 to 14 ailments compared to fewer than four on average for World War II and Korea. You are a broadcast journalist interested in developing a series of reports on invisible veterans of the wars in Iraq and Afghanistan and have made appointments with four physicians at a veteran's hospital to learn more about the nature and severity of these ailments, why the number is so high for these two most recent wars, the causes of these ailments, and ways these ailments can be reduced for future combat veterans.

A Career in the Commercial Space Industry

You entered a university studying aeronautical and astronautical engineering the year the space shuttles were retired and NASA shuttered many of its space launch facilities in Florida. During your sophomore year, the first commercial rocket sent a commercial vehicle to the international space station to take needed supplies and return with worn out and no longer needed equipment. In addition, all astronauts sent to and returned from the station now ride on Russian vehicles. You are going to interview two professors and two Ph.D. students in your major about future careers in the space program. The interviews will take place in the interviewees' offices at the university.

Political Campaign Directors

You are majoring in political science and have an interest in entering politics in the future, first at the local level. You want to discover what it is like running for political office at three levels: local (mayor or city council), regional (state or national representative), and state (governor, U.S. Senate). Specific concerns are funding, party support, getting nominated, conducting a campaign, working with the ever-present media, and the use of the Internet and social media. You have made arrangements through key informants to interview three persons who have managed local, regional, and state political campaigns.

Surviving Summer before Air Conditioning

Every year in July and August, you hear weather reports about how hot it was in the Midwest during the summers of 1936 and 1937. Most high temperature records were set in these two years before there was air conditioning. You've heard your grandparents born in these years talk about how many infants died shortly after birth and how the hospitals tried to cope with temperatures in the 100s. For an oral history project in a library science class, you have decided to interview four persons who experienced these conditions as teenagers or young adults to discover the problems they encountered, how they managed to work and sleep, and what they did to try to stay as cool as possible. The interviews will take place in a lounge area of a retirement facility.

Student Activities

1. Compare and contrast the sample attitude survey in Chapter 6 with the informational interview in this chapter. How are the openings similar and different? How are questions similar and different? What are the apparent question sequences? What schedules are used? How are the closings similar and different? What interviewing skills are required for the participants of each interview?

2. Interview a newspaper journalist and a broadcast journalist about their interviewing experiences and techniques. How does the nature of the medium affect interviewers and interviewees? How does the medium affect interview structure, questioning techniques, and note taking? What advice do they give about note taking and tape recording interviews? How do the end products differ? What constraints does each medium place on interviewers?

3. Record a televised press conference in which one person is answering questions from several interviewers. How is this situation similar to and different from one-on-one interviews? What stated or implied rules governed this interview? What skills are required of interviewers and interviewee? How did the interviewee recognize interviewers? What answering strategies did the interviewee use? What questioning strategies did interviewers use?

4. A growing number of interviewers are turning to the Internet to conduct probing interviews. Develop a moderately scheduled 20-minute interview on a topic that will require fairly lengthy answers and then conduct one face-to-face interview and one employing Skype. Identify the advantages and disadvantages of each with respect to relationship building, communication interactions, depth of answers, self-disclosure, probing questions, spontaneity, and ability or inability to observe and hear the interviewee's answers.

Notes

1. Bob Steele, "Interviewing: The Ignored Skill," http://www.poynter.org/column .asp?id=36&aid=37661, accessed September 25, 2006.

2. Sarah Stuteville, "13 Simple Journalist Techniques for Effective Interviews," http:// matadornetwork.com/bnt/13-simple-journalist-techniques-for-effective-interviews, accessed May 7, 2012.

3. Eric Nalder, *Newspaper Interviewing Techniques,* Regional Reporters Association meeting at the National Press Club, March 28, 1994, The C-SPAN Networks (West Lafayette, IN: Public Affairs Video Archives, 1994).

4. Steele.

5. Ken Metzler, "Tips for Interviewing," http://darkwing.uoregon.edu/~sponder/cj641/ interview.htm, accessed September 26, 2006.

6. Beverley J. Pitts, Tendayi S. Kumbula, Mark N. Popovich, and Debra L. Reed, *The Process of Media Writing* (Boston: Allyn and Bacon, 1997), p. 66.

7. Jaldeep Katwala, "20 Interviewing Tips for Journalists," http://www.mediahelpingmedia .org/training-resources/journalism-basics/475-20-interviewing-tips-for-journalists, accessed May 7, 2012.

8. Eric Steven Raymond and Rick Moen, "How to Ask Questions the Smart Way," http://www.catb.org/~esr/faqs/smart-questions.html, accessed September 26, 2006.

9. R. Thomas Berner, *The Process of Writing News* (Boston: Allyn and Bacon, 1992), p. 123.

10. Pitts, Kumbula, Popovich, and Reed, p. 64.

11. Raymond L. Gorden, *Interviewing: Strategy, Techniques, and Tactics* (Homewood, IL: Dorsey Press, 1980), p. 235.

12. Fred Fedler, John R. Bender, Lucinda Davenport, and Paul E. Kostyu, *Reporting for the Media* (Fort Worth, TX: Harcourt Brace, 1997), p. 227.

13. David Sparks, "30 Tips on How to Interview like a Journalist," http://www.sparkminute.com/2011/11/07/30-tips-on-how-to-interview-like-a-journalist, accessed May 11, 2012.

14. Eugene C. Webb and Jerry R. Salancik, "The Interview or the Only Wheel in Town," *Journalism Monographs* 2 (1966), p. 18.

15. Metzler.

16. Robert Ogles is a professor of mass communication at Purdue University.

17. Katwala.

18. Stuteville.

19. Nalder.

20. Carole Rich, *Writing and Reporting News: A Coaching Method* (Belmont, CA: Thomson/Wadsworth, 2005), p. 124; Berner, p. 127; The Missouri Group, *Telling the Story: Writing for Print Broadcast, and Online Media* (Boston: Bedford/St. Martin's, 2001), p. 51; Melvin Mencher, *Basic Media Writing* (Madison, WI: Brown & Benchmark, 1996), p. 231.

21. Henry Schulte and Michael P. Dufreshe, *Getting the Story* (New York: Macmillan, 1994), p. 24.

22. Metzler.

23. "Journalistic Interviews," http://www.uwgh.edu/clampitp/Interviewing/Interviewing%20lectures/Journalistic%20Interviews.ppt., accessed October 4, 2006.

24. Stephen Budiansky, "Truth Extraction," *The Atlantic Monthly,* June 2005, 32.

25. Tamar Weinberg, "Tips for Asking Questions During Journalistic Interviews," http://lifehacker.com/351399?tips-for-asking-questions-during-journalistic-interviews, accessed May 22, 2009.

26. Missouri Group, p. 58.

27. Originally cited in "The Point of View," a publication of the Alameda District Attorney's Office.

28. "Leading Questions," http://www.mediacollege.com/journalism/interviews/leading-questions.html, accessed October 4, 2006.

29. "Open-Ended Questions," http://www.mediacollege.com/journalism/interviews/open-endedquestions.html, accessed October 4, 2006.

30. William Zinsser, *On Writing Well* (New York: Harper Perennial, 1994), p. 70.

31. Missouri Group, p. 58. Tony Rogers, "Tips for Taking Good Notes," http://journalism.about.com/od/reporting/a/notetaking.htm?p=1, accessed May 21, 2012; Charlie

Bentson King, "The Importance of Note Taking in Interviews," http://www.trainingabc.com/The-Importance-of-Note-Taking-in-Interviewing-nid-30html, accessed May 21, 2012; Police Link, "Note Taking During an Interview," http://policelink.monster.com/training/articles/1915-note-taking-during-an-interview?print, accessed May 21, 2012.

32. "Oral History Project: Guidelines for Recording an Interview," *Alberta Online Encyclopedia,* http://www.youthsource.ab.ca/teacher_resources?oral_interview.html, accessed July 14, 2009; "How to Record Interviews," *Transcriptionlive,* http://www.transcriptionlive.com, accessed July 14, 2009.

33. Carole Rich, *Writing and Reporting News: A Coaching Method* (Belmont, CA: Wadsworth, 1997), p. 110; "A Practical Guide to Taping Phone Calls and In-Person Conversations in the 50 States and D.C.," The Reporters Committee for the Freedom of the Press, 2008, http://www.rcfp.org/taping/, accessed July 14, 2009; "Recording interviews: Legal issues," Knight Citizen News Network, http://www.kcnn.org/interviewing/resources_recording, accessed July 14, 2009.

34. See for example, "Chapter 21: Press & Media Conferences," The New Manual, http://www.thenewsmanual.net/Manual%201/volume1_21.html, accessed May 21, 2012.

35. Rogers.

36. "Interview Structure," http://www.mediacollege.com/video/interviews/structure.html, accessed October 4, 2006.

37. Dan McCurdy, "The Rules of Live Radio Broadcast Interviewing," http://danmccurdy.suite101.com/the-rules-of-live-radio-broadcast-interviewing-a226345, accessed May 23, 2012; Sparks; Rebekah Martin, "Broadcast Interview Techniques," http://www.ehow.com/way_5840219_broadcast-interview-techniques.html, accessed May 23, 2012; Teresa Botteron, "What Every Investigator Needs to Know to Avoid the Most Common Mistakes of the Recorded Interview," http://www.pimall.com/nais/nl/n.recordedinterview.html, accessed May 21, 2012.

38. "Framing Interview Shots," http://www.mediacollege.com/video/interviews/framing.html, accessed October 4, 2006; "Composing Interview Shots," http://www.mediacollege.com/video/interviews/composition.html, accessed October 4, 2006; "Studio Interview Settings," http://www.mediacollege.com/video/interviews/studio.html, accessed October 4, 2006.

39. Fedler, Bender, Davenport, and Kostyu, p. 224.

40. Bill Marimow, "Delicate Art of the Interview: Civility vs. Tenacity," http://www.npr.org/templates/story/story.php?storyId=6438613, accessed May 23, 2012.

41. "Video Interviewing: Tips for Interviews Using Video Cameras," http://www.bc.edu/offices/careers/skills/intrerview/video/, accessed September 30, 2006.

42. "Videoconference Interview Tips," Career Development and Experiential Learning, Memorial University, http://www.mun.ca/cdel/career_students/videoconference_interviewtips.php, accessed July 15, 2009.

43. Reporter and editor Wendell Cochran in Steele.

44. John R. Bittner and Denise A. Bittner, *Radio Journalism* (Englewood Cliffs, NJ: Prentice Hall, 1977), p. 53.

45. Travis Reed, "Did TV Interview Lead Woman to Kill Herself?" http://www.suntimes .com/news/nation/52533,CST-NWS-grace14.article, September 14, 2006.

46. Phillip H. Alt and Edwin Emery, *Reporting the News* (New York: Dodd, Mead, & Co., 1959), p. 125.

47. Stith, p. 2.

48. Joe Navarro and John R. Schafer, "Detecting Deception," *FBI Law Enforcement Bulletin,* July 2001, pp. 9–13, accessed on the Internet, July 20, 2009.

49. William T. G. Litant, "And, Were You Present When Your Picture Was Taken?" *Lawyer's Journal* (Massachusetts Bar Association), May 1996.

50. Steele.

51. Pat Stith, *Getting Good Stories: Interviewing with Finesse* (ProQuest Research Library, April 24, 2004), p. 2.

52. "Man Reads His Obituary in Paper," Lafayette, Indiana *Journal & Courier,* June 13, 1985, p. D4.

53. Diana Pisciotta, "How to Prepare for a Broadcast Interview," http://www.inc.com/ guides/2010/05/preparing-for-the-broadcast-interview.html, accessed May 21, 2012.

54. Pisciotta; "11 Tips for Broadcast Interviews," http://communitymediaworkshop.org/ npcommunicator/11-tips-for-broadcast-interviews, accessed May 21, 2012.

55. "EE's Perspective," http://www.uwgb.edu/clampitp/interviewing/interviewing %20Lectures/Journalistic%20Interviewsppt, accessed October 4, 2006.

Resources

Adams, Sally, Wynford Hicks, and Harriett Gilbert. *Interviewing for Journalists.* Florence, KY: Routledge, 2008.

Heritage, John. "Designing Questions and Setting Agendas in the News Interview," in *Studies in Language and Social Interaction,* Philip Glenn, Curtis LeBarob, and Jenny Mandelbaum, eds. Mahwah, NJ: Lawrence Erlbaum, 2002.

Metzler, Ken. "Tips for Interviewing," http://darkwing.uoregon.edu~sponder/j641/ Interview.htm.

Rich, Carole. *Writing and Reporting News: A Coaching Method.* Belmont, CA: Thomson/ Wadsworth, 2012.

Steele, Bob. "Interviewing: The Ignored Skill," http://www.poynter.org/column.asp? id=36&aid=37661.

Synge, Dan. *The Survival Guide to Journalism.* New York: McGraw-Hill, 2010.

"Videoconference Interview Tips." Newfoundland and Labrador, Canada: Memorial University of Newfoundland, 2009.

I f you feel inundated by survey requests from charities, political candidates, religious organizations, colleges, and companies, that's because you are. Research conducted by the Vovici Company in 2010 (through a survey, of course) revealed that American adults are asked to take part in surveys 7 billion times each year and that the 80 percent who claim to complete the surveys they start provide 2.6 billion responses.[1] Some of these surveys are conducted face-to-face at homes, malls, businesses, sporting events, and hospitals, but growing numbers are being conducted over the telephone and through the Internet. As the number of surveys has continued to escalate, so has the unwillingness to participate. Potential interviewees are concerned about confidentiality, privacy, telemarketers, survey accuracy, biases of survey organizations, and benefits to themselves and society. Authors of a recent study of "trends in surveys on surveys" conclude that "Overall, there has been a markedly negative shift in attitudes toward public opinion researchers and polls across several dimensions between the mid-1990s and the first decade of the 2000s."[2]

The objectives of this chapter are to provide you with guidelines for preparing, conducting, and evaluating results of survey interviews and to make your interviews productive and rewarding for both parties.

In Chapter 5, we discussed the *informational interview* in which **flexibility** and **adaptability** are essential characteristics and interviewers operate from interview guides or moderate schedules of questions that enable them to probe freely into answers. This chapter focuses on the *survey interview* in which **reliability** (assurance that the same types of information are collected in repeated interviews) and **replicability** (the duplication of interviews from respondent to respondent) are essential characteristics and interviewers operate from meticulously planned and highly structured interviews during which they may ask only *preplanned* probing questions.

> "Surveys reach out and touch everyone."

> Survey interviews are neither flexible nor adaptable.

Purpose and Research

> Survey interviews have multiple purposes.

Before you start thinking about questions or persons you might interview, determine precisely the purpose of your survey. The types of information you *need* to discover and *how* you will *use* this information determine whether you will conduct a **qualitative** or a **quantitative** survey.[3] You will use a qualitative approach if you want to explore ideas and feelings, dig deeply into issues, discover motivations, understand different perspectives, and understand behaviors. Your findings are presented in narrative form in which words are critical. You will use a quantitative approach if you want to determine frequencies of behavior, degrees of feelings, consensus of opinions or attitudes, causes and effects, preferences, averages, and make predictions or strategic decisions. Your findings are presented in quantitative form in which numbers are critical. Your needs and questions may be tempered by the optimum length of your interviews. They may be as brief as three to five minutes or as long as 15–20 minutes. Longer interviews cover more areas of interest (essential for qualitative surveys) and are more reliable, but they may be unnecessary or detrimental to quantitative surveys designed to determine a few attitudes or intentions.

> Longitudinal studies reveal trends and changes over time.

One additional factor—**time**—will shape your purpose. How soon must you complete your interviews to achieve your purpose? You may have to complete a survey almost overnight to determine reactions to an event such as a political debate or a court decision, and this limits your purpose to a few questions probably conducted over the telephone. Other topics or issues may require weeks or months and allow you to develop longer and more complex interviews that delve thoroughly rather than superficially into subject matter. Time also determines the type of survey you need to conduct. A **cross-sectional survey** takes a slice of what is felt, thought, or known during a narrow time span and is used when you need to determine how interviewees are reacting at present. A **longitudinal survey** determines trends in feeling, thought, or knowledge over time.

> Don't assume adequate knowledge of a topic.

As soon as you have a clearly defined purpose, investigate all aspects of the topic. Explore its past, present, and future as well as proposed and attempted solutions. Check resources such as organizational files and archives, correspondence and interviews with knowledgeable people, government documents, professional journals, books, previous surveys on this topic, the Internet, news magazines, and newspapers. Talk to people who have studied this topic or have been involved.

> Don't waste time learning what you already know.

Research reveals information already available in other sources that need not be gathered in your survey. Become an expert on the topic, particularly unique terminology and technical concepts. If you are going to deal with subject matter such as global warming, "right to stand your ground laws," or organic farming, you must determine the precise and understandable meaning of key terms so they are clear to interviewees and acceptable to those who may read or use your results to form opinions or take actions. Research will reveal past attitudes and opinions and speculations about current attitudes and opinions. A thorough knowledge of the topic provides insights into areas you need to explore, the complexities of the issue, and potential intentional and unintentional inaccuracies in answers during interviews.

ON THE WEB

Select a current international issue and do background research through the Internet. Use at least three different search engines, such as the United Nations (http://www.un.org), International Forum on Globalism (http://www.ifg.org/), global engineering (http://news.foodonline.com/pehanich/fpso11598.html). What types of information did you discover? What information is unavailable on the Internet? What does the search suggest for a survey on this issue: subtopics, areas of conflict, differing views of experts, public opinion, history of the issue, current developments?

Structuring the Interview

When you have determined a precise purpose and conducted necessary research, develop a highly structured interview.

Interview Guide and Schedule

An interview guide is essential for survey interviews because it dictates the topics and subtopics you will cover and primary and probing questions to be asked. Review carefully the suggestions for creating interview guides in Chapter 4.

Begin your **interview guide** by listing major areas. For example, if you are planning to survey Illinois educators on ways to reform the public schools in their state, major topics might include state-supported pre-schools, all-day kindergarten, parental involvement in the education process, elimination of state mandates and regulations, increased funding for technology in the classroom, year-round schools, aides to work one-on-one with students who are having difficulties, and separate classrooms for students with special needs. If you are conducting a **qualitative survey,** you may develop a highly scheduled interview that includes open-ended questions, planned probes, and the possibility of unplanned probes that depend upon interviewee responses. There is a degree of flexibility in questioning because you are more concerned about depth of information than with statistical compilation of data. The traditional interview guide (who, what, when, where, how, and why) may be adaptable to qualitative surveys, but surveys often require a more detailed guide and schedule that ensures complete coverage of a topic or issue and the manner of organizing, reporting, and interpreting answers.

> A detailed guide is easily transformed into a scheduled format.

If you are conducting a **quantitative survey,** you must elicit answers that are easy to record, tabulate, and analyze. The flexibility and adaptability of the qualitative survey may lead to difficulties in coding and tabulation of results, so you will rely on a highly scheduled, standardized format that ensures replicability of interviews and accurate compilation of findings.

> Standardization is essential for surveys.

The Opening

Although "each interview is unique, like a small work of art . . . with its own ebb and flow . . . , a mini-drama that involves real lives in real time,"[4] each respondent must go through as identical an interview as possible. Compose an opening that typically includes a greeting, name of the interviewer, the organization conducting the survey, subject matter of the interview, purpose, amount of time the survey will take, and assurance of confidentiality. Encourage interviewers to give this opening verbatim without reading it or sounding stilted. To make the opening sound more natural, you may allow skilled interviewers to create their own openings as long as each opening includes all of the elements you have stipulated. The following is a standardized opening for a survey and includes a qualifier question.

Good afternoon, I'm _____. The state Department of Natural Resources has hired my firm to conduct a survey of those who go boating on Michigan's lakes to determine how it can promote boating while maintaining the quality of the lakes and the areas surrounding them. The survey will take only ten minutes and your answers will be strictly confidential. (GO TO THE FIRST QUESTION.)

1. How frequently do you boat on lakes in Michigan? (*If the answer is less than 3 times a year, place an × by answer 1.1 and terminate the interview. If the answer is 3 or more times a year, go to Q.2.*)
   1.1 ____ less than 3 times a year
   1.2 ____ 3–5 times a year
   1.3 ____ 6–8 times a year
   1.4 ____ 9–11 times a year
   1.5 ____ 12 or more times a year

This opening identifies the interviewer and organization and states a general purpose and length of the interview. Notice that the interviewee is not asked to respond. The interviewer moves smoothly and quickly from orientation to the first question without giving the respondent an opportunity to refuse to take part. The first question determines the interviewee's qualifications. In this survey, respondents must boat on Michigan's lakes at least three times a year. The survey schedule provides instructions for the interviewer to follow and has precoded the question for ease of tabulating results when the survey is completed.

> **There are no icebreaker questions or small talk in surveys.**

The opening may not identify the group that is paying for it (a political candidate, a pharmaceutical company, special interest group, for instance) or the specific purpose (to determine which strategies to employ during a political, advertising, or lobbying campaign) because such information might influence how interviewees respond. When a newspaper such as the *New York Times* or the *Washington Post*, a cable or television network such as CBS or CNN, or a well-known polling group such as Harris or Gallup conducts a survey, the organization's name is used to enhance the prestige of the poll and the interviewer, to reduce suspicion that a candidate or corporation is behind the survey, and to motivate respondents to cooperate. Interviewers may have to show identification badges or letters that introduce them and establish their legitimacy as survey takers.

> **Simple incentives reduce rejections.**

Because of the increase of refusals to take part in surveys, particularly those on the Web, and the fact that the quality of survey results depends on response rates, creators of surveys have increasingly focused on incentives ranging from simple assurances to prepaid monetary offers as high as $40 per interview. Incentives tend to come during the opening minutes of the interview when the interviewer must motivate a contact to take part in the survey. Although some research indicates the obvious, that the higher the financial incentive the greater the likelihood of participation, even token incentives may improve response rates.[5] One study indicated that a simple prepaid, nonmonetary incentive (such as a ballpoint pen) made during the opening can increase response rates and result in greater completeness in answers during the early portion of survey interviews.[6] Non-monetary incentives include emphasizing how interviewees might benefit personally from the study, stressing the civic obligation to help others and to be active citizens, assuring privacy and confidentiality, focusing on respondent interest in the topic, establishing credibility of the organization conducting or sponsoring the survey, and stressing the brevity of the survey for those with little available time. Some survey researchers are concerned that emphasis on incentives may persuade some persons to take part to their detriment.[7]

The Closing

The closing is brief and expresses appreciation for the time and effort expended to aid the survey. For example:

> That's all the questions I have. Thank you very much for your help.

If the survey organizer wants a respondent's telephone number to verify that a valid interview took place, the closing might be:

> That's all the questions I have. May I have your telephone number so my supervisor can check to see if this interview was conducted in the prescribed manner? (gets the number) Thank you very much for your help.

If you can provide respondents with results of a survey, a common practice in research interviews, the closing might be:

> That's all the questions I have. Thank you for your help, and if you'll give me your address, I'll be sure that you receive a copy of the results of this study. (gets the address) Thanks again for your help.

Interviewees prefer anonymity.

Some interviewees are reluctant to give their telephone numbers or e-mail addresses to strangers. Be prepared to back off from either request if the interviewee appears anxious, suspicious, or very reluctant. Do not sacrifice the rapport and goodwill you created during the interview. When one of the authors was conducting polls for a political party, he discovered that many respondents did not want to give their telephone numbers for fear they would be deluged with calls from candidates during the campaign. With permission from the party, he stopped asking for telephone numbers, and closings went smoother.

Respondents may be curious about a survey or interested in the topic and want to discuss it. This can be a good relationship builder and motivator for taking part in future surveys, but do so only if time permits, the interviewee will have no opportunity to talk to future interviewees, and the survey organization has no objections.

Survey Questions

Interviewers cannot make on-the-spot adjustments.

Create each question carefully because you cannot rephrase, explain, or expand on questions during interviews without risking your ability to replicate interviews, an essential element of surveys. In quantitative surveys, all question phrasing and strategic decisions are made in the planning stage; none on the spot. In qualitative surveys, all primary questions and most probing questions are planned ahead of time.

Every word in every question may influence results.

Phrasing Questions

All interviewees must hear the same questions asked in the same phrasing and manner. A slight change in wording, vocal emphasis on a word, or facial expression can generate different answers. For example, in a religious survey, interviewers asked one set of respondents, "Is it okay to smoke while praying?" Over 90 percent responded "No." When they asked another set of respondents, "Is it okay to pray while smoking?" over 90 percent replied "Yes." Although these questions appear to be the same, respondents interpreted them differently. The first sounded sacrilegious, lighting up while praying. The second sounded like a good idea, maybe even necessary. Recall the discussion of *why questions* in Chapter 3 that illustrated how emphasis may change the focus and meaning of simple questions. This is critical in surveys in which you are striving for replicability.

A single word might alter significantly how people respond to a question, thereby altering the results of a survey. Researchers asked the following question to one group of respondents:

"Do you think the United States should allow public speeches against democracy?"

The results were "should allow" 21 percent and "should not allow" 62 percent. Then these researchers substituted a single word and asked respondents:

"Do you think the United States should forbid public speeches against democracy?"

The results were "should not forbid" 39 percent and "should forbid" 46 percent.[8] Respondents viewed the word "forbid" as a stronger and more dangerous action than "not allow"—perhaps un-American—even though the effect of the governmental policy would be the same.

Researchers David Yeager and Jon Krosnick recently compared attempts to measure attitudes and beliefs in survey interviews that employed ambiguous questions such as "Some people think that" and "Other people think that" with interviews that asked direct questions of interviewees. They discovered that validity was higher when using direct questions that presented response options and that ambiguously phrased questions took longer to ask and answer.[9] Make each question clear, relevant, appropriate to the respondent's level of knowledge, neither too complex nor too simple, neutral, and socially and psychologically accessible. This is not a simple task when respondents may be of both genders and differ widely in culture, age, income level, education, intelligence, occupation, geographical area, and experiences. The increasing diversity of the American population may result in your target population representing widely diverse continents, cultures, and nations. Be careful of using formal names or acronyms for persons or organizations with which your interviewees may not be familiar. Persons of different cultures may be fluent in English but be confounded with abbreviations, colloquialisms, aphorisms, jargon, euphemisms, and slang. Avoid ambiguous words and phrases such as a lot, often, much, large school, or recently discovered that have many and vague meanings.

> Adapt phrasing to all members of a target population.

> Be wary of negatively phrased questions.

Survey researchers warn against phrasing questions negatively because they can be misleading and confusing. For instance, Jack Edwards and Marie Thomas note that "a negative answer to a negatively worded statement may not be equivalent to the positive answer to a positively worded statement."[10] Even the explanation sounds confusing. They give this example: "Disagreeing with the statement 'My work is not meaningful' does not necessarily mean that the same individual would have agreed with the statement 'My work is meaningful.'" Forcing a respondent to disagree with a negative statement can be confusing. Think of the difficulties you've had with negatively phrased multiple-choice questions in examinations. Babbie warns that many respondents will fail to hear the word "not" in a question during an interview so those in favor of a statement such as "The U.S. should not establish diplomatic relations with Iran" might disagree with the statement. And those who actually disagree may answer the same way.[11] Edwards and Thomas warn, "you may never know which is which."

Sample Question Development

Questions evolve as you develop a schedule, particularly for a quantitative survey. Here is how a question concerning texting while driving might evolve during preparation.

> How do you feel about the state-imposed law against texting while driving?

Keep recording of answers in mind when phrasing questions.

Take a closer look at this seemingly neutral question. "State-imposed" may bias results because it may sound tyrannical and unconstitutional to some respondents. The openness of the question and the ambiguity of the word "feel" may result in a wide range of answers, some positive ("It makes me feel safer," "I'm generally for it," and "Whatever it takes to reduce car crashes") and some negative ("It's another effort of the nanny state to violate my constitutional rights," "Angry," and "Fearful of what's next"). Others may give lengthy answers for and against the law that will create recording and coding nightmares.

Try a second version that closes up the question and eliminates "*state-imposed.*"

> Are you for, against, or have no feelings about the state's law against texting while driving?
>
> _____ for
> _____ against
> _____ no feelings

This version eliminates the potential bias of the first (and resolves recording problems), but it may be too closed for qualitative and quantitative purposes. Interviewees may not be simply for or against the law or believe there should be exceptions or qualifications, perhaps allowing emergency texting. Intensity of feelings is not accounted for. The "No feelings" answer option may generate a great many undecided and don't know answers and either necessitate a lot of probing or reduce the impact of the question. Coding answers may be a problem.

Develop a third version such as the following:

> **2.** Do you strongly agree, agree, disagree, or strongly disagree with the state law against texting while driving?
> 2.1 ____ strongly agree
> 2.2 ____ agree
> 2.3 ____ disagree
> 2.4 ____ strongly disagree
> 2.5 ____ undecided (*Do not provide unless requested.*)
> 2.6 ____ Why? _____
> (Ask only of respondents choosing strongly agree or strongly disagree.)

This third option assesses intensity of feelings, is easy to record and code, leaves undecided as an unstated option, provides instructions for interviewers, and includes a built-in secondary *"Why"* question to discover reasons for strong approval or strong disapproval. The authors have discovered that those with moderate responses tend not to have ready explanations for agreeing or disagreeing, approving or disapproving, liking or disliking. They just have that general feeling.

> **Build in secondary questions for reasons, knowledge, level, and qualifiers.**

Work with each question until it satisfies phrasing criteria and is designed to obtain the information needed. Careful phrasing avoids confusion and inaccurate results. Later we will address the pretesting of surveys to detect potential problems with questions.

Probing Questions

Probing questions are less frequent and usually planned in survey interviews. For instance, if a respondent gives an unclear answer, you might ask, "What do you mean by that?" "How do you mean that?" or "What I hear you saying is . . . ; is this what you meant to say?" If a respondent provides a very brief answer or appears reluctant to elaborate, use a silent probe, a nudging probe such as "Uh-huh," or an informational probe such as, "Tell me more about. . . ." If you are unsure a respondent has told you everything of relevance to a question, use a clearinghouse probe such as, "Anything else?" or "Is there anything else you would like to add?" Remember to record probing questions and answers carefully, clearly, and accurately for later tabulation and analysis.

Your goal is to perform nearly identical survey interviews over and over. On-the-spot probing may result in interviewer bias if you or other interviewers phrase questions verbally or nonverbally in ways that suggest the answers you prefer or lead different respondents to provide different answers. If some interviewers ask probing questions and others do not, the amount and type of information attained will differ from one interview to the next, and result in unreliable data or data that is impossible to tabulate and analyze with a degree of confidence.

Question Strategies

There are five question strategies that enable interviewers to assess knowledge level, honesty, and consistency; reduce undecided answers; prevent order bias; and incorporate probing questions.

Filter Strategy

The **filter strategy** enables you to determine interviewee knowledge of a topic. For example:

Interviewer: Are you familiar with the water company's proposed rate increase for next year?

Interviewee: Yes I am.

Interviewer: What is the water company proposing?

If an interviewee says no, you go to the next question. If the interviewee says yes, you ask the interviewee to reveal the extent and accuracy of knowledge. This follow-up question may discover that the respondent is confused or is misinformed. Many interviewees will say yes to bipolar questions, even when they have no idea what the interviewer is talking about, to avoid appearing uninformed.

> Don't take "yes" as the final answer.

Repeat Strategy

The **repeat strategy** enables you to determine if an interviewee is consistent in responses on a topic, particularly a controversial one. You may ask the same question several minutes apart and compare answers for consistency. A variation of this strategy is to disguise the question by rephrasing it.

6. Do you supervise your children's use of computers at home?
6.1 ____ yes
6.2 ____ no

14. Do your children have free access to computers at home?
14.1 ____ yes
14.2 ____ no

Another example of a repeat strategy is to go from a moderately closed to a highly closed question, such as:

11. How often during a week do you drink alcoholic beverages?
_____

> Repeat questions must be essentially the same to determine consistency in answers.

20. I am going to read a list of how frequently you drink alcoholic beverages each week. Stop me when I read the frequency that best describes your drinking.
20.1 ____ less than once a week
20.2 ____ 1–2 times a week
20.3 ____ 3–4 times a week
20.4 ____ 5-6 times a week
20.5 ____ 7 or more times a week

Do not make the repetition too obvious or close to the initial question and be sure the rewording does not change the intent of the initial question.

Leaning Question Strategy

Respondents may be reluctant to take stands or make decisions, often because they do not want to reveal their feelings or intentions. Employ a *leaning* question, not to be confused with a *leading* question, to reduce the number of "undecided" and "don't know" answers. The following is a typical **leaning question strategy.**

9a. Do you plan to vote for or against the school referendum in the fall election?
(If undecided, ask Q. 9b.)
____ for
____ against

9b. Which way are you leaning today?

_____ for

_____ against

_____ undecided

The "undecided" option remains in question 9b because an interviewee may be truly undecided at the moment. A variation of the leaning question is, "Well, if you had to vote today, how would you vote?" Clearly stated "undecided" and "don't know" options may invite large percentages of these answers, particularly when a question asks for criticism of people, organizations, or products. However, some sources recommend that you always include "don't know" or "not applicable" answer options in all questions, unless all interviewees will have a definite answer, to reduce interviewee frustration and provide the most honest and accurate answers.[12]

Shuffle Strategy

The order of answer options in questions may affect interviewee responses. Research indicates that last choices in questions tend to get negative or superficial evaluations because interviewees get tired or bored but that interviewees also tend to select an option because it is the first mentioned or the last heard. The **shuffle strategy** varies the order of answer options from one interview to the next to prevent **order bias.** The method of rotation is carefully explained when training interviewers. Notice the built-in instructions to interviewers in the following example:

Now, I'm going to read you a list of the five most popular beers by sales volume in the United States. I want you to tell me if you have a highly favorable, favorable, neutral, unfavorable, or highly unfavorable attitude toward each. (_Rotate the order of the beers from interview to interview. Encircle answers received._)

	Highly Favorable	Favorable	Neutral	Unfavorable	Highly Unfavorable
Miller Light	5	4	3	2	1
Budweiser	5	4	3	2	1
Coors Light	5	4	3	2	1
Bud Light	5	4	3	2	1
Corona Extra	5	4	3	2	1

Potential order bias has resulted in strange events in political, persuasive, and advertising surveys. A political candidate in Indiana changed his name legally so it would begin with A. This placed him at the top of the ballot on election day, the belief being that voters select the top names in lists of candidates. He lost, but his and similar actions have led states to shuffle names on ballots.

Chain or Contingency Strategy

Highly standardized and highly scheduled formats allow for preplanned questions that enable you to probe into answers. This **chain or contingency strategy** is illustrated in the following series from a market survey. Notice the built-in instructions and precoding for ease of recording answers and tabulating data.

1a. During the past month, have you received any free samples of breakfast cereal?
(PLACE AN X BY THE ANSWER RECEIVED.)

Yes _____ 1—ASK Q. 1b.
No _____ 2—ASK Q. 2a.

1b. Which breakfast cereal did you receive?

Cheerios _____ 1
Frosted Flakes _____ 2
Special K _____ 3
Great Grains _____ 4
Shredded Wheat _____ 5

1c. (ASK ONLY IF GREAT GRAINS IS NOT MENTIONED IN Q. 1b; OTHERWISE SKIP TO Q. 1d.)

Did you receive a free sample of Great Grains?

Yes _____ 1—ASK Q. 1d.
No _____ 2—SKIP to Q. 2a.

1d. Did you use the free sample of Great Grains?

Yes _____ 1—SKIP to Q. 2a.
No _____ 2—ASK Q. 1e.

1e. Why didn't you use the free sample of Great Grains?

_____ _____ _____
_____ _____ _____

The chain or contingency strategy enables you to probe into answers while maintaining control of the process and ensuring that each interview is as identical as possible.

Question Scales

A variety of scale questions allow you to delve more deeply into topics and feelings than bipolar questions and to record and tabulate data more easily.

Interval Scales

Interval scales provide distances between measures. For example, **evaluative interval scales** (often called **Likert scales**) ask respondents to make judgments about persons, places, things, or ideas. The scale may range from five to nine answer options (five is most common) with opposite poles such as "strongly like . . . strongly dislike," "strongly agree . . . strongly disagree," or "very important . . . not important at all." Here is an evaluative interval scale:

> Do you strongly agree, agree, have no opinion, disagree, or strongly disagree with the university's plan to develop a three-semester school year starting in 2016?
>
> 5   Strongly agree   _____
> 4   Agree   _____
> 3   Neutral   _____
> 2   Disagree   _____
> 1   Strongly disagree _____

Provide aids for interviewee recall of answer options.

You may provide respondents with cards (color-coded to tell them apart) for complex questions or ones with many choices or options. A card eliminates the faulty-recall problem that respondents experience. They can study the answers or objects they are evaluating, rating, or ranking without trying to remember all of the options given orally. Here is an example of card use:

> Please use the phrases on this card to tell me how the recent television ads for the new water park at the Dunes National Sea Shore has affected your interest in visiting the park.
>
> 5   Increases my interest a lot   _____
> 4   Increases my interest a little _____
> 3   Will not affect my interest   _____
> 2   Decreases my interest a little _____
> 1   Decreases my interest a lot   _____

Frequency scales deal with number of times.

Frequency interval scales ask respondents to select a number that most accurately reflects how often they do something or use something. For example:

> How frequently do you eat pork?
>
> More than once a week _____
> Once each week   _____
> Every other week   _____
> Once or twice a month _____
> Less than once a month _____
> Rarely   _____

Numerical scales deal with ranges.

Numerical interval scales ask respondents to select a range or level that accurately reflects their age, income, educational level, or rank in an organization. For example:

> I am going to read several age groupings. Please stop me when I read the one that applies to you.
>
> 18–24   _____
> 25–34   _____
> 35–49   _____

50–64 _____
65 and over _____

Nominal Scales

Nominal scales provide mutually exclusive variables and ask respondents to name the most appropriate variable. These are self-reports and do *not* ask respondents to rate or rank choices or to pick a choice along an evaluative, numerical, or frequency continuum. Choices may be in any order. For example, you might ask:

Do you consider yourself to be a:

Democrat _____
Republican _____
Libertarian _____
Independent _____
Other _____

When you last ate dinner in a restaurant, did your entree consist of:

Beef _____
Pork _____
Lamb _____
Poultry _____
Fish _____
Other _____ (PLEASE WRITE NAME.)

In nominal questions, the options are mutually exclusive and include most likely options from which to choose. "Other" is the final option because the respondent must be able to choose one of the named options or provide an option.

Ordinal Scales

Ordinal questions ask respondents to rate or rank the options in their *implied* or *stated* relationship to one another. They do not name the most applicable option as in interval and nominal scales.

The following is a **rating ordinal scale:**

As you have traveled around the country during the past five years, I'm sure that you have stayed in a variety of hotels and motels. Please rate each of the following *applicable* hotels and motels as excellent, above average, average, below average, or poor.

Holiday Inn Express	Ex.	Abv. Av.	Av.	Bel. Av.	Poor	N/A
Hilton Garden Inn	Ex.	Abv. Av.	Av.	Bel. Av.	Poor	N/A
Hampton Inn	Ex.	Abv. Av.	Av.	Bel. Av.	Poor	N/A
Drury Inn	Ex.	Abv. Av.	Av.	Bel. Av.	Poor	N/A
Comfort Inn	Ex.	Abv. Av.	Av.	Bel. Av.	Poor	N/A
Courtyard	Ex.	Abv. Av.	Av.	Bel. Av.	Poor	N/A

Note that this rating scale generates six responses, including not applicable for an unused hotel or motel. The following is a **ranking ordinal scale:**

> On this card are the names of 5 news programs. Rank order them in terms of accuracy and dependability with 1 being highest and 5 being lowest.

Rank

ABC WorldNews   ____

CBS Evening News   ____

CNN Newsroom   ____

Fox Report   ____

NBC Nightly News   ____

The following ordinal question asks respondents to select from among options and rank them in order.

> On this card are several reasons cited frequently for granting school vouchers to poor grade school and high school students. Pick the three you think are most important and rank them in order of importance to you.

____ Fairness   ____ Reduction of union power

____ Competition   ____ Higher quality education

____ Cost   ____ Reduced government control

____ Parental involvement

Bogardus Social Distance Scale

The **Bogardus Social Distance Scale** determines how people feel about social relationships and distances from them. You want to know if a person's attitude or feeling changes as the issue comes closer to home. This scale usually moves progressively from remote to close relationships and distances to detect changes as proximity narrows. For example, you might use the following Bogardus Social Distance Scale to determine how interviewees feel about expanded oil drilling.

| **Bogardus scales measure effect of relational distances.** |

1. Do you favor expanded oil drilling in the   _____ Yes   _____ No
   United States?
2. Do you favor expanded oil drilling in the   _____ Yes   _____ No
   Midwest?
3. Do you favor expanded oil drilling in your state? _____ Yes   _____ No
4. Do you favor expanded oil drilling in your   _____ Yes   _____ No
   county?
5. Do you favor expanded oil drilling in this   _____ Yes   _____ No
   township?

In many questions, respondents are safely removed from the attitude or feeling they are expressing about a product, issue, action, or person. The Bogardus Social Distance Scale brings an issue ever closer to home so it is no longer something impersonal or one that affects others "over there."

Minimize guessing in surveys.

Question scales are designed to obtain a range of results and Level 2 and 3 disclosures, but respondents may try to "out psyche" survey takers. Students do this when taking standardized tests. For instance, respondents may try to pick "normal" answers in nominal and ordinal scales and safe, moderate, or middle options in interval scales. Rather than admit they do not know the correct answer, even when there is no correct answer, respondents may pick the option that stands out, such as the second in a list that includes 10 percent, 15 percent, 20 percent, 30 percent, and 40 percent. Respondents who first agree that a certain activity would make most people uneasy are less likely then to admit ever engaging in that activity and may attempt to change the subject.[13]

Anticipate confusion in scale questions.

Phrase scale questions carefully to avoid game playing, guessing, and confusion. Listen and observe reactions during pretesting interviews to detect patterns of responses, levels of interviewee comprehension, and hesitancy in responding. Long scales, complicated rating or ranking procedures, and lengthy explanations may confuse respondents, perhaps without either party realizing it at the time.

Question Sequences

Question sequences complement question strategies.

Review the question sequences discussed in Chapter 4. The tunnel sequence is useful when no strategic lineup of questions is needed. Gallup's quintamensional design sequence, or a variation of it, is appropriate when exploring intensity of attitudes and opinions. Funnel, inverted funnel, hourglass, and diamond sequences include open-ended questions, so answers may be difficult to record, code, and tabulate. They are appropriate for qualitative surveys because the wealth of information interviewers obtain from open questions is worth the problems involved. A study of the effects of question order suggests that general questions should come first followed by more specific questions. This is a funnel sequence.[14]

Selecting Interviewees

Interviewees are the sources of your data. The best schedule of questions is of little help if you talk to the wrong people at the wrong time or in the wrong place.

Defining the Population

The first step in selecting interviewees is to define the **population** you wish to study. The population may be small and similar such as members of a sales staff or large and diverse such as all employees of an auto plant. You may select a subset of a large population such as all employees over age 50 of a department store. The identified population should include all persons who are able and qualified to respond to your questions and about whom you want to draw conclusions.

If a target population is small (members of a fitness club), you may interview all of them. Most surveys, however, deal with populations that far exceed time, financial, and personal limitations—the 35,000 undergraduate students at a university or residents over the age of 18 in a city of 250,000. Dozens of interviewers could not reach, let alone interview, all of these people, so you interview a **sample** of them and extend findings to all of them. A common pitfall is not to spend the time necessary to ensure that the population from which the sample is drawn is complete and well defined.[15]

Steve Mason/Getty Images

■ *The first step in selecting interviewees is to define the population or target group you wish to study.*

Sampling Principles

The fundamental principle is that a sample must accurately represent the population or target group under study. Old-time watermelon sellers practiced this principle when they carefully cut out a triangular plug from a watermelon. This plug represented the entire watermelon.

Each potential respondent from a defined population must have an equal chance of being interviewed. You determine the probability that each person might be selected by deciding upon an acceptable **margin of error.** The precision of a survey is the "degree of similarity between sample results and the results from a 100 percent count obtained in an identical manner."[16] Most surveys attain a 95 percent **level of confidence,** the mathematical probability that 95 out of 100 interviewees would give results within 5 percentage points (margin of error) either way of the figures you would have obtained if you had interviewed the entire targeted population. Survey results reported in the media routinely state that a survey had a margin of error of 4 percent. This means that if 42 percent of respondents approve of the way Congress is doing its job, the real figure might be as low as 38 percent or as high as 46 percent.

A tolerable margin of error depends on the use of survey results. If you want to predict the outcome of an election or the effects of a new medical treatment, you must strive for a small margin of error, 3 percent or less. If you are conducting a survey to determine how employees feel about a new recreation facility, a higher margin of error is acceptable, 4 or 5 percent.

> A sample is a miniature version of the whole.

Determine **sample size** by the size of the population and the acceptable margin of error. Some survey organizations produce accurate national surveys with a margin of error in the 3 percent range from a sample of 1,500. Standard formulas reveal that as a population increases in size, the percentage of the population necessary for a sample declines rapidly. In other words, you must interview a larger percentage of 5,000 people than of 50,000 people to attain equally accurate results. Formulas also reveal that you must increase greatly the size of a sample to reduce the margin of error from 5 percent to 4 percent to 3 percent. The small reduction in the margin of error may not be worth the added cost of conducting significantly more interviews. Philip Meyer offers the following table that shows the sample sizes of various populations necessary for a 5 percent margin of error and a 95 percent level of confidence.[17]

> Margin of error determines the worth of a survey.

> A sample is the actual number of persons interviewed.

Population Size	Sample Size
Infinity	384
500,000	384
100,000	383
50,000	381
10,000	370
5,000	357
3,000	341
2,000	322
1,000	278

Creative Research Systems offers a sample size calculator as a public service.[18] You may employ its calculator once you know the confidence interval (margin of error of 3, 4, or 5 points), the confidence level (percentage of sureness you have in results such as 95 percent), and your target population size.

Sampling Techniques

Size of sample is important, but how you select the sample is of utmost importance to the validity of a survey. As W. Charles Redding warned years ago, "a bad survey is worse than no survey."[19] There are two general types of sampling, **probability** and **non-probability.**[20] In probability sampling, you know that each member of your population has a certain chance of being interviewed. In non-probability sampling, you do not know the chance that each member of your population will be interviewed. There are five common methods of probability sampling, the most accurate method of sampling.

Random Sampling

> **Random sampling is like "drawing names from a hat."**

Random sampling is the simplest method of selecting a representative sampling. For example, if you have a complete roster of all persons in a population, you place all names in a container, mix them thoroughly, and draw out one name at a time until you have a sample.

Table of Random Numbers

> **In skip interval you select every *n*th name from a list.**

A more complicated random sampling method is to assign a number to each potential respondent and create or purchase a **table of random numbers.** With eyes closed, place a finger on a number and read a combination up, down, across to left or right, or diagonally. Select this number as part of the sample or decide to read the last digit of the number touched (46) and the first digit of the numeral to the right (29) and thus contact respondent number 62. Repeat this process until you have the sample you need.

Skip Interval or Random Digit

In a **skip interval** or **random digit sampling,** you may choose every 10th number in a telephone book, every fifth name in a roster of clients, or every other person who walks into a supermarket. The Random Digital Dialing system now in wide use for conducting surveys "randomly generates telephone numbers in target area-code and prefix areas," "gives every telephone number in the area an equal chance of being called," and ensures anonymity because no interviewee names are used.[21] This common sampling technique may have some built-in flaws. For instance, a growing percentage of the population has unlisted phone numbers or relies on cell phones. On the other hand, a growing number of households have more than one telephone number, and this increases the probability that a particular household may be contacted more than once. A voter, customer, or membership roster might be outdated. Time of day, day of the week, and location may determine the types of persons available for interviews.

Stratified Random Sample

A stratified sample most closely represents the whole.

Random sampling procedures may not provide adequate representation of subgroups within a population. If a population has clearly definable groups (males and females; ages; education levels; income levels; and diverse cultural groups), employ a **stratified random sampling method.** This method allows you to include a minimum number of respondents from each group, typically the percentage of the group in the target population. For instance, if a targeted population consists of 30 percent first-year students, 25 percent sophomores, 20 percent juniors, 20 percent seniors, and 5 percent graduate students, your sample would represent these percentages.

Sample Point

A sample point is usually a geographical area.

A sample point represents a geographical area (a square block or mile, for instance) that contains specific types of persons (grain farmers or retired persons, for instance). Instructions may tell interviewers to skip corner houses (corner houses are often more expensive) and then try every other house on the outside of the four-block area until they have obtained two interviews with males and two with females. The U.S. Department of Agriculture uses aerial photographs of farm areas and crops to determine which farmers to interview to determine the amounts of various crops planted and possible yields of these crops each year. The **sample point** or **block sample** gives the survey designer control over selection of interviewees without resorting to lists of names, random digits, or telephone numbers.

There are two common methods of non-probability sampling, the least accurate forms of sampling. Survey interviewers employ them because they are convenient and inexpensive.

Self-Selection

Self-selection is the least representative of sampling methods.

The most inaccurate sampling method is **self-selection.** You see this voluntary method used nearly every day in radio and television talk shows, newscasts, and on the Internet. Who is most likely to call C-SPAN, Rush Limbaugh, or a television station? You guessed it—those who are very angry or most opposed to/most in favor of an action. Moderates rarely call or write. It is easy to predict how self-reporting surveys on gun control, health care reform, and labor unions will turn out.

Convenience

Convenience sampling is popular because respondents are numerous and easy to reach. Examples are interviewers stopping students as they exit a classroom building, shoppers as they walk through a shopping mall, or people as they walk down the street. The only criterion for selection is convenience for the interviewer. Randomness and representation of diverse elements of a target population built into probability forms of sampling are not considered.[22]

Selecting and Training Interviewers

Creating a survey instrument and developing a careful sample of interviewees are critical, but so is selecting interviewers and training them to conduct the interviews properly.

Number Needed

You can rarely do it all by yourself.

If you plan to interview a small number of persons and the interviews will be brief, one interviewer may be sufficient. Most often you will need several interviewers, particularly when interviews will be lengthy, the sample is large, time allotted for completing the survey is short, and interviewees are scattered over a large geographical area. Large and difficult interviewing assignments result in serious interviewer fatigue and decline in motivation;[23] both will reduce the quality of interviews and the data received.

Qualifications

Interviewers must follow the rules.

A highly scheduled, standardized interview does not require the interviewer to be an expert on the topic or skilled in phrasing questions and probing into answers. It does require a person who can learn and follow guidelines, read the questions verbatim and effectively, and record answers quickly and accurately. If you are using a highly scheduled interview format that requires skillful probing into answers, interviewers must have the ability to think on their feet, adapt to different interviewees, handle unanticipated interviewee objections and concerns, and react effectively and calmly to strange answers. In this type of interview, professionally trained interviewers are more efficient and produce more accurate results. A recent study in *Public Opinion Quarterly* discovered that "experienced interviewers obtain higher rates of acquiescent reports than do inexperienced interviewers, even after accounting for potential differences in interviewer and respondent characteristics. These differences across interviewers are not mediated by differential pace of the interview, as measured in interview length, implying that there may be differences in interview behaviors for experienced and inexperienced interviewers."[24]

Personal Characteristics

Interviewer credibility is critical in surveys.

Interviewers who are older, have a nonthreatening demeanor, and have an optimistic outlook get better response rates and cooperation, regardless of their experiences. Age generates credibility and self-confidence, and optimism motivates interviewees to cooperate.[25] One study discovered that personality and attitude of the interviewer are the most important elements in shaping interviewee attitudes toward surveys.[26]

Interviewee Skepticism

Nearly one-third of respondents believe that answering survey questions will neither benefit them nor influence decisions, that there are too many surveys, that surveys are too long, and that interviewers ask too many personal questions. Some 36 percent of

Interviewees are increasingly wary of surveys.

respondents in one study said they had been asked to take part in "false surveys," sales or political campaign interviews disguised as informational surveys. The authors of a report on how the Gallup Organization conducts public opinion polls note that "The public's questions indicate a healthy dose of skepticism about polling. Their questions, however, are usually accompanied by a strong and sincere desire to find out what's going on under Gallup's hood."[27] Clearly, survey interviewers must be aware of relational dimensions such as warmth, involvement, dominance, and trust and make every effort to establish a positive relationship with each respondent by appearing to be friendly, relaxed, and trustworthy.

Similarity of Interviewer and Interviewee

Similarity, but not a mirror image, may be important.

Similarity is an important relational dimension in survey interviews. You should dress similar to interviewees because if interviewers *look like me,* I am more likely to cooperate and answer appropriately. An in-group relationship with the interviewee (black to black, senior citizen to senior citizen, Hispanic-American to Hispanic-American) may avoid cultural and communication barriers and enhance trust because the interviewer is perceived to be safe, capable of understanding, and sympathetic. It may be essential that interviewers can speak to interviewees in their own language, including dialects or regional differences.[28]

Training Interviewers

Conduct training sessions with carefully written instructions for all interviewers, regardless of experience. Training results in greater use of appropriate probing questions, feedback, and giving instructions.

Poor execution can undo thorough preparation.

Discuss common interviewee criticisms of surveys and stress the importance of following the question schedule exactly as printed. Explain complex questions and recording methods. Be certain interviewers understand the sampling techniques employed. Emphasize the need to replicate interviews to enhance reliability and attain an acceptable margin of error and level of confidence. Describe the entire process and purpose. Discuss the nature and danger of interviewer bias. You may need to assist interviewers in reading maps and identifying households. Rehearse the interview, including the opening, asking questions and recording answers—critical if probing questions are included or interviewers will need to create them on the spot, and closing the interview. The following are typical instructions for interviewers.

Preparing for the Interview

Guard against interviewer bias.

Study the question schedule and answer options thoroughly so you can ask rather than read questions and record answers quickly and accurately. Dress appropriately, and be neat and well groomed. Do not wear buttons or insignia that identify you with a particular group or position on the issue to avoid biased responses. Choose an appropriate time of week and day.

Conducting the Interview[29]

Be friendly, businesslike, and interested in the topic. Speak clearly, at a good pace, and loudly enough to be heard easily. Maintain eye contact and don't be afraid to smile.

Ask all questions clearly, without hesitation, and neutrally. Adopt an informal speaking manner that avoids the appearance of reading or reciting openings, questions, and closings.

Opening the Interview

Motivate the interviewee from the moment the interview commences. State your name, identify your organization, and present your credentials if appropriate. Explain the purpose, length, nature, and importance of the study; then move to your first question without appearing to pressure the interviewee to take part.

Asking Questions

> No question can be altered in any way.

Ask all questions, including answer options, exactly as worded. You may repeat a question but not rephrase it or define words. Do not change the order of questions or answer options unless instructed to do so. If you are doing a qualitative study, probe carefully into answers to obtain insightful and thorough answers free of ambiguities and vague references.

Receiving and Recording Answers

> Maintain a pleasant "poker face" throughout.

Give respondents adequate time to reply, and then record answers as prescribed in your training and on the schedule. Write or print answers carefully. Remain neutral at all times, reacting neither positively nor negatively to responses.

Closing the Interview

When you have obtained the answer to the last question, thank the interviewee for cooperating and excuse yourself without being abrupt. Be polite and sensitive, making it clear that the interviewee has been most helpful. Do not discuss the survey with the interviewee.

Conducting Survey Interviews

With preparation completed, it's time to **pretest the interview** with a portion of the targeted audience to detect potential problems with questions and answer options.

Pretesting the Interview

> Lack of pretesting invites disaster.

The best plans on paper may not work during real interviews. Try out the opening, questions, recording answers, and closing.

Leave nothing to chance. For instance, in a political poll conducted by one of our classes, students deleted the question "What do you like or dislike about your major?" because it took too much time, generated little useful data, and posed a coding nightmare because of diverse replies. When interviewees were handed a list of political candidates during another project and asked, "What do you like or dislike about . . . ?" many became embarrassed or gave vague answers because they did not know some of the candidates. This question was replaced with a Likert scale from "strongly like" to "strongly dislike," including a "don't know" option, and interviewers probed into reasons for liking or disliking only for candidates ranked in the extreme positions on the scale. Respondents tended to know something about candidates they strongly liked or strongly disliked.

In a survey of mudslinging during political campaigns, one of the authors discovered that scale questions tended to confuse elderly respondents, so he added special explanations to complex questions.

Ask questions such as these when conducting pretests. Did interviewees understand what you needed and why? Did the wording of any question pose problems for some interviewees? Did interviewees react negatively or refuse to answer certain questions? Did each question attain the information desired? Did recording of answers pose any problems?

Leave nothing unquestioned.

Once you have studied the pretest results and made alterations in procedures, questions, and answer options, you are ready to conduct the full survey.

Interviewing Face-to-Face

Ideally, the survey interview would be conducted in a face-to-face "personal" interview, that obtains a good response rate because of the personal touch and interviewees can see and hear the interviewer and feel, touch, experience, and perhaps taste products. The face-to-face interview has a number of advantages over other forms of survey taking.[30] It is easier for the interviewer to establish credibility through physical appearance, dress, eye contact, and presentation of credentials. Interviewers can be sure of interviewing targeted responses, including "marginalized populations," in specific places at specific times. Respondents are more willing to take part in lengthy interviews that enable interviewers to ask more questions on complex issues and focus on in-depth attitudes and information. Face-to-face interviews allow interviewers to observe attitudes and reactions revealed through facial expressions, eye contact, gestures, and posture. Respondents are more likely to provide self-generated and more accurate answers because of the "naturalness" of the situation.

The face-to-face interview has some disadvantages. It is expensive, time-consuming, and slow. It requires a considerable number of thoroughly trained interviewers who may or may not interview the representative sample the survey requires. It may be impossible to do face-to-face interviews over a wide geographical area.

Interviewing by Telephone

Telephone interviews may be inexpensive in money but costly in results.

Because face-to-face survey interviews are expensive and time-consuming, and societal changes have made it difficult to predict when respondents might be available, the telephone survey interview—particularly with the advent of Random-Digit Dialing technology—has become dominant. But the telephone interview has its own set of problems.

While some studies indicate that telephone and face-to-face interviews produce similar results, researchers urge caution when selecting interviewing methods. One study discovered that many interviewers do not like telephone interviews, an attitude that may affect responses. Another found that fewer interviewees (particularly older ones) prefer the telephone, resulting in a lower degree of cooperation in telephone interviews.[31] People feel uneasy about discussing sensitive issues with strangers they cannot see, and it is difficult for interviewers to make convincing confidentiality guarantees when they are not face-to-face with respondents.[32] Those using answering machines, answering services, and call identifiers can filter out unwanted calls, including surveys.[33] The advent of the cell phone and the ever-increasing number of people who rely on cell phones rather than land lines has created problems for survey interviewers who could once rely on telephone books for sampling. This has led researchers to warn against coverage bias when cell phone-only respondents (often younger or of low economic status) are excluded.[34] Although some early studies suggested that responses in cell phone interviews might be less accurate than land line interviews, a recent study revealed "no evidence of a device effect."[35]

Regardless of the potential problems with telephone survey interviews, they have become dominant because of significant advantages.[36] The telephone is not only less expensive, but it also provides faster results, literally overnight if desired. There may be fewer interviewer effects such as interviewer bias because there is increased uniformity in manner and delivery and no effect from dress, appearance, mannerisms, facial expressions, and eye contact. Interviewers feel safer using the telephone than venturing into dangerous neighborhoods, particularly at night. Respondents provide fewer socially acceptable answers, perhaps because they feel safer (they need not admit strangers into their homes or businesses) and prefer the anonymity of the telephone when answering controversial or personal questions.

Here are guidelines for conducting interviews over the telephone.

Opening the Telephone Interview

Most refusals in telephone surveys occur prior to the first substantive question: one-third in the opening seconds, one-third during the orientation, and one-third at the point of listing household members. Speaking skills (pitch, vocal variety, loudness, rate, and distinct enunciation), particularly during the opening, are more important than content. One study concluded, "Respondents react to cues communicated by the interviewer's voice and may grant or refuse an interview on that basis."[37] Telephone interviewers must establish trust through vocal and verbal analogs to the personal appearance, credentials, and survey materials that enhance trust in face-to-face interviews.

A growing number of interviewers are turning to the telephone for easier and less expensive means of conducting surveys and polls.

Purestock/SuperStock

How to Use the Telephone

The literature on survey interviewing contains important advice for would-be telephone interviewers. These guidelines are equally relevant to face-to-face interviews.[38]

- *Do not give a person a reason or opportunity to hang up.* Develop an informal but professional style that is courteous (not demanding) and friendly (not defensive). Get the interviewee involved as quickly as possible in answering questions because active involvement motivates people to take part and cooperate.

Opening the telephone interview is critical.

Do nothing but ask and listen during telephone interviews.

- *Listen carefully and actively.* Give your undivided attention to what the interviewee is saying by not drinking, eating, sorting papers, or playing with objects on your desk. Don't communicate nonverbally with others in the room, and say nothing you do not want the interviewee to hear even if you believe you have the mouthpiece covered. Explain any pauses or long silences of more than a few seconds or signal you are listening with cues such as "Uh huh," "Yes," "Okay."
- *Use your voice effectively.* Talk directly into the mouthpiece. Speak loud enough, slowly, clearly, and distinctly because the interviewee must rely solely on your voice. State each answer option distinctly with vocal emphasis on important words and pause between each option to aid in comprehension and recall.
- *Use a computer-assisted telephone interview system* that enables you to dial random numbers quickly and to compile results within minutes of completing interviews.

Interviewing through the Internet

An increasing number of survey interviews are taking place through the Internet—e-mail, Web pages, and computer direct.[39] They are substantially less expensive and faster than either face-to-face or telephone interviews. A survey posted on a popular Web site may generate thousands of responses within hours.[40] Because they are highly flexible, Internet surveys can target large populations over great distances. A major problem of survey interviews—interviewees attempting to give socially acceptable answers—is lessened because of the anonymity and perceived safety of the Internet interview. A significant concern in face-to-face and telephone interviews, interviewer bias, is not a problem in Internet surveys. Respondents give more honest answers to sensitive topics. Unlike paper-and-pencil surveys, and even some face-to-face and telephone surveys, interviewees tend to provide more detail in answers to open-ended questions, perhaps because it is easy and quick to type lengthy answers on a keyboard and they can reply when it suits them.

On the other hand, the critical nonverbal communication that aids face-to-face and telephone interviews is lost when you use the Internet. Response rates may suffer because it is more difficult to establish the credibility of the survey and its source or to distinguish the survey interview from a slick telemarketer sales interview. While the Internet gives respondents time to think through answers, it may lose the spontaneity of interactions in face-to-face and telephone interviews; they are essentially electronic bulletin boards. However, "real-time chat" software can ensure spontaneity. It's nearly impossible to probe into answers or employ question strategies such as shuffle, leaning, and repeat. Evidence indicates that completion rates are lower for lengthy surveys; respondents grow tired of the process and simply log off.

It is difficult to target specific audiences you wish to sample in wide-ranging, Internet surveys, and you may not know who in a family, corporation, school, or state replied to your survey. Your sample, and thus your results, may be highly questionable. Those who feel most strongly about an issue, usually with negative attitudes, may overwhelm the results in self-selected Internet surveys. This has led researchers Chris Mann and Fiona Stewart to warn, "There is no doubt that the unrepresentativeness of current Internet access remains the greatest problem for data collection on-line."[41]

Coding, Tabulation, and Analysis

Once all interviews are completed, the final phase of the survey begins. This phase involves coding, tabulation, and analysis of the information received.

Coding and Tabulation

Begin the final phase of the survey by **coding** all answers that were not precoded, usually for open-ended questions. For instance, if question 20 is "You say you oppose amnesty as a means of handling the immigration issue created by the millions of immigrants who have entered this country illegally. Why do you oppose this as an option?" will elicit a wide variety of answers. If question 20 is coded #20, each answer can be coded 20 plus, 1, 2, 3, 4, etc., such as the following:

20-1	It would reward those who have entered this country illegally.
20-2	A new wave of illegal immigrants would enter this country.
20-3	It would not resolve illegal immigration as a divisive social and political issue.
20-4	Illegal immigrants would continue to take jobs from American citizens and lower wages for all workers.
20-5	Illegal immigrants and their children pose an overwhelming economic burden on cities and states.
20-6	Illegal immigrants increase the terrorist threat to the United States.

Record answers to open-ended questions with great care.

Answers to open-ended questions may require analysis and structuring before developing a coding system. For example, in a study of voter perception of mudslinging in political campaigns, the interviewer asked, "What three or four words would you use to describe a politician who uses mudslinging as a tactic?" Answers included more than 100 different words, but analysis revealed that most words tended to fit into five categories: untrustworthy, incompetent, unlikable, insecure, and immature.[42] A sixth category, "other," received words that did not fit into the five categories. All words were placed into one of these six categories and coded from one to six.

Analysis

Analysis is making sense of your data.

Once all answers are coded and the results tabulated, the **analysis** phase begins. This task can be overwhelming. One of the authors surveyed 354 clergy from 32 Protestant, Catholic, and Jewish groups to assess their interview training during college and seminary and since entering the ministry.[43] The 48 questions in the survey times 354 respondents provided 16,992 bits of information.

How can the survey interviewer handle massive amounts of information generated in most surveys? Charles Redding offered several helpful suggestions.[44]

- *Be selective.* Ask "What findings are likely to be most useful?" and "What will I do with this information once I get it?" If you have no idea, do not ask for it.
- *Capitalize on the potential of data.* Subject data to comparative breakdowns to discover differences between demographic subgroups.

- *Dig for the gold.* What is the really important stuff hidden within raw data and simple tabulations? For instance, in polls of registered voter attitudes, interviewers often discover that female respondents favor a candidate far less than male respondents and that Americans who have recently become citizens are likely to have very different views toward immigration than third or fourth generation Americans.

- *Look for what is missing.* What you do not find may be more important than what you do find. What information did you not obtain?

Know the limitations of your survey.

During analysis of data, ask these questions. What conclusions can you draw and with what certainty? For what segment of a target population can you generalize? What are the constraints imposed by the sample, schedule of questions, the interviewing process, and the interviewers? Why did people respond in specific ways to specific questions? What unexpected events or changes have occurred since the completion of the survey that might make this survey dated or suspect? What should be done with the "undecided" and "don't know" answers or blanks on survey forms?

Be careful in using survey results.

Caution is essential for all survey takers. For example, journalists must be cautious when writing headlines and making predictions. Organizations must be cautious when basing policy decisions on survey results. Voters must be cautious when casting votes according to candidate-preference polls. You might subject data to a statistical analysis designed to test reliability and significance of data. Babbie and other research methodologists (see resources) provide detailed guidelines for conducting sophisticated statistical analyses.

When the analysis of data is complete, determine if the purpose and objectives of your survey are achieved. If so, what are the best means of reporting the results?

The Respondent in Survey Interviews

The ever-growing number of surveys conducted throughout the world each day by government agents and agencies, political candidates and parties, advertisers and marketing representatives, special interest groups and activists, charities and religious organizations, colleges and students ensures your involvement in these highly structured interviews. They are rarely compulsory, so you are free to "just say no," but when you do, you may forfeit an opportunity to influence important decisions that affect you, your family, your field of work, and your community. Don't walk away, close the door, hang up the phone, or hit the delete button too hastily, but approach all survey requests cautiously and with a healthy skepticism.

The Opening

Understand what a survey is all about before participating.

Take an active part in the opening and discover through observing, listening, and asking questions the identity of the interviewer, the interviewer's credentials, the organization sponsoring the survey, the purpose of the survey, why and how you were selected to participate, the length of the interview, how the information you give will be used, and the confidentiality of your answers and your identity. Become thoroughly oriented prior to answering questions. If the interviewer does not provide important information, ask for it. When one of the authors was visiting his daughter and her family in Vancouver,

Washington, more than 2,000 miles from home, he was approached in a shopping mall by a market researcher. The researcher explained who she was, what she was doing, and why she was doing it. She did not state that he had to be a local resident. When asked if it made any difference that he was visiting from the Midwest, the interviewer said she wanted only those who regularly visited the mall. The interview ended.

The opening minutes enable you to determine if the interview is a survey or a slick persuasive interview under the guise of a survey. Is it a nonpartisan political survey being conducted by a nationally known and reputable polling organization or part of a political campaign for a specific candidate or party? When one of the authors responded to the doorbell at his home, a college-age person announced that she was conducting a survey of families with children for a summer internship. A few questions revealed that she was selling child-oriented magazines for a summer job, not an internship sponsored by her college as implied in her opening.

The Question Phase

Listen perceptively.

Listen carefully to each question, particularly to answer options in interval, nominal, and ordinal questions. If a question or option is difficult to recall, ask the interviewer to repeat the question slowly. If a question is unclear, explain why and ask for clarification. Avoid replays of earlier answers, especially if you think you "goofed." Do not try to guess what a question is going to be from the interviewer's first words. You might guess wrong and become confused, give a stupid answer, or needlessly force the interviewer to restate a perfectly clear question.

Think before answering.

Think through each answer to respond clearly and precisely. Give the answer that best represents your beliefs, attitudes, or actions. Do not permit interviewer bias to lead you toward an answer you think the interviewer wants to hear or how other respondents might answer.

You have rights as a respondent. You can refuse to answer poorly constructed or leading questions or to give data that seem irrelevant or an invasion of privacy. For instance, an interviewer recently asked one of the authors, "Do you favor boutique solutions to our energy needs such as wind farms or environmentally friendly nuclear power plants that can supply electricity to major industries and cities?" The word "boutique" clearly revealed the bias and agenda of the interviewer. Expect and demand tactful, sensitive, and polite treatment from interviewers. Insist on adequate time to answer questions. If you have agreed to a 10-minute interview and the interview is still going strong at the 10-minute mark, remind the interviewer of the agreement and proceed to close the interview unless only a few more seconds are required. Survey interviews can be fun, interesting, and informative if both parties treat one another fairly.

Summary

The survey interview is the most meticulously planned and executed of interviews. Planning begins with determining a clearly defined purpose and conducting research. The purpose of all survey interviews is to establish a solid base of fact from which to draw conclusions, make interpretations, and determine future courses of action. Only then does the survey creator structure the interview and develop questions with appropriate strategies, scales, sequences, coding, and recording methods. Selecting interviewees involves delineating a target population to survey and choosing a sample of this population that represents the whole. The creator of the survey chooses sampling methods, determines the size of the sample, and plans for an acceptable margin of error. Each choice has advantages and disadvantages because there is no one correct way to handle all survey situations.

Survey respondents must determine the nature of the survey and its purposes before deciding whether to take part. If the decision is to participate, respondents have a responsibility to listen carefully to each question and answer it accurately. Be sure you understand each question and its answer options. Demand enough time to think through answers. Feel free to refuse to answer obviously leading or poorly phrased questions that require a biased answer or choosing among options that do not include how you feel and what you prefer.

Key Terms and Concepts

The online learning center for this text features FLASHCARDS and CROSSWORD PUZZLES for studying based on these terms and concepts.

Bogardus Social Distance Scale	Likert scale	Random digital dialing
Chain or contingency strategy	Longitudinal survey	Random sampling
Convenience sample	Margin of error	Ranking ordinal scale
Coverage bias	Marginalized respondent	Rating ordinal scale
Cross-sectional survey	Nominal scale	Reliability
Evaluative interval scale	Non-probability sampling	Repeat strategy
Face-to-face interview	Numerical interval scale	Replicability
Filter strategy	Order bias	Sample point
Frequency interval scale	Ordinal scale	Sampling principles
Internet interview	Personal interview	Self-selection
Interval scale	Population	Shuffle strategy
Leaning question strategy	Probability sampling	Skip interval scale
Level of confidence	Qualitative survey	Stratified random sample
	Quantitative survey	Table of random numbers
	Precision journalism	Web survey

A Survey Interview for Review and Analysis

The purpose of this survey is to discover how parents with school-age children (kindergarten through 12th grade) perceive the problems of bullying their children and others are encountering in their daily lives, both inside and outside of the school setting. What should be done to assist children who are victims of bullying or the perpetrators, and who should assist them?

As you read through this survey schedule, notice the parts of the opening, including the opening and qualifying questions. Identify the question strategies, question scales, and question sequences. How are the built-in probing questions, instructions for interviewers, and precoded answers designed to aid the interviewer and ensure accuracy and replicability of the survey being conducted by many interviewers? What is included in the brief, planned closing?

How might the opening be improved, including the order and placement of demographic and qualifying questions? As a potential interviewee, what questions might you have for the interviewer before proceeding with the interview? Which questions could have been phrased more effectively? What problems might the open-ended questions pose for interviewers and interviewees? How well do the questions cover the areas of concern in this research survey? How might answer options have been precoded for ease of tabulation? How adequate is the closing?

Bullying Encountered by School-Age Children

Speak to any parent of school-age children (kindergarten through the 12th grade) residing in the household. Hello, my name is _____, a graduate student in counseling at ISU. I'm assisting with a national study of how parents of school-age children perceive the problem of bullying their children or the children of other parents are encountering in their daily lives. The results will be published in professional journals and released to the press. The interview will only take a few minutes.

1. I'm going to read you several age ranges. Stop me when I read the one that includes your age.

   18–24 _____
   25–34 _____
   35–49 _____
   50 and over _____

2. What was the last grade level of your formal education?

   8–11 years   _____
   12–15 years   _____
   High school graduate _____
   College graduate   _____
   Postgraduate work   _____

3. Are you a parent of a school-age child, kindergarten through 12th grade? (IF NO, ASK IF SUCH A PARENT RESIDES IN THE HOUSEHOLD. IF NO PARENT RESIDES IN THE HOUSEHOLD, TERMINATE THE INTERVIEW. IF YES, PROCEED TO Q. 3a).

3a. How many school-age children do you have?

   1–2 _____   5–6   _____
   3–4 _____   7 or more _____

3b. What are their ages?

   5–7   _____   14–16 _____
   8–10 _____   17–19 _____
   11–13 _____

4a. When you think of bullying and school-age children (child) today, what problem comes to mind first?

_____

4b. What do you see as the major cause of bullying?

_____

4c. What are other possible causes of bullying?

_____

_____

_____

5. Many parents tell us that bullying is a serious problem facing their school-age children (child) today. How would you rate the job parents are doing in addressing this problem? (CIRCLE ANSWERS IN THE SCALES PROVIDED AT THE END OF Q. 7.)

6. How would you rate the job the schools are doing in addressing bullying? (CIRCLE ANSWERS IN THE SCALES PROVIDED AT THE END OF Q. 7.)

7. How would you rate the job law enforcement is doing in addressing this bullying problem? (CIRCLE ANSWERS IN THE SCALES LISTED BELOW.)

	Parents	**Schools**	**Law Enforcement**
Excellent	1	1	1
Good	2	2	2
Average	3	3	3
Not so good	4	4	4
Poor	5	5	5

8. Do (Does) your children (child) have free access to the Internet?

Yes _____

No _____

9. Here is a card (HAND CARD TO INTERVIEWEE.) that lists some of the problems parents identify as major problems facing their school-age children. (ROTATE THE ORDER FROM ONE INTERVIEW TO THE NEXT.) Who do you think is likely to address these problems most effectively: parents, schools, law enforcement, or the government?

	Parents	**Schools**	**Law Enforcement**	**Government**
Drugs	1	2	3	4
Alcohol	1	2	3	4
Assault	1	2	3	4
Robbery	1	2	3	4
Gun violence	1	2	3	4
Rape	1	2	3	4
Sexual predators	1	2	3	4
Bullying	1	2	3	4
Suicide	1	2	3	4

10. Many parents tell us they are concerned about the bullying of their school-age children. This card (HAND CARD TO THE INTERVIEWEE.) lists several possible solutions to the bullying problem. Which one do you believe would be the most effective deterrent?

    More adult supervision in and near schools.   1

    Stiffer penalties for those bullying school-age children.   2

    Stiffer penalties for those who ignore bullying
        including parents.   3

    A law that requires teachers and principals to report all
        instances of bullying.   4

    Permanent expulsion of any student caught bullying
        other students.   5

11. Many parents we talk to feel that schools have become more violent and threatening since they were in school. This card (HAND CARD TO THE INTERVIEWEE.) gives often-cited causes of violence and threats facing our school-age children today. Which one of these causes do you feel is the greatest cause? (RECORD ANSWER.) Which is the next greatest cause? (RECORD ANSWER.) Which would be the next cause? (RECORD ANSWER). And which would be the next cause? (RECORD ANSWER.)

	First	Second	Third	Fourth
Lack of discipline in homes	1	2	3	4
Lack of adult supervision	1	2	3	4
Lack of discipline in the schools	1	2	3	4
Lack of supervision in the schools	1	2	3	4
Unlimited access to social media	1	2	3	4
Gang activity in schools and community	1	2	3	4
Violence in the home	1	2	3	4
Violence in society	1	2	3	4
Violence in the media	1	2	3	4

12. Some sources claim that the only way to reduce the bullying of school-age children today is to strengthen the traditional family in the United States. Tell me whether you strongly agree, agree, disagree, or strongly disagree with each of these recommended ways to strengthen the traditional family. (RECORD ANSWERS IN THE SPACES BELOW AND ROTATE THE ORDER IN WHICH THE STATEMENTS ARE GIVEN FROM INTERVIEW TO INTERVIEW.)

    a. Physical abuse should be the only grounds for divorce.
    b. Abortion should be illegal.
    c. A constitutional amendment should forbid same-sex marriages.
    d. New income tax deductions should enable more women to remain at home with their children.
    e. Adultery should be a felony.

f. The minimum wage should provide an adequate income for every family.

	a	b	c	d	e	f
Strongly agree	1	1	1	1	1	1
Agree	2	2	2	2	2	2
Don't know	3	3	3	3	3	3
Disagree	4	4	4	4	4	4
Strongly disagree	5	5	5	5	5	5

13a. Are you familiar with so-called "stand-your-ground" laws?

Yes _____ (IF YES, ASK Q. 12b.)

No _____

13b. What do you know about "stand-your-ground" laws?

_____

_____

14. Do you control your children's (child's) access to the Internet at home?

Yes _____

No _____

15a. Educational psychologists claim that bullying is one of the major problems facing school-age children today. Do you approve or disapprove of making bullying an illegal act that might lead to arrest and incarceration?

Approve _____
Disapprove _____

15b. Why do you feel this way?

_____

_____

15c. How strongly do you feel about this?

Strongly _____
Very strongly _____
Something about which you will never change your mind _____

16. With a growing concern for juvenile crime and the arrest of significant numbers of preteens and teenagers for adult crimes such as bullying, assault, robbery, rape, burglary, and the use of firearms in committing these crimes, many communities are building juvenile detention centers to house these young offenders.

a. Would you be in favor of building such centers in your state?
Yes _____   No _____

b. Would you be in favor of building such a center in your county?
Yes _____   No _____

c. Would you be in favor of building such a center in your city?
Yes _____   No _____

d. Would you be in favor of building such a center in your neighborhood?
Yes _____   No _____

That's all the questions I have. The survey results should be made public within five to six weeks.

Now I would like to ask you some personal questions so we can see how people with different backgrounds feel about the bullying problem facing their school-age children today.

17. Do you generally consider yourself to be a conservative, liberal, centrist, or other?

Conservative _____

Liberal _____

Centrist _____

Other _____

18. Do your children attend public schools, private schools, or are they homeschooled?

Public schools _____

Private schools _____

Homeschooled _____

19. I'm going to read several household income ranges. Stop me when I read the range that includes your current annual family income.

0 through $14,999 _____

$15,000 through $24,999 _____

$25,000 through $49,999 _____

$50,000 through $74,999 _____

$75,000 through $99,999 _____

Over $100,000 _____

That's all the questions I have. Thank you very much for participating in this important survey. The results should be made public within six months.

Survey Role-Playing Cases

Drinking on Campus

Drinking on college campuses is a growing concern nationwide with increasing numbers of assaults, accidental deaths, and shootings, particularly at off-campus housing and drinking establishments. The interviewer is chairing the Student Affairs Committee that has taken on the task of creating a survey of a cross section of faculty and students to discover their experiences with drinking issues on campus, their fears and concerns for student safety and that of others, and suggestions for making the campus safer in perception and reality.

Health Care Reform

In spite of the Supreme Court's upholding of the constitutionality of The Patient Protection and Affordable Care Act (derisively called Obamacare by its opponents), conflict over how to reform the health care system to control cost while sustaining quality continues unabated as it has for decades. A group of medical, governmental, and religious leaders has banded together to assess the problems, concerns, and attitudes of a cross section of adults (anyone 18 years or older) to guide their discussions and proposals for further health care reforms.

Need for a 24–7 Child Care Facility

You and four friends with experiences in local child care feel that there is a need for a facility that would provide 24–7 child care in your community. All local facilities open at 6:00 a.m. and close at 6 p.m., but a growing number of parents, including single parents, are working 4:00 p.m. to midnight and midnight to 8:00 a.m. shifts and need day care during these evening and nighttime periods. The five of you are considering building and staffing a 24–7 day care facility but need to assess the number of clients and children you might serve to make it financially feasible. You are both creating a survey instrument and trying to determine your target population.

A Fitness Center

You graduated from college ten years ago with a degree in physical therapy and have since worked at a number of rehabilitation and fitness centers on the West Coast. Although these positions have been rewarding and provided a great variety of experiences as both a therapist and a business administrator, you would like to get back to western Kentucky where your family lives and to settle down in a mid-sized city. You have decided to conduct surveys of residents in Bowling Green, Paducah, and Henderson to determine the feasibility and nature of creating your own rehabilitation and fitness center that would cater to the 40 and above population.

Student Activities

1. Serve as a volunteer interviewer for a survey being conducted on your campus or community. What instructions and training did you receive? How were interviewees determined? What problems did you encounter in locating suitable and cooperative interviewees? What problems did you have with the survey schedule? What is the most important thing you have learned from this experience? What advice would you give the organization you volunteered to serve?

2. Try a simple interviewer bias experiment. Conduct 10 short opinion interviews on a current issue, using an identical question schedule for all interviews. During five of them, wear a conspicuous T-shirt, button, or badge that identifies membership in or support of an organization that supports one side of the issue: a Republican elephant, or Democratic donkey, a crucifix or a Star of David, an organization's logo or a product slogan. Compare results to see if and how your identification with an organization on one side of the issue affected answers to identical questions.

3. Obtain a number of market survey schedules used in face-to-face, telephone, and Internet surveys. Compare and contrast these schedules. How are the openings similar and different? How are schedules and sequences similar and different? How

are question strategies and question scales similar and different? How are closings similar and different? What surprises did you discover in your comparisons?

4. Interview a person who has worked for one or more survey agencies that create and conduct surveys for a variety of clients such as politicians, universities, and manufacturers. Cover such topics as determining the purpose, conducting research, selecting the target population, determining the sampling method, arriving at an acceptable margin of error, creating and pretesting the interview schedule, selecting and training interviewers, and deciding upon the method: face-to-face interviews, telephone interviews, Internet interviews.

Notes

1. Jeffrey Henning, "Survey Nation: 7 Billion Survey Invites a Year," http://blog.vovici/blog/bid/51106/Survey-Nation-7-Billion-Survey-Invites-a-Year, accessed June 4, 2012.

2. Jibum Kim, Carl Gerschenson, Patrick Glaser, and Tom W. Smith, "Trends—Trends in Surveys on Surveys," *Public Opinion Quarterly* 75 (Spring 2011), pp. 165–191.

3. Leslie A. Baxter and Earl Babbie, *The Basics of Communication Research* (Belmont, CA: Wadsworth/Thomson, 2004), p. 22.

4. http://www.socialresearchmethods.net/kb/interview.htm, accessed September 29, 2006.

5. Morgan M. Millar and Don A. Dillman, "Improving Response to Web and Mixed-Mode Surveys," *Public Opinion Quarterly* 75 (Summer 2011), pp. 249–269; Jens Bonke and Peter Fallesen, "The impact of incentives and interview methods on response quantity and quality in diary- and booklet-based surveys," *Survey Research Methods* 4 (2010), pp. 91–101.

6. Diane K. Willimack, Howard Schuman, Beth-Ellen Pennell, and James M. Lepkowski, "Effects of a Prepaid Nonmonetary Incentive on Response Rates and Response Quality in Face-to-Face Survey," *Public Opinion Quarterly* 59 (1995), pp. 78–92.

7. Eleanor Singer and Mick P. Couper, "Do Incentives Exert Undue Influence on Survey Participation? Experimental Evidence," http://www.ncbi.nim.nih.gov/pmc/articles/PMC2600442, accessed June 6, 2012.

8. Stanley L. Payne, *The Art of Asking Questions* (Princeton, NJ: Princeton University Press, 1980), p. 57.

9. David Yeager and Jon Krosnick, "Does Mentioning 'Some People' and 'Other People' in an Opinion Question Improve Measurement Quality?" *Public Opinion Quarterly* 76 (Spring 2012), pp. 131–141.

10. Jack E. Edwards and Marie D. Thomas, "The Organizational Survey Process," *American Behavioral Scientist* 36 (1993), pp. 425–426.

11. Earl Babbie, *The Practice of Social Research* (Belmont, CA: Wadsworth/Thomson, 1995), p. 145.

12. Creative Research Systems, "The Survey System," file://C:DOCUME~1\stewart\
LOCALS\Temp\G2BBVAF.htm, accessed September 29, 2006.

13. Norman M. Bradburn, Seymour Sudman, Ed Blair, and Carol Stocking, "Question
Threat and Response Bias," *Public Opinion Quarterly* 42 (1978), pp. 221–234.

14. Sam G. McFarland, "Effects of Question Order on Survey Responses," *Public Opinion
Quarterly* 45 (1981), pp. 208–215.

15. "Common Pitfalls in Conducting a Survey," Fairfax County Department of Systems
Management for Human Services, April 2003.

16. W. Charles Redding, *How to Conduct a Readership Survey: A Guide for Organizational Editors and Communication Managers* (Chicago: Lawrence Ragan Communications, 1982), pp. 27–28.

17. Philip Meyer, *Precision Journalism* (Bloomington: Indiana University Press, 1979),
p. 123; Redding, pp. 31–36.

18. "Sample Size Calculator," http://www.surveysystem.com/sscalc.htm, accessed August
14, 2009.

19. Redding, p. 1.

20. "Survey Sampling Methods," http://startreck.com/survey-research/sampling-methods
.aspx, accessed June 10, 2012; "Probability and Nonprobability Sampling," http://
www.emathzone.com/tutorials-basic-statistics/probability-and-nonprobability-
sampling.html, accessed June 27, 2012.

21. "Designing the Survey Instrument and Process," http://www.airhealthwatch.com/
mdph_instrument.htm, accessed September 29, 2006.

22. "Sampling (Statistics)," http://en.wikipedia.org/wiki/sampling_%28statistics29,
accessed August 14, 2009.

23. Kristen Olson and Ipek Bilgen, "The Role of Interviewer Experience on Acquiescence,"
Public Opinion Quarterly 75 (Spring 2011), pp. 99–114.

24. Eleanor Singer, Martin R. Frankel, and Marc B. Glassman, "The Effect of Interviewer
Characteristics and Expectations on Response," *Public Opinion Quarterly* 47 (1983),
pp. 68-83.

25. Stephan Schleifer, "Trends in Attitudes toward and Participation in Survey Research,"
Public Opinion Quarterly 50 (1986), pp. 17–26.

26. Frank Newport, Lydia Saad, and David Moore, "How Polls Are Conducted," in *Where
America Stands,* John Wiley & Sons, 1997, http://www.janda.org/c10/Lectures/
topic05/GallupFAQ.htm, accessed June 11, 2012.

27. "Evaluation Tools for Racial Equity: Tip Sheets," http://www
.Evaluationtoolsforracialequity.org/, accessed September 29, 2006.

28. Jennifer Dewey, "Guidelines for Survey Interviewing," NCREL, September 14, 2000,
accessed June 10, 2012; William M.K. Trochim, "Interviews," Research Methods
Knowledge Base, 2006, http://www.socialresearchmethods.net/kb/interview.php,
accessed June 2, 2012.

29. Roger W. Shuy, "In-Person versus Telephone Interviewing," in *Inside Interviewing: New Lenses, New Concerns,* James A. Holstein and Jaber F. Gubrium, eds. (Thousand Oaks, CA: Sage, 2003), pp. 175–183.

30. Lawrence A. Jordan, Alfred C. Marcus, and Leo G. Reeder, "Response Style in Telephone and Household Interviewing," *Public Opinion Quarterly* 44 (1980), pp. 210–222; Peter V. Miller and Charles F. Cannell, "A Study of Experimental Techniques in Telephoning Interviewing," *Public Opinion Quarterly* 46 (1982), pp. 250–269.

31. William S. Aquilino, "Interview Mode Effects in Surveys on Drug and Alcohol Use," *Public Opinion Quarterly* 58 (1994), pp. 210–240.

32. Michael W. Link and Robert W. Oldendick, "Call Screening: Is It Really a Problem for Survey Research?" *Public Opinion Quarterly* 63 (Winter 1999), pp. 577–589.

33. John Ehlen and Patrick Ehlen, "Cellular-Only Substitution in the United States as Lifestyle Adoption: Implications for Telephone Survey Coverage," *Public Opinion Quarterly* 71 (2007), pp. 717–733.

34. Courtney Kennedy and Stephen E. Everett, "Use of Cognitive Shortcuts in Landline and Cell Phone Interviews," *Public Opinion Quarterly* 75 (Summer 2011), pp. 336–348.

35. DJS Research, "What Are the Pros and Cons of Data Collection Methods," http://www.marketresearchworld.net/index2.php?option=com_content&task=view&id=21, accessed June 26, 2012; Campbell Rinker, "Surveys," http://www.campbellrinker.com/surveys.html, accessed June 26, 2012.

36. Lois Okenberg, Lerita Coleman, and Charles F. Cannell, "Interviewers' Voices and Refusal Rates in Telephone Surveys," *Public Opinion Quarterly* 50 (1986), pp. 97–111.

37. Joe Hopper, "How to Conduct a Telephone Survey for Gold Standard Research," http://www.verstaresearch.com/blog/how-to-conduct-a-telephone-survey-for-gold-standard-research, accessed 26 June 2012.

38. "Personal Surveys vs. Web Surveys: A Comparison," http://knowledge-base.supersurvey.com/in-person-vs-web-surveys.htm, accessed September 29, 2006; Creative Research Systems, "The Survey System."

39. "Personal Interviews vs. Web Surveys: A Comparison," http://knowledge-base.supersurvey.com/in-person-vs-web-surveys.htm, accessed August 10, 2009.

40. "Online Survey vs. Telephone Survey," hppt://www.eventavenue.com/content/resources/online_surveys.php, accessed June 26, 2012; Dirk Heerwegh and Geert Loosveldt, "Face-to-Face versus Web Surveying in a High-Internet-Coverage Population: Differences in Response Quality," *Public Opinion Quarterly* 72 (2008), 836-846.

41. Chris Mann and Fiona Stewart, "Internet Interviewing," in Holstein and Gubrium, p. 243.

42. Charles J. Stewart, "Voter Perception of Mudslinging in Political Communication," *Central States Speech Journal* 26 (1975), pp. 279–286.

43. Charles J. Stewart, "The Interview and the Clergy: A Survey of Training, Experiences, and Needs," *Religious Communication Today* 3 (1980), pp. 19–22.

44. Redding, pp. 119–123.

Resources

Conrad, Frederick G., and Michael F. Schober, eds. *Envisioning the Survey Interview of the Future.* San Francisco: Wiley-Interscience, 2007.

Fink, Arlene. *How to Conduct Surveys: A Step-by-Step Guide.* Thousand Oaks, CA: Sage, 2012.

Gwartney, Patricia A. *The Telephone Interviewer's Handbook.* San Francisco: Jossey-Bass, 2007.

Holstein, James A., and Jaber F. Gubrium, eds. *Inside Interviewing: New Lenses, New Concerns.* Newbury Park, CA: Sage, 2003.

Meyer, Philip. *Precision Journalism.* Lanham, MD: Rowman & Littlefield, 2002.

Scheuren, Fritz. *What Is a Survey?* Alexandria, VA: American Statistical Association, 2004.

7

The Recruiting Interview

Recruiting employees is a critical task for every organization because their futures depend on it. Tom Peters, in his book titled *Re-Imagine,* writes that today "talent rules," so management must be obsessed with attracting and retaining new talent.[1] Others echo Peters's predictions. William Lewis writes that finding talent at a reasonable cost and developing that talent is the ultimate difference between success and failure.[2] A senior manager told the authors, "Anyone can buy technology, but the critical element in competing globally is the *people!*"

The task of recruiting high-quality people is not easy. It is hard work. As a search firm executive told the authors, "You can't know enough, learn enough, or experience enough" in a single interview. The process entails multiple contacts. It is an elaborate courtship process fraught with all sorts of interpersonal problems between two complex parties and susceptible to bias and distortion. In spite of such problems, the interview remains a critical component of the selection process because recruiters must become keenly aware of and probe into the skills, attitudes, behaviors, and abilities that may make an applicant an ideal **fit** for the **organization** and **position.**[3]

Luke Collard, a senior consultant at Scott Recruitment Services, contends that "If the interview is done by an experienced professional who knows what they are looking for, has the ability to ask the right questions, and get beyond the fluffy stuff they will come away with justified reasons as to why an individual either is or isn't suitable."[4]

A common and faulty belief is that Human Resources (HR) personnel recruit new employees for organizations. In truth, HR personnel typically play minor roles in the recruiting process because it is far too important and complex to assign to a single element of any organization, particularly when the need is for highly trained personnel such as sales representatives, educators, attorneys, physicians, engineers, therapists, research scientists, and financial managers to name only a few. You may have already taken part in recruiting activities while a college student, and you certainly will when you graduate regardless of your career path. We have seen many of our students return to campus within a year of graduation to aid in recruiting talent for their organizations because they can identify readily with their alma mater and its students.

The objectives of this chapter are to introduce you to the fundamental principles of successful employee recruiting. These include locating high-quality applicants, preparing for the recruiting process, obtaining and reviewing information on applicants, structuring interviews, conducting interviews, and evaluating interviews. Learning and applying these principles will make you a valuable asset to your organization while enhancing the quality of your future colleagues.

Where to Find Good Applicants

There are numerous resources available to locate quality applicants in virtually all fields from college graduates to senior citizens. Your social and professional networks are excellent sources for identifying experienced applicants who have drawn attention to themselves because of their performance and accomplishments. Check your file of "potentials," persons who have come to your attention in the field and at professional meetings and might be quality applicants for your opening. Don't overlook current or past interns as potential full-time employees or as contacts for quality applicants. Interns are excellent recruiters because they can sing your praises without seeming to be part of your establishment and readily identify with college-age students. College career centers enable you to make contacts with soon-to-be college graduates and alumni and to arrange for interviews.

Attend **job or career fairs** on college campuses, at malls, in host cities such as Chicago and Seattle, and ones coinciding with professional meetings and conferences. Personal contacts, attractive booths, and promotional materials such as brochures, book bags, and inexpensive pens get your name before a large number of potential applicants and help them recall who and what you are. Be sure those who staff your booth have excellent interpersonal skills, enjoy meeting people, and are able to conduct interviews on-the-spot if these can be arranged. If you are not currently hiring, be honest about it. Be sure to bring along carefully phrased job descriptions to attract those interested in and qualified for the opening(s) you have. Have application forms and sign-up sheets handy to keep track of quality applicants, take notes, and collect resumes. Make follow-up contacts shortly after attending a career fair with those who seem best qualified and most interested in your position(s) and organization.[5]

> Merely publishing an opening is not sufficient.

Your organization might decide to hire a **staffing firm** (sometimes called placement agencies, employment agencies, or head hunters) to locate quality applicants and perhaps to conduct initial screening interviews. Select such firms carefully to determine their success rates and suitability for your organization and the position(s) you wish to fill. The American Staffing Association offers important guidelines for making the best choice, including shopping around, type of staffing help you need, impressions of your initial interactions with the firm, how the staffing firm selects its employees (screening, testing, and training), and how well the firm understands your organization and your needs.[6]

> Web sites have not replaced personal contacts.

Many organizations, particularly in retail, have in-store terminals and kiosks to attract people who might not apply otherwise. This allows them to establish and update "a prospective database every minute the store is open" and to sort through applications to locate the most qualified applicants.[7] There are many resume databases you can use if in-store terminals and kiosks are inappropriate or unavailable for your organization. These include the National Resume Database, Regional Database, Local Resume Database, Category Focus that includes 22 career fields, the Office of Federal Contract Compliance Programs (OFCCP), and CareerBuilder.com.[8]

There are literally hundreds of Internet and electronic sources available to locate quality applicants. These include Web sites of colleges and universities, religious organizations, senior citizen clubs, political parties, and special interest groups. Here are a few key sources:

- CareerBuilder.com
- Kennedy's *The Directory of Executive and Professional Recruiters* (support@RecruiterRedbook.com)
- Monster (http://jobsearch.monster.com)
- Monster (www.monster.com)
- Wall Street Journal Careers Main (http://wsj.com)

Most organizations are striving to diversify their workforces, particularly among ethnic groups. Joyce Gioia suggests that you advertise in ethnic media (such as alternate language newspapers, magazines, Web sites, radio, and television) and in movie theaters that attract a highly diverse clientele.[9] Think globally, Gioia writes, because recruiting employees from diverse ethnic groups "holds opportunities for companies beyond their wildest dreams."

Don't overlook your Web site because the majority of prospective applicants will check this site to determine if your organization is attractive and a good fit. One study revealed that one in two potential applicants consider the employer's Web site to be "important" and that one in four would reject a potential employer on the basis of a poor Web site.[10] Your site should be easy to read, interesting, and sophisticated. A simple reality check is to log onto your site *as a potential employee* to see if it meets these criteria.

Preparing the Recruiting Effort

Since the recruiting interview remains the central component of attracting and selecting employees, recruiters must approach the process systematically and learn how to prepare for, participate in, and evaluate it. Professionally conducted interviews not only select better employees but also present good impressions of organizations.[11] "The key to a successful interview and selection process is good planning. Planning helps you to learn the necessary information about each applicant while at the same time avoid potential legal pitfalls of the process."[12]

Reviewing EEO Laws

Start the recruiting process by carefully reviewing **equal employment opportunity (EEO)** laws, including those of the states in which you will be recruiting that may be more stringent than federal laws. Although such laws (and executive orders) can be traced back to the Civil Rights Act of 1866, you must know six laws thoroughly.[13]

> Unintentional violations are still violations.

- The Equal Pay Act of 1963 requires equal pay for men and women performing work that involves similar skill, effort, responsibility, and working conditions.
- The Civil Rights Act of 1964, particularly Title VII, prohibits the selection of employees based on race, color, gender, religion, or national origin, and requires employers to discover discriminatory practices and eliminate them.

Review EEO laws carefully.

© Stockbyte/Veer

- The Age Discrimination in Employment Act of 1967 prohibits employers of 25 or more persons from discriminating against persons because of age.

- The Rehabilitation Act of 1973 (Sections 501 and 505) orders federal contractors to hire persons with disabilities, including alcoholism, asthma, rheumatoid arthritis, and epilepsy.

- The Civil Rights Act of 1991 (often referred to as the 1992 Civil Rights Act) caps compensation and punitive damages for employers, provides for jury trial, and created a commission to investigate the "glass ceiling" for minorities and women and reward organizations that advance opportunities for minorities and women.

- The Americans with Disabilities Act of 1990 (effective July 25, 1992), Title I and Title V, prohibits discrimination against persons with physical and mental impairments that substantially limit or restrict the condition, manner, or duration under which they can perform one or more life activities and requires reasonable accommodation by employers.

Understanding and complying with EEO laws is good for business. For instance, aging baby boomers and senior citizens, rather than being a drag on organizations as previously thought, bring valuable experiences to positions; know what they can and cannot do; are willing to take the initiative; are loyal; exhibit a willingness to learn, adjust, and adapt as they have for many years; show patience and a willingness to "hang in there" when facing difficult situations and relationships; are good listeners; and have the ability to get the job done.[14] Not hiring these people in the first place because of age is not only unlawful but may deprive your organization of valuable resources.

Compliance with EEO Laws

Although EEO laws have been in effect for decades, interviewers continue to violate them knowingly and unknowingly. One study reported that 70 percent of 200 recruiters for Fortune 500 companies thought at least 5 of 12 unlawful questions were "safe to ask."[15] Another study found that 12 percent thought it was acceptable to ask questions about political beliefs, 27 percent about family background, 30 percent about the candidate's spouse, and 45 percent about the candidate's personal life.[16] Job discrimination cases rose to an all-time high (more than 95,000) during the recession of 2008–2010 due in large part to mass layoffs and scarce hiring. The leading charges were race, gender, age, and disability discrimination.[17]

Numerous EEO laws would seem to complicate the employee recruiting/selecting process, but complying with them is simple. Everything you do, say, or ask during the selection process must pertain to **bona fide occupational qualifications (BFOQs),** requirements essential for performing a particular job. BFOQs *include* work experiences, training, education, skills, conviction records, physical attributes, and personality traits that have a direct bearing on one's ability to perform a job effectively. BFOQs *exclude* gender, age, race, religion, marital status, physical appearance, disabilities, citizenship, place of birth, ethnic group, veteran status, military records, military discharge status, and arrest records that have no bearing on one's ability to perform a job effectively.

> BFOQs are the keys to non-discriminatory hiring.

Exceptions to laws and orders are made when an employer can demonstrate that one or more normally unlawful traits are essential for a position. For example, appearance may be a BFOQ for a modeling position, religion for a pastoral position, age for performing certain tasks (serving alcohol, operating dangerous equipment), physical abilities such as eyesight and manual dexterity for pilots, physical strength for construction workers, the legal right to be employed in the United States, and English language skills for an English teacher.

> EEO violations are easy to avoid.

You can avoid EEO violations, and possible lawsuits for your employer, if you take advantage of the training your organization offers, review sources readily available in professional journals and on the Internet, and take an online course designed to help you comply with EEO laws and guidelines.[18]

They offer practical suggestions such as shaking hands with a person who is disabled, not pushing a wheelchair unless asked, identifying yourself and others involved in the interview if the applicant is blind, and using physical signals, facial expressions, and note passing if an applicant has a hearing impairment.[19] Sources help you keep up-to-date in laws and situations. For instance, a number of our students from the military reserve and active military units that were called to duty in the wars in Iraq and Afghanistan have informed us that recruiters have asked them about the type of military discharge they received. This is an unlawful question because it is not a job-related question and may delve into an applicant's medical record or disability.[20]

A few guidelines will help you avoid most EEO violations and lawsuits. First, meet the **test of job relatedness** by establishing legally defensible selection criteria. Second, be sure *all questions* are related to these selection criteria. Third, standardize the interview by asking the *same questions* for all applicants for a position. If you ask specific questions only of applicants who are female, disabled, older, or minority, you are undoubtedly asking unlawful questions. Fourth, be cautious when probing into answers because a significant number of EEO violations occur in these created-on-the-spot questions. Fifth, be cautious of innocent chit-chat during the informal parts of interviews, usually the opening and closing or the minutes following the formal interview. This is when you are most likely to ask or comment about family, marital status, ethnic background, and nonprofessional memberships. Sixth, focus questions on what an applicant *can do* rather than on what an applicant *cannot do*. Seventh, if an applicant begins to volunteer unlawful information, tactfully steer the person back to job-related areas.

> Focus on the positive, not the negative.

> Treat applicants as you would want to be treated.

Exercise #1—Testing Your Knowledge of EEO Laws

Test your knowledge of EEO laws and selection interviews by rating each question below as *lawful* (can be asked), *depends* (may be asked under certain circumstances), or *unlawful* (cannot be asked). Explain why it is lawful, unlawful, or depends.

	Lawful	Unlawful	Depends

1. I see that you are in the National Guard. What are your chances of being called to active duty?
2. How fluent are you in French?
3. Have you ever been arrested?
4. What software programs did you develop at MicroTek?
5. Do you have a legal right to work in the United States?
6. Did you lose your hand while in Iraq?
7. Are you married?
8. What professional organizations do you belong to?
9. Do you drink alcoholic beverages?
10. Which religious holidays do you observe?
11. Do you go by Charles or Charlie?
12. Would there be a problem for you to relocate to another state?
13. I noticed that you walk with a limp.
14. How soon do you plan to retire?
15. Weinberg . . . . is that Jewish?

Keep these rules in mind when recruiting.

> **Accepting or keeping unlawful information creates liability for the company even if the information was not requested.**

- Federal laws supersede state laws unless the state laws are more restrictive.
- The Equal Employment Opportunity Commission (EEOC) and the courts are not concerned with *intent* but with *effect*.
- Advertise each position where all qualified applicants have a reasonable opportunity to learn about the opening.
- Your organization is liable if unlawful information is maintained or used even if you did not ask for it.
- Do not write or take notes on the application form. Doodling on an application form may appear to be a discriminatory code.

- Three recent concerns have arisen in the law: domestic partners, same-sex marriage, and hearing as a disability. An appropriate response is, "We hire persons based on what they know and how well they can do the job, not on personal preferences or disabilities." Organizations should be prepared to enhance volumes on phones and computers.
- EEO laws generally pertain to all employers of 15 or more people.

Developing an Applicant Profile

> The profile must be a composite of BFOQs.

With EEO laws in mind, conduct a thorough analysis to develop a **competency-based applicant profile** for the position for which you are recruiting. This profile of the ideal employee typically includes specific skills, abilities, education, training, experiences, knowledge levels, personal characteristics, and interpersonal relationships that enable a person to fulfill a position with a high degree of excellence.[21] The intent is to measure all applicants against this profile to ensure that recruiting efforts meet EEO laws, are as objective as possible, encourage all interviewers to cover the same topics and traits, and eliminate (or at least minimize) the **birds of a feather syndrome** in which recruiters favor applicants who are most like themselves—traditionally this has favored male applicants.

> The profile is the ideal by which all applicants are measured.

> Is past performance the best predictor of future performance?

A rapidly growing number of organizations are employing a **behavior-based** selection technique to ensure that each interviewer asks questions that match each applicant with the applicant profile. Behavior-based interviewing rests on two interrelated principles: past behavior in specific job-related situations is the best predictor of future behavior and past performance is the best predictor of future performance. Interviewers ask interviewees to describe situations in which they have exhibited specific skills and abilities.[22] A National Institutes of Health publication states that the behavior-based interview technique "seeks to uncover how a potential employee actually did behave in a given situation; not on how he or she might behave in the future."[23] The behavior-based techniques begins with a needs and position analysis to determine which behaviors are essential for performing a particular position. Behaviors might include:

develops and implements	conducts
monitors and facilitates	establishes
applies	builds
stays current	understands and utilizes
advises and consults	recommends

Other organizations have modified this approach into a **trait-based** or **talent-based** system in which specific traits or talents rather than behaviors are identified in a position analysis. For instance, traits might include:

achievement	dependability	oral communication
ambition	initiative	people-oriented
assertiveness	listening	responsibility
competitiveness	motivation	responsiveness

Can nondomi-
nant group
applicants
match your
profile?

Regardless of the means you use, check each profile behavior or trait carefully. Is each essential for excellent job performance? Is leadership necessary for an entry-level position? Can you measure the behavior or trait? Are you expecting recruiters to act as psychologists? Will some targeted behavior or traits adversely affect your organization's diversity efforts and discriminate unintentionally? For example, traits such as competitiveness, aggressiveness, direct eye contact, forcefulness, and oral communication skills may run counter to the upbringing and culture of many nondominant groups.[24] Traits and behaviors being sought must be position-related—BFOQs—and clearly defined so that all interviewers are looking for the same ones.

Once you have developed an applicant profile, write a clear description that "encapsulates requirements for a given position." Karen O'Keefe writes, "Ultimately, the job description is the inspiration for any subsequent interview so defining the position up front will make finding the right person for the job much easier."[25] Being underprepared is the biggest mistake you can make.

Assessing What Applicants Want

Times and people are changing.

Since recruiting interviews are as much about attracting as selecting outstanding employees, it is imperative that you understand the targets of your search.

What Do Applicants Desire in a Position and Career?

Young, college-educated applicants are very different from those of 10 or 20 years ago. While they are interested in career paths and steady employment, the thought of remaining with one organization until receiving the gold watch is unrealistic to most. Applicants are more interested in strong reputations than in brand name.

While specifics on salary and benefits are of concern to young job applicants, they are no longer the keys to job and organization attraction they once were. Young applicants today are more interested in the environment and culture an organization provides, mentoring, stress training programs, tuition assistance for graduate work toward a MBA for instance, and career development opportunities.[26] They want extensive information about positions and organizations prior to interviews.

Applicants are increasingly information-driven.

The new workforce fully understands that diversity is reality. They expect and welcome working with a range of educations, ages, races, and ethnic groups. Political and geographical boundaries pose few obstacles since many have traveled, studied, or worked abroad.

What Do Applicants Desire in an Interviewer?

Applicants have clear preferences in interviewers. Their decisions are significantly affected by their satisfaction with the communication that takes place, and their attraction to the interviewer is the strongest predictor of their attraction to an organization.[27] They view the recruiter's behavior as a model of what to expect from the employer, so a negative experience may eliminate an organization from further consideration.

The recruiter is the organization in the applicant's eyes.

Applicants expect interviewers to be friendly, attentive, sensitive, warm, honest, enthusiastic, straightforward, personable, and genuinely interested in them. They do not want to be pressured or interrupted. They prefer interviewers to act and talk naturally without reading questions, being stuck to a schedule, or giving canned presentations.

Applicants want interviewers to be professionals who know what they are talking about. In one survey, 93 percent reported they like to meet with and learn the experiences of

Select recruiters with applicant traits in mind.

relatively new employees rather than veteran representatives determined to sell their organizations.[28] Nondominant group applicants (women, minorities, lower class) report they are more comfortable and communicate more openly with and feel better understood and evaluated by interviewers more like them. On the other hand, this openness and relief may turn to confusion, anger, and guarded interactions if they feel scrutinized by "one of their own."[29]

Applicants want interviewers to ask them relevant, open questions and give them opportunities for self-expression. They like interviewers to offer limited self-disclosures to avoid shifting the focus away from the applicant.[30] And applicants want detailed information that is relevant to the position and organization.

Obtaining and Reviewing Information on Applicants

With planning completed and the recruitment under way, gather as much information as possible about each applicant through application forms, resumes, letters of recommendation, objective tests, and social networking Web sites. Review this information carefully to gain a clear view of your relationship with the applicant. It is your first opportunity to determine how well this person fits the position you have open and your organization's unique culture.[31] This review reveals areas to probe during the interview, perhaps comparing oral and written answers to similar questions. Fredric Jablin and Vernon Miller discovered that employers who review applicant credentials thoroughly ask more questions, a wider variety of questions, and probe more into answers.[32] The result is a better determination of applicant fit.

Application Forms

Modify application forms to fit the applicant profile.

Design **application forms** with EEO laws and the applicant profile in mind. Avoid traditional categories that violate EEO guidelines such as gender, age, race, ethnicity, national origin, marital status, physical characteristics, arrest records, type of military discharge, and request for a picture. Include a few open-ended questions similar to ones you will ask during the interview. Be sure to provide adequate space for applicants to answer all questions thoroughly. Look for what is and is not reported on the form, how applicants respond to open-ended questions, and gaps in dates of employment and education.

Cover Letters

The cover letter is often your initial contact with an applicant. Read it carefully. Is it addressed to a specific and appropriate person in your organization, or is it an all-purpose "To whom it may concern" salutation that required no work on the applicant's part? Is the letter modeled to address your position and organization? If so, the applicant has expended energy in research and shows real interest in working for you. Does the letter reveal career goals and qualifications for the position you have open? Too often applicants send out dozens or hundreds of letters seeking interviews for positions for which they are not qualified in education or experience. Is the letter written professionally free of spelling, grammar, and punctuation errors? Susan Heathfield, a human resources specialist, admits that she may be "an old fuddy-duddy," but claims that such errors "are indicative of what you can expect from the candidate as an employee. Looking for careless, sloppy, or unconcerned? I doubt it. Your evidence is sitting before you on your desk or on your computer screen."[33]

Ryan McVay/Getty Images

■ *Review the applicant's credentials prior to the interview so you can devote full attention to the applicant during the interview.*

Resumes

A resume is usually enclosed with the cover letter or attached as an e-mail. Review it thoroughly *prior to the interview*. Patricia Buhler writes that "reading the resume for the first time in front of the applicant sends a clear message about a lack of preparedness and a lack of importance."[34] Delete unlawful information from the resume (picture, age, marital status, religious organizations, and so on) before any person involved in the recruitment effort can see it. If you keep this information (even though you did not request it), you can be held liable for possible discrimination.

Does the applicant's career objective meet the applicant profile? If so, assess how well the applicant's education, training, and experiences complement the stated career objective and the applicant profile. Healthfield identifies a number of "red flags" recruiters should look for in resumes. These include employment gaps without specific dates, lack of attention to details (such as missing words, typos, cut-and-paste errors, wrong dates), lack of customization to your job posting, overqualified for the position, and unusual employment history.[35]

Some applicants do not match their resumes.

Consider a scanner if you attract hundreds of applicants.

The cover letter is often your first opportunity to "see" an applicant.

Be aware that a significant percent of applicants cheat on their resumes. In a survey conducted by Careershop.com, 73 percent of respondents admitted that they had lied on their resumes. Lies included college degrees they did not have, inflated job titles, made up experiences, inaccurate years of work, padded dates to mask employment gaps, fictitious employers, exaggerated current salaries, inflated job responsibilities and achievements, and claims of sole responsibility for team accomplishments.[36] False claims on resumes of high military decorations or medals, including the Congressional Medal of Honor, led Congress to pass The Stolen Valor Act in 2006 to make such claims a federal crime. In a 2012 decision, the Supreme Court declared this act to be unconstitutional because it infringed on protected speech guaranteed by the First Amendment.[37] Incentives to lie on resumes include the publicity and admiration of valor exhibited in wars in Iraq and Afghanistan, long-term unemployment, being trapped in a miserable job, and not having the education, experiences, and skills increasingly required of applicants in the twenty-first century, and the Peter Principle in which people have been promoted to their levels of incompetence and now face the proverbial glass ceiling, demotion, or dismissal.

If you are hiring a number of new staff or your postings will receive a large volume of resumes, you might be wise to use appropriate applicant tracking software programs.

These will scan resumes quickly and efficiently while identifying applicants best suited to your opening and organization so your interviews are a manageable number. They can also store a large volume of resumes if you need to scan the pool again. The Capterra Web site lists 244 software programs from which you can choose the one or ones best suited to your needs.[38] Scanning software typically sorts applicants based on key words, skills, interests, and experiences. You need to load these carefully to minimize losing excellent applicants. For instance, if candidates use the word personnel or purchasing instead of human resources or procurement management, they will be eliminated from the pool. The same is true if they use abbreviations that do not match those in the system, headers the system doesn't recognize, spaces between the letters of their names for graphical purposes that cannot be accurately parsed out, and font sizes and typefaces the software finds less readable.[39] It would be wise to identify guidelines in your advertisements and recruiting literature for preparing scannable resumes so all candidates are on the same playing field.

Letters of Recommendation and References

Review **letters of recommendation** with skepticism because they are written by friends or admirers. They rarely contain negative information. Letters do reveal people an applicant knows who will write letters and add bits of information about how well the applicant fits the profile.

References are usually persons applicants choose carefully to guarantee a favorable recommendation. Calls to references, however, allow you to ask open-ended questions and probe into answers to get beyond the superficial or guarded words and phrases of a letter. Unfortunately, fears of lawsuits have led many organizations to formulate policies that allow them to give only the dates on which the applicant attended school or was employed. Organizations may require interviewers to get permission from applicants before contacting letter writers or references. Bob Ayrer recommends calling references once a short list is determined and picking out those with a medium range relationship to the applicant—"not close enough to lie for them, but close enough to have an opinion" of the applicant's worth.[40]

> Fears of lawsuits are hampering reference checks.

Standardized Tests

> Choose tests cautiously.

An ever-growing number of organizations are employing standardized tests as a supplement to reviewing credentials and conducting interviews. It's becoming a standard practice in the recruiting process. Some sources claim that the behavior-based interview that is so widely used today is more effective "when combined with employment tests, many of which are now administered online."[41] An industry has developed to meet this demand and companies claim their products deliver results, measure the fit between the job and candidate, and avoid the subjective bias of the interview. Before choosing any test for use in your hiring process, be sure it is job-related or tailored, validated on a cross-section of the population, and non-discriminatory. If a test appears to screen out one group more than another, don't use it. The EEOC has investigated complaints that some tests "have an adverse impact on black and Latino applicants," require "a proficiency in English that could discriminate against candidates who are not native speakers," and violate the Americans with Disabilities Act by requiring

> All tests must be carefully pretested.

pre-employment medical examinations or detecting conditions such as depression and paranoia.[42] There are four common types of tests used in recruiting: aptitude, personality, basic skills, and honesty/integrity.

Aptitude tests identify the abilities of a potential employee and attempt to predict how well and quickly a person is likely to learn tasks required in the position you wish to fill. General aptitude tests are sometimes called IQ or Intelligence tests. One criticism of aptitude tests is that they do not measure the all-important and elusive variable called "common sense."[43]

Personality tests assess people skills along with personality traits and personality types. Perhaps the best known personality test, the Myers-Briggs Type Indicator (MBTI), was created in 1943 and has been perfected by research and by assessing millions of applicants over the years.[44] This test and ones such as the Wilson Analogy Test and the Miller Analogies Test also identify the reasoning and critical thinking skills of applicants.

Basic skills tests measure mathematics, measurement, reading, and spelling skills. These skills are essential when individuals or teams are required to write up problems with machines or groups. Some tests pose a problem and require the applicant to write five to seven sentences describing the problem. Test monitors use a common formula to check spelling, sentence structure, verb tense, clarity, and readability.

Honesty tests are designed to assess the ethics, honesty, and integrity of applicants through paper and pencil tests or **integrity interviews.** There are a variety of pencil and paper tests on the market, and some reveal disturbing results. For example, Julia Levashina and Michael Campion, developers of the Interview Faking Behavior (IFB) Scale, discovered that 90 percent of undergraduate job applicants were guilty of "faking" (intentionally distorting answers) ranging from exaggerations, embellishments, omissions, and concealments to outright lies that included colleges attended, fictitious degrees, job titles, previous salaries, experiences, responsibilities, and employment dates.[45] Be cautious when using these tests. Researchers of the American Psychological Association reviewed over 200 studies pertaining to honesty tests and concluded that they identify individuals with a *high propensity* for stealing in the workplace, but this finding left others wondering about applicants who fall in the *moderate* to *low* ranges.[46] Robert Fitzpatrick, a Washington attorney who specializes in employment law, warns, "While they [honesty tests] might screen out some undesirable job candidates, they also screen out [like the old polygraph tests] a tremendous percentage of perfectly honest, upstanding citizens."[47] If you use honesty tests, be sure they have been thoroughly validated on a cross-section of the American population to avoid charges of discrimination.

Integrity interviews may assess the honesty or integrity of prospective employees.[48] Truthful applicants tend to acknowledge the probability of employee theft, reply without hesitation, reject the idea of leniency for dishonesty, and expect favorable test results. Interviewers have reported a strange phenomenon called *outguessing* in which applicants cheerfully admit to unethical activities because they believe they are normal and "everyone does it."[49] Two formats are used most frequently. The first consists of highly structured interviews that focus on ethics and integrity by delving into previous work experience directly related to the position available. Work-related questions result in applicants having positive feelings toward the integrity interview and the organization.

> Few tests assess common sense.

> Basic skills appear to be declining when they are more important than ever.

> Honesty tests may appear intrusive, but they are here to stay.

> Probing deeply into answers is essential in assessing honesty.

O N   T H E   W E B

Integrity interviews are becoming more common during the selection process as employers attempt to assess the integrity of potential employees in an age when honesty often seems the exception rather than the norm. Many employers and researchers are raising serious questions about the accuracy and value of honesty tests in the employment selection setting. Search the Internet for discussions of the uses and concerns raised by written and oral honesty tests. These sources should get you started on your search: Infoseek (http://www.infoseek.com), PsycInfo (http://www.psycinfo.com), The Monster Board (http://www.monster.com/), CareerBuilder (http://www.careerbuilder.com/), and PsychLit (http://www.psychlit.com/).

Focus on real or hypothetical work situations.

Second, if previous work experience is unavailable, the interviewer poses situational questions using specific dimensions of ethical and honest behavior. Donna Pawlowski and John Hollwitz have developed a structured situational interview "based on the assumption that intentions predict behaviors."[50] Interviewers ask interviewees to respond to hypothetical scenarios and employ a 5-point scale with an agreed upon definition of the dimension. Other dimensions are relationship manipulation, interpersonal deception (lying), security violation (giving out trade secrets), and sexual harassment (telling dirty jokes or displaying nude pictures).

Social Media

Probe into social media with caution.

A significant percentage of applicants use blogs and Web sites such as MySpace and Facebook that reveal a great deal about them. Much of this information has nothing to do with their qualifications for a position with organizations, but it may tell you a great deal about how well they would fit into your organizational culture, including their motivations, work habits, attitudes, and future plans. It's easy to access this information, and some employers routinely ask applicants for their social networking passwords. Be careful. Congress tried unsuccessfully in 2012 to pass legislation that would make it illegal for employers to ask for passwords. Some states are now considering their own legislation. Tread lightly. Snooping into Web sites is likely to reveal personal characteristics such as age, race, gender, disabilities, marital status, and sexual orientation that violate EEO laws. Brian Libby suggests that "you ask in advance if the candidate has any online presence they'd like you to check out."[51]

Conducting the Interview

Once you have obtained and reviewed extensive information on applicants, you are ready to conduct the interview.

The Atmosphere and Setting

Establish an environment that is conducive to sharing information as well as feelings, attitudes, and motivations. Ideally, you should conduct the recruiting interview in a comfortable, quiet, and private location that eliminates or minimizes noise and interruptions. Choose seating that maximizes interpersonal communication. Close the door and turn off telephones, cell phones, computers, and beepers. In reality, however, you may not have access to such a quiet location. The authors have conducted recruiting interviews in hotel lobbies, on hotel steps, in hotel hallways, in restaurants and bars, at open houses in ballrooms, and on park benches at outdoor career and job fairs. Make the best with what you are dealt with.

Approach each interview as if it is your day's top priority. Be positive and attentive because it may be a major event in the applicant's life, even if it is merely routine for you and your sixth interview of the day, and it plays a critical role in attracting and selecting quality employees. Patricia Buhler writes: "The interview is a two-way street. While the interviewer is screening applicants for fit with the organization and position, the applicant is 'interviewing' the company for fit as well. The interview, then, should also be viewed as a public relations tool." She warns that "Bad publicity travels quickly."[52] Applicants do not distinguish you from your organization. Quality applicants are more likely to accept offers if they perceive you to be a good representative of your organization. Be open and honest. This is what you demand of applicants. Give a realistic picture of the position and organization. Practice a **conscious transparency** in which you share information with applicants, explain the purpose of questions, and promote dialogue through a supportive climate.[53]

> The atmosphere may make or break an interview.

The Interview Parties

The recruiting interview has traditionally involved two persons, the recruiter and the applicant. A variation of this is the **chain format** in which one recruiter may converse with an applicant for 15 or 20 minutes, perhaps developing a general impression of the applicant's background, and then passes the applicant along to a second recruiter who probes into specific job skills. A third recruiter may then take over and assess the applicant's technical knowledge. The chain format is common in "plant" or "on site" and determinate interviews that follow the screening process. A series of interviews may take more than a day, including lunch and dinner with additional members of the organization.

Some organizations are experimenting with a **team, panel, or board** of two to five recruiters who interview an applicant at the same time. Panel members, for instance, may divide up an applicant's application and resume with one member asking about work experiences, a second asking about education and training, a third asking about technical knowledge, and a fourth asking about job-related skills. Research indicates that a panel is more effective in predicting job performance than the one-on-one interviews, but recruiters and applicants prefer the traditional approach.[54] A panel or team seems advisable when conducting cross-cultural interviews to eliminate bias and assure communication and understanding.

> Employers are experimenting with a variety of formats.

Group interviews that involve several members of an organizational sub-set such as faculty of an academic department, public relations staff from a medical center, or IT specialists in a company are common when an applicant appears for a determinate set of interviews on what is called a "plant trip." This approach gives a wide variety of potential colleagues an opportunity to ask questions and listen to answers before they may have to vote on a hiring decision. They all hear the same answers to the same key questions and may reduce the problem of different recruiters claiming that they received or interpreted answers quite differently in their one-on-one contacts.

A **seminar** format in which one or more recruiters interview several applicants at the same time takes less time than single interviews, enables an organization to see several applicants replying and reacting to the same questions at the same time, and may provide valuable insights into how applicants might work with one another as a team. If conducted with skill, applicants will not see the interview as a competition but as an opportunity to build upon others' comments while revealing their qualifications and experiences. If you are looking for leaders, an applicant who is overwhelmed by this format and remains generally silent may not be a good fit.

Opening the Interview

Involve the applicant in the opening.

The opening is a critical part of each recruiting interview. It sets the tone for the interview and creates the all-important first impression of you and your organization.

Establishing Rapport

Begin the interview by greeting the applicant by name in a warm, friendly voice and with a firm but not crushing handshake to create **rapport.** Introduce yourself and your position with the organization. Do not ask the applicant to call you by your first name if this is a first interview because few applicants will feel comfortable doing so. Rapport building is particularly important in cross-cultural interviews. Establish a relationship "that is based on trust, understanding, and acceptance" from the first moments of the interview, and bear in mind "that speaking the same language does mean sharing the same culture."[55]

Do not delay the inevitable.

Engage in a bit of small talk about a noncontroversial issue, but do not prolong casual conversation or fall into overworn questions such as "What do you think of this weather?" or "How was your trip?" that elicit few meaningful responses and add nothing to rapport with the applicant. Prolonged idle chatting may heighten tension by creating anxiety and suspense.

Orientation

Proceed to the orientation phase of the opening in which you tell the applicant how the interview will proceed. Traditionally this has meant recruiters asking questions, recruiters providing information on the position and organization, and then applicants asking questions.

Be systematic and creative.

Giving information first delays active involvement of the applicant and may communicate that the recruiter intends to dominate the interview. You might tell the applicant how long the interview will take and approximately how long you will devote to each part. If the interview is taking place during an on-site or plant trip, provide the applicant with an agenda for the visit and the names and positions of people who will be involved in the selection process.

Share control with the applicant.

While the traditional approach has been interviewer-controlled, recruiters are recommending an interviewee-controlled approach. For instance, Bob Ayrer, who specializes in hiring salespersons, recommends an extensive orientation period. "At this point SHUT UP!" he writes. "Allow the prospective salesperson to take control (that is what you are hiring them to do in the field, isn't it?)."[56]

The Opening Question

The **opening question** is the transition to the body of the interview. This open-ended, easy-to-answer first question gets the applicant talking about a familiar subject (education, experiences, background, recent internship). It sets the tone for the interview—the applicant talking and the recruiter listening and observing.

> Begin with an open question, but not too open.

Plan the opening question carefully, and avoid always starting with the same question. Adapt it to what you have learned in previewing information. The most common opening question, "Tell me about yourself," is so open that applicants often do not know where to begin or how much information to give. Do they start with birth, grade school, high school, college, or current/recent positions? Do they talk about hobbies, education, work experiences, major events? This highly open, generic question neither relaxes the applicant nor gets the applicant talking about meaningful subjects. A better opening question is "Tell me about your duties (or responsibilities) in your current position."

> Do not set up the applicant for an early failure.

Do not put the applicant on the spot too early because interviewers tend to put more weight on negative information, and the earlier it comes in the interview, the more devastating it may be. Pose an easy-to-answer, reasonably open question to get the applicant talking and ready to answer more difficult questions.

The Body of the Interview

> Unstructured interviews do not recruit top-quality applicants.

Sources differ on how structured the body of the recruiting interview ought to be, but research indicates that the validity of recruiting highly qualified applicants is most successful when organizations utilize highly structured formats.[57] The old "seat of the pants," "off the top of the head," and "my gut tells me" interviews lead to numerous hazards. An unstructured, rambling, unfocused interview tells the interviewer almost nothing about job candidates.[58] For instance, interviewers talk more than applicants in unstructured interviews rather than the 80 percent for applicants to 20 percent for recruiters rule of thumb. Interviewers tend to make their decisions within the first three to four minutes, long before answers to critical and thought-provoking questions. They cover factual and biographical information that is readily available on application forms and resumes, are more susceptible to stereotyping and biases, and more likely to ask questions that violate EEO laws. Many highly qualified applicants do not make good first impressions, but they will "grow on you" as they answer questions about experiences and goals, reveal technical knowledge and awareness of your organization's specific needs and future plans, and exhibit how they are good fits for your organizational culture.

Highly Structured Interviews

> Highly structured interviews are more reliable but less flexible and adaptable.

A growing number of recruiters advocate highly scheduled interviews in which all questions are prepared and tested ahead of time and posed to each applicant without variation. Highly structured interviews are more reliable because all applicants are asked the same or very similar questions and recruiters must pay close attention throughout the interview instead of the first few minutes. Organizations may employ a highly structured interview centered on specific traits in the applicant profile (interpersonal skills, computer expertise, team experience) or an interview guide (can the person do the job, will the person do the job, will the person fit into the organization).

Fit with the position and organization is critical because well-qualified applicants who do not match the organization's culture result in poor performance and high turnover rate. Some interviews cover topics such as company environment, management influence, and co-workers.

Behavior-based methods focus on job-related skills.

Behavior-based recruiting is very common. An organization may develop a highly structured interview that provides for skillful patterning and selecting of questions, recording of responses, and rating of applicants on behaviorally defined dimensions. In the following example, the interviewer employs a five-point scale to rate answers according to the degree to which it exhibits or gives information about one or more behaviors: 5 = strongly present and 1 = minimally present.

Rating	Behavior	Question
_____	Initiative	Give me an example of when you have resolved conflicts between employees.
_____	Energy	How many times have you done this?
_____	General intelligence	What was the outcome?
_____	Decisiveness	How did you feel about the results you got?
_____	Adaptability	When faced with intransigence, what did you do?

Build in insightful secondary questions.

While listening to the answer to the first question, look for the kinds of conflicts the applicant has addressed and their complexity. Preplanned probing questions probe deeper into the experience, including methods used, and success the applicant had in resolving conflicts. The answer may reveal a number of other characteristics such as communication ability, sensitivity, fairness, and ability to follow prescribed procedures.

While the highly scheduled interview may lessen the influence of stereotypes, recruiter-applicant dissimilarity, and the possibility of lawsuits for EEO violations, it has shortcomings:[59] It enhances recruiter control and may be detrimental to underrepresented group members. The applicant may have little opportunity to introduce job-related information. Recruiters have little opportunity to adapt to specific applicants, to probe into answers, or to share information when thought necessary. The organization dominates what should be a mutual activity between recruiter and candidate.

Place the applicant in realistic work settings.

William Kirkwood and Steven Ralston argue that the highly structured interview bears little resemblance to situations applicants will face on the job. Thus, the interviewee is unable to demonstrate and the recruiter is unable to observe the applicant's skills in realistic settings.[60] Any process that stifles the recruiter's ability to probe into answers is likely to result in fewer insights into the applicant as a person and potential employee. We recommend a moderately scheduled interview that allows both parties the flexibility necessary for meaningful interactions and a maximum of self-disclosure in a real-life setting.

Question Sequences

Select one or more **question sequences** appropriate for the interview and the applicant; normally this means funnel, inverted funnel, or tunnel sequences. Interviewers

Get the applicant talking as quickly as possible.

tend to use the inverted funnel sequence by asking closed primary questions during the early minutes of the interview and open-ended probing questions in the later minutes.[61] The inverted sequence enables recruiters to test applicants and then switch to a funnel sequence with applicants they perceive to be most qualified. Since applicants tend to give short answers to closed questions while they feel out the interviewer and longer answers and more information to open questions, interviewers may make snap judgments within the first few minutes of interviews based on very little information. Also, the best way to relax an applicant is to get the person talking. Begin with a funnel or tunnel sequence to get the interviewee talking, relaxed, and giving maximum information.

Closing the Interview

The closing must sustain the positive tone of the interview.

If you are conducting **screening interviews** at job fairs, campus career centers, conferences, or on site, you are unlikely to terminate further consideration of applicants. It is a fishing expedition to decide on the quality of the applicant pool and who tends to stand out among a number of interviewees. You will determine later whether to have additional interviews. Your closing will be a variation of the following example:

> Jackie, I've enjoyed talking with you this morning. (pause to let the applicant talk) We are recruiting on several midwestern campuses for this position at our Kansas City facility. We plan to invite four or five candidates to Kansas City for additional interviews within a few weeks. You will be hearing from us within the next 10 days about whether you will be invited for these interviews. Do you have any final questions for me? (pause to let the applicant talk) If you need to contact me or you have additional questions, here is my card with my cell phone and office telephone numbers and e-mail address.

Do not encourage or discourage applicants needlessly.

If you are conducting **determinate interviews** that follow up on one or more screening interviews, then your decision may be whether or not to terminate further consideration. You are unlikely to indicate this during the interview however. Be honest and candid with applicants. If you have many excellent applicants for a position, do not give each the impression that he or she is at the top of the list.

Watch what you do, say, and ask following the formal closing as you walk with the person to the door or to the parking lot, or escort the person to meet another member of your organization. These informal times can lead to EEO violations. Do not do or say anything that adversely affects the relationship you have developed carefully during the interview.

Make decisions and notify all applicants as soon as possible.

Follow up on all prospects. You or your representative should sign all letters and phrase each to give them a personal touch. When rejecting applicants, do not "string them along" needlessly or give them false hope. Let them down gently, but do not try to give explanations that only raise questions and arguments. Recruiters use a variation of "We had a large number of excellent applicants" and "We tried to pick the one who seemed to be the best fit for this position." Strive to maintain feelings of goodwill toward your organization by communicating that you gave each applicant an equal chance of being selected.

Asking Questions

Questions are your primary tools for obtaining information, assessing how well the applicant matches the applicant profile, determining fit with your organization, and discovering what the applicant knows about the position and organization.

Keep your questions open-ended.

Use open-ended, neutral, insightful, and job-related questions. Open-ended questions encourage applicants to talk while you listen, observe, and formulate effective probing questions. Applicants give longer answers to open-ended questions and feel greater satisfaction with interviews that are dominated by open-ended primary and probing questions.[62]

Common Question Pitfalls

Be on guard for pitfalls in primary and probing questions.

Recruiters create or rephrase questions to detect relevant behaviors and probe for details, clarity, and implied meanings. This spontaneity makes the interview a lively and insightful conversation but makes it susceptible to common question pitfalls. In addition to question pitfalls discussed in Chapters 3 and 5 (bipolar trap, open-to-closed switch, double-barreled inquisition, leading push, guessing game, yes/no response, curious probe, quiz show, don't ask, don't tell), there are three particularly relevant to the recruiting interview.

Evaluative responses will lead to safe, superficial answers.

1. *The evaluative response:* The interviewer expresses judgmental feelings about an answer that may bias or skew the next response.

    Boy, I'll bet you regret that decision.
    That wasn't a good reason to quit a job, was it?
    That was a mistake, wasn't it?

2. *The EEO violation:* The interviewer asks an unlawful question.

    How often do you attend church?
    How does your prosthetic leg hamper you in driving long distances?
    What will you do if your husband gets transferred?

Do not ask for information you already have.

3. *The resume or application form question:* The interviewer asks a question that is already answered on the resume or application form.

    Where did you get your degree in criminology?
    Have you studied abroad?
    What internships have you had?

Traditional Questions

The following are **traditional recruiter questions** that avoid pitfalls and gather important job-related information.

- Interest in the organization

    Why would you like to work for us?
    What have you read about our organization?
    What do you know about our products and services?

- Work-related (general)

  Tell me about the position that has given you the most satisfaction.
  How have your previous work experiences prepared you for this position?
  What did you do that was innovative in your last position?

- Work-related (specific)

  Describe a typical strategy you would use to motivate people.
  What criteria do you use when assigning work to others?
  How do you follow up on work assigned to subordinates?

- Teams and teamwork

  How do you feel when your compensation is based in part on team results?
  What does the word *teamwork* mean to you?
  How would you feel about working on cross-functional teams?

- Education and training

  Tell me about the computer programs you have used.
  How has your education prepared you for this position?
  If you had your education to do over, what would you do differently?

- Career paths and goals

  If you join us, what would you like to be doing five years from now?
  How do you feel about the way your career has gone so far?
  What are you doing to prepare yourself for advancement?

- Performance

  What do you believe are the most important performance criteria for a project
    engineer?
  All of us have pluses and minuses in our performance. What are some of your
    pluses (minuses)?
  How do you make difficult decisions?

- Salary and benefits

  What are your salary expectations?
  Which fringe benefits are most important to you?
  How does our salary range compare to your last position?

- Career field

  What do you think is the greatest challenge facing your field?
  What do you think will be the next major breakthrough in your field?
  How do you feel about environmental regulations in your field?

The trend is toward on-the-job questions.

Nontraditional Questions

When recruiters came to realize that most traditional questions fail to assess how an applicant has dealt effectively with work-related situations, they began to develop and implement a variety of new "on-the-job" question strategies. These question strategies also enable interviewers to counter impression management tactics used by nearly all applicants such as self-promotion (designed "to evoke attributions of competence") and ingratiation (designed "to evoke interpersonal liking and attraction"). Both of these tactics have proven to be "positively related to interviewer evaluations."[63]

Behavior-Based Questions

Interviewers conducting behavioral-based interviews ask questions about past experiences in which applicants have handled situations that are related to the position. For instance, recruiters may ask:[64]

- Tell me about an idea of yours that was implemented primarily through your efforts.
  How did you handle a past situation when the rules were changed at the last minute?
- Tell me about your most difficult relationship with a team member. How did you handle it?
- Describe a time when you experienced a setback in a class, in a sport, or on the job. How did you handle it?
- Tell me about a situation in which you had to handle an irate customer or client.
- Give me an example of how you sold an unpopular idea to fellow workers.

Critical Incident Questions

In **critical incident questions,** recruiters select actual incidents that are occurring or have occurred on the job within their organizations and ask applicants how they would handle or would have handled such incidents. For instance:

> **Critical incident questions assess how applicants would handle real work situations.**

- We are experiencing a growing problem of waste in our milling operation. How would you handle this if we hired you?
- Last year there was a lot of strife among our sales staff. If you had been with us, what would you have done?
- Like many firms, we are experiencing a decline in sales of our traditional products. What would you suggest we do about it?
- We have traditionally faced difficulties in recruiting a diverse staff because most of our plants are located in small cities in rural areas of the west. How would you suggest we improve our recruiting efforts? . . .

Hypothetical Questions

Hypothetical questions are often criticized because they have posed unrealistic, even silly situations such as, "How would you go about counting all of the golf balls in the United States?"[65] Hypothetical questions, like critical incident questions, can be valuable tools in the recruiting interview. Justin Menkes writes that questions such as these are useful because they "raise questions and situations that the candidate has never confronted" and for which the candidate cannot be prepared in advance.[66] In hypothetical questions, a recruiter creates highly realistic but hypothetical situations and asks applicants how they would handle each.

Suppose you are suspicious that some workers are doctoring their time cards. What
would you do?

If your company suddenly announced the closing of your facility by January 1, what
would you do?

If a female employee came to you claiming sexual harassment, how would you
handle it?

A Case Approach

> **A case approach is the most realistic on-the-job question format.**

In a case approach, an applicant is placed into a carefully crafted situation that may
take hours to study and resolve. It could be a personnel, management, design, or production problem. Some are elaborate simulations that require role playing and may
involve several people, including other applicants.

Probing Questions

No matter how well you phrase a traditional, behavior-based, critical incident, or hypothetical question, it is seldom enough to accept an initial response and move on to your
next primary question. Observe, listen carefully to what *is* and *is not* said, and then
probe. Silent and nudging probes may be effective because applicants feel less threatened and more respected when interviewers respond with simple verbal and nonverbal
signals that do not interrupt them. Often you need to "drill down" for specifics with
carefully phrased probing questions to explore suggestions and implications, clarify
meanings, force applicants to move beyond safe, superficial Level 1 answers to get at
feelings, motivations, preferences, knowledge, and expertise. Use all available questioning tools to get the information needed to select the best applicants.

> **Probing questions produce insights.**

Dig beneath the surface of rehearsed and planned answers to locate the real person
who might work for you. Behavior-based questions, not to mention traditional questions, have been around long enough for applicants to figure out what recruiters are
looking for and what they want to hear. Applicants have career counselors, Web sites,
seminars, and experienced persons in their networks that literally coach them on how
best to respond to a wide variety of questions. **Remember there are always two applicants in each interview, the real and the make-believe.** Your task is to determine
how much of what you see and hear is a façade and how much is genuine. For instance,
when MBAs were asked to tell about a time when they faced a challenge, six gave identical answers about serving on a fund-raising committee. Later investigation revealed
that none of the six had been on such a committee.[67]

Some recruiters have become so concerned with dishonest and rehearsed answers
to behavioral-based questions that they have resorted to weird questions such as the following for which they hope applicants will have to give honest answers: "If you were
a character in fiction, who would you be?" "If you were a salad, what kind of dressing
would you be?" "If you were a fruit, what kind of fruit would you be?" If we ignore the
total irrelevance of such questions to any job, it's only a matter of time before applicants will soon hear about them and prepare ready-made answers. A better strategy is to
probe into answers to behavior-based and other "on-the-job" types of questions. When
one of the authors asked Dana Olen, a recruiter for Stryker (a Fortune 500 company
that employs a behaviorally based interviewing approach), what she would do if an

applicant provided a suspicious answer to a behavior-based question, perhaps one that seemed too good to be true, she immediately provided six probing questions she might ask. These included "Who did you work with on this project?" If a company-sponsored project: "What company was this?" and "How did that company's structure integrate into the project?" If a class project: "Describe this class for me." "How many people were you working with?"

Unfortunately, extensive probing is not without pitfalls. In their studies of applicant faking behavior, Levashina and Campion discovered that "follow-up questioning increased faking in both situational and past behavioral structured interviews." During informal debriefing, participants revealed that standardized follow-up questions (e.g., "Could you please elaborate?") were perceived as cues signaling that the requested information was important for the interviewer and prompting more detailed answers that encouraged respondents to fake.[68] Before you rethink the advisability of probing into answers, these researchers also discovered that "past behavioral interviews with no follow-up questioning were the most resilient to faking." The solution seems to be more specific probing questions such as those suggested by Olen rather than simply "Tell me more." The goals of probing are to get detailed information on an applicant's experiences and abilities while determining the truthfulness of replies. Be prepared to react quickly if your probing starts to elicit information that may violate EEO laws. Rochelle Kaplan relates an incident in which an applicant replied to a question about the greatest challenge in undergraduate school by stating, "Coming out as a gay male to my friends and family."[69] Other applicants have delved into politics and religion.

Closing Thoughts on Use of Questions

All on-the-job questions (behavior-based, critical incident, hypothetical, case) are based on the belief that the best way to assess ability to perform a job is to observe the applicant doing the job. Many applicants can tell you about the theories and principles they would use, but they are unable to put these theories and principles into practice. It is one thing to say how you might confront a hostile employee but quite another to do it.

Remember two additional factors when asking on-the-job questions. First, experienced applicants have a wealth of examples from which to draw, while soon-to-be college graduates and those with little experience have few. Try to provide a level playing field when you are interested in a variety of levels of experience. Second, behavioral, critical incident, and hypothetical questions favor those who can tell good stories in positive and likeable manners. They may measure social skills and storytelling rather than intelligence and ability to perform well on the job.[70]

Avoid becoming a cheerleader, as many of our student interviewers tend to do, by saying "Great!" "Very good" or "Awesome!" after every answer. Applicants will come to expect the praise and become concerned if it stops. Maintain a pleasant, supportive poker face that never reveals whether you believe an answer is very good, negative, or outrageous.

Giving Information

Giving information before and during the interview is a major determinant of applicant satisfaction. Before you begin to give information, however, ask two important transition questions: *What do you know about this position? What do you know about our organization?"* Answers to these questions show, first, how much homework the applicant has done, revealing the applicant's level of interest and work ethic. Second, they tell you what the applicant already knows about the position and organization so you can begin where the person's knowledge leaves off. This prevents you from giving information the applicant already has or is readily available on your Web site.

Give adequate information to facilitate the **matching process** between the organization and the applicant. Information about your organization's reputation, organizational environment, the position, typical work day, and advancement opportunities are the most important factors in acceptance of job offers. You may compare your organization to your competitors', but do not be negative.

Sell the advantages of your position and organization. Avoid exaggerating, intentionally hiding negative aspects of the position or organization, or inflating applicant expectations. These practices result in high rates of employee dissatisfaction and turnover. Avoid gossip. Do not talk too much about yourself, a common turn-off in selection interviews.

While you want to inform applicants thoroughly, your information giving must not dominate the interview. Studies have found that applicants speak for only 10 minutes in a typical 30-minute screening interview.[71] Reverse this figure. You will learn more about the applicant by listening than by talking. Review the guidelines for information giving in Chapter 12 and follow these suggestions.

> **Minimize "you" in the interview.**

> **Rule #1: Keep your ears open and your mouth shut.**

- Practice good communication skills because applicants may judge the "authenticity" of information by how it is communicated verbally and nonverbally.

- Encourage applicants to ask questions about information you are giving so you know it is being communicated accurately and effectively.

- Do not overload applicants with information.

- Organize your information systematically and logically.

Evaluating the Interview

> **Record your impressions and reactions immediately.**

Take notes during interviews because note-taking increases recall and judgment accuracy.[72] Review your thoughts and notes carefully, and then record your reactions to each applicant as soon as possible. Build in time between interviews for this purpose. Organizations may provide recruiters with standardized evaluation forms to match applicants with the applicant profile for each position.

The **interview evaluation** often consists of: a set of standardized questions and space for comments. See the sample interview evaluation form in Figure 7.1. The standardized part should consist of bona fide occupational qualifications for each position that enable you to determine how well the applicant matches these qualifications. Focus on the applicant's qualifications, not irrelevant factors. A study at the University of North Texas revealed that recruiters often chose applicants on the basis of voices and regional accents. Those identified with specific regions by accent were less likely to be chosen for "high profile jobs" and more likely to be assigned, if hired, to lower-skilled and lower-contact positions.[73]

Figure 7.1   *Interview Evaluation Report*

Candidate Evaluation Report

Interviewer _____   Date _____

Candidate _____   Position _____

Rating Scale: 5 = Exceptional, 4 = Above Average, 3 = Average, 2 = Below Average,
1 = Unsatisfactory

Education/Training	5	4	3	2	1
Comments:					
Work Experiences	5	4	3	2	1
Comments:					
Interpersonal Skills	5	4	3	2	1
Comments:					
Technical Skills	5	4	3	2	1
Comments:					
Motivation/Initiative	5	4	3	2	1
Comments:					
Working with Others/Teams	5	4	3	2	1
Comments:					
Knowledge of the Company	5	4	3	2	1
Comments:					
Interest in the Company	5	4	3	2	1
Comments:					

The following are open-ended questions you might address in your postinterview evaluation:

- What are the applicant's strengths for this position?
- What are the applicant's weaknesses for this position?
- How does this applicant compare to other applicants for this position?
- What makes this applicant a good or poor fit with our organization?

Assess the performance of both interview parties.

Use the evaluation stage to assess your interviewing skills and performance. How successful was I at creating an informal and relaxed atmosphere that encouraged the applicant to speak openly and freely? How effectively did I listen and observe and then probe insightfully into answers? How well did I provide information on the position and organization not readily available to the applicant in other sources? Did I reserve adequate time for the applicant to ask questions, and did I respond effectively to these questions?

How successful was I at closing the interview positively and leaving a good impression of the process and organization?

Summary

The recruiting interview can be an effective means of selecting employees, but it takes preparation that includes knowledge of state and federal EEO laws, an applicant profile, review of information on applicants, and developing a carefully structured interview. Preparation must be followed by a thoroughly professional interview that includes an effective opening, skillful questioning, probing into answers, thorough information giving, honest and detailed answers to questions, and an effective closing. You must practice communication skills that include language selection, nonverbal communication (silence, voice, eye contact, facial expressions, posture, and gestures), listening, and empathy.

When the interview is concluded, conduct evaluations of the applicant and yourself. The first focuses on the applicant's suitability and fit and the second on your effectiveness as recruiter and evaluator.

Key Terms and Concepts

The online learning center for this text features FLASH CARDS and CROSSWORD PUZZLES for studying based on these terms and concepts.

Basic skills tests
Behavior-based
    selection
Birds of a feather
    syndrome
Board interview
Bona fide occupational
    qualification (BFOQ)

Career fairs
Chain format
Competency-based
    applicant profile
Conscious transparency
Cover letters
Critical incident questions
EEO laws

Honesty tests
Integrity interviews
Interview evaluation
Job fairs
Matching process
Scanning softare
Talent-based selection
Trait-based selection

A Recruiting Interview for Review and Analysis

Trent Douglas is applying for an entry-level management position with TBD Electronics that produces parts for several automobile manufacturers. Elizabeth Prohosky, a recent college graduate, is a college recruiter for TBD and is spending the week interviewing management, supervision, and organizational communication majors at California State University at Long Beach.

How satisfactory are the rapport and orientation stages of the opening? How well do the recruiter's questions meet EEO guidelines and avoid common question pitfalls? How effectively does the recruiter *probe into* and *react to* answers? What evidence is there that the employer has an ideal applicant profile in mind? How adequate is the employer's information giving? Does the employer control the interview too much, too little, or about right? How satisfactory is the closing?

1. **Recruiter:** Hi! I'm Elizabeth Prohosky from TBD Electronics.

2. **Applicant:** Hi. I'm Trent Douglas.

3. **Recruiter:** I'm glad we could meet this afternoon. Please call me Liz.

4. **Applicant:** Uh, okay.

5. **Recruiter:** How's your semester?

6. **Applicant:** It's been a very difficult semester.

7. **Recruiter:** Uh huh. Well, let's get to it. I'm going to ask you some questions to see how you fit the position we have open in management at TBD; then I will tell you a little bit about TBD; and finally, I'll answer a few questions if you have any. Okay?

8. **Applicant:** Certainly. I've really been looking forward to this interview with TBD.

9. **Recruiter:** Great. First, why did you switch from Cal. State at Fullerton to Cal. State at Long Beach after your first year?

10. **Applicant:** Well, to be honest, it was because my girlfriend was at Long Beach.

11. **Recruiter:** I see. That was the *only* reason for switching universities?

12. **Applicant:** That was the clincher, but I did look into the management program at Long Beach and it looked pretty good, about the same as Fullerton.

13. **Recruiter:** That's good. How people-oriented are you?

14. **Applicant:** That's one of my strong suits. I've always been people-oriented, joined lots of clubs, been active in my fraternity, served as social secretary for the Future Manager's Club, things like that, you know.

15. **Recruiter:** Good. Good. What experience have you had working on teams?

16. **Applicant:** Well, I have been a three-year member of the speech team and, during my second year, I played on the rugby team. Of course, we work as teams in most of my management courses, particularly strategic management courses. I just seem to gravitate to teams.

17. **Recruiter:** Awesome. How about internships, co-ops, and study abroad experiences?

18. **Applicant:** As I put on my resume, I had an internship at a TRW plant back home that made gears for cars and trucks. I spent part of a summer break touring Mexico.

19. **Recruiter:** Very good. Tell me about one of the most difficult problem-solving situations you have been involved with.

20. **Applicant:** Let's see. I guess I would pick a time when the speech team coach asked me to assign research tasks to each team member with the idea that we would put all of this research together so we could prepare for upcoming extemporaneous speaking contests. Two of the team members were not doing their assignments and this was making it impossible to prepare a final resource book.

21. **Recruiter:** Wow. What did you do?

22. **Applicant:** I got all of us together in the Union café and said it was to all of our advantages to get the research completed and compiled because it would help or hurt all of us in future tournaments. We got the job done.

23. **Recruiter:** How did your coach react to your involvement in this situation?

24. **Applicant:** He didn't say much.

25. **Recruiter:** Uh huh. If you were doing this again, what would you do differently?

26. **Applicant:** I've thought about that a ton. I think I would try to meet first with the slackers before involving all of the team.

27. **Recruiter:** Uh huh.

28. **Applicant:** Some of the people were embarrassed and took my criticism personally. It did affect our relationship for the rest of the year.

29. **Recruiter:** I'm sure it did. By the way, where was your next speech tournament?

30. **Applicant:** Let me think. I believe it was at San Diego State . . . or maybe at Concordia. We did okay; I remember that.

31. **Recruiter:** What was the focus of your research?

32. **Applicant:** I think it was . . . uh, it had something to do with controlling investment firms, something like that.

33. **Recruiter:** I see. Tell me, Trent, what interests you most in a management position with TBD Electronics.

34. **Applicant:** Well, I like your locations in the West and I've always been interested in cars and in the auto industry.

35. **Recruiter:** So, Trent, why should we hire you over other applicants?

36. **Applicant:** That's a tricky question. First, I have a good GPA in management from a strong management program. Second, I have a ton of experience working with people. And, third, I'm really interested in the auto industry.

37. **Recruiter:** Of course. By the way, what is your overall GPA?

38. **Applicant:** My GPA in management courses is a 2.9 on a 4.0 scale.

39. **Recruiter:** And what about your overall GPA?

40. **Applicant:** It's around a 2.1.

41. **Recruiter:** Okay. What do you know about TBD Electronics?

42. **Applicant:** Let's see. I know you have plants in Denver, Boise, and Seattle—and some others—that make electronic parts for several auto manufactures, both foreign and domestic.

43. **Recruiter:** (Silence.)

44. **Applicant:** I think I read somewhere that TBD started out making electronics for the military, maybe the Army.

45. **Recruiter:** Good guess. Actually we started out making electronics for the Navy and some small aircraft manufacturers. In 1994 we began to switch to the auto industry, focusing on antilock braking and traction control systems. Ford and GM were our first auto customers, and we now work with Chrysler, Honda, Kia, and Hyundai. We have developed revolutionary new ignition and GPS systems. We are headquartered in San Diego because of our early Navy connection. We have some time left for a question or two.

46. **Applicant:** How has the value of TBD stock fared in the economic downturn?

47. **Recruiter:** Like most stock of companies dealing with the auto industry, we took a hit early on, particularly when GM made major cuts and Chrysler essentially shut down for a few months. We're doing okay now.

48. **Applicant:** What is your research focusing on today?

49. **Recruiter:** We are working very hard on early warning systems that would alert drivers when they are closing in on another vehicle or another vehicle is closing in on them from the side or rear.

50. **Applicant:** That sounds great.

51. **Recruiter:** Well, Trent, our time's about up. It's been good talking to you. We will get back to you within two weeks. If you've not heard from us by then, you can e-mail me at the address on this card.

52. **Applicant:** I'm really looking forward to hearing from you. Thanks for the interview.

53. **Recruiter:** (shakes hand) I'm glad to hear that and good luck with your job search.

Recruiting Role-Playing Cases

Aircraft Maintenance Supervisor

You are one of three chief aircraft maintenance supervisors for a major airline conducting screening interviews at a career fair in Chicago. You are seeking to fill two aircraft maintenance supervisor positions for your national maintenance facility in Denver. Your specific targets are recent graduates of maintenance programs in schools of technology at major universities and military personnel with experience in maintaining aircraft like or similar to those used by your airline. Hands-on experience with aircraft and previous supervisory experience are essential.

A Sales Position

Your home improvement firm is seeking salespersons to call on homeowners who have expressed an interest in purchasing new doors, windows, or siding when responding to cold calls from a calling center. The positions require experience in sales, good interpersonal skills, and knowledge of building materials and remodeling methods and problems. Although your firm handles two well-known manufacturers of doors, windows, and siding, candidates must have the ability to become thoroughly familiar with several manufacturers to respond adequately to customers' questions and concerns. A bachelor's degree or two-year degree in building construction technology is preferred, but highly experienced candidates will be considered.

A Sportscaster

You are the new owner-manager of radio station WPRZ in a city of 75,000 people. The station has changed owners a number of times during the past 15 years, and a new format has come with each new owner: classic rock, syndicated talk shows, a mixture of everything, and most recently country and western. You want to maintain the current format (country and western) because you feel that it fits the community best, but you also want to hire a sportscaster who would focus on local college and high school teams and begin some live broadcasting for football and basketball games. You want to hire a first-rate, on-air sportscaster who can establish good relations with the community, the college, and the schools in the city and county. You face two problems: you have limited funds for salary and benefits and many applicants will see your city and station as "out in the sticks."

Student Activities

1. Many recruiters believe that incentive is critical to a good hire. Contact your campus career center and ask permission to pose two questions to a dozen recruiters: What questions do you ask that pertain to incentive? How do you assess incentive from applicant credentials, applicant answers, and applicant questions?

2. Contact a number of recruiters from different career fields and ask them to discuss the pluses and minuses of hiring recent college graduates. Probe for specifics and illustrations (without names). What changes have they seen in recent college graduates during the past 10 years?

3. Contact a number of recruiters to see how many employ a behavior-, trait-, or talent-based approach to recruiting new employees. If they do not use or have abandoned one of these approaches, what are their reasons for doing so? What differences can you detect among the three approaches? How do recruiters using one or more of these approaches detect dishonest answers?

4. Do a Web-based search of sources on EEO laws and regulations and the recommendations these sources make to recruiters to ask lawful questions and to applicants for recognizing and replying to unlawful questions. What changes have affected employment interviews during the past five years? What are the most controversial and often violated EEO laws and regulations? Which state laws tend to be more stringent than federal laws?

Notes

1. Tom Peters, *Re-Imagine: Business Excellence in a Disruptive Age* (London: Dorling Kindersley, 2003), pp. 18 and 81.

2. William W. Lewis, *The Power of Productivity: Wealth, Poverty, and the Threat to Global Stability* (Chicago: University of Chicago Press/McKinsey and Company, 2004).

3. Patricia M. Buhler, "Interviewing Basics: A Critical Competency for All Managers," *Supervision* 66 (March 2005), pp. 20–22; Adam Agard, "Pre-employment Skills Testing: An Important Step in the Hiring Process," *Supervision* 64 (June 2003), pp. 7–8.

4. Luke Collard, "Interviews Are a Waste of Time?" http://www.recruitingblogs.com/profiles/blogs/interviews-are-a-waste-of-time, accessed July 11, 2012.

5. Curtis Burk, "Finding Suitable Job Candidates at Career Fairs," http://job.ezinemark.com/finding-suitable-job-candidates-at-career-fairs-- 7d366fc25c1f.htmo, accessed July 11, 2012.

6. "How to Select a Staffing Firm," http://www.american staffing.net/staffing customers/select.cfm, accessed July 10, 2012.

7. Roger Herman and Joyce Gioia, "You've Heard of E-Business . . . How About E-Recruiting?" The Workforce Stability Institute, http://www.employee.org/article_you_heard_of_e-business.html, accessed September 14, 2006.

8. "Find Quality Candidates in the Resume Database," http://www.careerbuilder.com/jobposter/staffing-recruiting/page.aspx?pagever=RBU_ProdSearch, accessed July 10, 2012.

9. Joyce Gioia, "Special Report: Changing the Face(s) in Your Recruiting Efforts," Workforce Stability Institute, http://www.employee.org/article_changing_the_face.html, accessed September 14, 2006.

10. Joyce Gioia, "Are Prospective Applicants Saying 'No'—Based on Your Website?" Workforce Stability Institute, http://www.employee.org/article_prospective_saying_no.html, accessed September 14, 2006.

11. Michael A. McDaniel, Deborah H. Whetzel, Frank L. Schmidt, and Steven D. Mauer, "The Validity of Employment Interviews: A Comprehensive Review and Meta-Analysis," *Journal of Applied Psychology* 79 (1994), pp. 599–616.

12. "The Interview and Selection Process," LSU AgCenter Research & Extention, http://www.Lsuagcenter.com/...Interview-Selection-Process-08-06.pdf, accessed July 13, 2012.

13. "Federal Laws Prohibiting Job Discrimination Questions and Answers," http://www.hum.wa.gov/FAQ/FAQEEO.html, accessed July 12, 2012.

14. Roger Herman, "Older Workers—A Hidden Treasure," Workforce Stability Institute, http://www.employee.org/article_older_workers_hidden_treasure.html, accessed September 14, 2006; "Old, Smart, Productive," *BusinessWeek Online,* June 27, 2005, http://www.businessweek.com, accessed September 11, 2006.

15. Junda Woo, "Job Interviews Pose Risk to Employers," *The Wall Street Journal,* March 11, 1992, pp. B1 and B5.

16. Clive Fletcher, "Ethics and the Job Interview," *Personnel Management,* March 1992, pp. 36–39.

17. "Job Discrimination Claims Rise to Record Levels," http://www.msnbc.com/id/29554931/, accessed March 13, 2009.

18. "Human Resource Training Curriculum on CD-ROM," http://www.bizhotline.com/html/interviewing_skills_laws_gove.html, accessed September 18, 2009; "EEOC Is Watching You: Recruitment Discrimination Comes to the Forefront," http://www.multicultural/advantage.com/recruit/eeo-employment-law/EEOC-is-watching, accessed September 18, 2009; "The Do's and Don'ts of Interviewing," University of Minnesota, http://www.dumn.edu?~kgilbert/rec4315-/InterviewDos&donts.pdf, accessed July 12, 2012.

19. "Etiquette for Interviewing Candidates with Disabilities," *Personnel Journal* supplement, September 1992, p. 6.

20. Personnel Policy Service, "You Can't Ask That: Application and Interview Pitfalls," http://www.pps.publishers.com/articles/application_interview.htm, accessed September 18 2009; University of Connecticut, Office of Diversity and Equity, "Unlawful Questions," http://Web.uconn/uwode/quest.html, accessed October 18 2007; U.S. Equal Opportunity Commission, "New and Proposed Regulations," http://www.eeoc.gov/policy/regs/index.html, accessed September 18, 2009.

21. Kevin Wheeler, "Interviewing Doesn't Work Very Well," *Electronic Recruiting Exchange,* http://www.ere.net, accessed September 14, 2006; West Virginia Bureau of Employment Programs, "Guidelines for Pre-employment Inquiries," http://www.wvbep.org/bep/Bepeeo/empinqu.htm, October 18, 2007.

22. University of Minnesota, College of Liberal Arts, "Behavior-Based Interviewing," http://www.cclc.umn.edu/interviews/behavior.html, accessed February 26, 2009; Katharine Hansen, "Quintessential Careers: Behavior Interviewing Strategies," http://www.quintcareers.com/printable/behavioral_interviewing.html, accessed February 26, 2009; About.com.Job Searching, "Behavioral Interview," http://jobsearch.about.com/cs/interviews/a/behavioral.htm?p=1, accessed February 26, 2009.

23. "Behavior Interview Guide," National Institutes of Health, Equal Employment Opportunity Specialist, GS – 260," hr.od.gov/hrguidance/employment/interview/... 260-intrerview.do..., accessed July 12, 2012.

24. Patrice M. Buzzanell, "Employment Interviewing Research: Ways We Can Study Underrepresented Group Members' Experiences as Applicants," *Journal of Business Communication* 39 (2002), pp. 257–275; Patrice M. Buzzanell and Rebecca J. Meisenbach, "Gendered Performance and Communication in the Employment Interview," in *Gender and Communication at Work,* Mary Barrett and Marilyn J. Davidson, eds. (Hampshire, England: Ashgate Publishing, 2006), pp. 19–37.

25. Karen O'Keefe, "Five Secrets to Successful Interviewing and Hiring," http://www.writingassist.com, accessed September 14, 2006.

26. Troy Behrens, "How Employers Can Ace Their Campus and Site Interviews," *Journal of Career Planning & Employment,* Winter 2001, pp. 30–32; Deborah Shane, "52% of US Companies Say Job Applicants Are NOT Qualified?" http://www.deborahshaneroolbox.com/millions -of-jobs-and-no-qualified-applicants-how-can-that-be/, accessed July 13, 2012.

27. Steven M. Ralston and Robert Brady, "The Relative Influence of Interview Communication Satisfaction on Applicants' Recruitment Decisions," *Journal of Business Communication* 31 (1994), pp. 61–77; Camille S. DeBell, Marilyn J. Montgomery, Patricia R. McCarthy, and Richard P. Lanthier, "The Critical Contact: A Study of Recruiter Verbal Behavior during Campus Interviews," *The Journal of Business Communication* 35 (1998), pp. 202–224.

28. Behrens, pp. 30–32.

29. Patrice M. Buzzanell, "Tensions and Burdens in Employment Interviewing Processes: Perspectives of Nondominant Group Applicants," *Journal of Business Communication* 36 (1999), pp. 134–162.

30. DeBell, Montgomery, McCarthy, and Lanthier, pp. 204–224.

31. Louis Rovner, "Job Interview or Horror Movie?" *Occupational Health & Safety*, February 2001, p. 22.

32. Fredric M. Jablin and Vernon D. Miller, "Interviewer and Applicant Questioning Behavior in Employment Interviews," *Management Communication Quarterly* 4 (1990), pp. 51–86.

33. Susan M. Heathfield, "5 Resume Red Flags for Employers," http://humanresources.about.com/od/hire-employees/tp/resume-red-flags-for-employers.html, accessed

July 13, 2012; M. Susan Heathfield, "5 More Resume Red Flags for Employers," http://human resources.about.com/od/hire-employees/tp/five-more-resume-red-flags. html, accessed July 13, 2012.

34. Buhler.

35. Susan M. Heathfield, "Gone in Thirty Seconds: How to Review a Resume," http://humanresources.about.com/od/selectemployees/a/resume_review_2.html, accesses July 9, 2012.

36. Wayne Tomkins, "Lying on Resumes Is Common; Catching It Can Be Challenging," Lafayette, Indiana *Journal and Courier,* September 1, 2000, p. C7; Landy Chase, "Buyer Beware: How to Spot a Deceptive Sales Resume," *New Orleans City Business,* November 4, 2002, p. 22; Kim Isaacs, "Lying on Your Resume: What Are the Career Consequences?" http://career-advice.monster.com/resumes-cover-letters/resume-writing-tips/lying-on-your-resume/article.aspx, accessed July 13, 2012.

37. Tejinder Singh, "Court Holds Stolen Valor Act Unconstitutional, Dismisses First American Financial v. Edwards," http://www.scotusblog.com/2012/06/court-holds-stolen-valor-act-unconstitutional-dismisses-first-american-financial-v-edwards, accessed July 13, 2012.

38. "Applicant Tracking Software Programs," http://www.capterra.com/applicant-tracking-software?gclid=CObNx17GmbECFbEBQAodEQkCeg, accessed July 14, 2012.

39. "Creating a Scannable Resume," http://careerempowering.com/resume-empower/creating-a-scannable-resume.html, accessed July 14, 2012; Toni Bowers, "Quick resume tip: Negotiating resume scanning software," http://www.techrepublic.com/blog/career/quick-resume-tip-negotiating-resume-scanning-software/1950, accessed July 9, 2012.

40. Bob Ayrer, "Hiring Salespeople—Getting behind the Mask," *American Salesman,* December 1997, pp. 18–21.

41. Stephanie Clifford, Brian Scudamore, Andy Blumberg, and Jess Levine, "The New Science of Hiring," *Inc* 28 (August 2006), pp. 90–98, http://www.wf2la7.webfeat .org, accessed September 13, 2006; Bill Angus, "Uses of Pre-Employment Tests in Selection Procedures," http://www.psychtest.com/PreEmploy.html, accessed July 16, 2012.

42. Rochelle Kaplan, "Do Assessment Tests Predict Behavior or Screen Out a Diverse Work Force?" *Journal of Career Planning & Employment,* Spring 1999, pp. 9–12; "Employers Aim to Measure Personality, Skill," http://www.brainbench.com/xml/bb/business/newsletter/050606/050606article.xml, accessed July 16, 2012.

43. Angus.

44. "Myers Briggs Test: What Is Your Myers Briggs Personality Type?" http://www .personalitypathways.com/type_inventory.html, accessed July 16, 2012.

45. Julia Levashina and Michael A. Campion, "Measuring Faking in the Employment Interview: Development and Validation of an Interview Faking Behavior Scale," *Journal of Applied Psychology* 92 (2007), pp. 1638–1656.

46. Wayne J. Camara, "Employee Honesty Testing: Traps and Opportunities," *Boardroom Reports,* December 15, 1991.

47. Carol Kleiman, "From Genetics to Honesty, Firms Expand Employee Tests, Screening," *Chicago Tribune,* February 9, 1992, p. 8–1.

48. Donna R. Pawlowski and John Hollwitz, "Work Values, Cognitive Strategies, and Applicant Reactions in a Structured Pre-Employment Interview for Ethical Integrity," *The Journal of Business Communication* 37 (2000), pp. 58–75.

49. Pawlowski and Hollwitz, pp. 58–75.

50. Pawlowski and Hollwitz, p. 61.

51. Brian Libby, "How to Conduct a Job Interview," http://www.cbsnews.com/8301-505125_162-5105294/how-to-conduct-a-job-interview, accessed July 9, 2012; Dirk Stemerman, "Dirk Stemerman: Social Media and Job Applicants," http://www.montereyherald.com/business/ci_20381226/dirk-stemerman-social-media-and-..., accessed June 25, 2012.

52. Buhler.

53. Kirkwood and Ralston, pp. 69–71.

54. Marlene Dixon, Sheng Wang, Jennifer Calvin, Brian Dineen, and Edward Tomlinson, "The Panel Interview: A Review of Empirical Research and Guidelines for Practice," *Public Personnel Management* 31 (2002), pp. 397–428.

55. Choon-Hwa Lim, Richard Winter, and Christopher C.A. Chan, "Cross-Cultural Interviewing in the Hiring Process: Challenges and Strategies," *The Career Development Quarterly* 54 (March 2006), p. 267.

56. Ayrer, pp. 18–21.

57. Arthur H. Bell, "Gut Feelings Be Damned," *Across the Board,* September 1999, pp. 57–62; Allen I. Huffcutt and Winfred Arthus, "Hunter and Hunter (1984) Revisited: Interview Validity for Entry-Level Jobs," *Journal of Applied Psychology* 79 (1994), pp. 184–190; Karen I. van der Zee, Arnold Bakker, and Paulien Bakker, "Why Are Structured Interviews So Rarely Used in Personnel Selection?" *Journal of Applied Psychology* 87 (2002), pp. 176–184.

58. Clifford, Scudamore, Blumberg, and Levine.

59. Buzzanell, pp. 134–162.

60. William G. Kirkwood and Steven M. Ralston, "Inviting Meaningful Applicant Performances in Employment Interviews," *The Journal of Business Communication* 36 (1999), p. 66.

61. Craig D. Tengler and Fredric M. Jablin, "Effects of Question Type, Orientation, and Sequencing in the Employment Screening Interview," *Communication Monographs* 50 (1983), pp. 245–263.

62. Jablin and Miller, pp. 51–86; Gerald Vinton, "Open versus Closed Questions—an Open Issue?" *Management Decision* 33 (1995), pp. 27–32.

63. Aleksander P. J. Ellis, Bradley J. West, Ann Marie Ryan, and Richard P. DeShon, "The Use of Impression Management Tactics in Structured Interviews: A Function of Question Type," *Journal of Applied Psychology* 87 (2002), pp. 1200–1208.

64. Randy Myers, "Interviewing Techniques from the Pros," *Journal of Accounting* 202 (August 2006), pp. 53–55; "Using Behavioral Interviewing to Help You Hire the Best

of the Best," *HR Focus* 81 (August 2006), p. 56; Slippery Rock University, "Behavior Based Interview Questions," http://www.sru.edu/pages/11217.asp, accessed February 26, 2009.

65. Myers.

66. Menkes.

67. Jim Kennedy, "What to Do When Job Applicants Tell . . . Tales of Invented Lives," *Training*, October 1999, pp. 110–114.

68. Levashina and Campion, pp. 1650–1651.

69. Kaplan, pp. 9-12.

70. Justin Menkes, "Hiring for Smarts," *Harvard Business Review* 83 (November 2005), pp. 100–109.

71. Thomas Gergmann and M. Susan Taylor, "College Recruitment: What Attracts Students to Organizations?" *Personnel* 61 (1984), pp. 34–36; Fredric M. Jablin, "Organizational Entry, Assimilation, and Exit," *Handbook of Organizational Communication* (Beverly Hills, CA: Sage, 1987).

72. Catherine Houdek Middendorf and Therese Hoff Macan, "Note-Taking in the Employment Interview: Effects on Recall and Judgments," *Journal of Applied Psychology* 87 (2002), pp. 293–303.

73. "If They Say Tomato, and You Say To-Mah-To, What Then?" Workforce Stability Institute, http://www.employee.org/article_tomato.html, accessed September 14, 2006.

Resources

Barrett, Mary, and Marilyn J. Davidson, eds. *Gender and Communication at Work*. Hampshire, England: Ashgate Publishing, 2006.

Bunting, Sandra. *The Interviewer's Handbook*. London, England: Kogan Page, 2005.

Lynn, Adele. *The EQ Interview*. New York: AMACOM, 2008.

Powell, Larry, and Jonathan H. Amsbary. *Interviewing: Situations and Contexts*. Boston: Pearson Education, 2005.

Yeung, Rob. *Successful Interviewing and Recruitment*. London, England: Kogan Page, 2008.

The Employment Interview

Searching for a position that meets your desires, needs, and future plans has never been easy, even in the best of times, but the economic reality that you face today and during the next four or five years is truly daunting. The position you are seeking is out there, but competition is stiff and employers can afford to be choosy. There are no simple formulas, magic acts, or short cuts to locate and land one of your dream jobs, just a lot of hard work. You must approach this search systematically and analytically.

The objectives of this chapter are to work you through a series of stages in the employment search process. Start with a thorough analysis of yourself and proceed to doing your homework, conducting the search, preparing credentials, creating a favorable first impression, answering questions, asking questions, closing the interview, evaluating each interview while looking toward the next, and dealing with inevitable rejections. Let's begin with a systematic self-analysis.

Analyze Yourself

> You cannot sell you if you don't know you.

You can determine which career, position, and organization is the best *fit* for you only if you **know yourself**. Recruiters ask questions designed to discover who *you* are, what *you* have done and can do, and how well *you* fit a specific position in a specific organization's plans and culture. You can answer questions insightfully and persuasively only if you know who you are. You are literally selling you in every employment interview, and if you don't know you—the product you are selling—you won't sell yourself to the recruiter. It's that simple. Let's get started.

Questions to Guide Your Self-Analysis

Self-analysis is painful because few people want to probe deeply and honestly into their strengths and weaknesses, successes and failures. No one needs to see your self-analysis but you, so be painfully honest with yourself. Your future depends on it. The following questions and traits can serve as a preflight checklist prior to launching your job search in earnest.[1]

- What are my *personality* traits?

____ Motivated	____ Willing to take risks
____ Open-minded	____ Assertive
____ Adaptive	____ Able to work under pressure
____ Flexible	____ Open to criticism

- How *trustworthy* am I?
  - ____ Honest   ____ Tolerant
  - ____ Reliable   ____ Sincere
  - ____ Ethical   ____ Self-controlled
  - ____ Fair   ____ Even tempered

- What are my *intellectual* strengths and weaknesses?
  - ____ Intelligent   ____ Analytic
  - ____ Creative   ____ Rational
  - ____ Organized   ____ Critical
  - ____ Planner

- What are my *communicative* strengths and weaknesses?
  - ____ Oral communication skills   ____ Interpersonal skills
  - ____ Written communication skills   ____ With diverse people
  - ____ New media skills   ____ With subordinates, co-workers,
  - ____ Listening skills   superiors

- What are my *accomplishments* and *failures?*
  - ____ Academic   ____ Professional
  - ____ Extracurricular activities and   ____ Goals set and met
    interests
  - ____ Work

Focus on
strengths and
weaknesses.

- What are my *professional* strengths and weaknesses?
  - ____ Formal education   ____ Experiences
  - ____ Informal education   ____ Skills
  - ____ Training

- What do I want in a *position?*
  - ____ Responsibility   ____ Contact with people
  - ____ Independence   ____ Security
  - ____ Authority   ____ Variety
  - ____ Prestige   ____ Salary
  - ____ Type of work   ____ Benefits
  - ____ Decision making

- What are my most valued *needs?*
  - ____ Home and family   ____ Free time
  - ____ Income   ____ Recreation opportunities

____ Possessions ____ Feeling of success and accomplishment

____ Geographical location

- What are my *professional* interests?

Why and how have you made past decisions?

____ Short-range goals ____ Growth

____ Long-range goals ____ National/international recognition

____ Advancement

- Do I have a *mature and realistic perception* of my field?

____ History ____ Developments

____ Trends ____ Areas of specialization

____ Challenges ____ Current problems

____ Future problems ____ Essential education/training

____ Essential experiences ____ Employment opportunities

When you have answered these questions thoroughly and honestly, you should know who you are, what you are qualified to do, what you would like to do, and what you want in life. Above all, you will "have identified what sets you apart from other candidates" so you can present your uniqueness through your résumés, cover letters, and interviews.[2]

Do Your Homework

Researching your field, the positions for which might apply, the organizations you might contact, current events, and the employment interviewing process is stage two in the search process. Executive recruiter Eric Larson claims "There's no such thing as too much preparation."[3] And Alison Green, an authority on career and job search issues, writes that "Whoever said 80 percent of success is just showing up wasn't thinking about job interviews. Thoroughly preparing for an interview makes a huge difference in how well you do. (And it can also make you a lot less nervous.)"[4]

Research Your Field

Knowing your field is essential for selecting organizations and scheduling interviews.

Discover everything you can about your field from its past to its future and everything in between. It is essential that you develop a mature, realistic perception of what your field is like and what people do during typical workdays.

You don't want to discover that you hate your field the first day on the job. Internships, cooperative arrangements, part-time positions, observational visits, shadowing members of the profession, and volunteer activities enable you to discover what a field is all about. There are numerous published and Internet resources on every major career field from acting and advertising to visual arts and writing. Simply click on Google for sources such as:

Careers.org

CareerOne-Stop

Campus Explorer

AOL. Jobs

Peterson's Job Opportunities

Occupational Outlook Handbook

WetFeet.com

Vault.com

> **Research enables you to answer and ask questions insightfully.**

Recruiters expect applicants to know why they chose a particular career field, to have positive attitudes toward this field, to know why they want a career in this field, and to be aware of the opportunities and limitations of careers in this field. They also expect applicants to be acquainted with organizational life.

Research the Position

> **How closely do you match this position?**

Once you have located a position in your field that appears to be what you are looking for, learn everything you can about *this* position. Check the job description word by word to see how well you *match* or *fit* the requirements specified: education and training, experiences, skills, responsibilities, travel involved, location, and starting date. You need not be a perfect fit for the position, but you must be close enough for the recruiter to consider your application seriously. If the description lists three-to-five years of experience and you have a little over one year of outstanding experience, give it a go. If you have a degree in building construction technology and the description for a construction engineering manager specifies a degree in civil engineering, check it out. On the other hand, if the description specifies a degree and experience in social work while your degree is in English and your experience is limited to editing manuscripts for a publisher, don't waste the recruiter's time or yours. If you have no intention of moving from the Upper Peninsula of Michigan and the position is in Boston, check it off your list. Alison Green recommends that once you have studied the position thoroughly, "picture yourself doing the job."[5] A thorough understanding of the position prepares you to answer questions effectively and ask meaningful questions when the interviewer invites you for an interview.

Research the Organization

> **Research enables you to answer key questions effectively.**

Learn everything you can about each organization to which you apply. This used to be an arduous task, but the Internet has changed all of that. Nearly every organization, tiny to huge, has a Web site. For example, if you learned of a position at Wabash National Corporation, a leading manufacturer of semi-trailers, that sounds relevant to your career interests, a few clicks on its Web site will provide information "about us" that includes careers, investors, history, vision, mission, values, products, locations, news and events, and number of "associates." Only through careful research can you answer effectively two inevitable interview questions, "What do you know about us?" and "Why do you want to work for us?"

Other sources will give insights not readily available on organizational Web pages designed to impress readers. Such topics include downsizing plans, potential mergers, financial status, reputation in the field, recent setbacks, and culture. Talk to current and former employees, clients, professors, friends, and relatives. Check out newspaper articles, discussions in trade journals, and your local or campus library. Valuable resources include *American Business Disc, Dun's Electronic Business Directory, Hoovers: Your Fastest Path to Business Information, Standard and Poor's Corporate Records,* and *Thomas Register of American Manufacturers.*

You cannot overestimate how important it is to learn everything you can about the organization ahead of time. A poor answer to an early question such as "Tell me what you know about us" can destroy an interview. Knowing too little about the position and organization is a major turnoff by recruiters. In a survey of 188 recruiters, John Cunningham discovered that 68 percent said "researching the company and position is the most important step in preparing for an interview." This resulted in "lack of awareness about company and position" being number one in a list of thirty-three ways to slip up during the interview.[6]

Research the Recruiter

When possible, get to know the interviewer ahead of time.

If you are able to identify the recruiter ahead of time, talk to friends, associates, professors, career center personnel, members of the interviewer's organization, and use social media such as Linkedin and Twitter for a wealth of personal and professional information. Discover the interviewer's position, professional background, organizations to which the interviewer belongs, personality, and interviewing characteristics. An interviewer may have a dry sense of humor, come from a different culture, or be "all business." It helps to know the person you will interact with prior to the interview. If the person is all business, you might want to avoid small talk, lengthy answers, and attempts at humor.

Research Current Events

Keep abreast of what is happening in the world and in your field.

Keep up to date with what is going on in the world. *Newsweek, Time, BusinessWeek, Fortune, The Wall Street Journal,* and online news sources are excellent for current developments. Employers expect mature applicants to be aware of what is going on around them and in the world—local, state, national, international—and to have formed intelligent, rational positions on important issues.

Be informed about current trends, changes, developments, research, and mergers that are affecting the organization to which you are applying, your field, and your career path. If you are interested in a position as a high school music teacher, you need to be aware of educational "reforms" taking place in many states and state budget problems that are resulting in "downsizing" music programs, including bands, orchestras, and choral groups. If you are interested in the pharmaceutical field, you need to be aware of new products, promising research, and controversies concerning new drugs and cost to consumers. If you are interested in working in another country such as China, India, or Greece, you need to be aware of the country's relations with the United States, cultural differences, cost of living, and policies affecting noncitizen workers.

Research the Interview Process

Rely on no single source about employment interviews.

Discover everything you can about what takes place during the employment interviewing process. The goal is to avoid or at least minimize mistakes and surprises. Begin your research by reviewing Chapter 7 on the recruiting interview, then talk to peers in your field who have been through the process recently, professors who are actively involved in interviewing and keep abreast of what is taking place in your field, and recruiters. The Internet will provide a wealth of information and insights into all aspects of the interviewing process. Ask questions such as "What's the most important thing I can do to prepare for an interview?" "How important is appearance?" "What kinds of questions do recruiters ask?" "What do recruiters look for in answers?" "What types of information do recruiters provide about their organizations and the openings they have?" "What kinds of questions should I ask?" "How are plant trip interviews different from screening interviews?"

As you gather input into the recruiting process, be aware that there is no "typical" or "standard" way to conduct interviews. If you talk to four or five recruiters, even from the same organization, you are likely to get four or five versions of interviewing. Students often asked us why we didn't bring a recruiter to class "to show us how it's done." Our response was always the same: It would take dozens of recruiters, not one, to show how it's really done. Some recruiters employ behavior-based or trait-based interviews, and some don't. Some employ highly structured or moderately structured interviews, and some don't use either. Some probe extensively into answers, and others seldom use probing questions. Some provide extensive information on the organization and position, and some don't give any information. Some will give you several minutes to ask questions, and some won't give you any time to ask questions. Your goals should be to avoid being surprised by what happens in an interview and to be ready for anything.

Integrity is essential for all positions.

As we discussed in Chapter 7, a consistent concern of recruiters is to determine the **honesty** of applicants. A highly educated, trained, and skilled employee without honesty, morals, and sincerity will quickly become a detriment to the organization. A recruiter may ask you to take a written and/or oral honesty test designed to determine degrees of honesty or conduct (taking a pencil or some paper home versus taking expensive printer cartridges or a laptop home). A recruiter may conduct an **integrity interview** or incorporate questions into an interview to assess honesty. An important rule is to be honest in all of your preinterview materials (application form, cover letter, résumé) and in every answer during an interview. Any hint of dishonesty or evasiveness will result in a rejection notice.

Expect the unexpected.

Your research into the interview process may produce surprising results. For example, recent studies reveal that 50 percent of "speech acts" in sample interviews were declarative statements rather than questions and answers. Most interviewers have no training in interviewing. In a study of 49 interviews, 10 interviewers did not give applicants opportunities to ask questions. Recruiters are increasingly viewing the interview as a *work sample* and look for relevant job behaviors from applicants: can you do the job, will you do the job, and how well will you *fit* into the organization? A shocking finding in this depressed economy with high unemployment is that employers are finding it difficult to find enough qualified applicants to fill the openings they have in their organizations. In the United States, the shortage jumped from 14 percent in 2010 to 52 percent in 2011.[7]

Conducting the Search

Now that you have analyzed yourself and completed your research, it's time to begin the process of looking for specific positions with specific organizations. Do not overlook any source that will enable you to locate openings that appear to match your qualifications and interests and to arrange interviews.

Networking

Since sources claim that the majority of jobs are never advertised but are filled by word-of-mouth, **networking** appears to be the best means of locating positions. Surveys support this claim by reporting that from 41 to 80 percent of applicants attain their positions through networking.[8] How do you go about networking?

> **Leave no potential source off your network tree.**

Begin by starting a **network tree** of primary contacts, people you know personally. These may include relatives, friends, colleagues, acquaintances, neighbors, co-workers, former employers, internship directors, teachers and professors, and persons you know from high school, college, church, or the fitness center. Write down each person's telephone numbers (land line and cellular), mailing address, and e-mail address. Now start the branches of your network tree by identifying those you don't know personally: friends or associates of your personal contacts such as the boss of your best friend, a former roommate's spouse, your dentist's neighbor, and fellow members of a veteran's organization. As you get involved in your job search, continue to expand your network tree and prune those who have provided no contacts.

> **Keep your network complete and up-to-date.**

When you have your network tree reasonably developed, reestablish your relationship with each. Contact each directly, and don't rush into asking for help. Carry on a pleasant conversation in which you describe your situation and goals, emphasizing where you want to go in your career and not where you are or have been. Make your request for help as specific as possible—"I'm looking for a position as manager of a high-end restaurant," not a generic request such as—"I'm looking for a different job, do you know of any openings?" When you get a lead, write down the lead's full name, position, organization, and telephone number under the contact's name so you know who suggested the lead and ask if you can use the contact's name. The *who* may be a major factor in a lead's interest in helping you. If a contact has no leads for you, ask for three or four names who might know of career opportunities. Add these to your network tree.

Be sure to maintain your network. Ask for advice and help with your career search, perhaps with your résumé, but do not ask for a job. Be sure to keep in touch with your contacts. Keep them informed about what you are doing and the progress you are making. Prepare them for calls and e-mails they might be receiving from organizations you have contacted. Let them know when you have an offer and particularly when you have accepted an offer. Be sure to send thank you notes for their assistance. Be willing to assist members of your network when they are searching for positions. Networking is a mutual process.

Social Media

Social media expand your network.

The widespread use of social media such as LinkedIn, Facebook, and Twitter is now blurring the line between traditional and online networking.[9] For instance, you might contact a friend online and then talk to the friend in person about your job search. You can literally jump-start your search by reaching out to people on your printed network tree and those in your electronic network to let them know that you are looking for a job and the type of job you want. Social media allow you to create and post a profile, keep contacts up-to-date on the status of your search, reconnect to people in your past, and reach out to people you don't know. On LinkedIn you can add a professional headline such as "consultant" or "online teacher." Alexis Grant, in a MONEY post entitled "10 Smart Ways to Use Social Media in Your Job Search," recommends joining industry chats on Twitter to keep up-to-date on your industry, make useful contacts, and showcase your expertise in your field.[10]

Although job candidates report that they are 50 percent more likely to apply for a position they find on Facebook and readily use social media to check out organizations, careers, and recruiters, they send mixed signals about potential employers asking for their Facebook passwords or trolling their Web sites. They want to sustain their privacy while using social media.[11] Job seekers cannot have it both ways. Potential employers will increasingly access your use of social media such as Facebook, MySpace, Blogger, LinkedIn, and Friendster. You may feel safe and private in what you share with others—recordings of yourself acting goofy, at drunken parties, in sexually explicit poses, using profanity, and bragging about sexual exploits and taking part in drunken escapades—and certain that employers will not see them or that you can delete them easily. One source warns that "The Web may seem ephemeral, but what you casually post one night might just last a digital eternity."[12]

Use social media with caution.

Employers are concerned about how you will fit into their culture, perform your job maturely, and present a positive image of the organization within the community. A study by Kimberly Shea and Jill Wesley of Purdue University's Center for Career Opportunities discovered that over a third of recruiters routinely run applicant names through search engines to see what is "out there." Nearly half use some sort of technology to screen applicants, and 75 percent of these indicate that what they find influences their decisions, 50 percent negatively.[13] Other organizations employ college students and interns to search sites their peers use most often. Shea and Wesley urge you to think before inserting images and stories online and ask yourself, "Would you be willing to share your Web site/blog/Facebook profile with your grandparents?"

Web Sites, Classified Ads, and Newsletters

Overlook no source.

Nearly every organization has a Web site, and each is likely to include a section on careers and positions they wish to fill. Identify organizations for which you would like to work and check out their sites. Many organizations place classified ads in local,

ON THE WEB

Select a position you will be interested in when you complete your education or training. Search at least three Internet resources to discover the availability of such positions, geographical areas in which they are located, organizations that are seeking to fill them, and the nature of the positions being offered. Check resources such as Job Hunt (http://www.job-hunt.org), CareerBuilder Center (http://www.careerbuilder.com), MonsterTrak (http://www.monstertrak.com). After collecting this information, develop a list of interview questions to which you would need answers before making a decision to accept one of these positions.

regional, and national newspapers. These ads not only attract candidates but also satisfy the EEOC test of making openings known to all who might be interested and qualified. Join your professional organizations to show you are truly a professional and to keep abreast of what's happening in your field but also to take advantage of newsletters these organizations send out in print and online. Many have job listings in your field.

Career Centers and Employment Agencies

> **Your campus center is a goldmine.**

Nearly every college and university operates a center for career opportunities that is available to all of its students, often to alumni as well, and they are free. Your center can help you determine which careers are best suited to your interests, education, and experiences and it will have a wealth of materials on organizations and suggestions for doing online research. Counselors will help you develop résumés appropriate for your career interests and qualifications and assist you in writing effective cover letters. Most important, perhaps, centers can provide contacts for interviews in a variety of fields, many of which will take place on your campus to eliminate travel expenses and time. If you are an alumnus and interested in changing a position or career, a trained counselor can help you to determine a future direction.

There are hundreds of employment or placement agencies, sometimes referred to as head hunters, that can help you locate positions and arrange interviews.[14] Some agencies specialize in specific career fields such as health care, teaching, management, communication, engineering, and government positions. When you sign up with an agency, it "becomes your advocate and 'represents you'—a relationship that starts whenever you apply for a job through" it and by "listing and submitting your résumé."[15] An employment agency may perform tasks similar to those provided in college career centers.

> **If it sounds too good to be true, it probably is.**

Percentage agencies will help place you for a fee, often a percentage of your first year's salary, payable upon assuming a position they helped you obtain. Most agencies have **fee-paid positions,** which means that an organization has retained them on a fee basis to locate quality applicants. You pay nothing. If you use a percentage agency, be aware that they may charge a registration fee to process your credentials. Most agencies are ethical and want to find excellent positions for their clients, but use reasoned skepticism. If they want a great deal of money in advance just to process your résumé or make claims of placing nearly all of their applicants in highpaying positions, go elsewhere. Be careful of agencies that want to produce videotapes and other expensive credentials.

The Career/Job Fair

Career or job fairs held on your campus, a local mall, or around the country are excellent for meeting several employers at one location, finding out what positions are available, networking, and on-the-spot, face-to-face interviews. Some fairs are designed for specific fields or majors such as health care, the aircraft industry, engineering, agriculture, liberal arts, education, or pharmacy. Large corporations or government agencies may conduct their own fairs. Some career fairs are limited to specific groups such as military veterans or those recently displaced when a company closes a large facility.

When you attend a career fair, be thoroughly prepared. There are a variety of resources that can guide your preparation. For example, Virginia Tech's Division of Student Affairs has posted an excellent resource entitled "How to prepare for a job fair/career fair."[16] It addresses such questions and headings as, "Should I go to a career fair?" "Why go?" "Before you go," "At the career/job fair," "How can I be successful at the job or career fair?" and "What if I'm not ready to look for a job?" Here are some guidelines.

Know your career goals, who you want to talk to, and what you are looking for in a career or the interaction will be a waste of time for you and the recruiter. Recruiters expect you to have a clear career focus or objective. Allison Doyle recommends that you prepare a "one minute commercial" that stresses your strong points, goals, and where you would like to go within the company.[17]

When you attend a fair, be professionally dressed and have copies of résumés with you. Scout the terrain by noting who is there, where they are in a crowded maze of tables and organizational banners, and whether they are conducting interviews or merely handing out information.[18] Gather printed information and listen and observe as you walk about and stand in line. Is this an organization for which you would like to work, and are you qualified for the types of positions they are talking about? If not, don't waste both your and the recruiter's time.

When you come face-to-face with a recruiter, be aware that this person is sizing you up quickly by noting your appearance, communication skills, and professionalism. Strive to be assertive, enthusiastic, and calm. The worst question you can ask is "What are you offering/hiring for?"

Ryan McVay/Getty Images

Where is your clear career goal? The worst answer to a question such as "What are you looking for?" is "A job." This might be cute, but it is an immediate turnoff.[19]

If there are no job fairs in your area or you want to cast a larger net, Web sites can help locate fairs around the country.

If attractive fairs are too far to visit in person, consider virtual job fairs. Don Best of Unisfair writes that "A virtual job fair is just like a regular job fair, with different employer booths and chances to talk to employers about jobs."[20] Prepare for these like you would for a face-to-face interaction even though the conversation is in text form. Be prepared and make an immediate good impression, making certain that grammar and spelling are without error. Answer questions thoroughly and have intelligent, mature questions ready for employers.

Knocking on Doors

> No single résumé is suitable for all positions.

If there are no advertised openings in your area or in your field, you might use the old-fashioned way of seeking a job, knocking on doors. For instance, if you are looking for a position in broadcast journalism, sales, health care, teaching, or landscaping, pick an organization of interest that might have need or use for a person who is uniquely qualified and able to contribute immediately to its products or services. Organizations are always on the lookout for talented and experienced staff. Knock on the door. Identify the type of position you are seeking, what you have to offer them, and what makes you unique. The organization may not be able to offer you a position now, but it might later. At the least, this organization might identify openings in your field of which they are aware or recommend you to a friend. This person becomes part of your network. Be persistent. Nearly every employer has a story about a person who kept coming to the office time after time until finally the employer, impressed with the person's persistence and qualifications, created an opening to use this person's tenacity and abilities.

> Knocking on doors works.

Presenting Yourself to the Employer

Up to this point in your search for a career, you have studied yourself, your field, organizations, recruiters, and where the jobs are. In essence, you have been off stage. Now it's time to present yourself to potential employers, not yet face-to-face but through a branding process in the social media, résumés, portfolios, and cover letters.

Branding

> Your brand is uniquely you.

Branding is not merely an early twenty-first century "buzz word" but also refers to a carefully crafted image you present to potential employers through the social media. The goal is to differentiate yourself from the hundreds of others who are graduating with your major or who have similar professional experiences and interests. You must *demonstrate* and *not just tell* why you are of value to an employer. Your "brand" emphasizes your talents, strengths, and expertise—what sets you apart from others—that are carefully aligned with the employer's needs.[21] As Dan Schawbel, author of the best-selling book *ME 2.0: Four Steps to Building Your Future,* states, "Personal branding is the process by which you uncover what makes you special and desirable in the marketplace, and then communicate your value to the right audience."[22] Your brand, then, "is a distillation of who you genuinely are—and how you must appear to your current and potential employers."[23] You need to express your passion for your career, emphasize your strengths, and identify your long- and short-range goals. Schawbel urges you "to target your online presence toward the jobs you're really passionate about."

Earlier in this chapter, we focused on using social media for networking and locating positions, and we warned about the possible negative impact of what you include in such media. Now it's time to emphasize the positive impact of your use of social media. Barbara Stefani, owner of Career Savers, writes that "over 90 percent of recruiters perform Internet searches on candidates before making a hiring decision, and over half of employers solidify their decision to hire based on a strong online presence."[24] Sources on branding encourage applicants to expand and enhance their online visibilities by creating their own Web site, having a blog, using video promotion, posting social media updates, and taking part in online conversations pertinent to their fields and career interests. Share your thoughts on trends and news by answering questions, responding to postings, and writing your own postings. If you are inexperienced at producing online materials, a variety of resources—such as Brand-Yourself.com—are available to assist.[25]

> **Recruiters do online searches.**

Résumés

Preparing the perfect résumé gets so much attention in print and on the Internet that you may believe the résumé is the *magic bullet* that will launch or further your career. Hold on a moment. The résumé's *only purpose* is to obtain an interview that may lead to more interviews and eventually to a position in your field. Notice that the *perfect résumé* is singular, but you are much less likely to land a job if you produce only one version of your résumé. Experts on résumés agree on this point: you must *customize* your résumé to meet the specific words of the job announcement and the needs of the employer.[26]

Your résumé is your *silent sales representative*, and it is often the first opportunity a prospective employer has to *see* you. Most recruiters will spend only seconds scanning the résumé you send them, so it must gain and sustain a positive impression, one that will motivate them to read further. It is most impressive when it is tailored to a specific position and appears to be highly professional. James Campion recommends that you "think like the boss" if you want the job.[27] Would *you* hire *you?*

Segments of Résumés

> **Make it easy for interviewers to locate you.**

> **Phrase career objectives with great care.**

Although there is considerable disagreement about what exactly a résumé should include, exclude, and look like, there is no shortage of Web sites and publications that claim to offer "award-winning résumés" or "the perfect résumé." Richard Bolles, author of the famous book entitled *What Color Is Your Parachute?*, updated annually, claims he collects such résumés and shows them to his employer friends. Inevitably they declare that each award-winning and perfect résumé would never get a job for anyone.[28] With such diverse preferences in mind, we will offer suggestions that apply to most situations. Don't forget, of course, that each position will require you to do some customizing of your résumé. What may work for one organization or field may be totally inappropriate for another. In other words, develop a *targeted résumé*.

Contact Information: Place your *full name* at the top center of the page in larger font than the remainder of the résumé and in bold print. Do not use nicknames. Provide one or two mailing addresses with ZIP codes and the e-mail address you access most often. Provide a landline telephone number and a cell phone number with area codes. The goal is to make it easy for the recruiter to reach you quickly. Do not have silly, immature material on your answering machine unless your career goal is to become a comedian. If you provide a campus telephone number, place a date when it may no longer be operable. List a business telephone number only if it is appropriate for prospective employers to use.

Career Focus: Your unique branding continues beyond the Internet, and the statement of your career focus (sometimes labeled profile, professional overview, professional background, professional summary, summary of qualifications, career objective, or simply objective) is an ideal place to use branding to catch the employer's attention quickly. Since the employer is likely to spend only seconds scanning your résumé, you must stand out by designing a headline or focus that shows you are what the employer is looking for and motivates the employer to continue reviewing your résumé. Some sources recommend that you not include the traditional "Objective" because it focuses on what *you* want, not what the *employer wants*. The key, regardless of label, is to make it *employer* rather than *self-directed*.[29]

Be brief but include key words used in the ad for the position. For example, if the ad for a position in landscape design specifies a degree in landscape architecture with a focus on housing and real estate development in an urban setting, your profile should identify interests, training, and experiences that match this description. Don't include words advertisers refer to as "puffery" that sound impressive and mean nothing. Avoid clichés that everyone uses such as "I'm a team player," "I have great communication skills," "I'm a problem solver," "I am highly motivated," and "I give 110 percent."[30] Puffery and clichés will send your résumé to the rejection pile. Remember, the remainder of your résumé must live up to your claims and branding in your career focus.

Education and Training: If you are in the process of completing your education and training or recently did so and your work experiences are minimal or unrelated to the position, your educational record usually comes next. In a survey of 188 college recruiters conducted by John Cunningham, 57 percent preferred education to be listed first, even when the college applicant had significant work experiences.[31] Indicate specifically how your education and training are *a fit* for the position you are seeking in this organization. List your degrees or training **in reverse chronological order** so the employer can detect quickly what you are *doing now* or recently completed. List degree, diploma, certificate or license, date of graduation or completion, school, location of the school if name is insufficient for accurate identification (many universities have multiple campuses or use the same name), and majors and minors. You might provide a *selective list of courses* relevant to the opening, particularly if you are short on experience. List your grade point average (GPA) if it is a B or better, and indicate the numerical system used at your college, for example: 3.35 (4.0 scale) or 3.35/4.0. Do not use abbreviations for courses, majors, or degrees. An interviewer may not know if Eng. refers to English or engineering.

Job-Related Experiences: The next résumé segment presents your experiences that are relevant to this position with this organization. Eighty-eight percent of recruiters in one study rated job-related experiences as very important or above average in importance.[32] If you are young and just completing your education and training, you may have had limited work or salaried positions in your field, but you should have relevant experiences you can showcase. These may be co-op programs through your university, internships (paid and unpaid), research or teaching assistantships, and volunteer activities. If for instance you are seeking a position in building construction, having experience in building a Habitat for Humanity home or a program to rehabilitate homes for the poor and elderly can be impressive. The study cited above found that recruiters rated the following as very important or above average in importance: leadership roles in student organizations 86 percent and volunteer community service 58 percent. All organizations are seeking leaders and doers, so make these stand out in your résumé.

Emphasize your job-related experiences.

Activities: The next section after experiences, or education/training if you have years of experience in your career field or are changing fields, lists activities and organizational memberships. These typically include college, professional, and community activities and groups. Be selective and continually update your résumés. High school activities are excluded for college graduates, and college organizations and activities are excluded once you have an established record in your career. Potential employers are interested in *doers* rather than *joiners*, so a long list of organizations minus leadership roles gives a negative impression. Include honorary organizations, professional, and pre-professional organizations in your field (such as the Public Relations Student Society of America). Provide a brief description for any organization that may not be familiar to an employer.

Recruiters look for leaders.

Volunteer Experiences: If you have significant volunteer experiences that may not be directly related to a position but reveal important information about you, list them as a segment in your résumé. If these are few in number or significance, include them as part of your activities.

Provide only relevant information.

There are items that you should exclude from your résumé. Do not list references; employers assume you will provide references if they want them. Exclude personal information (ethnicity, age, marital status, parental status, health or disabilities, height, and weight), a photo, and political, religious, and ethnic memberships and activities that may pose EEOC problems for employers if they maintain or act on it. You do not break laws if you do so, but you are providing information that generally is not a bona fide occupational qualification (BFOQ).

Types of Résumés

There are basically two types of résumés, chronological and functional. If you are developing a **chronological format,** the most common résumé, list your experiences (including internships, co-op arrangements, assistantships, unpaid positions, organizational activities) in *reverse* chronological order so the employer can see quickly what you have been up to most recently. See Figure 8.1 for a sample chronological format résumé. List organization, title of your position or positions, dates, and what you did in each position. Emphasize the skills and experiences most relevant for the

Figure 8.1   *Chronological résumé*

Nancy A. McWilliams

1214 Maple Drive,
Shelbyville, IN 46176
(317)226-3499/(317)413-2679
namcwilliams@hotmail.com

Objective:	A position as a family case manager with a child services agency that allows me to work with families and children in need of services.
Education:	**Indiana University Purdue University Indianapolis (August, 2010 to present)**
	Bachelor of Social Work
	Minor in Psychology
	GPA: 3.17/4.0 overall and 3.4/4.0 in major
Experience:	Court-Appointed Special Advocate for children (CASA) September 2012 to present
	Marian County, Indiana

- Acted as Educational Surrogate Parent for four children.
- Worked with DCS Family Case Managers.
- Counseled parents on following court orders.
- Worked with Children in Need of Services (CHINS).
- Consulted with school and psychological counselors.
- Wrote reports for Juvenile Court hearings.

Volunteer at the Crisis Center for Women
June 2010 to August 2012

Plainfield, Indiana

- Registered women who came to the shelter.
- Coordinated play activities for the children.
- Assisted in maintaining security from 8:00 p.m. to 12:00 a.m.

Horse Therapist at Bar Q Ranch
Summers of 2009, 2010, 2011, 2012

Batesville, Indiana

- Worked as horse therapist for special needs children.
- Conducted orientation sessions to inform and relax the children.
- Guided the children in riding activities.

Activities:	Vice-President and President of the Bachelor of Social Work Student Association 2012 to present

- Planned activities.
- Conducted monthly meetings.
- Coordinated the annual fundraiser.

opening. The primary concern of recruiters is applicant achievement and accomplishment. A chronological résumé is easy to write and organize, emphasizes relevant experiences and skills, and is preferred by employers because they can scan it quickly.

If you are developing a **functional format,** most appropriate for creative positions and those in which writing is important, place your experiences under headings that highlight your qualifications for the position (see Figure 8.2). Typical headings are management, sales, advertising, training, counseling, team building, organizational development, recruiting, finance, teaching, administration, supervision, project manager, and marketing. You can include a variety of experiences from different positions, internships, and organizations under each heading, an advantage when you have had few paying positions or positions directly related to the opening.

If you are using a functional format, you may list organizations or include them within various major headings under experience, or blend them within your skills and experiences. Your outside activities may indicate motivation, communication skills, ability to work with people, work ethic, ability to lead, and indicate that you are not a narrow specialist.

| Select the résumé format best suited to you.

A chronological format, such as the one in Figure 8.2, is easy to write and organize, emphasizes experiences, is most common, and is easy for an employer to scan for relevant experiences.

A functional format focuses attention on relevant skills to match the ideal applicant profile and seemingly unrelated positions and education are not highlighted. A functional résumé does not repeat the same skills and experiences under different positions, so it can be tighter and shorter. Many employers do not like functional résumés because they typically do not identify dates for education and training or, more importantly, for work experiences. Employers cannot detect gaps in employment to ask for explanations. Chronological résumés are also easier to read and review. Some résumés are blends of the two formats.

Guidelines for Résumés

| Pay attention to content and appearance.

Regardless of the résumé type you select, follow several guidelines to make them precise, informative, and persuasive. Above all, be honest.

| Dishonesty is a candidate killer.

Honesty Is the Best Policy: A conservative estimate is that one in six college students lies on résumés and application forms, but some experts on résumés claim that the percentage is as high as 50 percent.[33] Applicants claim experiences they have not had, courses they have not taken, graduation indexes they have not achieved, and degrees they have not received. The sad fact is that the higher a person goes in an organization, the more likely the person is to lie about employment gaps, job titles, job responsibilities and achievements, claiming sole responsibility for team efforts, and making up fictitious employers.[34] Michael Josephson, president of the Josephson Institute of Ethics, warns that "Lies are like potato chips. You can't tell just one."[35]

While some applicants have something to hide, many believe that a little "puffery," a euphemism for lying, will get them a position and advancement. Employers and ethicists agree that this is a **bad idea** with potentially **bad results.** One source warns that "When fitted onto résumés, falsehoods can sit undetected indefinitely. Or, they can

Figure 8.2 *Functional résumé*

Nancy A. McWilliams

1214 Maple Drive,
Shelbyville, IN 46176
(317)226-3499/226-3499
namcwilliams@hotmail.com

Objective:	A position as a family case manager with a child services agency that allows me to work with families and children in need of services.
Education:	Indiana University Purdue University Indianapolis (August, 2010 to present) Bachelor of Social Work Minor in Psychology GPA: 3.17/4.0 overall and 3.4/4.0 in major
Experience:	**Consulting**

Consulting

- With school systems as an Educational Surrogate Parent
- With DCS Family Case Managers
- With school and psychological counselors

Counseling

- Parents on following court orders
- Children in Need of Services
- Girls experiencing interpersonal conflicts
- Horse therapist for special needs children

Coordinating

- Play activities for children
- Aquatic activities for girls
- An annual fundraiser

Conducting

- Monthly meetings
- Registration at a women's shelter
- Orientation sessions to inform and relax special needs children for horse therapy

Writing

- Reports for Juvenile Court Hearings

Activities: Vice-President and President of the Bachelor of Social Work Association detonate at any moment, proving fatal to careers and credibility."[36] Scott Reeves writes bluntly: "A solid résumé will get you in the door. A lie on the résumé will get you kicked down the stairs."[37]

Select words with care.

Choose Words Carefully: Choose every word and phrase with care because many are immediate turnoffs for employers. For instance, employers say they find these words and phrases to be meaningless: proven track record, responsible for, hard-working, goal-oriented, well-organized, and ambitious. They prefer action verbs such as the following that show you are a *doer*:

administered	facilitated	oversaw
advised	fashioned	performed
arbitrated	formulated	persuaded
arranged	founded	planned
built	generated	recommended
budgeted	improved	reconfigured
coached	increased	researched
consulted	instructed	sold
counseled	led	solved
created	maintained	supervised
designed	managed	tested
directed	modified	trained
edited	negotiated	updated
eliminated	operated	wrote
evaluated	organized	

Each of these action verbs, of course, must be backed by examples and facts, not fluff.

Proofread thoroughly.

Proofread and Then Proofread Some More: Proofread every word and phrase for correct spelling and grammar and check every comma, semicolon, colon, and period. Look for the ever-present typo that is so easy to overlook. Danielle Lorenz, a specialist on job hunting and résumés writes that "I would say as they see a spelling, grammatical or typographic error the résumé will get tossed right away."[38] Debra Auerbach, AOL jobs coordinator, reports that when employers were asked about guaranteed deal-breakers, 61 percent identified typos as the top reason for dismissing a candidate from consideration.[39] Mistakes such as the following are legendary among recruiters:[40]

"Ruining an eight-person team."

"I am very interested in the newspaper add for the accounting position."

Under abilities: "Speak English and Spinach."

"I am a very capable proofreader."

"Deetail-oriented."

Don't rely on spell check to do the job for you. If you not a skilled proofreader, ask for help from someone who is.

Make your
résumé easy
to review.

Take Mechanics Seriously: Pay attention to appearance and layout. Print your résumé on white, off-white, light gray, or light beige bond paper. Pay attention to how the résumé is blocked so it looks neat, attractive, organized, carefully planned, and uncrowded. Employers like white space on résumés, so indent sections carefully, double-space parts, and leave at least one-inch margins all around. Center your name at the top in bold letters so it stands out. Use different printer fonts so headings guide the reader through important information about you. Employers prefer résumés with bullets that separate and call attention to important information because this helps them scan the résumé more efficiently. If you provide two addresses, place one on each side under your name. If you provide one address, place it in the center or on the right side away from staples and paper clips.

Most employers prefer a single-page résumé. However, a two-page or longer résumé is acceptable if it is necessary to provide valuable information, experiences, and insights. Don't try to say too much about too little. Don't try to adhere to the one-page rule by using a tiny font or narrow margins to fit everything onto a single page. Employers prefer a less crowded two-page résumé. If you develop a two-page résumé, print it front to back on one sheet of paper because a second page may get misplaced or ripped off when your résumé is taken from a file or briefcase. Signal with a page number or notation that there is more on the back. Repeat your name at the top on the left and a page number on the top right.

Be professional in everything you say and do in the résumé. Don't try to be cute or "creative." Control your urges to use script résumé fonts or to employ several font sizes and styles. Keep color and graphics to a minimum unless you are applying for a position that places a high value on creativity such as advertising, video production, and graphic design. Don't include a picture of your pet or decorate the résumé with cute bunnies or kittens. Don't print your name in two-inch high letters to get attention and be remembered. These things have happened in the zany world of job seeking.

The Electronically Scanned Résumé

Electronically
scanned
résumés must
be different.

Organizations are turning increasingly to résumé scanning software to save time and money. If you know that an organization will receive dozens or hundreds of applications for a position it is seeking to fill, assume that the employer will scan your résumé electronically. Follow these basic rules for mechanics and wording of the scanned résumé.

Key words
are critical in
electronically
scanned
résumés.

Mechanics of electronically scanned résumés are of critical importance because the scanner must be able to **read** your résumé.[41] Use black ink and only one side of 8 ½ inch white paper. Do not staple. Margins should be at least 1.6 inches on both sides, and characters should be 75 or fewer per line. Do not use boxes or columns. Employ size 11 to 14 fonts because the scanner may not read smaller print. Most recommended typefaces are Times Roman Numeral, Arial, and Times New Roman. Avoid fancy fonts. Use virtually no punctuation because punctuation may confuse a scanner, but you may use bold face or all capital letters. Do not employ bullets (solid or hollow), italics, underlining, graphics, or spaces between the letters of your name.

While mechanics are important so a scanning system can read your résumé, **key words** are most important because they will determine if an employer will set up an interview or discard your résumé. Include words pertinent to the job posting so the scanner is able to locate what the employer programmed it to look for.[42] Since some employers scan career objectives to sort résumés into files for different positions, be sure to have a clearly identifiable objective or profile linked to the description of the position you are seeking. Joyce Lain Kennedy, an authority on the electronic job search, recommends, "The more keyword marketing points you present about yourself, the more likely you are to be plucked from an electronic résumé database now, in six months, or a year from now."[43] The Purdue Online Writing Lab recommends replacing action verbs with nouns that are easier to scan. For example, change manufacturing to manufacturing supervisor, design to design assistant, production to production manager, and injection molding to injection molding inspector.[44] Be sure your résumé contains up-to-date terms, labels, and names the scanner is programmed to detect. The following are samples of correct and incorrect terms for scannable résumés:

Yes	No
human resources	personnel
administrative assistant	secretary
sales associate	sales clerk
information systems	data processing
environmental services	housekeeping
accountant	bookkeeper
facilities engineering	maintenance
inside sales	customer relations

Terms and labels are critical in scannable résumé:

Organizations may reject candidates with less than 50 percent of the required skills.

Organizations are now accepting or asking for résumés to be sent electronically to save time and to create electronic files on applicants. Be sure your software system will send your résumé in an attractive format. Instructors and students at some universities have reported that organizations have requested all applicant files be sent on CD-ROMs. Paper files are unacceptable. On the other hand, many organizations are being inundated with hundreds of e-résumés from unqualified applicants. They find such résumés to be sloppy, impersonal, and mass-mailed rather than customized for a particular position with a particular organization. Unless told to do otherwise, include a cover letter that clearly identifies the position you are applying for and stresses how you are a good fit. Always bring a copy of your cover letter and résumé to the interview.

Online Résumés

With the Internet an integral part of our lives, organizations and entrepreneurs have created online sites for posting résumés and seeking positions. The advantages are that it is easy and you have the potential of reaching a wide variety of potential employers in career fields worldwide.

Use online services with caution.

Unfortunately, the ease of posting résumés online has made applicants easy prey for unscrupulous Web searchers who act as fake employers to take your money and your identity. Heather Galler of Carnegie Mellon University has developed a computer program called "Identity Angel" that searches online job boards for what she calls the "holy trinity" of information thieves love to attain: name, address, and Social Security number. If it locates such information, it sends a warning to the potential target of online thieves and frauds.

Galler offers these suggestions:[45] First, read the privacy policy carefully to determine how long your résumé will be active and how you can delete it. "If there's no privacy policy, forget it." Second, be aware of fake recruiters, particularly if they ask for a driver's license or other personal information under the pretense of needing this for background checks. Ask the "recruiters" for references and check to see if they are members of local or national recruiter's associations. Third, set up an alternative e-mail address, use a cell phone, and provide a P.O. box as your address for job hunting. Fourth, if you want to see if your personal information is online, type in your name and the last four digits of your Social Security number. By providing more information, you may outsmart yourself because thieves can use spyware to get more of your personal information.

The Portfolio

> Your portfolio shows you in action.

Portfolios are essential if you are in fields such as photography, advertising, public relations, art and design, journalism, architecture, teaching, and professional writing. Your **portfolio** should be a small yet varied collection of your best work. Organize your portfolio thematically. Make it visually attractive. Have excellent copies of your work—not faded, soiled, marked-up, graded, or wrinkled samples. Employers want to see how well you write, design, photograph, edit, and create, and the well-designed and presented portfolio is the best means of doing this.

If you are going into broadcasting, your portfolio must contain an audio or videorecording of selections that illustrate your best oral and video work. Quality, not quantity, is what sells.

Some colleges and universities are encouraging or requiring students to create electronic portfolios that can include a wide variety of materials in an attractive, compact, and highly usable package. In addition to revealing what a candidate has done and can do, the e-portfolio demonstrates knowledge of and ability to apply new technologies.

The Cover Letter

> The all-purpose form letter is rarely taken seriously.

> Design and target letters to specific positions and organizations.

Your cover letter is often the first contact you have with an employer, so be positive and to the point. The fundamental purposes of your cover letter are *to gain this employer's attention* and *to entice this employer* to read your résumé. The first purpose requires you to make a good impression by revealing a positive attitude and pleasant personality. You must appear motivated and enthusiastic. The second purpose requires you to include highlights of your education, training, and experiences that show you are interested in and qualified for a specific position open in the employer's organization. Never send a résumé without attaching a cover letter.

Mechanics of the Cover Letter: Your letter should be brief, usually three or four paragraphs in length, and never more than one page. See Figure 8.3. Provide margins of 1.5 inches left and right and adjust top and bottom margins to balance your letter on the page. If you have difficulty placing all information you feel is absolutely necessary to include on a single page, adjust the margins to keep the letter to one page. Use simple

Figure 8.3   *Cover letter*

1214 Maple Drive
Shelbyville, IN 46176
March 14, 2014

Mr. Scott Dempsey
Indiana Department of Child Services
1783 W. 3rd Street
Bloomington, IN 47404

Dear Mr. Dempsey:

I am writing in response to the FCM position posted on your Web site last week and understand that the person selected for this position would begin work on or about June 14, 2014. I am very interested in this position because it matches my career focus, education, and experiences.

I will graduate from IUPUI in May of this year with a Bachelor of Social Work Degree. In my job as a CASA in Marian County since 2009, I have worked closely with a number of FCMs in several cases involving CHINS. This has enabled me to observe their work with parents and children and to appreciate how critical their roles are in maintaining families when possible and seeing that children are placed in safe and loving environments when the family is no longer a viable option. I believe that my experience as a CASA, a volunteer at the Crisis Center for Women, and as a horse therapist for children with special needs makes me uniquely qualified for a position as FCM in the Department of Child Services.

I look forward to meeting with you to discuss my interest and background in a position as a FCM. Enclosed is a copy of my résumé that provides additional details about my qualifications and experiences. Feel free to contact me at either of the telephone numbers listed on my résumé or by e-mail at namcwilliams@hotmail.com. I would be available for an interview at your convenience.

Sincerely,

Nancy A. McWilliams

Enclosure: résumé

to read fonts of 10 to 12 points. A Virginia Tech Web site suggests that you ask another person to read your résumé. If the person mentions the font, change it.[46] Your letter must be neat, printed on white bond paper, and be professional with no typos, grammatical errors, punctuation errors, or misspellings. One of our former journalism students applied for an editing position with the Cincinnati *Enquirer* and misspelled Cincinnati in the cover letter. The student did not get the job, but the editor did send an irate letter, along with the student's original letter, to the student's academic department head.

Content of the Cover Letter: Tailor each cover letter to the position and organization. Form letters impress no one. Try to address your letter to a specific person involved in the hiring process, and spell this person's name correctly. Be careful when you address the person as Mr. or Ms. For instance, first names such as Jordan and Chris may be a man or woman. Letters addressed "To Whom It May Concern" or "Dear Sirs" rarely get positive responses. Organize your letter into three paragraphs.[47] In the *first* paragraph, tell the employer why you are writing, in which position you are interested, and why this particular position with this particular organization appeals to you. Reveal how you discovered this opening and what you know about this organization. Show you have researched both position and organization. In the *second* paragraph, explain briefly how your education, training, and experiences—your qualifications—make you an ideal fit for this position, with this organization, at this time. *Be persuasive!* You may refer to your résumé, but do not merely repeat it. In the *third* paragraph, restate your enthusiasm for this position and ask for an interview opportunity or chance to talk about it and the organization. Indicate when and where you will be available for an interview. Mention enclosures and offer to send additional information if needed. Be sure to express appreciation for the employer's consideration.

> Show interest and enthusiasm or do not apply.

Creating a Favorable First Impression

As you approach the interview, realize that your **attitudes** are a critical ingredient in your success or failure.[48] Be thoroughly prepared. Anxiety is heightened when you feel you do not know enough about the position or organization, are unready to answer tough questions, and do not know what questions to ask. If you feel you are not going to do well in an interview, you won't.

Approach the employment interview as a sales process, and you are the product. Know yourself thoroughly. If you cannot sell you to you, how can you sell you to the recruiter? Be *positive* about yourself, current and past employers, associates, professors, and clients. Be professional and ethical throughout the interview. Never bad-mouth others or reveal confidences. One study revealed that good **first impressions** lead interviewers to show positive regard toward applicants, give important job information, sell the organization to them, and spend less time gathering information.[49]

> Avoid self-fulfilling prophecies.

If the interview will be over the telephone, avoid common "interruptions" such as flushing toilets, cleaning dishes, barking dogs, and answering e-mail messages.[50] Find a quiet place and give your full attention to the interaction. Avoid the cell phone when possible because the signal may fade and it's often difficult to hear clearly on cell phones.

> Know how and when to share control of the interview.

Relationship of the Interview Parties

Assess the *relationship* that is likely to exist between you and the interviewer. How will control be shared? Control may be determined by the job market and the organization's need to fill the position. *Successful applicants* dominate interviews but also know when to let the interviewer control the conversation. *Unsuccessful applicants* are submissive or try to dominate when the employer clearly wants to do so.

Do you want to take part in this interview? You may find it difficult to "get fired up" for an interview if you have been turned down a number of times during previous

© Digital Vision/Getty Images

months or you are not really interested in this position or organization. Are you interviewing for a sales position only because you cannot get into management?

What is the degree of affection (mutual trust, respect, friendship) between you and the interviewer as revealed in previous encounters, telephone contacts, and letters? How similar are you to the interviewer in age, gender, race, ethnic group, background, education, and profession? Research reveals that candidates racially similar to interviewers (black and white) receive higher interviewer ratings.[51]

Dress and Appearance

Understand and adapt to the relationship with the recruiter.

Dress and *appearance* are critical elements in a favorable first impression. In a survey of college recruiters, 95 percent cited professional image as *important* or *very important.*[52] They see clothes and accessories as "making a strong visual statement" that suggests confidence and "gives the interviewee a competitive edge." Your appearance shows interest in the position and organization, respect for the interviewer, attentiveness to details, and knowledge of what is appropriate dress and appearance for a formal business setting. While many companies are now promoting business casual at the workplace, 81 percent of respondents in this survey prefer formal business attire for formal interviews "to see how applicants would present themselves in a business meeting or presentation." Mary Dawne Arden, an executive coach and president of Arden Associates in New York, states that "No one can fault you for being too formal in an interview. But being sloppy, or even too casual, will kill your prospects."[53]

Dress for a formal business occasion.

Neatness costs nothing and pays dividends.

Remember that, "When you look good, you feel good and when you feel good you are more likely to articulate intelligent and well thought out answers to questions."[54] David A. McKnight, a management and image consultant, claims that "Nine out of 10 employers say, when all else is equal, they select the most attractive candidate or the candidate that presents themselves best."[55]

Advice for All Applicants

For most employment interviews you would be wise to wear a conservative, professional, solid-color suit. *Think* competence, communication, respect, and appropriateness rather than *fashion*. It's better to be overdressed than underdressed.[56] Kate Middleton, president and founder of a national career counseling and placement firm, recommends the rule of thumb "that you dress one or two levels higher than the job that you're going for."[57] A tragic mistake is to dress too casually because our society has become remarkably casual.

Although these dress guidelines apply to most employment interviews, you must know the industry into which you hope to enter. Each organization has its own unique culture and environment.[58] If you have questions about the formality of interview dress, ask your professors, members of professional associations, and people employed in this industry. Do not hesitate to contact the organization conducting the interview and ask discretely about how you should dress for the interview. As a rule of thumb, organizations in finance, government, human resources, banking, sales, and hospitality prefer formal dress. Organizations in advertising, public relations, graphic design, technology, and the trades may prefer less formal dress such as business casual, Dockers, and a buttoned shirt. Do not assume that because employees of an organization dress in business casual or less formally that this is appropriate for an interview. Dress up unless told to do otherwise.

You need not spend a fortune on your interview attire, but invest in quality, well-fitting clothing that will remain pressed and unwrinkled. Be neat, clean, and lint free. Polish your shoes. Be sure there are no missing buttons or un-removed tags. Do not carry a book bag or backpack. Brush your teeth, comb your hair, take a breath mint, and clean your hands and fingernails.

Your want your dress and appearance to play a significant "supporting role" in the selection process.[59] However, you do not want to be remembered for how you looked but for your presentation skills, interpersonal communication, answers to questions, and—above all—for your qualifications for this position with this organization at this time.

Advice for Men

Be on the conservative side in dress and appearance.

Standard interviewing apparel for men is a two-piece dark suit (blue, gray, black) with a white or pastel solid shirt and a contrasting but not "wild" tie. Wear conservative, professional apparel to the interview, even if the interviewer (who has a job by the way) may be dressed informally. Wear a long-sleeved shirt even during the summer. Do not wear a turtleneck shirt. Wear leather, laced business shoes with leather soles, preferably black or cordovan, and not clunky looking. Your belt should match your shoes.

Try the sit-down test to check for fit. Almost anyone can wear clothes that are a bit too tight when standing, but sitting down quickly reveals if the jacket, waistband, seat, or collar is too tight or the shirt gaps at the waist. Insert one finger into the collar of your shirt. If the collar is too tight, you need a larger shirt; if it is too loose, you need a smaller shirt to avoid the sloppy look of a drooping collar.

Coordinate colors carefully.

Wear dark socks that complement your suit and cover at least half a leg so when you sit down and cross your legs, no skin is visible. Tie size and design depend upon what is in style, but it is always safe to wear a wide stripe, small polka dot, or conservative pattern that is blue, red, gray, or burgundy.

When in doubt, ask for help.

Choose clothing that is appropriate for your body shape: regular, thin or slender, heavy or muscular, and tall or short. For example, a heavy, muscular male should choose dark shades with small pinstripes. A thin or slender male may wear a greater variety of clothing, and some plaids might add size and depth to the physical appearance.

Bonnie Lowe writes that "your goal is to look professional and conservative."[60] A sport court or blazer is nearly always too casual except for informal gatherings or dinners associated with the selection process. Your hair should be trimmed and neatly combed or brushed. Facial hair is generally accepted (if neat and trimmed), but know your industries preferences. Professional and conservative also applies to watches, ballpoint and fountain pens, briefcases, earrings, tattoos, and cologne. In today's job market, it is wise to play it safe and to seek every advantage.

Advice for Women

Makeup, hairstyle, and clothing are personal decisions that reveal a great deal about your personality—who you are, your self-concept, and what you think of others. Take them seriously. No makeup is probably too little, but if makeup calls attention to itself, it is too much. Recruiters suggest small (not dangling) earrings with one per ear, one ring per hand, and no bracelets. Coloring is essential, and a cosmetic counselor can help determine what is professionally appropriate for you. Keep perfume to an absolute minimum or use none at all. You do not want to be recalled for your smell.

> **Appearance should not call attention to itself.**

Wear a tailored two-piece suit with skirt or slacks and in navy, black, dark gray, or brown. Skirt length should be to the bottom of the knees when standing and cover your thighs when seated.[61] If you must tug at your skirt when you sit down, it is too short. Avoid skirts with long slits. Select a tailored, conservative blouse that matches your suit while avoiding "see through" blouses or ones with plunging necklines. Wear clear or plain styled stockings appropriate for your outfit. Low, closed-toe, and comfortable pumps are more appropriate than high heels. Carry a simple handbag and a professional-looking briefcase.

> **Provocative clothing can end your candidacy.**

Nonverbal Communication

Nonverbal communication (voice, eye contact, gestures, and posture) are important ingredients throughout selection interviews. Scott Reeves reports a typical example in which an applicant looked very strong on paper but "offered a deadfish handshake, slouched and fidgeted in his chair, failed to make eye contact with the interviewer and mumbled responses to basic questions." He was not hired.[62] Arden cites a study that found "a first impression is based on 7% spoken words, 38% tone of voice, and 55% body language."[63] Interviewers react more favorably toward applicants and rate them higher if they smile, have expressive facial expressions, maintain eye contact, and have clear, forceful voices. Technology plays important roles in the employment process, but recruiters interview applicants because they prefer "high touch" to "high tech" when selecting people who will join and influence the futures of their organizations. They want to see, hear, and observe you in action.

> **Be alive and dynamic.**

Dynamism and energy are communicated through the way you shake hands, sit, walk, stand, gesture, and move your body. Try to appear (and be) calm and relaxed, but sharp and in control. Avoid nervous gestures, fidgets, movements, and playing with pens or objects on the interviewer's desk. Respond crisply and confidently with no sign of arrogance. When replying to questions, maintain eye contact with the recruiter. If there are two or more recruiters in the room, glance at the others when answering a question but focus primarily on the questioner, particularly as you complete your answer.

> **Good communication skills are important in all positions.**

Speak in a normal conversational tone with vocal variety that exhibits confidence and interpersonal skills. Interviewers prefer standard accents. If English is your second language or you have an accent developed since birth, work on your accent and pronunciation so interviewers can understand you clearly and effectively.

Do not hesitate to pause before answering difficult questions, but frequent pauses may make you appear hesitant, unprepared, or "slow." Interviewers interpret pauses of one second or less as signs of ambition, self-confidence, organization, and intelligence.

Interview Etiquette

Arrive for the interview a few minutes ahead of time. If you are not on time for the interview, will you be on time for work? Is this a sign of the importance you place on this interview? Do not arrive too early. The recruiter may have other tasks to perform or interviews to conduct and does not want to assign staff to entertain you until the scheduled interview. Be courteous to everyone you meet.

> **Be on time and ready to interact.**

Greet the employer pleasantly and dynamically. Do not use the interviewer's first name unless invited to do so. Don't extend your hand first.[64] Shake hands if and when the interviewer offers to do so. Then use a firm but not crushing handshake. The interviewer will want to use that hand during the interview. Sit when asked to do so and never sit down before the interviewer does. Be an active participant during the opening. You will become relaxed once you get into the flow of the interview, so respond to opening, icebreaker questions as you would in a normal conversation. How you handle yourself during the first few minutes with a stranger tells the interviewer a great deal about your interpersonal communication and people skills.

Place your briefcase and other belongings on the floor, not on a table or desk. Avoid playing with or rearranging items on a desk. Do not place your feet on any item of furniture. Be sure your cell phone is turned off. Don't interrupt the interviewer, look at your watch, peruse your résumé, or check your BlackBerry for messages. Give your full attention to the interaction. Refrain from telling jokes, using swear words, and employing slang. Never badmouth a former employer. If you are interviewing over a meal, be sure to use proper eating etiquette. Never start eating until everyone at the table has been served. One senior recruiter we talked to related that he took applicants out to nice restaurants to see if they knew how to use the appropriate silverware, how to place the napkin, how to eat soup, and when and how to pass food to others at the table. Don't order alcohol unless invited to do so and then sip one drink during the interview. If you do not drink alcoholic beverages, politely decline the offer. One slip of the lip can end your candidacy for a position. Be sure to say thank you at the close of every interview.

Answering Questions

> **Decisions are made on the total interview.**

We are now ready to discuss the meat of the interview, answering and asking questions. If your first impression has been favorable, now is your opportunity to reveal the substance of your product—you.

Preparing to Respond

Be ready and eager to answer questions effectively. Nervousness will lessen when you concentrate on answering confidently and thoroughly. Successful applicants are prepared to handle frequently asked questions such as:

- Tell me about yourself.
- Why do you want to work for us?

Be ready to handle traditional questions.

- What are your greatest strengths? Weaknesses?
- What are your short-range career goals? Long-range goals?
- Why did you leave your position with _____?
- What did you like best in your position at _____? Like least?
- Why should we select you over the other applicants for this position?
- What do you know about our organization?

These traditional questions play major roles in selection interviews, particularly during the opening minutes. Interviewers use them to get applicants talking and relaxed, and to learn about them as human beings and budding professionals.

The nature of questioning in employment interviews has changed. Interviewers are asking more challenging questions about your experiences in specific situations (behavior-based questions) and placing applicants in **joblike situations** to see how they might fit in and function as employees. The philosophy is simple: employers can determine best how applicants might operate in specific positions by placing them in these positions during the interview. Task-oriented questions assess thinking and communication abilities and reveal how well you can operate in stressful or surprise situations. Here are common on-the-job question strategies:

Welcome on-the-job questions to show what you can do.

- *Behavior-based questions:*

  "Tell me about a time when you operated as part of a team to solve a vexing technical problem."

- *Current critical incident questions:*

  "We are facing a situation in which we . . . If you were on our team, what would you recommend we do to resolve this situation?"

- *Historical critical incident questions:*

  "Two years ago we had a conflict between . . . If you had been the supervisor in this situation, what would you have done?"

- *Hypothetical questions:*

  "Suppose you had a customer who claimed his computer hardware was damaged in shipment. How would you handle this?"

- *Weird hypothetical questions:*

  "If you were a vegetable, what kind of vegetable would you like to be?"

- *Task-oriented questions:*

  "Here's a sheet of paper. Write a policy statement for the assignment of overtime." Interviewers have been known to take out a ballpoint pen and say, "Sell this to me."

Many employers are requiring would-be teachers to teach, salespersons to sell, engineers to engineer, managers to manage, and designers to design. Job simulations, role-playing, presentations, and day-long case studies challenge applicants to demonstrate their knowledge, skills, experiences, maturity, and integrity.

Structuring Answers

Questions that place applicants in job-like situations—behavior-based, current and historical critical incidents, hypothetical—typically require them to tell narratives about experiences or would-be experiences. Ralston, Kirkwood, and Burant write, for instance, that behavioral questions require you to tell stories that are critical to successful interviews. They list several criteria for good stories.[65] Good stories are internally consistent, consistent with the facts employers hold to be true, relevant to questions asked and the applicant's claims, provide details that support claims, and reflect the applicant's beliefs and values. Try one or more of these patterns to structure your answers in a way that tell your stories effectively.

> **Structure answers strategically.**

Mini-speech method: Approach questions, particularly ones that require you to tell stories, as if you were giving a brief speech. This method is a good way to approach critical incident and hypothetical questions that *do not focus* specifically on your *past experiences.* Your speech would be in three traditional parts.

Introduction: Tell recruiters what you are going to tell them.

Body: Tell them.

Conclusion: Tell them what you told them.

STAR Method: The S.T.A.R. method is highly recommended for answering behavior-based questions because it zeroes in on behaviors and skills exhibited in *past experiences* that are highly relevant to the specific position being sought.[66] It has four parts adding up to the word "star."

Situation: Describe the setting or background including when, where, and with whom.

Task: What needed to be done, why, and with what expectations?

Action: What action did you take and how did you do it?

Results: What were the results, accomplishments, consequences?

PAR Method: The P.A.R. method is a variation of the STAR approach and is recommended for behavioral-based questions.[67] Each method shares the goal of focusing on your past performance while emphasizing experiences, skills, leadership, and ability to get a job done. It has three parts.

P: The problem or task you were assigned

A: The actions you took solving the task or problem

R: The results or consequences of your actions

When you are asked a difficult behavior-based, critical incident, hypothetical, or task question, think through your answer carefully, and consider the future ramifications for you and the organization. Ask for additional details about the situation and the problem and determine the authority you would have to act in this situation. Such queries will impress the recruiter with your maturity, professionalism, and understanding of organizational policies and procedures.

Responding Successfully

Listen and think, then respond.

Successful interviewees play active roles in openings and closings. They *listen* carefully to the *whole* question, *think* through each answer carefully, and then respond *succinctly* and *specifically* to the *point* of the question. If, for instance, a recruiter asks, "Why would you like to work as a production supervisor for Caterpillar?" you focus on the specifics of the position open at Caterpillar and why Caterpillar is an ideal fit for your interests and qualifications. Emphasize what you can do for Caterpillar. Answer questions thoroughly, but know when to stop talking. This is particularly important in telephone interviews because you do not have the usual interviewer nonverbal cues (leaning forward, looking at notes, nodding of the head, facial expressions, and gestures) present in face-to-face interviews to tell you when enough is enough.

Think before you speak.

Successful interviewees provide answers that are not only carefully structured with clear arguments and relevant content but also consist of good grammar, choice of words, and action verbs that show you a *doer*. Michael Skube, a journalism professor, has discovered a number of simple and common words that frequently stump college students. These include impetus, ramshackle, lucid, advocate, derelict, satire, brevity, novel, and afflicted vs. afflict.[68] These "potholes in exchanges" turn off recruiters. When asking you a question about working in teams, the recruiter may be listening for the pronouns you use. If you work well in teams, you will speak of *us, we,* and *our*; if you work better alone (perhaps this is your preference), you will speak of *I, me,* and *mine.*

Avoid evasiveness.

Successful interviewees are honest, sincere, and ethical in all that they do during interviews. They are not evasive. They provide responses that appear to be unscripted and unrehearsed. They do not provide answers that merely sound good. Beware of Internet sources that purport to offer sure-fire answers that will impress all recruiters. There is *no single correct answer* to any question. Five different interviewers from the same organization may seek different answers to the same questions.

Successful interviewees are enthusiastic and dynamic. They show interest in this position with this organization. They speak positively about their education and experiences. They demonstrate the characteristics of the organization's ideal applicant profile through interpersonal communication skills, answers, questions, and actions. They know when to follow up questions with questions, paraphrase questions in their own words, ask for clarification, and seek more information or background.

Responding Unsuccessfully

Unsuccessful interviewees play passive and limited roles in both openings and closings. They do not identify with the needs of the organization, perhaps because they know little about either the position or the organization, and show little interest or enthusiasm in this position with this organization. Interviewees appear uncertain about the kind of position they want or where they plan to be in the future. They seem to have unclear or unrealistic goals. During the closing, they do not ask for the position.

Weak applicants are cautious and evasive.

Unsuccessful interviewees are evasive or appear to be trying to tell recruiters what they think recruiters want to hear. Perhaps they are trying to give the "perfect" answers they found on the Internet. Being evasive may lead the recruiter to see the interviewee as dishonest. Unsuccessful interviewees are inflexible in the position they want and seem unwilling to bend a little to fit this position or organizational needs and desires.

Unsuccessful interviewees exhibit poor attitudes. They seem pessimistic about their futures and whether they will be considered fairly. Applicants may badmouth former employers or disparage their schools and the educations they received. Recruiters know that if an applicant badmouths a former employer, they will get this treatment next if they hire this person. Applicants may appear arrogant or cocky and their verbal and nonverbal messages communicate they believe the recruiter is very fortunate to have an opportunity to interview them.

Unsuccessful interviewees have poor listening and thinking skills and blurt out answers they will regret. They use their mouths instead of their heads. For example, when asked "Why should I hire you?" one applicant replied that he would be a great asset to the company softball team while another said he was bored watching TV.[69] Every recruiter can relate interview ending comments such as the following:[70]

Listen and think before acting and talking.

Sorry for yawning; I usually sleep until my soap operas are on.

I am quitting my job because I hate to work hard.

My résumé might look like I am a job hopper. But I want you to know that I never left any of those jobs voluntarily.

Recruiters also tell stories of hard-to-believe actions during interviews such as these:

An applicant stretched out on the floor to fill out the application form.

An applicant wore an iPod and said she could multitask during the interview.

An applicant said she had not had lunch and proceeded to eat a hamburger and fries during the interview.

When asked about his hobbies, an applicant stood up and danced around the office.

Unsuccessful applicants are poor communicators.

When an alarm clock went off in his briefcase, the applicant shut it off, and asked the interviewer to hurry up with his questions because he had to leave for another interview.

As the saying goes, "Don't be a statistic." Think about what you are saying and doing. Unsuccessful interviewees have poor communication skills. They use fewer concrete and active words and do not use technical jargon that exhibits experiences and knowledge of their fields and the positions for which they are interviewing. Their responses tend to be nonassertive and include the following:

Qualifiers such as "perhaps," "maybe," and "sort of."

Meaningless slang such as "you know," "know what I'm sayin'," and "know what I mean."

Nonfluencies such as "ummm" or "uh."

Vague phrases such as "and stuff like that" or "and that sort of thing."

Know what
not to do
during
interviews,
and then do
not do it.

A Marist College poll discovered that words such as "actually," "whatever," "awesome," "literally," "like" and phrases such as "twenty four seven," "Am I making sense," "It is what it is," and "At the end of the day" are among the most annoying and irritating to Americans.[71] Imagine how recruiters feel. We would add to this list "ton of," as in "I have a ton of experience." How do you measure experience in pounds?

Responding to Unlawful Questions

Do not be
surprised
by unlawful
questions.

Applicants, particularly women, are still asked unlawful questions even though federal and state laws have existed for decades and most organizations train employees to follow EEO guidelines. Violations range from mild infractions such as "What does your husband do?" to sexual harassment. Some are accidental during informal chatting with applicants and some are due to curiosity, tradition, lack of training, or ignorance of the laws.

Unlawful questions pose dilemmas for applicants. If you answer an unlawful question honestly and directly, you may lose the position. If you refuse to answer an unlawful question (almost impossible to do graciously), you may lose a position because you are uncooperative, evasive, or "one of those."

Review EEO
laws and your
rights.

Be prepared to answer unlawful questions tactfully and effectively. First, review the EEO laws and exercise in Chapter 7 so you can determine when a question is unlawful.

Exercise #1—Which Questions Are Unlawful and Why?

If you are a Hispanic, female college graduate interviewing for a management position for a national retail chain, which of these questions would be unlawful? Why? How might you reply?

1. Where are you from?

   _____

2. Any marriage plans?

   _____

3. Tell me about your internship at Macy's.

   _____

4. Where do you hope to be in your career in five years?

   _____

5. How long would you expect to work for us?

   _____

6. How well do you speak Spanish?

   _____

7. Which religious holidays do you observe?

   _____

8. Do you have a significant other?

   _____

9. What do you do after work?

_____

10. I see you have a hearing aid; how might that affect your work with us?

_____

Second, be aware of tricks recruiters use to get unlawful information without appearing to ask for it.[72] For example, a low-level clerk may ask you which health insurance plan you would choose if hired; your answer may reveal that you are married and have children, that you are a single parent, or that you have a serious medical problem. During lunch or dinner or a tour of the organization's facilities when you are least expecting serious questions, an employer, perhaps a female, may probe into child care under the guise of talking about her own problems: "What a day! My daughter Emily woke up this morning with a fever, my husband is out of town, and I had an eight o'clock conference downtown. Do you ever have days like this?" You may begin to tell problems you have had with your children or family members and, in the process, reveal a great deal of irrelevant, unlawful, and perhaps damaging information without knowing it. Employers have learned how to get unlawful information through lawful questions. Instead of asking, "Do you have children?" an employer asks, "Is there any limit on your ability to work overtime (evenings, weekends, holidays)?" Others use coded questions and comments.

> **Beware of recruiter tricks to get unlawful information.**

- "Our employees put a lot into their work" means "Older workers like you don't have much energy."
- "We have a very young staff" means "You won't fit in."
- "I'm sure your former company had its own corporate culture, just as we do here" means "Hispanics need not apply."
- "We are a very traditional company" means "We don't hire women beyond clerical staff."

Third, determine how important the position is for you. Your primary goal is to get a good position, and if you are hired, you may be able to change organizational attitudes and recruiters' practices. You can do nothing from the outside. If questions are gross violations, consider reporting the recruiter to his or her superior or to the career center. If this person is typical of the organization or a person you would report to if hired, you might be wise to look elsewhere.

> **Consider your needs and desires before responding.**

Fourth, practice using a variety of answer tactics. For example, try a tactful refusal that is more than a simple "I will not answer that question because it is unlawful."

1. Interviewer: How old are you?

> **Be tactful!**

   Interviewee: I don't think age is important if you are well qualified for a position.

2. Interviewer: Do you plan to have children?

   Interviewee: My plans to have a family will not interfere with my ability to perform the requirements of this position.

Use a _direct, brief_ answer, hoping the interviewer will move on to relevant, lawful questions.

1. **Interviewer:** What does your wife do?

   Interviewee: She's a pharmacist.

2. **Interviewer:** Do you attend church regularly?

   Interviewee: Yes, I do / No, I don't.

Pose a *tactful inquiry* such as the following that skirts the question and attempts to guide the recruiter away from the unlawful inquiry with a job-related question.

1. **Interviewer:** What does your husband do?

   Interviewee: He's in construction. Why do you ask?

2. **Interviewer:** You seem confined to a wheelchair; how might this affect your work performance?

   Interviewee: I am quite mobile in my chair. How is my disability relevant for a position as a computer software designer?

Try to *neutralize* the recruiter's obvious concern.

1. **Interviewer:** Do you plan on having a family?

   Interviewee: Yes, I do. I'm looking forward to the challenges of both family and career. I've observed many of my women professors and fellow workers handling both quite satisfactorily.

2. **Interviewer:** What happens if your husband gets transferred or needs to relocate?

   Interviewee: The same that would happen if I would get transferred or asked to relocate. We would discuss location moves that either of us might have to consider and make the best decision.

Try to *take advantage* of the question to support your candidacy.

Make unlawful questions work for you.

1. **Interviewer:** Where were you born?

   Interviewee: I am quite proud that my background is _____ because it has helped me work effectively with people of diverse backgrounds.

2. **Interviewer:** Are you married?

   Interviewee: Yes, I am, and I believe that is a plus. As you know, studies show that married employees are more stable and dependable than unmarried employees.

You might try what Bernice Sandler, an authority on discrimination in hiring, calls a **tongue-in-cheek test response** that sends an unmistakable signal to the recruiter that he or she has asked an unlawful question. This tactic must be accompanied by appropriate nonverbal signals to avoid offending the interviewer.

Be careful when being clever.

1. **Interviewer:** Who will take care of your children?

   Interviewee: (smiling, pleasant tone of voice) Are you trying to see if I can recognize an unlawful question in the selection process?

2. **Interviewer:** How long do you expect to work for us?

   Interviewee: (smiling, pleasant tone of voice) Is this a test to see how I might reply to an unlawful question?

Asking Questions

While you may pore over lists of recruiter questions and formulate appropriate answers, you may spend little time planning questions *you* will ask. Most recruiters will give you an opportunity to ask questions. Take full advantage of this opportunity.

Guidelines for Asking Questions

Your questions help you not only get information to make an important life decision but also reveal your preparation, maturity, professionalism, interests, motivation, and values. You control this part of the interview; make the most of it.

Asking good questions results in more than information.

A major mistake is not having any or too few questions to ask. Your questions can convince the recruiter that you are the ideal person for a position and organization or destroy the favorable impression you made during the opening and while answering questions.

If you have a number of questions prepared but the interviewer answers all of them during the information-giving stage of the interview, do not ask a question merely to ask a question. There is a good likelihood it will be a poor one because you have not considered it carefully.

Ask insightful and mature questions.

Successful applicants ask more questions than unsuccessful applicants. And the questions of successful applicants are open-ended and probe into the position, organization, and recruiter's opinions to get complete and insightful answers.

Successful applicants ask probing questions.

In addition to the guidelines presented in Chapter 3 for effective questions, here are specific guidelines for employment questions.

- Avoid the "me . . . me . . . me . . ." syndrome in which all of your questions inquire as to what you will get, how much you will get, and when you will get it. These questions indicate that you are *self-centered* and care little about others, including future colleagues and organizations. Organizations expect you to be team-oriented and organization-centered with a healthy desire for rewards and advancement.

Ask your most important question first.

- Avoid questions about salary, promotion, vacation, and retirement during screening interviews and never pose them as your first questions. If salary is your primary concern when choosing a position and organization, the recruiter will turn to others. Recruiters expect you to be interested in rising to higher levels within their organizations, but they also expect you to be interested in and dedicated to the position for which you are interviewing. If time away from work is a primary concern, then perhaps you have little interest in *working* for them.

- Do not waste time asking for information that is readily available on the organization's Web site or in the library. If answers to your questions are readily available on Web sites and company literature, you have obviously made little effort to research either the position or the organization.

Question Pitfalls

When asking questions, you may tumble into the common question pitfalls discussed in previous chapters: double-barreled, curious probe, leading, yes/no response, bipolar, guessing game, and open-to-closed switch. In addition to common question pitfalls, applicants have some pitfalls of their own. These are centered on common wording that can produce a *negative impression* at a critical time late in the interview.

Exercise #2—Applicant Pitfalls

Rephrase each bad question below to make it a good question.

1. *The have to question* may sound like you will be an unhappy and uncooperative employee.

> *Bad:* Would I have to travel much?
>
> *Good:*

> **Prepare a schedule to avoid question pitfalls.**

2. *The typology question* focuses on type rather than explanation that is desired.

> *Bad:* What type of training program do you have?
>
> *Good:*

3. *The pleading question* (often a series of them) seems to beg for answers.

> *Bad:* Could you please tell me about your expansion plans?
>
> *Good:*

4. *The little bitty question* may indicate lack of interest in detailed information, perhaps asking a question merely to ask a question.

> *Bad:* Tell me a little bit about your facility in Atlanta.
>
> *Good:*

5. *The uninformed question* may exhibit lack of maturity or background study prior to the interview.

> *Bad:* Tell me about benefits and stuff like that.
>
> *Good:*

Prepare a moderate schedule of carefully phrased questions. Order them according to importance because you may not get the opportunity to ask five or six questions in a 20- to 25-minute interview, particularly if your questions are open-ended and you probe into answers. Also, the recruiter will assume that you will ask your most important questions first or second. If these are salary and benefits, this is a major turnoff.

> **How you ask may be more important than what you ask.**

Sample Applicant Questions

The following sample applicant questions show interest in the position and the organization, are not overly self-centered, and meet question guidelines:

> **Adapt your questions to each position and organization.**

- Describe your ideal employee for me.
- Tell me about the culture of your organization.
- How does your organization encourage employees to come up with new ideas?

- How much choice would I have in selecting geographical location?
- What is a typical workday for this position?
- What is the possibility of flexible working hours?
- How does your organization evaluate employees?
- What characteristics are you looking for in applicants for this position?
- How might your organization support me if I wanted to pursue an MBA?
- How often would I be working as part of a team?
- What, in your estimation, is the most unique characteristic of your organization?
- How might an advanced degree affect my position in your organization?
- Tell me about where other persons who have held this position have advanced within the organization.
- What do you like most about working for this organization?
- Tell me about the merger with TelEx.
- I noticed in *The Wall Street Journal* last week that your stock has risen almost 4 percent during this economic recession. What explains this increase?
- Tell me about the people I would be working with.
- Tell me about your training program.
- What major departmental changes do you anticipate during the next five years?
- What is the most important criterion for selecting a person for this position?

The following questions may help with a variety of positions in new and startup organizations:

- Which of your products are most in demand?
- Who are your major competitors?
- How much collective experience do your top officers have in the field?
- What are your plans for going public?
- Who are the major regulators of your business?

The Closing

Be aware of everything you say and do.

The closing stage of the employment interview is usually brief. Do not say or do anything that will detract from an impressive performance. Play an active role in the closing. Express your interest in the position and organization. And discover what will happen next, when, and whom you should contact and how if you need to get in touch about the position. Ask for the position tactfully.

The interview "Is not over 'til it's over." If a member of the organization walks you to the outer office, the elevator, or the parking lot, the interview is not over. If a person takes you on a tour of the organization or the area, it is not over. If a person takes you to lunch or dinner, it is not over. The employer will note everything you do and say. Positions are lost because of the way applicants react during a tour, converse informally, meet other people, eat dinner, or handle alcoholic beverages.

Evaluation and Follow-Up

Debrief yourself immediately following each interview. Jot down your answers to tough questions, information the recruiter provided, and the recruiter's answers to your questions. Make a list of pros and cons of the position and organization and what you don't know that would be critical in making a decision. Do you think you did well or not so well? Be careful not to overreact. Your perceptions of what took place during the interview may be greatly exaggerated toward the positive or the negative.

Ask questions such as these during your postinterview debriefing:

- How adequate was my preparation?
- How effective was I during the opening?
- How appropriate were my dress and appearance?
- What opportunities to sell myself did I hit and miss?
- How thorough and to the point were my answers?
- How well did I adapt my questions to this organization and position?
- How effectively did I show interest in this organization and position?
- Did I obtain enough information on this position and organization to make a good career decision?

> Remember: the interview is more art than science.

> Be thorough in your debriefing.

> Quality applicants write thank-you notes.

Follow up the interview with a brief, professional letter thanking the interviewer for the time given you. Promptness is less important than content. Avoid firing off letters with little thought. Lisa Ryan, managing director for recruiting at Heyman Associates of New York, tells the story about walking a person to the elevator and finding an e-mail thank-you note waiting for her when she returned to her office moments later. The candidate had e-mailed her from the elevator. She recommends that you "put some substance into your thank-you note."[73] Emphasize your interest in this position and organization. The thank-you letter provides an excuse to contact the interviewer, keeps your name alive, and includes additional information that might help the organization decide in your favor.

Handling Rejection

All applicants will face rejection, even when they feel interviews went well. Potential employers reject applicants for a variety of reasons, often because of fit or because another applicant has a valued experience or skill. They may interview dozens of people for a single position and must make difficult choices. You will never hear from some recruiters.

How you handle rejections influences your attitudes, attitudes that may lead to further rejections. One writer warns: "**Don't be a victim.** The worst thing tired and frustrated job seekers can do is to conclude that employer reps and hiring managers are out to get them, that the job search process is out of their control, and that they're the victims of some evil, monolithic power."[74] Don't take rejection personally.

> Learn from rejections.

Use each interview as a learning process. Ask what you might do differently in the next interview. How did you handle behavioral-based and critical incident questions?

What was the nature of the questions you asked? How might you have prepared more thoroughly? What did you do that might have turned off the recruiter? Was this a position for which you were highly qualified, or was it a stretch?

Summary

Technology has allowed us to communicate instantly and to send and check information immediately. The scanning of résumés and the use of the Internet as sources for positions and résumé storage are changing the face of searching for positions. Personality, integrity, and drug tests are adding a new dimension to the process.

We have become a part of the global economy and are undergoing a second industrial revolution moving from a manufacturing to a service- and information-oriented society. The best positions in the future will go to those who understand and are prepared for the selection process. You must know yourself, the position, and the organization to persuade an employer to select you from hundreds of other applicants. The job search must be extensive and rely more on networking and hard work than merely appearing at your college career center for an interview. Your résumés and cover letters must be thorough, professional, attractive, adapted to specific positions with specific organizations, and persuasive.

Interviewing skills are increasingly important because employers are looking for employees with communication, interpersonal, and people skills. You can exhibit these best during the interview. Take an active part in the opening, answer questions thoroughly and to the point, and ask carefully phrased questions about the position and the organization. Take an active part in the closing, and be sure the interviewer knows you want this position. Close on a high note.

Follow up the interview with a carefully crafted thank-you letter that expresses again your interest in this position and organization. And do an insightful postinterview evaluation that addresses strengths and weaknesses with future interviews in mind.

Key Terms and Concepts

The online learning center for this text features FLASHCARDS and CROSSWORD PUZZLES for studying based on these terms and concepts.

Appearance	Follow-up	Research
Arrival	Functional format résumé	Résumé
Attitudes	Honesty tests	Screening interview
Behavior-based	Integrity interview	Self-analysis
Branding	Joblike situations	Social media
Career/job fair	Mini-speech method	STAR method
Career objective	Network tree	Successful applicants
Chronological format résumé	Networking	Talent-based
Cover letter	Nonverbal communication	Trait-based universal
Determinate interview	PAR method	Universal attitudes
Dress	Percentage agencies	Universal skills
Electronically scanned	Placement agency	Unsuccessful applicants
Fee-paid positions	Portfolio	
First impression	Relationship	

An Employment Interview for Review and Analysis

This interview is between a senior in computer technology and a college recruiter for Software Specialties, Inc., a firm that creates computer software for the aircraft industry. SS has been growing rapidly as more sophisticated aircraft have come on line and security against terrorism has become a critical concern since 9/11.

How active and effective is the applicant during the opening? What image does the applicant present during the interview? How appropriate, thorough, to the point, and persuasive are the applicant's answers? Has the applicant done adequate homework? How persuasively does the applicant demonstrate an interest in and fit for the position as a production supervisor for SS? How well do the applicant's questions meet the criteria presented in this chapter? How active and effective is the applicant during the closing?

1. **Recruiter:** Good afternoon, Carolyn. (shaking hands) Please be seated.

2. **Applicant:** Thanks.

3. **Recruiter:** I hope you have met some of our people here at the computer science job fair.

4. **Applicant:** Yes, I have. I talked to Jane Fox and Jack Short.

5. **Recruiter:** Good. And you've had an opportunity to look through some of our materials?

6. **Applicant:** Yes.

7. **Recruiter:** Good. I want to talk to you for about 20 to 25 minutes. Let me begin by asking why you chose computer science at Texas Tech.

8. **Applicant:** I've always been a Tech fan, and I wanted to go to a large university close to home.

9. **Recruiter:** And why computer technology?

10. **Applicant:** Well, during my first year, I realized that I was both hands-on and theory-oriented. The computer technology program is very hands-on. After taking some CS classes and talking to students and faculty, I decided to switch majors.

11. **Recruiter:** Describe what you would consider to be an ideal position for you.

12. **Applicant:** I guess it would be like my internship with Microsoft. It would give me an opportunity to work on interesting projects, do some troubleshooting, and stuff like that.

13. **Recruiter:** What do you include in "stuff like that"?

14. **Applicant:** Well, you know, interesting stuff like handheld computers and working on problems with new software.

15. **Recruiter:** Tell me about the most difficult work situation you have ever faced.

16. **Applicant:** It was when my father had a heart attack during my second year.

17. **Recruiter:** How did you handle it?

18. **Applicant:** I leaned sort of on my mom and my older sisters.

19. **Recruiter:** How did you lean on them?

20. **Applicant:** I talked to them a lot, hung out with them more often. They were awesome.

21. **Recruiter:** What about your most difficult *work* experience?

22. **Applicant:** Oh, that's when the Burger Barn burned down.

23. **Recruiter:** Uh huh?

24. **Applicant:** Well, I lost my job and everything.

25. **Recruiter:** What did you do?

26. **Applicant:** I got another job.

27. **Recruiter:** I see. How do you feel about geographical location?

28. **Applicant:** I like to travel and find people very friendly everywhere. Know what I mean?

29. **Recruiter:** Are you saying that you have no geographical preferences?

30. **Applicant:** Pretty much. I guess I would prefer a warm climate.

31. **Recruiter:** What experience have you had working with teams?

32. **Applicant:** I've had a ton of experience with teams.

33. **Recruiter:** Tell me about some of these experiences.

34. **Applicant:** I was involved in teams and group work in most of my CT classes. And I worked with teams often during my internship.

35. **Recruiter:** How often was that?

36. **Applicant:** Oh, I'd say a couple of times a week; sometimes more than that.

37. **Recruiter:** Tell me about a difficult team project.

38. **Applicant:** Well, that was in a design class, and the group was not getting the job done. I had to step in and take charge by calling meetings, assigning specific tasks, and things like that.

39. **Recruiter:** And then?

40. **Applicant:** We managed to meet the deadline and get an A– on the project.

41. **Recruiter:** So this ended up being your project rather than a team project.

42. **Applicant:** Oh no. I served as leader and instigator, but we all did our parts.

43. **Recruiter:** Why would you like to work for SS?

44. **Applicant:** Well, everything I have read indicates that you are one of the fastest growing computer software companies, and I'm really interested in developing software for aircraft and national security.

45. **Recruiter:** Anything else?

46. **Applicant:** Yes. You're located in Atlanta, Georgia, just a few miles from Marietta where Lockeed Martin is developing the F35 Lightening II with versions that can take off conventionally from runways, from carrier decks, or vertically. This may offer great opportunities for SS employees.

47. **Recruiter:** That's true. Why should we hire you for this position?

48. **Applicant:** Well, I have received an excellent education at Tech, and I think my experiences have prepared me thoroughly for this job.

49. **Recruiter:** What do you know about SS?

50. **Applicant:** You were originally started by Robert Cabrini. You went public in the early 90s and formed Software Specialties, Inc. You now have facilities in Georgia, Oregon, Washington, and Nevada.

51. **Recruiter:** We have nearly 1,500 employees with facilities in the states you named and have plans for a facility near Boston. What questions do you have?

52. **Applicant:** What is the salary range for this position?

53. **Recruiter:** It would depend upon the location, but we are very competitive with the industry.

54. **Applicant:** Tell me about the stock-sharing plan mentioned in one of your brochures.

55. **Recruiter:** After you've been with us for six months, you are eligible to purchase stock in the company. We believe this is a good way for all of us to have a stake in what we do.

56. **Applicant:** Would I have to relocate often?

57. **Recruiter:** Not often.

58. **Applicant:** Tell me about the culture of SS. How diverse is your research staff?

59. **Recruiter:** Our research staff includes people from 12 different countries. Any other questions?

60. **Applicant:** Not right now.

61. **Recruiter:** Good. We hope to make a decision in about two or three weeks. It's been good talking with you and getting acquainted.

62. **Applicant:** Thanks for the interview. I'm very interested in a position with SS.

63. **Recruiter:** You're welcome. We'll be in touch.

Employment Role-Playing Cases

A Career in Computer Technology

You are a recent graduate with a degree in computer science and media technology and design. Although you are confined to a wheelchair because of a swimming accident while in high school, you have managed to get around a large university campus for four years and played in a wheelchair basketball league. Your interest is in a computer design position that would require you to travel to a variety of locations in the United States and Japan to confer with other designers and check out technological developments.

Managing a Corporate Farm

You grew up on a 700-acre grain farm in eastern Kansas and will graduate this spring in the animal science department at Kansas State University. Since there is no opportunity to manage the family farm and your interests are in livestock rather than grain, you are interviewing for positions with corporate farms. You have an appointment with a recruiter for Prairie Farms, a corporation that owns both grain and livestock farms in the Midwest and Southwest. The opening is for a manager of Bar Y farms in South Dakota that includes herds of beef cattle and bison. It is a major supplier for specialty steak restaurants in the Midwest, particularly Omaha, Kansas City, Minneapolis, and Chicago.

A Buyer for a Major Department Store

You are in your mid-twenties and have worked with a specialty women's clothing store since graduating from college three years ago with a degree in retail management. You have a good record as a sales associate, and many of your customers seek you out for assistance. Your real professional interest is serving as a buyer rather than a career primarily in sales. You are interviewing in Chicago for a buyer position with Macy's. This would be your dream job.

A Public Relations Position

You recently graduated from college with a major in general communication rather than a specialty because you weren't sure what you wanted to do. The position you are applying for is with a public relations and advertising agency. Its advertisement specified a degree and experience in public relations. While you only took a couple of public relations courses in college, you have worked with local politicians on their campaigns and with the intercollegiate communications office. You helped write press releases and organize events.

Student Activities

1. Contact five college recruiters from different corporations of diverse sizes. See if they use a behavior-based, talent-based, or trait-based system. If so, why do they use this system and how have they modified it over time to suit their specific needs? If they do not use such a system, why have they decided not to do so? If they have abandoned one of these systems after trying it for a few years, why did they abandon it?

2. Visit your college career center to discover the services and materials they offer. How do they counsel students who are trying to determine careers they might be interested in and qualified for? How can they help you arrange and prepare for interviews?

3. Take the Myers-Briggs Personality Indicator. How do the results compare to your self-perceptions? How might these results help determine career paths and positions?

4. Interview five recent college graduates with your major. How large were their networks, and how did they use these networks to locate positions? Who on their networks proved most helpful? How many interviews were involved in the hiring process for their current positions? Did they experience panel interviews as well as traditional one-on-one interviews? How did screening interviews differ from determinate interviews? What were the most critical questions they were asked? What were the most critical questions they asked?

Notes

1. Charles J. Stewart, *Interviewing Principles and Practices: Applications and Exercises* (Dubuque, IA: Kendall/Hunt, 2011); Lois J. Einhorn, Patricia Hayes Bradley, and John E. Baird, *Effective Employment Interviewing: Unlocking Human Potential* (Glenview, IL: Scott, Foresman, 1981).

2. J. Craig Honaman, "Differentiating Yourself in the Job Market," *Healthcare Executive*, July–August 2003, p. 66.

3. Wendy Rose Gould, "How to Prepare for the Job Interview," http://www.ehow/how_1721_prepare-job-interview.html, accessed July 25, 2012.

4. Alison Green, "How to Prepare for a Job Interview," http://money.usnews.com/money/blogs/outside-voices-careers/2011/02/07/how-to-prepare-for-a-job-interview, accessed July 25, 2012.

5. Green.

6. John R. Cunningham, *The Inside Scoop: Recruiters Tell College Students Their Secrets for Success in the Job Search* (New York: McGraw-Hill, 1998), pp. 120 and 184.

7. Deborah Shane, "52% of U.S. Companies Say Job Applicants Are NOT Qualified?" http://www.deborahshanetoolbox.com/millions-of-jobs-and-no-qualified-applicants-how-can-that-be, accessed July 13, 2012.

8. Barbara Safani, "The Ultimate Guide to Job Searching," http://jobs.aol.com/articles/2011/01/24/ultimate-guide-to-job-searching, accessed July 25, 2012; Susan Adams, "Networking Is Still the Best Way To Find a Job, Survey Says," http://www.forbes.com/sites/susanadams/2011/1/06/07/networking-is-still-the-way-to-find-a-job-survey-says, accessed July 27, 2012.

9. Adams; Rachel Levy, "How to Use Social Media in Your Job Search," http://jobsearch.about.com/od/networking/a/socialmedia.html, accessed July 27, 2012; Alexis Grant, "10 Smart Ways to Use Social Media in Your Job Search," http://money.usnews.com/money/careers/slideshows/10-smart-ways-to-use-social-media-in-your-job-search/4-1, accessed July 28/2012.

10. Grant.

11. Grant; Joe Light, "Recruiters Troll Facebook for Candidates They Like," http://online.wsj.com/article/SB10001424053111903885604576490763256558794.html, accessed January 6, 2012.

12. Brad Stone, "Web of Risks," Newsweek, August 28, 2006, p. 77.

13. Kimberly Shea and Jill Wesley, "FaceBook, and Friendster, and Blogging—Oh My! Helping Students to Develop a Positive Internet Presence," Center for Career Opportunities, Purdue University, unpublished manuscript, 2006.

14. "Headhunters Directory.com," http://www.headhuntersdirectory.com, accessed July 30, 2012.

15. "Top Ten Tips for Using Employment Agencies," http://www.libgig.com/toptenemployment agencies, accessed July 30, 2012.

16. "How to Prepare for a Job Fair/Career Fair," http://www.career.vt.edu/JobSearch-Guide/JobCareerFairPrep.html, accessed July 30, 2012.

17. Allison Doyle, "Job Fair Participation Tips," http://jobsearch.about.com/od/jobfairs/a/jobfairs.htm?p=1, accessed October 2, 2009.

18. "The Walkabout Technique," College Grad.com, http://www.collegegrad.com/job-search/Job-Fair-Success/The-Walkabout-Technique, accessed October 2, 2009.

19. "Job Fair Success," College Grad.com, http://www.collegegrad.com/jobsearch/Job-Fair-Success/, accessed October 2, 2009.

20. Anita Bruzzese, "Virtual Job Fairs Expand Search Options for Those Seeking Work," Lafayette, IN, *Journal & Courier*, July 30, 2008, p. D2.

21. Lindsay Olson, "On Careers: How to Brand Yourself for the Job Hunt," http://money. usnews.com/money/blogs/outside-voices-careers/2011/12/06/how-to-brand-yourself-for-the-job-hunt, accessed July 30, 2012; Gallup, "It's Time to Brand Yourself," http:// business-journal.gallup.com/content/121430/time-brand-yourself.aspx, accessed July 30, 2012.

22. Tim Estiloz, "The Key to Job Search Success? Try Branding Yourself!" http://jobs.aol. com/articles/2011/01/11/hranding-yourself-in-2011, accessed July 30, 2012.

23. "It's Time to Brand Yourself."

24. Barbara Safini, "Hot Job Site: Brand-Yourself.com," http://jobs.aol.com/ articles/2011/01//10/hot-job-site-brand-yourself-com, accessed July 30, 2012.

25. Safani.

26. "Tips for Success—The Resume," http://www.worksmart.ca.gov/tips_resume.html, accessed July 9, 2012.

27. "Extra Touches Help Resume Dazzle," Lafayette, IN, *Journal & Courier,* May 21, 1995, p. C3.

28. Richard N. Bolles, *What Color Is Your Parachute? 2010* (Berkeley, CA: Ten Speed Press, 2010), p. 53.

29. Barbara Safani, "The Ultimate Guide to Resumes," http://jobs.aol.com/ articles/2011/01/25ultimate-guide-to-resumes/?icid=main%7Chp-deskt, accessed January 28, 2011; Evelyn U. Salvador, *Step-by-Step Resumes* (Indianapolis: JIST Works, 2006), p. 138.

30. Wes Weller, "5 Tips for Turning Your Resume into an Interview," http://blog.hiredmy-way.com/5-tips-for-turning-your-resume-into-an-interview, accessed August 3, 2012; Fleur Bradley, "10 phrases to Ban from Your Resume," http://www.msnbc.com/id 37219334/ns/business-careers/t/phrases-ban-your-resume, accessed August 3, 2012.

31. Cunningham, p. 68.

32. Robert Reardon, Janet Lenz, and Byron Folsom, "Employer Ratings of Student Partici-pation in Non-Classroom-Based Activities: Findings from a Campus Survey," *Journal of Career Planning and Employment,* Summer 1998, pp. 37–39.

33. Kim Isaacs, "Lying on Your Resume," https://career-advice-monster.com/resumes-cover-letters/resume-writing-tips/lying-on-your-resume/article.aspx, accessed July 13, 2012.

34. Isaacs.

35. Kris Frieswick, "Liar, Liar—Grapevine—Lying on Resumes," *CFO: Magazine for Senior Financial Executives,* http://www.findarticles.com, accessed October 2, 2006.

36. "Lying on Resumes: Why Some Can't Resist," *Dallas Morning News,* The Integrity Center, http://www.integctr.com, accessed October 2, 2006.

37. Scott Reeves, "The Truth About Lies," http://www.forbes.com, accessed October 2, 2006.

38. Danielle Lorenz, "Job Hunting and Career Building," http://talentegg.ca/discuss-view-topic/how-do-employers-conduct-a-primary-scan-of-resumes, accessed July 9, 2012.

39. Debra Auerbach, "Incredibly Dumb Resume Mistakes That Hiring Managers Hate," http://jobs.aol.com/articles/2012/07/11/incredibly-dumb-resume-mistakes-that-hiring-managers-hate, accessed August 7, 2013.

40. Jeff Wuorio, "5 ways to make your resume shine," *USA Weekend*, September 16-18, 2011, p. 4; "Proofread Your Resume," http://www.cvtips.com/resumes-and-cvs/proofread-your-resume.htm, accessed August 7, 2012.

41. Toni Bowers, "Quick Resume Tip: Negotiating resume scanning software," http://www.techrepublic.com/blog/career/quick-resume-tip-negotiating-resume-scanning-software/1950, accessed July 9, 2012; "Preparing a 'Scannable Resume'," http://www.buffalostate.edu/offices/edc/scannable.html, accessed August 7, 2012; "What You Need to Know about Scannable Resumes," http://www.moneyinstructor.com/art/scanresume.asp, accessed July 9, 2012.

42. Tom Washington and Gary Kanter, "Creating a Scannable Resume," http://careerempowering.com/resume-empower/creating-a-scannable-resume. html, accessed July 14, 2012

43. "The New Electronic Job Search Phenomenon," an Interview with Joyce Lain Kennedy, Wiley, http://archives.obs-us.com/obs/german/books/kennedy/JLKInterview.html, accessed December 2, 2008.

44. "Scannable Resumes Presentation," https://owl.english.purdue.edu/owl/resource/700/1, accessed August 7, 2012.

45. Annette Bruzzeze, "Online Resumes Can Trigger Identity Theft," Lafayette, IN, *Journal & Courier*, August 30, 2006, p. D3.

46. "Cover Letters: ypes and samples," http://www.career.vt.edu/jobsearchguide/coverlettersamples.htm, accessed August 8, 2012.

47. Cover letters: types and samples; Louise M. Kursmark, Best Resumes for College Students and New Grads (Indianapolis: JIST Works, 2012).

48. Benjamin Ellis, "The Four A's of the Successful Job Search," *Black Collegian*, October 2000, p. 50.

49. Thomas W. Dougherty, Daniel B. Turban, and John C. Callender, "Confirming First Impressions in the Employment Interview: A Field Study of Interviewer Behavior," *Journal of Applied Psychology* 79 (1994), pp. 659–665.

50. Sarah E. Needleman, "Four Tips for Acing Interviews by Phone," *The Wall Street Journal,* http://www.career;journal.com, accessed September 11, 2006.

51. Amelia J. Prewett-Livingston, Hubert S. Field, John G. Veres III, and Philip M. Lewis, "Effects of Race on Interview Ratings in a Situational Panel Interview," *Journal of Applied Psychology* 81 (1996), pp. 178–186.

52. Karol A. D. Johansen and Markell Steele, "Keeping Up Appearances," *Journal of Career Planning & Employment,* Summer 1999, pp. 45–50.

53. Scott Reeves, "Is Your Body Betraying You in Job Interviews?" http://www.forbes.com, accessed October 20, 2006.

54. "Interview Appearance and Attire," http://www/career.vt.edu/Interviewing/InterviewAppearance.htm, accessed August 10, 2012; Carole Martin, "The 2-Minute

Drill," http://career-advice.monster.com/job-interview/interview-appearance/the 2-minute-drill/article.aspzx, accessed August 10, 2012.

55. Robert DiGiacomo, "Six Style Tips for Interview Success," http://career-advice-monster.com/job-interview/interview-appearance-stype-tips-for-interview-success-hot-jobs/articls.aspzx, accessed August 10, 2012.

56. Carole Martin, "10 Interview Fashion Blunders," http://career-advice.monster.com/job-interview/interview-appearance/10-interview-fashion-blunders/article.aspx, accessed August 10, 2012; Thad Peterson, "Dress Appropriately for Interviews," http://career-advice.monster.com/job-interview/interview-appearance/appropriate-interview-dress/article.aspx, accessed August 10, 2012.

57. Thad Peterson, "Dress Appropriately for Interviews," http://career-advice.monster.com/job-interview/Interview-Appearance/Appropriate-Interviews, accessed October 2, 2009.

58. Peterson; Carole Martin, "Casual or Casualty?" http://career-advice.monster.com/job-interview/interview-appearance/casual-or-casualty/article.aspx, accessed August 10, 2012.

59. "Interview Appearance and Attire."

60. Bonnie Lowe, "Job Interviews: Plan Your Appearance to Make a Great First Impression," Ezine Articles, http://ezinearticles.com/?Job-Interview:-Plan-Your-Appearance-to-Make-a-Great-First-Impression, accessed October 2, 2009.

61. "How to Dress for an Interview," http://www.123getajob.com/jobsearch2.html, accessed October 2, 2009; Cheryl Ferguson, "Recruiting Roundtable: Interview Fashion and Grooming Tips," http://career-advice.monster.com/job-interview/inetrview-appearance/recruiter-roundtable-fashion-grooming-tips-hot-jobs/article.aspx, accessed August 10, 2012; DiGiacomo.

62. Reeves, "Is Your Body Betraying You in Job Interviews?"

63. Reeves, "Is Your Body Betraying You in Job Interviews?"

64. Penny Kiley, "Business etiquette and the job interview," hppt://gradireland.wordpress.com/2011/11/07/business-etiquette-and-the-job-interview, accessed August 10, 2012; Margaret Page, "Outclass the Competition with Simple Interview Etiquette," http://etiquettepage.com/business-etiquette/outclass-the-competition-eith-simple-interview-etiquette, accessed August 10, 2012; Didi Lorillard, "Business Etiquette & Manners: Job Interviews," http://www.golocalprov.com/business/business-etiquette-manners-job-interviews, accessed August 10, 2012.

65. Steven M. Ralston, William G. Kirkwood, and Patricia A. Burant, "Helping Interviewees Tell Their Stories," Business Communication Quarterly, September 2003, pp. 8–22.

66. "STAR Method of Answering Questions," https://www.cco.purdue.edu/Student/Job SearchSkillsBehavioralInterviewing.shtm, accessed August 10, 2012; Nagesh Belludi, "The 'STAR' Technique to Answer Behavioral Interview Questions,"http://www.right-attitudes.com/2008/07/15/star-technique-answer-interview-questions, accessed July 9, 2012; Lindsay Browning"P.A.R. Interview Technique," http://www.lindsaybrowning.ie/2010/08/23/p-a-r-interview-technique, accessed July 9, 2012.

67. Korey Dowling, "Interview Tips: Using the S.T.A.R Method," http://www.adventis-templolyment.org.au/items/interview-tips-using-the-s-t-a-r-method, accessed July 9, 2012; "Nurse Interview Questions and Answers – Part 2," http://www.job-interview-site.com/nurse-interview-questions-and-answers-part-2.html, accessed August 28, 2012; Maureen Malone, "Behavior-Based Interview Tips," http://www.ehow.com/list_6520299_behavior_based-interview-tips.html, Accessed August 28, 2012.

68. Michael Skube, "College Students Lack Familiarity with Language, Ideas," Lafayette, IN, *Journal & Courier*, August 30, 2006, p. A5.

69. "Why Should I Hire You?" *Afp Exchange,* November–December 2003, p. 8.

70. "Run That One by Me Again: You Did What at Your Last Job?" *Barron's,* January 13, 2003, p. 12.

71. Marist Poll, "12/16: Whatever, Still Most Annoying Word, You Know. Like, Seriously? Just Sayin'." http://maristpoll.marist.edu/1216-whatever-still-most-annoying-word-you-know-like-seriously-just-sayin'/, accessed August 31, 2012.

72. William Poundstone, "Why Are Manhole Covers Round (and How to Deal with Other Trick Interview Questions)," *Business,* July 2003, p. 14.

73. Kris Maher, "The Jungle: Focus on Recruitment, Pay and Getting Ahead," *The Wall Street Journal,* January 14, 2003, p. B10.

74. "Job Seekers, Take Heart—and Control," *BusinessWeek Online,* http://www.businessweek.com, accessed September 11, 2006.

Resources

Bolles, Richard N. *What Color Is Your Parachute? 2010: A Practical Manual for Job-Hunters and Career-Changers.* Berkeley, CA: Ten Speed Press, 2013.

Enelow, Wendy S., and Shelly Goldman. *Insider's Guide to Finding a Job*. Indianapolis, IN: JIST Works, 2005.

Kursmark, Louise M. *Best Resumes for College Students and New Grads.* Indianapolis: JIST Works, 2012.

Martin, Carole. *Perfect Phrases for the Perfect Interview*. New York: McGraw-Hill, 2005.

Salvador, Evelyn U. *Step-by-Step Resumes*. Indianapolis: JIST Works, 2006.

Yate, Martin. *Knock 'Em Dead: The Ultimate Job Seekers Guide*. Adam, MA: Adam Media Corp., 2006.

The Performance Interview

There are few processes more important to modern organizations than reviewing the performance of its employees. A few years ago a senior executive of a major high-tech company told the authors that "Today everyone has the same computers, technology, and buildings, so the major difference is people and their creative contribution. My job is to attract, develop, empower, and retain the best minds and creative spirits that I can find." An important key to developing, empowering, and retaining employees is the performance review. However, after completing an exhaustive review of the literature and research on the "appraisal process," Michael Gordon and Vernon Miller conclude, "Despite the fact that it was created for good and valuable purposes, performance appraisal is the source of widespread dissatisfaction."[1] Many of its detractors have called for the elimination of the appraisal process. Gordon and Miller counter this argument by citing "serious literature that offers ample and persuasive evidence that performance appraisal is worth the effort and is an indispensable management responsibility."[2] Those of us who have been intimately involved in performance reviews can also relate that it may be the most trying of management responsibilities.

Gordon and Miller report their literature review and research in *Conversations About Job Performance: A Communication Perspective on the Appraisal Process*. Their key principle is the concept that "the appraisal interview is a conversation about performance," what they refer to as "the defining moment in the appraisal process."[3] They also claim, however, that the interview "remains the Achilles' heel of the performance appraisal process" and "the greatest source of dissatisfaction with the process."[4] A major cause of this dissatisfaction is that few parties in performance review interviews are trained in conducting or taking part in these critical conversations.

The objectives of this chapter are to introduce you to the notion of the performance review interview as a *coaching process*, to ways of preparing effectively for these critical *organizational conversations*, to a variety of *review models*, to the principles of *conducting* and *taking part* in performance interviews, and to the performance *problem* interview. Let's begin by approaching the performance interview as a coaching event.

Approaching the Interview as a Coaching Opportunity

A new vision for organizations with an emphasis on developing, empowering, and retaining the best talent is coinciding with a new vision of the performance interview or, in the words of Gordon and Miller, "conversation about performance."

Management consultant Garold L. Markle calls this vision "catalytic coaching." Catalytic coaching is:

> A comprehensive, integrated performance management system built on a paradigm of development. Its purpose is to enable individuals to improve their production capabilities and rise to their potential, ultimately causing organizations to generate better business results. It features clearly defined infrastructure, methodology and skill sets. It assigns responsibility for career development to employees and establishes the boss as developmental coach.[5]

Catalytic coaching is *future* rather than *past* centered, places responsibility on the employee rather than the superviser, and deals with salary indirectly. The supervisor is a coach rather than evaluator. Markle declares that this approach spells "the end of the performance review" as we have known it.

When we reviewed several performance review models designed to develop employees and enhance performance, the notion of coaching—effective communication in a nonjudgmental atmosphere—was the centerpiece of each. Former pro-football coach Don Shula and former pro-football player Ken Blanchard have developed a set of basic principles that appropriately spell out the word "coach."[6]

- Conviction driven—Never compromise your beliefs.
- Overlearning—Practice until it's perfect.
- Audible ready—Respond predictably to performance.
- Consistency of leadership—Consistency in performance.
- Honesty based—Walk the talk.

Markle and the Shula-Blanchard duo emphasize the importance of commitment to excellence, honesty, responsibility, and teamwork that result in effective interpersonal communication, a review that provides meaningful feedback, and an enhanced level of performance.

The philosophy of coaching rather than judging performance has heightened the need for more frequent and improved performance interviews, discussions, and development. Frequent communication between supervisors and employees results in more favorable job-related performance ratings.[7] Kenneth Wexley claims that "If a manager provides coaching on an ongoing basis, the [appraisal interview] becomes a review of issues that have already been discussed by the manager and employee in the past."[8]

Create a supportive climate that involves the interviewee.

Organizations are conducting various forms of performance interviews on a more frequent basis and are connecting them closely to developmental and coaching plans. Employees prefer a **supportive climate** that includes mutual trust, subordinate input, and a planning and review process. They want to be treated sensitively by a supportive, nonjudgmental interviewer. They want to contribute to each aspect of the review, get credit for their ideas, know what to expect during the interview, have the ability to do what is expected, receive regular feedback, and be rewarded for a job well done.

Above all, the employee must see "fairness" in the performance interview, and it's "the nature of the communication that takes place during the appraisal interview" that is "especially critical in creating a sense of fairness about the process."[9]

You can create a relaxed, positive, and supportive climate by continually monitoring the employee's progress, offering psychological support in the forms of praise and encouragement, helping correct mistakes, and offering substantial feedback. Base your review on performance, not on the individual. Provide performance-related information and measure performance against specific standards agreed upon during previous reviews. Employees see supervisors as helpful, constructive, and willing to help them solve performance-related problems when these supervisors encourage them to express their ideas and feelings and to participate equally in performance review interviews.[10]

> **"Too seldom" is a common complaint.**

Providing feedback on a regular basis can avoid formal, once-a-year "tooth-pulling" reviews dreaded by both parties. Evaluate poor performance immediately before damage to the organization and the employee is irreparable. Avoid surprises during the interview caused by withholding criticisms until the formal review session. Conduct as many sessions as necessary to do the job right.

Preparing for the Performance Interview

> **Be careful of judging what you cannot measure.**

Training is essential for successful reviews. You must know how to create a genuine dialogue with the interviewee. Be a good listener by not talking when the other wants to talk and by encouraging the employee to speak freely and openly.[11] Be an active listener by asking appropriate and tactful questions, not a passive listener who lets the other party talk with little guidance or support. Avoid *"Why"* questions that place the interviewee on the defensive because they may intentionally or unintentionally communicate disapproval, disbelief, or mistrust. Playing the role of evaluator reduces the two-way communication process and negatively affects your relationship. Interviewees perceive interviewers who know how to handle performance-related information, assign goals, and give feedback to be equitable, accurate, and clear during performance interviews, in other words to be credible.

Reviewing Rules, Laws, and Regulations

There are no laws that address the performance review directly, but several EEO laws and guidelines pertain to the review process. You need to be keenly familiar with laws such as the following to avoid charges of unlawful practices during reviews: Title VII of the 1964 Civil Rights Act as amended, the Age Discrimination in Employment Act of 1967, and the Americans with Disabilities Act of 1990 that forbid discrimination based on age, race, color, gender, religion, national origin, and physical and mental impairments. All elements of the employment process are covered by civil rights laws and EEO guidelines, including hiring, training, compensating, promoting, transferring, and discharging.

Be careful of assessing traits such as honesty, integrity, appearance, initiative, leadership, attitude, and loyalty that are difficult to rate objectively and fairly.

Supervisors at all levels have found it useful to talk periodically with each subordinate about personal and work-related issues.

© John A Rizzo/Pixtal/SuperStock

"Using unreliable and unvalidated performance appraisal" systems may cause serious legal problems because personal preferences, prejudices, and first impressions may lead to intentionally inflating or deflating performance ratings to get even, punish employees, or promote them to another department.[12]

Laws do not require performance reviews, but ones conducted must be standardized in form and administration, measure work performance, and be applied equally to all employees. Goodall, Wilson, and Waagen warn that communication between "superiors" and "inferiors" in the review process leads to ritual forms of address "that are guided by commonly understood cultural and social stereotypes, traditional etiquette, and gender-specific rules."[13] If this is so, do not be surprised if you violate EEO laws and guidelines. The American workforce is increasingly older, and age discrimination is becoming the most prominent area of litigation even though older workers perform better than younger workers.[14]

Diane Chinn and Maurice Baskin, two authorities on performance reviews and EEO laws, offer a variety of suggestions to make all reviews conform to the law and avoid lawsuits.[15] All supervisors who conduct performance reviews must receive detailed written guidelines and instructions and be trained in conducting all aspects of reviews, particularly the interview. They must follow these guidelines to the letter. Have two or more staff review employees separately as cross-checks on accuracy and avoidance of bias. Be sure performance appraisals are reviewed with employees, making sure employees have the opportunity to offer suggestions and raise concerns before signing them. Employees should have full access to all records pertaining to their work.

> **Age will play an ever-greater role as baby boomers turn 50 and 60 in ever-greater numbers.**

Selecting Review Model

Theorists and organizations have developed performance review models to meet EEO laws and to conduct fair and objective performance-centered interviews applicable to different types of positions and organizations. Their goals are to establish competencies, set goals and expectations, monitor performance, and provide meaningful feedback.[16]

> **The BARS model focuses on skills.**

Behaviorally Anchored Rating Scales (BARS) Model

In the **behaviorally anchored rating scales** (BARS) model, skills essential to a specific position are identified through a position analysis and standards are set, often with the aid of industrial engineers. Typical jobs for which behaviors have been identified and standards set include telephone survey takers (at so many telephone calls per hour), meter readers for utility companies (at so many meters per hour), and data entry staff or programmers (at so many lines of entry per hour). Job analysts identify specific skills and weigh their relative worth and usage. Each job has specific measurable skills that eliminate game-playing or subjective interpretation by interviewers.

Employees report high levels of review satisfaction with the BARS model because they feel they have greater impact upon the process and see interviewers as supportive.[17] They know what skills they are expected to have, their relative worth to the organization, and how their performance will be measured. However, not every job has measurable or easily identifiable skills, and arguments often arise over when, how, and by whom specific standards are set. Gordon and Miller have also discovered that "Raters distort the evaluations they make on subjective instruments in order to achieve goals other than providing an accurate assessment of the employee's performance (e.g., maintaining interpersonal relationships and group harmony)."[18]

Management by Objectives (MBO) Model

The **management by objectives** model involves a supervisor and an employee in a mutual (50-50) setting of results-oriented goals rather than activities to be performed.

> **The MBO model focuses on goals.**

Advocates of the MBO model contend that behaviorally based measures can account for more job complexity, be rated directly to what an employee does, and minimize factors the employee cannot control. This model is designed to be less role ambiguous and subjective than person-based measures by making clear which behaviors are required for a specific job. It facilitates performance feedback and goal setting by encouraging employer-employee discussions regarding strengths and weaknesses.

> **The MBO model applies four criteria to each position: quality, quantity, time, and cost.**

The MBO model classifies all work in terms of four major elements: inputs, activities, outputs, and feedback.[19] Inputs include equipment, tools, materials, money, and staff needed to do the work. Activities refer to the actual work performed: typing, writing, drawing, calculating, selling, writing, shipping. Outputs are results, end products, dollars, reports prepared, or services rendered. Feedback refers to subsequent supervisor reaction (or lack of it) to the output. When you act as a performance review interviewer using a MBO model, keep several principles in mind.

1. Always consider quality, quantity, time, and cost. The more criteria you use, the greater the chances that the measurement will be accurate.

2. State results in terms of ranges rather than absolutes. Allow for freedom of movement and adjustment.

> **Do not consider too many objectives.**

3. Keep the number of measurable objectives critical to performance to no more than six or eight, and set a mutual environment.

> **Beware of setting complex objectives.**

4. Try for trade-offs between mutually exclusive aims and measures. An objective that is too complex may be self-defeating. For example, attempts to reduce labor and decrease cost at the same time may create more problems than you solve.

5. When the value of the performance is abstract, initiate practices that make it measurable.

6. If you cannot predict conditions on which performance success depends, use a floating or gliding goal that enables you to adapt to changing circumstances. Unfortunately the strengths of the MBO model, including its interactive nature and adaptability to complex positions, have led many organizations to abandon it because of "the large number of meetings required and the amount of documentation necessitated."[20] Gordon and Miller write that unlike other models, it cannot be standardized to facilitate comparisons "across individuals or organizational units."

Universal Performance Interviewing Model

William Cash developed the **universal performance interviewing model** and tested it in more than 40 organizations. This model begins with four basic questions that can serve as guidelines for fairness and comparisons among employees. Interviewers must be able to specify what is missing or not being done well so they can provide feedback to institute change.

The UPI model focuses on performance and work requirements.

1. What is not being done that should be?
2. What expectations are not being met at what standard?
3. Could the person do it if motivated?
4. Does the individual have the skills to perform as needed?

Understand why performance is lagging.

Narrow each problem to a coachable answer. For example, maybe no one has emphasized that getting 100 percent of customers' numbers at the beginning of calls is critical because the customer number drives the system and makes it easier to access billing and other information under that number. Maybe the employee knows the customer's number by heart and intends to place it in the correct position on the screen after the customer hangs up. The observation judgment dilemma has always been a problem for performance reviewers.

The four questions in conjunction with six key words shown in Figure 9.1 enable interviewers to make several observations about performance. This model can be employed with others (such as the popular 360-degree review process) or with separate observations by supervisors, peers, and customers (internal and external) that can be compared to one another for consistency, trends, and rater reliability.

Figure 9.1   *Six key words in the universal performance interviewing model*

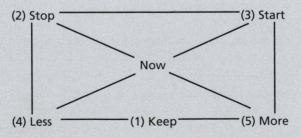

A sheet of paper with the four questions in columns can provide the bases for coaching sessions that take place weekly for production workers and monthly for professionals. A summary session may be done quarterly with an annual review to set goals for the coming year, review progress, and look at developmental needs.[21]

Once you have answered the four basic questions, start on the model with *keep*. When an employee is doing something well, make sure the person knows you appreciate a job well done. Then go to *stop*, followed by *start, less, more,* and finishing with a time frame for improving performance. The word *now* emphasizes the importance of making appropriate changes immediately. Define *now* specifically in terms of weeks or perhaps months.

The universal performance interviewing model enables you as coach to start with positive behavior you wish the employee to maintain, followed by behaviors you wish corrected now. This begins the interview on a positive note. Your *stop* list should be the shortest and reserved for behaviors that are qualitatively and procedurally incorrect, place an employee at risk, or are destructive to others in the workplace.

You can present each of the four questions and the six words at different verbal and nonverbal levels, including hints, suggestions, and corrections. For example, you might say:

I want you to stop doing . . .	You must do more of . . .
I want you to start doing . . . now	You must do less of . . .

Interviewers may spend too much time on the analytical end and too little time on a specific behavior to be altered and how. If you cannot provide a specific alternative behavior, there is no need for a performance review.

Let's use the customer service representative mentioned earlier as an example. Assume that the representative knows many customer numbers because of the frequency of calls from them and has the numbers memorized. She thinks it is unnecessary to log each number into the system until she has finished discussing specific problems with customers. Use one of the following styles to present the problem without making it a bigger problem.

- *Hint:* (smiling pleasantly) I noticed you were busy this morning when I stopped by to observe you. I just thought it might be easier for you to record each customer's number at the beginning of your conversation.

- *Suggestion:* (neutral facial expression and matter-of-fact vocal inflections) Just one idea came to mind from my observation this morning. I'd like to see you record each customer's number early so it doesn't get lost in the shuffle of answers to other callers.

- *Correction:* (stern voice and face) Based on my observation this morning, you must be sure to record each customer's number before you do anything else on the system for that number. This number drives our entire system, and problems result when it is not recorded immediately.

The purpose of every performance interview is to provide accurate feedback to the employee about what must be altered, changed, or eliminated and when. Most employees want to do a good job, and the performance mentor or coach must provide direction for resolving the problem.

Another part of the model, crucial in performance interviews, are the two Ss—*specific* and *several*. Performance interviews must not be guessing games. The two Ss enable interviewers to provide specific examples to show the problem is not a one-time incident but a trend.

Figure 9.2 includes all parts of the universal performance interviewing model. It allows you to measure or observe on-the-job behavior and either compare it to goals or quickly correct the smallest error.

The 360-Degree Approach

The **360-degree approach** to performance review has gained widespread acceptance, particularly among Fortune 500 companies. It "enables organizational members to receive feedback on their performance, usually anonymously, from all major constituencies they serve": supervisors, peers, subordinates, subcontractors, customers, and so on.[22]

Each firm employs a somewhat unique 360-degree process, questionnaires, and interview schedules, but we can describe the typical process. An employee works with a supervisor to select a number of evaluators, such as a direct supervisor, staff at the same level as the employee, colleagues, and individuals from departments the employee interacts with on a regular basis. The 360-degree model requires team and interpersonal skills. Questionnaires covering skills, knowledge, and style are sent to each of the evaluators. The completed questionnaires are summarized and, in some cases, scores are displayed on a spreadsheet. The manager selects individuals from the original group to serve as a panel to conduct a feedback interview. The interviewer/facilitator may take the raw data from the questionnaires and interview the evaluators. The employee receives the data in advance of the meeting. Each participant comes with coaching or behavior change input. The purpose is not to attack or blame the employee but to provide objective, behavior-based feedback with suggestions where necessary for improvement. The employee may not need much improvement, so compliments are acceptable.

> Vague comments and suggestions may harm relationships and fail to improve performance.

> The 360-degree approach involves multiple observers.

> The interviewee plays a role in selecting evaluators.

Figure 9.2   *The universal performance interviewing model*

(2) Stop ——————————— (3) Start

Specific
Several   Now   Hints
                                          Suggestions
                                          Corrections

(4) Less ——————— (1) Keep ——————— (5) More
(Training)   (Motivation)

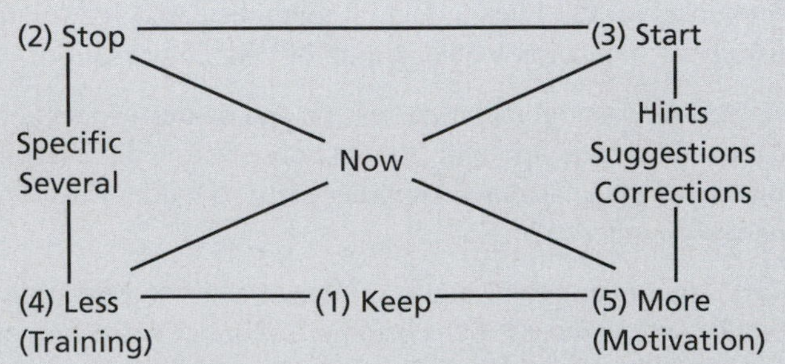

The 360-approach uses a group feedback interview.	The interviewer/facilitator may ask the employee to start the meeting with reactions to the data, then ask open questions with neutral probes. For example:

- Tell me about your responsibilities in R&D.

    Tell me more.

    Explain it to me.

    Describe your frustrations with the consultants' training manual.

Employ open questions and probe into answers.	- If you were going to take on a similar project, what would you do more or less of? - When you identified people in accounting as "bean-counters" what did you mean?

How did they behave?

What did they say?

What did they do?

A plan for improvement is essential.	Once the feedback session is completed, both parties formulate a plan for improvement.

The use of **multisource feedback** for employee development works best in organizations that use a goal-setting process from the top down.[23] The 360-degree approach has a number of advantages. The questionnaires and interview provide objective data and feedback necessary for employee improvement and development because this feedback emanates from multiple sources: supervisors, peers, subordinates, and customers. The employee not only has control over who gives feedback but is able to read, hear, and discuss the data that provides documentation for dealing with performance problems.

Be aware of pluses and minuses of each review model.

Although the 360-degree approach is widely popular, it is not without its critics. Jai Ghorpade writes that it is fraught with five significant paradoxes.[24] (1) Although it is designed for employee development, "it gets entangled with the appraisal process." (2) Multiple raters may increase the scope of information provided to the employee but not better information. (3) Anonymous ratings may be inaccurate, incompetent, and biased. (4) "Quantitative and structured feedback on generic behaviors is easy to acquire, score, and disseminate," but it may have serious problems of accuracy, fairness, and interpretation because it is difficult to control rater tendencies. (5) "Involving persons in authority may taint the process and reduce its credibility." Angelo DeNisi and Avraham Kluger recognize many of the same problems with the 360-degree feedback approach and write that although most feedback reviews lead to improvement in performance, 38 percent of effects are negative.[25] They offer suggestions such as: (1) Use this system for development rather than decision-making purposes, (2) help employees interpret and react to ratings, (3) minimize the amount of information given to employees, (4) do not have performance review team members evaluate employees in all areas, and (5) use the 360-degree system on a regular basis rather than once or occasionally. Vernon Miller and Fredric Jablin cite different scores from raters, including the employee, the involvement of untrained raters or ones with inexperience in areas they are rating, and the assumption that increasing the number of raters results in feedback quality.[26]

ON THE WEB

As you begin to think seriously about specific careers and organizations, investigate how organizations assess the performance of employees. Use the Internet to discover the types of performance review models used by employers in which you have a career interest. Access two types of resources. First, research employers through general resources such as CareerBuilder (http://www.careerbuilder.com), MonsterTrak (http://www.monstertrak.com/), and Monster (http://www.monster.com/). Second, check the Web sites of specific organizations such as Pricewaterhousecoopers (http://www.pwc.com), Ford (http://www.ford.com/), and Electronic Data Systems (http://www.eds.com).

Garold Markle writes that the 360-degree approach is highly inefficient because it is enormously time-consuming on the part of both interviewer and interviewee and takes weeks or months in turnaround time. This delay may result in both parties forgetting what they had to say during the process.[27]

Critics of the 360-degree approach recognize its strengths as well as its deficiencies and recommend solutions to make it a more efficient and reliable method of reviewing and enhancing performance.[28] Use the 360-degree model as a regular part of performance reviews and for decision making only. Do not use this approach as the "primary mechanism for delivering downward feedback." Provide training and guidance for all raters, emphasizing objectivity in ratings to lessen bias, and limit raters to their areas of expertise. Do not assume that more raters equal quality feedback, and be careful of overloading employees with data.

Choosing what appears to be the best performance review model for your organization and employees is important to the review process, but the best model will fail if the performance interview is not conducted skillfully and if either party is dissatisfied with its nature and outcome. Studies indicate that organizations often try one system after another and may adopt the system others are abandoning.[29] Be aware that the communication that takes place during the interview or interviews is critical in every system.

Conducting the Performance Interview

Study the employee's past record and recent performance reviews. Review the employee's self-evaluation. Understand the nature of the employee's position and work. Pay particular attention to the fit between the employee, the position, and the organization. Identify in advance the primary purpose of the interview, especially if it is one of several with an employee. Prepare key questions and forms you will use pertaining to measurable goals.

Select and understand the perspective of the interview.

Know yourself and the employee as persons. Are you aware of your potential biases and how you can minimize or eliminate them in the interview? Will you approach the interview from an appraisal or a developmental perspective? From an **appraisal perspective,** you may see the interview as required and scheduled by the organization, superior-conducted and directed, top-down controlled, results-based, past-oriented, concerned with *what* rather than *how,* and organizationally satisfying. By contrast, from a **developmental perspective,** the interview is initiated by individuals whenever needed, subordinate-conducted and directed, bottom-up controlled, skill-based, now- and future-oriented, concerned with *how,* cooperative, and self-satisfying. Select a developmental approach, Markle's "catalytic coaching," rather than an appraisal approach.

> **Relationship influences both parties and the nature of the interview.**

Understand the relationship that exists between you and the employee. What is your relational history? Are you the best person for the interviewer role? Would the interviewee prefer someone else? How motivated is each party to take part in the process? How will control be shared? Research reveals that two or more reviewers often evaluate the same employee differently because their relationships differ.

Schedule the interview several days in advance so that both parties can prepare thoroughly. Prepare a possible action plan to be implemented following the interview.

Opening the Interview

Put the interviewee at ease with a pleasant, friendly greeting. Get the person seated in an arrangement that is nonthreatening and not superior-subordinate. Fear of what performance interviews might yield interferes with communication between parties and keeps the review process from achieving its full potential.[30]

> **Be prepared but flexible in opening the interview.**

Establish rapport by supporting the employee and engaging in a few minutes of small talk. Orient the employee by giving a brief outline of how you want the interview to proceed. If there is something the employee wants to talk about first, do it. An alteration of your interview plan is worth the improved communication climate. Encourage the employee to ask questions, bring up topics, and participate actively throughout the interview.

Discussing Performance

> **Use all of your listening skills.**

Communication skills are essential to successful performance interviews. Be aware of your own nonverbal cues and observe those emanating from the interviewee. It is not so much *what* is said but *how* it is said. Listen carefully to the interviewee and adapt your listening approach to the changing needs of the interview, listening for comprehension when you need to understand, for evaluation when you must appraise, with empathy when you must show sensitivity and understanding, and for resolution when developing courses of action to enhance performance.

"Be an active listener" is good advice and common sense, but Goodall, Wilson, and Waagen warn that interviewers must know *why* they are listening actively: "Motives may include a desire to exhibit efficient appraisal behavior, to show a concern for the interviewee's well-being, or to collect evidence that may be used for or against the subordinate at a later date."[31] The first two are positive, but the third may be detrimental to the interview and future interactions.

> **Feedback is central in performance interviews.**

Maintain an atmosphere that ensures two-way communication beyond Level 1 by being sensitive, providing feedback and positive reinforcement, reflecting feelings, and exchanging information. Feedback may be your most important skill. Use a team of interviewers rather than a single interviewer. Research indicates that the panel approach produces higher judgment validation, better developmental action planning, greater compliance with EEO laws, more realistic promotion expectations, and reduced perception of favoritism.

Make the discussion full and open between both parties with the goal of improving individual and organizational performance. Keys to success are your abilities to communicate information effectively and encourage open dialogue. Strive to be a coach in career management and development.

Discuss the interviewee's total performance, not just one event. Begin with areas of excellence so you can focus on the person's strengths. Strive for an objective, positive integration of work and results. Cover standards that are met and encourage the interviewee to identify strengths. Communicate factual, performance-related information and give specific examples.

Either excessive praise or criticism may create anxiety and distrust. Employees expect and desire to discuss performance weaknesses. An employee who receives no negative feedback or suggestions of ways to improve will not know which behavior to change. Discuss needed improvements in terms of specific behaviors in a constructive, nondirective, problem-solving manner. Employees are likely to know what they are not doing, but unlikely to know what they should be doing. Let the employee provide input.

Probe tactfully and sensitively for causes of problems. On the other hand, do not heap criticism upon the employee. The more you point out shortcomings, the more threatened, anxious, and defensive the employee will become. As the perceived threat grows, so will the person's negative attitude toward you and the review process. It is often not what is intended that counts but what the other party believes is intended.

Terry Lowe identifies seven ways to ruin a performance review.[32] The **halo effect** occurs when you give favorable ratings to all duties when the interviewee excels in only one. The **pitchfork effect** leads to negative ratings for all facets of performance because of a particular trait you dislike in others. The **central tendency** causes you to refrain from assigning extreme ratings to facets of performance. The **recency error** occurs when you rely too heavily on the most recent events or performance levels. The length of service of an interviewee may lead you to assume that present performance is high because past-performance was high. The **loose rater** is reluctant to point out weak areas and dwells on the average or better areas of performance. The **tight rater** believes that no one can perform at the necessary standards. And **competitive raters** believe no one can perform higher than their levels of performance.

Summarize the performance discussion and make sure the employee has had ample opportunity to ask questions and make comments before establishing goals. Use reflective probes and mirror questions to verify information received and feedback given. Use clearinghouse questions to be sure the employee has no further concerns or comments.

Setting New Goals and a Plan of Action

Goal-setting is the key to successful performance reviews and should constitute 75 percent of the interview. Focus on future performance and career development. Hill writes that "Although it is important to evaluate on the basis of past performance, it is just as important to anticipate future growth, set goals, and establish career paths."[33]

Follow these guidelines when discussing and setting goals. Review previous goals before setting new ones because both parties must be able to determine when goals have been met and why. Make goals few in number, specific and well-defined rather than ambiguous, practical, neither too easy nor too difficult, and measurable. Avoid either-or statements, demands, and ultimatums. Combining feedback and employee suggestions with clear goal setting—while avoiding intentional or unintentional imposition of goals—produces the highest employee satisfaction. Decide upon follow-up procedures with the employee and how goals will be implemented.

> **The interviewee must be an active participant.**

Closing the Interview

Do not rush the closing. Be sure the interviewee understands all that has transpired. Conclude on a note of trust and open communication. End with the feeling that this has been an important session for interviewee, interviewer, and the organization. If you have filled out a required form sign off on the agreements. If organizational policy allows, permit interviewees to put notes by items they feel strongly about. Provide a copy of the signed form as a record of the plan for the coming performance period.

> **Close with the perception that the interview has been valuable for both parties.**

The Employee in the Performance Review

Maintain complete, detailed, accurate, and verifiable records of your career activities, initiatives, accomplishments, successes, and problem areas.[34] Make a list of goals set during the last performance review. Keep letters and e-mails that contain positive and unsolicited comments from supervisors, co-workers, subordinates, clients, customers, and management. Analyze your strengths and weaknesses and be prepared for corrective actions with ideas to improve on your own. Self-criticism may soften criticism from others.

> **Do a self-evaluation before the interview.**

At least half of the responsibility for making the performance interview a success rests with you. Approach the interview as a valuable source of information on prospects for advancement, a chance to get meaningful feedback about how the organization views your performance and future, and an opportunity to display your strengths and accomplishments. Be prepared to give concrete examples of how you have met or exceeded expectations. Prepare intelligent, well-thought-out questions. Be ready to discuss career goals.

> **Approach the interview with a positive attitude.**

Maintain a productive, positive relationship with the interviewer and do not become defensive unless there is something to become defensive about. If the interviewer puts you on the defensive, maintain direct eye contact and clarify the facts before answering charges. Ask, "How did this information come to your attention?" or "What are the exact production figures for the third quarter?" This gives you time to formulate thorough and reasonable responses based on complete understanding of the situation. Answer all questions thoroughly. Ask for clarification of questions you do not understand. Offer explanations, not excuses. Assess your performance and abilities reasonably, and be honest with yourself and your supervisor. Realize that what you are, what you think you are, what others think you are, and what you would like to be may describe different people.

> **Avoid unnecessary defensiveness.**

<table>
<tr><td>

A good offense is better than a good defense.

</td><td>

The performance review interview is not a time to be shy or self-effacing. Mention achievements such as special or extra projects, help you have given other employees, and community involvement on behalf of the organization. Be honest about challenges or problems you expect to encounter in the future. Correct any of the interviewer's false impressions or mistaken assumptions. Do not be afraid to ask for help.

</td></tr>
</table>

The performance review interview is not a time to be shy or self-effacing. Mention achievements such as special or extra projects, help you have given other employees, and community involvement on behalf of the organization. Be honest about challenges or problems you expect to encounter in the future. Correct any of the interviewer's false impressions or mistaken assumptions. Do not be afraid to ask for help.

If you are confronted with a serious problem, discover how much time is available to solve it. Suggest or request ways to solve your differences as soon as possible. The interviewer is not out to humiliate you, but to help you grow for your own sake and that of the organization. Keep your cool. Telling off your supervisor may give you a brief sense of satisfaction, but after the blast, the person will still be your supervisor and the problem will be worse. Do not try to improve everything at once. Set priorities with both short- and long-range goals.

During the closing, summarize or restate problems, solutions, and new goals in your own words. Be sure you understand all that has taken place and the agreements for the next review period. Be certain that the rewards fit your performance. Close on a positive note with a determination to meet the new goals.

The Performance Problem Interview

When an employer has problems with an employee, the situation may range from excessive absences, failure to follow rules and procedures, and insubordination with supervisors to actions that threaten the well-being of fellow employees and supervisors, the organization, or customers and clients. The current practice is to handle all but extreme cases as a performance problem that requires coaching and to avoid the use of the term *discipline* that *implies guilt*. In many states, employers must show *just cause* for disciplining or terminating an employee.

Determine Just Cause

Just cause "means a legally sufficient reason" for an action that a litigant can prove in court to the satisfaction of a judge.[35] When it pertains to employment, just cause means that an employer must have sufficient justification for disciplining an employee to improve performance (rather than as punishment) or to terminate employment because of "misconduct irreconcilable or inconsistent with the contract of employment."[36] The opposite of just cause is *at will* which means that "either party may terminate the employment relationship at any time for any reason."[37]

In 1966, Carroll Daugherty of Northwestern University developed Seven Tests for Just Cause to be used in grievance arbitration between union workers and their employers.[38] They have since become the standard criteria employed in both union and nonunion discipline and termination actions.[39] The following seven tests or criteria for just cause can serve as guides when conducting performance problem interviews.

• *Was the employee given clear and unambiguous warning of possible disciplinary consequences for failure to follow a rule or directive?*

Follow an oral warning with a written warning within a short time.

- *Was the rule or directive reasonably related to the orderly, efficient, and safe operation of the organization?*

  This rule or directive must be applied routinely and equally to all similar employees.

> **Treat all employees fairly and equally.**

- *Before taking action, was the alleged incident investigated timely to determine if the employee had in fact disobeyed a rule or directive?*

  Timely usually means that an investigation occurred within one to three days.

- *Was the investigation conducted fairly, objectively, and in an impartial manner?*

  Did the employer interview all parties involved and obtain all necessary proof and documentation?

- *Was adequate evidence and documentation gathered to prove that a violation of a rule or directive had occurred?*

  Write down the problem in detail and obtain necessary proof and records before arranging for a performance problem interview.

> **The punishment must fit the infraction.**

- *Were all employees determined to be in violation of a rule or directive given equal treatment?*

  Each organizational investigation of a performance problem must be conducted in exactly the same manner with no evidence of discrimination.

- *Is the penalty applied reasonably related to the seriousness of the problem and the employee's total performance record?*

  Penalties must be appropriate for the performance problem and progressive rather than regressive in nature.

Prepare for the Interview

> **Practice before conducting the real thing.**

Prepare for performance problem interviews by taking part in realistic role-playing cases. These rehearsals can lessen anxiety and help you anticipate employee reactions, questions, and rebuttals. The variety of situations and interviewees encountered can help you refine your case-making, questioning, and responding.

Role-playing cases, literature reviews on performance problem situations, and discussions with experienced interviewers will help you learn what to expect. For example, Monroe, Borzi, and DiSalvo discovered four common responses from employees that occurred in 93 percent of incidents.[40]

1. *Apparent compliance:* overpoliteness and deference, apologies, promises, or statements of good intentions.

> **Be prepared for common reactions and responses.**

2. *Relational leverage:* statements that they have been with the organization longer than the interviewer and therefore know best, that they are the best and you can't fire or discipline them, reference to friends or relatives within the organization, or reference to your close relationship to them.

3. *Alibis:* claims of tiredness, sickness, being overworked, budget cuts, family problems, it's someone else's fault, or poor instructions or information.

4. *Avoidance:* disappearing on sick leave or vacation, failure to respond to memos or phone calls, or failure to make an appointment.

What evidence do you have of the infraction?

Review *how* you know the employee has committed an infraction that warrants an interview. Did you see the infraction directly, as in the case of absenteeism, poor workmanship, intoxication, harassing another employee, or insubordination? Did you find out indirectly through a third party or by observing the results (such as lateness of a report, poor quality products, or goals unmet)? Were you anticipating an infraction because of a previous incident, behavior, or stereotype? For example, African-Americans and other minorities are often watched more closely than others because supervisors believe they are more likely to violate rules. On the other hand, supervisors tend to be lenient with persons they perceive as likable, similar to themselves, or possessing high status or exceptional talent. Supervisors may avoid confronting persons they know will "explode" if confronted. Not confronting is the easy way out.

Distinguish between the severity of infractions.

Next, decide whether the perceived problem warrants a review. Absenteeism and low performance are generally considered more serious than tardiness and horseplay. Determine the cause of the infraction because this will affect how you conduct the interview and what action to take.

Review the employee's past performance and history. Two basic reasons for action are poor performance or a troubled employee. When a person's performance gradually or suddenly declines, the cause may be motivational, personal, work-related, or supervisory. Drops in performance may be indicated by swings in the employee's behavior. Keep an eye on performance indicators such as attendance, quality or quantity of work, willingness to take instructions, and cooperation.

A troubled employee may have an alcohol or drug dependency, a marital disturbance, problem with a child, or an emotional problem such as depression. An employee may be stealing from your organization to support a gambling habit, drug or alcohol addiction, or a boyfriend or girlfriend. These employees need professional counseling.

Relational dimensions are critical in performance problem interviews.

For principles applicable to the performance problem interview, see the performance portion of this chapter and Chapter 11 on the counseling interview. Consider the relational dimensions discussed in Chapter 2. Often neither party wants to take part, and you may have delayed the interview until there is no other recourse and multiple problems have piled up. As a specific problem comes to a head, you and the employee may come to dislike and mistrust one another, even to the point of verbal and nonverbal abuse.

Keep Self and the Situation under Control

Uncontrolled anger can destroy an interaction.

While you want to head off a problem before it becomes critical, do not conduct a performance problem interview when you are angry. You will be unable to control the interview if you are unable to control yourself. Trust, cooperation, and disclosure are difficult to attain in a threatening environment.

When one or both parties may have difficulty containing their anger or animosity, follow these suggestions.

- *Hold the interview in a private location.* Meet where you and the employee can discuss the problem freely and openly.

- *When severe problems arise, consider delaying a confrontation and obtaining assistance.* Let tempers cool down. You may want to consult a counselor or call security before acting.
- *Include a witness.* The witness should be another supervisor because using one employee as a witness against another employee is dangerous for all parties involved. Follow to the letter all procedures spelled out in the union contract and organizational policies.

Focus on the Problem

> Deal with facts rather than impressions and opinions.

Deal in specific *facts,* such as absences, witnesses, departmental records, and previous disciplinary actions. Do not allow the situation to become a trading contest: "Well, look at all the times I have been on time" or "How come others get away with it?"

> Avoid unsupported accusations.

- *Record all available facts.* Unions, EEOC, and attorneys often require complete and accurate records. Take detailed notes, record the time and date on all material that might be used later, and obtain the interviewee's signature or initials for legal protection. Establish a **paper trail**.

- *Do not be accusatory.* Avoid words and statements such as troublemaker, drunk, thief, and liar. You cannot make medical diagnoses so avoid medical terms.

- *Preface remarks carefully.* Begin comments with phrases such as "According to your attendance report . . . ," "As I understand it . . . ," and "I have observed . . ." These force you to be factual and avoid accusing an employee of being guilty until proven innocent.

> Ask questions that draw out the interviewee.

- *Ask questions that enable the employee to express feelings and explain behavior.* Begin questions with "Tell me what happened . . . ," "When he said that, what did you . . . ," "Why do you feel that . . . ?" Open-ended questions allow you to get facts, feelings, and explanations from the employee.

© Digital Vision

■ *Never conduct a performance review interview when you are angry, and conduct the interview in a private location.*

Avoid Conclusions during the Interview

A hastily drawn conclusion may create more problems than it solves. Some organizations train supervisors to use standard statements under particular circumstances. If you are sending an employee off the job, you may say:

> "I do not believe you are in a condition to work, so I am sending you home. Report to me tomorrow at . . ."

"I want you to go to medical services and have a test made; bring me a slip from the physician when you return to my office."

"I'm sending you off the job. Call me tomorrow morning at nine, and we can discuss what action I will take."

Be slow to draw conclusions.

Such statements give you time to talk to others, think about possible actions, and provide a cooling-off period for all concerned.

Closing the Interview

Conclude the interview in neutral. If discipline is appropriate, do it. Realize, however, that delaying action may enable you to think more clearly about the incident. Be consistent with organizational policies, the union contract, and all employees. Refer to your organization's prescribed disciplinary actions for specific offenses.

Summary

Review an employee's performance on the basis of standards mutually agreed upon ahead of time. Apply the same objectives equally to all employees performing a specific position. Research and good sense dictate that performance, promotion, and problem issues are discussed in separate interview sessions. Performance review interviews should occur at least semiannually, while promotion, salary, and performance problem interviews usually take place when needed. Deal with performance problems before they disrupt the employee's work or association with your organization. Select a performance review model most appropriate for your organization, employees, and positions.

For both employer and employee, flexibility and open-mindedness are important keys in successful performance review interviews. Flexibility should be tempered with understanding and tolerance of individual differences. The performance process must be ongoing, with no particular beginning or end. Supervisors and subordinates are constantly judged by the people around them. By gaining insights into their own behavior and how it affects others, both parties can become better persons and organization members.

Key Terms and Concepts

The online learning center for this text features FLASHCARDS and CROSSWORD PUZZLES for studying based on these terms and concepts.

360-degree approach	Competitive rater	Recency error
At will	Halo effect	Supportive climate
Behavior-based feedback	Just cause	Tight rater
Behaviorally anchored rating scales	Loose rater	Universal performance interviewing model
Catalytic coaching	Management by objectives	
Central tendency	Multisource feedback	
	Pitchfork effect	

A Performance Interview for Review and Analysis

Living in the Great Outdoors, Inc. is a rapidly expanding general merchandise chain in the upper Midwest that caters to those who live, work, and play in the outdoors. It offers full lines of outdoor clothing for children and adults, outdoor gear for fishing, hunting, hiking, and skiing, and furnishings for cabins and second homes. Melissa Swenson is manager of a Living in the Great Outdoors mega-store near Duluth, Minnesota. Gabe Johansen has been the dock manager for a little over a year. This is a semi-annual performance review interview. The interview is taking place in the manager's office at 3:30 p.m. on a Friday afternoon shortly before Gabe is scheduled to get off work for a three-day weekend.

How effective is rapport building and orientation? Is the climate supportive or defensive? How effectively do manager and production supervisor deal with positive aspects of performance before getting to negative aspects? Does either party dominate a specific phase of the interview? How effectively do the parties set goals for the next review period? How effectively is the interview closed? How skilled is the manager, as a coach?

1. **Interviewer:** Good afternoon Gabe, have a seat.

2. **Interviewee:** Thanks. It's a great fall day with a three-day weekend.

3. **Interviewer:** Any plans?

4. **Interviewee:** Yes. Andy's home from North Dakota State, and we're planning some hiking along Lake Superior.

5. **Interviewer:** Great! What a wonderful way to spend some time with your son. Any questions before we get started on the fall review?

6. **Interviewee:** Not really. We've been discussing my performance and the delivery dock's problems from time to time.

7. **Interviewer:** That helps doesn't it? As I've said before, we are really pleased with your performance as dock manager. Before you took over, it was not unusual for us to take more than a day to unload a truck, and this meant a driver staying overnight and his rig being out of use for an extra day.

8. **Interviewee:** I've never figured out why it took so long. You just move things along in an orderly manner.

9. **Interviewer:** That's right. It's not unusual now that you unload a truck in a half-day.

10. **Interviewee:** A lot of this credit belongs to my crew that has really bought into the new procedures and assignments. Frankly, I'm afraid with the cost cutting going on that our record may not be as good during the next quarter.

11. **Interviewer:** Don't worry about that. I've got your back.

12. **Interviewee:** That's good to hear, but don't stand too far back (laughs).

13. **Interviewer:** I won't (smiles). We are concerned about an increase in breakage with house wares. Our records indicate that there has been a slow but steady increase in breakage as unloading times decline. Care to comment about this?

14. **Interviewee:** Well . . . I wasn't aware of the increase in breakage. When you're moving thousands of items from truck to store to floor, it's inevitable that something

will get dropped, particularly when taking fragile items out of containers and placing them on shelves.

15. **Interviewer:** The breakage is occurring for the most part from truck to floor, not truck to store or placing merchandise on shelves and displays.

16. **Interviewee:** How do you know that?

17. **Interviewer:** I've instructed our stockers to contact me when they open a container and discover damaged goods. Nearly all damage occurs from truck to floor. I've seen very little damage of items being placed on shelves or displays.

18. **Interviewee:** Perhaps some of this damage, maybe a lot of it, is happening when trucks are being loaded. They really jam things in there with forklifts.

19. **Interviewer:** All items are now carefully checked before being loaded into containers, and a supervisor signs off on items and observes their loading.

20. **Interviewee:** I see. When were you going to tell me about this problem?

21. **Interviewer:** I was making sure that I had all of the information I needed and that could be documented before confronting you. I'm not blaming you, personally, of course. I certainly don't believe that you have personally broken items, but you need to supervise your dock crew more carefully both when unloading trucks and when transporting items to the floor.

22. **Interviewee:** Well, it's not easy to be in two places at once. We have drastically reduced the time it takes to unload and turn around our delivery trucks because I'm right there throughout the process. If I leave the unloading area and wander throughout the store, I'm concerned about the speed of unloading.

23. **Interviewer:** Gabe, you need to pick people you can trust to do what is needed without your constant supervision. I don't expect you to unload trucks and supervise at the same time. You're the manager, not the crew.

24. **Interviewee:** I see what you're saying, but I've always been a hands-on type. I think my crew respects me because I'm not afraid to get my hands dirty.

25. **Interviewer:** You must find the right balance between being manager and crew member. Work on reducing your supervision and relying on people you feel you can trust with more responsibility. You picked your crew so now you must pick the leaders among them.

26. **Interviewee:** Okay. What else?

27. **Interviewer:** Not much really. I'd like you to be a little more flexible with work assignments.

28. **Interviewee:** What do you mean by that?

29. **Interviewer:** Well . . . when you do not have a truck scheduled, we do need for you to help out in other areas.

30. **Interviewee:** Such as? I've got my hands full most of the time on the dock. And I am dock manager.

31. **Interviewer:** Yes, you are, and I know you are very busy when a truck is in. However, we could use you in displays and, at times, placing merchandise on the floor. You don't seem to be very happy when asked to help in other areas.

32. **Interviewee:** I don't recall any of these people volunteering or being asked to help us on the dock. I'm not sure most people could find their way to the dock.

33. **Interviewer:** I understand your feelings, but work on being less agitated when asked to help elsewhere.

34. **Interviewee:** I'm agitated?

35. **Interviewer:** Well, let's end on a positive note. I am very pleased with your performance as dock manager, your primary position. All I'm asking is that you be a bit more vigilant to reduce breakage and to be a little more willing to help in other areas when you have the time.

36. **Interviewee:** Okay. I can do that. Anything else?

37. **Interviewer:** Nope, that's it. Have a great weekend hiking with your son.

Performance Review Role-Playing Cases

An Aircraft Maintenance Specialist

The interviewer is the Maintenance Supervisor at the central maintenance repair facility for Mid-American Airlines, a regional carrier. He is conducting a quarterly performance review interview with a maintenance specialist who joined the airline three years ago right out of a university aviation technology program. His record has been excellent with only a few minor problems that appear to have been resolved. Unfortunately, the airline has suffered from a great deal of bad publicity following two recent incidents in which rows of seats came unbolted during flights. No injuries have occurred, but the FAA and consumer advocacy groups are demanding answers. Since the interviewee is primarily responsible for checking and repairing passenger seats, the interviewer will probe into reasons for these potentially deadly occurrences and discover what the interviewee has done and plans to do to make certain no seats come loose in flight again.

A Volleyball Coach

The interviewer is the Athletic Director at Forbes College and reviews the performance of all coaches prior to the start of their seasons in late August and when seasons end from January to May. The interviewee is the head coach of the women's volleyball team that has won 54 percent of its games each of the past three years. This year is expected to be the break-out year because the team is loaded with experience and has two highly recruited players. This interview will focus on the prospects for a stellar season and how the coach is working at motivating the team individually and as a whole. Her teams traditionally start strong and then fade near the end of the season. Degree of success this season may determine the coach's future at Forbes College.

A Retail Manager

The interviewer is the manager of a large department store and conducts performance reviews with the departmental managers semi-annually. The employee is the Women's Department Manager. She is forty-two years old and a single mother of four children ages thirteen to nineteen. The interviewee does an excellent job. She anticipates problems, thinks of a variety of appropriate solutions for every problem, and is highly professional in manner and dress. Unfortunately, she is starting to come in late for work rather frequently and seems to have ready-made excuses for each occasion, some of which are barely believable. The interviewer must determine how to approach this manager about the effects her tardiness are causing in her department without affecting her outstanding work. She does not want to lose this manager, but she must help her to correct this problem.

A Troubleshooter

The interviewer is the vice president of a large paper products manufacturer that has plants throughout the United States and in several other countries. He oversees plant managers and engineering troubleshooters who travel weekly to different plants to resolve production problems, set up and troubleshoot new computer systems, and train personnel in operating new production equipment. The interviewee, a former plant manager, is an excellent troubleshooter, but he is becoming unhappy with the constant travel and being away from his family. This performance interview is aimed at keeping the interviewee happy and on the job as well as reviewing performance.

Student Activities

1. Interview a human resources director at a medium to large organization about performance reviews. Ask questions such as: Which performance review system or model do you employ? Why did you select this system? How did you adapt this model to your organization? How do you train interviewers to be coaches rather than judges? How do you address potential bias in performance reviews?

2. Compare and contrast Garold Markle's "catalytic coaching" approach to performance review with the behaviorally anchored rating scales model, the management by objectives model, and the universal performance interviewing model. How might the catalytic coaching approach alter each and improve each?

3. Contact supervisors at three different types of organizations: industrial, academic, and religious. Ask about the types and severity of behavioral problems they have encountered among employees during the past three years. What were the causes of these problems? How did they use performance interviews to address these problems? Who were involved in these interviews? How were interviews adapted to type and severity of behavioral problems? How effective were the interviews in resolving the problems short of dismissal?

4. Terminating employees is always a difficult decision for organizations to make and is fraught with problems ranging from an angry employee, to lawsuits for unfair and unjustified termination, to violence following termination. Interview three people who have experience in terminating employees to discover how they prepare cases for termination, conduct performance problem interviews that will result in termination, and how they attempt to safeguard against lawsuits and potential violence.

Notes

1. Michael E. Gordon and Vernon D. Miller, *Conversations About Job Performance: A Communication Perspective on the Appraisal Process* (New York: Business Expert Press, 2012), p. 6.

2. Gordon and Miller, p. 7.

3. Gordon and Miller, p. x.

4. Gordon and Miller, pp. ix and 7.

5. Garold L. Markle, *Catalytic Coaching: The End of the Performance Review* (Westport, CT: Quorum Books, 2000), p. 4.

6. Taken from *Everyone's a Coach* by Don Shula and Ken Blanchard. Copyright 1995 by Shula Enterprises and Blanchard Family Partnership. Used by permission of Zondervan Publishing House (http://www.zondervan.com).

7. K. Michele Kacmar, L. A. Witt, Suzanne Zivnuska, and Stanley M. Gully, "The Interactive Effect of Leader-Member Exchange and Communication Frequency on Performance Ratings," *Journal of Applied Psychology* 88 (2003), pp. 764–772.

8. Kenneth N. Wexley, "Appraisal Interview," in R. A. Berk (ed), *Performance Appraisal: Methods and Applications* (Baltimore: Johns Hopkins Press, 1986), p. 168.

9. Gordon and Miller, pp. 25–26.

10. Ronald J. Burke, William F. Weitzell, and Tamara Weir, "Characteristics of Effective Employee Performance Review and Development Interviews: One More Time," *Psychological Reports* 47 (1980), pp. 683–695; H. Kent Baker and Philip I. Morgan, "Two Goals in Every Performance Appraisal," *Personnel Journal* 63 (1984), pp. 74–78.

11. "Guidelines for Conducting the Performance Interview," http://www.lcms.org, accessed December 19, 2006.

12. "Performance Appraisal," Answer.com, http://www.answers.com/topic/performance-appraisal?&print=true, accessed October 9, 2009.

13. H. Lloyd Goodall, Jr., Gerald L. Wilson, and Christopher F. Waagen, "The Performance Appraisal Interview: An Interpretive Reassessment," *Quarterly Journal of Speech* 72 (1986), pp. 74–75.

14. Gerald R. Ferris and Thomas R. King, "The Politics of Age Discrimination in Organizations," *Journal of Business Ethics* 11 (1992), pp. 342–350.

15. Diane Chinn, "Legal Implications Associated With a Performance Appraisal," http://www.eHow.com/info_8038194_legal-implications-associated-performance-appraisal.htm, accessed September 28, 2012; Maurice Baskin, "Legal Guidelines for Associations for Conducting Employee Evaluations and Performance Appraisals," http://www.asaecenter.org/Resources/whitepaperdetail.cfm?itemnumber=12208, accessed September 28, 2012.

16 David Martone, "A Guide to Developing a Competency-Based Performance-Management System," *Employment Relations Today* 30 (2003), pp. 23–32.

17. Stanley Silverman and Kenneth N. Wexley, "Reaction of Employees to Performance Appraisal Interviews as a Function of Their Participation in Rating Scale Development," *Personnel Psychology* 37 (1984), pp. 703–710.

18. Gordon and Miller, pp. 21 and 23.

19. This explanation comes from a booklet prepared by Baxter/Travenol Laboratories titled *Performance Measurement Guide*. The model and system were developed by William B. Cash, Jr., Chris Janiak, and Sandy Mauch.

20. Gordon and Miller, p. 25.

21. Jack Zigon, "Making Performance Appraisals Work for Teams," *Training,* June 1994, pp. 58–63.

22. Jai Ghorpade, "Managing Five Paradoxes of 360-Degree Feedback," *The Academy of Management Executive* 14 (1993), p. 140.

23. Anthony T. Dalession, "Multi-Source Feedback for Employee Development and Personnel Decisions," in *Performance Appraisal: State of the Art in Practice,* James W. Smitter, ed. (San Francisco: Jossey-Bass, 1998).

24. Ghorpade, pp. 140–150.

25. Angelo S. DeNisi and Avraham N. Kluger, "Feedback Effectiveness: Can 360-Degree Appraisals Be Improved?" *The Academy of Management Executive* 14 (1993), pp. 129–139.

26. Vernon D. Miller and Fredric M. Jablin, "Maximizing Employees' Performance Appraisal Interviews: A Research and Training Agenda," paper presented at the 2003 annual meeting of the National Communication Association at Miami Beach; correspondence with Vernon Miller, December 12, 2008.

27. Markle, pp. 76, 78.

28. Miller and Jablin; DeNisi and Kluger, pp. 136–137; Ghorpade, pp. 144–147; Markle, p. 79; Gordon and Miller, pp. 23–24.

29. Gordon and Miller, pp. ix and 17.

30. Goodall, Wilson, and Waagen, pp. 74–87; Arthur Pell, "Benefiting from the Performance Appraisal," *Bottomline* 3 (1996), pp. 51–52.

31. Goodall, Wilson, and Waagen, p. 76.

32. Terry R. Lowe, "Eight Ways to Ruin a Performance Review," *Personnel Journal* 65 (1986), pp. 60–62.

33. Hill, p. 7.

34. "Powering Up Your Annual Performance Reviews," July 23, 2009, *Executive Career Insights,* http://www.executivecareerinsights.com/my_weblog/performance-reviews/, accessed October 8, 2009.

35. "Just Cause & Legal Definition," http://definitions.uslegal.com/j/just-cause, accessed October 4, 2012.

36. "Just Cause Definition," http://www.duhaime.org/LegalDictionary/J/JustCause. aspx, accessed October 4, 2012; Diane Chinn, "Standard of Proof in an Employee's

Discipline Case," http://smallbusiness.chron.com/standard-proof-employees-discipline-case-14236.html, accessed October 4, 2012.

37. Kirk A. Johnson and Elizabeth Moser, "Improvement #4: Limit 'Just Cause' Discipline and Discharge Clauses," http://www.mackinac.org/4915, accessed October 4, 2012.

38. Chinn, "Standard of Proof in an Employee's Discipline Case."

39. "What Is Just Cause?" http://www.hr.ucdavis.edu/supervisor/Er/copy_of-Justcause, accessed October 4, 2012; "Seven Tests of Just Cause," http://hrweb.berkeley.edu/guides/managing-hr/er-labor/disciplinary/just-cause, accessed October 4, 2012; Diane Chinn, "Standard of Proof in an Employee's Discipline Case"; Improvement #4.

40. Craig Monroe, Mark G. Borzi, and Vincent DiSalvo, "Conflict Behaviors of Difficult Subordinates," *Southern Communication Journal* 54 (1989), pp. 311–329.

Resources

Fletcher, Clive. *Appraisal, Feedback, and Development: Making Performance Work.* New York: Routledge, 2008.

Harvard Business Review Staff. *Harvard Business Review on Appraising Employee Performance.* Cambridge, MA: Harvard Business School Press, 2005.

Markle, Garold L. *Catalytic Coaching: The End of the Performance Review.* Westport, CT: Quorum Books, 2000.

Gordon, Michael E., and Vernon D. Miller. *Conversations About Job Performance: A Communication Perspective on the Appraisal Process.* New York: Business Expert Press, 2012.

Winter, Graham. *The Man Who Cured the Performance Review.* New York: John Wiley, 2009.

10

The Persuasive Interview

T his chapter focuses on the *persuasive interview* in which the essential purpose is to influence how parties *think*, *feel*, and/or *act*. It is a *mutual* interaction in which both parties must play active and critical roles because persuasion is *done with* not *to* another. You take part in persuasive interviews every day as a customer or sales person, client or attorney, patient or physician, student or professor, voter or candidate, recruit or recruiter, child or parent. The pervasiveness of persuasion in our daily lives leads Roderick Hart, dean of the College of Communication at the University of Texas, to write, "one must only breathe to need to know something about persuasion."[1]

> You cannot avoid persuasion in our society.

The objectives of this chapter are to help you understand, first, the ethical issues and responsibilities pertaining to both parties in the persuasive process and, second, the fundamentals of how to prepare for and take part in persuasive interviews. These fundamentals include being thoroughly informed about the other party, the situation, and the issue; being thoroughly prepared for the interaction; and being a critical but open-minded participant.

The Ethics of Persuasion

More than 2000 years ago the Greek theorist Isocrates wrote that it is not enough to learn the mere techniques of persuasion; we must also be aware of the moral responsibilities when attempting to alter or reinforce the beliefs and behavior of others.[2] Isocrates' concerns about the state of ethics in ancient Greece are reflected in our twenty-first century society. A recent Gallup poll on "Honesty/Ethics in Professions" found that fewer than 20 percent of respondents see practitioners of the following professions, listed in descending order, as very high or high in ethics: lawyers, business executives, labor union leaders, stockbrokers, advertising practitioners, telemarketers, lobbyists, members of Congress, and car salespeople.[3] This perceived dishonesty in our society led political scientist David Callahan to write a book entitled *The Cheating Culture: Why Most Americans Are Doing Wrong to Get Ahead.*[4]

> Ethics and persuasion are interrelated.

Since the persuasive interview is a mutual activity, both parties share ethical imperatives. Richard Johannesen, a leading authority on ethics and persuasion, writes that "As receivers and senders of persuasion, we have the responsibility to uphold appropriate ethical standards of persuasion."[5] Herbert Simons, the author of several books on persuasion, suggests, "In your role as communicator and recipient of persuasive messages, ask yourself: What ethical standards should guide my conduct in this particular case? What should I expect of others?"[6]

What Is Ethical?

Johannesen writes that "**Ethical issues** focus on value judgments concerning degrees of right and wrong, virtue and vice, and ethical obligations in human conduct."[7] Notice the word *degrees*. It's easy to agree that a person trying to sell a fraudulent investment scheme or home repair rip-off, particularly to a vulnerable or desperate person, is unethical. Other situations are not so easy. For instance, you may criticize a politician or insurance sales representative for using extreme fear appeals and then use these same appeals to persuade a friend to stop smoking or a child not to get into a car with a stranger. What about a "stealth strategy" in which an "undercover" person pretends to be a tourist, fellow student, or concerned citizen rather than a skilled persuader? Even single, carefully selected words may tip the balance: depression for recession, socialist for government-funded institution, terrorism for all violent acts, excuse for explanation, propaganda for information.

<aside>**When do we cross ethical boundaries?**</aside>

Every strategy and tactic discussed in this chapter, even careful analysis and adaptation to the other party, may be misused and identified as *manipulative* and, therefore, unethical.

Fundamental Ethical Guidelines

Kenneth Andersen writes that "although we do not wish to force a given system of values or ethical code upon the reader, we do argue that he [she] has a responsibility to form one. We believe that it is desirable both for the immediate practical reasons of self-interest and for more altruistic reasons that a person accept responsibility for what he [she] does in persuasion both as receiver and as source."[8] The age-old "golden rule" remains relevant for your ethical conduct: "Do unto others as you would have them do unto you." While it is difficult to develop a code of ethics applicable to all persuasive situations and agreeable to all, Gary Woodward and Robert Denton offer us a starting point when they write, "ethical communication should be fair, honest, and designed not to hurt other people."[9]

<aside>**What are the implications of the golden rule?**</aside>

Be Honest: Most of us are basically honest and seldom tell outright lies, but we might "fib" a bit about missing a class or being late for work, "exaggerate" a little to gain approval or sympathy, or "fudge" on a desire or motive. If we are truly honest, however, we will *not* attempt to conceal our true motives, compromise our ideas and ideals to gain an advantage, fail to divulge disbelief in what we advocate, or camouflage unwillingness to fulfill commitments and promises. Herbert Simons suggests that we ask two questions to assess our honesty: "How will I feel about myself after this communicative act? Could I justify my act publicly if called on to do so?"[10]

Be Fair: If you follow the golden rule, fairness will not be a problem. Ask yourself questions that address fairness. How vulnerable is the other party because of status difference (authority, expertise, age, health, finances, position held)? How serious are the possible consequences of this interview? How adequate and fair are my arguments, facts, language, tactics, and claims? Am I stockpiling objections and grievances until late in the interview? Am I throwing in irrelevant, trivial, or far-fetched ideas and arguments to derail the interview?[11] Strong and sometimes emotional disagreements are common in persuasive interviews, but unfair tactics may result in irreparable harm to this and future interactions with this party.

<aside>**Being fair is the basis of ethical persuasion.**</aside>

Be Skeptical: Have a healthy trust of others, but don't be gullible. Every con artist depends on your assistance and gullibility.[12] Balance your trust with skepticism. Don't let greed or getting something for nothing make you a willing accomplice. Be wary of simplistic assertions, claims, promises, and solutions that guarantee quick fixes and really good deals. Slick operators such as Bernie Madoff who bilked family and friends as well as highly respected investors, celebrities, and fortune hunters out of $50 billion dollars succeeded for years because their clients asked few questions, did no research, and refused to listen to those who preached caution.

Be Thoughtful and Deliberate in Judgment: Many witnesses at Madoff's trial related that they were skeptical of his investment scheme, but mere skepticism was not enough. The "buyer beware" notion of ethics, alive and well in Ponzi schemes epitomized by Madoff's ventures, places the burden of proof on you, the persuadee. Listen, think, question, synthesize, and research, then decide whether or not to accept a person, idea, or proposal.[13] Both parties in the persuasive interview should ask critical questions and demand answers backed by solid evidence. Research indicates that we are typically more interested in appearance than substance. If we like the other party who looks like us, acts like us, sounds like us, talks like us, and appears to have the *right connections* (persons, religions, businesses, political parties, financial institutions), we assume proposals are logical and acceptable.[14] The *appearance* of reasoning may be more important than substance. We tend to accept sources and "experts" as long as they agree with our preconceived beliefs, attitudes, and values. Johannesen claims that "an essential element in responsible communication, for both sender and receiver, is the exercise of thoughtful and deliberate judgment."[15]

> Appearance too often outweighs substance.

Be Open-Minded: Being open-minded does not mean that you do not have strong beliefs, attitudes, and values or commitments. It does mean that you do not *automatically assume* that persuaders of certain professions, political parties, religions, races, genders, ages, or cultures are trustworthy/untrustworthy, competent/incompetent, caring/uncaring. This amounts to "persuader profiling." Likewise, do not automatically accept or reject proposals that challenge the ways things have always been done or that appear to be new. "Be open to dissent and opinions of others."[16]

> Be open to opposing views.

Be Responsive: Provide verbal and nonverbal feedback to the other party so they can understand your needs, limitations, and perceptions of what is taking place and being agreed to. Reveal what you are thinking and how you are reacting. Be actively involved in the interview from opening through closing. Johannesen writes that "persuasion can be seen as a transaction in which both persuaders and persuadees bear mutual responsibility to participate actively in the process."[17]

With ethical issues and responsibilities clearly in mind, we are now ready to discuss the roles of persuader and persuadee and how each should prepare for and take part in persuasive interviews.

Part 1: The Interviewer in the Persuasive Interview

Selecting Interviewees

In many persuasive situations, your interviewee is predetermined: parent, instructor, employer, member of a team, acquaintance. This is the only person you must persuade because this person alone can grant a wish, solve a problem, complete a task, or meet a financial need.

In other situations, you must select from among potential interviewees or locate interviewees in your university, community, city, state, or country. Professional persuaders call this **prospecting.** Start with your own network of persons with whom you have had previous connections and have established a relationship. They may be family members, friends, fellow alumni, clients, associates, church members, customers, contributors, and supporters. Contact sources in your network who are not potential interviewees but may help you locate good prospects.

Prospecting is a numbers game because you may need to locate dozens or hundreds of interviewees, but try to avoid **cold calls** in which you contact a list of strangers with no connection to you or one of your sources. Some sources estimate that only 5 to 10 people in 100 cold calls will listen, two or three may be interested in what you are "selling," and only one will "buy."[18] This failure rate can be demoralizing. All persuaders face rejection, and you must learn to deal with it. Eric Adams recommends that you "See rejection as a necessary evil in the process and be ready to move on. Or think of it this way; a quick 'no' is often better than uncertainty or delaying tactics that result in a 'no' much later, after you have invested time and money in a proposal."[19] Darrell Zahorsky warns that making an appointment does not mean the prospective interviewee will keep the appointment or be a good prospect. Some people "find it easier to agree to an appointment rather than saying they are not interested."[20]

The next step is to purge your list of prospects. Quality is more important than quantity. Although there is no guarantee of success in any persuasive interview, the possibility of success is increased if your interviewee meets five criteria.

1. *Your proposal creates or addresses a need, desire, or motive for this interviewee.* If there is no need, desire, or motive, there will be no persuasion.

2. *Your proposal and you (including your profession and organization) are consistent with the interviewee's values, beliefs, and attitudes.* Lack of compatibility, trust, or respect results in failure to persuade.

3. *Your proposal is feasible, practical, or affordable for this interviewee.* Possibility is critical in persuasion.

4. *Your proposal's advantages outweigh its disadvantages for this interviewee.* You must acknowledge and neutralize stated and unstated objections.

5. *There is no better course of action for this interviewee.* Your proposal is the best among choices.

Once you have trimmed your list of interviewees, start preparing for the interview by analyzing each prospect.

Analyzing the Interviewee

Learn everything you can about the interviewee so you can tailor your message to this person rather than create a generic approach that is "sort of" adapted. Seek answers to four questions. What are the interviewee's personal characteristics? What are the interviewee's educational, social, and economic backgrounds? What are the interviewee's cultural differences? What are the interviewee's values, beliefs, and attitudes? What are the interviewee's feelings?

Personal Characteristics

Take into consideration relevant personal characteristics such as age, gender, race, size, health, disabilities, physical fitness, appearance, and intelligence. Any one or a combination of these characteristics may affect what a person is *able to do* or *wants to do.* Avoid all too frequent societal stereotypes such as all elderly people are slow and gullible, blonds are dumb, Hispanics are illegal aliens, women are technically challenged, and those with poor health lead unhealthy lives. Each one of us is a composite of personal characteristics that is impossible to stereotype. Research does indicate, however, that level of intelligence tends to make interviewees less receptive to persuasion. Highly intelligent interviewees are more influenced by evidence and logical arguments and tend to be highly critical. Both factors make them more difficult to persuade.[21]

Tailoring requires knowing.

Educational, Social, and Economic Backgrounds

The level of educational attainment may affect interviewees in significant ways. For example, studies indicate that college graduates tend to be more involved in public affairs, the sciences, and cultural activities, to have good jobs with good incomes and to like them, to hold fewer stereotypes and prejudices, and to be more critical in thinking, flexible, and independent in attitudes.[22] Socioeconomic background includes the interviewee's memberships and are important because our attitudes are strongly influenced by the groups we belong to. The more committed an interviewee is to various groups, the less likely you are to persuade this person with an effort that appears to conflict with group norms. Charles Larson writes that one of two major determinants of behavior intention is "the normative influence on an individual and its importance to the individual. **Normative influence** is a person's belief that important individuals or groups think it is advisable to perform or not to perform certain behaviors."[23] Know the interviewee's occupation, income, avocations and hobbies, superior/subordinate relationships, marital status, dependents, work experiences, and geographical background because these affect frames of reference—their ways of viewing people, places, things, events, and issues.

Memberships may be powerful outside forces.

Culture

You need to understand cultural differences that may affect your interview. For instance, Western cultures, such as the United States, tend to be "me" centered and stress the importance of individual accomplishment, leadership, and accumulation of awards and things. Others, particularly in Asia, are "we" centered and stress the importance of the group or team and see those who stress self and claim individual achievement as distasteful and offensive. Some cultures consider bribery a normal part of business. Others feel it is necessary to give gifts as part of the process. Bargaining is an essential part of persuasion in many cultures, often preceded by a relationship-building period over dinner or tea. In the United States, "time is money," so Americans expect others to be on time. In Great Britain it is considered "correct" to be 5 to 15 minutes late, and in Italy a person may arrive two hours late and not understand why you are upset.[24]

Values/Beliefs/Attitudes

Each culture has a set of generally accepted **values**—fundamental beliefs about ideal states of existence and modes of behavior that motivate people to think, feel, or act in particular ways.[25] Values, often referred to as "hot buttons" by college recruiters, sales representatives, and politicians, are the foundations of beliefs and attitudes. The following scheme of values includes those central to the American value system, the hot buttons that motivate interviewees to think, feel, or act in certain ways at certain times. Determine which ones are most relevant to your interviewee.

> **Values are the "hot buttons" we push in persuasive interviews.**

Survival Values

Peace and tranquility	Preservation of health
Personal attractiveness	Safety and security

Social Values

Affection and popularity	Generosity
Cleanliness	Patriotism and loyalty
Conformity and imitation	Sociality and belonging

Success Values

Accumulation and ownership	Material comfort
Ambition	Pride, prestige, and social recognition
Competition	Sense of accomplishment
Happiness	

Independence Values

Equity and value of the individual	Freedom from restraint
Freedom from authority	Power and authority

Progress Values

Change and advancement	Quantification
Education and knowledge	Science and secular rationality
Efficiency and practicality	

As you review this list of values, recall recent experiences urging you to contribute to a Habitat for Humanity home, help victims of a flood, or change health care plans. Appeals of these persuaders may have centered on values such as prestige, generosity, considerateness, security, belonging, peace, and salvation. Determine which values are most relevant to this interviewee in this situation and with this issue.

> **Values are the foundations of our belief systems.**

Political, economic, social, historical, and religious **beliefs** emanate from values. Determine which of these beliefs relate to a topic and proposal. If equity and value of the individual are important values, an interviewee is likely to support equal rights and opportunities for women, African-Americans, and Hispanics. If education and knowledge are important values, a person is likely to support increased funding for schools, give to college fund-raising campaigns, and be interested in books and computer databases.

Attitudes are relatively enduring combinations of beliefs that predispose people to respond in particular ways to persons, organizations, places, ideas, and issues. If you are a conservative, you are likely to react predictably to things you consider to be liberal. The reverse is true if you are a liberal. Attitudes come from beliefs that come from cherished values. Determine the interviewee's probable attitude toward the need or desire you will develop and the proposal you will make.

> **Attitudes tend to predict actions.**

Consider the other party's probable attitudes along an imaginary scale from 1 to 9 with 1, 2, and 3 indicating strongly positive; 4, 5, and 6 indicating neutrality or ambivalence; and 7, 8, and 9 indicating strongly negative.

Strongly for			Undecided/neutral			Strongly against		
1	2	3	4	5	6	7	8	9

From what you know about this interviewee, where along this scale is this person's attitude likely to rest? If on positions 1 or 2, little persuasive effort may be required. If on positions 8 or 9, persuasion may be impossible beyond a small shift in feeling or thinking. If the attitude is on positions 4, 5, or 6, theoretically you should be able to alter ways of thinking, feeling, or acting with a good persuasive effort. This may not be the case, however, if an interviewee is strongly committed to remaining neutral, undecided, or noncommitted.

> **Know what is possible, likely, and impossible.**

Persuasion theorists from Aristotle in ancient Greece to the present day have claimed that the interviewee's attitude toward the interviewer (ethos, credibility, image) is the most important determinant of success.[26] You must assess the interviewee's attitudes toward you, your profession, and the organization you represent. Several dimensions determine your credibility, including *trustworthy/safe* (honest, sincere, reliable, fair), *competent/expert* (intelligent, knowledgeable, good judgment, experienced), *goodwill* (caring, other-centered, sensitive, understanding), *composure* (poised, relaxed, calm, composed), and *dynamic/energetic* (decisive, strong, industrious, active).[27] Think of your previous experiences with this person. If an interviewee dislikes you, distrusts your organization, or sees your profession as dishonest or untrustworthy, you must alter these attitudes during the interview. To create and maintain high credibility with an interviewee, your appearance, manner, reputation, attainments, personality, and character must communicate trustworthiness, competence, caring, composure, and dynamism. People tend to react more favorably to highly credible interviewers who are similar to them in important ways and appear to share their values, beliefs, and attitudes. While they want interviewers to be similar to them, they also expect them to be wiser, braver, more knowledgeable, more experienced, and more insightful.[28] Consider these factors prior to the interview.

> **Low credibility may undermine the best effort.**

> **Perceived similarities may enhance receptivity.**

> **How we feel may determine what we do.**

Emotions

Emotions, sometimes called feelings or passions, significantly influence how people think, feel, and act. Along with values, emotions are "hot buttons" you need to discover and push if you hope to persuade. Some emotions are necessary for *survival* including

Figure 10.1 *The relationship of values, beliefs, attitudes, and emotions*

```
                              E
                         V    m                          Persons
                         a    o                          Places
          Values } Beliefs } Attitudes }  u   i  } Judgment/Action }  Things
                         e    o                          Ideas
                         s    n                          Acts
                              s
```

hate, fear, anger, love, and sexual attraction. Others are necessary for social involvement: pride, shame, guilt, sympathy, pity, humor, joy, and sadness. You must be aware
of the other party's mood, why the party feels that way, and how it is likely to affect the
interview. With mood of the interviewee in mind along with topic, situation, and purpose, determine which emotions you must appeal to in this interview.

What, then, is the relationship of values, beliefs, attitudes, and emotions in persuasive interviews? As indicated in Figure 10.1, the process begins with values (our
fundamental beliefs about existence and behavior), which lead to *specific beliefs*
(judgments about what is probably true or believable), which form *attitudes* (organizations of relevant beliefs that predispose us to respond in particular ways), which
may result in *judgment or actions* toward persons, places, things, ideas, proposals, and acts. Specific values and emotional appeals serve as triggering devices for
judgments and actions. Altering or reinforcing an interviewee's thinking, feeling, or
acting is a complex process.

Analyzing the Situation

The interview situation is a total context of persons, relationships, motives, events,
time, place, and objects.

Atmosphere

The "why" of the interview may vary significantly between parties.

Study carefully the atmosphere in which the interview will take place. Know why
the interview is occurring at this time: a regularly scheduled event, an emergency, a
moment of opportunity, a major event, or a routine interaction. Will the climate be hostile, friendly, ambivalent, or apathetic?

Timing

Timing may be everything.

Timing may be critical. When is an ideal time to conduct the interview? When would
be too early or too late? Contacting a potential United Way donor months in advance of
the annual campaign may be too early for the interviewee to think about making a commitment but the day after the campaign ends is too late. What events have preceded this

© ONOKY–Photononstop / Alamy

▪ *The persuasive situation is a total context of persons, relationships, events, time, place, and objects.*

interview such as visits from your competitors? You would not want to be the fourth employee of the day to ask for a raise from an employer who has just discovered a serious financial problem. What events will take place following the interview, such as a competing fund-raiser, an annual sale, or a budget meeting? Certain times of the year (vacation time, tax time, Christmas season) are great for some interviewers and terrible for others.

Physical Setting

Provide for privacy and control interruptions, especially telephone calls. Make an appointment if it is difficult to guess how much time an interview will take.

Will you be the host (the interview is in your office or residence); a guest (the interview is in the interviewee's place of business or residence); or on neutral ground (a conference room, restaurant, hotel, club)? If you are trying to recruit a student for your university, you might prefer to get the interviewee on campus during a beautiful fall day when leaves are red and gold, perhaps following a football victory. If you are selling a life insurance policy, you might want the interview to take place in the interviewee's home surrounded by family members, furnishings, and valued possessions the family would want protected in case of an accident or death.

> On whose turf will the interview take place?

Outside Forces

> Outside influences may wage counter-persuasive efforts.

Consider the influence of **outside forces.** For instance, organizational or professional policies may prescribe what you can and cannot do in a sales interview. You may be trying to convince a friend to attend your college while another college is recruiting this person with a full-ride scholarship, mom and dad want the interviewee to attend their alma mater, and a significant other wants the interviewee to attend a local college. Awareness of outside influences may determine how you open an interview, select appeals and evidence, develop proposals, and address counterpersuasion.

Researching the Issue

Be the best informed and most authoritative person in each interview. Investigate all aspects of the topic, including events that may have contributed to the problem, reasons for and against change, evidence on all sides of an issue, and possible solutions. Search for solid, up-to-date information. You are taking part in a persuasive interview, not giving a speech to an audience of one, so the interviewee can demand support, challenge assumptions, generalizations, and claims, and ask for documentation of a source at any moment during an interview. Parties are impressed with persuaders who reply to inquiries with facts and documentation rather than generalities and evasions. Try to determine prior to the interview what the interviewee knows about an issue and attitudes held toward the issue and possible solutions.

You must have the facts and know how to use them.

Sources

Do not overlook any potentially valuable source of information: the Internet, e-mail, interviews, letters, pamphlets, questionnaires, surveys, unpublished studies, reports, newspapers, periodicals, professional journals, and government documents. Use your own experiences and research. Know the sources available to the interviewee.

Types of Evidence

Search for a variety of evidence to support your need and proposal. Collect *examples,* both factual and hypothetical, to illustrate your points. People like good *stories* that make problems real. Gather *statistics* on relevant areas such as inflation, growth rates, expenses, benefits, insurance coverages, profits and losses, causes and effects. Collect *statements* from acknowledged *authorities* on the topic as well as *testimonials* from those who have joined, attended, purchased, signed, or believed. Look for *comparisons and contrasts* between situations, proposals, products, and services. Locate clear and supportable *definitions* for key terms and concepts.

Gather and use a variety of evidence.

Distinguish *opinion* (something that is assumed, usually cannot be observed, can be made at any time, and either is or should be believed tentatively) from *fact* (something that can be or has been observed, is verifiable, and is thought of as securely established). Present your evidence effectively, including thorough documentation of your sources. The substance of your persuasive interview enhances the long-term effect of your interview and is particularly important if a decision will not be made for weeks or months.

The effect of a well-supported interview lasts longer than a poorly supported one.

Planning the Interview

After analyzing the interviewee, studying the situation, and researching the topic, you are ready to plan the interview.

Determine Your Purpose

If you know the interviewee will be a "hard sell" because of a value, belief, and attitude system, then your purpose may be merely to influence thinking or feeling in a minor way. Getting the interviewee to think about an action or to admit there is a problem may be a major success for a first interview. Later you might move the interviewee toward a more significant change or action. On the other hand, if an interviewee contacts you and tells you he or she wants to change auto insurance companies, is interested in an investment, or would like to take a tour of China, you may move quickly through need and desire to solutions with a good chance of success.

Be realistic but not defeatist.

Set a realistic goal for an interview. Significant changes come in increments after a series of interviews. Do not assume after one interview that an interviewee is not interested or will not change. Authorities on sales interviews claim that it typically takes five contacts before a sale is made. Be patient.

Select Main Points

> Do not make
> the need too
> complicated.

Select reasons to establish a need or desire. Do not rely on a *single* reason because the interviewee may see little urgency in a problem that is so simple or unidimensional or find it relatively easy to attack or reject *only* one point. Research indicates that more points also enhance the effectiveness of persuasion over time.[29] On the other hand, six or eight points may make an interview too long and superficial as you rush through so many points. An interviewee may become overloaded with information and complex arguments and end up confused or bored.

> Know the
> strength of
> each point
> and intro-
> duce it
> strategically.

After selecting and developing reasons for a change, ideally three or four, determine the strength of each for this interviewee in this situation. This will determine the order in which you present points. Assume that you are trying to recruit a top merit scholar for your university and research indicates that this interviewee has three major criteria for choosing a university, ranked in this order: available majors, academic reputation, and financial aid. Introducing your strongest point first or last (available majors) is about equal in effect. If there's any possibility you might run out of time or be interrupted before you can present all of your points or reasons, start with your strongest point.

Develop Main Points

Develop each point into what the interviewee will see as a valid and acceptable logical pattern. Effective interviews are a carefully crafted blend of the logical and the psychological. You have choices to make.

Arguing from accepted belief, assumption, or proposition involves three explicitly stated or implied assertions (statements you believe and clearly want others to believe). For instance, a fire inspector might argue this way:

> Your assertions
> must
> lead to your
> conclusion.

Assertion #1: All students living in apartments should have renters insurance.
Assertion #2: You live in an apartment.
Point: You should have renters insurance.

You need not state all three parts of this pattern if the interviewee is likely to provide the missing assertion or conclusion. Regardless, your argument rests on the first assertion that is the critical belief, assumption, or proposition. For instance, you might leave the second assertion unstated and let the interviewee provide it. This involves the interviewee in the process and encourages self-persuasion. This strategy is possible with all patterns of argument.

Assertion #1: All students living in apartments should have renters insurance.
Assertion #2: (left unstated)
Point: You should have renters insurance.

You might state your assertions and let the interviewee draw the conclusion.

Assertion #1: All students living in apartments should have renters insurance.
Assertion #2: You live in an apartment.
Point: (left unstated)

Arguing from condition is based on the assertion that if something does or does not happen, something else will or will not happen. You might reason this way with a student.

> *Assertion #1:* If you continue to drink and drive, you're going to lose your driver's license.
>
> *Assertion #2:* You're going to continue drinking and driving.
>
> *Point:* You're going to lose your driver's license.

Weigh conditions carefully and be able to support them effectively. As with arguing from accepted belief, you may invite the interviewee to fill in a missing part or parts.

Arguing from two choices is based on the assertion that there are only two possible proposals or courses of action. You delete one by establishing that it will not work or resolve a problem, and conclude the obvious.

> *Assertion #1:* You can take the plane or drive to your interview in Philadelphia.
>
> *Assertion #2:* Driving the 700 miles to Philadelphia will require you to miss the final exam in Psychology 495.
>
> *Point:* You ought to fly to Philadelphia.

Your evidence must warrant your conclusion.

This argument rests, first, on being able to limit the choices and, second, convincing the interviewee that one is unacceptable so yours is the only one remaining.

Arguing from example leads to a generalization about a whole class of people, places, things, or ideas from a sample of this class. For instance, an interviewer attempting to persuade a university administrator of the dangers of binge drinking on campus, might use this argument from example:

> *Sample:* In a recent survey of college students conducted by the University of New Mexico, it was discovered that 69% of 500 respondents admitted to binge drinking at least once.
>
> *Point:* The majority of your students take part in binge drinking.

The quality of the sample, as in the survey interview, is critical in argument from example.

Arguing from cause-effect is related to example because interviewers often use a sample as proof of a causal relationship. Unlike the argument from example that leads to a generalization, this argument attempts to establish what caused a specific effect. For instance:

Beware of false causes.

> *Evidence:* In a study of 100 auto accidents, law enforcement officers reported that nearly a third occurred while drivers were texting, about the same as when drivers had been drinking alcoholic beverages.
>
> *Point:* Texting while driving causes as many accidents as drinking alcoholic beverages.

You must convince the other party that the evidence leads to the only or major cause of effect.

Arguing from facts reaches a point that explains best a body of facts. This is how investigators argue when attempting to explain a phenomenon. For instance:

> *Facts:* While investigating the storm damage caused in a two-county area on August 5, we noted that the storm had moved in a nearly straight line. In open

areas, there was no evidence of a twisting motion in grass and weeds. Trees and small buildings were knocked down but not twisted. No one heard the tell-tale freight train sound of a tornado.

Point: It's obvious that the storm damage was the result of straight line winds and not a tornado.

Unlike argument from example, the interviewer in this case is arguing from a variety of facts, not a sample of a class of things.

Arguing from analogy occurs when you point out that two things (people, places, objects, proposals, ideas) have important characteristics in common and draw a conclusion based on these similarities. For example, a coach might argue like this:

Points of comparison: Like North Side, West Lake High has a veteran quarterback who is an excellent runner as well as passer. Their line is anchored by four seniors who are both large and quick. Their pass defenders have made six interceptions this year. And they have a junior kicker who has made fields goals from as far out as 46 yards.

Point: West Lake High will be hard to beat, just like North Side two weeks ago.

The number of significant similarities are critical in developing and selling this argument.

> How similar are the similarities?

Select Strategies

> When you think theories, think strategies.

Once you have chosen main points and persuasive patterns, select psychological strategies to make them persuasive. A number of theories explain how you might bring about changes in thinking, feeling, and acting. These theories explain complex human activities through careful observation of what happens in the real world and may serve as persuasive strategies.

Identification Theory

Kenneth Burke, arguably the leading rhetorical theorist of the twentieth century, claims that you persuade by identifying with the interviewee. Strive to establish **consubstantiality** (a substantial similarity) with the interviewee. The overlapping circles representing the interview parties in our model in Chapter 2 are based on Burke's notion that to communicate or persuade, you must talk the other party's language "with speech, gesture, tonality, order, image, attitude, *identifying*" your ways with theirs.[30] There are several ways to identify with a person and establish common ground.[31]

> Appearances are important in perceiving common ground.

- *Associating* with groups to which you both belong, shared cultural heritage or regional identification, programs you both support.
- *Disassociating* from groups, cultures, regions, or programs the interviewee opposes or is distant from.
- Developing *appearance and visual symbols* that establish identification such as dress, hairstyle, makeup, jewelry, political buttons, or religious symbols.

- Sharing *language* such as jargon, slang, colloquialisms, and in-group words and phrases.

- Employing *content and values* important to the interviewee.

Strive for real identification, not a fabrication to initiate the change you desire.

Balance or Consistency Theory

According to **balance and consistency theories**, human beings strive for a harmonious existence with self (values, beliefs, and attitudes) and experience psychological discomfort (dissonance) when aspects of existence seem inconsistent or unbalanced.[32] You may experience source-proposition conflict when you like persons but detest their positions on issues or dislike persons but favor their products or services. You experience attitude-attitude conflict when you oppose government involvement in your life but want the government to outlaw hate speech and require prayer in the public schools. You experience perception-perception conflict when you see Mexico as a beautiful but dangerous place to vacation. You experience a behavior-attitude conflict when you believe strongly in law and order but use a fake ID to get into bars.

> Not all interviewees are happy with harmony.

You may create psychological discomfort (dissonance) by attacking a source or pointing out attitude, perception, and behavioral conflicts. Then you show how the interviewee can bring these inconsistencies into balance by providing changes in sources, attitudes, perceptions, and behaviors. If you detect that an interviewee is experiencing psychological discomfort, you may bring about balance or consistency by helping the interviewee see no inconsistency, perceive the inconsistency to be insignificant, or tolerate inconsistency.

> An interviewer may create or resolve dissonance.

Inoculation Theory

According to **inoculation theory** it's more effective to prevent undesired persuasive effects from occurring than using damage control afterward.[33] For example, a few years ago one of the authors received a telephone call from the state police warning him of solicitors who were claiming to be representatives of a state police sponsored charity for children and relating what solicitors were telling contributors. The caller hoped the preemptive call would prevent the author from being victimized and maintain the credibility of legitimate state police charities.

> An inoculation strategy immunizes an interviewee from future persuasion.

In this strategy, you forewarn the interviewee, perhaps by exposing the interviewee to small "doses" of a potential persuader's language, arguments, and evidence so the interviewee can resist the effort. Or you might provide arguments and evidence the interviewee may use to mount an effective countereffort if confronted by an interviewer against whom he or she is being immunized.

Induced Compliance Theory

According to the **induced compliance theory,** you may change an interviewee's thinking, feeling, or acting by inducing her or him to engage in activities counter to values, beliefs, and attitudes.[34] Participation in counteractivities may bring about self-persuasion. Apply enough pressure so an interviewee will comply without feeling there is no choice. Feeling coerced may prevent change.

> There are many ways to trigger self-persuasion.

There are a variety of ways to induce compliance. You might induce an interviewee to *espouse* a belief or counterattitude to understand or appreciate the other side of an issue, such as a liberal position on sex education or a conservative position on health care reform. You might induce an interviewee to *take part* in an unaccustomed or unattractive activity, such as going to a religious service or helping at a homeless shelter. You might induce an interviewee to *play an opposite role,* such as a superior instead of a subordinate, teacher instead of a student, parent instead of a child. You might induce a party to act to *receive a reward* or *avoid a punishment,* such as tickets to a concert or a speeding ticket.

Psychological Reactance Theory

> **Restricting behavior may lead to persuasion or resentment.**

According to **psychological reactance theory,** people react negatively when someone threatens to restrict a behavior they want to engage in.[35] They may value the restricted behavior more and want to engage in it more frequently. People may devalue alternatives because they feel they are stuck with them and may resent the restricting agent. Organizations produce limited editions of books, stamps, coins, and cars to enhance demand for them. Tickets to the NCAA basketball Final Four are of great value because they are scarce. Interviewees may be less in favor of giving to the college development fund or joining their athletic booster clubs if they feel they are being forced. Whenever possible avoid real or perceived pressure on the other party to think, feel, or act differently. Make your proposal attractive, make scarcity or a deadline known without appearing to threaten, develop a serious need without excessive appeals to fear, and offer choices.

Conducting the Interview

Be flexible, adaptable, and cautious about assumptions. You are conducting an interview, not giving a speech. Plan how you will involve the interviewee throughout the interview.

> **Do not use routine openings even for routine interviews.**

Opening

Your opening must gain attention and interest, establish rapport, and motivate the interviewee to take part. The major advantage of the interview over public or mass persuasion is the opportunity to tailor your message to a single party. Adapt the opening to each interviewee and setting. Don't rely on a standard or traditional formula. When insufficient information is available or you have no opportunity to study the interviewee ahead of time, use the first few minutes of the interview to discover how you can best adapt to this person. *Take note of* the interviewee's dress, appearance, and manner. *Ask a few questions* designed to discover background, interests, and attitudes critical to this interview. *Listen* to what the interviewee "says" verbally and nonverbally. If the party consists of more than one person, *detect* who is the leader or spokesperson.

> **If the opening fails, there may be no body or closing.**

The majority of persuasive interactions fail in the first few seconds, during the attention step in the opening, so choose your language and nonverbal actions carefully.[36] Think of openings in sales calls made to your home and how you reacted. Persuaders trying to convince you to give to a charity are often trained to recite a prescribed opening regardless of your age, gender, income, background, or level of interest. You may dislike this charity; it makes no difference to the persuader. Little wonder that few of these "cold" calls succeed.

Review the opening techniques and principles discussed in Chapter 4. Select the techniques suitable for this party and situation. Begin with a warm greeting and use the interviewee's name. If the person is a stranger, do not make your greeting sound like a question: "Good evening, Mrs. Walsh?" This suggests that you are unsure of the person's name or identity, unsure of yourself, and not prepared.

If you know the interviewee well and both the situation and your relationship warrant it, use the person's first name. As a general rule, do not greet a stranger, superior, or person in a formal setting by first name or nickname unless you are asked to do so.

It may be necessary to introduce yourself (name, position, title, background), your organization (name, location, nature, history, products, services), and the purpose of the interview. Orientation is essential when there is no relational history between parties and no appointment or arrangements made ahead of time. Be brief.

You may begin with a sincere inquiry about family or mutual friends or small talk about the weather, sports, highway construction, or campus facilities. Do not prolong this rapport stage. Be conscious of the interviewee's situation and preferences. If a person replies immediately after the greeting, "What can I do for you?" the person wants to get down to business.

Cultures differ in amount of acceptable small talk and socializing. Most Americans want to "get to the point" and "get the job done." Japanese and other cultures desire to get acquainted, to follow "interaction rituals," and to go slower in making commitments and decisions.[37] Do not prolong the rapport stage.

Involve all members of the other party from the start so each person will play an active role throughout the interaction. American persuaders and persuadees, particularly males, tend to take turns unevenly during interactions and to speak at length during each turn. Japanese and others take turns evenly and make shorter statements.

Use the opening to create mutual interest in the interview and establish trust and degree of affection or liking between the parties. Each party should understand the purpose of the interview and how they will share control.

> **Neither rush nor prolong the opening.**

> **Reduce reticence by involving the interviewee immediately and often.**

> **The opening should be a good fit with the whole interview.**

Need or Desire

Create a need or desire by developing in detail the three or four points you selected in the preparation stage. Introduce them in the order you have determined will be most effective, strongest point first or last with weaker points in the middle.

Develop One Point at a Time

Explain a point thoroughly. Provide sufficient evidence that is factually based, authoritative, recent, and well documented. Use a variety of evidence (examples, stories, authority, statistics, comparisons, definitions) so the interviewee is neither buried under an avalanche of figures nor bored with one story after another. Incorporate the values, beliefs, and attitudes important to this interviewee.

Encourage Interaction

> **Don't lecture; interact.**

This is an interview, not a speech. You are more likely to persuade when the interviewee is actively involved. Stress how each point affects this interviewee's needs and desires.

Do not go to your next point until there has been some sort of agreement. With one point developed and agreed upon, move to point two, then three, and so on. Do not rush through a point or jump to the next one if the interviewee raises objections or poses questions. Move on when the interviewee seems ready to do so. Be patient and persistent.

Questions

Although you rarely come to a persuasive interview with a schedule of questions, questions serve a variety of functions in persuasive interviews. Never *tell* when you can *ask* because this involves the interviewee as an active participant rather than a passive recipient. Ask and then listen. You cannot plan on a series of questions to get the job done, particularly if an interviewee sees no need, has no desire, or is unaware of options.

> **Questions play unique roles in persuasive interviews.**

Information-Gathering Questions

Ask questions to determine knowledge level and to draw out concerns and objections. Listen carefully to responses and probe for accuracy and details. For example:

> **Use questions to analyze the interviewee.**

- Tell me what concerns you about your liability insurance coverage.
- What do you know about the compensation programs for installing windmills on your property?
- How frequently do you travel between Pittsburgh and Philadelphia?

Verification Questions

Use reflective, mirror, and clearinghouse questions to check the accuracy of assumptions, impressions, and information obtained before and during an interview. You may assume you have answered an objection satisfactorily or gotten an agreement when you have not. Be certain an interviewee understands what you are saying and grasps the significance of your evidence and points. Silence on the interviewee's part can indicate confusion or disagreement as well as understanding and agreement. Ask:

> **Questions can clarify and verify interactions.**

- Does that answer your concerns about the length of our MBA program in strategic management?
- You seem to be most concerned about scholarship money available for your daughter.
- Are we in agreement that a laptop computer would serve your needs and financial situation best?

Encouraging Interaction Questions

Questions early in interviews warm-up both parties and set the tone for the interview. Encourage the interviewee to play an active role in the interview. An interviewee feels freer to ask questions and provide meaningful feedback once he or she plays an active part in the process and understands what you expect. Use questions to discover how a quiet or noncommittal interviewee is reacting.

> **Questions can stimulate interactions.**

- How was your tour of the production facility?
- What do you think of the new ad campaign?
- What are your thoughts about the year-around school calendar?

Attention and Interest Questions

Use questions to keep interviewees tuned in and alert to what you are saying. They may be busy or preoccupied with other concerns and their minds may wander. Interesting, challenging, and thought-provoking questions maintain interest and attention. For example:

- How would you feel if your insurance company would refuse to cover your new child born with a physical problem?
- Do you remember the winter of 2002 when your power went out for six days?
- What would you do if your company suddenly went out of business?

Agreement Questions

Use questions to obtain small agreements that lead to bigger agreements. Getting agreement after each point leads to agreement at the end of the need so you can move effectively to establishing criteria for solutions. Do not ask for agreement or commitment before you have developed or supported a point thoroughly. A barrage of generalizations and claims will not prove a point or establish a need. Use a yes-response question (often in the form of a statement) to control the interview and lead to agreement after thoroughly developing one or more points and small agreements.

- With the market rebounding, this is a great time to invest, don't you agree?
- I know you understand that limiting bonuses this year is the best way to meet the recession.
- I'm sure you don't want to risk your child's future.

Objection Questions

Use questions to respond tactfully to objections and draw out unstated questions and objections. Get these on the table at the proper time. Questions can also discover what an interviewee knows about an issue and reveal the importance or reasons behind objections.

- You say cost is a major concern in purchasing a hybrid SUV, but what would you pay over the next five years for gasoline in a standard SUV?
- You seem hesitant about your trip to China; what is your major concern?
- What information do you need to remove doubts about this proposal?

Don't ask questions prematurely that call for agreements when you have established nothing upon which to agree. Use leading and loaded questions sparingly because high-pressure tactics turn off interviewees. A series of questions are unlikely to persuade; you must present good reasons supported by information and evidence.

Adapting to the Interviewee

Tailor the persuasive interview to the values, beliefs, and attitudes of the interviewee. Determine the probable disposition of the interviewee, and select appropriate tactics and strategies.

Indecisive, Uninterested Interviewees

> **The inter-viewee may see no personal need or relevance.**

If an interviewee is indecisive, uninterested, or uncertain, help the person see the reality and urgency of the problem, issue, or need. Use opening techniques to get the interviewee's attention and generate interest in the problem. Lead off with your strongest point and provide a variety of evidence that informs and persuades. Use questions to draw out feelings and perceptions and involve the interviewee.

Emphasize the urgency of the problem and the necessity of acting *now*. Use moderate fear appeals to awaken the interviewee to dangers to self, family, or friends. Appeal to values such as preservation of health, safety and security, freedom from restraint, ownership, and value of the individual. Show *how* the interviewee can make a difference.

Hostile Interviewees

> **Do not assume there will be hostility.**

If an interviewee may be hostile, be sure your impression is accurate. Do not mistake legitimate concerns or objections or a gruff demeanor for hostility. If a person is truly hostile, determine why; then consider a common ground approach.

- A **yes-but approach** begins with areas of agreement and similarity and gradually leads into points of disagreement. It lessens hostility and disagreement later by establishing common ground early on.
- A **yes-yes approach** gets an interviewee in the habit of agreeing when you reach apparent disagreements, the person may be less likely to disagree.
- An **implicative approach** withholds an explicit statement of purpose or intent to avoid a knee-jerk negative reaction from the interviewee. You hope the interviewee will see the implications of what you are saying, perhaps feeling they came up with the concerns and solution.

> **You must get to the point in a reasonable amount of time.**

Regardless of the common ground approach, listen, be polite, and avoid defensiveness or anger when working with hostile interviewees. Hostility often results from lack of information, misinformation, or rumors. Respond with facts, expert testimony, examples, stories, and comparisons that clarify, prove, and resolve issues between parties. Be willing to accept minor points of disagreement and to admit your proposal is not perfect; no proposal is. Employ **shock-absorber** phrases that reduce the sting of critical questions: "Many residents I talk to feel that way, however . . ." "That's an excellent question, but when you consider . . ." "I'm glad you thought of that because. . . ."

Closed-Minded and Authoritarian Interviewees

> **Select evidence most appropriate for each party.**

A **closed-minded or authoritarian interviewee** relies on trusted authorities and is more concerned about who supports a proposal than the proposal itself. Facts alone, particularly statistics, will not do the job. Show that the interviewee's accepted authorities support your persuasive efforts. The closed-minded and authoritarian person has strong, unchangeable central values and beliefs, and you must be able to identify yourself and your proposal with these values and beliefs.

Do not bypass hierarchical channels or alter prescribed methods. Authoritarians react negatively to interviewers who don't belong or appear to be out of line, and may demand censure or punishment for appearing to violate accepted and valued norms.[38]

Skeptical Interviewees

If the interviewee is skeptical, begin the interview by expressing some views the interviewee holds—a yes-but or yes-yes approach. Maintain positive nonverbal cues such as a firm handshake, good eye contact, a warm and friendly manner, and appropriate appearance and dress. If the interviewee feels you are young and inexperienced, allude tactfully to your qualifications, experiences, and training and provide substantial and authoritative evidence. Be well prepared and experienced without bragging. Avoid undue informality and a cocky attitude. If the interviewee sees you as argumentative, avoid confrontations, attacks on the person's position, and demands. If the interviewee thinks you are a know-it-all, be careful when referring to your qualifications, experiences, and achievements. If the interviewee has concerns about your organization, you might withhold its name until you have created personal credibility with the interviewee. If the name must come out early in the interview, try to improve its image by countering common misperceptions, relating how it has changed, or identifying its strengths. You may have to distance yourself from some elements or past practices of your organization.

> Image or credibility may be the major cause of failure.

Shopping-Around Interviewees

Interviewees may shop around before making a major purchase or decision and will face **counterpersuasion** from other interviewers. When meeting with a shopper or an undecided interviewee, forewarn and prepare the interviewee. Provide the interviewee with supportive arguments, evidence, and responses to questions or points others are likely to raise. Give small doses of the opposition's case (inoculation theory) to show the strengths and weaknesses of both sides. Develop a positive, factual, nonemotional approach that addresses the competition when necessary but dwells primarily on the strengths of *your* position and proposal.

> Be prepared for interviewees facing counterpersuasion.

Intelligent, Educated Interviewees

The highly **intelligent or educated interviewee** tends to be less persuasible because of knowledge level, critical ability, and faculty for seeing the implications behind arguments and proposals. Research indicates that such interviewees "are more likely to attend to and comprehend the message position but are less likely to yield to it."[39] For example, they are likely to see through the good guy–bad guy approach used in many sales situations.

> A two-sided approach addresses but does not advocate each side.

When working with highly intelligent and educated interviewees, support your ideas thoroughly, develop arguments logically, and present a two-sided approach that weighs both sides of issues. Minimize emotional appeals, particularly if the interviewee is neutral or initially disagrees with your position and proposal. Encourage the interviewee to ask questions, raise objections, and be an active participant.

If an interviewee is of low intelligence or education, develop a simple, one-sided approach to minimize confusion and maximize comprehension. A complex, two-sided approach and intricate arguments supported by a variety of evidence may confuse the interviewee. Use examples, stories, and comparisons rather than expert testimony and statistics.

The Solution

When you have presented the need, summarized your main points, and gotten important agreements, you are ready for solutions.

Establishing Criteria

Begin the solution phase by establishing criteria (requirements, standards, rules, norms, principles) that any solution should meet. If the interviewee is obviously ready to move into this phase of the interview before you have presented all of your points, move on.

Establish a set of criteria *with the interviewee* for evaluating possible solutions. This process is natural to us. For example, when selecting a college major, you may have considered courses, core requirements, specialties, careers, faculty, availability of internships, and marketability when you graduate. In simple decisions such as selecting a place to eat, you have criteria in mind, such as type of food and beverage, cost, distance, location, atmosphere, music, availability of large screen television for watching a football game, and preferences of others. Use this natural process in persuasive interviews.

As you think of criteria prior to the interview and develop them with the interviewee during the interview, realize that not all criteria are of equal importance. For example, admissions directors at state universities have found that quality of school is the most important criterion for out-of-state applicants while cost is number 1 and quality is number 2 for in-state students. The situation can influence criteria. For instance, cost may override all other criteria during economic recessions.

Establishing a set of criteria with the interviewee involves the interviewee in the process; shows that you are attempting to tailor your proposal to his or her needs, desires, and capabilities; provides a smooth transition from the need to the solution; and reduces the impression that you are overly eager to sell your point. Agreed-upon criteria enable you to build on a foundation of agreements, provide an effective means of comparing and assessing solutions, and deal with objections.

> Establishing criteria is natural but often unconscious.

> All criteria are not created equally.

> Criteria are designed to evaluate and to persuade.

Considering the Solution

Present your solution in detail. Do not assume the interviewee will understand the details and nature of the solution you have in mind unless this becomes clear during the interview. It's best to err on the side of too much information rather than too little.

If you consider more than one solution, deal with one at a time. Explain a solution in detail and use whatever visual aids might be available and appropriate: booklets and brochures, drawings and diagrams, graphs, letters, pictures, slides, computer printouts, sketch pads, swatches of materials, objects, and models. Interviewees may remember only about 10 percent of *what they hear* but 50 percent of *what they do* and 90 percent of *what they both see and do.*[40]

Approach the solution positively, constructively, and enthusiastically. Believe in what you are presenting and show it. Emphasize the strengths and benefits of your proposal rather than the weaknesses of the competition. Avoid **negative selling** unless the competition forces you to do so as a matter of self-defense. The interviewee is likely to be more interested in the advantages of your proposal than the disadvantages of another.

> Seeing is believing.

Help interviewees make decisions that are best for them. Encourage questions and active involvement. Use repetition, what one writer calls the "heart of selling," to enhance understanding, aid memory, gain and maintain attention, and make the interviewee aware of what is most important.[41] Educate interviewees about options, requirements, time constraints, and new features.

Handling Objections

You cannot address an objection you do not hear.

Perhaps nothing seems more threatening than the thought of an interviewee raising unexpected or difficult objections. It's best to encourage the interviewee to voice objections to reveal the interviewee's concerns, fears, misunderstandings, and misinformation. Do not assume agreement because the interviewee raises no questions or objections. Watch for nonverbal clues such as restlessness, fidgeting, poor eye contact, raised eyebrows, confused expressions, signs of boredom, or silences. Find out what is happening within.

Objections are numerous and often issue, goal, situation, or interviewee specific.

Anticipate common objections.

- *Procrastination: Never do today what you can put off until tomorrow.*
  Let me think about it.
  I've still got three weeks before that paper is due.
  My old truck is doing fine, so I'll wait awhile.

- *Cost: That's a lot of money.*
  That iPhone is too expensive for me.
  I didn't expect remodeling to cost that much.
  That's pretty expensive for a two-day conference.

- *Tradition: We've always done it this way.*
  That's how we've always done business.
  We've always had our reunions in Eagle River.
  My grandfather chose that line of clothing when he opened the business in 1924.

- *Uncertain future: Who knows what tomorrow will bring.*
  My job is rather iffy right now.
  The economy is struggling, so I'm reluctant to hire new staff.
  At my age, I don't buy green bananas.

- *Need: What's the problem?*
  We've got good investments, so we don't need life insurance.
  The current performance review system is working just fine.
  We don't have much crime around here, so we don't need an alarm system.

How to Approach Objections

Meeting objections requires thought, understanding, tact, and substance.

Anticipate objections to eliminate surprises. Think about handling each objection as a series of steps.

Plan how to respond to reduce surprises.

Listen carefully, completely, and objectively, never assuming you understand the other person's point or concern until you have heard it.

Clarify the objection, making sure you understand exactly what it is and its importance before you respond.

Respond appropriately, tactfully, and seriously. *If an objection is serious to the interviewee, it is serious*. There are four common strategies for handling objections.

Minimize the Objection

Reduce the importance of the objection.

Minimize an objection by restating it to make it less important or by comparing it to other weightier matters. Provide evidence to reduce its importance.

1. **Interviewee:** We've always thought it would be great to live downtown in a loft like this, but we're afraid of the crime rate in downtown areas.

2. **Interviewer:** That was true a few years ago, but crime is declining in the centers of cities and spreading to outlying areas where there are fewer police officers. For example, in this area during the past three years, robberies and theft have declined by 23 percent, assaults by 43 percent, and shootings have all but disappeared. At the same time, in the outlying areas of this city, robberies and theft have increased by 27 percent, assaults by 12 percent, and shootings by 15 percent.

Capitalize on the Objection

Take advantage of the objection.

Capitalize on an objection to *clarify* your point, *review* the proposal's advantages, *offer* more evidence, or *isolate* the motive behind the objection. Convert a perceived disadvantage into an advantage.

1. **Interviewee:** We'd like to purchase a house instead of continuing to pay rent on an apartment, but the housing market seems really bad with all the foreclosures and banks being reluctant to make home loans right now.

2. **Interviewer:** Actually, this is a great time to purchase a home. The mortgage rates at 3 percent are the lowest in almost 50 years; the market is flooded with excellent homes in all price ranges; and the government has special programs for first-time home buyers. All of this will change within the next few months as the recession lessens and more buyers enter the market.

Deny an Objection

If you deny it, you must prove it isn't so.

Deny an objection *directly* or *indirectly* by offering new or more accurate information or by introducing new features of a proposal. You cannot deny an objection by merely denying it; *prove it*.

1. **Interviewee:** I've heard that your group, Parents for a Quality Education, wants to raise our property taxes by 25 percent and are against the school voucher program that enables many of us to send our children to faith-based schools.

2. **Interviewer:** Actually we are proposing a 2.5 percent increase in property taxes to prevent the loss of quality teachers in our schools, busing for high school students, and advanced courses essential for our children to compete for college scholarships. We are not against the voucher program in principle but are concerned about the fairness of faith-based schools being exempt from the many state regulations imposed on public schools. We believe it should be a level playing-field if the state truly believes in fair competition among school systems.

Confirm an Objection

Confirm an objection by agreeing with the interviewee. It is better to be honest and admit problems than to offer weak defenses.

1. **Interviewee:** I've been looking at a number of e-readers, particularly the Nook, but they're pretty pricey.

2. **Interviewer:** The e-readers do seem pricey when you look only at the initial cost. A low-end Nook costs about $99.00, and the top of the line tablet runs about $200.00. This seems pricey, but books are considerably cheaper on the e-reader than in print. If you read ten books over the next couple of years, you will save more than your Nook cost, even the top of the line version.

Closing

Approach the closing positively and confidently. Do not pressure the interviewee or appear too eager. Interviewers may hesitate to close, fearing they may fail to persuade, while interviewees fear they will make a wrong decision. Sales professionals, for instance, cite hesitation to ask for a sale as the major cause of failure to sell.[42]

The closing consists of three stages: (1) trial closing, (2) contract or agreement, and (3) leave-taking.

Trial Closing

Close as soon as possible and don't continue talking if the interviewee is sold on your proposal. You may talk yourself out of an agreement.

As you approach the end of the solution phase, watch and listen for verbal and non-verbal cues that the interviewee is moving toward a decision. Verbal cues include questions and statements such as "How soon will the new software be available?" "Your idea appears sound." "This looks like a great tour." Nonverbal cues include enthusiastic vocal expressions, head nods, smiles, exchange of glances between interviewees as if to verify interest or agreement, or handling brochures, pictures, and written reports.

Yes-response and leading questions verify that the interviewee is ready to close: "I'm sure you can see this is the best way to go." "You want this condo, don't you?" "Do you want to face a lawsuit?" After you ask a trial closing question, *be quiet!* Give the interviewee time to think and self-persuade. Silence communicates confidence and gives the interviewee an opportunity to raise unanswered questions and objections.

If you get a no to your trial closing question, ask why. You may need to review the criteria, compare advantages and disadvantages of acting now, or provide more information. An interviewee may not be ready to act. Fear of possible consequences and how others may react (outside forces) may overcome a need or desire.

If you get a yes to your trial closing question, lead into the contract or agreement stage: "We can sign off on this today." "We can have this equipment installed within two weeks." "It would be a relief to have this decision made."

Contract or Agreement

After a successful trial closing, move to the contract or agreement stage. This is a critical time because the interviewee knows the closing and a commitment are coming.

The contract or agreement stage is critical because the interviewee knows a commitment is imminent.

Jupiterimages/Getty images

Be natural and pleasant. Maintain good communication. Consider closing techniques appropriate for this stage.

- An *assumptive close* addresses part of the agreement with a phrase, such as "I assume that you prefer . . ."

- A *summary close* summarizes agreements made as a basis for decisions.

- An *elimination of a single objection close* responds to the single objection that stands in the way of an agreement.

- An *either-or close* limits the interviewee's choices, then shows that the solution you advocate has the most advantages and the fewest disadvantages.

> **Select closing techniques most appropriate for this interview and interviewee.**

- An *I'll think it over close* acknowledges the interviewee's desire to think about a decision. Try to discover the level of interest and why the interviewee is hesitating.

- A *sense of urgency close* stresses why an interviewee should act now.

- A *price close* emphasizes the savings possible or the bottom line of the offer.

Leave-Taking

When the contract or agreement is completed, no agreement or contract can be reached, or another interview is necessary, conclude pleasantly and positively. Do not let the **leave-taking** phase be **abrupt** or **curt.** You may undo the rapport and trust you worked so hard to establish.

> **Leave-taking should reinforce all you have accomplished.**

Adapt the verbal and nonverbal leave-taking techniques discussed in Chapter 4 or combine them to suit each interviewee. Be sincere and honest in this final closing phase, and make no promises you cannot or will not keep because of personal or authority limitations, organizational policies, laws, or time constraints.

Summary Outline

This outline summarizes the elements in the structure of a persuasive interview that covers need/desire and solution.

I. Opening the interview
    A. Select the most appropriate techniques from Chapter 4.
    B. Establish rapport according to relationship and situation.
    C. Provide appropriate orientation.

II. Creating a need or desire
    A. Provide an appropriate statement of purpose.

      B. Develop a need point-by-point with maximum involvement of and careful adaptation to the other party.
1. Use appropriate argument patterns
2. Provide a variety of evidence.
3. Employ effective strategies.
4. Appeal to important values and emotions.
5. Obtain overt agreements as you proceed, being sure to point out how the interviewee party is involved or must be concerned.

      C. Summarize the need or problem and attain overt agreements from the interviewee.

III. Establishing criteria
    A. Present the criteria you have in mind, explaining briefly the rationale and importance of each criterion.
    B. Encourage the interviewee to add criteria.
    C. Involve the interviewee in the discussion of criteria.
    D. Summarize and get agreement on all criteria.

IV. Presenting the solution
    A. Present one solution at a time.
1. Explain the solution in detail using visual aids when possible.
2. Evaluate the solution using agreed-upon criteria.
    B. Respond to anticipated and vocalized objections.
    C. Get agreement on the appropriateness, quality, and feasibility of the preferred solution.

V. Closing the interview
    A. Begin a trial closing as soon as it seems appropriate to do so.
    B. When the trial closing is successful, move to a contract or agreement with the interviewee.
    C. Use appropriate leave-taking techniques discussed in this chapter and Chapter 4.

There is no set pattern for all persuasive interviews.

You will not develop all parts of this outline in every interview. If an interviewee agrees with the need or problem prior to the interview, merely summarize the need in the opening and move directly to criteria. An interviewee may see the need but not agree with your proposed solution. Or an interviewee may feel constraints make any move now impossible. Feasibility is the central concern in this interview, not need or a specific proposal. The interviewee may like your proposal but see no personal need.

Part 2: The Interviewee in the Persuasive Interview

Two key principles in this chapter are (1) that persuasion is *done with* and *not to* another and (2) that both parties are responsible for making the interview a success. With these principles in mind, we now turn our focus to the interviewee in the persuasive interview.

Be an Informed Participant

Unlike interviewers who often are trained and experienced in the ways of altering how people think, act, and feel, interviewees often have little or no training in persuasion and may have scars from failed persuasive encounters. The remainder of this chapter introduces you to the *tricks of the trade* to level the persuasive playing field.

Psychological Strategies

We may act automatically during persuasive interviews.

Interviewers use strategies designed to create psychological discomfort—dissonance—to alter your ways of thinking, feeling, and/or acting.[43] For instance, **standard/learned principles** may automatically guide an action or decision. You may believe, for example, that:

You get what you pay for.

If it's expensive, it's got to be good.

Sales save money.

If an expert says so, it must be true.

If it meets industry standards, it's safe.

Upscale retailers depend on these standard/learned principles to move expensive, high-quality items ranging from jewelry to automobiles.

Look for real differences.

In the **contrast principle**, interviewers know that if a second item is fairly different from the first in attractiveness, cost, or size, it seems *more different* than it actually is. If I want to rent you an apartment, I may show you a rundown one first and then a somewhat better apartment. You may see the second apartment as substantially rather than moderately better. If a sales associate can sell you an expensive suit first, then expensive ties, shirts, and belts seem inexpensive in comparison.

We feel obligated to return favors.

The **rule of reciprocation** instills in you a sense of obligation to repay in kind what another provides. For instance, if a person gives you a free soft drink and then asks you to buy a raffle ticket, you feel obligated to buy the ticket even though it may cost more than the soft drink. This process is at work every time you open your mail and discover yet another packet of personalized address labels. You are likely to send in a donation or not use the labels even though you did not request them. Research reveals that if you use the labels and do not send in a donation you may experience psychological discomfort and fear shame if someone discovers your action.

One concession deserves another, or not.

In a **reciprocal concessions** strategy, you feel a sense of obligation to make a concession in response to a concession. Parties employ this psychological strategy in labor–management negotiations when one party, for example, concedes on health care and the other then feels obligated to concede on retirement benefits. You encounter this strategy in everyday interactions such as when a roommate agrees to provide the car for an outing and you feel obligated to pay for the gas.

Persuaders may ask for a lot and settle for less.

A **rejection then retreat** strategy begins with a proposal that may make a second more acceptable. The idea is that after you reject the first you will feel both obligated and somewhat relieved to agree to the second. One study discovered that if Boy Scouts asked persons to purchase $5 circus tickets and were turned down, the same persons were likely to say yes to a second proposal of a $1 chocolate bar. The Boy Scouts gained either way, and the persuadees felt good about helping out for a lesser amount. Salespersons often start with the top of the line and then retreat to a fallback position *if* necessary.

In **undercover** or **stealth marketing**, an interviewer party of two or more persons pretends to be a friendly, disinterested party and not a sales representative. For example, two people appearing to be tourists or visitors ask a person passing by if she will take their picture. The cooperative passerby agrees and just happens to notice that the couple has a very interesting and attractive digital camera. She asks about it and the party, who just happen to be undercover sales reps for this camera company, gladly comply. The persuadee has no idea that a sales interview is taking place.

Be a Critical Participant

Language Strategies

<aside>Seek the meanings of symbols.</aside>

Woodward and Denton write that language "is far more than a collection of words and rules for proper usage. Language is the instrument and vehicle of human action and expression."[44] Skilled interviewers are keenly aware of the power and manipulation of verbal symbols, but too many of us see these symbols as merely words and rules. Larson warns that "as receivers, we need to get to the bottom of persuasive meanings; carefully analyzing the symbols used or misused by persuaders can help us get there."[45] An important first step in this analysis is to identify common language strategies.[46]

Framing and Reframing

<aside>Jargon is not harmless.</aside>

Persuaders use language to frame or construct the way you see people, places, things, and objects. For instance, **jargon** substitutes peculiar words for common words. While some jargon seems harmless enough (schedule irregularity for airline flight delay), others can hide the truth (terminological inexactitude for lie), make something sound more technical than it is (emergency exit light for a flashlight), more valuable than it is (garment management system for one hook and two hangers), or less severe (collateral damage for the killing of civilians during military actions). Woodward and Denton warn that jargon may "require special interpretations and make us dependent on attorneys [physicians, engineers, professors, consultants] for help, advice, and action."[47]

<aside>Ambiguities say little but sound like a lot.</aside>

Strategic ambiguities are words with multiple or vague meanings. Persuaders assume you will interpret the words according to their specific needs or perceptions without asking embarrassing, negative, or insightful questions. If a politician claims to be a conservative or moderate, what exactly is this person? What is a lifetime guarantee or a limited warranty? What is an affordable apartment or a top salary? What is free-range poultry or poultry raised the old-fashioned way? Studies show that we will pay a premium price for lite, diet, natural, and low-carb products without knowing how these differ from ones that are not.

<aside>Imagery substitutes for experiences.</aside>

Imagery—word pictures—contains multisensory words to color what you have experienced, will experience, may experience, or experience indirectly. A representative of a travel agency, with the aid of leaflets, posters, and Web sites, will help you visualize skiing in Switzerland, visiting the Aztec ruins in Mexico, surfing in Hawaii, seeing the wildlife of Kenya, or enjoying the theater in New York. On the other hand, an interviewer might employ the same tactics to paint a negative picture complete with apocalyptic images and dire predictions if you vote for a political opponent, purchase a competing product, join a different religious group, accept a scholarship with another school, or travel to Egypt instead of Kenya.

Euphemisms substitute *better sounding* words for common words. Cadillac was the first to substitute preowned for used cars, emphasizing ownership rather than use. You might find an inexpensive interview suit but not a cheap one and purchase it from a sales associate rather than a clerk. A lifelike Christmas tree sounds better than a fake or artificial one. Women's size is a common substitution for large size, but you will not find petite sizes in a men's department. You might order a lite beer at your favorite campus hangout, but would you order a diet beer? We are all attracted by pleasant sounding words, names, and labels.

Euphemisms replace substance with sound.

Differentiation is not an attempt to find a better sounding word but to alter how you see *reality*. For example, when an animal rights advocate wants you to become an animal guardian instead of an animal owner, this person wants to change how you see your relationship with your pet. Calling female members of an organization, women, is not "political correctness"—a euphemism—but an effort to change perceptions of the abilities, capabilities, and maturity of women compared to girls. The purposes of euphemisms and differentiation are very different; the first wants to make something *sound better* while the second seeks to change your *visions of reality*.

Words may alter reality.

Appealing to the People

Interviewers may appeal to your historic faith in the rule and wisdom of "the people," following Lincoln's adage that "you can fool all of the people some of the time and some of the people all of the time, but you can't fool all of the people all of the time." The *ad populum* tactic claims to speak on behalf of the people—the alleged majority—such as voters, students, employees, college athletes, consumers, and small business owners. It's the "common folk," of course, not the elite, the government, the administration, or the executives. When, for instance, an attorney claims that he's "here for the people," who are these people?

For many of us, the majority rules.

The **bandwagon** tactic urges you to follow the crowd, to do what everyone else is allegedly doing, buying, wearing, attending, or voting. It appeals to your desire to belong and conform, often accompanied by a note of urgency: "My course is filling up very quickly." "The concert tickets are being snapped up."

Listen for important qualifiers such as nearly, probably, almost, and majority. Ask for numbers or names of those who have signed a petition, agreed to a change, or joined an organization. Be cautious of phrases such as experienced investors, people in the know, and those who are on the move that are designed to pressure and flatter.

Have an inquiring mind.

Simplifying the Complex

Interviewers attempt to reduce complex problems, issues, controversies, and situations to their simplest elements. The **thin entering wedge**, also known as the **domino effect** or the **slippery slope**, claims that one decision, action, or law after another is leading toward disastrous consequences. Talk to a person who is against censorship, gun control, or same-sex marriages and you are likely to hear how censorship of books in public schools is one more step toward censoring all reading materials, how the

Fear of chain reactions may stifle any action.

registration of handguns is yet another step toward outlawing and confiscating all guns, and how same-sex marriage is a slippery slope toward the destruction of the home and the family. Look for evidence of a related, intentional string of actions that are tipping dominos, producing wedges, or sliding down a dangerous slope.

Slogans are clever words or phrases that encapsulate positions, stands, or goals.

Slogans are clever phrases and more.

They are a vague but powerful means to alter the way you think, feel, or act because they are catchy and entice you to fill in the meaning—to self-persuade. Interviewers rely on slogans to attract customers, recruits, contributors, and loyalty and may change them to communicate different messages. For instance, when Purdue University changed its slogan from "Touching tomorrow today" and then "Discover Purdue" with "Purdue: It's Happening Here," President Martin Jischke explained that "there is a tremendous amount of excitement around campus. . . . I think this theme is just trying to capture that sense of energy, momentum and pride that we have at Purdue."[48] Ask what slogans mean and if they truly represent a person, organization, campaign, or solution.

Polarizing limits our choices and our thinking.

An interviewer may **polarize** people, organizations, positions, or courses of action by claiming that you have only a choice of two: conservative or liberal, friend or foe, Chevy or Ford, wind power or nuclear power, for gun control or against gun control. It's a simplistic, but often persuasive, view of the world. Are there really only two choices? For instance, are you either conservative or liberal, a mixture of each, or something else?

Dodging the Issue

Attacking a source does not address the issue.

Interviewers may attempt to dodge critical issues, questions, or objections. **Ad hominem** (getting personal) dodges undesired challenges by discrediting a source because of age, culture, gender, race, affiliation, or past positions, statements, or claims. A parent may tell a child to "just consider the source" when the child is called a name or has a belief challenged. An acquaintance may urge you to ignore research conducted by a known conservative or liberal, government agency or corporate association, religious or secular organization. Insist that the interviewer address the issue, point, or substance of the research.

Sharing guilt does not remove guilt.

You have used the *tu quoque* tactic since childhood to dodge an issue or objection by revolving it upon the challenger or questioner: "You're one too," "It takes one to know one," or "So do you." These are classic *tu quoque* responses. If you question a political candidate about taking money from special interests, the person may reply, "All politicians take money from special interests" or "Your candidate has accepted money from labor unions and trial lawyers."

Blaming others is an attempt to dodge responsibility.

Interviewers may dodge issues by **transferring guilt** to others, making the accuser, victim, or questioner the guilty party. Cheating on an exam is the professor's fault; failing to report all income on a tax report is the IRS's fault; parking illegally is the college's fault for not providing enough parking places. Defense attorneys turn victims of crimes into the guilty parties, particularly in rape or abuse cases. Do not allow attribution of guilt to others without addressing questions, concerns, and objections.

Logical Strategies

The logical and psychological are inseparable.

As discussed earlier, persuaders develop arguments into what appear to be valid and acceptable patterns. It is important to recognize and challenge these common logical patterns.[49]

Argument from example is a statement about the distribution of some characteristic among the members of a whole class of people, places, or things. It's based on a sample of this class. If you recognize this pattern, ask:

> Always check the sample from which generalizations come.

- What is the total amount of this sample?
- What is the nature of this sample?
- When was the sample taken?
- What is the interviewer asserting from this sample?

Beware of the *hasty generalization* in which the persuader generalizes to a whole group of people, places, or things from one or a few examples. For instance, a friend may warn you against dining at a particular restaurant because he had a bad meal there once.

Argument from cause-to-effect addresses what caused an effect. Ask questions such as:

> Be careful of coincidences seen as causes.

- Was this cause able to generate this effect?
- Was this cause the only possible cause?
- Was this cause the major cause?
- What evidence is offered to establish this causal link?
- Is a coincidence mistaken for the cause?

> Just because B followed A, it does not mean that A caused B.

Beware of the *post hoc* or **scrambling cause-effect** fallacy that argues simply because B followed A, A must have caused B. For instance, I got the flu the day after I got that flu shot, so the shot gave me the flu.

Arguing from fact or hypothesis offers the best accounting or explanation for a body of facts and is the type of reasoning investigators use in murder mysteries. For instance, a football coach might argue that because he has a senior quarterback who has started for three years, has a veteran defensive line, has three outstanding linebackers, and has a pre-season all-American field goal kicker that this will be the team's breakout year. Ask these questions during an interview when hearing an argument from fact:

> Be a super-sleuth when encountering hypotheses.

- How frequently is this hypothesis accurate with these facts?
- Is the body of facts sufficient?
- What facts would make the claim more or less convincing?
- How simple or complex is the hypothesis?

Arguing from sign is a claim that two or more variables are related in such a way that the presence or absence of one may be taken as an indication of the presence or absence of the other. For example, you may note that the flag on the post office is at half-mast and reason that someone of importance has died. Ask these questions when hearing an argument from the sign:

> A sign may have many meanings or no meanings.

- What is the relationship between the variables?
- Is the presence or absence verifiable?
- What is the believability or reliability of the sign?

Arguing from analogy or comparison is based on the assumption that if two people, places, or things have a number of similarities they also share significant others. For instance, a salesperson might argue that since a moderately priced SUV has many of the same features as a luxury SUV (V8 engine, room for six adults, equal cargo space, video system for rear seat occupants, leather seating, and four-wheel drive), you should lease the less expensive SUV because it is of the same quality. Ask these questions:

> Look for important differences as well as important similarities.

- How similar are the similarities?
- Are enough similarities provided?
- Are the similarities critical to the claim?

Arguing from accepted belief, assumption, or proposition is based on a statement that is thought to be accepted or proven. The remainder of the argument follows from this assertion, such as: Smoking causes cancer. You are a smoker. Therefore you will get cancer. Ask these questions:

> Identify the major assertion upon which the argument rests.

- Do you accept the foundational assertion?
- Do the other assertions follow logically from this assertion?
- Does the claim necessarily follow from these assertions?

Beware of argument based on alleged self-evident truths that cannot be questioned or disputed because they are "fact."

In argument from condition, an interviewer asserts that if something does or does not happen, something else will or will not happen. The central focus is the word *if*. Ask these questions:

> "If" arguments may ignore obvious or unpredictable conditions.

- Is the condition acceptable?
- Is this the only condition?
- Is this the major condition?

Evidence

Look closely at the evidence an interviewer offers (or does not offer) to gain attention and interest, establish credibility and legitimacy, support arguments, develop a need, and present a solution.[50] Evidence may include examples, stories, authorities or witnesses, comparisons and contrasts, statistics, and key definitions. Use these questions to assess the acceptability of the interviewer's evidence.

> Assess the reliability and expertise of sources.

- *Is the evidence trustworthy?* Are the persuader and the persons and organizations being cited unbiased and reliable? Are the sources of the evidence (newspapers, reports, Internet, publications) unbiased and reliable?
- *Is the evidence authoritative?* What are the training, experience, and reputation of the authorities or witnesses being cited? Were they in positions to have observed the facts, events, or data?

- *Is the evidence recent?* Is it the most recent available? Are newer statistics or findings available? Have authorities changed their minds?

- *Is the evidence documented sufficiently?* Do you know where and how the statistics or results were determined? Who determined them? Where and when were they reported?

- *Is the evidence communicated accurately?* Can you detect alterations or deletions in quotations, statistics, or documentation? Is the evidence cited in context?

- *Is the evidence sufficient in quantity?* Are enough authorities cited? Enough examples given? Enough points of comparison made? Adequate facts revealed?

- *Is the evidence sufficient in quality?* Are opinions stated as facts? How satisfactory is the sample used for generalizations and causal arguments? Does proof evidence (factual illustrations, statistics, authority, detailed comparisons) outweigh clarifying evidence (hypothetical illustrations, paid testimonials, figurative analogies, and metaphors)?

> **Insist on both quantity and quality of evidence.**

> **Be an active and critical player in the interview.**

Be active in the interview. Each interview has the potential of altering or reinforcing the way you think, feel, or act, including the money you spend, the votes you cast, the relationships you establish or maintain, the possessions you protect, the work you do, and the life you lead.

Ask a variety of questions during each interview. Informational questions, for example, enable you to obtain information and explanations, probe into vague and ambiguous words and comments, and reveal feelings and attitudes that may lie hidden or merely suggested. There are no foolish questions, only questions you foolishly fail to ask.

The Opening

> **Play an active role in the opening because it initiates the persuasive process.**

Be alert and active from the first moments of each interview. If the interview is a "cold call" in which you have no time to prepare, use carefully phrased questions to discover the identity, position, and qualifications of the interviewer. Discover the real purpose and intent of the interview. Use the opening to play an active, critical, and informed role in the interview. It all starts with the opening.

Too many persuadees play passive roles during openings. Here is a typical example from an interview in one of our classes. The persuadee is head of surgery at this hospital, believes in following strict hierarchies with surgeons at the top, feels physicians rather than nurses will detect and address any real problems, and is all business.

Persuader: Dr. Smalley, I'm Lilly McDowell, one of the surgical nurse supervisors.

Persuadee: Hi Lilly, have a seat.

Persuader: I'd like to talk to you about the problems we are having with surgical patients after they leave the hospital and a solution to this problem.

Persuadee: Okay.

Persuader: Well, we have discovered that . . .

The interviewee does not exhibit personality or attitudes and learns little about the purpose of this interview, how long it will take, or the nature of the problem. He allows the interviewer to launch into the need without question even though the interviewee appears to be encroaching on his authority and status, his area of expertise and responsibility, and does not explain the nature of the problem or how it was determined.

Need or Desire

> Ask questions, challenge arguments, and demand solid evidence.

If an interviewer attempts to conduct an interview without a clear purpose and in which the need is a collection of generalizations and ambiguous claims, insist on a point-by-point development with each point crafted carefully and logically, supported with adequate evidence, and adapted to *your* values, beliefs, and attitudes. Beware of fallacies and tactics that dodge your questions and objections. An interviewer may attempt to introduce another point rather than address your concerns about a point. Insist on answers to your questions and objections and get agreements before delving into another point.

Weigh evidence carefully and be on guard against psychological strategies designed to manipulate your reactions and make you feel obligated to reply in kind. Do not tolerate negative selling or mudslinging. Insist on getting agreements on the need before going into criteria or a solution.

Criteria

> Criteria enable you to weigh solutions.

Establishing criteria with the interviewer that any solution should meet is a critical part of the persuasion process. An interviewer may come to an interview with a list of criteria, and this helps the process and shows planning. Take an active part in establishing criteria. Are the criteria clear? Do you wish to modify some criteria? Which are the most important criteria? Are there criteria you wish to add?

Solution

> Be sure the solution meets the need and is the best available.

An interviewer may claim there is only *one* obvious solution to the need or desire agreed upon. There is rarely only one solution to any problem. Insist upon a detailed presentation of each possible solution. Ask questions and raise objections. Be sure the criteria are applied equally to each solution to determine which is best for you in this situation. If possible, insist on seeing, feeling, hearing, or experiencing the product or proposal.

When you have agreed upon a solution or course of action, beware of qualifiers or "add-ons" such as guarantees, rebates, accessories, processing fees, and commitments. What exactly is a "lifetime" warranty or guarantee? The persuader may hope that since you have made the *big* decision, you will agree to *small* decisions—the contrast principle discussed earlier. What are you getting that's "free"?

The Closing

> Take your time when making a final decision.

Do not be rushed into making a decision or commitment. You have little to gain and much to lose through haste. A common tactic is to create a psychological reaction by claiming the possibility of censorship or the scarcity of a product. An organization may produce a limited number of books, coins, cars, or positions to make them more in demand, to urge you to act quickly before it is too late or an agency steps in to prevent you from acting.

Take time to think about a decision; sleep on it. Be sure all of your questions and objections are answered satisfactorily. Be aware of the possible ramifications of your decision. Consider getting a second or third opinion. Talk to persons who have relevant expertise or experiences. Check out competing products, candidates, offers, and programs. When coming to a new community, check out several neighborhoods before buying a home or renting an apartment; visit several universities before deciding where to pursue a graduate or professional degree; try out several laptops before deciding which to purchase.

ON THE WEB

Assume you are going to purchase a new car upon graduation. You want to be thoroughly informed and prepared when you contact sales representatives so you can make an intelligent decision and get a good deal. Use the World Wide Web to access information on brands, models, features, comparative prices, and assessments by automotive experts. Sample manufacturer sites are Toyota (http://www.toyota.com), Acura (http://www.acura.com), Mazda (http://mazdausa .com), Buick (http://www.parkavenue.com), and Chrysler (http://www.chryslercars.com). What information is readily available on the Internet, and why is this so? What information is not included on the Internet, and why is this so? What are common persuasive tactics used on the Internet? What questions does your research suggest you pursue during interviews?

Summary

Good persuasive interviews are ones in which both parties are actively involved, not speeches given to an audience of one but interpersonal interactions in which both parties must speak and listen effectively. The guiding principle is that persuasion is *done with* not *done to* another party.

Good persuasive interviews are honest endeavors conducted according to fundamental ethical guidelines. They are not games in which the end justifies the means or *buyer beware* is a guiding principle. The appeal should be to the head and the heart rather than relying on emotional hot buttons that will override critical thought and decision making.

Good persuasive interviews are carefully researched, planned, and structured, yet they remain flexible enough to meet unforeseen reactions, objections, and arguments. The interviewer adapts the persuasive effort to *this persuadee;* develops, supports, and documents important reasons for a change in thinking, feeling, or acting; and presents a detailed solution that meets criteria agreed upon by both parties. Persuasion often entails several contacts in which the persuader and persuadee reach incremental agreements.

Good persuasive interviews involve the interviewee as a responsible, informed, critical, and active participant who plays a central not passive role in the interview. The interviewee acts ethically, listens carefully, asks insightful and challenging questions, raises important objections, challenges evidence and arguments, recognizes common persuasive tactics for what they are, and weighs solutions according to agreed upon criteria.

Key Terms and Concepts

The online learning center for this text features FLASHCARDS and CROSSWORD PUZZLES for studying based on these terms and concepts.

Ad hominem	Differentiation	Psychological strategies
Ad populum	Domino effect	Reciprocal concessions
Agreement questions	Dissonance	Rejection then retreat
Analyzing the interviewee	Encouraging interaction	Rule of reciprocation
Arguing from accepted belief	questions	Scrambling cause-effect
Arguing from analogy	Ethics	Self-evident truths
Arguing from cause-effect	Evidence	Shock-absorber phrases
Arguing from condition	False dichotomy	Shopping-around
Arguing from example	Framing	interviewee
Arguing from facts	Hasty generalization	Skeptical interviewee
Arguing from two choices	Hostile interviewee	Slippery slope
Argument from sign	Identification theory	Slogans
Attention and interest	Implicative approach	Socioeconomic
questions	Indecisive interviewee	background
Attitude-attitude conflict	Induced compliance	Solution
Attitudes	theory	Source-perception
Balance or consistency	Intelligent interviewee	conflict
theory	Interrelated conditions	Standard/learned principles
Bandwagon tactic	Motives	Stealth marketing
Behavior-attitude conflict	Name-calling	Strategic ambiguities
Beliefs	Normative influence	Thin entering wedge
Buyer beware	Objection questions	Transferring guilt
Closed-minded or authori-	Objections	*Tu quoque*
tarian interviewee	One-sided approach	Trial closing
Cold calls	Open-minded	Two-sided approach
Consubstantiality	Polarization	Undercover marketing
Contract or agreement	*Post hoc fallacy*	Values
closing	Prospecting	Verification questions
Contrast principle	Psychological discomfort	Yes-but approach
Criteria	Psychological reactance	Yes-yes approach
Culture	theory	

A Persuasive Interview for Review and Analysis

This interview is between Josh Molinsky, a member of the County Council, and Susan Dawson, president of the Chamber of Commerce, in which Josh will attempt to convince Susan of the need to implement a highly controversial Local Option Highway User Tax, better known as a wheel tax. Susan has expressed concerns about the need for such a tax and the potential negative impact of this tax on businesses located or doing business in the county, particularly if surrounding counties do not adopt a wheel tax. Josh feels that Susan's support is critical in selling the idea of a user tax to other segments of the community and hopes this interview will be a first step in changing her mind. No action is desired.

How thoroughly has the interviewer done his homework, including analyzing the persuadee? How does the relationship of the parties affect the interview? How satisfactory are the opening, need, and closing? How satisfactory is the evidence in support of reasons for a change? How effectively does the persuader respond to objections and questions? Since persuasion is done with and not to an interviewee, how effectively does the interviewee make this a mutual interaction? How active and critical is the interviewee in the opening, the need step, analyzing arguments and evidence, establishing criteria any solution should meet, weighing the advantages and disadvantages of the proposed solution or solutions, and closing the interview?

1. **Interviewer:** Good morning, Susan. (cheerful and smiling) How are the kids?

2. **Interviewee:** Hi, Josh. They're fine, thanks. (shakes his hand) Jamie will graduate from high school in a few weeks.

3. **Interviewer:** That's great. My kids are doing well, too. The twins are in eighth grade and Julie is in fifth. Didn't I see you at the Chamber of Commerce Convention in Nashville a couple of weeks ago?

4. **Interviewee:** Yes. It was a great opportunity to share ideas on what is impacting businesses, particularly small ones like mine.

5. **Interviewer:** I always find the sharing of ideas and concerns at conventions to be helpful. Just to discover you're all in the same boat helps at times.

6. **Interviewee:** That's true. (looks at her watch) What can I do for you?

7. **Interviewer:** Did the Local Option Highway User Tax come up during any of your meetings?

8. **Interviewee:** Yes, it did. (frowning) It's not very popular among Chamber members or their communities. Is that what you want to talk to me about? I know the County Council is considering it.

9. **Interviewer:** Yes, that's why I'm here this morning. I'm well aware of the unpopularity of the so-called wheel tax. Letters to the *Constitution* and call-ins on local radio shows are running 3 to 1 opposed to the idea. As you know, several of us on the County Council feel it's the lesser of two evils.

10. **Interviewee:** Uh huh. And what does that have to do with me or the Chamber of Commerce?

11. **Interviewer:** Well . . . frankly . . . we feel it is essential to have you on board on this issue if we're going to sell it to business leaders and employers.

12. **Interviewee:** That's not going to happen until our members change their minds, which is unlikely. You see . . .

13. **Interviewer:** (cuts in) I'd like to explain why we've changed our minds during the past year and maybe why you ought to reconsider it.

14. **Interviewee:** I find this need for new money rather curious since you were the leader of the faction that opposed taking any of the federal economic stimulus money specifically designated for road repair and building projects. Other communities have taken advantage of this money while we are looking for new taxes.

15. **Interviewer:** Well, as they say, that's water under the bridge and we are facing some big decisions.

16. **Interviewee:** Well, as they also say, that's money over the dam that might have prevented some of these big decisions.

17. **Interviewer:** I hear you, but I'm still against taking any so-called stimulus money from the feds. It's a matter of principle.

18. **Interviewee:** I also think not adding a new tax is a matter of principle.

19. **Interviewer:** At the time, we hoped the state legislature would provide supplemental appropriations and perhaps a small increase in the gas tax to provide needed highway funding. Because of opposition to raising taxes of any kind and then the catastrophic recession the past three years, the legislature cut funding. We're now in a bind with new projects and necessary repairs far exceeding the funds available.

20. **Interviewee:** I think, in times like this, all agencies must live within their means. Even if that seems painful to some. As I recall, that was the point you made when running for election to the County Council. It helped you defeat the long-time Council member you opposed.

21. **Interviewer:** I guess it depends upon who's feeling the pain, or "whose ox is being gored" so to speak.

22. **Interviewee:** I don't follow that metaphor at all. All of us were gored during the recession and all of us felt the pain of budget cuts. Metaphors are interesting but don't prove anything.

23. **Interviewer:** Well, the Chamber has been pushing the county to make Karber Road four lanes instead of two because of the rapidly growing development on the south side. The cost of this improvement, with necessary curbs, sidewalks, and storm sewers, will be more than $1 million per lane per mile. This limits us to a quarter-mile of a four-lane Karber Road per year. That's a long time to complete this much-needed five-mile stretch of road.

24. **Interviewee:** The federal stimulus money was designed for projects like this that would have employed dozens, maybe hundreds, of workers, most of them unemployed. We in the county must live with the past principled actions of its leaders. I think it's time to prioritize projects. Those of us in *business* (vocal emphasis) have to do that all the time.

25. **Interviewer:** And so do those of us in government positions. The problem is that many projects seem to be at the top of the priority list. For instance, the Karber Road project is highly important, but so are the replacement costs of 15 bridges in the area that the state is demanding we repair or replace. The cost is more than a million a bridge just for repair work.

26. **Interviewee:** A lot of the stimulus money was earmarked for bridge repair and replacement, particularly after the disaster in Minneapolis. Those could have been at the top of the county's list.

27. **Interviewer:** (sounds exasperated) Susan . . . The past is past, and debating past decisions will not solve any of our problems. The average life for a paved road is

about 15 years, and a great many new roads built in the county in the booming 1990s are reaching that age. Do you know what it costs just to repave a road?

28. **Interviewee:** No (laughing), but you're going to tell me.

29. **Interviewer:** That's right. (not smiling) Last year it cost $50,000 to resurface a mile of road that required no other repairs. Since we rely primarily on asphalt that is oil based, the cost this year with the rise in oil prices is likely to exceed $55,000 a mile, not including gas price increases for running our equipment.

30. **Interviewee:** I can appreciate this fact, but you'll just have to delay some resurfacing until the economy and tax revenue improve. Or . . . you could apply for a federal grant for matching funds. Many counties in this state are doing this.

31. **Interviewer:** That *sounds* (vocal emphasis) like a good idea until you figure in the added cost of a deteriorated road that requires more than resurfacing. The cost could jump to $75,000 a mile. We have over $650 million invested in county roads.

32. **Interviewee:** Josh, it's priority again. Prioritize the important projects and reduce or eliminate other costs. You can do this until you hear from the government about your application for a matching funds grant.

33. **Interviewer:** Okay, that sounds like *good business* (vocal emphasis). We can do this by eliminating culvert repairs, guardrail improvements, signage, snow plowing, salting of icy roads, mowing during the summer, picking up dead animals, and patching of potholes. Would you and county residents be in favor of this after the first snowfall or severe damage to tires and suspensions because of potholes and ruts?

34. **Interviewee:** I'm not proposing the elimination of these *essentials* (vocal emphasis). You have conveniently ignored my suggestion of applying for a federal grant for matching funds for essential bridge or road projects.

35. **Interviewer:** I will not sacrifice the principle I ran on; we will not ask for federal funds. The federal government needs to live within its means as we do.

36. **Interviewee:** You do not seem to have a problem asking me to sacrifice *my principle* that a wheel tax would burden our county residents but not those driving in from surrounding counties.

37. **Interviewer:** (sounding incredulous) You're president of the Chamber of Commerce, and you're concerned about those who bring their business and their money into this county?

38. **Interviewee:** Of course not (sounds a bit testy). We have many programs designed to encourage working and shopping here. I'm just concerned about fairness. When we all but begged you and the council to accept stimulus money, you told us you could not and would not sacrifice your principles. Well, my principle is no new taxes, and now you're begging me to sacrifice my principles to make up for the problems largely caused by your principles.

39. **Interviewer:** I hear you and can appreciate what you're saying, but short of tollbooths on every road, there is no way to charge a road tax on those coming in, and we both agree we want them to continue coming in.

40. **Interviewee:** That's not what I had in mind. It's ridiculous.

41. **Interviewer:** Real or imagined tollbooths won't be necessary because I suspect that surrounding counties will soon have a Local Option Highway User Tax of their own. In fact, Jefferson and Henry counties to our west will institute such a tax this fall. Like us, they see no other choice.

42. **Interviewee:** Well, I'm not sold on the idea of a new tax yet, but I will think about it and then talk to you about the nature of the tax plan you would initiate, such as a sunset provision that would end it after three years.

43. **Interviewer:** That's all I wanted to do this morning, to encourage you to think about the idea and the problems we face. Can we meet on Thursday morning around 9:00?

44. **Interviewee:** That time is open on my calendar, but I'd like to see a breakdown of the highway budget for this year before then to see where our road money is going.

45. **Interviewer:** The County Council committee on option taxes is meeting Wednesday night, and I might have some ideas to share the next morning. I'll get you a copy of the budget.

46. **Interviewee:** Okay. See you then. We do pay a price for our principles, don't we?

47. **Interviewer:** Yes, we do, but what else do we have to live by?

Persuasion Role-Playing Cases

Acquiring a Commuter Airline Service

The interviewer is the manager of a university-operated airport that had provided commercial passenger service to the area since the 1950s. Unfortunately, the convenience and limo service every two hours to an international airport just 65 miles away and the cost of commuter airline tickets resulted in several airlines coming and going over the years because of lack of passengers. Nighthawk Air is the only airline continuing to serve the airport with two morning and two afternoon flights to Detroit. It has announced that it will discontinue service on December 1. The interviewer is scheduling interviews with several commuter airlines in an effort to persuade them to begin service in December.

The interviewee is chief of operations for Eastern-Southern, a four-year-old commuter airline serving Delaware, Maryland, Virginia, and North Carolina. Its long-range plans are to extend service to Pennsylvania and Ohio. Competition from large airlines, a steep rise in fuel bills, and a severe economic recession have made these plans tenuous at best. She is willing to listen to the interviewer from a service area that might be in the airline's future, but she is well aware of the number of airlines that have come and gone from his airport. There would have to be guarantees of reasonable passenger numbers and some financial incentives. The interviewer has a good background in the aviation industry but little management experience or success in selling commuter service to his campus and community.

Adoption of the New Line of Clothing

The interviewer is 24 years old and is the assistant manager of Abbey's, a women's clothing store in a shopping mall close to a college campus. The three lines of clothing and the selection of jewelry clearly appeal to "mature" women in their late 30s and older, not the college customer but her mother. The interviewer wants to persuade the owner–manager to eliminate at least one line of clothing and replace it with one or ones that will attract the teenage and young adult clientele. The selection of jewelry would be mixed in appeal. The interview is taking place in the interviewee's office at 8:00 a.m. before the shop opens at 9:30.

The interviewee has owned Abbey's for nearly 20 years and has been satisfied with sales and the number of repeat customers she attracts. Ego involvement is high because the interviewee personally selected the shop's brands and jewelry and travels to Chicago, San Francisco, and New York to make stock selections. She sees Abbey's as offering a distinct alternative, one of the very few remaining in the area, to all of the "teeny-bopper" stores that populate the local mall that have nothing for women over 30. The interviewer is seen as a very hard worker with excellent communication skills but highly interested in her own tastes in clothing and jewelry. She is part of her generation, but this does not prevent her from interacting with and selling to women several years older.

A Drought-Resistant Seed Corn

The interviewer is a sales representative for Millennium Hybrids, which has developed a new drought-resistant seed corn that has proven highly successful in tests in drought-prone areas of the midwestern states and Colorado. It was developed following the disastrous summer of 2012 when widespread drought reduced corn production by some 53 percent. It is more expensive than traditional hybrids, but predictions are for more summers like that of 2012 over the next several years. The interviewer first met the interviewee, a farmer-owner of a 3,000-acre grain farm in western Iowa, when he was doing research on seed corn at Iowa State University.

The interviewee has used seeds from Millennium Hybrids in the past but switched to King Hybrids after he lost more than 80 percent of his crop in 2012. He believed King's seed corn was more drought resistant. Although he is willing to talk about the new Millennium hybrid, he has been happy with the King Hybrids and its sales representative who has worked very closely with him during the past two years.

Preserve a Historical Home

The Harrison home was built in the country west of New Goshen in the early 1850s and remained in the family until 1932, when it was willed to the Jefferson County Historical Society along with many of its original furnishings. Since then, it has served as a historical attraction, a place to house and exhibit the Society's wealth of artifacts, and a space for offices. Many of the materials used to build this home were imported from Italy, Switzerland, and Germany and then transported up the Mississippi and Ohio Rivers before being loaded onto wagons for their trip to the building site seven miles from New Goshen. Recently the Historical Society announced that the Harrison home was now too small for all of its holdings and that it could no longer afford the upkeep of the aging building. It plans to sell it and move into the former Jefferson County Academy, a much larger building that is also of significant historical value. The interviewer, a retired college history teacher, hopes to persuade the director of the State Department of Historic preservation to provide a grant that would enable the Historical Society to maintain the home.

The director of the State Department of Historic Preservation has read a detailed proposal from the persuader and is sympathetic. However, her agency is swamped with requests to preserve old homes, schools, and buildings throughout the state. Each request seems to have merit but funds are limited and efforts to reduce the federal budget have eliminated or greatly reduced funds for preservation of structures. The director is interested in how much money the persuader is willing to invest in the Harrison home and what efforts he is willing to undertake to raise additional funds.

Student Activities

1. Locate a professional (sales representative, recruiter, fund-raiser) who conducts persuasive interviews on a regular basis and spend a day on the job with this person. Observe how this person prepares for each interview, selects strategies, opens interviews, develops needs and solutions, closes interviews, and adapts to interviewees.

2. Select three persons in different career fields (e.g., sales, medicine, athletics, lobbying, recruiting, advocacy) who have extensive experience in persuasive interviewing. Probe into how they prepare for and try to persuade three of the following types of interviewees: indecisive, hostile, closed-minded, skeptical, shopping around, highly educated. Which do they find most difficult? What are their most effective strategies for each? Which value and emotional appeals do they use most often and why?

3. Identify an acquaintance or family member who is known for driving hard bargains. Go with this person to a persuasive interview; it need not be a sales situation. Observe the role this person plays in the opening, how this person handles the need or desire, the information this person obtains, objections and questions raised about the solution, and how this person negotiates a final decision. If this interviewee threatens to go to a competitor or a person higher up in an organization, how does the interviewer react?

4. Keep a log over a two-week period of the telephone and e-mail solicitations you receive. How well are these adapted to you as a person and to your needs, desires, and motives? Which values and emotions do they use as triggering devices? How ethical are their tactics? Which types of evidence do they employ? How do they react when you raise questions or objections? How do they close the interviews?

Notes

1. Roderick P. Hart, "Teaching Persuasion," in *Teaching Communication: Theory, Research, and Methods,* John A. Daly, Gustav W. Friedrich, and Anita L. Vangelisti, eds. (Hillsdale, NJ: Lawrence Erlbaum, 1999), p. 133.

2. Isocrates, "Against the Sophists," in *The Rhetorical Tradition: Readings from Classical Times to the Present,* Patricia Bizzell and Bruce Herzberg, eds. (New York: Bedford/St. Martins, 2001), pp. 72–75.

3. "Honesty/Ethics in Professions," http://www.gallup.com/poll/1654/honesty-ethics-professiona.aspx, accessed September 7, 2012.

4. David Callahan, *The Cheating Culture: Why More Americans Are Doing Wrong to Get Ahead* (New York: Harcourt, 2004).

5. Richard L. Johannesen, "Perspectives on Ethics in Persuasion," in Charles U. Larson, *Persuasion: Reception and Responsibility* (Belmont, CA: Wadsworth/Cengage Learning, 2013), p. 41.

6. Herbert W. Simons, *Persuasion in Society* (Thousand Oaks, CA: Sage, 2001), p. 374.

7. Johannesen, p. 41.

8. Kenneth E. Andersen, *Persuasion: Theory and Practice* (Boston: Allyn and Bacon, 1971), p. 327.

9. Gary C. Woodward and Robert E. Denton, Jr., *Persuasion and Influence in American Life* (Long Grove, IL: Waveland Press, 2009), p. 350.

10. Simons, p. 374.

11. Johannesen, p. 43.

12. Omar Swartz, *Persuasion as a Critical Activity: Application and Engagement* (Dubuque, IA: Kendall/Hunt, 2009), pp. 321–322.

13. Woodward and Denton, p. 361.

14. James Price Dillard and Michael Pfau, eds., *The Persuasion Handbook: Developments in Theory and Practice* (Thousand Oaks, CA: Sage, 2002), pp. 4–14.

15. Johannesen, p. 43.

16. Woodward and Denton, p. 361.

17. Johannesen, p. 46

18. Charlie Lang, "Making Cold Calls Enjoyable . . . Impossible?" *Articlebase,* http://www.articlebase.com/business-articles/making-cold-calls-enjoyable-impossible-46, accessed October 17, 2009.

19. Eric J. Adams, "The Art of Business: Client Prospecting for Creative Pros Who Hate Prospecting," http://www.creative pro.com/article/the-art-of-business-client-prospecting-for-creative-pros, accessed October 15, 2009.

20. Darrell Zahorsky, "Myths of Sales Prospecting," *About.com,* http://sginformation .about-com/cs/sales/a/prospect.htm?p=1, accessed October 15, 2009.

21. Deirdre Johnston, *The Art and Science of Persuasion* (Madison, WI: Brown & Benchmark, 1994), p. 185; Sharon Shavitt and Timothy Brock, *Persuasion: Psychological Insights and Perspectives* (Boston: Allyn and Bacon, 1994), pp. 152–153.

22. "College and Its Effect on Students: Early Work on the Impact of College, Nine Generalizations, Later Studies, Pascrella and Terenzini," http://education.stateuniversity.com/pages1844/College-its-Effect-on-Students.html, accessed September 10, 2012.

23. Larson, p. 91.

24. Michael Argyle, "Intercultural Communication," in *Intercultural Communication: A Reader,* Larry A. Samovar and Richard E. Porter, eds. (Belmont, CA: Wadsworth, 1988), pp. 35–36.

25. Milton Rokeach, *Beliefs, Attitudes, and Values* (San Francisco: Jossey-Bass, 1968), p. 124.

26. Aristotle, *Rhetoric,* W. Rhys Roberts, trans. (New York: The Modern Library, 1954), Bk. I, Chap. 2, p. 25.

27. Robert H. Glass and John S. Seiter, *Persuasion, Social Influence, and Compliance Gaining* (Boston: Pearson, 2007), p. 77; Larson, pp. 276–277.

28. Woodward and Denton, Jr., pp. 107–119; Swartz, p. 207.

29. Daniel J. O'Keefe, *Persuasion: Theory and Research* (Thousand Oaks CA: Sage, 2002), p. 150.

30. Kenneth Burke, *A Rhetoric of Motives* (Berkeley: University of California Press, 1969), p. 55.

31. Burke, pp. 21–45; Charles J. Stewart, Craig Allen Smith, and Robert E. Denton, Jr., *Persuasion and Social Movements* (Prospect Heights, IL: Waveland Press, 2012), pp. 144–148.

32. Woodward and Denton, pp. 143–146; Larson, pp. 218–219.

33. Kathleen Kelley Reardon, *Persuasion in Practice* (Newbury Park, CA: Sage, 1991), pp. 54–55; O'Keefe, pp. 246–250; Erin Alison Szabo and Michael Pfau, "Nuances of Inoculation: Theory and Applications," in *The Persuasion Handbook: Development in Theory and Practice,* James Price Dillard and Michael Pfau, eds. (Thousand Oaks, CA: Sage, 2002), pp. 233–258.

34. O'Keefe, pp. 88–94.

35. Michael Burgoon, Eusebio Alvaro, Joseph Grandpre, and Michael Voulodekis, "Revisiting the Theory of Psychological Reactance," in *The Persuasion Handbook: Development in Theory and Practice* (Sage, 2002), pp. 213–232.

36. "Opening Statements," *JUSTSELL*, http://www.justsell.com/opening-statements, accessed September 14, 2012.

37. William B. Gudykunst and Tsukasa Nishida, *Bridging Japanese/North American Differences* (Thousand Oaks, CA: Sage, 1994), pp. 68–73; Judith N. Martin and Thomas K. Nakayama, *Experiencing Intercultural Communication* (New York: McGraw-Hill, 2011), pp. 261–262 and 321–322.

38. Stewart, Smith, and Denton, pp. 200–208; Robert N. Bostrom, *Persuasion* (Englewood Cliffs, NJ: Prentice Hall, 1983), pp. 181–182.

39. Shavitt and Brock, pp. 152–153.

40. Larson (2007), p. 295.

41. Tom Hopkins, *How to Master the Art of Selling* (Scottsdale, AZ: Champion Press, 2005).

42. Lee Iacocca, *Iacocca: An Autobiography* (New York: Bantam Books, 1984), p. 34.

43. Kelton V. Rhoads and Robert B. Cialdini, in Dillard and Pfau, pp. 514–517; Robert B. Cialdini, *Influence: Science and Practice* (New York: HarperCollins, 1993), pp. 19–44.

44. Woodward and Denton, p. 50.

45. Larson (2004), pp. 103–104.

46. Woodward and Denton, pp. 69–73; Larson (2013), pp. 120–142; Swartz, pp. 273–291.

47. Woodward and Denton, p. 72.

48. West Lafayette, IN, *The Exponent*, August 22, 2003, p. B1.

49. Woodward and Denton, pp. 85–95; Larson (2013), pp. 238–243.

50. Simons, pp. 167–171.

Resources

Cialdini, Robert B. *Influence: Science and Practice*. Boston: Allyn and Bacon, 2008.

Dillard, James Price, and Michael Pfau, eds. *The Persuasion Handbook: Developments in Theory and Practice*. Thousand Oaks, CA: Sage, 2002.

Johannesen, Richard L., Kathleen Valde, and Karen Whedbee. *Ethics in Human Communication*. Long Grove, IL: Waveland Press, 2008.

Larson, Charles U. *Persuasion: Reception and Responsibility*. Belmont, CA: Thomson/Wadsworth, 2013.

Swartz, Omar. *Persuasion as a Critical Activity: Application and Engagement*. Dubuque, IA: Kendall/Hunt, 2009.

Woodward, Gary C., and Robert E. Denton. *Persuasion and Influence in American Life*. Long Grove, IL: Waveland Press, 2009.

The Counseling Interview

T his chapter focuses on the counseling interview, one of the most sensitive of interviews because it occurs only when a person feels incapable or unsure of handling a *personal problem*. The problem may be work performance, grades, finances, a relationship, health, or a host of other situations. The purpose of the counseling interviewer is to *assist* a person in gaining insight into and ways of coping with the problem, not to *resolve* the problem. Ultimately the person with the problem must resolve it. That's why many sources refer to the counseling interview as the *helping interview*.

> **Be a helper not a problem solver.**

Relatively few people are highly trained counselors or therapists, but nearly all of us counsel or help co-workers, friends, family members, students, neighbors, and fellow members of organizations when they approach us with a problem or concern and ask us to listen, offer a bit of advice, or help them cope with a situation. Your formal training in counseling may range from none to several hours in training sessions and workshops to prepare you for your helping role as a member of the clergy, a physician, a teacher, a lawyer, or a funeral service director. Experts in crisis management claim that in a time of crisis, "everyone is a resource."[1] The so-called *lay counselor* with minimal training has proven to be quite successful, partly because people seeking help trust people similar to them and appear to be open, caring, and good listeners.[2] For instance, nearly every state has a CASA (Court Appointed Special Advocate) program in which carefully selected volunteers undergo several hours of training and then become advocates for children who have been abused and neglected. They get to know these children thoroughly and serve as their "voice in court."[3]

The objectives of this chapter are to introduce you to the basic principles of counseling including your ethical responsibilities when you consent to help another person, the important steps in preparing for a counseling interview, nondirective and directive interviewing approaches, structuring the interview, and the critical ingredients of a successful counseling interview. This chapter will prepare you to help those who turn to you for assistance with day-to-day problems in their personal and work lives. **It does not prepare you to be a psychotherapist or to handle critical problems such as drug or alcohol abuse, severe psychological problems, or legal issues.**

Ethics and the Counseling Interview

Ethics is at the heart of every counseling interview, and it's not unusual for counselors to face difficult ethical dilemmas such as maintaining appropriate boundaries with subordinates and knowing when to say no to a request for help. The preamble to the "Code of Ethics" of the American Counseling Association (ACA) specifies that "Through a chosen ethical decision-making process and evaluation of the context of the situation, counselors are empowered to make decisions that help expand the capacity of people to grow and develop."[4] A variety of resources on counseling offer numerous guidelines for this decision-making process.[5] We will focus on seven that are of special importance to the counseling interview.

> **Know when to say no.**

Establish and Maintain Trust

You must establish trust with the party you wish to help, what the ACA identifies as "the cornerstone of the counseling relationship."[6] Sherry Cormier and her colleagues agree with the ACA when they write that, "The potential value of a sound relationship base cannot be overlooked because the relationship is the specific part of the process that conveys the counselor's interest in and acceptance of the client as a unique and worthwhile person and builds sufficient trust for eventual self-disclosure and self-revelations to occur."[7] Of all the dimensions of relationship discussed in Chapter 2, trust/safety is clearly the most important because it is the "core trait" or essential element of the counseling interview. Without trust, no interview is likely to occur.[8] One study found that persons not yet contemplating change (compared to those who were contemplating change, already engaged in change, or maintaining previous changes) have significantly lower expectations of help and the interviewer's acceptance, genuineness, and trustworthiness.[9]

> **Trust is the keystone of effective counseling.**

To establish and sustain trust, you must show that you are trustworthy. Be genuinely interested in the person seeking help and prove that you respect the person's privacy. Keep interactions strictly confidential so the interviewee can disclose his or her innermost thoughts and concerns without fear that you will relate these to others. Honor all commitments you make.

Act in the Interviewee's Best Interests

All of your efforts to help must be in the other's best interests. Know if the interviewee is capable of making sound choices and decisions. Encourage interviewees to make decisions within their personal beliefs, attitudes, and values. Respect the other's dignity as you strive to promote this person's welfare. Some authorities on counseling claim that an interviewer's self-disclosure of personal experiences and background helps the interviewee to gain insights and new perspectives for making changes because of an equalized relationship and reassurance.[10] On the other hand, others warn that while sharing personal stories may be powerful, this sharing may appear to be self-indulgent to the interviewee and detract from the interviewee's own experience.[11]

> **Respect the other party's dignity and worth.**

Provide information necessary for the interviewee to make informed decisions and choices. This requires you to be well-informed about relevant information on this person's socio-economic status, education, work history, family background, group memberships, medical and psychological histories, test results, and past problems and courses of action. Talk to people who know the interviewee well (instructors, employers, counselors, family members, friends, and co-workers) to gain insights into the interviewee that will guide you when conducting the counseling interview.

> **Beware of preconceptions.**

Assess information from others carefully. Do they have reasons to lie or exaggerate? All of us have formed negative, defensive, or wary attitudes toward a person because of what others have told us only to discover the opposite was true when we interacted directly with the person. Beware of preconceptions that may lead you to pre-judge an interviewee or formulate a defensive or antagonistic approach. Be particularly cautious when working with children.

Understand Your Limitations

> **Know your limits.**

Be realistic about your counseling skills and limitations, and do not try to handle situations for which you have neither the training nor the experience. Sherry Cormier, Paula Nurius, and Cynthia Osborn write that, "Self-awareness is an important aspect of competence and involves a balanced assessment of our strengths and limitations."[12] Know when to refer the interviewee to a person with greater counseling skills and expertise. For instance, a teacher must be able to detect when a student needs psychological or medical rather than academic help.

> **Listening is your critical skill.**

Skilled counselors are open-minded, optimistic, self-assured, relaxed, flexible, and patient. They are people-centered rather than problem-centered. They are sensitive to others' needs and are able to communicate understanding, warmth, comfort, and reassurance. They give interviewees undivided and focused attention. They provide appropriate verbal and nonverbal responses, and they are excellent listeners. Jeffrey Kottler, author of *A Brief Primer of Helping Skills,* writes, "I'll say that again: *Listening is the most crucial helping skill.*"[13]

How comfortable are you when a person reveals an embarrassing problem or incident or expresses intense feelings of sorrow, anxiety, fear, or anger? Society provides us with euphemisms for vagina, breasts, penis, masturbation, intercourse, and even rape. How comfortable are you with using proper terms and names for conditions, actions, and body parts? Your unease is likely to become apparent to the interviewer and stifle disclosure and communication.

Do Not Impose Your Beliefs, Attitudes, and Values

> **Can you reveal your motives and agenda?**

You bring your entire self to each counseling interview, including your personality, beliefs, attitudes, values, and experiences. For example, be aware of the importance of the values you hold and how they compare to the values of the interviewee. The values of both parties may affect all aspects of the counseling interview. How comfortable are you with disclosing your motives and personal agenda? Can you guide the direction and flow of the interview without ordering, prescribing, or persuading? In other words, can you restrain your personal beliefs, needs, and attitudes so as not to become argumentative and defensive and not to impose your will on the interviewee? You must be able to work jointly in devising plans and courses of action.

Helen Cameron warns, "Anyone who feels they can operate from a *value neutral* perspective is deeply mistaken."[14] You transmit your values through dress, appearance, eye contact, manner, and words. Although it is impossible to be value neutral or free, you must strive to understand and respect the interviewee's values that may be very different from your own. Can you "set aside" your values or "suspend judgment" so you can conduct a successful helping interview?

Respect Diversity

You must understand and respect the interviewee's culture and how it differs from your own because cultural differences may have a variety of effects on your counseling interview. Merely being culturally aware is inadequate. Paul Pedersen claims that "Culture controls our lives and defines reality for us, with or without our permission and/or intentional awareness."[15] When you think of the word "culture," you may focus on gender, race, ethnicity, and national origin, but Cormier, Nurius, and Osborn "recommend that helpers regard *all* conversations with clients as 'cross-cultural.'"[16] Add sexual orientation, socioeconomic class, geographical area, religion or spirituality, physical and mental abilities, and family form to your list.

> Strive to be more than "culturally aware."

If you feel that you are inadequately prepared for cross-cultural counseling interviews, seek training and assistance from skilled counselors. A study of white racial identity in counseling interviews recommended that interviewers "who are racially unaware must obtain sufficient training in becoming multiculturally competent." Such training should "emphasize racial and cultural self-awareness, knowledge about other racial and cultural groups in the context of interpersonal interactions (e.g., counseling relationships), and skill development in terms of intervening with clients in a culturally appropriate manner."[17] Improve your cultural awareness by avoiding generalizations and stereotypes such as all Asian students are high academic achievers, all Hispanics are illegal immigrants, all poor people are lazy, and all women are nurturing. There is diversity among diversity. Try to meet people where they are, not where you think they ought to be. Don't assume the "correct values" belong to your culture exclusively. Research indicates that when there is a match of worldviews between interviewer and interviewee, good working relationships are established and interviewees feel more understood. A mismatch may hinder the relationship, particularly when counseling Asian-Americans.[18] On the other hand, do not assume that cultural differences override all other considerations in counseling interviews. Research indicates that qualities intrinsic to the personalities, attitudes, and nonverbal behavior of interviewers—rather than gender or ethnic group membership—largely account for counseling effectiveness.[19]

> We all value our values.

Maintain Relational Boundaries

You must maintain an appropriate relationship with the interviewee, particularly when you have an administrative, supervisory, or evaluative role. Be cautious when you are trying to help a student, a person of the opposite gender, or a subordinate. As a teacher, Big Brother or Big Sister, or a CASA, for example, your goal is to help this child deal with an academic, social, or family problem, not to become a surrogate parent. Avoid doing or saying anything that may be interpreted as sexual or authoritative harassment. Maintain respect with the client and realize that any form of intimacy may pose major problems for both of you.

> Know where the boundaries are.

Maintain an emotional distance. Some sources warn that it is an easy step from emotional to sexual involvement. We see this too often in the news when male or female teachers have affairs with under-aged students. Thousands of men and women helped families, friends, and co-workers following the tragedy of September 11, 2001. In some cases, the helpers became emotionally and sexually involved to the extent that they destroyed their own families while trying to help other families.

Do No Harm

We have saved this code of ethics until last because, in a very real sense, it encompasses all of the others. Be aware of dangers in trying to help others. Always act within the boundaries of your competence to avoid giving bad or ill-informed advice. Regardless of the advice you give, you may be blamed for outcomes or lack of them. Behave legally, morally, and ethically at all times. Know when to refer the interviewee to a professional with greater counseling and specialized skills. The National Board for Certified Counselors offers this rule of conduct that is particularly relevant in light of recent violent attacks and sexual molestation in organizations, schools, businesses, theaters, and shopping centers perpetrated by disturbed individuals who had sought counseling or revealed intentions to others. Though addressed to certified counselors, it is a wise rule for all of us to follow: "When a client's condition indicates that there is a clear and imminent danger to the client and others, the certified counselor must take reasonable action to inform potential victims and/or inform responsible authorities."[20]

> Do no harm!

Prepare Thoroughly for the Counseling Interview

Anticipate Questions and Responses

If you know an interviewee thoroughly prior to the interview, you may anticipate and respond effectively to common questions and comments such as the following:

> Be prepared for rejections of offers to counsel.

If I need help, I'll let you know.

I can take care of myself.

I need to get back to work.

Why should I discuss my personal problems with you?

You wouldn't understand.

Don't tell Mom and Dad.

Just tell me what I should do.

No one knows how I feel.

You don't know what it's like being a student (parent, patient, teenager).

Get off my back.

I can't afford to take time off.

The more thoroughly you have analyzed the interviewee, the more likely you are to know *why* a person is reacting in a particular way and how to reply effectively.

> Listen rather than talk.

If an interviewee asks for help without notice or explanation and you have no relational history with this person, rely on your training and experiences to discover what is bothering the person and how you might help. Do not assume you know why a person is calling, showing up at your door, or bringing up a topic. Ask open-ended questions that enable the interviewee to explain the purpose of the interview. Listen carefully for information and insights that will enable you to help this person.

Consider Interviewing Approaches

Determine which interviewing approach introduced in Chapter 2 (directive and nondirective) is the most suitable for this interviewee and situation. Each has its advantages and disadvantages. The sensitive and potentially explosive nature of the counseling interview necessitates a careful selection of approach.

Directive Approach

When using a **directive approach,** you control the structure of the interview, subject matter, pace of interactions, and length of the interview. You collect and share information, define and analyze problems, suggest and evaluate solutions, and provide guidelines for actions. In brief, you serve as an expert or consultant who analyzes problems and provides guidelines for actions.

Know when to maintain control and when to let go.

The interviewee is a reactor and recipient rather than an equal or major player in the interaction. The directive approach is based on the assumption that you know more about the problem than the interviewee and are better suited to analyze it and recommend solutions. The accuracy of this assumption, of course, depends upon you, the interviewee, and the situation.

Nondirective Approach

Is the interviewee capable of or willing to take control?

In the **nondirective approach,** the interviewee controls the structure of the interview, determines the topics, decides when and how they will be discussed, and sets the pace and length of the interview. You assist the interviewee in obtaining information, gaining insights, defining and analyzing problems, and discovering and evaluating solutions. You listen, observe, and encourage but do not impose ideas. Most sources prefer a nondirective approach to counseling and emphasize the interviewer's role as engaging, exploring, encouraging, listening, understanding, affirming, reassuring, and validating rather than ordering, confronting, directing, warning, threatening, cautioning, and judging.[21]

The nondirective approach is based on the assumption that the interviewee is more capable than you of analyzing problems, assessing solutions, and making correct decisions. The interviewee must implement recommendations and solutions. The accuracy of this assumption, like the directive assumption, depends on you, the interviewee, and the situation.

Do not assume the problem is lack of information.

The interviewee may know nothing about the problem or potential solutions, or worse, may be misinformed about both. The interviewee's problem may not be lack of information or misinformation but the inability to visualize a current or future problem or make sound decisions. You serve as an objective, neutral referee, presenting pros and cons of specific courses of action. Distinguish between when you are serving as expert advisor and when, perhaps subtly and unintentionally, you are imposing personal preferences.

The interviewee may prefer a directive (highly structured) approach. A study of Asian-American students discovered that when career counselors used a directive approach, students saw them as more empathetic, culturally competent, and providing concrete guidance that produced immediate benefits.[22]

■ *Provide a climate conducive to effective counseling, which is a quiet, comfortable, private location, free of interruptions.*

© Digital Vision

Combination of Approaches

Many counseling interviewers employ a combination of directive and nondirective approaches. You may begin with a nondirective approach to encourage the interviewee to talk and reveal the problem and its causes. Then you may switch to a more directive approach when discussing possible solutions or courses of action. A directive approach is best for obtaining facts, giving information, and making diagnoses, while a nondirective approach tends to open up large areas and bring out a great deal of spontaneous information.

Select a Structure

> Be flexible in choosing and changing approaches.

There is no standard structural format for the counseling interview, but Hartsough, Echterling, and Zarle's "sequential phase model" is applicable to most counseling situations.[23] They developed this structure originally for handling calls to campus and community crisis centers. Figure 11.1 illustrates their sequential phase model.

Figure 11.1 *Phases of counseling interviews*

Affective	Cognitive
1. Establishment of a helpful climate	**2.** Assessment of crisis
a. Making contact	*a.* Accepting information
b. Defining roles	*b.* Encouraging information
c. Developing a relationship	*c.* Restating information
	d. Questioning for information
3. Affect integration	**4.** Problem solving
a. Accepting feelings	*a.* Offering information or explanations
b. Encouraging feelings	*b.* Generating alternatives
c. Reflecting feelings	*c.* Decision making
d. Questioning for feelings	*d.* Mobilizing resources
e. Relating feelings to consequences or precedents	

The affective or emotional phases, boxes 1 and 3, involve the interviewee's feelings of trust in the counselor, feelings about self, and feelings about the problem. A nondirective approach is usually best for the affective phases of the interview. The cognitive or thinking phases, boxes 2 and 4, involve thinking about the problem and taking action. A directive or combination of approaches is usually best for the cognitive phases.

The typical counseling interview begins with establishing rapport and a feeling of trust (phase 1), proceeds to discovering the nature of the interviewee's problem (phase 2), probes more deeply into the interviewee's feelings (phase 3), and comes to a decision about a course of action (phase 4). Except in emergencies, you should not move from phase 1 to phase 4, or omit phase 3, without careful thought. If you do not discover the depth of the interviewee's feelings, you may not be able to understand the problem or possible solutions.

Do not expect to move through all four phases in every counseling interview or to proceed uninterrupted in numerical order. You may go back and forth between phases 2 and 3, or between phases 3 and 4, as different aspects of the problem are revealed or disclosed, feelings increase or decrease in intensity, and a variety of solutions are introduced and weighed. Unless the interviewee wants specific information (where to get medical or housing assistance, how to drop or add a course, how to get an emergency monetary loan), you may not get to phase 4 until a second, third, or fourth interview. Be patient.

Select the Setting

Consider carefully the climate and tone of the interview. Each will affect the levels of communication that take place and the willingness to disclose feelings and attitudes.

Provide a climate conducive to good counseling—a quiet, comfortable, private location, free of interruptions. An interviewee will not be open and honest if other employees, students, workers, or clients can overhear the conversation. Select a neutral location such as a lounge, park, or an organization's cafeteria where the interviewee might feel less threatened and more relaxed. Some interviewees feel comfortable or safe only on their own turf, so consider meeting in the person's room, home, office, or place of business.

> Do not underestimate the importance of location and seating.

When possible, arrange the seating so that both parties are able to communicate freely. You may want to sit on the floor with a child, perhaps playing a game, drawing pictures, or looking at a book. Studies suggest that an optimal interpersonal distance is 3.5 feet. Many students comment that an interviewer behind a desk makes them ill at ease, as though the "mighty one" is sitting in judgment. They prefer a chair at the end of the desk—at a right angle to the interviewer—or in chairs facing one another with no desk in between.

> A round table is a traditional arrangement for problem solving.

Arrangements of furniture can contribute to or detract from the informal, conversational atmosphere so important in counseling sessions. Counseling interviewers discovered that a round table, similar to a dining room or kitchen table, is preferred by interviewees because it includes no power or leader position. Interviewees like this arrangement because they often handle family matters around the dining or kitchen table.

Conducting the Interview

As you approach the interview, keep important principles in mind. Realize that you are "investing in people" and that people can change, grow, and improve. You must be able to accept the person as the person is, so don't approach the interview as an opportunity to remodel an individual to your liking. The interview is a learning process for both parties and is unlikely to be a one-shot effort.[24]

The Opening

Want to help and show it.

The first minutes of a counseling session set the verbal and psychological tone for the remainder. Greet the interviewee by name in a warm, friendly manner, being natural and sincere. Show you want to be involved and to help. Do not be condescending or patronizing. You might want to say, "It's about time you showed up!" or "What have you done this time?" Stifle your frustration or irritation. Accept the interviewee as he or she is and try to understand "the client's world from inside the client's frame of reference."[25]

Initial Comments and Reactions

Do not try to second-guess the interviewee's reason for making an appointment or dropping by. It is tempting to make statements such as:

Are you still fighting with your roommate?

I assume you want to be excused from class again.

I suppose this is about money.

I know why you're here.

A person may not have initiated this interview for any of these reasons but may feel threatened or angry by your comment and attitude. Your interruption and comment may ruin an opening the interviewee has prepared that would have revealed why the interviewee has turned to you for help.

Be tactful and neutral but not indifferent.

Avoid tactless and leading reactions all too common in interactions with family members, children, friends, and associates. All of us have been on the receiving end of such statements as:

Why did you pierce your tongue?

You look awful.

You've been turning work in on time, haven't you?

Looks like you've put on a few pounds.

When did you get red hair?

Such comments and questions can destroy the climate and tone necessary for a successful counseling interview and destroy the interviewee's self-confidence and self-esteem.

Rapport and Orientation

The counseling interview may consume considerable time getting acquainted and establishing a working relationship, even when your relationship with the interviewee has a long history. This relational history may be positive or negative because both parties monitor previous interactions and enter a new exchange with high or low expectations. The counseling interview is often more threatening than other interactions. An interviewee may begin by talking about the building, books on the shelves, pictures on the walls, the view out the window, or the weather. Be patient. The interviewee is sizing up you, the situation, and the setting and may be building up nerve to introduce an issue.

The **rapport** stage is your chance to show attention, interest, fairness, willingness to listen, and ability to maintain confidences. In other words, it's a critical stage in establishing trust with the interviewee. You can discover the interviewee's expectations and apprehensions about the interview and attitudes toward you, your position, your organization, and counseling sessions.

When rapport and orientation are completed, let the interviewee begin with what seems to be of most interest or concern. It is the first step toward revealing the precise nature of the problem the interviewee has been unable to face or resolve. Do not rush this process. Observe the nonverbal cues that may reveal inner feelings and their intensity.

Encourage Self-Disclosure

Disclosure of beliefs, attitudes, concerns, and feelings determines the success of the counseling interview and is a major factor in the interviewee's decision to seek or not seek help.[26] Studies reveal that "self-disclosing is a very complex process that involves intricate decision making."[27] The climate conducive for disclosure begins during the opening minutes of the interaction. Research suggests that the situation is the most important variable in determining level of self-disclosure. If positive, it creates a trusting relationship and engenders "feelings of safety, pride, and authenticity." The interviewee may come to see that keeping secrets "inhibits" the helping process "whereas disclosing produces a sense of relief from physical as well as emotional tension."[28] During this stage, focus attention on strengths and achievements rather than weaknesses and failures and what is most in need of attention. This approach builds confidence and a feeling that it is safe to disclose beliefs, attitudes, and feelings.

Encourage interviewee disclosure by disclosing your feelings and attitudes, ensuring confidentiality, and using appropriate humor.[29] Although full self-disclosure is a desirable goal, an interviewee may be less tense and more willing to talk to you by hiding some undesirable facets of themselves.[30]

If you initiate the counseling session, state clearly and honestly what you want to talk about. If there is a specific amount of time allotted for the interview, make this known so you can work within it. The interviewee will be more at ease knowing how much time is available. Quality is more important than the length of time spent with an interviewee.[31] Attire and role behavior significantly affect the interviewee's perceptions of attractiveness and level of expertise and determine how closely the person will be drawn to you and the level of self-disclosure.

You can enhance self-disclosure through appropriate reactions and responses. Prepare carefully to reduce surprises, and don't be shocked by what you see and hear. Release tensions with tasteful humor but don't appear to minimize the interviewee's problem. Speak as little as possible, and don't interrupt the interviewee. Listen empathically. Be sure your voice, facial expressions, eye contact, and gestures communicate

Accept seemingly irrelevant opening comments.

Work within a known time frame.

a confident, warm, and caring image. Avoid highly directive responses until you have established a close, working relationship based on tactfulness and honesty.

Culture is a major determinate of the extent of self-disclosure in counseling interviews. A study of African-Americans engaging in counseling at a community health agency discovered that African-Americans in this setting "engaged in an ongoing assessing process." Initially, they assessed client-therapist match [white or black], which was influenced by three factors: salience of Black identity, court involvement, and ideology similarity between client and therapist. These clients then assessed their safety in therapy and their counselor's effectiveness simultaneously." They used this information to monitor and manage their degree of self-disclosing along a continuum.[32] Another study supported the importance of counselor self-disclosure in cross-cultural counseling—particularly their reactions to and experiences of racism or oppression. Such counselor self-disclosure typically improved the counseling relationship and made clients feel more understood.[33] Other research has revealed how different cultures see the authority of counselors. In some Eastern cultures, people see counselors as authority figures and may find a nondirective approach unsettling because the authority has turned the interview over to them to control.[34] They feel much more comfortable when counselors use a directive, interviewer-centered approach.

Gender may also play a significant role in determining self-disclosure. Females tend to disclose significantly more about themselves and their problems than do males, especially on intimate topics such as sex, and a person's self-disclosure history often affects disclosure in other interviews.[35] Males often have psychological defenses to protect themselves from feelings of weakness and to restrict emotional reactions.[36]

Listen

Listening is the most important skill to master. Listen for empathy so you can reassure, comfort, express warmth, and try to place yourself in the interviewee's situation and world. Listen for comprehension so you can be patient, receive, understand, and recall interactions accurately and completely. Avoid listening for evaluation that judges and may openly criticize. Directly or indirectly moralizing, blaming, questioning, and disagreeing are major roadblocks to effective counseling.[37] To get to the heart of a problem, give undivided attention to the interviewee's words and their implications and to what is intentionally or unintentionally left unmentioned.

> Focus on the interviewee and the interviewee's problem.

Do not interrupt or take over the conversation. Beware of interjecting personal opinions, experiences, or problems. Too often, a person may want to talk about a serious illness of a father or mother, but the counselor takes over with a story about his or her own family illness.

If the interviewee pauses or stops talking for a few moments, use silence to encourage the interviewee to continue talking. Rebecca Leonard suggests several nonverbal behaviors that communicate a willingness to listen: lean toward and face the other person squarely, maintain good eye contact, and reflect attention through facial expressions.[38] Interviewees interpret smiles, attentive body postures, and gestures as evidence of warmth and enthusiasm.

Observe

Observe how the interviewee sits, gestures, fidgets, and maintains eye contact. Pay attention to the voice for loudness, timidity, evidence of tenseness, and changes. These observations provide clues about the seriousness of the problem and the interviewee's state of mind. Deceptive answers may be lengthier, more hesitant, and with long pauses. People maintain eye contact longer when they lie.

> **Look for nonverbal signals but interpret them cautiously.**

If you are going to take notes or record the interview, explain why, and stop if you detect that either activity is affecting the interview adversely. People may be hesitant to leave a recording that others might hear. They are willing to confide in you, not others.

Question

Questions play important roles in counseling interviews, but asking too many questions is a common mistake. Questions may interrupt the interviewee, change topics prematurely, and break the flow of self-disclosure. Numerous questions reduce the interviewee to a mere respondent and may stifle the interviewee's own questions.

> **Do not ask too many questions.**

Open-ended questions encourage interviewees to talk and express emotions. Both are important for encouraging, reflecting, and questioning about feelings and restating and probing for information.[39] Ask one question at a time because doublebarreled questions result in ambiguous answers with neither portion answered clearly and thoroughly. Use encouragement probes such as:

> **Keep your questions open-ended.**

And?	I see.
Uh-huh?	Go on.
Then what happened?	And then?

Use *informational probes* for clarification, explanation, and in-depth information.

Why do you think that happened?

How did she react?

What do you mean he "overreacted"?

Tell me more about your confrontation with Professor Barger.

The *clearinghouse probe* can ensure that you have obtained all necessary information about an incident or problem.

What happened after that?

Are these all of the important details?

Anything else you would like to talk about?

Have I answered all of your questions?

Some questions can help interviewees *make meanings* of situations. Steele and Echterling provide these examples:

What worries you most right now?

What do you think you can learn from this?

What scares you most now?

They also provide examples of what they call *getting through* questions that help interviewees manage their emotions.[40]

How did you get through that?

How are you finding it possible to get through this family crisis?

What did you do to feel better about this?

Phrase all questions with care.

Avoid **curious probes** into feelings and embarrassing incidents, especially if the interviewee seems hesitant to elaborate. Beware of questions that communicate disapproval, displeasure, or mistrust that make the interviewee less open and trusting. Avoid leading questions except under *unusual* circumstances. Counselors working with children may go through intensive training in programs such as "Finding Words" that stress the use of nonleading questions. Avoid *why* questions that appear to demand explanations and justifications and put the interviewee on the defensive. Imagine how an interviewee might react to questions such as, *Why* weren't you on time? *Why* did you do that? *Why* confront Doug? *Why* do you think that?

Respond

A client-centered approach focuses the interview on the interviewee.

Selecting appropriate responses to questions and information requests may be difficult. The emphasis in this chapter is on a client-centered approach to the counseling interview in which the focus is on what the interviewee is saying verbally and nonverbally and what the interviewee is feeling. This approach suggests appropriate responses to elicit and identify feelings about self, feelings about the problem, and feelings of trust in the interviewer.[41]

Center the interview on this interviewee, no one else.

Interviewers may respond to interviewee information, questions, comments, and feelings in a variety of ways. These responses are on a continuum from highly nondirective to nondirective, directive, and highly directive.

Highly Nondirective Reactions and Responses

Highly nondirective reactions give total control to the interviewee.

Highly nondirective reactions and responses encourage interviewees to continue commenting, analyze ideas and solutions, and be self-reliant. The interviewer offers no information, assistance, or evaluation of the interviewee, the interviewee's ideas, or possible courses of action.

Remain silent to encourage interviewees to continue or to answer their own questions.

1. **Interviewee:** I'm thinking of quitting the team.

2. **Interviewer:** (silence)

3. **Interviewee:** I'm not getting much playing time and the long practices make it difficult for me to study at night.

Review the interviewee's file prior to the interview so you can devote full attention during the interview.

Ingram Publishing

Encourage interviewees to continue speaking by employing semi-verbal phrases.

1. **Interviewee:** Nothing I do seems to make my supervisor happy.

2. **Interviewer:** Um-hmm.

3. **Interviewee:** She's always on my case even when I'm on time and don't visit with my friends much.

When reacting and responding in a highly nondirective manner, be aware of your *nonverbal behaviors*. Face, tone of voice, speaking rate, and gestures must express sincere interest and reveal empathy. Interviewees look for subtle signs of approval or disapproval, interest or disinterest. Ruth Purtilo discusses five kinds of smiles, each of which may send a message you do not intend to send: I know something you don't know; poor, poor you; don't tell me; I'm smarter than you; and I don't like you either.[42]

Holding one's hand or a simple touch may reassure a person and show caring and understanding.

Simple nonverbal reactions such as rolling your eyes, raising an eyebrow, crossing your arms, and sitting forward on your chair may adversely affect an interview. Do not prolong silence until it becomes awkward. If an interviewee seems unable to continue or to go it alone, switch to a different response.

A variety of question techniques serve as highly nondirective responses, including silent, nudging, and clearinghouse probes. Restate or repeat an interviewee's question or statement instead of providing answers or volunteering information, ideas, evaluations, or solutions. Urge the person to elaborate or come up with ideas.

You may *return* a question rather than answer it to encourage the interviewee to analyze problems and select from among possible solutions. A return question looks like this:

> **Use questions that force the interviewee to formulate answers and solutions.**

1. **Interviewee:** Should I file a formal grade appeal for the D in French?

2. **Interviewer:** How do *you* feel about that?

Do not continue to push a decision back if you detect that the individual has insufficient information or is confused, misinformed, genuinely undecided, or unable to make a choice.

Invite the interviewee to discuss a problem or idea.

1. **Interviewee:** I'm beginning to doubt that I can handle this.

2. **Interviewer:** Want to talk about it?

The invitational question asks if the person is *willing* or *interested* in discussing, explaining, or revealing. Do not intrude with more demanding questions such as, "Tell me about it" or "Such as?" Avoid a *why* question that may communicate criticism or impatience.

Reflective and mirror questions make sure you understand what the interviewee has just said or agreed to. They are designed to *clarify* and *verify* questions and statements, not to lead a person toward a preferred point of view.

> **Use questions to determine what a person is and is not saying.**

1. **Interviewee:** I can't seem to get motivated this semester.
2. **Interviewer:** Are you saying that your classes are not as challenging as last semester?

Reflective questions often begin with phrases such as: "Is it accurate to say . . . ?" "I feel you are saying . . . ?" "If I understand what you're saying, you're . . . ?" and "Let me see if I understand what you're saying . . . ?" They require careful listening and a concerted verbal and nonverbal effort not to lead the interviewee.

Nondirective Reactions and Responses

> **Be an informer rather than a persuader.**

Nondirective reactions and responses inform and encourage with no imposition of either intended.

1. **Interviewee:** What are my options?
2. **Interviewer:** The university offers you two options at this point of the semester. You may take my course pass/fail so you need to earn only a C grade or you can withdraw from the course by midsemester with a passing grade.

Be specific in answers. If you do not have the information, say so and promise to get it or refer the interviewee to a better-qualified source. Encourage and reassure the interviewee by noting that certain feelings, reactions, or symptoms are normal and to be expected.

1. **Interviewee:** I've been back from Afghanistan for six months, and I still duck or drop to the ground when I hear a loud noise. My family gets embarrassed, particularly when it happens in public.
2. **Interviewer:** This happened to me when I returned from two years in Iraq. It will take time, but you will gradually adjust and recognize these for what they are.

> **A thoughtless comment or two can damage a relationship.**

There are quick ways to lose the trust and respect of an interviewee facing a difficult situation. You may give unrealistic assurances such as, "There's nothing to worry about," "I'm sure everything will be just fine," or "Everything works for the best." You may preach to the person with "in the old days" comments such as, "You think you have it tough? When I was your age, I had to . . ." or "When we were first married, we faced . . ." Avoid clichés "like the plague."

Every cloud has a silver lining.

We all have to go sometime.

It's always darkest before the dawn.

No pain, no gain.

Be careful of falling into the *we* trap. Think of when you experienced common *we'isms* from counselors, teachers, health care providers, parents, and others.

How are *we* doing this afternoon?

We can handle it.

Let's take it one day at a time.

Are *we* ready for the exam?

You may have felt like shouting, "What do you mean *we*? I'm the one taking the test (getting the shot, undergoing therapy, overcoming grief)!"

Directive Reactions and Responses

Directive reactions and responses go beyond encouragement and information to mild advice and evaluations or judgments. In the following interchange, the interviewer supports the interviewee's ideas and urges action:

> Directive responses advise and evaluate but do not dictate.

1. **Interviewee:** I'm terrible at math and don't think I can handle the required course in quantitative research methods.
2. **Interviewer:** I understand your concern, but why don't you try the 200 level course first and see how it goes?

A directive response may mildly question the interviewee's comments or ideas. Be tactful and cautious.

1. **Interviewee:** My supervisor is talking about scheduling me to work on weekends, and that would keep me from visiting my grandmother who raised me.
2. **Interviewer:** Why don't you talk to her about it?

The interviewer may provide information and personal preference when asked.

1. **Interviewee:** If you were in my shoes, what would you do?
2. **Interviewer:** I would work on completing my high school education and then take some courses at the local community college to prepare me for today's workforce.

Mild directive reactions and responses may challenge an interviewee's actions, ideas, or judgments, or urge the person to pursue a specific course or to accept information or ideas. Employ directive responses only if nondirective responses do not work.

Highly Directive Reactions and Responses

Reserve **highly directive reactions** and responses for special circumstances. Suggestions and mild advice are replaced with ultimatums and strong advice. The following illustrate highly directive responses and reactions:

Exhaust all less
directive means
first.

1. **Interviewee:** I don't think I can stop drinking; maybe cut back a bit but not go cold turkey.

2. **Interviewer:** Then how do you expect to get your children back?

3. **Interviewee:** I can be a good mother and drink a bit less.

4. **Interviewer:** You've proven several times that you cannot do both. Your only option is to join an AA group and stop drinking. Otherwise, you'll never get your children back.

Highly directive responses are most appropriate for simple behavioral problems and least appropriate for complex ones based on long-time habits or firmly held beliefs and attitudes. Be a helper, not a dictator. The change or solution must come from the interviewee.

Research reveals that interviewees who receive positive feedback comply more with the interviewer's requests and recommendations, return more often for counseling, and arrive earlier. These findings led the researcher to conclude that "How interviewers respond seems to make a crucial difference."[43] Interviewees are more likely to implement interviewer recommendations when there is a good match between the recommendation and the problem, the recommendation is not too difficult to implement, and the recommendation is built on the interviewee's strengths.[44]

The Closing

If interviewees feel they have imposed on you or been pushed out the door as though on an assembly line, progress made during the interview may be erased, including the relationship fostered so carefully throughout.

The verbal and nonverbal leave-taking actions discussed in Chapter 4 explain how interviews are closed both consciously and unconsciously. Decide which means or combination of means best suits you and the other party.

Involve the
interviewee
as an active
participant in
the closing.

The interviewee should be able to tell when the closing is commencing. Don't begin new topics or raise new questions. Don't expect to meet all expectations or finish with a neat solution. Be content that you have stirred thought and enabled the interviewee to discuss problems and express feelings. Leave the door open for further interactions.

Evaluate the Interview

Think carefully and critically about each counseling interview in which you take part. Perceptive analysis will improve your helping interactions with others. Be realistic. They are interactions between complex human beings, at least one of whom has a problem and may not know it, want to admit it, or desire to do what it takes to resolve the problem.

Review all
you did and
did not do and
accomplish.

How prepared
were you
for this
interaction?

As you review the counseling interview, ask yourself questions such as these. How adequately did I review the interviewee and the interviewee's problem beforehand? How conducive were the location and climate to openness and disclosure beyond Level 1? How appropriate were my directive and nondirective responses? How skillful were my questions in quality and quantity? How insightfully did I listen? How effectively did I help the interviewee to gain insights into problems and make decisions? Did I agree or disagree too readily? What did I do to enhance the likelihood of interviewee compliance with suggested actions?

ON THE WEB

Selecting counseling approaches and responses most appropriate for a particular interviewee and problem may be critical to the outcome of the interview. Philosophies and practices differ among counselors and counseling agencies. Use the Internet to explore the interviewing approaches currently advocated and illustrated by researchers, practitioners, and agencies when dealing with a variety of clients and problems. Useful sources are the Pamphlet Page (http://uhs .uchicago.edu/scrs/vpc/virtulets.html), the Counseling Center Village (http://ub-counseling.buffalo.edu/ccv .html), and Counseling and Psychological Services at Purdue University (http://www.purdue.edu/caps).

Your perceptions of how the interview went and how the interviewee reacted may be exaggerated or incorrect. You will be greatly surprised by your successes and your failures in attempting to help others. Some of each are short-lived.

The Telephone Interview

Many counseling interviews take place over the telephone, perhaps a cell phone while one or both parties are walking to class, driving to work, having dinner, working in an office, or relaxing after class or during a vacation. Crisis centers have used telephones effectively for many years.

Telephone interviews are common because they are inexpensive, convenient, allow for anonymity (may be "safer" than a face-to-face interaction), can give one a sense of control (you can hang up at any time), and can take place over long distances and at any time of the day or night. Unfortunately, telephone interviews may come at very inconvenient times when a counselor is too busy to talk, is in a different time zone, or is counseling another person. This often happens during office hours. The telephone invites "multitasking" because a party can do other things while "listening" to you.

A recent study of telephone counseling revealed that respondents found "telephone counseling was helpful for both global and specific improvement and that they were satisfied with the counseling they received. Respondents also rated the counseling relationship and level of interpersonal influence similar to face-to-face counseling studies measuring the same attributes."[45] The authors of this study noted the absence of visual contact between interview parties and recommended training for counselors to use their voices as substitutes for place, clothes, nonverbal cues such as eye contact and gestures, and physical appearance.

Summary

You take part in a counseling interview whenever you try to help a person gain insight into a physical, career, emotional, or social problem and discover ways to cope. The counseling interview is a highly sensitive interview because it usually does not occur until a person feels incapable of handling a problem or a counselor decides that a helping session is needed.

Preparation helps to determine how to listen, question, inform, explain, respond, and relate to each interviewee. No two interviews are identical because no two interviewees and situations are identical. Thus, there are many suggestions but few rules for selecting interview approaches, responses, questions, and structures.

Key Terms and Concepts

The online learning center for this text features FLASHCARDS and CROSSWORD PUZZLES for studying based on these terms and concepts.

Client-centered approach	Directive approach	Highly directive reactions
Cognitive phase	Directive reactions	Nondirective approach
Compliance	Expressed feelings	Lay counselor
Curious probes	Getting through questions	Make meaning questions
		Sequential phase model

A Counseling Interview for Review and Analysis

This counseling interview is between a college student and a professor who taught her in a macro economics course the previous semester. The student is currently enrolled in a political economics course taught by the professor's wife who is highly active in the Republican Party at the local and state levels. With a presidential election in full swing, the course often turns to the presidential candidates and their economic positions and policies. The student feels that her professor's political preferences and activities often lead her to make comments that are blatantly Republican and disparage the Democratic and Libertarian candidates and positions. The student fears that her obvious preference for the Democratic candidate will jeopardize her final grade. She is turning to her former professor for help.

How well does the interviewer comply with the ethics of counseling? How do the location of the interview and the atmosphere appear to impact this interview? Which counseling approach does the interviewer employ? How would you assess the relationship between the parties and its influence on the interview? How does this interview match the sequential phases of counseling interviews? How well does the interviewer assess the student's crisis, deal with feelings, and help to resolve the student's problem? How does the interviewer deal with the apparent conflict of interest since the student's problem pertains to his wife?

1. **Interviewer:** Hi Emily! Come in and have a seat. Would you like a cup of tea?

2. **Interviewee:** No, thank you. I just had lunch.

3. **Interviewer:** How's your semester going?

4. **Interviewee:** Okay . . . for the most part.

5. **Interviewer:** Good. Good. I'm always glad to hear how my former students are doing. Did you have a chance to get away during October Break?

6. **Interviewee.** Yes. I have a problem I want to talk to you about.

7. **Interviewer:** Okay. You're not still concerned about the grade I gave you on your research project.

8. **Interviewee:** No. I think you were right.

9. **Interviewer:** Are you here about the global economics course that was cancelled?

10. **Interviewee:** No. I am applying for a fellowship at the London School of Economics instead.

11. **Interviewer:** Awesome! You certainly deserve a fellowship with your grades and the tough courses you have taken.

12. **Interviewee:** I do have a problem.

13. **Interviewer:** Okay. Tell me about it.

14. **Interviewee:** Well, I'm not sure I should be here because it involves Professor McWerter and her political economics course.

15. **Interviewer:** I see. You're having a problem in my wife's course?

16. **Interviewee:** Yes, I am.

17. **Interviewer:** Does it have to do with the workload or the theoretical nature of the course?

18. **Interviewee:** No, those make the course challenging.

19. **Interviewer:** Are you having a grade problem?

20. **Interviewee:** Not yet.

21. **Interviewer:** What does that mean?

22. **Interviewee:** Well . . . to put it bluntly, I'm afraid that your wife's outspoken political biases in the course will put many of our grades in jeopardy if we don't agree with her.

23. **Interviewer:** Oh, I don't think that would ever happen. She is a strong Republican and I am a strong Democrat, but we've co-existed for thirty years. Her alleged biases won't affect your grade.

24. **Interviewee:** That's not what I hear from students who have taken her political economics course. One student who took her course last spring during the primary elections is taking his grade to the College Grade Appeals Committee. They have agreed to hear his appeal.

25. **Interviewer:** Is the student accusing my wife of political bias as a reason for his grade appeal?

26. **Interviewee:** I'm not sure, but I think so.

27. **Interviewer:** Well, that's neither here nor there. Do you think any of the grades you have received so far are unfair for whatever reason?

28. **Interviewee:** No, not yet, but most of our grades have come from objective tests.

29. **Interviewer:** I appreciate you coming to see me, but you do realize that I have a problem with your professor being my wife.

30. **Interviewee:** I know, but I needed someone to talk to and you always encouraged us to come see you.

31. **Interviewer:** That's true, and I'd like to help. You need to make an appointment with Marabeth and tell her your concerns.

32. **Interviewee:** I think she will deny that her party bias will affect her grading, and I might be in worse trouble for bringing this up.

33. **Interviewer:** She's taught for many years and does like to argue politics, but I've never seen it compromise her professionally. Go see her. Tell her you feel very uncomfortable in her class, even threatened by her personal politics. Ask her what you can do.

34. **Interviewee:** Could you talk to her?

35. **Interviewer:** I'm afraid that would be crossing the line. I cannot interfere with her teaching or question what she is doing when I have not observed her class.

36. **Interviewee:** Okay, if I do that and feel even more threatened, then what? I've thought about going to the department head or the dean. So have some other students, particularly one student who is President of the Young Democrats.

37. **Interviewer:** That would be unfair to her. She has a right to know your concerns before going over her head. Talk to her first and, if that doesn't work, then you can go to the next level. Try to resolve this by confronting the problem as you see it. I doubt that she is aware of how some of you feel. Make her aware of your feelings.

38. **Interviewee:** Okay. I'll set up an appointment. Maybe another student or two will come along to show it's not just my concern.

39. **Interviewer:** That's a good idea. There is strength in numbers as long as you don't appear to be ganging up on her.

40. **Interviewee:** Thanks, Professor Walsh. Please don't mention that I have come to see you.

41. **Interviewer:** Of course not. I will keep this between you and me. Just do it soon so you can get on with your semester. Fortunately, the presidential election is just a few weeks away.

Counseling Role-Playing Cases

Changing Jobs

The interviewee, Denise, is a recently divorced mother of four and has been working at a Macy's department store for about five months. Her supervisor is very pleased with Denise's work and has been training and assigning work to her that involves several parts of the store including loading dock manager. Denise is very happy with her job and is enjoying the support of her supervisor and store manager. A neighbor approached her a few days ago with a possible position in the office of a small construction firm. The position pays much better than her position with Macy's and offers the possibility of full benefits. She is trying to decide if a considerable, immediate salary increase and benefits would outweigh the longer term potential with a large corporation such as Macy's.

She has decided to talk to her older brother Jack who has years of experience in large and small construction firms to see what he would suggest she do. They have always had a great relationship, and Denise values his opinion highly. The problem is her potential willingness to do whatever Jack suggests. Jack will have to be very careful in offering his advice. He must be a good listener rather than a problem solver and help Denise make what she believes is in her best interests and those of her children.

Dating and Religion

The interviewee is 24 years old and a graduate student at the University of South Dakota. She has been dating a classmate from South Dakota State University for several months, and both are beginning to get serious about a future together. She is Catholic and he is Jewish, and their religious faiths are very important to them. While neither sees religion as a major problem, neither of them is willing to change faiths or to commit themselves to raising future children in the other's religious tradition. They have talked about attending each other's worship services "on occasion."

The interviewee has decided to meet with a neighbor back home, Sheri Prohofsky, during Thanksgiving break to get some suggestions. Sheri is married with three children, and her husband is Jewish. She and her husband have seemed to work out their religious differences quite well with each remaining active in their church and temple. They have allowed their children to decide which faith tradition they will follow, if any.

A Case of Sexual Harassment

The interviewee, Marty, is a very attractive thirty-four-year-old new car salesman at a large GMC dealer on the West Coast. He has been doing quite well and has been Sales Associate of the Month three times in the last year-and-a-half. He enjoys his position and has had a good working relationship with Sally, the sales manager, until the past few weeks. During that time, Sally has been asking him to go out with her, sending him suggestive e-mail messages, and touching him suggestively when they are alone. Marty is engaged, is not attracted to Sally, and has been trying not to be alone with her. He is hesitant to go to the dealer's owner because he does not want to jeopardize his position, and he fears that the owner will find a male claiming sexual harassment to be funny or ludicrous.

The interviewee has decided to go to the female pastor of his church, Elizabeth Zwier, who has dealt with sexual harassment issues within the church, the church school, and religious-based community organizations. The interviewer must be careful not to blame Marty directly or indirectly for Sally's advances. Doing so will end any chance she has to help him and to maintain their positive relationship.

A Child in a Foster Home

The interviewer is a newly sworn-in Child Advocate and has been assigned a case involving 10-year-old Joey Spitzer who was taken away from his mother two years ago because of her drug addiction problem that caused her to disappear on several occasions from the apartment she shared with her boyfriend and Joey. The interviewer has reviewed documents on the case and is meeting Joey and his foster parents for the first time.

Joey has never met his father and has now been in three foster homes, having been removed from the previous two because of altercations with the foster parents. A month ago he ran away from his third foster home and was found by police three days later. Things seem to be going better, and his foster parents, the owners of a large dairy farm, have tried to make him comfortable in a rural setting. Joey had never seen a dairy operation until moving in with this third set of foster parents, and he is fascinated by the machinery and computer-driven milking operation. The purpose of this interview is to get acquainted with Joey and to explain the relationship between Child Advocates and their assigned children. The interviewer is particularly interested in discovering how Joey feels about his living situation and foster parents.

Student Activities

1. Visit a crisis center in your community or on your campus. Talk with counselors about their training techniques and self-evaluations. Ask about the code of ethics they are expected to follow and what ethical issues they have encountered when taking crisis calls. Which approach, directive or nondirective, do they find most useful? What roles do questions play in the counseling interview? How do they maintain focus on the interviewee and the interviewee's problems? Observe how volunteer counselors handle telephone counseling. How does telephone counseling differ from face-to-face counseling?

2. Interview three different types of counselors, such as a marriage counselor, a student counselor, a financial counselor, or a legal counselor. How are their approaches and techniques similar and different? What kinds of training have they had? How much training do they consider essential? In their estimation, what makes a "successful" counselor?

3. Pick one of the counseling role-playing cases and develop a complete approach to the case, beginning with setting and furniture arrangement. How would you begin the interview? What questions would you ask? How much would you disclose about yourself—training, background, experiences, and so on? What kinds of reactions and responses would you use? What solution would you suggest? What would you do and not do to aid interviewee compliance? How would you close the interview?

4. Interview an experienced CASA/GAL (Court Appointed Special Advocate for children or Guardian Ad Litum). Explore the training that is required to become a CASA. What kinds of cases has this volunteer handled? Which have proven to be the most difficult? How do CASAs attempt to establish relationships with their assigned children? What may threaten the relationships they establish? How do they communicate with different-age children? How do they adapt to children from cultures very different from their own? What is the most important skill they have learned about counseling?

Notes

1. William Steele, "Crisis Intervention: The First Few Days—Summary of Dr. Lennis Echterling's Presentation," reprinted from *Trauma And Loss: Research and Interventions* V4 N2 2004, http://www.tlcinst.org/crisisint.html, accessed July 5, 2010.

2. Donald R. Atkinson, Francisco Q. Ponce, and Francine M. Martinez, "Effects of Ethnic, Sex, and Attitude Similarity on Counselor Credibility," *Journal of Counseling Psychology* 31 (1984), pp. 589–591.

3. GAL (Guardian Ad Litum) in some locations.

4. "ACA Code of Ethics" (American Counseling Association, 2005).

5. "Code of Ethics" (National Board of Certified Counselors, 2005); "Ethical Tips for School Counselors" (American School Counseling Association), http://www.schoolcounselor.org/content.asp&sl=136&conteid=166, accessed October 17, 2012; "Ethical Standards School Counseling," http://www.slideshare.net/cailhubert/ethical-standards-school-counseling," accessed October 17, 2012.

6. "ACA Code of Ethics."

7. Sherry Cormier, Paula S. Nurius, and Cynthia J. Osborn, *Interviewing and Change Strategies for Helpers: Fundamental Skills and Cognitive Behavioral Interventions* (Belmont, CA: Brooks/Cole, 2009), p. 5.

8. Cormier, Nurius, and Osborn, p. 82; Helen Cameron, *The Counseling Interviewing: A Guide for the Helping Professions* (New York: Palgrave Macmillan, 2008), p. 23; Jeffrey A. Kottler, *A Brief Primer of Helping Skills* (Thousand Oaks, CA: Sage, 2008), p. 53.

9. William A. Satterfield, Sidne A. Buelow, William J. Lyddon, and J. T. Johnson, "Client Stages of Change and Expectations about Counseling," *Journal of Counseling Psychology* 42 (1995), pp. 476–478.

10. Sarah Knox, Shirley A. Hess, David A. Petersen, and Clara E. Hill, "A Qualitative Analysis of Client Perceptions of the Effects of Helpful Therapist Self-Disclosure in Long-Term Therapy," *Journal of Counseling Psychology* 44 (1997), pp. 274–283.

11. Kottler, p. 58.

12. Cormier, Nurius, and Osborn, p. 17.

13. Kottler, p. 73.

14. Cameron, p. 14.

15. Paul B. Pedersen, "Ethics, Competence, and Professional Issues in Cross-Cultural Counseling," in *Counseling Across Cultures*, Paul B. Pedersen, Juris G. Draguns, Walter J. Lonner, and Joseph E. Trimble, eds. (Thousand Oaks, CA: Sage), p. 5.

16. Cormier, Nurius, and Osborn, p. 25.

17. Madonna G. Constantine, Anika K. Warren, and Marie L. Miville, "White Racial Identity Dyadic Interactions in Supervision: Implications for Supervisees' Multicultural Counseling Competence," *Journal of Counseling Psychology* 52 (2005), p. 495.

18. Bryan S. K. Kim, Gladys F. Ng, and Annie J. Ahn, "Effects of Client Expectation for Counseling Success, Client-Counselor Worldview Match, and Client Adherence to Asian and European American Cultural Values on Counseling Process with Asian Americans," *Journal of Counseling Psychology* 52 (2005), pp. 67–76.

19. Barbara Goldberg and Romeria Tidwell, "Ethnicity and Gender Similarity: The Effectiveness of Counseling for Adolescents," *Journal of Youth and Adolescents* 19 (1990), pp. 589–603.

20. "Code of Ethics."

21. Steele p. 355; Cameron, pp. 2, 45–49; Kottler, pp. 40, 57.

22. Lisa C. Li and Bryan S. K. Kim, "Effects of Counseling Style and Client Adherence to Asian Cultural Values on Counseling Process with Asian American College Students," *Journal of Counseling Psychology* 51 (2004), pp. 158–167.

23. Lennis G. Echterling, Don M. Hartsough, and H. Zarle, "Testing a Model for the Process of Telephone Crisis Intervention," *American Journal of Community Psychiatrists* 8 (1980), pp. 715–725.

24. "Effective Counseling," http://www2.ku.edu/~coms/virtual_assistant/via/counsel.html, accessed October 12, 2006; "Counseling Interviews," http://www.uwgb.edu/clampit/

interviewing/interviewing%20lectures/counseling%Interviews%.html, accessed October 12, 2006.

25. Cameron, p. 23.

26. David L. Vogel and Stephen R. Wester, "To Seek Help or Not to Seek Help: The Risks of Self-Disclosure," *Journal of Counseling Psychology* 50 (2003), pp. 351–361.

27. Earlise C. Ward, "Keeping It Real: A Grounded Theory Study of African American Clients Engaging in Counseling at a Community Mental Health Agency," *Journal of Counseling Psychology* 52 (2005), p. 479.

28. Barry A. Farber, Kathryn C. Berano, and Joseph A. Capobianco, "Client's Perceptions of the Process and Consequences of Self-Disclosure in Psychotherapy," *Journal of Counseling Psychology* 51 (2004), pp. 340–346.

29. Bryan S. K. Kim, Clara E. Hill, Charles J. Gelso, Melissa K. Goates, Penelope A. Asay, and James M. Harbin, "Counselor Self-Disclosure, East Asian American Client Adherence to Asian Cultural Values, and Counseling Process," *Journal of Counseling Psychology* 50 (2003), pp. 324–332.

30. Anita E. Kelly, "Clients' Secret Keeping in Outpatient Therapy," *Journal of Counseling Psychology* 45 (1998), pp. 50–57.

31. Paul R. Turner, Mary Valtierra, Tammy R. Talken, Vivian I. Miller, and Jose R. DeAnda, "Effect of Session Length on Treatment Outcome for College Students in Brief Therapy," *Journal of Counseling Psychology* 43 (1996), pp. 228–232.

32. Ward, p. 471.

33. Alan W. Burkard, Sarah Knox, Michael Groen, Maria Perez, and Shirley A. Hess, "European American Therapist Self-Disclosure in Cross-Cultural Counseling," *Journal of Counseling Psychology* 53 (2006), p. 15.

34. Cormier, Nurius, and Osborn, p. 73.

35. Timothy P. Johnson, James G. Hougland, and Robert W. Moore, "Sex Differences in Reporting Sensitive Behavior: A Comparison of Interview Methods," *Sex Roles* 24 (1991), pp. 669–680; Judy Cornelia Pearson, Richard L. West, and Lynn H. Turner, *Gender and Communication* (Madison, WI: Brown & Benchmark, 1995), pp. 149–152.

36. James R. Mahalik, Robert J. Cournoyer, William DeFranc, Marcus Cherry, and Jeffrey M. Napolitano, "Men's Gender Role Conflict and Use of Psychological Defenses," *Journal of Counseling Psychology* 45 (1998), pp. 247–255.

37. Cameron, pp. 45–49.

38. Rebecca Leonard, "Attending: Letting the Patient Know You Are Listening," *Journal of Practical Nursing* 33 (1983), pp. 28–29; Ginger Schafer Wlody, "Effective Communication Techniques," *Nursing Management,* October 1981, pp. 19–23.

39. Echterling, Hartsough, and Carle, pp. 715–725.

40. Steele and Echterling.

41. Sherry Cormier and Harold Hackney, *Counseling Strategies and Interventions* (Boston: Pearson, 2008), pp. 136–141; Cameron, pp. 51–58; Kottler, pp. 86–89.

42. Ruth Purtilo, *The Allied Health Professional and the Patient: Techniques of Effective Interaction* (Philadelphia: Saunders, 1973), pp. 96–97.

43. Peter Chang, "Effects of Interviewer Questions and Response Type on Compliance: An Analogue Study," *Journal of Counseling Psychology* 41 (1994), pp. 74–82.

44. Collie W. Conoley, Marjorie A. Padula, Darryl S. Payton, and Jeffrey A. Daniels, "Predictors of Client Implementation of Counselor Recommendations: Match with Problem, Difficulty Level, and Building on Client Strengths," *Journal of Counseling Psychology* 41 (1994), pp. 3–7.

45. Robert J. Reese, Collie W. Conoley, and Daniel F. Brossart, "Effectiveness of Telephone Counseling: A Field-Based Investigation," *Journal of Counseling Psychology* 49 (2002), pp. 233–242.

Resources

Cameron, Helen. *The Counseling Interview: A Guide for the Helping Professions.* New York: Palgrave Macmillan, 2008.

Cormier, Sherry, Paula S. Nurius, and Cynthia J. Osborn. *Interviewing and Change Strategies for Helpers: Fundamental Skills and Cognitive Behavioral Interventions.* Belmont, CA: Brooks/Cole, 2009.

Hill, Clara E. *The Helping Skills: Facilitating Exploration, Insight, and Action.* Washington, DC: American Psychological Association, 2009.

Kottler, Jeffrey A. *A Brief Primer of Helping Skills.* Thousand Oaks, CA: Sage, 2008.

Pedersen, Paul B., Juris G. Draguns, Walter J. Lonner, and Joseph E. Trimble, eds. *Counseling Across Cultures.* Thousand Oaks, CA: Sage, 2008.

The Health Care Interview

T his chapter focuses on the health care interview, arguably the most sensitive of interviews because it deals with the mental and physical well-being of the interviewee. Interviewers have a wide variety of medical training, practices, specialties, competencies, and experiences, and their interactions with patients may range from routine checkups, inquiries about health concerns, treatment for minor illnesses, and minor surgeries to critical, life-threatening situations that seriously impair the patient's ability to communicate effectively. The purposes of the health care interview are to assess a person's mental or physical health, provide this person with relevant and accurate information, and prescribe courses of action that will meet the person's health needs and concerns.

> **Each health care interview serves a variety of purposes.**

Whether or not you are planning a career in health care, you have and will take part in health care interviews with varying degrees of seriousness throughout your life span. The growing emphasis on preventive medicine will increase the frequency of such interviews, and you are likely to establish long-term relationships with a wide range of health care professionals, some of whom may be your neighbors or colleagues.

The objectives of this chapter are to introduce you to the ethical responsibilities of the health care interviewer, the growing emphasis on patient-centered care (PCC), ways to create a collaborative relationship in the health care interview, the critical role of patient perceptions of the interviewer's communication and competence, the principles of gathering and sharing information, and ways to counsel and persuade to reach agreements and motivate the interviewee to comply with prescribed courses of action.

Ethics and the Health Care Interview

> **Ethics and the health care interview are intertwined.**

Nurit Guttman writes that "Ethical issues are involved in most, if not all, decisions that relate to the goals, design, implementation, and evaluation of any health care intervention." And "these ethical issues," he concludes, "are often implicit and embedded in subtle decision-making processes, and their delineation requires an assessment of unintended impacts."[1] It's difficult to create and apply a single code of ethics to complex health care interventions and assessments that pertain to specific individuals with specific needs, problems, and abilities in specific situations, and with specific health care providers who may range from licensed practical nurses and emergency medical technicians, to highly trained specialists in practices such as neurology, oncology, and psychiatry. The effort to develop a suitable code of ethics is important because, as Guttman claims, "Interventions that are sensitive to ethical concerns are more likely to gain the trust and respect of intended populations and collaborators."[2] Codes developed by a variety of health care associations provide us with a core of ethical principles or standards appropriate for the health care interview.[3]

**Do no
harm.**

The centuries old adage of *do good* and do *no harm* is considered the "paramount" or "foremost ethical maxim for health care providers and includes physiological, psychological, social, and cultural aspects of harm" and good.[4] Unfortunately, the intention to do good may result in harm. For example, recommended physical activities or medications may result in injuries or health complications. To do good while avoiding harm, then, includes such principles as being competent as a health care provider, remaining within your area of competence, communicating truthfully, assuming responsibility for individual and professional actions, and reporting health care professionals who appear to be deficient in character or competence. Guttman writes that "Truthful communication also requires that all relevant information should be provided, as indicated by the ethical standard of *completeness*" and accuracy.[5]

Health care providers must *respect the rights* and *dignity* of each patient. The Code of Ethics of Emergency Physicians, for example, claims that U.S. public policy and medical ethics recognize that "access to quality emergency care is an individual right that should be available to all who seek it."[6] The vulnerability of patients is of particular concern. Vicki Lachman, a clinical professor and director in Advanced Practice Nursing at Drexel University, writes that "Caring defines nursing, as curing often defines medicine. The nurse attends to the vulnerability of the patient, principally because the patient's needs have the potential to create dependency."[7] Health care providers must safeguard the patient's rights of *confidences* and *privacy*, and should "disclose confidential information only with the consent of the patient or when required by an overriding duty such as the duty to protect others or to obey the law."[8]

**Respect the
rights and
dignity of
every patient.**

Health care providers must *respect diversity* of patients and avoid any act that excludes, segregates, or demeans the dignity of the patient. For example, the code for emergency medical technicians says its providers must "encourage the quality and equal availability of emergency medical care."[9] They must provide "services based on human need, with respect for human dignity, unrestricted by consideration of nationality, race, creed, color, or status." Other codes include characteristics such as ethnic origin, age, socioeconomic status, and sexual orientation.[10] There may be built-in problems with meeting this standard. For instance, Guttman warns that "the obligations to promote people's health by encouraging them to adopt health promoting behaviors may conflict with the obligation to respect their autonomy."[11] People "have an intrinsic right to make decisions for themselves," and "health care providers may come from different ethnic groups, whose values and life circumstances differ from those" of their patients.[12] Mohan Dutta (2007) advocates a "culturally-centered" approach that provides "marginalized groups with opportunities to engage in critical dialogues and have their voices heard by their own community."[13]

Health care providers must maintain appropriate boundaries in the provider-patient relationship. For instance, "The Principles of Medical Ethics" of the American Psychiatric Association state that "the psychiatrist shall be ever vigilant about the impact that his or her conduct has upon the boundaries of the doctor-patient relationship."[14] It warns that "the inherent inequality in the doctor-patient relationship may lead to exploitation of the patient." The relationship of the provider and patient is critical to the health care interview, so we will proceed to treat this relationship in considerable depth.

Patient-Centered Care (PCC)

Patient-centered care is both new and very old.

The perceptions and practice of health care are undergoing significant changes in the twenty-first century as health care practitioners and patients espouse a collaborative partnership, a mutual participation in health care. Patient-centered care (PCC) places an emphasis on patients and providers as "coagents in a problem-solving context."[15] This new trend, or what some sources argue dates to ancient Greece, assures that patient "needs, preferences, and beliefs are respected at all times."[16] Debra Roter and Judith Hall write that:

> Partnership-building communication assists patients in assuming a more active role in the medical dialogue, either through active enlistment of patient input (e.g., asking for the patient's opinion and expectations, use of interest cues, paraphrasing and interpreting the patient's statement to check for [physician] understanding, and explicitly asking for patient understanding) or passivity by assuming a less dominating stance within the relationship (e.g., being less verbally dominant).[17]

Advocates of co-agency contend that when patients are more actively involved as partners, rather than passive bystanders, they are more satisfied with their care, receive more patient-centered care such as information and support, are more committed to treatment regimens and managing health issues, have a stronger sense of control over their health, and experience better health.[18]

A reciprocal relationship is key.

Patient-centered health care can advance in the United States if both parties share control and actively seek to reduce *relational distance*. While both parties in the health care interview are unique in some ways, they share many perceptions, needs, values, beliefs, attitudes, and experiences. Both should strive to maintain dignity, privacy, self-respect, and comfort. The goal of the health care interaction is to "develop a reciprocal relationship, where the exchange of information, identification of problems, and development of solutions is an interactive process."[19] The relationship between patient and provider may be "the most critical component of the health care delivery process."[20] Establishing a collaborative relationship tends "to ensure that health decisions respect patient's wants, needs, and preferences" and that patients have the information and support to make effective decisions to take part in their health care.[21] How patients perceive their relationships with their providers influence how they take part in health care interviews.[22]

Both parties must strive to reduce relational distance.

While reducing the relational distance between the interview parties is central to patient-centered care, neither party should rush this relationship too quickly. Each party must try to know and understand one another because mutual understanding reduces relational distance. Both parties may enhance the relationship by trying to be relaxed and confident, showing interest in one another as unique persons, maintaining objectivity, being sincere and honest, treating one another with respect, paying attention to verbal and nonverbal messages, remaining flexible, and maintaining appropriate degrees of control.[23]

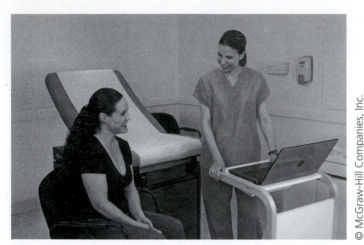

The development of positive relationships between health care providers and receivers is essential for effective communication and health care.

© McGraw-Hill Companies, Inc.

Although it takes two parties to form a productive relationship, providers and patients continue to believe the provider has the burden to make the relationship work.[24] This finding leads Hullman and Daily to conclude that the health care provider's "ability to be flexible and adaptable is extremely important in medical encounters."[25] On the other hand, the American Medical Association claims that "The patient-physician relationship is of greatest benefit to patients when they bring medical problems to the attention of their physicians in a timely fashion, provide information about their medical condition to the best of their ability, and work with their physicians in a mutually respectful alliance."[26] This would be collaboration at its best.

Sharing Control

Sharing control is the first step in forming a collaborative relationship. Traditionally, power and authority have been lopsided in the health care interview. The provider is highly trained, sees the situation as routine, speaks in scientific terms and acronyms few patients understand, appears to be in control of self and the situation, is emotionally uninvolved, and is fully clothed in a suit or uniform. Control gravitates to the provider because this party chooses and controls the setting, timing, and structure of the interview. Closed questions, limited reactions, changing of topics, and interruptions signal who is in charge. When patients challenge this situation, providers may quickly reassert their "authorial presence" or ignore the challenge.[27] A recent study of patients' presentation of Internet research findings during health care interviews reveals that physicians may dismiss such research as "face threatening" and assert their authority. Male patients in particular perceived that physicians "felt a loss of control" when they mentioned Internet research, perhaps because they feared they would be proven wrong or didn't know enough.[28]

> Both parties must share control.

The patient is often uninformed, sees the situation as a crisis, is emotionally involved, has little medical knowledge, has little control over what happens in an unfamiliar and threatening environment, and may be partially nude, highly medicated, or in severe pain. Patients are partly to blame for the parent–child relationship that may exist in the interview by dutifully taking on a subordinate role in the relationship and remaining compliant.[29] While a majority of patients, particularly younger ones, want to be actively involved in the process, some prefer a "paternalistic model of health care" in which the provider maintains control.[30] They may fail to ask questions at critical times during interviews. A patient may appear to be compliant while employing subtle

> Patients must be active and responsive.

control strategies, such as changing topics, asking numerous questions, giving short, unrevealing answers to open questions, withholding vital information, or talking incessantly. A patient may demonstrate relational power through silence rather than conversational dominance or agree with a provider during an interview and then ignore prescriptions, regimens, and advice afterward.

While there is considerable agreement on what constitutes competent physician communication, there is little evidence of what constitutes competent patient communication. One study revealed that "From the physician's perspective, the communicatively competent patient is well prepared," "gives prior thought to medical concerns," educates himself or herself about the illness, comes to the interview with an agenda (and remains focused on it), provides "detailed information about his or her medical history, symptoms, and other relevant matters," and seeks information by asking questions about the diagnosis and treatment.[31] The patients' perspective in this study mirrored the physicians'. While these results are encouraging, this study also discovered that there was not "a significant correlation between perceptions of competence and patients' actual discourse, that "perceptions of communication in a medical interview do not necessarily match what is actually said." What physicians and patients think they see and hear often does not match reality.

Both parties must negotiate and share control "as partners striving for a common goal."[32] As a provider, develop positive relational climates by showing interest in the patient's lifestyle, nonmedical concerns, and overall well-being. Supportive talk that includes statements of reassurance, support, and empathy demonstrates interpersonal sensitivity and sincere interest in the patient as a person.

Empathy is "an essential element of the physician-patient relationship," and a showing of empathy increases patient satisfaction and reduces time and expense. Carma Bylund and Gregory Makoul write that "Empathy is not just something that is 'given' from physician to patient. Instead, a transactional communication perspective informs us that the physician and patient mutually influence each other during the interaction."[33] They discovered that while some patients provided repeated opportunities for empathic responses, others provided little or none. When patients did so, physicians in their study "had a clear tendency for acknowledging, pursuing, and confirming patients' empathic opportunities." This is a positive trend in physician–patient interactions.

As a provider, encourage the patient to express ideas, expectations, fears, and feelings about the medical problem and value the patient's expertise. The goal is to treat one another as equals. As a patient, come to each interview well informed about the health problem and ready to provide detailed information as honestly and accurately as possible, express concerns, respond effectively to the provider's questions, and state your opinions, suggestions, and preferences.

> It takes two to form an effective relationship.

Appreciating Diversity

Diversity among patients and providers is a reality both parties must recognize and address. We understand intuitively that patients, particularly those from other cultures, experience and react differently to health care interviews, but few of us are aware that providers also experience stress and anxiety when dealing with different types of patients and those from other cultures.[34] There may be a "significant association between physicians' ethnicity and their perceptions of patients."[35]

Gender

Women are more concerned about health than men and more verbal during interactions. This may be a learned difference because more health care information in the media is aimed at women than men. Women spend more communication time with providers and are more active communicators during these visits, but their providers take their concerns less seriously. On the other hand, male patients tend to be more domineering than females regardless of the gender of the provider.[36] A by-product of more females entering the fields of obstetrics and gynecology is the significant percentage of women patients choosing female physicians. This has led male physicians to work on improving their interpersonal communication skills.[37]

> **Age and sex influence communication and treatment.**

Age

Age is a growing factor as life expectancy increases and the baby boomer generation reaches retirement age. Older patients are more reluctant to "challenge the physician's authority" than younger patients, often with good reason. Providers who are mostly under 55 are "significantly less egalitarian, less patient, and less respectful with older patients," perhaps reflecting society's changing attitudes toward "aging" and the wisdom of our elders. Providers are "less likely to raise psychological issues with" older patients.[38] Younger patients are more comfortable with "bothering" health care providers and less awed by authority and credentials. If a patient is incapacitated, often because of age, it may be wise to involve a surrogate (spouse or child) or a health care proxy who may have important information to share with the physician and be able to collaborate about the patient's care.[39]

Culture

> **Health communication differs in the global village.**

There are approximately 47 million people in the United States who speak a language other than English at home, and this does not include the millions of international travelers who come to the United States each year.[40]

Globalization and its accompanying cultural differences affect interpersonal communication in many ways. African-American and Puerto Rican patients have indicated that their race, ethnicity, and lower economic status impacted negatively on their information seeking (particularly HIV-related information) and health care.[41] Patients of a lower social class may be openly reluctant to challenge physicians so they attempt to control the relationship.[42] Arab cultures practice close proximity and kissing among men; both actions may be seen as offensive in American or European health care interactions. Native American and Asian cultures prize nonverbal communication, while American and German cultures prize verbal communication. Latinas are a good fit with patient-centered health care providers because they value interactions with physicians more than European- and African-Americans.[43] Many societies, particularly Asian, are less assertive.

Kreps and Thornton identify the differences in medical philosophies in different countries and suggest the difficulties these might pose for nonnative health care providers and patients:[44]

- French physicians tend to discount statistics and emphasize logic.
- German physicians tend to be authoritarian romantics.
- English physicians tend to be paternalistic.
- American physicians tend to be aggressive and want to "do something."

These differences affect communicative roles and control sharing in medical interviews. Providers must be culturally sensitive to differences in reporting pain, understanding informed consent, using appropriate language, and disclosing information that may rely on cultural knowledge, modesty, and comfort. Alice Chen, in an article titled "Doctoring Across the Language Divide," relates an instance when she was treating a Muslim woman and ordered an X-ray to assess for arthritis. A male X-ray technician wanted to lift up the horrified woman's hijab so he could position the equipment properly. Chen referred her to a different facility with a notation that the patient needed a female technician.[45]

Stereotypes

> "Good" patients get better health care.

Stereotypes affect the way providers see and treat patients. Perception of the patient as childlike is revealed in condescending attitudes and baby talk with adults. One study indicated that 20 percent of staff interactions in nursing homes qualifies as *baby talk,* a speech style common when speaking to infants that has a "slower rate, exaggerated intonation, elevated pitch and volume, greater repetition, and simpler vocabulary and grammar."[46] Health care providers use *elderspeak* when addressing older adults. Examples include "Hi *sweetie*. It's time for *our* exercise," "Good girl. You ate all of your dinner," and "Good morning *big guy*. Are *we* ready for *our* bath?" The results of such "inappropriately intimate and childish" baby talk and elderspeak are "decreased self-esteem, depression, withdrawal, and the assumption of dependent behaviors congruent with stereotypes of frail elders."

The stereotypical *good patient* is cooperative, quiet, obedient, grateful, unaggressive, considerate, and dispassionate. *Good patients* tend to get better treatment than *bad patients*. Patients seen as lower class get more pessimistic diagnoses and prognoses. Overweight patients are deemed *less* likable, seductive, well educated, in need of help, or likely to benefit from help and *more* emotional, defensive, warm, and likely to have continuing problems.

Creating and Maintaining Trust

> Confidentiality and trust go hand in hand.

Trust is essential in health care interactions because they deal with intimate and sensitive personal information and must maximize self-disclosure. Trust comes about when both parties "see one another as legitimate agents of knowledge and perception."[47] Breaches of confidentiality may lead to discrimination, economic devastation, or social stigma. Trust is destroyed and with it any hope of building or maintaining a productive relationship. Breaches of confidentiality may be intentional or unintentional and occur in many places: elevators, hallways, cafeterias, providers' offices, hospital rooms, cocktail parties, or over the telephone, particularly the ubiquitous cell phone. Maria Brann and Marifran Mattson relate an instance in which a patient tried to keep the reason for her appointment confidential by handing the provider a written note; the provider insisted that the patient read the note aloud. In another situation, a patient tried to answer confidential questions quietly; the provider proceeded to ask questions about her situation in a loud voice.[48] Solutions include talking and answering questions in soft tones, exchanging information only with providers who have a need to know, and conducting interactions in private, audibly secure locations.

Providers and patients co-create trust.

Trust is established in the early minutes of interviews when each party is determining if this is a person he or she can trust. It is further negotiated as both parties "enact behaviors" that construct "shared expectations of a trusting relationship."[49] Humor, for instance, can "facilitate positive patient–provider interactions" and "create a patient-centered environment" that affects "patients' positive attitude and happiness."[50] The results are positive perceptions of caregivers that enhance trustworthiness and lead to better health outcomes, increased compliance with providers' advice, and fewer malpractice suits.[51] Spontaneous humor is most effective. Providers can enhance trust through supportive talk that increases patient participation in interviews and by eliciting full disclosure of information, clarifying information, and assessing social and psychological factors involved in illness.[52]

Skills training is the first step.

Communication is clearly central to patient-centered care and to establishing a productive relationship between health care provider and patient. Observable communication skills, however, may not be sufficient to achieve either. Moira Stewart and her colleagues conclude their study of "The Impact of Patient-Centered Care on Outcomes" by warning that: "The differences in interviewing skills may not be associated with patient responses. Physicians may learn to go through the motions of patient-centered interviewing without understanding what it means to be truly attentive and a responsive listener."[53] They write that "the education about communication should go beyond skills training to a deeper understanding of what it means to be a responsive partner for the patient" and to create a meaningful and insightful common ground between the interview parties. Matthew Swedlund and his colleagues studied the connection between patient relationship and satisfaction and "identified four specific aspects of ongoing relationships that were significantly associated with satisfaction, namely, the relationship between the parent and the physician, the relationship between the child and the physician, the parent's comfort asking the physician questions, and the parent's trust in the physician."[54]

Opening the Interview

The opening of the health care interview, when and where it takes place, and who initiates it have significant impact on the remainder of the interview. Neither party should see it as routine.

Enhancing the Climate

The opening sets the tone for the entire interview.

The provider should create an atmosphere in which the patient feels free to express opinions, feelings, and attitudes. Both parties rely heavily on interviews to get and give information, but the process is often taken for granted. Parties fail to realize that cooperation is essential for sharing information and attitudes toward courses of action.

Location and setting promote collaborative interactions.

Select a comfortable, attractive, quiet, nonthreatening, and private location free of interruptions in which interactions will remain confidential. Check out a typical pediatrics area and one for adults of all ages and conditions. The first is designed thoughtfully in every detail (pictures, aquarium, toys, plants, books) for the young patient and parents to minimize fear and anxiety and maximize cooperation and communication. The second is likely to be a stark waiting room with a television and a few magazines. The adult patient is then typically called to a treatment room, given a few perfunctory tests, asked to put on a hospital gown (open in the back and drafty), and then left alone for several minutes with an examining table, a variety of medical gadgets, and a few charts of the human's insides. This is not a setting likely to decrease anxiety and tension.

Establishing Rapport

Individualize your opening. In a study of provider–patient satisfaction, Mohan Dutta-Bergman discovered that "open physician-patient communicative style is not the universal solution to patient needs. Instead, the fundamental message that emerges from this research is the need for tailoring the health care providers' communicative styles depending on the needs of the patient."[55]

Use the opening to reduce apprehension.

Begin the interview with a pleasant greeting and by introducing yourself and position if you are unacquainted with the patient or family. If you address the patient by first name (Hi Sally) while you address yourself by title (I'm Dr. Percifield), you create a superior-to-subordinate relationship from the start. If you are acquainted with the patient, open with a personal greeting that acknowledges your relationship. The patient must return the greeting and take an active part in the opening.

Neither rush nor drag out the opening.

Employ small talk, humor, or self-disclosure to relax the patient, show interest, increase trust, and enrich the relationship. This patient-centered approach enhances patient satisfaction.[56] Reduce apprehension by carefully explaining procedures, being attentive and relaxed, treating patients as equals, and talking to them in their street clothes rather than hospital gowns. Rapport building and orientation are strengthened if the provider reviews the patient's file before entering the examination room so the interview can begin on a personal and knowledgeable level. Neither rush nor prolong the opening unless trust is low because both parties prefer to get to the point after establishing a personal connection.

If a patient has been waiting for some time because you are behind schedule, apologize for the inconvenience and explain the reason for it. Simple politeness and courtesy—treating people the way you want to be treated—can defuse an angry or impatient interviewee and show you value the person's time and are sensitive to perceptions and needs. Judith Spiers has shown the relevance of *politeness theory* and how it can improve communication in the health care interaction. She writes that:

Politeness breeds politeness.

> Politeness is used primarily to ease social interaction by providing a ritualistic form of verbal interaction that cushions the stark nature of many interactions such as requests, commands, or questioning. Politeness provides a means for covering embarrassment, anger, or fear in situations in which it would not be to one's advantage to show these emotions either as a reflection of one's self or because of the reaction of the other.[57]

This is excellent advice for helping health care receivers to "save face" in a threatening situation over which they have little control.

Studies indicate that perception of "time pressures and medical terminology influence patient participation and the development of rapport in medical encounters."[58] When "medical professionals spent more time in consultations and used little terminology, patients reported being more willing to ask for additional information as they felt a good physician-patient relationship had been established." The opening questions health care providers ask and how quickly they ask them after an interview begins are important to establishing a relationship, building and maintaining rapport, and getting adequate and insightful information. When a patient initiates an interview without explanation, the provider's opening question is most likely to be a "general-inquiry" such as, "What brings you in this morning?" "What seems to be the problem?" or "What can I do for you today?" If a patient has mentioned a reason when making an appointment or told the physician's assistant or nurse about a problem, the provider's opening question is likely to be a "confirmatory" question such as, "I understand you're having some sinus problems today?" "What kind of difficulties are you having with your knee?" or "Tell me about the stress you are experiencing." Some health care providers use electronic interviews with patients prior to in-person visits. Patients select from a list of medical complaints and then reply to a series of questions phrased in language they will understand. When the provider enters the treatment room for the face-to-face interview, he or she has reviewed the information and both provider and patient are ready to begin the interview. One physician relates, "My total focus is on the patient, and it's unusual for me to need to look at the computer."[59]

A second type of confirmatory question focuses on specific symptoms, such as, "Is the pain mainly on the left side of your head?" or "Does the dizziness occur most often when you focus rapidly on near and far objects and then near objects again?" John Heritage and Jeffrey Robinson discovered that general-inquiry questions elicit longer problem presentations, including more current symptoms. More restrictive closed questions, a second form of confirmatory question, constitutes "a method for initiating problem presentation and distinctively communicates physicians' readiness to initiate, and enforce the initiation, of the next phase of the visit: information gathering."[60] The physician takes control and dictates where the interview is heading.

If the provider initiates the interview, the opening question may be open-ended, such as "How has your health been during the past year?" or specific such as "Have you experienced any side effects from the medication for your cholesterol?" What takes place after the opening question depends upon the reason for the visit. If it is an annual routine checkup, the provider is likely to orient the patient as to what will take place and then launch into the body of the interview with questions and examinations. If it is a follow-up session, the provider may move to the body of the interview with a series of questions directed toward a specific problem or results of a previous treatment.

Orient the patient.

Getting Information

Health care providers and patients devote significant portions of interview time seeking information. Information exchange is a major component of competence in provider–patient interactions. This is not an easy task, so let's begin by identifying barriers to sharing information and then by offering suggestions for gathering information effectively and efficiently.

Barriers to Getting Information

Physical and emotional factors often make it difficult for patients to recall or articulate information accurately and completely. Their concern is why they are ill rather than what they can do about it. Frightened and anxious patients leave out significant parts of their medical histories and they may camouflage the real problem by making allegorical statements such as, "You know how teenagers are." Patients say they don't want to be judged about smoking, weight, or over-the-counter drugs, so they tell "harmless little white lies" and are not particularly concerned about the potential consequences.[61] Some overestimate the risk of a problem. For instance, research indicates that "many women overestimate their percentage risk of breast cancer, even after they have received careful estimates from health care professionals." They resist the information received.[62] One way to reduce this problem appears to be a "social comparison strategy" in which patients are asked to compare their risk to others. However, even after using this strategy, women continued to see their risk as "50 percent when the actual risk was closer to 14 percent."[63] Mothers recall only about half of their children's major illnesses.

> **Do not assume patients will provide accurate information.**

Self-disclosure is critical to the information gathering process. It is imperative that the communication interactions between caregiver and patient reach Level 3 rather than incomplete and superficial Levels 1 and 2. Studies indicate that it is all too common for patients to withhold information or to give less than honest information to avoid embarrassment, feeling uncomfortable, getting bad news, or receiving a lecture from the health care provider. A recent study revealed that five physician characteristics significantly improve self-disclosure and honesty. These include "physician gender, lack of hurriedness, use of first-name introduction, use of open-ended questions, and friendliness."[64] This study also discovered that "open-ended questions might demonstrate to the patient that they are communication partners who prioritize the relationship and this co-ownership." They "facilitate trust and comfort with patients because they encourage patient questions and they demonstrate the listening skills of the physician." Another study found that patients find it very difficult to give others depressing news such as when a disease is "progressing or is stigmatized" and believe that sharing such news may "have a more negative impact on their receiving support."[65] Checton and Greene found that "uncertainty plays a prominent role in people's disclosure decisions."[66] They assess "what reaction they are likely to receive prior to sharing and if unsure about potential responses or outcomes, weigh this factor into decisions" before disclosing information. One solution is for the patient "to share a small piece of information to assess the receiver's response," sort of testing the waters, before being willing to share fully.[67]

> **Self-disclosure is central in the health care interview.**

> **Ask obviously relevant questions as soon as possible.**

The traditional history-taking portion of interviews is often longer than discussions of diagnostic and prognostic issues. The manner tends to be impersonal, with many questions having little or nothing to do with the patient's current problem or concern. One patient remarked, "He spent so long on things not wrong with me—two pages of lists—that it made me feel the interview had nothing to do with my illness at all."[68] Patients in great pain or psychological discomfort may become angry or numbed by endless, closed questions, what one researcher calls "negative weakening." One of the authors witnessed this wearing down process while visiting a family member in a nursing home in Florida. An elderly, ill, confused, and angry patient had just been admitted to the same room as the author's mother-in-law. Two medical personnel entered soon thereafter and began to ask a lengthy list of questions. Many would have taxed a medically fit person, and it did not take long before the patient was exhausted and obviously confused. The interview droned on, even though one of the questioners remarked to the other, "I don't know why we don't do this over two or three days. It's not like she's going anywhere." The interview continued with diminishing returns.

Provider dominance deadens interactions.

A series of rapid-fire closed questions (sometimes referred to as the Spanish inquisition approach) clearly sets the tone for the relationship: the provider is in charge, wants short answers, is in a hurry, and is not interested in explanations. One study revealed that 87 percent of questions were closed or moderately closed and that 80 percent of answers provided only solicited information with no volunteering.[69] Providers control interactions through closed questions, content selection, and changing of topics. They routinely ask questions such as: Do you have regular bowel movements? Do you feel tired? Are you ever short of breath? Any chest pains? What does *regular* mean? Who doesn't feel *tired*? Who hasn't been *short of breath* from time to time or experienced an occasional *chest pain*? What does a yes or no answer to any of these questions tell the health care provider?

Explain medical terms and procedures.

Many health care providers assume familiarity with medical *jargon* and *acronyms* that are useful only for interactions with other medical professionals. One study discovered that 20 percent or more of respondents did not know the meaning of such common terms as abscess, sutures, tumor, and cervix, and the percentages escalated with more uncommon words such as edema and triglyceride. Persons over 65 are less knowledgeable than ones between 45 and 64, and more educated respondents are most familiar with medical terms.[70] Patients seldom ask for clarification or repetition of questions or terminology. They feel it is the provider's responsibility as the expert and one in charge.[71]

Researchers are beginning to focus on "health literacy" and its potentially adverse effects on information giving and processing. One study that used structured interviews with patients discovered that "lower health literacy predicted lower self-efficacy, which predicted feeling less well informed and less prepared, being more confused about the procedure and its hazards, and wanting more information about risks."[72] Similarly, Maria Dahm's research that studied "Tales of Time, Terms, and Patient Information-Seeking Behavior" revealed that patients' impressions about medical terms in interviews aligned with guidelines that promoted use of lay language and more detailed explanations.[73] She discovered that, contrary to these guidelines, "physicians often sought to clarify (semitechnical) terms by adopting topic controlling strategies such as using closed questions or taking extended histories." These tactics limit "patients' opportunity to speak and therefore can have effects on partnership building and, in turn, on the patient-physician relationship."

Ways to Improve Information Getting

Both parties can improve information getting in health care interviews; the key being to find ways to foster exchanges that create a collaborative effort. Providers should promote turn-taking so patients will feel free to ask questions, provide more details, and react to what they are saying. Nonverbal cues such as pauses, eye contact and head nods and verbal signals invite interactions instead of monologues. Be careful of verbal

Encourage turn-taking.	routines that give patients false cues for turn-taking. These include "Okay?" "Right?" and "Uh-huh" that only appear to invite reactions. Patients see them as false cues that invite agreement rather than questions or competing notions.

Research indicates that patients who take an active part in medical interviews provide more details about their symptoms and medical history, get more thorough answers to their questions, and prompt health care providers to volunteer more information and use "significantly more supportive utterances."[74] Donald Cegala and his colleagues believe that high patient participation "helps the physician to more accurately understand the patient's goals, interests, and concerns, thus allowing the physician to better align his or her communication with the patient's agenda."[75]

Ask and Answer Questions

Use a funnel sequence that begins with open questions to communicate interest, encourage lengthy, revealing responses, and show trust in the patient as a collaborator to provide important information, including information you might not think to ask for. Open questions that are free of interviewer bias and invite rather than demand answers give patients a greater feeling of control.

The funnel sequence gives a sense of sharing control.	Use an inverted funnel sequence with caution because closed questions asked early in an interview may set a superior-to-subordinate tone and communicate the desire of the provider to seek brief answers while maintaining control. Patients will give short answers that reveal little information and hide fears, feelings, and symptoms. Patients may be unable or unwilling to adjust to open-ended questions that come later in the inverted sequence.

Vary listening approaches.	Listen carefully and actively for hidden as well as obvious requests and responses. Listen for evidence of confusion, hesitation, apprehension, or uncertainty. Patients should prepare lists of questions prior to interviews when they can think about concerns without the pressure of interactions with providers. Don't hesitate to ask the other party to repeat or rephrase an unclear question. You cannot reply sufficiently if you do not

understand what is being asked. Dr. Nancy Jasper, a clinical professor at Columbia University's College of Physicians and Surgeons, illustrates the need to probe into answers, particularly when patients are "fudging with the truth."

> I always ask my patients whether they smoke. . . . A lot of women will say, "No but I am a social smoker." And I say, "You'll have to define that for me because I have no idea what that means." They'll say they only smoke on the weekends. But you start to uncover more when you ask: "How many cigarettes do you smoke in a week?"[76]

Both parties must listen carefully to understand what one another is really saying before proceeding with the interview.

Tell Stories

Encourage storytelling and listen.	What patients want most is an opportunity to tell their stories, and these narratives are "essential to the diagnostic process" and the most efficient approach to eliciting necessary information.[77] Gary Kreps and Barbara Thornton write:

> Stories are used by consumers of health care to explain to their doctors or nurses what their ailments are and how they feel about these health problems. . . . By

listening to the stories a person tells about his or her health condition, the provider can learn a great deal about the person's cultural orientation, health belief system, and psychological orientation toward the condition.[78]

Susan Eggly writes that both parties must cocreate the illness narrative so they can influence one another and shape the narrative as it is told.[79] She identifies three types of stories: "narratives that emerge through the co-constructed chronology of key events, the co-constructed repetition and elaboration of key events, and the co-constructed interpretation of the meaning of key events." Collaboration in storytelling is important because patients routinely omit valuable information from narratives they think is unimportant, do not feel safe in revealing, or assume the provider would not be interested.[80] Roter and Hall write that "From the patient perspective . . . the opportunity to relate the illness narrative and reflect on experience, perspective, and interpretation of symptoms and circumstances may hold therapeutic value, and, consequently, patients' disclosure, especially in the psychological realm, can be viewed as an indicator of the visit's patient-centered focus."[81]

> **The less you talk, the more you may say.**

Avoid interruptions during narratives and answers, especially when patients become overwhelmed with emotion. The success of the interview may be due to the number of words the provider does *not say* or the numbers of questions *not asked*. Some researchers use the phrase "empathic opportunity terminator" to identify interactions that redirect interviews and cut off further revelations of patients' emotional concerns.[82] In the first interaction below, the physician changes the subject.

Patient: I'm in the process of retiring . . .

Physician: You are?

Patient: Yeah. I'll be 73 in February.

Physician: How's your back?

In this interaction, the physician retreats to an earlier, less emotional concern.

Patient: And right now I'm real nauseous and sick. I lost 10 pounds in six days.

Physician: Okay. You lost 10 pounds.

Patient: And I'm getting, and I'm getting worse. I'm not getting any better.

Physician: Okay . . . and right now you are not able to eat anything, you said?

Older patients tend to give significantly longer presentations and narratives than younger patients, but they do not reveal more current symptoms. They do offer more information about a symptom, "engage in more painful self-disclosure," and disclose more about seemingly irrelevant matters such as family finances.[83] Providers must be patient and probe for relevant specifics and explanations. Caplan, Haslett, and Burleson write that "It is particularly critical to understand how communication processes change and how older adults communicate their concerns and feelings."[84] They discovered that when older patients discussed a loss in later life, they "shifted from a primarily factual mode (what the loss was, how the loss occurred, etc.) to a focus on the impact of this loss on their lives (e.g., handling new tasks and expressions of emotions)."

Listen, Observe, and Talk

Be patient and persistent.

As a provider, be patient and use nudging probes to encourage patients to continue with a narrative or answer. Avoid irritating interjections such as *right, fine, okay,* and *good.* Avoid guessing games. Ask, "When does your back hurt?" not "Does it hurt when you first get up? When you stand a lot? When you sit for a while?" Avoid double-barreled questions such as "And in your family, has there been high blood pressure or strokes? Diabetes or cancer?" Employ reflective and mirror questions to check for accuracy and understanding. Listen for important cues in answers, what patients are suggesting or implying verbally and nonverbally. Make it clear to parents, spouses, relatives, or friends present that the patient must answer questions if physically and mentally able to do so.

Use leading questions with caution.

Leading questions such as "You're staying on your diet, aren't you?" signal that you want agreement, a yes answer, and that is likely what you will get even if it's false. At times you may need to use leading questions to persuade patients to follow regimens and take medicines properly. Annette Harres discusses the importance of "tag questions" to elicit information, summarize and confirm information, express empathy, and provide positive feedback.[85] "You can bend your knee, can't you?" "You've been here before, haven't you?" "I'm sure it's been a very difficult adjustment since your husband Paul died."

Addressing the Language Barrier

Health care professionals have long recognized that "**communication** breakdowns are the most common root cause of **health errors** that harm patients," and this problem is exacerbated by an estimated "95 million people" who "do not have the fundamental literacy skills in English to understand even the most basic" health information such as how and when to take medication.[86] Nearly half of this number have little or no command of the English language. The misinterpretation of a single word, such as "irritate," may lead to delayed care and medical errors. Studies indicate that Latino patients who prefer to speak Spanish rather than English may "experience higher levels of decision dissatisfaction and decision regret than those from other cultural and ethnic groups."[87]

Providers have tried a variety of solutions, some successful and some not. For example, family and friends may speak the patient's native language or be more fluent in English, but they may not repeat all of a provider's questions or explanations or be able to translate or explain medical terms accurately into the patient's native language or at the patient's level of understanding.[88] Children as interpreters pose problems because their command of the parents' native language may be minimal, "their understanding of medical concepts tends to be simplistic at best," and "parents can be embarrassed or reluctant to disclose important symptoms and details to their child."[89]

Successful programs have included comprehensive interpreter services in a language such as Spanish, creation of a course to teach Spanish to health care professionals, and use of specific phrases in Spanish to assess acute pain. They are limited, of course, to a single language. Some large medical facilities include a number of interpreters who are fluent in languages they encounter most often. A national system of interpreters fluent in many languages and trained in health care, similar to the one operated by the Australian government on a 24/7 basis, would be ideal.

Giving Information

Patients
remember
little and
follow less.

It is essential that both parties in the health care interview provide sufficient informa-tion that is insightful and accurate and leads to diagnoses and prognoses that address the patient's health concern and problem. Giving information seems simple enough with one party sending information and one party receiving it, but this process is deceptively difficult in real life. No matter how adequate and accurate information might be, it is fruitless if the receiver cannot recall it in similar fashion. Patients find "it difficult to remember information discussed during medical interviews."[90] One study revealed that patients, on average, could recall only about 52 percent of treatment recommendations within minutes following their interviews. A second discovered that within 10 to 80 minutes, less than 25 percent of patients remembered everything they were told, and patients who remembered most had received only two items of informa-tion. Another discovered that within a short time, 10 patients showed significant distor-tions of information received and 4 showed minimum distortions.[91]

Causes for Loss and Distortion of Information

There are three root causes for failure to give and to recall information accurately: atti-tudes of medical providers, problems of patients, and ineffective transmission methods.

Attitudes of Providers

Both parties
contribute
to loss and
distortion.

Health care providers place greater emphasis on getting information than giving it even though the strongest predictor of patient satisfaction is how much information is given on a condition and treatment. In a typical 20-minute interview, less than 2 minutes is devoted to information giving. Providers may be reluctant to provide information because they do not want to get involved, fear patients' reactions, feel they (particularly nonphysicians) are not allowed to give information, or fear giving incorrect information. Nurses, for instance, are often uncertain about what a physician wants the patient to know or has told the patient.

Beware
of faulty
assumptions.

Providers underestimate the patient's need or desire for information and overesti-mate the amount of information they give. On the other hand, patients cite insufficient information as a major failure of health care and are turning to the Internet in rapidly increasing numbers.[92] A study of cancer patients revealed that barely over 50 percent of those who wanted a *quantitative* prognosis got one and over 60 percent of those who did not want a *qualitative* prognosis got one.[93] Many providers assume patients understand what they tell them, including subtle recommendations and information laced with medical jargon and acronyms.[94] Metaphors such as "We're turning a corner," "There's light at the end of the tunnel," and "The Central Hospital family is here to help" require patients to complete the implied comparison, and the result may be con-fusion and anxiety rather than comfort and reassurance. Providers tend to give more information and elaborate explanations to educated, older, and female patients.

As patients turn increasingly to the Internet for information, health care profes-sionals are disturbed that 72 percent of patients believe all or most of what they read on the Internet, regardless of source.[95] This is particularly true for so-called seeker patients with higher educations and incomes, who are younger, and who are actively involved in interpersonal networks. They are "health conscious" and like the active "involvement in the processing of information."[96] It is less true for so-called nonseeker patients who are older, have less education, and come from low income groups. They "intentionally avoid information that may cause them anxiety or stress."[97]

Problems with Patients

Patients too often exaggerate their abilities to recall information accurately and completely without taking notes or other aids and, if they cannot recall information (what they assume is a simple task), they may be embarrassed to admit they cannot do so.[98] On the other hand, they may choose to protect themselves from unpleasant experiences by refusing to listen, or they may interpret information and instructions according to their personalities. For instance, if a provider says, "You have six months to a year to live," a pessimist may tell friends, "I have less than six months to live," while an optimist may relate cheerfully, "The doctor says I might live for years."

> **Patients may hear what they want to hear.**

Patients may not understand or comprehend information because they are untrained or inexperienced in medical situations. They can be confused by conflicting reports, studies, and the media. For instance, in the fall of 2009, the U.S. Preventive Services Task Force recommended that women over 40 should undergo screening mammography only every two years instead of the traditional every-year testing. This created a major controversy among health professionals and organizations with many stating their conflicting opinions through the media. Such controversies pose particular problems for older patients who have less knowledge and understanding of medical situations and greater difficulties in giving information.[99] Patients are bombarded with unfamiliar acronyms (IV, EKG, D & C) and jargon (adhesions, contusions, nodules, cysts, benign tumors). The names of pharmaceuticals are nearly impossible to pronounce, let alone understand. A study by Hagihara, Tarumi, and Nobutomo investigated the common phenomenon in which physicians' and patients' understanding and evaluation of medical test results and diagnoses differ markedly. They recommend that "To avoid either a failure on the part of the patient to understand the explanation, or a patient misunderstanding the physician's explanation, physicians should pay more attention both to the topic under discussion and to their patients' questions and attitudes."[100]

> **Use acronyms cautiously.**

The aura of authority may inhibit patients from seeking clarification or explanation. A woman who did not understand what *nodule* meant did not ask questions "because they all seem so busy, I really did not want to be a nuisance . . . and anyway she [nurse] behaved as though she expected me to know and I did not want to upset her."[101] The hope for a favorable prognosis leads patients to oversimplify complex situations or misinterpret information. Others are afraid they will appear stupid if they ask questions about words, explanations, problems, or procedures. For a variety of reasons, "patients routinely pass up, or actively 'withhold,' an opportunity to" ask about "the nature of the illness, its relative seriousness or the course it is likely to follow."[102]

> **Authority and setting may stifle collaboration.**

Many of us rely on **lay theories** to communicate and interpret health problems. Common "theories" include: All *natural* products are healthful. If I no longer feel bad, I do not need to take my medicine. If a little of this medicine helps, a lot will do more good. If this medication helped me, it will help you. And radiation and chemicals are bad for you.

> **A little knowledge can be dangerous.**

Katherine Rowan and Michele Hoover write that "scientific notions that contradict these and other powerful lay theories are often difficult for patients to understand because patients' own lay alternatives seem irrefutably commonsensical."[103]

Some information is lost or distorted because of how it is given and how it is received. Providers may rely on a single medium, such as oral information giving, but research reveals that about one-third of patients remember oral diagnoses while 70 percent recall written diagnoses.[104] Oral exchanges are often so brief and ambiguous that they are confusing or meaningless. A provider made this comment: "Now, Mr. Brown, you will find that for some weeks you will tire easily, but you must get plenty of exercise."[105] How long is "some weeks"; what does "tire easily" mean; and how much is "plenty of exercise"? Health care professionals routinely prescribe medications to be taken four times a day without telling the patient what that means: every six hours, every four hours with a maximum of four doses within 24 hours, or as needed, not to exceed four a day. Health care providers *overload* patients with data, details, and explanations far beyond their abilities to comprehend and recall. Ley discovered that within a few hours 82 percent of patients could recall two items of information, but the percentage dropped to 36 percent for three or four items, 12 percent for five or six items, and 3 percent for seven or more items.[106]

> **Avoid information overload.**

Giving Information More Effectively

Perhaps the most effective means of helping patients to recall information and treatment recommendations is to develop relationships in which they play an active rather than a passive role in the health care interview. Mary Politi and Richard Street remind us that "medical decision making is much more than a cognitive process. It is also a social event, one defined by the nature of the communication and the relationship between the clinician and the patient/family."[107] Both patient and provider give information that focuses on what is relevant to this patient, and this effort not only aids patient recall of information but also greater compliance with treatment recommendations.[108] Nonverbal communication is too often ignored in research studies, but it can aid in giving information more effectively.[109] When giving information orally, place vocal emphasis on important words, dates, figures, warnings, and instructions. This is a substitute for the underlining, bold lettering, highlighting, and italicizing you employ in printed materials to indicate what is most important.

If you detect patients adhering to one of the lay theories mentioned earlier, help them recognize their theory and its apparent reasonableness and show its fallacies and potentially dangerous results. Encourage patients to ask questions by building in pauses and inviting inquiries, not at the end of a lengthy one-sided presentation. A silent patient may feel intimidated, hopelessly confused, or believe it is the provider's responsibility to provide adequate and clear information. Ask patients to repeat or explain what you have said and look for distortions, missing pieces, and misunderstandings.

> **An inquisitive patient is an informed patient.**

Avoid overloading patients with information. Discover what they know and proceed from that point. Eliminate unnecessary materials. Reduce explanations and information to common and simple terms. Define technical terms and procedures or translate them into words and experiences patients understand. Present information in two or more interviews instead of one lengthy interview. As a rule, provide only enough clearly relevant information to satisfy the patient and the situation.

Involve others in the process. Include family members and friends so they can help retain and interpret information and aid in compliance with instructions. A common practice is for the attending physician to fill out a prescription order and explain what it is, what it is for, how it should be taken, and its potential side effects. Then the pharmacist who fills the prescription repeats the same information. Others in this process are nurses, technicians, patient representatives, and receptionists. Make sure all participants in the organizational hierarchy are thoroughly informed about the patient so each is aware of what the patient knows, needs to know, and can be told.

> The more heads, the better.

Organize information systematically to aid recall. Present important instructions first so they do not get lost in reactions to a diagnosis. Repeat important items strategically two or more times during the interaction so they are highlighted and easy to recall.

Use a variety of media, including pamphlets, leaflets, charts, pictures, slides, DVDs, the Internet, models, and recordings. Dentists, for example, use models of teeth and jaws to explain dental problems and DVDs to show the benefits of flossing and brushing frequently. Emergency medical technicians use mannequins to teach CPR. Never hand a pamphlet or leaflet to a patient and say, "This will answer all of your questions." Patients say they are helpful but admit they seldom read them.

> Employ a variety of resources.

The telephone, particularly with the widespread use of cell phones, accounts for nearly 25 percent of all patient–provider interactions.[110] Nurse call centers that integrate assessment, advice, and appointment systems are increasing rapidly and have transitioned from "nurse advice" to "telephone risk assessment." If nurses and other practitioners can satisfy patients and physicians that they are effective information conduits as part of a health care triad, the result will be timeliness, accuracy, quantity, and usefulness of information. Perceptions of accuracy and reliability—trust—are best when the telephone provider is seen as a reinforcer.[111] The telephone provider must note time, date, information, and recommendations for the file and pass on information to other providers in the triad.

> The telephone accounts for one-fourth of health care interviews.

Counseling and Persuading

Health care providers tend to be *task oriented* and expect patients to follow their recommendations because they have the authority, expertise, and training. Unfortunately, patient compliance has been notoriously low, as low as 20 percent for prescribed drugs and as high as 50 percent for long-term treatment plans. With these compliance problems and the ever-greater emphasis on treating the whole person, providers must be more than information conduits. They must also act as **counselors** to help patients understand and deal with problems and **persuaders** to convince patients to follow recommendations accurately and faithfully.

> Information giving does not ensure compliance.

Barriers to Effective Counseling and Persuading

> Watch for hints and clues about real problems.

Patients may make the health care interaction difficult by remaining silent, withdrawing, or complaining about a physical problem rather than admitting a psychological one. One of our students reported that she had missed an examination and several class sessions because she had cancer. Only later did we learn through a third party that the student had long suffered from severe depression and suicidal tendencies. She felt it was

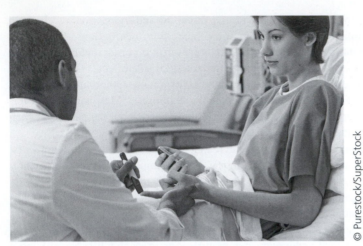

© Purestock/SuperStock

■ *Health care professionals may spend little time talking with patients because they are task oriented rather than people oriented.*

> **Providers may try to dodge unpleasant exchanges.**

more acceptable to have a physical than a mental problem. A provider may dismiss a patient with a diagnosis of stress, nerves, or overactive imagination.

Health care providers may spend little time talking with patients because there are many tasks to perform and talking is a social rather than a medical activity. Predictably, providers fail to detect subtle cues and hints that a patient wants to talk about a different and more serious medical issue.

Health care providers employ a variety of **blocking tactics** to avoid counseling and persuading. Researchers and practitioners have identified several common tactics.

Providers may attempt to dodge an issue by using humor, pursuing a less threatening line of conversation, providing minimal encouragement, denying the severity of the problem, pretending to have a lack of information, or rejecting the patient's source of information such as the Internet or popular magazines. On the other hand, providers may try to avoid an issue entirely by pretending not to hear a question or comment, ignoring a question or comment, changing the subject, becoming engrossed in a physical task, hiding behind hospital rules, passing the buck to another provider, or leaving the room. The nurse in the following exchange exhibits common blocking tactics.[112]

Nurse: There you are, dear. Okay? (gives a tablet to the patient)

Patient: Thank you. Do you know, I can't feel anything at all with my fingers nowadays?

Nurse: Can't you? (minimal encouragement)

Patient: No, I go to pick up a knife and take my hand away and it's not there anymore.

Nurse: Oh, I broke my pencil! (walks away)

The patient desperately wants to talk to the nurse about a frightening and worsening condition, but the nurse is determined not to get involved or discuss the problem.

Effective Counseling and Persuading

Review the principles and guidelines presented in Chapters 10 and 11 that are highly relevant to the health care setting. Parties should plan for each interview with five relational factors in mind: empathy, trust, honesty, mutual respect, and caring. Source credibility has long been recognized as a key ingredient in the counseling and persuasion process, and a study by Paulsel, McCroskey, and Richmond discovered that "perceptions of physician, nurse, and support staff competence and caring were positively correlated with patients' satisfaction with the care they received and their physician."[113]

Select an Appropriate Interviewing Approach

Providers have traditionally tried two approaches. The first is a paternalistic approach in which the provider assumes the patient will see the wisdom of advice provided and alter attitudes and behavior accordingly. The second is an advise and educate approach that explains the medical reasons why and hopes for the best. Neither approach has produced results beyond 50 percent compliance. Telling patients what to do when they don't want to do it does not motivate them to act, and repeating unwanted advice may alienate them and produce resistance. Deborah Grandinetti advises that "change isn't an event; it's a process."[114] Let's focus on the process.

Select an approach that is collaborative and best suited to this patient at this time. Barbara Sharf and Suzanne Poirier use a theoretical framework that psychiatrists Szasz and Hollender developed to teach medical students how to select appropriate interview approaches.[115]

- An active (directive approach) is recommended when a patient is passive and unable to participate.
- An advisory (nondirective) approach is recommended when a patient is compliant because of acute illness and thus not at full capacity.
- A mutual participation (combination directive-nondirective) is recommended when gathering data, solving problems, and managing an illness of a patient who can participate fully.

Regardless of approach, strive for **collaboration** during the interview by showing respect for the patient's agenda and encouraging mutual sensitivity. Adherence to medication and instructions is most likely when communication is optimal. Patients often have logical reasons for not complying: too embarrassing, painful, costly, dangerous side effects, ineffectiveness, or time-consuming. Discover this logic, present good counter-reasons, and employ tactful counter arguments to improve compliance.

Provide an Appropriate Climate

The patient should set the pace of the interaction. Significant changes come about over time and through a series of stages. Do not rush ahead or skip stages before either party is ready. A smoker, drinker, or overweight person is unlikely to change in one giant step. Be aware of how your voice and manner may influence patients.

A researcher discovered, for instance, that when one physician emphasized the danger of swallowing medication for a canker sore in a direct and dire manner, the patient did not get the prescription filled. Another physician employed self-deprecating humor and a lighter tone when prescribing acne medication, and it was filled.[116] The effects of humor are well documented. Humor facilitates an open, personal, and caring climate; helps patients lose their patient role; and enables parties to convey thoughts and feelings in a nonthreatening and productive manner. If humor is insensitive or used ineffectively, it may embarrass, hurt, or mock the other party.

Tradition is not always best.

No approach is useful all of the time.

Work for a team effort.

Humor is an effective facilitator.

Encourage Interaction

Encourage patients to talk. If you share your experiences and feelings, the patient is more likely to confide in you. This promotes self-disclosure. Employ nonverbal communication to show that you care and want to listen. Listen with comprehension so that you understand what the patient is saying and implying. Listen with empathy so you can see the situation as the patient does. Don't ask too many questions. Richard Botelho uses question sequences such as the following to get the interviewee talking about a problem and its seriousness.[117]

> **Sharing and caring are essential.**

Interviewer: If you developed a complication from smoking, say lung disease, do you think you would quit smoking?

Interviewee: Yes, I think so.

> **Make each question count.**

Interviewer: Do you want to wait until you get a complication to decide to change?

Interviewee: No, I don't think so.

Interviewer: Why wait?

Use a range of responses and reactions (from highly nondirective to highly directive). Give advice only when the patient lacks information, is misinformed, does not react to less directive means, or challenges information and recommendations. Avoid blaming or judging that may create an adversarial relationship. Fear appeals may lead to patient denial or avoidance of regimens, medications, and checkups. Guttman and other researchers claim that fear appeals "mainly scare those who are already scared" and do not produce "desired protective practices or norms."[118] Offer praise for past performance and compliance.

Consider Solutions

Approach a solution when the patient is ready to listen and comply. Only 10 percent of providers feel they are successful in "helping patients change any health-related" behavior.[119] Compliance is low "when instructions are 'preventive,' when patients are without symptoms, and when the treatment regimen lasts for a long period of time."[120]

> **Collaborate to achieve incremental changes.**

Jointly construct a plan of action that recognizes social, psychological, and financial constraints. Present strategies in the context of the patient's life; share the logic behind health care decisions; enable patients to create their own narratives about their health; encourage patients to assume accountability for their decisions; identify short-term goals; and collaborate in naming resources and examining alternative options.[121] Lisa Maher writes that providers should "have patients voice their own reasons for change. The patient—not the physician—must articulate the reasons for making—or not making—a change."[122] These recommendations promote **self-persuasion**.

Present specific instructions and demonstrate how easy they are to follow. Express hope and recall challenges the patient has met in the past. The goals are to encourage patients, give them hope, and provide good reasons for complying with *mutually* agreed upon recommendations. You may have to persuade the patient they will work, are doable, and are effective. You cannot resolve the patient's problem; only the patient can do that.

Closing the Interview

During the closing of the health care interview, both parties must understand completely and accurately what they have discussed, the information they have exchanged, the recommendations made, and agreements reached. Clearinghouse probing questions are essential as an initial closing device: "Is there anything else you wanted to discuss today?" "Are there any other concerns we haven't addressed?"

Although the opening may focus on a single concern, patients may hold back information or concerns until the closing minutes of the interview. They may ask questions during the final minutes when the provider is busy writing out prescriptions, information, or regimens and is paying less attention. The real purpose of the patient's visit may get lost in the closing.

The summary phase of the interview "must not only make sense to the patient, but also must make sense in terms of the medical care the physician can offer."[123] Make it thorough but not overwhelming. Ask questions to be certain the patient understands what has taken place, what has been agreed to, and what will happen next, particularly the patient's responsibilities and tasks. Ask patients to tell you these in their words to reveal confusions, misunderstandings, intentions, and successful information exchange.

Close the interaction on a positive and productive note that communicates understanding, empathy, trust, and caring. How each party closes the interview will enhance or detract from the relationship and influence the nature of the next interaction and whether or not there will be a next interaction. A recent study revealed that "Patients' postvisit satisfaction with physicians' communication is important because it is positively associated with objective measures of physician's task proficiency, patients' adherence to medical recommendations, and patients' continuity of care."[124]

Summary

The health care interview is common, difficult, and complex. Situations vary from routine to life-threatening and the perceptions of both parties influence the nature and success of interviews. For a health care interview to be successful, it must be a collaborative effort between provider and patient, and this requires a relationship based on high ethical standards, trust, respect, sharing of control, equality of treatment, and understanding. A collaborative and productive relationship will reduce the anxiety, fear, hostility, and reticence that often accompany health care interviews. Provider and patient must strive to be effective information getters, information givers, and counselor–persuaders.

Providers (from receptionist to physician) and patients (including families and friends) must realize that good communication is essential in health care interviews and that communication skills do not come naturally or with experience. Skills require training and practice. Each party must learn how to listen as well as speak, understand as well as inform, commit to as well as seek resolutions to problems. Communication without commitment is fruitless. Both parties must follow through with agreements and prescribed regimens and medications.

Key Terms and Concepts

 The online learning center for this text features FLASH CARDS and CROSSWORD PUZZLES for studying based on these terms and concepts.

Assumptions	Elderspeak	Politeness theory
Baby talk	Face threatening	Relational distance
Blocking tactics	General inquiry questions	Self-persuasion
Climate	Information overload	Stereotypes
Co-agency	Jargon	Stories/narratives
Collaboration	Lay theories	Task oriented
Confirmatory questions	Patient-centered care	Trust
Counselors	Persuaders	

A Health Care Interview for Review and Analysis

This interview is between a nurse practitioner and a 19-year-old student who was mugged and robbed at 3:30 a.m. on his way back to his residence from a night of bar-hopping near campus. His roommate has helped him to the emergency room of the university health center. The patient is bruised and has a large bump on his forehead but does not appear to have any broken bones. He has a number of aches and pains and has been admitted to a treating room.

Assess the relationship between provider and patient. How collaborative is this interaction? How effectively do provider and patient get and give information? How effectively does the provider counsel and persuade the patient? How appropriate is the blend of directive and nondirective reactions and responses? How effectively do provider and patient use questions? How does the friend of the patient help and hinder the interview process?

1. **Provider:** Sam Perkowitz?

2. **Patient:** Yes.

3. **Provider:** What happened to you?

4. **Patient:** I got mugged.

5. **Provider:** On campus?

6. **Patient:** Sort of.

7. **Provider:** What do you mean sort of?

8. **Patient:** Well, it was near my apartment just south of campus on Stadium Street.

9. **Provider:** Are you a student?

10. **Patient:** Yes, I'm a sophomore in aviation technology.

11. **Provider:** What is your student ID number?

12. **Patient:** 707-765-695.

13. **Provider:** Have you been to the University Health Center before?

14. **Patient:** Yeah, a couple of times.

15. **Provider:** What for?

16. **Patient:** The flu and a bad cold.

17. **Provider:** Have you notified the police about the mugging?

18. **Patient:** Not yet.

19. **Provider:** Why not?

20. **Patient:** I'm really hurting and decided to come here first.

21. **Provider:** Well, we'll notify the police immediately.

22. **Patient:** Okay.

23. **Provider:** When did this happen?

24. **Patient:** About 3:30.

25. **Provider:** Was anyone with you?

26. **Patient:** No, I was alone.

27. **Provider:** You were walking in that area alone at 3:30 a.m.?

28. **Patient's friend:** He has a bad bump on his head and may have some broken ribs.

29. **Provider:** I'm talking to the patient.

30. **Patient's friend:** I know that, but he needs some medical help.

31. **Provider:** You were walking alone?

32. **Patient's friend:** Yeah, he left the party early.

33. **Provider:** So you were all alone. Do you have a headache?

34. **Patient:** Yes.

35. **Provider:** Are you nauseous?

36. **Patient:** Sometimes.

37. **Provider:** Are you experiencing dizziness?

38. **Patient:** Yeah, particularly when I bend over.

39. **Provider:** Okay. First, let's take a look at the bump and cut on your head. They look nasty. Have you experienced any blurred vision?

40. **Patient:** Mainly at first and less so now. I feel sort of light-headed.

41. **Provider:** Had you been drinking?

42. **Patient:** Uh, yeah, a little.

43. **Patient's friend:** A little! He was staggering around like it was Saturday night after a big football game.

44. **Provider:** How do you feel now? A little woozy? A little light-headed? A bit disoriented?

45. **Patient:** Sorta like that, maybe.

46. **Provider:** You're not sure?

47. **Patient's friend:** He's always like that.

48. **Provider:** Well, I'll clean that bump and cut for you.

49. **Patient:** Will I need stitches?

50. **Patient's friend:** He's afraid of stitches.

51. **Provider:** Maybe a few. Does that bother you a great deal?

52. **Patient:** I guess so because I've never had stitches before.

53. **Provider:** It's nothing; you'll hardly feel it.

54. **Patient's friend:** Hey, man, I've had a lot of stitches. It's not fun . . .

55. **Provider:** (to the friend) Why don't you have a seat in the waiting room? Sam will be out soon.

56. **Patient's friend:** Thanks, but I want to stay with my buddy.

57. **Provider:** Okay. Are you allergic to any medications?

58. **Patient:** I don't think so.

59. **Provider:** Okay. I'll prescribe a painkiller that I want you to take four times a day.

60. **Patient:** Whenever I need to take one?

61. **Provider:** No. Take one every four to six hours. I want you to place an ice pack on your head for the next couple of hours.

62. **Patient:** I live off campus a few blocks. And I've got to get to my history exam at 10:00.

63. **Patient's friend:** He could come over to my chem lab. We've got ice there.

64. **Provider:** I would like him to remain here for an hour or so until we know he is okay. We need to do some X rays to see if you have any broken ribs. Take a deep breath and let me know how that feels.

65. **Patient:** Oww! That hurts a lot about here.

66. **Provider:** Okay, I want one of our staff to take you down to the X-ray department. Then, he will bring you back up here so we can give you an ice pack and wait on the X-ray results.

67. **Patient:** I can walk okay.

68. **Patient's friend:** Yeah. He walked over here.

69. **Provider:** I'm sure you feel you can, but we don't want to take any chances on your falling. Take this form with you to the X-ray area, and I'll see you soon.

70. **Patient's friend:** That's good because both of his parents are attorneys.

71. **Provider:** Uh-huh. See you in a few minutes. You won't need an attorney, just your X-ray form.

Health Care Role-Playing Cases

A Bicycle Accident

Gloria Tyler was riding her bicycle on campus after class heading back to her residence hall. When passing a parked car, the driver suddenly opened the car door and Gloria ran into the door and went over the handle bars onto the street. EMTs arrived within a few minutes after the driver called 911. Gloria is experiencing pain in her lower back and left arm that may be broken. The EMTs are asking her questions about the pain she is experiencing and the problem with her arm. A campus police officer has arrived and wants to ask questions about the cause of the accident. In essence, Gloria is taking part in two interviews simultaneously.

A Gunshot Victim

The patient was hunting rabbits with a friend, and the friend spun around trying to get a good shot at a rabbit. He didn't see his companion who was walking about 25 yards to his left. The patient's face was struck by at least a dozen shots, one in his left eye. While his wounds are being cleaned and the shot removed from his face before surgery on his eye, a nurse must get his medical history and determine if he is allergic to any medications or anesthesia. The patient is in a great deal of pain and wants to get on with the surgery.

A Possible Heart Attack

Kirk Abbott has been working long hours and most weekends for several weeks trying to meet a design problem for his company. Around 9:00 p.m. as he was trying to get home before his young children went to bed, he began to experience a pain in his jaw and pain down his felt arm. There is a history of heart problems in his family. His father died of a heart attack at the age of 32, and his grandfather had major heart surgery in his early 40s. Kirk has driven himself to the emergency room of a nearby hospital.

An Annual Checkup

The patient, age 48, has scheduled an annual checkup with his long-time primary caregiver. They were college roommates and kept in touch as the patient became a well-known aeronautical engineer and the caregiver a widely recognized specialist in internal medicine. The patient's family has a history of heart problems; his father and two uncles died of heart attacks in their early fifties. The physician has been urging the patient to exercise more and lose weight for a number of years. The stress caused by the increasing difficulty of securing government grants for aerospace projects is beginning to take a toll on the patient.

Student Activities

1. Nurse practitioners are becoming common in health care, often seeing patients instead of physicians. Interview an experienced nurse practitioner and discuss how she establishes and maintains relationships with patients and other members of her health care organization: receptionists, technicians, nurses, and physicians. How does the nurse practitioner deal with patients who clearly expect to see a physician rather than a "nurse"? How does she deal with physicians who see her as encroaching on their turf?

2. Interview three different health care providers (e.g., an EMT, a nurse, a nurse practitioner, a physician, a surgeon, an optometrist) about the problems they encounter when giving information to patients. Which techniques have worked well and which have

failed? How do they approach giving information to patients of different cultures, ages, genders, levels of education, and health status? What kinds of information tend to get lost or misinterpreted most often? Why does this happen?

3. Visit a pediatric ward of a hospital. Observe how child-life specialists address and interact with young patients. Talk with them about their training in communication with small children. What communication problems do they experience that are unique to different ages of children?

4. Your campus, like most in the United States, is likely to have students and families from many different countries. Visit the campus health center or a local hospital and discuss how they interact effectively with patients who speak little or no English. What types of interpreters have they used: family, hospital, volunteer, or telephone interpreters? Which do they use most often? What problems have they encountered with interpreters?

Notes

1. Nurit Guttman, "Ethics in Communication for Health Promotion in Clinical Settings and Campaigns," in Teresa L. Thompson, Roxanne Parrott, and Jon F. Nussbaum (eds.), *The Routledge Handbook of Health Communication* (New York: Routledge, 2011), p. 632.

2. Guttman, p. 633.

3. "AAMA Medical Assistant Code of Ethics," http://www.aama-ntl.org/about/code_creed.aspx?print=true, accessed October 31, 2012; "Principles of Medical Ethics," AMA, http://www/ama.assn.org/ama/pub/physician-resources/medical-ethics/code-medical-ethics, accessed October 31, 2012.

4. Guttman, p. 633; *The Principles of Medical Ethics* (Arlington, VA: American Psychiatric Association, 2009), p. 3.

5. Guttman, p. 634.

6. "Code of Ethics for Emergency Physicians," http://www.acep.org/Content.aspx?id=29144, accessed October 31, 2012.

7. Vicki D. Lachman, "Applying the Ethics of Care to Your Nursing Practice," *MDSURG Nursing* 21 (March–April 2012), p. 113.

8. "Code of Ethics for Emergency Physicians."

9. "EMT Oath and Code of Ethics," http://www.naemt.org/about_us/emtoath.aspx, accessed October 31, 2012.

10. *The Principles of Medical Ethics.*

11. Guttman, p. 633.

12. Guttman, pp. 633–635.

13. Mohan J. Dutta, "Communicating about Culture and Health: Theorizing Culture-Centered and Cultural Sensitivity Approaches," *Communication Theory* 17 (August, 2007), pp. 304–328.

14. *"The Principles of Medical Ethics."*

15. Amanda Young and Linda Flower, "Patients as Partners, Patients as Problem-Solvers," *Health Communication* 14 (2001), p. 76.

16. Bruce L. Lambert, Richard L. Street, Donald J. Cegala, David H. Smith, Suzanne Kurtz, and Theo Schofield, "Provider–Patient Communication, Patient-Centered Care and the Manage of Practice," *Health Communication* 9 (1997), pp. 27–43; Silk, Westerman, Strom, and Andrews, p. 132; "Opinion 10.01—Fundamental Elements of the Patient-Physician Relationship," http://www.ama-assn.org/ama/pub/physician-resources/medical-ethics/code-medical-ethics/opinion1001.page?, accessed October 25, 2012; Moira Stewart, Judith Belle Brown, Anna Donner, Ian R. McWhinney, Julian Oates, Wayne Weston, and John Jordan, "The Impact of Patient-Centered Care on Outcomes," *The Journal of Family Practice* 49 (September 2000), pp. 796–804.

17. Debra L. Roter and Judith A. Hall, "How Medical Interaction Shapes and Reflects the Physician-Patient Relationship," in *The Routledge Handbook of Health Communication*, p. 57.

18. Richard L. Street, Jr., and Bradford Millay, "Analyzing Patient Participation in Medical Encounters," *Health Communication* 13 (2001), p. 61; Christina M. Sabee, Carma L. Bylund, Rebecca S. Imes, Amy A. Sanford, and Ian S. Rice, "Patients' Attributions for Health-Care Provider Responses to Patients' Presentation of Internet Health Research," *Southern Communication Journal* 72 (July–September 2007), pp. 265–266.

19. Young and Flower, p. 71.

20. Laura L. Cardello, Eileen Berlin Ray, and Gary R. Pettey, "The Relationship of Perceived Physician Communicator Style to Patient Satisfaction," *Communication Reports* 8 (1995), p. 27; Rubin, p. 107.

21. Kami J. Silk, Catherine Kingsley Westerman, Renee Strom, and Kyle R. Andrews, "The Role of Patient-Centeredness in Predicting Compliance with Mammogram Recommendations: An Analysis of the Health Information National Trends Survey," *Communication Research Reports* 25 (May 2008), p. 132.

22. Chas D. Koermer and Meghan Kilbane, "Physician Sociality Communication and Its Effects on Patient Satisfaction," *Communication Quarterly* 56 (February 2008), p. 81.

23. Marie R. Haug, "The Effects of Physician/Elder Patient Characteristics on Health Communication," *Health Communication* 8 (1996), p. 256; Hullman and Daily, p. 317; Ashley P. Duggan and Ylisabyth S. Bradshaw, "Mutual Influence Processes in Physician-Patient Communication: An Interaction Adaptation Perspective," *Communication Research Reports* 25 (August 2008), p. 221.

24. Diana Louise Carter, "Doctors, Patients Need to Communicate," Lafayette, IN *Journal & Courier,* February 22, 2004, p. E5.

25. Hullman and Daily, p. 321.

26. "Opinion 10.01—Fundamental Elements of the Patient-Physician Relationship."

27. Kandi L. Walker, Christa L. Arnold, Michelle Miller-Day, and Lynne M. Webb, "Investigating the Physician-Patient Relationship: Examining Emerging Themes," *Health Communication* 14 (2001), p. 54.

28. Sabee, Bylund, Imes, Sanford, and Rice, pp. 268, 278–282.

29. Walker, Arnold, Miller-Day, and Webb, pp. 51–52; Merlene M. von Friederichs-Fitzwater and John Gilgun, "Relational Control in Physician-Patient Encounters," *Health Communication* 3 (2001), p. 75.

30. Sabee, Bylund, Imes, Sanford, and Rice, p. 266; Silk, Westerman, Strom, and Andrews, p. 139.

31. Donald J. Cegala, Carmin Gade, Stefne Lenzmeier Broz, and Leola McClure, "Physicians' and Patients' Perceptions of Patients' Communication Competence in a Primary Care Medical Interview," *Health Communication* 16 (2004), pp. 289–304.

32. Walker, Arnold, Miller-Day, and Webb, p. 56.

33. Carma L. Bylund and Gregory Makoul, "Examining Empathy in Medical Encounters: An Observational Study Using the Empathic Communication Coding System," *Health Communication* 18 (2005), pp. 123–140.

34. Kelsy Lin Ulrey and Patricia Amason, "Intercultural Communication between Patients and Health Care Providers: An Exploration of Intercultural Communication Effectiveness, Cultural Sensitivity, Stress, and Anxiety," *Health Communication* 13 (2001), pp. 454 and 460.

35. Donald J. Cegala, "An Exploration of Factors Promoting Patient Participation in Primary Care Medical Interviews," *Health Communication* 26 (2011), p. 432.

36. Haug, pp. 253–254; Anne S. Gabbard-Alley, "Health Communication and Gender," *Health Communication* 7 (1995), pp. 35–54; von Friederichs-Fitzwater and Gilgun, p. 84.

37. Carma Bylund, "Mothers' Involvement in Decision Making During the Birthing Process: A Quantitative Analysis of Women's Online Birth Stories," *Health Communication* 18 (2005), p. 35.

38. Haug, pp. 252–253; Connie J. Conlee, Jane Olvera, and Nancy N. Vagim, "The Relationship among Physician Nonverbal Immediacy and Measures of Patient Satisfaction with Physician Care," *Communication Reports* 6 (1993), p. 26.

39. G. Winzelberg, A. Meier, and L. Hanson, "Identifying Opportunities and Challenges to Improving Physician-Surrogate Communication," *The Gerontologist* 44 (October 2005), p. 1.

40. Michael Greenbaum and Glenn Flores, "Lost in Translation," *Modern Healthcare,* May 3, 2004, p. 21.

41. Karolynn Siegel and Victoria Raveis, "Perceptions of Access to HIV-Related Information, Care, and Services among Infected Minority Men," *Qualitative Health Care* 7 (1997), pp. 9–31.

42. von Friederichs-Fitzwater and Gilgun, p. 84.

43. Silk, Westerman, Strom, and Andrews, p. 140; Mary Politi and Richard L. Street, Jr., "Patient-centered Communication during Collaborative Decision Making," in *Routledge Handbook of Health Communication*, p. 410.

44. Gary L. Kreps and Barbara C. Thornton, *Health Communication: Theory and Practice* (Prospects-Heights, IL: Waveland Press, 1992), pp. 157–178. See also Gary L. Kreps, *Effective Communication in Multicultural Health Care Settings* (Thousand Oaks, CA: Sage, 1994).

45. Alice Chen, "Doctoring Across the Language Divide," *Health Affairs,* May/June 2006, p. 810.

46. Kristine Williams, Susan Kemper, and Mary Lee Hummert, "Improving Nursing Home Communication: An Intervention to Reduce Elderspeak," *The Gerontologist,* April 2003, pp. 242–247.

47. Young and Flower, p. 72.

48. Maria Brann and Marifran Mattson, "Toward a Typology of Confidentiality Breaches in Health Care Communication: An Ethic of Care Analysis of Provider Practices and Patient Perceptions," *Health Communication* 16 (2004), pp. 230 and 241.

49. Walker, Arnold, Miller-Day, and Webb, p. 57.

50. Juliann Scholl and Sandra L. Ragan, "The Use of Humor in Promoting Positive Provider–Patient Interaction in a Hospital Rehabilitation Unit," *Health Communication* 15 (2003), pp. 319 and 321.

51. Jason H. Wrench and Melanie Booth-Butterfield, "Increasing Patient Satisfaction and Compliance: An Examination of Physician Humor Orientation, Compliance-Gaining Strategies, and Perceived Credibility," *Communication Quarterly* 51 (2003), pp. 485 and 495.

52. Taya Flores, "Humanistic Medicine: Compassion and Communication Vital to Patients," Lafayette, IN *Journal & Courier*, March 31, 2009, p. D1.

53. Stewart, Brown, Donner, McWhinney, Oates, Weston, and Jordan, pp. 796–804.

54. Matthew P. Swedlund, Jayna B. Schumacher, Henry N. Young, and Elizabeth D. Cox, "Effect of Communication Style and Physician-Family Relationships on Satisfaction with Pediatric Chronic Disease Care," *Health Communication* 27 (2012), p. 503.

55. Mohan J. Dutta-Bergman, "The Relation Between Health Orientation, Provider–Patient Communication, and Satisfaction: An Individual-Difference Approach," *Health Communication* 18 (2005), p. 300.

56. Koermer and Kilbane, pp. 70–81.

57. Judith Ann Spiers, "The Use of Face Work and Politeness Theory," *Qualitative Health Research* 8 (1998), pp. 25–47.

58. Maria R. Dahm, "Tales of Time, Terms, and Patient Information-Seeking Behavior—An Exploratory Qualitative Study," *Health Communication* 27 (2012), pp. 682 and 688.

59. "Improving Care with an Automated Patient History," Online CME from Medscape, *Family Practice Medicine* (2007), pp. 39–43, http://www.medscape.com/viewarticle/561574 + 3, accessed December 2, 2008.

60. John Heritage and Jeffrey D. Robinson, "The Structure of Patients' Presenting Concerns: Physicians' Opening Questions," *Health Communication* 19 (2006), p. 100.

61. Delthia Ricks, "Study: Women Fudge the Truth with Doctors," *Indianapolis Star*, April 1, 2007, p. A21.

62. Amanda J. Dillard, Kevin D. McCaul, Pamela D. Kelso, and William M. P. Klein, "Resisting Good News: Reactions to Breast Cancer Risk Communication," *Health Communication* 19 (2006), p. 115.

63. Dillard, McCaul, Kelso, and Klein, p. 123.

64. Cara C. Lewis, Deborah H. Matheson, and C.A. Elizabeth Brimacombe, "Factors Influencing Patient Disclosure to Physicians in Birth Control Clinics: An Application of the Communication Privacy Management Theory," *Health Communication* 26 (2011), pp. 508–509.

65. Kathryn Greene, Kate Magsamen-Conrad, Maria K. Venetis, Maria G. Checton, Zhanna Bagdasarov, and Smita C. Banerjee, "Assessing Health Diagnosis Disclosure Decisions in Relationships: Testing the Disclosure Decision-Making Model," *Health Communication* 27 (2012), p. 365.

66. Maria G. Checton and Kathryn Greene, "Beyond Initial Disclosure: The Role of Prognosis and Symptom Uncertainty in Patterns of Disclosure in Relationships," *Health Communication* 27 (2012), p. 152.

67. Greene, Magsamen-Conrad, Venetis, Checton, Bagdasarov, and Banerjee, p. 366.

68. Allen J. Enelow and Scott N. Swisher, *Interviewing and the Patient* (New York: Oxford University Press, 1986), pp. 47–50; A. D. Wright et al., "Patterns of Acquisition of Interview Skills by Medical Students," *The Lancet*, November 1, 1980, pp. 964–966.

69. Kelly S. McNellis, "Assessing Communication Competence in the Primary Care Interview," *Communication Studies* 53 (2002), p. 412.

70. Carol Lynn Thompson and Linda M. Pledger, "Doctor–Patient Communication: Is Patient Knowledge of Medical Terminology Improving?" *Health Communication* 5 (1993), pp. 89–97.

71. Julie W. Scherz, Harold T. Edwards, and Ken J. Kallail, "Communicative Effectiveness of Doctor–Patient Interactions," *Health Communication* 7 (1995), p. 171.

72. Erin Donovan-Kicken, Michael Mackert, Trey D. Guinn, Andrew C. Tollison, Barbara Breckinridge, and Stephen J. Pot, "Health Literacy, Self-Efficacy, and Patients' Assessment of Medical Disclosure and Consent Documentation," *Health Communication* 27 (2012), p. 581.

73. Dahm, pp. 686–687.

74. Donald J. Cegala, Richard L. Street, Jr., and C. Randall Clinch, "The Impact of Patient Participation on Physician's Information Provision during a Primary Care Interview," *Health Communication* 21 (2007), pp. 177 and 181.

75. Cegala, Street, and Clinch, p. 181.

76. Ricks, p. A21.

77. Susan Eggly, "Physician–Patient Co-Construction of Illness Narratives in the Medical Interview," *Health Communication* 14 (2002), pp. 340 and 358.

78. Kreps and Thornton, p. 37.

79. Eggly, p. 343.

80. Young and Flower, p. 87.

81. Roter and Hall, p. 57.

82. Marlene von Friederichs-Fitzwater, Edward D. Callahan, and John Williams, "Relational Control in Physician–Patient Encounters," *Health Communication* 3 (1991), pp. 17–36.

83. Heritage and Robinson, p. 100.

84. Scott E. Caplan, Beth J. Haslett, and Brant R. Burleson, "Telling It Like It Is: The Adaptive Function of Narratives in Coping with Loss in Later Life," *Health Communication* 17 (2005), pp. 233–252.

85. Annette Harres, "'But Basically You're Feeling Well, Are You?': Tag Questions in Medical Consultations," *Health Communication* 10 (1998), pp. 111–123.

86. "American Medical Association Report Provides Guidelines for Improved Patient Communication," *U.S. Newswire,* June 19, 2006, accessed October 25, 2006.

87. Politi and Street, p. 410.

88. Greenbaum and Flores, p. 21.

89. Chen, p. 812.

90. Patrick J. Dillon, "Assessing the Influence of Patient Participation in Primary Care Medical Interviews on Recall of Treatment Recommendations," *Health Communication* 27 (2012), pp. 62–63.

91. P. Ley, "What the Patient Doesn't Remember," *Medical Opinion Review* 1 (1966), pp. 69–73.

92. Sabee, Bylund, Imes, Sanford, and Rice, pp. 265–284.

93. Stan A. Kaplowitz, Shelly Campo, and Wai Tat Chiu, "Cancer Patients' Desires for Communication of Prognosis Information," *Health Communication* 14 (2002), p. 237.

94. Silk, Westerman, Strom, and Andrews, p. 141.

95. Sabee, Bylund, Imes, Sanford, and Rice, p. 267.

96. Mohan Dutta-Bergman, "Primary Sources of Health Information: Comparisons in the Domain of Health Attitudes, Health Cognitions, and Health Behaviors," *Health Communication* 16 (2004), p. 285.

97. Shoba Ramanadhan and K. Viswanath, "Health and the Information Seeker: A Profile," *Health Communication* 20 (2006), pp. 131–139.

98. Dillon, p. 63.

99. S. Deborah Majerovitz, Michele G. Greene, Ronald A. Adelman, George M. Brody, Kathleen Leber, and Susan W. Healy, "Older Patients' Understanding of Medical Information in the Emergency Department," *Health Communication* 9 (1997), pp. 237–251.

100. Akihito Hagihara, Kimio Tarumi, and Koichi Nobutomo, "Physicians' and Patients' Recognition of the Level of the Physician's Explanation in Medical Encounters," *Health Communication* 20 (2006), p. 104.

101. Patricia MacMillan, "What's in a Word?" *Nursing Times*, February 26, 1981, p. 354.

102. Jeffrey D. Robinson, "An Interactional Structure of Medical Activities during Acute Visits and Its Implications for Patients' Participation," *Health Communication* 15 (2003), p. 49.

103. Katherine E. Rowan and D. Michele Hoover, "Communicating Risk to Patients: Diagnosing and Overcoming Lay Theories," in *Communicating Risk to Patients* (Rockville, MD: The U.S. Pharmacopeial Convention, 1995), p. 74.

104. Carter, p. E5.

105. F. S. Hewitt, "Just Words: Talking Our Way through It," *Nursing Times*, February 26, 1981, pp. 5–8.

106. Ley, pp. 69–73.

107. Politi and Street, p. 400.

108. Dillon, p. 62.

109. Rotter and Hall, p. 58.

110. Thomas K. Houston, Daniel Z. Sands, Beth R. Nash, and Daniel E. Ford, "Experiences of Physicians Who Frequently Use E-Mail with Patients," *Health Communication* 15 (2003), p. 516.

111. Gerald R. Ledlow, H. Dan O'Hair, and Scott Moore, "Predictors of Communication Quality: The Patient, Provider, and Nurse Call Center Triad," *Health Communication* 15 (2003), pp. 437 and 457.

112. Jill M. Clark, "Communication in Nursing," *Nursing Times,* January 1, 1981, p. 16.

113. Michelle L. Paulsel, James C. McCroskey, and Virginia P. Richmond, "Perceptions of Health Care Professionals' Credibility as a Predictor of Patients' Satisfaction with Their Health Care and Physician," *Communication Research Reports* 23 (2006), p. 74.

114. Deborah Grandinetti, "Turning No to Yes: How to Motivate the Reluctant Patient," *Medical Economics*, June 15, 1998, pp. 97–111.

115. Barbara F. Sharf and Suzanne Poirier, "Exploring (UN)Common Ground: Communication and Literature in a Health Care Setting," *Communication Education* 37 (1988), pp. 227–229.

116. Roxanne Parrott, "Exploring Family Practitioners' and Patients' Information Exchange about Prescribed Medications: Implications for Practitioners' Interviewing and Patients' Understanding," *Health Communication* 6 (1994), pp. 267–280.

117. Grandinetti, pp. 97–111.

118. Guttman, p. 637.

119. Lisa Maher, "Motivational Interviewing: What, When, and Why," *Patient Care*, September 15, 1998, pp. 55–60.

120. Shelley D. Lane, "Communication and Patient Compliance," in *Explorations in Provider and Patient Interaction*, Loyd F. Pettegrew, ed. (Louisville, KY: Humana, 1982), pp. 59–69.

121. Young and Flower, pp. 69–89.

122. Maher, pp. 55–60.

123. Manning and Ray, p. 467.

124. Jeffrey D. Robinson, Janice L. Raup-Krieger, Greg Burke, Valerie Weber, and Brett Oesterling, "The Relative Influence of Patients' Pre-Visit Global Satisfaction with Medical Care on Patients' Post-Visit Satisfaction with Physicians' Communication," *Communication Research Reports* 25 (February 2008), p. 2.

Resources

Kar, Snehendu B. *Health Communication: A Multicultural Perspective.* Thousand Oaks, CA: Sage 2001.

Murero, Monica, and Ronald E. Rice. *The Internet and Health Care: Theory, Research and Practice.* Mahwah, NJ: Lawrence Erlbaum, 2006.

Ray, Eileen Berlin, ed. *Health Communication in Practice: A Case Study Approach.* Mahwah, NJ: Lawrence Erlbaum, 2005.

Thompson, Teresa L., Roxanne Parrott, and Jon F. Nussbaum. *The Routledge Handbook of Health Communication.* New York: Routledge, 2011.

Wright, Kevin B., and Scott D. Moore, eds. *Applied Health Communication.* Cresskill, NJ: Hampton Press, 2008.

GLOSSARY

Abrupt or curt: short and often rude responses or curtailing of interactions.

Accidental bias: when an interviewer unintentionally leads respondents to give answers they feel the interviewer wants to give rather than their true feelings, attitudes, or beliefs.

Ad hominem: an effort to dodge an issue or challenge by discrediting the source that raised it.

Ad populum: an appeal to or on behalf of the majority.

Ambiguity: words to which interview parties may assign very different meanings.

Analysis: a careful examination of the nature and content of answers and impressions noted during an interview.

Appearance: how you look to the other party in the interview, including dress and physical appearance.

Applicant profile: the required knowledge, experiences, skills, and personal traits necessary to perform a job satisfactorily.

Application form: a form created by an organization to gather basic information about applicants, including their backgrounds, experiences, education, and career interests.

Appraisal perspective: the performance interview is seen as required, scheduled, superior-conducted and directed, adversarial, evaluative, and past-oriented.

Arguing from accepted belief: argument based on an accepted belief, assumption, or proposition.

Arguing from analogy: argument based on common characteristics of two people, places, objects, proposals, or ideas shared.

Arguing from cause-effect: an argument that attempts to establish a causal relationship.

Arguing from condition: an argument based on the assertion that if something does or does not happen, something else will or will not happen.

Arguing from example: an argument based on a sampling of a given class of people, places, or things.

Arguing from facts: an argument based on a conclusion that best explains a body of facts.

Arguing from two choices: arguing that there are only two possible proposals or courses of action and then eliminating one of the choices.

Arrival: the point at which one interview party encounters the other to initiate an interview.

Assumptions: assuming that something is true or false, is intended or unintended, exists or does not exist, is desired or undesired, will or will not happen.

Attitude: relatively enduring combinations of beliefs that predispose people to respond in particular ways to persons, organizations, places, ideas, and issues.

At will: an employment situation in which either party may terminate the employment relationship at any time and for any reason.

Baby talk: speaking to elder patients as if they were infants, including slower rate, exaggerated intonation, and simpler vocabulary.

Balance or consistency theory: a theory based on the belief that human beings strive for a harmonious existence with self and others and experience psychological discomfort (dissonance) when they do not.

Balanced scorecard approach: compensation, measurement, and performance are tied to coaching and improved performance.

Bandwagon tactic: a tactic that urges a person to follow the crowd, to do what everyone else is doing.

Basic skills tests: tests that measure mathematics, measurement, reading, and spelling skills.

Behavior-based selection: selection based upon the behaviors desired in a position and behaviors exhibited by applicants.

Behavior-based selection technique: a selection technique that begins with a needs and position analysis to determine which behaviors are essential for performing a particular job and proceeds to match applicants with this analysis.

Behaviorally anchored rating scale (BARS) model: a performance review model that identifies essential skills for a specific job and sets standards through a job analysis.

Belief: the trust or confidence placed in social, political, historic, economic, and religious claims.

Bipolar question: a question that limits the respondent to two polar choices such as yes or no, agree or disagree.

Bipolar trap: a bipolar question phrased to elicit a yes or no response when the questioner wants a detailed answer or specific information.

Birds of a feather syndrome: the selection of employees most similar to interviewers.

Blocking tactics: efforts of interviewers to avoid counseling or getting involved with interviewees, particularly in the health care setting.

Board interview: when two to five persons representing an organization may interview an applicant at the same time.

Bogardus Social Distance scales: questions that determine how respondents feel about social relationships and distances from them.

Bona fide occupational qualifications (BFOQ): requirements essential for performing a particular job.

Branding: when an applicant presents a carefully crafted image to potential employers through social media.

Broadcast interview: an interview that takes place live over radio or television or will be played all or in part at a later time.

Built-in bias: interviewer bias that is intentionally or unintentionally built into a schedule of questions.

Career/Job fairs: gatherings of organizations and companies, often at malls or on college campuses, during which job seekers may make contacts with representatives and gather information about employment opportunities.

Career objective: a brief, concise statement of a targeted career goal.

Case approach: when an applicant is placed into a carefully crafted situation that takes hours to study and resolve.

Catalytic coaching: a comprehensive, integrated performance management system based on a paradigm of development.

Cause-to-effect sequence: interview sequence that addresses causes and effects separately but relationally.

Central tendency: when interviewers refrain from assigning extreme ratings to facets of performance.

Chain or contingency strategy: a strategy that allows for preplanned secondary questions in survey interviews.

Chair format: when one recruiter for an organization converses with an applicant for several minutes and then passes the applicant along to another recruiter for the organization who probes into job skills, technical knowledge, or another area.

Chronological format résumé: a résumé that lists education, training, and experiences in chronological order.

Clearinghouse probe: a question designed to discover whether previous questions have uncovered everything of importance on a topic or issue.

Client-centered approach: a counseling approach that focuses on the client rather than content or situation.

Closed-minded or authoritarian interviewees: parties with unchangeable central beliefs who rely on trusted authorities when making decisions.

Closed question: a question that is narrow in focus and restricts the respondent's freedom to determine the amount and kind of information to offer.

Closing: the portion of an interview that brings it to an end.

Coaching: helping to improve performance rather than judging or criticizing performance.

Cognitive phase: the thinking and assessing phase of a counseling interview.

Cold calls: persuasive interview contacts made without an appointment or prior notice.

Collaboration: a mutual effort by both parties to inform, analyze, and resolve problems.

Collectivist culture: a culture that places high value on group image, group esteem, group reliance, group awareness, and group achievement.

Combination schedule: a question schedule that combines two schedules, such as highly scheduled and highly scheduled standardized.

Communication interactions: verbal and nonverbal exchanges that take place during interviews.

Comparison tactic: a person points out a few similarities between two places, people, or things and then draws conclusions from this superficial comparison.

Competitive rater: an interviewer who believes that no one can perform higher than his or her level of performance.

Complement: to complete, support, or repeat.

Complex interpersonal communication process: the assumption that one-to-one communication is simple is belied by the many variables that interact in this process.

Complexity vs. simplicity: questions that are either complex in wording and options or simple in wording and options.

Compliance: when an interviewee follows assessments and courses of action agreed to during a counseling interview.

Confirmatory questions: questions designed to verify understanding of an interviewee's (typically medical patients) concerns, problems, or statements.

Connotations: positive and negative meanings of words.

Conscious transparency: sharing information with applicants, explaining the purpose of questions, providing a supportive climate, and promoting unrestricted dialogue between interview parties.

Consubstantiality: the effort to establish a substantial sameness or similarity between interviewer and interviewee.

Contrast principle: if a second item or choice is fairly different from the first, it seems more different than it actually is.

Control: the extent to which one or both interview parties directs an interview.

Convenience sample: a sample taken when and where it is most convenient for the interviewee.

Conversation: an unstructured interaction between two or more people with no predetermined purpose other than enjoyment of the process.

Counselors: those who help interviewees to gain insights into and to cope with problems.

Counter persuasion: persuasion aimed at an interviewee by a persuader's competitor or antagonist following a persuasive interview.

Cover letter: a letter an applicant sends to a prospective employer that expresses interest in and qualifications for a position.

Coverage bias: occurs when cell phone only users who are often younger or of low economic status are excluded from a survey sample.

Critical incident question: a question that asks applicants how they might resolve a current problem the recruiter's organization is facing.

Cross-sectional study: a study that determines what is known, thought, or felt during a narrow time span.

Culture: shared customs, norms, knowledge, attitudes, values, and traits of a racial, religious, social, or corporate group.

Curious probe: a question that is irrelevant to the interview and satisfies only the interviewer's curiosity.

Defensive climate: a climate that appears threatening to one or both parties in an interview.

Determinate interviews: an interview designed to determine whether or not to make a job offer to an applicant.

Developmental model: the performance interview is initiated by individuals when needed, subordinate-conducted and directed, now and future oriented, cooperative, and self-satisfying.

Dialectical tensions: the result of conflicts over opposing needs and desires or between contrasting "voices" in an interview.

Dialogic listening: a means of focusing on ours rather than mine or yours to resolve a problem or task.

Diamond sequence: a question sequence that places two funnel sequences top to top.

Differentiation: an attempt through language to alter how a person sees reality by renaming it.

Directive approach: an interview in which the interviewer controls subject matter, length of answers, climate, and formality.

Directive reactions: when an interviewer reacts to a client with specific evaluations and advice.

Disclosure: the willingness and ability to reveal feelings, beliefs, attitudes, and information to another party.

Dishonesty: lying to or deceiving another interview party.

Don't ask, don't tell: a question that delves into information or an emotional area that a respondent may be incapable of addressing because of social, psychological, or situational constraints.

Double-barreled inquisition: a question that contains two or more questions.

Downward communication: an interview in which a superior in the organizational hierarchy is attempting to interact as an interviewer with a subordinate in the hierarchy.

Dyadic: an interaction that involves two distinct parties.

EEO laws: state and federal laws that pertain to recruiting and reviewing the performance of employees.

EEO violation question pitfall: when an interviewer asks an unlawful question during a recruiting interview.

Elderspeak: speaking to elder patients as if they were children, including addressing them as sweeties, girl or boy, and honey and employing the collective pronoun *our* (e.g., "it's time for our bath").

Electronic interviews: interviews conducted over the telephone, through conference calls, by video talkback, or over the Internet.

Electronically scanned résumé: a résumé designed in format and wording to be scanned electronically by recruiters.

E-mail interviews: interviews conducted through electronic e-mail rather than face-to-face.

Equal Employment Opportunity Commission: the agency assigned the task of overseeing and carrying out EEO laws.

Equal Employment Opportunity (EEO) laws: laws that pertain to employment and performance review interviews.

Ethical issues: issues that focus on value judgments concerning degrees of right and wrong, goodness and badness, in human conduct.

Euphemism: the substitution of a better sounding word for a common one.

Evaluative interval scales: questions that ask respondents to make judgments about persons, places, things, or ideas.

Evaluative response question pitfall: when an interviewer expresses judgmental feelings about an answer that may bias or skew the next answer.

Evasive interviewee: an interviewee who evades questions and gives indirect answers.

Evidence: examples, stories, comparisons, testimony, and statistics that support a claim.

Exchanging: a sharing of roles, responsibilities, feelings, beliefs, motives, and information during an interview.

Expressed feelings: feelings an interviewee expresses overtly and openly during a counseling interaction.

Face-to-face interview: an interview in which both parties are present physically in the same space during an interview.

Face threatening: interview interactions in which questions and answers may threaten the power or credibility of the interviewer or the interviewee.

Failed departure: when an interview has come to a close and parties have taken leave of one another only to come in contact accidentally later, often with a degree of communicative awkwardness.

False assumptions: assuming incorrectly that something is true or false, intended or unintended, exists or does not exist, desired or undesired, will or will not happen.

False closing: when verbal and nonverbal messages signal the closing of the interview is commencing but a party introduces a new topic or issue.

Feedback: verbal and nonverbal reactions of an interview party.

Feelings: emotions such as pride, fear, love, anger, and sympathy.

Fee-paid positions: when an organization retains a placement agency to locate qualified applicants and pays fees the agency would normally charge applicants.

Filter strategy: a question strategy that enables the interviewer to determine an interviewee's knowledge of a topic.

First impression: the initial impression one makes on another as a result of appearance, dress, manner, and quality of communication.

Flexibility: the ability to adapt during interviews to unexpected exchanges, answers, information, or attitudes.

Focus group interviews: a small group of people (6 to 12) act as an interviewee party with a highly skilled interviewer who asks a carefully selected set of questions that focus on a specific topic.

Frequency interval scales: questions that ask respondents to select a number that most accurately reflects how often they do or don't use or do something.

Functional résumé format: a résumé in which an applicant places experiences under headings that highlight qualifications for a position.

Funnel sequence: a question sequence that begins with a broad, open-ended question and proceeds with ever-more restricted questions.

Gender: how interview parties being female or male affects interview interactions.

General inquiry questions: an opening question that determines why an interviewee (often a medical patient) has initiated an interview.

Generic message: a persuasive message designed for a variety of audiences rather than a specific targeted audience.

Getting through questions: questions in counseling interviews designed to enable interviewees to manage their emotions.

Global relationships: relationships between parties from different countries and cultures.

Goal oriented: an interaction in which the interviewer is goal or task oriented rather than people oriented.

Ground rules: rules governing an interview agreed to by both parties.

Group interview: an interview in which there are multiple interviewers, such as several journalists at a press conference.

Guessing game: when a questioner attempts to guess information instead of asking for it.

Halo effect: when an interviewer gives favorable ratings to all job duties when an interviewee excels in only one.

Hasty generalization tactic: a person generalizes to a whole group of people, places, or things from only one or a few examples.

Highly closed questions: questions that can be answered with a single word or short phrase, most often a yes or no.

Highly directed reactions and responses: when an interviewer offers ultimatums and strong advice.

Highly nondirective reactions and responses: when an interviewer offers no information, assistance, or evaluations but encourages the interviewee to communicate, analyze, and be self-reliant.

Highly scheduled interview: a schedule in which the interviewer prepares all questions and their exact wording prior to an interview.

Highly scheduled standardized interview: a schedule in which the interviewer prepares all questions and their exact wording as well as answer options prior to an interview.

Historical critical incident question: a question that asks applicants how they would have resolved a problem the recruiter's organization faced in the past.

Honesty tests: tests designed to assess the ethics, honesty, and integrity of job applicants.

Hourglass sequence: a question sequence that begins with open questions, proceeds to closed questions, and ends with open questions.

Hyperpersonal revelations: highly personal (perhaps intimate) revelations of a person during an interview that reveals too much information.

Hypothetical question: a hypothetical but realistic question that asks respondents how they would handle a situation or problem.

Identification theory: a theory that persons persuade others by identifying with them in a variety of ways.

Idioms: expressions unique to a culture or nation likely to be misunderstood by a person from a different culture or nation.

Imagery: creating pictures or images in a person's mind through highly descriptive language.

Implicative approach: an approach that withholds an explicit statement of purpose or intent until the interviewee sees the implications and suggests a course of action.

Individualist culture: a culture that places high value on self-image, self-esteem, self-reliance, self-awareness, and individual achievement.

Induced compliance theory: a theory designed to change thinking, feeling, or acting by inducing others to engage in activities counter to their values, beliefs, or attitudes.

Inform: to provide information or knowledge to another party.

Information: stories, illustrations, comparisons, experiences, quotations, statistics, definitions, and explanations that apprise interview parties of problems, solutions, situations, and events.

Information-gathering interviews: interviews designed to obtain facts, opinions, data, feelings, attitudes, beliefs, reactions, advice, or feedback.

Information-giving interview: interviews designed to exchange data, knowledge, direction, instructions, orientation, clarification, or warnings.

Information overload: when interviewees are provided with more information than they can process or recall.

Informational probe: a question designed to obtain additional information when an answer appears to be superficial, vague, or ambiguous or to suggest a feeling or attitude.

Initiating the interview: the process by which an interview is arranged and started.

Inoculation theory: a theory based on the belief that it is often more effective to prevent undesired persuasion from occurring than trying damage control afterward.

Integrity interviews: interviews designed to assess the honesty and integrity of prospective employees.

Intelligent or educated interviewee: an interviewee with high levels of intelligence or informal and formal education.

Interactional: the exchanging or sharing of roles, responsibilities, feelings, beliefs, motives, and information.

Internet interview: an interview that takes place solely through the Internet.

Interpersonal communication process: a complex and often puzzling communication interaction with another party.

Interval scales: survey question scales that provide distances between measures.

Interview: an interactional communication process between two parties, at least one of whom has a predetermined and serious purpose, and involves the asking and answering of questions.

Interview evaluation: the formal or informal process of evaluating applicants following recruiting interviews.

Interview guide: a carefully structured outline of topics and subtopics to be covered during an interview.

Interview schedule: a list of questions an interviewer prepares prior to an interview.

Interviewee: the party who is not in basic control of the interaction, such as a respondent in a survey interview or an applicant in a recruiting interview.

Interviewer bias: when respondents give answers they feel questioners want them to give rather than express their true feelings, attitudes, or beliefs.

Inverted funnel sequence: a sequence that begins with closed questions and proceeds toward open questions.

Jargon: words that organizations or groups alter or create for specialized use.

Job/career fairs: gatherings of recruiters from a variety of organizations on college campuses or malls in which applicants can obtain information, make contacts, and take part in interviews.

Joblike situations: simulated job situations through questions or role playing that enable the recruiter to perceive how an applicant might act on the job.

Joint actions: when interview parties understand that what each does will impact the other and act in the other's party's interest.

Journalist's interview guide: a guide that focuses on who, what, when, where, how, and why.

Just cause: the fair and equitable treatment of each employee in a job class.

Key informant: a person who can supply information on situations, assist in selecting interviewees, and aid in securing interviewee cooperation.

Knowledge workers: workers that create and access information rather than manufacture products and are valued for their knowledge, ability to motivate others, and teamwork.

Law of recency: people tend to recall the last thing said or done in interviews.

Lay counselor: a person with little or no formal training in counseling.

Lay theories: commonsense theories patients hold about health care that often resist scientific notions and research findings.

Leading push: a question that suggests how a person should respond.

Leading question: a question that suggests implicitly or explicitly the expected or desired answer.

Leaning question strategy: a question strategy that enables interviewers to reduce the number of undecided and don't know responses in surveys.

Learning organization: an organization that places high value on knowledge, skills, competencies, opportunities for learning, and employees as intellectual capital.

Leave-taking: the effort to bring an interview to a close.

Length of service error: when an interviewer assumes that present performance is high because past performance was high.

Letters of recommendation: letters sent by references to prospective employers on behalf of persons applying for specific positions.

Level 1 interactions: interactions that are relatively safe and nonthreatening.

Level 2 interactions: interactions that require a moderate degree of trust and may be moderately threatening because of exchange of beliefs, attitudes, values, and positions on issues.

Level 3 interactions: interactions that require a great deal of trust because parties disclose fully their feelings, beliefs, attitudes, and perceptions on intimate and controversial topics.

Level of confidence: the mathematical probability that the survey is within an accepted margin of error.

Level of information: the amount and sophistication of information an interviewee has to offer.

Likert scale: interval scale questions that ask respondents to make judgments about persons, places, things, or ideas.

Listening: the deliberate process of receiving, understanding, evaluating, and retaining what is seen and heard.

Listening for comprehension: receiving, understanding, and remembering messages as accurately as possible.

Listening for empathy: a method of communicating an attitude of genuine concern, understanding, and involvement.

Listening for evaluation: a means of judging what is heard and observed.

Listening for resolution: a means of mutually resolving a problem or task.

Loaded question: a question with strong direction or dictation of the answer desired through the use of name calling or emotionally charged words.

Longitudinal study: a study to determine trends in what is known, thought, or felt over a period of time.

Loose rater: an interviewer who is reluctant to point out weak areas and dwells on the average or better areas of performance.

Make meaning questions: questions in counseling interviews designed to determine what an interviewee is most concerned about in an interview.

Management by objectives (MBO) model: a performance review model that involves a manager and a subordinate in a mutual (50-50) setting of results-oriented goals rather than activities to be performed.

Margin of error: the degree of similarity between sample results and the results from a 100 percent count obtained in an identical manner.

Marginalized respondent: a respondent who is unlikely to be surveyed because of culture, demographics, or lack of a telephone or easily accessed telephone number or residential address.

Matching process: the process of matching an applicant with a specific position and organization.

Meaning making: actions and questions designed to evoke meaning.

Metaphorical questions: questions that include metaphors, such as "establishing a level playing field" or addressing a company as a "family."

Mirror probe: a question that summarizes a series of answers to ensure accurate understanding and retention.

Moderately scheduled interview: a schedule in which the interviewer prepares all major questions with possible probing questions under each prior to an interview.

Motives: values such as security, belonging, freedom, ambition, and preservation of health.

Multisource feedback: feedback from a number of sources.

Mutual product: when the results of interviews depend upon the contributions of both parties.

Naming: the labeling of people, places, or things to make them appear different, to alter perceptions of reality.

Negative face: the desire to be free of imposition or intrusion.

Negative politeness: an effort to protect another person when negative face needs are threatened.

Negative selling: the attempt to persuade by attacking another or another's proposal rather than supporting yourself or your proposal.

Network tree: a listing of names, addresses, and telephone numbers of primary contacts who can provide leads for job openings and additional contacts.

Networking: creating a list of contacts for possible employment positions.

Neutral question: a question that allows a respondent to determine an answer with no overt direction or pressure from the questioner.

Neutralize: any effort to remove an obstacle to making a favorable impression or attaining a position, including recruiter questions that violate EEO laws.

Nexting: verbal and nonverbal signals from one party that it is time for the other party to enter into the interaction or to become silent.

Noise: anything that may interfere with the communication process, such as machinery, ringing telephones, doors opening and closing, others talking, traffic, and music.

Nominal scales: questions that provide mutually exclusive variables and ask respondents to pick or name the most appropriate.

Nondirective approach: an interview in which the interviewee controls subject matter, length of answers, climate, and formality.

Nondirective reaction: when an interviewer reacts to a client without giving advice or specific direction.

Non-probability sampling: when a survey taker does not know the chance each member of a population has of being interviewed.

Nonscheduled interview: an interview guide of topic and subtopics with no prepared questions prior to an interview.

Nontraditional forms: newer forms of interviewing such as focus groups, videoconferences, e-mail interviews, and virtual interviews.

Nonverbal closing actions: nonverbal actions that signal a closing is commencing, such as leaning forward, uncrossing legs, breaking eye contact, and offering to shake hands.

Nonverbal communication: nonverbal signals such as physical appearance, dress, eye contact, voice, touches, head nods, hand shakes, and posture.

Nonverbal interactions: nonverbal signals such as physical appearance, dress, eye contact, voice, touches, head nods, hand shakes, and posture.

Normative competence: when an interview party understands the parts each party will play in a relationship and develops workable rules and norms.

Normative influence: a person's beliefs of which behaviors important individuals or groups think are advisable or inadvisable to perform.

Nudging probe: a word or brief phrase that urges a respondent to continue answering.

Numerical interview scales: questions that ask respondents to select a range or level that accurately reflects an age, income level, educational level, and so on.

Observing: paying close attention to surroundings, people, dress, appearance, and nonverbal communication.

Off the record: information that cannot be reported following an interview.

Open question: a question that allows the respondent considerable freedom in determining the amount and kind of information to offer.

Open-to-closed switch: when a questioner asks an open question but changes it to a closed question before a respondent can reply.

Opening: the first minutes of an interview in which the interviewer attempts to establish rapport and orient the interviewee.

Opening question: the initial question during the body of an interview.

Opening techniques: verbal and nonverbal signals that establish rapport and orient the interviewee.

Order bias: possible influence on how interviewees respond due to the order of answer options in survey questions.

Ordinal scales: questions that ask respondents to rate or rank options in their implied relationship to one another.

Orientation: the portion of the opening in which the interviewer explains the purpose, length, and nature of the interview.

Outside forces: influential others such as family, friends, employers, and agencies who are not part of the interview but may affect one or both parties before, during, or after an interview.

Overt identification: an attempt to establish a "we are one and the same" perception.

Panel interview: when two to five persons representing an organization may interview an applicant at the same time.

Paper trail: written materials that allow the tracing of an individual or organization's actions or opinions.

PAR method: when an applicant structures an answer by addressing an assigned problem or task, actions taken to solve the assigned problem or task, and the results or consequences of actions taken.

Party: the interviewer or interviewee side in an interview.

Patient-centered care (PCC): when a patient's needs, preferences, and beliefs are respected at all times.

Percentage agencies: placement agencies whose fee for finding positions for clients is a specific percentage of the first year's salary.

Perceptions: the ways people see and interpret themselves, other people, places, things, events, and nonverbal signals.

Personal interview: a survey interview that takes place face-to-face.

Personal space: an imaginary bubble around us that we consider almost as private as our body.

Personality tests: tests designed to assess the people skills of applicants.

Persuaders: interviewers who attempt to alter the ways interviewees think, feel, and/or act.

Persuasive interviews: an interview designed to change an interviewee's way of thinking, feeling, and/or acting.

Pitchfork effect: when an interviewer gives negative ratings to all facets of performance because of a particular trait the interviewer dislikes in others.

Placement agency: an agency that provides services such as career counseling, résumé preparation, employer contacts, and interview opportunities for those seeking positions.

Placement interviews: interviews designed to assign employees to positions or to move them from one position or location to another.

Polarizing: the attempt to limit choices or positions to polar opposites.

Politeness theory: a theory that claims all humans want to be appreciated, approved, liked, honored, and protected.

Population: all persons able and qualified to respond in a particular survey.

Portfolio: a small and varied collection of an applicant's best work.

Positive attention: attention that generates recruiter interest in an applicant.

Positive face: the desire to be appreciated, approved, liked, and honored.

Positive politeness: an effort to show concern by complimenting and using respectful forms of address.

Post hoc or scrambling cause-effect tactic: basing a cause-effect relationship on coincidence, a minor cause, or a single cause.

Power speech: words that express certainty, challenges, verbal aggression, and metaphors.

Powerless speech: words and nonfluencies that express apologies, disclaimers, excuses, and uncertainty.

Precision journalism: journalistic reports based on survey research data.

Predetermined: planned in advance of an interaction.

Press conference: a setting in which multiple interviewers interview one interviewee.

Pretest: the test of an interview schedule with a small sample of respondents prior to a survey to detect possible problems that might result during the survey.

Primary question: a question that introduces a topic or new area within a topic and can stand alone out of context.

Privacy: freedom from unwanted intrusion into or access to interview interactions.

Probability sampling: when a survey taker knows that each member of a population has a certain chance of being interviewed.

Probing: the attempt to discover additional information and understanding.

Probing question: a question that attempts to discover additional information following a primary or secondary question and cannot stand alone out of context.

Problems of the interviewee's behavior interviews: interviews designed to review, separate, correct, or counsel interviewees for their behavior.

Problems of the interviewer's behavior interviews: interviews designed to receive complaints, grievances, or suggestions concerning the interviewer's behavior.

Problem-solution sequence: an outline divided into problem and solution phases.

Problem-solving interviews: interviews designed to discuss mutually shared problems, receive suggestions for solutions, or implement solutions.

Process: a dynamic, continuing, ever changing interaction of variables.

Prospecting: a systematic selection of interviewees who are good prospects for persuasive interviews.

Proximity: the physical distance between interview parties.

Psychological reactance theory: a theory based on the claim that people react negatively when someone threatens to restrict or does restrict a behavior they want to engage in.

Purpose: the reason or goal for a party conducting or taking part in an interview.

Qualitative survey: a survey in which findings are presented in textual form, usually words.

Quantitative survey: a survey in which findings are presented in numerical form, such as percentages and frequencies.

Question: any statement or nonverbal act that invites an answer.

Question pitfall: a slight alteration of questions, often unintentional, that changes them from open to closed, primary to secondary, and neutral to leading.

Question sequence: the strategic interconnection of questions.

Quintamensional design sequence: a five-step sequence designed to assess the intensity of a respondent's opinions and attitudes.

Quiz show pitfall: a question above or beneath the respondent's level of knowledge.

Random digit dialing: a system that randomly generates telephone numbers in target area codes and prefix areas for selecting a survey sample.

Random sampling: selecting respondents randomly from a container, a list, or group.

Ranking ordinal scale: questions that ask respondents to rank options in their implied relationship to one another.

Rapport: a process of establishing and sustaining a relationship by creating feelings of goodwill and trust.

Rating ordinal scale: questions that ask respondents to rate options in their implied relationship to one another.

Real setting: an interview setting with all of its defects and problems.

Reasoning from accepted belief, assumption, or proposition: reasoning based on the assertion that a belief, assumption, or proposition is true and without question.

Reasoning from analogy: reasoning based on points of similarity that two people, places, or things have in common.

Reasoning from cause-effect: reasoning based on a causal relationship.

Reasoning from condition: reasoning based on the assertion that if something does or does not happen, something else will or will not happen.

Reasoning from example: reasoning based on a generalization about a whole class of people, places, or things from a sampling of the class.

Reasoning from facts: reasoning that offers a conclusion as the best explanation for available evidence.

Reasoning from sign: a claim that two or more variables are related so the presence or absence of one indicates the presence or absence of the other.

Recall: the ability of an interview party to remember and report accurately what took place during an interview, including agreements, information exchanged, attitudes, and climate.

Recency error: when an interviewer relies too heavily on the most recent events or performance levels.

Reciprocal concessions: the effort to instill a sense of obligation in another to make a concession after the other party has made one.

Recording: taking mental or physical note of what is taking place during an interview.

References: names of persons applicants give to prospective employers who can provide assessments of their qualifications for positions.

Reflective probe: a question that reflects the answer received to verify or clarify what the respondent intended to say.

Reinforce: strengthening or making stronger.

Rejection then retreat: the persuader retreats to a second or fall back option if the interviewee rejects the preferred proposal.

Relational: an interpersonal connection between two parties or persons.

Relational dimensions: critical dimensions such as similarity, inclusion, affection, and trust that determine the nature of relationships.

Relational distance: the closeness of the relationship between interview parties.

Relational history: the past, present, and future connections between two parties or persons.

Relational memory: what interview parties remember from previous encounters with one another.

Relational uncertainty: when either party is unaware of the degree of warmth, sharing of control, or level of trust that will exist during an interview.

Relationship: an interpersonal connection between parties that influences their interest in the outcome of the interview.

Reliability: the assurance that the same information can be collected in repeated interviews.

Repeat question strategy: a question strategy that enables the interviewer to determine interviewee consistency in responses on a topic.

Replicability: the ability to duplicate interviews regardless of interviewers, interviewees, and situations.

Report: a formal or informal recording of the information attained during an interview.

Reproducibility: the ability to duplicate interviews regardless of interviewer, interviewee, and situation.

Research: a careful search for background materials, information, facts, and theories pertaining to a subject, person, or organization.

Restatement probe: a question that restates all or part of the original question that remains unanswered.

Résumé: a brief accounting of an applicant's career goal, education, training, and experiences.

Résumé or application form question pitfall: asking a question that is already answered on the résumé or application form.

Reticent interviewee: an interviewee who seems unwilling or unable to talk and respond freely.

Role competence: the ability of an interview party to play the roles of interviewer and interviewee effectively.

Rule of reciprocation: instills in an interviewee a sense of obligation to repay in kind what another provides.

Sample point or block sampling: preassigned numbers and types of respondents are chosen from assigned geographical areas.

Sample size: the number of persons interviewed during a survey when the whole population is too large to interview.

Sampling principles: principles that create a sample that accurately represents the population under study.

Sanitized setting: an interview setting without time constraints, interviewee problems, or situational problems such as noise, interruptions, inappropriate seating, or uncomfortable temperatures.

Scannable résumé: a résumé designed specifically to be scanned effectively by electronic software used by recruiters.

Scanning software: computer software that enables recruiters to scan résumés electronically to reduce the time required to select applicants to be interviewed.

Screening interviews: interviews designed to select applicants for additional interviews.

Secondary question: a question that attempts to discover additional information following a primary or secondary (probing) question and cannot stand alone out of context.

Selection interview: an interview in which the purpose is to select a person for employment or membership within an organization.

Self: focus of the interviewee on the interviewee during a counseling interview.

Self-analysis: a careful, thorough, and insightful analysis of self an applicant conducts prior to taking part in interviews.

Self-concept: how a person perceives self physically, socially, and psychologically.

Self-disclosure: the willingness and ability to disclose information pertaining to oneself.

Self-esteem: positive and negative feelings a person has of self.

Self-evident truth: a claim that a question or issue is not arguable because it is settled by rule or fact.

Self-fulfilling prophecy: a prediction that comes true because a person expects or predicts it will be so.

Self-identity: how, what, and with whom people identify themselves.

Self-persuasion: a situation in which a persuader encourages a person to persuade self rather than being persuaded by another.

Self-selection: when respondents alone determine if they will be included in a survey sample.

Seminar format: an interview format in which one or more recruiters interview several applicants at the same time.

Sequential phase model: a counseling model that centers on four phases based on affective (emotional) and cognitive (thinking) functions.

Sex: the genders of interview parties.

Shock-absorber phrases: phrases that reduce the sting of critical questions.

Shuffle strategy: a question strategy that enables interviewers to avoid responses based on the order rather than the content of answer options.

Silence: the absence of vocal communication from one or both parties in an interview.

Silent probe: when an interviewer remains silent after an answer and may use nonverbal signals to encourage the respondent to continue answering.

Similarity: characteristics, experiences, interests, beliefs, attitudes, values, and expectations interview parties have in common.

Situation: a total interview context that includes events prior to and after, time, place, and surroundings.

Situational schema: a schema that includes all of the different types of interviews.

Skip interval or random digit sample: a sampling method in which every predetermined number on a list is selected, such as every 10th name in a directory.

Skype: a program that enables interviewers and interviewees to communicate instantly over the Internet by using a microphone and webcam.

Slang: unofficial jargon that groups use.

Slogan or tabloid thinking: a clever phrase that encapsulates a position, stand, or goal of a persuader.

Sound-alikes: words that sound alike but have different meanings.

Space sequence: an outline that arranges topics and subtopics according to spatial divisions such as left to right, north to south.

Standard/learned principle: principles people learn through life that automatically guide actions and decisions.

STAR method: when an applicant structures an answer in four parts by addressing the situation, the task, the action taken, and the results of this action.

Status difference: the difference in social or organizational hierarchy between interviewer and interviewee.

Stealth marketing: when a sales representative pretends to be a friendly, disinterested party rather than a sales representative.

Strategic ambiguities: the strategic use of words with multiple or vague meanings to avoid specific definitions or explanations.

Strategic answers: when interviewees answer questions to their advantage.

Stratified random sampling: a sampling method that selects the number of respondents according to their percentages in the target population.

Structure: a predetermined arrangement of parts or stages into a meaningful whole.

Supportive climate: a climate in which there is trust and respect between parties.

System: a degree of structure or organization that guides a planned interaction between two parties.

Table of random numbers: a sample of respondents selected by assigning each respondent a number and using a table of random numbers for picking a sample.

Talent or trait-based selection process: a recruiting interview in which all interviewer questions focus on specific talents or traits included in the applicant profile.

Talkative interviewee: an interviewee who gives overly long answers and talks too freely.

Task oriented: an interviewer who is more concerned with performing a task efficiently and effectively than in communicating effectively with an interviewee.

Team interview: when two to five persons representing an organization may interview an applicant at the same time.

Telephone interview: an interview that is conducted over the telephone rather than face-to-face.

Tell me everything: an extremely open question with no restrictions or guidelines for the respondent.

Territorial markers: an imaginary bubble around us that we consider nearly as private as our body.

Territoriality: the physical and psychological space in which an interview takes place.

Test of job relatedness: effort to meet EEO laws by establishing legally defensible selection criteria, asking questions related to these criteria, asking the same questions of all applicants, being cautious when probing into answers, being cautious during informal chit-chat, focusing questions on what applicants can do, and steering applicants away from volunteering unlawful information.

The 360-degree approach: a performance review model that obtains as many views of a person's performance as possible from observers who interact with the person on a regular basis.

Thin entering wedge (domino effect or slippery slope) tactic: an argument that one decision, action, or law after another is leading inevitably toward some sort of danger.

Tight rater: an interviewer who believes that no one can perform at the necessary standards.

Time sequence: an outline that treats topics and subtopics in chronological order.

Tongue-in-cheek test response: a pleasant, perhaps humorous response that sends a signal to a recruiter that he or she has asked an unlawful question.

Topical sequence: an outline sequence that follows the natural divisions of a topic or subtopic.

Traditional forms: standard types of interviews such as informational, survey, employment, performance review, counseling, and health care.

Traditional recruiter questions: common questions generations of recruiters have asked, such as where do you plan to be five years from now.

Transfer interviews: interviews designed to promote employees, to assign them to positions, or to move them from one position or location to another.

Transferring guilt: an effort to dodge an issue by turning the accuser, victim, or questioner into the guilty party.

Trial closing: the attempt to determine if an interviewee is ready to close an interview with an agreement of some sort.

Tunnel sequence: a series of similar questions that are either open or closed.

Tu quoque: an effort to dodge an issue or objection by revolving it upon the challenger or questioner.

Two parties: an interviewer and an interviewee party consisting of one or more persons with distinct roles and purposes such as getting and giving information, counseling and being counseled, persuading and being persuaded, recruiting and being recruited.

Undercover marketing: when a sales representative pretends to be a friendly, disinterested party rather than a sales representative. Also called stealth marketing.

Unipolar question: a question that has only one obvious or desired answer.

Universal performance interviewing model: a performance review that focuses on coaching by starting with positive behavior a manager wants the employee to maintain and then moving to behaviors that need to be corrected.

Unsanitized setting: a real-world interview setting with all of its problems, crises, interruptions, and unexpected happenings.

Upward communication: an interview in which a subordinate in an organizational hierarchy is attempting to interact as interviewer with a superior in the hierarchy.

Values: fundamental beliefs about ideal states of existence and modes of behavior.

Verbal interactions: words (arbitrary connections of letters) that serve as symbols for people, places, things, events, beliefs, and feelings.

Videoconference: technology that enables interview parties to see and hear one another and to interact in real time.

Virtual interview: an electronic interview employed most often for practice and simulation.

Web survey: a survey that is conducted over the Internet rather than face-to-face or over the telephone.

Webinar: a presentation to an audience on the web that may become an interview if it is a collaborative exchange between two parties who ask questions and provide answers to one another.

Yes (no) response: a question that has only one obvious answer.

Yes-but approach: an approach that begins with areas of agreement and approaches points of disagreement after goodwill and a supportive climate are established.

Yes-yes approach: the attempt to get another party in the habit of saying yes so agreements may continue.

AUTHOR INDEX

SUBJECT INDEX

Notes

Notes

Notes

Notes

Notes